**DO NOT REMOVE
CARDS FROM POCKET**

The Promises We Keep

Also by William Korey

The Soviet Cage
The Key to Human Rights—Implementation
Human Rights and the Helsinki Accord

The Promises We Keep

Human Rights, the Helsinki Process, and American Foreign Policy

William Korey

Foreword by
Daniel Patrick Moynihan

St. Martin's Press
New York
in association with the
Institute for EastWest Studies, New York

INSTITUTE FOR EASTWEST STUDIES

© Institute for EastWest Studies 1993

First published in the United States of America 1993
Printed in the United States of America

ISBN 0-312-09118-4

Library of Congress Cataloging-in-Publication Data

Korey, William, 1922-
  The Promises We Keep : Human Rights, the Helsinki Process, and
  American Foreign Policy / William Korey
    p.   cm.
  Includes bibliographical references (p.   ) and index.
  ISBN 0-312-09118-4
  1. Human rights—Europe—History. 2. Europe—Foreign relations-
  United States.   3. United States—Foreign relations—Europe.
  I. Institute for EastWest Studies.   II. Title.
KJC5132.K67   1993
323'.094—dc20   92-46156
                                                         CIP

To Es, Alix, and Eileen

Table of Contents

Acknowledgments

This work has been ten years in the making. It began with a three-month stay as Guest Scholar at the Woodrow Wilson International Center for Scholars in early 1983. In 1986, the Ford Foundation awarded me a three-year travel and research grant that was subsequently extended for an additional 12 months. And, in 1991, the Institute for EastWest Studies named me as an Adjunct Scholar, permitting me to complete the writing of the volume.

Study of the Helsinki process was by no means an easy task. The absence of a secretariat for the Conference on Security and Cooperation in Europe and the closed character of most of the CSCE meetings meant that no independent stenographic or documentary record for its numerous meetings existed. To do research on the process, even a limited part such as America's role in it, meant extensive interviewing of those involved directly or indirectly in CSCE. This, of course, was supplemented by the reading of every speech made by a US Helsinki delegate and every official or unofficial published paper reflecting the US role.

Encouragement to pursue this often Sisyphean task came from five persons, to each of whom I am profoundly indebted. Seymour Reich, former President of B'nai B'rith, provided me with every form of assistance so that the research could be initially undertaken. Ambassador Max M. Kampelman extended a vast amount of his time for interview purposes and brought me to the attention of the Wilson Center. The late Bayard Rustin, the distinguished civil rights leader, early on recognized the international human rights potential of the Helsinki process and helped obtain important support for the project. Ambassador William vanden Heuvel, President of the Franklin and Eleanor Roosevelt Institute, expressed keen interest in the subject and recommended me to the Ford Foundation. And Rita Hauser, whose commitment to the human rights aspects of the project was as strong as her faith in its outcome, provided significant funding through the Hauser Foundation.

Numerous other individuals and institutions played crucial, at times invaluable, roles. Frances Guilbert, Ambassador Arthur Goldberg's long-time secretary, made available a most significant source on the Belgrade Follow-Up Meeting—the unpublished memoirs of the Ambassador's wife, Dorothy Goldberg. Mrs. Carroll Sherer, the wife of the US Ambassador to the Helsinki talks in Geneva and later deputy head at Belgrade, Albert Sherer, Jr., was kind enough to provide an archive of her husband's papers.

From 1980 on, each US head of delegation (and his staff as well) offered the essential oral documentation of what simply could not be obtained otherwise. Ambassador Kampelman was a remarkably impressive reservoir of insight at Madrid, and later at the human dimension talks in Copenhagen and in Moscow. His successor at the Vienna Follow-Up Meeting, Ambassador Warren Zimmermann, gave literally hours of his time to me in valuable office discussions, transatlantic telephone calls, and in various visits to New York.

Ambassador Michael Novak was unsparing in his assistance at the Bern human contacts experts' meeting, as was Ambassador Morris Abram at the Paris meeting of the Conference on the Human Dimension. Permission to attend staff meetings and, at times, NATO caucus sessions added considerably to my knowledge. Appointment as a public member of the US delegation to several meetings enabled me to have access to highly pertinent background information.

Richard Schifter, former Assistant Secretary of State for Human Rights and Humanitarian Affairs, was a constant source of informed background and perspective. Numerous other State Department officials provided help, as did US Information Agency employees who were attached to the delegations. One who was unusually cooperative was Edward Alexander.

Especially valuable, indeed indispensable, were the files of the US Helsinki Commission. Its extensive reports, studies, hearings and correspondence constituted a bonanza of information. I am grateful to the staff director of the Commission, Ambassador Sam Wise, for making the contents available to me as well as for offering his own informed insights. His predecessor, R. Spencer Oliver, later staff director of the House Committee on Foreign Affairs, extended every possible assistance and encouragement to my research project and gave of his time for lengthy interviews.

The staff of the Commission is an unusually talented group, and I am indebted to each of them for information, advice, suggestions, and criticism. Erika Schlager offered an extraordinarily useful critique with innumerable recommendations. Among those who were particularly helpful, too, were Orest Deychak, Robert Hand and Heather Hurlburt. Former Commission staffer Lynn Davidson, who later worked in the State Department's Policy Planning Staff, was a major source of know-how and guidance.

A vital source of documentation was the almost daily reportorial accounts filed by correspondents of Radio Free Europe/Radio Liberty, most notably Roland Eggleston. This vast, extremely useful resource was made available through the efforts of Joel Blocker, formerly news director of RFE in Munich.

Deep appreciation must also be extended to the Joyce Mertz-Gilmore Foundation for invaluable supplementary assistance, and to the Carnegie Council on Ethics and International Affairs for making its facilities available. I am also grateful to the Memorial Foundation for Jewish Culture and to James Rapp for helpful funding of special parts of the project.

Thanks must also go to a number of heads of foreign delegations to CSCE meetings, who, through interviews, broadened the perspective of the research and writing. Particularly helpful were Ambassadors William Bauer of Canada, Rudolf Torovsky of Austria and Hans Meesman of the Netherlands. Long-time CSCE veteran of the United Kingdom, Philip Hurr, offered most helpful insights. The distinguished Swiss Permanent State Secretary, Edouard Brunner, provided pertinent and illuminating background.

I benefited greatly from colleagues in the non-governmental community. US Helsinki Watch shared with me its extensive reports and studies, as well as its frequent briefing and policy meetings. Of considerable value was Ludmilla Alexeyeva, an original member of the Moscow Helsinki Group, whose recollections and advice were much appreciated. The World Conference on Soviet Jewry was a rich repository of research documentation. Especially pertinent advice and encouragement came from Professor Stephen Marks of Columbia University Law School, formerly my program officer at the Ford Foundation. I am also grateful to Joshua Dorosin for research assistance during 1988.

A very special word of thanks goes to Richard Levitt, Director of Publications at the Institute for EastWest Studies, who was in charge of all the editing and production arrangements for this book and was ably assisted by Michelle Boyd and Amy Lew. His creative labors have given the volume a much-needed shape and clarity. The final text, like the final responsibility, is, however, my own.

Foreword

"Wherever the standard of freedom and independence has been or shall be unfurled, there will be America's heart." So said John Quincy Adams in 1821 in as clear a declaration of this country's interest in human rights as ever a president has uttered. Yet he followed with "but she does not go abròad in search of monsters to destroy." The tension between America's commitment to human rights and its desire to remain apart was present at the creation.

Few aspects of America's international outlook have generated as much controversy at home and abroad as human rights. The controversy is perhaps understandable because promoting human rights is a very—some would argue uniquely—American concept. No other nation's political rhetoric—let alone diplomacy—has been so generously informed by the vocabulary of human rights.

The Declaration of Independence refers to "unalienable rights"—rights inherent in the individual, not granted by the state. James Madison—next to Thomas Jefferson, the prime rhetorician of America's founding—did not initially rely on the power of the state to protect these rights. In fact, he saw the power of the state as a potential threat to them. Writing in *The Federalist* in 1788, he advised the young republic to keep government power as diffuse as possible and to rely more on the often-conflicting individual pursuit of self-interest on the part of its citizens as the ultimate guarantor of their rights. Understanding, however, that neither governments nor individuals are innately disposed to respect the rights of others, America's founders soon promulgated the Bill of Rights—enjoining government to take an active role in protecting personal freedom. Government was then to be the protector of liberty, even from government. But does one government have the right to promote the liberty of those subject to another? And, if so, by what means can it legitimately act?

Does the United States have a particular claim on the right to promote liberty? Perhaps it does. The United Nations Charter rather obviously echoes our own constitutive documents ("We the Peoples of the United Nations") and the Bill of Rights inspired the United Nations General Assembly to adopt the Universal Declaration of Human Rights in 1948. Yet the aspirational language of the Declaration (e.g., "Everyone has the right to a standard of living adequate for the health and well-being of himself and of his family . . .") needed to be translated with enforceable precision into potentially binding international instruments. The General Assembly did so nearly 20 years later in the International Covenants on Human Rights. Not everyone agrees that each particular article in the Covenants is a legitimate right, and fewer agree about the wisdom of trying to enforce even those rights, but the Covenants represent evolutionary progress withal; so does the recent decision of the United States to ratify the Covenant on Civil and Political Rights.

The spectrum of views on the American policy of promoting human rights is a broad one. Proponents argue that US human rights policy is grounded in a moralism and commitment to the rule of law that view policy objectives in universal rather than strictly national terms. Some critics agree, and argue that this is precisely what is wrong—not right—with the policy. Thus, in his celebrated 1951 lectures at the University of Chicago, George Kennan derided those who promoted a "legalistic-moralistic approach to international problems." With some justification, Woodrow Wilson is either hero or villain to these proponents and critics because he believed, as I have written elsewhere, that patriotism was "first of all the duty to defend and, where feasible, to advance democratic principles in the world at large."

Other observers see less lofty motives behind the US human rights policy. They point to the selective attention America paid during the Cold War to human rights abuses abroad. There was no doubt about the message of Secretary of State George Marshall's 1948 address to the UN General Assembly, when he argued that "governments which systematically disregard the rights of their own people are not likely to respect the rights of other nations and other people and are likely to seek their objectives by coercion and force." Yet the US could ignore pernicious abuses in countries which shared its geopolitical interests or whose caudillos were equally afraid of "the worldwide communist conspiracy." This selective defense of human rights, critics argued, evidenced less an overarching attachment to the concept than an appreciation of its tactical value.

However, no study of America's human rights policies would be truly convincing if its author offered such a simple "moralism" versus "realism" dichotomy. First of all, Woodrow Wilson and others who championed international law and the policy of promoting democracy and human rights would maintain that the dichotomy is a false one. It is the ultimate act of self-interest, they would argue, for the United States to help bring about the growth of democracy around the globe. Moreover, there are simply too many variables for this simple bifurcation to capture reality. Even the "mere" 20 years of history of the Helsinki process (the period under study in this book) is too long a period, with too many vicissitudes, to be judged on the basis of only one pair of opposing views. For instance, many personalities—representing many viewpoints—were critical to the evolution of policy, and what might have been true of a Secretary of State in 1975 was most definitely not true in regard to his successor at Foggy Bottom in 1992, or even 1977. In addition, despite the sometimes personal nature of policy development which helps explain events, the impersonal, the structural, bureaucratic aspects of governance are often more critical and must be considered as well. They are certainly more lasting.

William Korey has not permitted his trenchant analysis to become the captive of any single viewpoint. With full appreciation for nuance and complexity, the importance of both individuals and structures, he has shown how US human rights policy evolved in the years 1972-92 within the context of the Helsinki process, which is generally identified with the Conference on Security and Cooperation in Europe. Korey demonstrates how this policy—these policies, really—developed as a synthesis of the various strains of American history and political practice. At various times, human rights policy has been developed according to a Wilsonian calculus; at other times, sometimes at the same time, it was realpolitik that dictated a highly public commitment to promoting personal freedom.

The Helsinki process reflects these divergent strains. CSCE for so many years relied on consensus, an almost Madisonian process of melding the competing interests of individual countries into, if not accord, then at least confluence. With the end of the Cold War (whose demise Korey credits in no small part to the Helsinki process) and new challenges facing Europe, many saw a need for bureaucratization. Over the last several years, more formal structures evolved, a tendency the US at first opposed. The distinguished public servant and long-serving US CSCE Ambassador, Max Kampelman—a hero of this fascinating account—objected to the creation of rigid bureaucratic formulae and the promulgation of documents ("wordsmithing," he called it) divorced from concrete action on specific abuses. Yet, in striking similarity to the decision 200 years earlier to create a Bill of Rights, he had led the US government to the forefront of CSCE's efforts to create what some called "a constitution for Europe."

George Kennan argued that "governing is not a moral exercise, but rather the practical function of maintaining order and discipline in the interest of social stability." Some years later, President Carter responded that if the United States ignored human rights, it would "lose influence and moral authority in the world." Korey shows that through the Helsinki process, US policy reconciled these two statements by pursuing a practical, disciplined moralism.

Daniel Patrick Moynihan

Prologue and Perspective

International agreements at times have had consequences totally unanticipated, indeed, the very opposite of what their drafters intended or expected. The Helsinki Final Act of August 1, 1975, a product of three years of negotiations, is a paradigm of such diplomatic and political irony. When the Conference on Security and Cooperation in Europe (CSCE) was launched 20 years ago, its principal sponsor, the Soviet Union, saw in it and in the agreement it produced the legitimation of the existing territorial and political arrangements in Eastern Europe and, therefore, of Soviet domination of the area. Instead, what happened in consequence of the unfolding "Helsinki process," including the accord's crucial human rights features, was the very crumbling of those arrangements and the collapse of the political and ideological structure upon which they rested.

Intimately related to these momentous dialectical transformations was the role of the United States. That role, like the Helsinki accord itself, was to undergo a remarkable reversal. The United States began as a passive player severely criticized by powerful forces at home for even being involved in the process at all, but through several presidential administrations it moved into an active leadership role centering on the dynamic human rights elements of Helsinki, focusing dramatic public attention upon them and thereby allowing them to exert their maximum influence. No one, whether in or out of the US government, could have expected the ultimate result: the disintegration of the Soviet and communist system in Europe. But that is precisely what did happen. US Helsinki policy eventually, and without specific intention, helped bring about the demise of the Cold War enemy in Eastern Europe.

But America's role in bringing about the political earthquake that shook the European communist world only complemented the small groups of activists, dissenters, and democrats in Eastern Europe who saw in Helsinki, not those security provisions of the Final Act that seemingly froze the status quo, but rather the human rights provisions that would eventually undermine the existing order of things. These activists were the prime movers and shakers, the real heroes of the revolutions of 1989. The US simply gave voice to their criticism, acting as a megaphone for sensitizing great masses of people.

The "new thinking" in Mikhail Gorbachev's glasnost policy was another vital factor in the transformation of Eastern Europe. The extraordinary revolutions in Eastern Europe would simply not have been tolerated by a Kremlin geared to a policy of "old thinking." Nor would trends toward free elections, pluralism, and the rule of law have taken place within the USSR itself without perestroika and new thinking, which to a significant degree were products of the Helsinki process, its language, and its concepts.

What was to be the formal expression of the Helsinki process came into existence on July 3, 1973, when the Conference on Security and Co-operation in Europe was created. It comprised all 33 countries of Europe except Albania, along with the United States and Canada, which by virtue of their membership in NATO had an obvious stake in European security. (It should be noted that the Baltic republics of Estonia, Latvia, and Lithuania had been incorporated into the Soviet Union in 1940, but the United States had never recognized this action.)

It was a resplendent and glittering assemblage of 35 foreign ministers in Helsinki's stark Finlandia House that launched CSCE.[1] Not since the Congress of Vienna in 1815 had so many foreign ministers gathered under one roof to discuss European issues. For over four days—until July 7—the white granite building echoed with speeches sounding the themes of détente. Not only were the NATO and Warsaw Pact powers repre-sented; every neutral and non-aligned country in Europe sent official del-egates. Even tiny San Marino and Liechtenstein were present (as was the Holy See).

Occupying center stage at the stellar gathering was the Soviet Foreign Minister, Andrei A. Gromyko. His speech opened the session, and he had no hesitancy about speaking 50 minutes, twice as long as the agreed-upon time limit. Nor was it surprising that he assumed the leading role, for the conference was a Soviet idea whose time had finally come. It had been initially proposed in 1954 by then Foreign Minister Vyacheslav M. Molo-tov, but fell by the wayside as the East and West military blocs consoli-dated. In 1966, Communist Party General Secretary Leonid Brezhnev resurrected the concept and made it his own, transforming it into the principal objective of the Warsaw Pact meeting in Bucharest that year.

At the core of the concept was the legitimization of Soviet domination of Eastern Europe through Western acceptance of post-war borders in the region. At Helsinki, Gromyko hammered on the theme for a code of conduct that would guarantee respect for "the territorial integrity of all European states in their present frontiers." He also spoke at some length about the need for increased economic cooperation between communist and capitalist countries.

Not surprisingly, Gromyko's speech said nothing about liberalizing daily contacts between the people of East and West, which had been a NATO aim ever since it first started to respond positively to Soviet soundings for a CSCE. At the 35-member preparatory discussions on CSCE begun in Helsinki in November 1972, which had lasted almost two hundred days, the Soviet Union and its allies had indicated a willingness to approve such human contacts. Were they now retreating from this acquiescence? If so, it could mean a stillborn CSCE.

Sir Alec Douglas-Home, the British Foreign Secretary, raised the issue. "If we do not improve the life of ordinary people at the conference," he observed, "we shall be asked—and with justice—what all our fine words and diplomatic phrases have achieved." Sir Alec recalled the great hope of one of his predecessors, Ernest Bevin: ". . . to be able to go down to Victoria Station in London, buy a ticket and go wherever I like without anybody demanding to see my passport." The "freer movement of people and ideas" was to be the key phrase that would symbolize the Western perspective on human rights at CSCE. Greater contacts by freer movement of people were central to the theme of cooperation. (It cannot be too strongly stressed how modest were initial Western objectives, yet "freer movement of people" would become an issue of enormous transcendence in the Helsinki process until 1989.)

But it was not enough for the British simply to make the point about freer movement. Sir Alec warned the Soviets that if progress on human contacts were not achieved, "there will be no alternative but to disperse, acknowledging that the conference was premature." He was supported by other Western foreign ministers, who linked border recognition to greater human contacts. The West German Foreign Minister, Walter Scheel, acidly observed that "the inviolability of frontiers only assumes its full meaning if frontiers do not disturb natural ties and if it is possible to maintain and establish contacts across frontiers." And the Dutch Foreign Minister, Max van der Stoel, went even further, making it clear that the gamut of contacts extended to information and ideas: "We should spare no effort to remove barriers which artificially limit man's own capability."

In contrast to the toughness of the Europeans, and especially the British, US Secretary of State William P. Rogers' presentation was mild. While he supported the West Europeans and emphasized that freedoms were "a fundamental aspect" of the conference, he avoided challenging the USSR and said nothing about negative repercussions for the entire process should progress not be made on human rights matters. Indeed, the White House, guided by National Security Adviser Henry A.

Kissinger, looked upon the CSCE with considerable skepticism and perceived the human rights issue as either inconsequential or unwarrantedly threatening to the Soviet Union.

The restrained performance with respect to human rights of Secretary of State Rogers at the CSCE founding was hardly surprising. President Richard Nixon had viewed relations with Moscow in terms of arms control and economic agreements, not human rights. The "Declaration on Basic Principles of US-Soviet Relations," which he signed in Moscow with Brezhnev on May 29, 1972, carried not a single reference to human rights.[2] Nixon told the US Congress on his return from the Soviet capital that these "Basic Principles" offered a "solid framework for the future development of better American-Soviet relations."[3]

The top State Department official dealing with the proposed CSCE structure, Assistant Secretary Martin Hillenbrand, in testimony before a congressional panel shortly before the Nixon visit to Moscow, carefully avoided any explicit reference to human rights. Instead, he told the subcommittee on Europe of the House Foreign Affairs Committee that "we believe that the [proposed] conference can constitute a modest step forward within a broader and long-range process of negotiation intended to lead to more stable East-West relations. . . ."[4] But these "stable" relationships had no human rights component. Hillenbrand went so far as to publicly dampen hopes for a significant breakthrough by the contemplated conference. "Representatives of some 30 states of diverse interests and regimes," he said, "cannot directly address the central problems of European security."

But the candor of the British carried the day—and the conference. The parties eventually agreed to establish three commissions, one each for security, economic cooperation and "humanitarian contacts," to draw up recommendations for the agenda of the 35-member "permanent" conference to begin that September in Geneva. For unlike the Congress of Vienna, which finalized the structure of post-Napoleonic Europe, the Conference of Helsinki constituted, in the words of Denmark's Knud Andersen, only "a beginning, not an end." Whether the Geneva deliberations would cap the aspirations for détente and move toward freer movement of peoples and ideas remained an open question. Walter Scheel put it bluntly: "If it were shown clearly in the course of our discussions that the gap between our views is still too wide, then I think it would be a dictate of honesty to say so unambiguously."

Two years would elapse before the Helsinki Final Act emerged from the CSCE deliberations. The 40,000-word document signed by the heads of state on August 1, 1975, carried a potential revolutionary theme for Eastern Europe, even if no one was yet fully aware of its implications. For the very first time in an international agreement, respect for human rights and fundamental freedoms was accorded recognition as a fundamental "principle" for regulating relations between states. Elaboration of the principle and of the so-called Basket III, which was designed to give a certain concreteness to the formula "freer movement of people and ideas," added greatly to the power of the revolutionary theme itself.

For political democracies, the concept and language of the Helsinki accord were rather modest. There was no discussion of pluralism and the rule of law—Western standards that define democracy. Civil liberties were not explicitly addressed. Still, for totalitarian structures, where human rights were best characterized by conspicuous absence, the Helsinki accord references could be explosive.

The USSR, unsurprisingly, resisted the language and specifics of human rights at every step of the negotiating process, and the intensity of the opposition of the Soviet Union and its Warsaw Pact allies often led to a softening or a circumscribing of the human rights language, although never to its evisceration. If, in the end, Moscow accepted the language of human rights, it was only because this was the quid pro quo for the West's formal acceptance of post-war territorial arrangements—the "inviolability of borders" and other principles dealing with security.

Even so, the Kremlin was less than enthusiastic about how its negotiators in Helsinki agreed to human rights language.[5] Presumably, they had acquiesced too quickly on certain Western human rights concepts. The principal Soviet negotiator was "punished" by not receiving an expected appointment to an important Communist Party organ. More significantly, as a recent disclosure in a leading Soviet journal made clear, the Kremlin had no intention in 1975 or afterward of honoring the Helsinki accord's references to human rights.[6] Instead, Soviet rulers had reached the decision to "pigeonhole" the human rights obligations. According to the journal, the "conceptual political content" of Helsinki, as related to human rights, would be "practically disregarded."

Meanwhile, the United States played a narrow and limited role in the negotiating process in Helsinki. A major work by a European participant and scholar called the US presence one of detachment, totally consistent with Kissinger's negative outlook on the process.[7] And while there were those in the State Department delegation who recognized the significance of various human rights provisions, only at the end did President Gerald Ford suggest that the White House had a certain awareness of the potential of the Helsinki document. In his address at the formal signing, the President emphasized that it was not the "promises we make" but rather the "promises we keep" that would determine the value of Helsinki.[8]

Ford's closing comment, if it suggested Helsinki's potential, also indicated the lack of Western certainty that the communist East would adhere to the obligations, the "promises" it had undertaken. There is nothing in Kissinger's speeches or writings that expresses the slightest interest in or expectation from the human rights provisions of the Final Act. In his two volumes of memoirs covering the White House years, he dealt with Helsinki only in the context of security considerations, never with respect to human rights.[9] This was not altogether strange, inasmuch as the subject of human rights was alien to his conception of foreign policy. He perceived diplomacy as related to external balance of power considerations, not to the internal conduct of governments.

Indeed, Kissinger considered the US role in the CSCE negotiating process to be largely oriented to "damage control," to preventing agreements between Western Europe and the Soviet Union that could negatively affect perceived US interests. Besides, he characteristically preferred dealing with Moscow in bilateral negotiations, not through multilateral discussions. He very much feared an excessive focus on human rights issues, which could lead to a direct confrontation with the USSR. That would jeopardize his prized bilateral relationship, which was oriented to restricting Moscow's expansion into Africa, Asia, and Central America (as well as seeking its assistance in ending the conflict in Vietnam). As a result of his perception of Helsinki's significance, or rather of its relative insignificance, the State Department, from a public relations viewpoint, deliberately played down the Helsinki Final Act.[10]

President Ford's planned trip to the Finnish capital to join the CSCE heads of state for the Final Act's signature ceremony on August 1 became the focus of a large-scale anti-détente, anti-Soviet and anti-Helsinki public campaign. Mail to the White House ran 10 to 1 urging Ford not to go.[11] A number of the major news media, led by the respected *Wall Street Journal*, editorialized in the same vein.[12] Powerful conservatives from both parties spoke out against Ford's participation; two vocal opponents—both presidential aspirants—were Ronald Reagan, the Republican Governor of California, and the popular Democratic Senator from Washington State, Henry M. Jackson.

Other observers, including the famed Russian novelist Aleksandr Solzhenitsyn, then living in the United States—he had been forcibly exiled from the USSR in violation of clear legal standards—saw Helsinki as a "betrayal" of the peoples of the Soviet Union and of the "captive nations" of Eastern Europe. Some assumed—erroneously—that the signing of Helsinki meant that the United States no longer recognized the independence of Lithuania, Latvia, and Estonia.[13] These opponents saw the Helsinki accord, not in the context of its human rights provisions with their potential revolutionary ramifications, but rather as sanctioning existing territorial and political arrangements.

Much has happened since 1975. George Bush's Secretary of State, James A. Baker III, conspicuously invoked the Helsinki process and CSCE as a major "pillar" of the new "architecture" of Europe and of the "new world order."[14] Hardly anyone speaks any longer of the Helsinki process in hostile terms. Even the consistently acerbic columnist William Safire has stopped attacking Helsinki and has even issued a kind of apologia, rare for him.[15]

By 1990, the letters "CSCE" assumed a prominent place in public discourse on international affairs. If earlier few knew what the initials stood for, now they had become "the sexiest new acronym in international diplomacy," as a prominent informed Washington commentator roguishly observed.[16] Foreign service officers, especially those of the new democracies in East Europe, became absorbed, even obsessed, with the question, Whither CSCE? NATO discussions in Brussels about CSCE were so extensive that one informed diplomat reported that fully one-half of the Brussels agenda was devoted to it.[17] And in 1991 within the splintered former Soviet Union—by then a commonwealth—a high Russian Foreign Ministry official spoke of the need for an "internal CSCE."[18]

Yes, "something" had happened between 1975 and the early 1990s. The United States, at best indifferent to the process at its inception, and the Russians/Soviets, extremely cynical sponsors, had come to clearly embrace Helsinki. How these extraordinary changes have come about is the subject of this study. The focus throughout remains always upon human rights and US policy. Security concerns are examined largely as they bear upon this central nexus, whether explicitly or implicitly. Economic and other aspects of the Helsinki process are largely excluded. Examination of the Helsinki accord, particularly its human rights provisions, is followed by systematic analysis of each Helsinki follow-up meeting—Belgrade (1977-78), Madrid (1980-83), and Vienna (1986-89)—with particular attention to the US role. Prior to Vienna, special human rights experts' meetings were held at Ottawa and Bern. Particular attention has been devoted to each, and some discussion has been given over to other Helsinki experts' meetings. Finally, close attention has been paid to the three meetings of the "Conference on Human Dimension" mandated by the Vienna review meeting—Paris (1989), Copenhagen (1990), and Moscow (1991).

The unique, mainly congressional institution, the Commission on Security and Cooperation in Europe (often referred to as the US Helsinki Commission), played a major role in the early transformation of American policy. Its importance in shaping and affecting US policy, especially in the early years, must not be underestimated; it warrants the fairly lengthy examination given in Chapter 2 and later sections.

The Commission's origins are found in the growing criticism by Congress and the public at large of Kissinger's subordination of human rights to other foreign policy goals. But even as it rejected Kissinger's pragmatic realpolitik, the Commission denied the arguments of the conservative opponents of Helsinki who cried "betrayal." The creators of the Commission, notably Congresswoman Millicent Fenwick and Congressman Dante Fascell, saw in the Final Act the opportunity for exposing human rights violations in Eastern Europe.

Kissinger's opposition to legislation creating the Commission and its effective functioning once in existence was hardly surprising. But a demoralized "Imperial Presidency" following Watergate and the post-Vietnam syndrome of public anger against the administration weakened his resistance, further undermined by the blatancy of Moscow's human rights violations. The Commission, staffed by talented professionals, would come to play a major role in affecting, especially in toughening, and implementing US Helsinki policy. Tension with State Department career officers was inevitable, although with time it would diminish.

The Commission was not only engaged in a large-scale function oriented to foreign policy; it also involved itself in domestic matters when issues related to Helsinki human rights questions were at stake. It successfully helped win a pardon for the "Wilmington Ten" (blacks convicted of a firebombing in Wilmington, North Carolina),[19] publicly advocated US ratification of the Genocide Convention and, more recently, the Covenant on Civil and Political Rights,[20] and played a crucial role in the legislative struggle to kill provisions of the McCarran-Walter Act that denied visas to various categories of foreigners seeking to visit the United States.[21] These initiatives were undertaken in part to counter Soviet arguments made at Helsinki review meetings that the United States could hardly charge others with human rights violations when it was itself engaged in rights abridgements. The Commission also prepared studies of US shortcomings in the human rights field so that they might be rectified;

its 1990 study of homelessness, for example, was a most useful survey of the problem.

But the Commission's major and distinctive mark was made in foreign affairs. It has been an extraordinary institution, unique in the history of American foreign-policy making and unique, too, in the Helsinki community; no other CSCE state created such a body.

There were counterparts of sorts, though—the monitoring Helsinki groups in Eastern Europe, most notably the Moscow Helsinki Watch Group, Charter 77 in Czechoslovakia, and, later, Solidarity in Poland. The way in which these non-governmental organizations (NGOs) and individuals stirred the conscience of the West, partly through the assistance of the Commission, is examined in this study (as are references to the various American non-governmental human rights organizations which worked closely with the Commission, particularly US Helsinki Watch). At the very beginning, some democrats and activists in Eastern Europe hardly rushed to embrace the Helsinki banner. Andrei Sinyavsky, the author of powerful novels of dissent created under the marvelous pseudonym Abram Tertz, related that he wept bitter tears when he first read the Helsinki document. Creative minds among the dissenters, however, soon recognized the significant lever offered by Helsinki's human rights provisions. Sinyavsky himself quickly came to this realization.

Had Gerald Ford won the presidential election in 1976, the impact of the Commission would likely have been modest. With the election of Jimmy Carter, however, human rights immediately became a major element in US foreign policy. Washington reversed its posture on Helsinki from passive and detached observation to activist championing of human rights. Carter's relationship with the Helsinki Commission was close and intimate. To give expression to the new government stance, Carter chose former Supreme Court Justice Arthur Goldberg to represent the United States at Helsinki's first review conference in Belgrade. It was an accidental choice; Goldberg had been initially invited to serve the administration in a different ambassadorial capacity.[22] Only when powerful opposition and infighting within the highest level of the administration's foreign policy establishment killed the initial plan did Carter decide upon the Helsinki-Belgrade appointment.

Although no diplomatist, Goldberg made breakthroughs at Belgrade that proved historic for the Helsinki process. When reviewing implementation practices by all governments, he insisted on the naming of names and the citing of specific cases of human rights violations. Previously, the mentioning of names had been considered taboo in international forums.

Diplomatic tact required presentation of the issue in general terms with, at most, only a hint of which country was the culprit. Goldberg eschewed such niceties in favor of a strategy considered harmful by NATO allies and by career officers in the State Department who worked with NATO (as well as by others who were strong advocates of détente). Additionally, the Justice's abrasiveness, and a certain arrogance, did not endear him to his NATO and delegation colleagues.

Still, Goldberg's accomplishment, in setting a standard of toughness, was considerable. The actual number of specific cases he and his colleagues mentioned at the plenary and in working groups was modest, less than a dozen, although they included major names such as Andrei Sakharov, Yuri Orlov, Anatoly Shcharansky, and the Charter 77 group. But a principle was established and recognized, and no one was surprised when Goldberg's successor named literally hundreds of repressed persons.

If Goldberg failed to reach an agreement with the USSR at Belgrade, it had little to do with his human rights strategy and much to do with Soviet indifference to advancing any reasonable offer that could lead to a trade-off between security and human rights questions. The Soviet Ambassador at the Belgrade talks, Yuli Vorontsov, concentrated largely on propaganda declamations. His attitude to Goldberg had a contemptuous ring; he repeatedly referred to his US counterpart as "the juh-udge,"[23] extending the consonants and vowels to evoke condescension for the former jurist, who presumably did not understand the ways of diplomacy. In private discussions with Goldberg and in public sessions, Vorontsov reflected the hard-line view that Moscow had nothing to learn from the West with respect to human rights questions.[24] More recently, as Mikhail Gorbachev's and then Boris Yeltsin's Ambassador to the UN, Vorontsov has spoken in the accents of glasnost and enlightenment, in sharp contrast to his previously brutish language.

With Max Kampelman's 1980 appointment to lead the US delegation to the Madrid follow-up meeting, America's policy of championing human rights reached a new level of sophistication and effectiveness. He enormously extended the process of mentioning names and cases. Indeed, Kampelman transformed the Helsinki process, which had no formal implementing organ (just as it had no institutional apparatus), into a kind of mechanism of compliance. The repeated, continuous, and precise recitation of examples of repression during the Madrid session held violators of human rights up to public scorn and contempt. Extensive media coverage, especially by the European press, and the almost daily broadcasts into Eastern Europe by Western transmitters, especially Radio Liberty and Radio Free Europe (even if jammed), magnified the negative image.

The impact on public opinion in Europe during the three-year Madrid session cannot be underestimated. Pro-communist and pro-Soviet sentiment was mitigated as reported cases of human rights violation mounted. The ad hoc implementation mechanism played an undefined but significant part in neutralizing popular sentiment in Western Europe against the installation of Pershing II and cruise missiles, deployed to offset the huge Soviet arsenal of SS-20s emplaced in Eastern Europe during the 1970s.[25] The "better red than dead" syndrome in sections of West European public opinion was certainly dealt a strong blow by information emerging from Madrid.

Kampelman's toughness was matched by considerable and natural diplomatic skills which helped him, unlike his predecessor, win over NATO allies to US strategy. He was assisted by Moscow's desire to negotiate an agreement on a French proposal for a CSCE conference on confidence-building measures that would lead to disarmament. (It would be formally entitled CDE—Conference on Disarmament in Europe.) Although the proposal had strong NATO-European support, the US was much more hesitant about it, especially when Ronald Reagan assumed the presidency. But Kampelman eventually used it as a lever to win limited human rights concessions from the Soviet Union.

Two ironies characterize Kampelman's service at Madrid. First, Arthur Goldberg sought to discourage him from accepting the Carter appointment.[26] In Goldberg's opinion, Helsinki had already ceased to be the promise and hope earlier contemplated. The Soviet invasion of Afghanistan in December 1979, the crackdown on dissenters (including Helsinki monitors), and the virtual halting of Jewish emigration constituted a dangerous threat to the Helsinki process. Moreover, he regarded the French proposal not as a potential bargaining chip, but rather as a means of undermining the human rights emphasis of Helsinki. Kampelman rejected the Goldberg plea (just as he rejected a similar recommendation from Kissinger).[27]

Second, in 1975, Kampelman had belonged to the camp of those Democrats led by Senator Henry Jackson who opposed President Ford's signing of the Helsinki Final Act.[28] Carter's National Security Adviser, Zbigniew Brzezinski, found Kampelman's tough anti-communism especially attractive and recommended him for the job.[29] Thus, an initial Helsinki opponent eventually became its most effective partisan. Kampelman's trick was in learning how to use and exploit its provisions. Significantly, Soviet officials at Madrid worked cooperatively with Kampelman even when the Communist Party press in Moscow launched hostile salvos against him.

Kampelman's original negative perception of Helsinki corresponded with the attitude of Ronald Reagan, who, during his election campaign, had urged the United States to boycott the Madrid meeting. Once in office, however, Reagan continued Kampelman's service at Madrid's CSCE talks. Most other ambassadors chosen by Carter, not surprisingly, were not reappointed. Reagan, like Kampelman himself, became a partisan and, by 1988, a strong champion of the Helsinki process. Indeed, during the early 1980s, the third-highest official in the State Department, Lawrence Eagleburger, in formal testimony before the Helsinki Commission, declared Helsinki to be a central element in US foreign policy.[30]

Thus, even during the 1983-86 interval between the end of the Madrid follow-up meeting and the start of the Vienna meeting, when progress in Helsinki's human rights provisions was in a virtual stalemate—indeed, a serious regression had set in—US CSCE policy remained firm. Soviet Jewish emigration, a metaphor for Helsinki's freer movement of people and ideas, was plummeting (as were Soviet German and Soviet Armenian emigration). At the same time, the number of refuseniks and "prisoners of conscience" was rising—although some, like Shcharansky, were released—while a general repression embraced the entire Soviet-dominated East European area.

The negative developments once again reinforced early anti-Helsinki views among some conservative sectors of opinion. Within Congress and even within the Helsinki Commission, voices were raised urging US withdrawal from CSCE. It required favorable testimony on Helsinki to the Commission by the released Shcharansky, a major public hero of the struggle for human rights, to help stymie the "dump Helsinki" trend.

Reflection of the East-West stalemate on human rights could be found in three CSCE meetings specifically on human rights issues—Ottawa, Budapest, and Bern. No agreement was reached at any for a concluding document, although Bern came close to adopting one. The proposed document at Bern appeared to carry some new positive elements, compared with the previous meetings, but in the context of a generally poor human rights *performance* by the USSR, the United States, after a certain confusion, decided at the last minute to veto it, to the dismay of most of its NATO allies. Even with the deadlock, however, the US succeeded in convincing Moscow to allow the emigration for family reunion of several hundred Soviet citizens who were closely related to Americans.

Washington's posture toward Helsinki remained favorable not only because of the modest family reunion achievement, but also as a result of surprising positive developments in 1986 at a CSCE conference on confidence-building measures in Stockholm. In this security area, agreements were reached for reducing the risk of surprise attacks. US policy makers saw Gorbachev's willingness to accede to unprecedented verification procedures, together with his call for a renewal of conventional arms reduction talks that could be brought under the Helsinki umbrella, as the possible opening of a new era in the security field.

But even more was at stake: Washington recognized that the Soviet desire to move more rapidly in the arms control field provided leverage that could be used to stimulate positive steps in the human rights field. If Ottawa, Budapest, and Bern were without results, it was largely because no trade-offs were possible with their strictly human rights agendas. US Secretary of State George Shultz considered that a strategy of linkage between arms control and human rights could produce significant progress at the forthcoming Vienna follow-up meeting. He sold his NATO colleagues on that strategy in December 1986.[31]

Gorbachev's new thinking, which absorbed the language and concepts of Helsinki in the human rights field as it had done in security, partly provided a basis for the success of linkage strategy. The opportunity was further enhanced when Moscow proposed holding a human rights conference in the Soviet capital. If the Soviet Union wanted such a conference badly enough, and if it also anxiously sought conventional arms reduction talks with the West, it would necessarily have to respond to Western demands on human rights. Not until the summer of 1988, after Gorbachev had succeeded in overcoming the powerful opposition of conservative forces in the party, was he able to make his desiderata patently evident.[32]

Implementing US strategy at Vienna was a protégé of Kampelman's, Warren Zimmermann, a highly skilled career officer. The results of Vienna in the human rights field were enormously impressive. Never before in Helsinki's history was so much progress realized. First, with respect to performance—the principal US priority—extremely significant compliance from the USSR was obtained on emigration levels, freeing of political prisoners, and ending foreign radio jamming. (Radio jammers would also soon be shut down by Czechoslovakia and Bulgaria, the principal holdouts among other Warsaw Pact countries.)

Second, the Vienna concluding document was so full of details concerning obligations of the participating states with respect to achieving the historic aim of "freer movement of peoples and ideas" that it far surpassed the Helsinki Final Act, let alone the follow-up Madrid document. What emerged was a document that bordered on "free" movement, especially with respect to movement of people. Very few encumbrances remained. In addition, the Vienna statement provided for the first time in Helsinki history a detailed set of religious and ethnic-cultural rights that could serve as a model for all of Eastern Europe.

Third, Vienna created unprecedented implementation provisions which, although quite modest and limited, nonetheless firmly challenged the traditional argument advanced by the communist powers since the beginning of Helsinki that internal affairs, including a country's human rights practices, were not the concern of the international community. Now the Helsinki signatories acknowledged, if only indirectly, that the issue of human rights was a legitimate concern of the international community.

These signal achievements were very much a triumph of US diplomatic strategy and of its chief architect, George Shultz. The Helsinki Commission would have held out for more concessions from the Soviets in the area of performance, but Shultz was adamant that to press Moscow too hard could have been counterproductive. His timing carried the day, as did his commitment to human rights, which stood 180 degrees away from that of Kissinger.

The new and far higher level of Helsinki standards helped trigger the revolutions in Central and Eastern Europe during the late summer and fall of 1989. The right of anyone to leave any country—the newly accepted standard at Vienna that the United States had insisted upon—became the justification for Hungary's communist government to refuse demands by the East German communist regime that its "vacationing" citizens in Hungary, who were really seeking to travel to West Germany, be returned. The resulting mass exodus of East Germans to the West rocked the supposedly impregnable Berlin Wall and torpedoed Communist Party rule in East Berlin itself.

In Sofia, Bulgaria, democrats and dissidents used the occasion of a Helsinki process meeting on the environment for significant demonstrations that led to the overthrow of Todor Zhivkov's rule. In Czechoslovakia, the talented dramatist Vaclav Havel and his Charter 77 group, which had been brought into existence by the Helsinki accord, guided a great public uprising, the Velvet Revolution, in the democratic seizure of power. Moscow, absorbed in its own new thinking and perestroika, including, in part, adherence to the new Helsinki standard, chose to avoid interfering in the momentous political earthquake which shook its entire East European communist domain, and, a year later, even Albania.

The "inviolability of borders" commitment could not maintain permanently the stability and integrity of communist rule, as Moscow had once imagined it would when it pressed for the Helsinki accord. Governmental stability rested, to a great extent, upon meaningful human rights—such was the ultimate lesson of Helsinki. Just as peace, in the last analysis, was the matter of human rights—as John F. Kennedy once observed—so were stability and legitimacy.

By 1990, the United States pressed for an even higher purpose for Helsinki. A democratic order must stand at the heart of a stable Europe. Without free elections, political pluralism, and the rule of law, societies might once again succumb to totalitarian rule. With Washington's encouragement, the Helsinki process focused on elaboration of a constitutional structure of democratic rights which would safeguard "the new world order."

This was accomplished at the Copenhagen human dimension meeting in June, with Kampelman serving as the principal draftsman of what would come to be called a "Magna Carta" for Europe when sanctioned by a CSCE summit held in Paris in November. The summit also contributed an elaborate institutional structure through which the Helsinki process would henceforth function. If the US had at the very beginning rejected the institutionalization of CSCE (and neither the Helsinki Commission nor Kampelman himself were enthusiastic about the idea, lest it diminish the flexibility of the process), the administration had come to accept the view that the seismic political changes dictated the advisability of incorporating a formalized and regularized structure to the process.

Interwoven into the regularization and institutionalization of the Helsinki process was a vigorous US presence. As early as March 1982, Undersecretary of State Eagleburger had enunciated as central to US policy the theme that Helsinki "gives us a place in a forum which discusses European issues, . . . [which] . . . are in fact American issues as well."[33] As part of the regularization of the Helsinki process, it was agreed to have the heads of state or government meet at summit level at least once every two years, with the first one scheduled for the Helsinki follow-up meeting in 1992. When contrasted with past practice, the frequency of the planned target summit dates highlighted how CSCE had come to occupy a far higher level of prominence: the ceremony of the Helsinki Final Act on August 1, 1975, constituted the initial heads-of-state summit; 15 years elapsed before the second summit was held on November 19-21, 1990.

Equally significant, the foreign ministers of CSCE states would meet as a powerful, policy-making council at least once a year, with the first meeting scheduled for Berlin in June 1991. The previous year—October

1990—the CSCE foreign ministers had met in New York City to approve the agenda of the summit in Paris the following month. But that American session was not termed a council meeting. It was significant in that it constituted the first CSCE meeting on US soil. In earlier years, the foreign ministers never met as a formal group, but did appear on several occasions at the follow-up meetings in Madrid and Vienna. (They did not appear at Belgrade, and some appeared at the beginning of the first human-dimension meeting in Paris in June 1989; all assembled at Copenhagen and Moscow.) The scheduling heretofore had been uncertain and unpredictable. Now its sessions would take on regularity and precision. The upgrading was further enhanced by the establishment of a committee of senior officials from the signatories to prepare the meetings of the council and carry out its decisions. In addition, the committee would review current issues, take appropriate decisions, and make recommendations to the council.

To service the new structure with its regularized meetings, a secretariat for CSCE was created with headquarters in Prague. The new Helsinki bureaucracy would not only organize the frequent meetings; it would also maintain an archive, circulate documents, and provide information to individuals, non-governmental organizations, international organizations, and non-participating states. An administrative apparatus had never existed previously within the Helsinki process; rather, the host countries of summits, follow-up meetings and experts' conferences had provided on an ad hoc basis a small number of functionaries from their respective foreign ministries.

Two additional bureaucracies were created. One, called the Conflict Prevention Center, to be situated in Vienna, was to focus on security and military concerns. The object of the Center was the promotion of confidence in security matters and of predictability and transparency in military questions. Exchanges of military information, including reports about unusual military activities, would be a key element in the furtherance of this aim. In addition, the Center would facilitate the conciliation of disputes between CSCE members. A second apparatus, entitled the Office for Free Elections, to be housed in Warsaw, was set up to facilitate election practices in East European countries and serve as a clearinghouse on electoral procedures.

The democratic human rights objective was to be augmented by the creation of some type of parliamentary framework. As all East European countries had now embraced representative systems, a mechanism to facilitate involvement and exchanges among parliamentarians was projected. However, the framework would be structured not by governments per se, but rather through contacts between parliamentary bodies.

CSCE had become an instrumentality in virtually continuous session. Follow-up meetings, a vital feature of the Helsinki accord, would be maintained. But instead of three-year intervals between follow-up meetings, they would now be held at two-year intervals. The duration of each session was to be not more than three months. Longer sessions need no longer be held, as CSCE would itself be continuous.

Still, for the United States, the extension and reinforcement of democracy retained the highest priority. At Moscow in September-October 1991, where the last of Helsinki's human-dimension meetings was held, a final burial of the old order was effected. A principal achievement of the conference was acceptance of a US proposal for creating an "Office for Democratic Institutions," to encompass and supersede the Office of Free Elections. When implemented several months later, it was called the Office for Democratic Institutions and Human Rights, which clearly demonstrated America's perspective for the future.

Another problem, however, preempted most of the attention at Moscow and during the prior twelve-month period. The demise of the communist system had brought in its wake a long-suppressed but now explosive nationalism. One coefficient of the new xenophobia was a virulent racism which saw the Jew or Gypsy or immigrant worker as the target for national hate. The predominant expression of intense national outbursts in multinational societies—notably in Yugoslavia and the USSR—was a drive for self-determination which inevitably meant secession or conflict or both.

To cope with the escalating racism and deepening nationalism, the Moscow meeting formally sanctioned an elaborate mechanism of mediation and fact finding that more deeply interred the long-standing and questionable Soviet claim alleging criticism of domestic practices to be unacceptable intervention in the internal affairs of states. Even as the mechanism was formulated, it was designed to also embrace serious human rights problems. The United States stood very much in the forefront of the initiative, particularly insofar as mediation was concerned.

What is stunningly evident is that two fundamental, almost axiomatic, features of the Helsinki process had all but been discarded by the end of 1991. First, no longer can a CSCE state claim that the Helsinki Final Act precludes criticism of domestic human rights situations. At Moscow, it was agreed—and emphatically so—"issues relating to human rights, fundamental freedoms, democracy and the rule of law are of international concern."[34] Therefore, the CSCE states "categorically and irrevocably de-clare" that Helsinki human rights commitments, both old and new, are the "legitimate concern of all participating states and do not belong ex-clusively to the internal affairs of the state concerned."

Even more significant was the inroad made into the sacred principle of consensus that had guided all previous CSCE decisions, resolutions, and actions. Any single state could veto a near-unanimous agreement. Now, if the issue involves the condition of human or minority rights in a particu-lar CSCE country, a group of other CSCE states, ranging from six to ten, can mandate sending a special fact-finding and observation mission from outside the area. Even when the targeted state objects, it cannot prevent the initiative.

The inroad was further extended by a decision taken at the level of the Council of Foreign Ministers of CSCE with reference to the calling of "emergency" meetings of the executive authority—the Committee of Senior Officials (CSO). A CSO emergency session can be called when a single CSCE state, backed by 12 others, deems the situation in a particu-lar state warrants it. Such "emergency" sessions have been called to deal with the military conflict in Yugoslavia. Not surprisingly, the mechanism would come into play as self-determination assumed a major feature of the European scene and of Helsinki debates. Eventually, the views of a gross violator of minority rights would be disregarded altogether in deci-sion making, and the violator could even be suspended from the process.

Self-determination, if an indirect consequence of a burgeoning nation-alism, was at the same time intimately linked to two aspects of the Helsinki process. For one thing, the right of self-determination was spelled out in the basic principles of the Helsinki accord, although the West had initially "translated" that right to mean the prevention of fur-ther application of the "Brezhnev Doctrine." For another, and here the sanction was clearer, the Helsinki process's canonization of free elections as the highest value virtually guaranteed cries for self-determination in multinational states.

Yet, what the self-determination drive produced could have the conse-quence of striking at the basic foundations of the stability that was now rooted in a democratic structure and system. (In some instances, self-determination, by easing an otherwise explosive nationalism, might have the effect of promoting stability.) And it could thereby severely challenge the significance and strength of the new institutional apparatus, which was too embryonic to have acquired the means for coping with the po-tency of the nationalist challenge. Whether and how nationalist impulses could be effectively dealt with so that stability can be restored or maintained is an open question for which there is an uncertain future. While the Helsinki process has been the tocsin of freedom in the past, it was by no means certain that it will continue to be so in the future.

The United States, through Woodrow Wilson, was the intellectual source of self-determination aspiration and ideology. But in the Helsinki process, Washington found it difficult, if not impossible, to systematically apply the Wilsonian logic, lest it subvert the democracy-based stability with which it now sought to replace the old totalitarian status quo. Frequent wavering and contradictions prior to and during the Moscow meeting characterized US Helsinki policy on this issue, in contrast to a fundamental consistency that had distinguished America's human rights policy.

The Moscow meeting, coming so soon after an abortive right-wing coup in the USSR, provided participants and observers alike with an unsettling view of the not-too-distant future. How would the CSCE be affected by the breakup of the Soviet state, the initiator of the CSCE process, into 15 separate republics? Already, with the admission of Estonia, Latvia, and Lithuania at the beginning of the meeting, the 35 members of the Helsinki process became 38. How would it cope with the quite sizable addition of former Soviet republics and former Yugoslav states? Aside from the unwieldiness of the membership, there was the question of what Kampelman called the "chemistry" resulting from the new ingredients. The tradition of democracy and human rights, the centerpiece of the Helsinki process, is not very deep in the most western parts of the former USSR; in the six successor Moslem republics of Central Asia and the Caucasus, the tradition is even more tenuous.

For the United States, the guideline for the admission of successor states would be their adherence to "five fundamental principles" propounded by Secretary of State Baker in his address at Moscow (and repeated in December 1991 in a major address at Princeton University). First, a country must conduct itself in accordance "with democratic values and practices." Second, it must "respect existing borders, internal and external," with any changes made "by peaceful and consensual means." Third, it must support "the rule of law" and achieve "peaceful change" through "democratic processes, especially elections." Fourth, it must "safeguard human rights," including "the equal treatment of minorities." (Specified here is the point that "leaders at all levels of government must forthrightly condemn and combat racial and ethnic hatred [and]-anti-Semitism. . . .") And, finally, it must respect "international law and obligations, especially adherence to the provisions of the Helsinki Final Act and the Charter of Paris."

If the US initially waffled on the self-determination issue, it remained consistent on the issue of human rights and democracy. That consistency was capped by the triumphant phrase Baker used to characterize the Moscow meeting—"Democracy's Season." He made the phrase the very title of his speech. It could be sharply contrasted with the speech of a predecessor, William Rogers, at the founding CSCE session in Helsinki nearly two decades earlier. Not once did the latter use the word "democracy," while the phrase "human rights" was mentioned only in passing. Nor did these terms enter into the discourse of President Nixon or his principal foreign policy adviser, Henry Kissinger, when commenting upon Helsinki at its birth. An entire eon had been traversed in the course of a rather short time frame.

The climactic "Democracy's Season" symbolized the new challenges posed by Europe that had been transformed by CSCE. The first stage of Helsinki was over; its second stage was beginning. New promises were being made; would they, could they, be kept?

▪1▪

Origins of the Helsinki Accord and US Policy[1]

onathan Swift's satiric novel *Gulliver's Travels* provided the source for the key question asked about the Helsinki Final Act at the very beginning. Was the 60-page, 40,000-word document adopted on August 1, 1975, at a summit of European and North American leaders of the Conference on Security and Cooperation in Europe Brobdingnag or Lilliput? Such was the query posed by a State Department legal insider who had played a role in the drafting of the Act.[2] After a lengthy, scholarly analysis, he was scarcely certain as to whether the document would be regarded by future generations as a giant "historical event" or a mere Lilliputian incident.

Certainly, the summit itself lent a Brobdingnagian quality to the Final Act. Researchers at *Time* found the stellar character of the gathering in Helsinki totally unprecedented; never before had there assembled in one place so many chiefs of state and principal national leaders for a single purpose.[3] Every European state except Albania—33 in all—was represented by its highest or dominant political figure. To this total were added the Prime Minister of Canada and the President of the United States, both present by virtue of their respective nations' membership in NATO.

In stunning contrast to this extraordinarily impressive assemblage was the US media presentation of the solemn ceremony. In important sections of the press, the Helsinki Final Act was treated as either meaningless or a betrayal of United States interests, as well as of the interests of the people of Eastern Europe. On the eve of the Helsinki meeting, the headline in the lead editorial of the respected *Wall Street Journal* read "Jerry, Don't Go!" That perspective, urging President Gerald Ford not to attend, was echoed in other major press organs, as well as by leading public figures and, indeed, by much of the public at large, if one is to judge by the mail received by the White House.[4] Conventional wisdom held the

Helsinki accord to be "a defeat for the West." The words were those of a top US diplomatic establishment figure, George Ball, but it could have been uttered by numerous other American political and diplomatic authorities.[5]

Judgment in the United States about the meaning and significance of the Helsinki accord at the time was largely based upon the belief that the Final Act gave the Kremlin precisely what it had sought—a freezing of the status quo in Eastern Europe—without extracting any important concession in return. Few were aware of the valuable, even historic, sections on human rights in the Final Act; indeed, the largest single segment in the various "Principles" of the agreement was devoted to human rights. In addition to Principle VII specifying "human rights and fundamental freedoms," a crucial section on "human contacts" in Basket III had considerable rights implications.

Little public attention had been paid to what were, in any case, the closed deliberations over a three-year period in Geneva and Helsinki which had led to the Final Act. Thus, the potential significance of human rights in the document went unnoticed. To deepen the prevailing ignorance further, the State Department, under the direction of Secretary of State Henry Kissinger, consciously and deliberately played down both the significance of the Final Act and how it served US purposes. The official minimization of Helsinki was done on both a private and public level.

Reasons for the downplaying varied. Kissinger had never been enthusiastic about the Helsinki process, and saw US diplomacy related to the process largely as "damage control." Secondly, détente, of which the Helsinki accord was a quintessential expression, had appeared to have run its course. The fall of Saigon and the collapse of the South Vietnam regime brought bitterness and confusion in their wake. A communist victory in Asia was seemingly compounded by the threat of a possible communist takeover of Portugal in Western Europe. The very word "détente" was taboo in administration circles. Finally, lest excessive expectations about the Helsinki accord be raised publicly, official Washington thought the less said the better.

A private conversation among Western diplomats at Helsinki several hours after the solemn signing ceremonies testifies to the uncertainty of how Helsinki would be viewed in history. As recorded by an American participant, one said: "Well, they signed it." Another said: "And now it will be buried and forgotten." "No," responded a colleague, "you are wrong. We have started something."[6]

The "something" turned out to be revolutionary. The Helsinki process contained within it the human rights ideas which, when effectively grasped and utilized, would ultimately topple the totalitarian structures of Eastern Europe together with the Berlin Wall which had partitioned East from West. A decade after the formation of CSCE, Secretary of State George Shultz glimpsed the potential outcome of the process: "In the most profound sense, the Helsinki process represents an historic effort to erode the cruel divisions between East and West in Europe."[7] He added that it is the purpose of the "process" to bring "freedom" and "human dignity" to all people. He could have further noted that stability of regimes and borders, which some perceived as a major objective of Helsinki, rested in the last analysis upon human rights.

At the core of the new continental system that would emerge following the revolutions of 1989 stood the sanctity of human rights, as enunciated in Helsinki documents. It would be augmented by an elaborate structure of democracy, including political pluralism and the rule of law, as provided by the unfolding Helsinki process. Inherent in that process was the aspiration for self-determination which would unite two separate Germanys, even as it would shortly afterward split asunder multinational Yugoslavia and torpedo the centralized Soviet empire.

But in August 1975 few perceived the amazing possibilities offered by the Final Act and the Helsinki process. The Helsinki accord's milestone character was simply not comprehended in the West. If there was exultation anywhere, it was found in the Kremlin and among its Warsaw Pact allies.

Izvestiia hailed it as the greatest event since the defeat of Hitler's armies, terming the Final Act "a law of international life."[8] Leonid Brezhnev spoke of its "historic significance," in which "millions upon millions of people" are conscious of its "political sweep." Polish Communist Party boss Edward Gierek called it a "major historic event"; Czechoslovak leader Gustav Husak said it was "unique in history in its significance"; Bulgarian ruler Todor Zhivkov called it "remarkable"; and Erich Honecker, party chief in East Germany, called it a victory of "reason."[9]

Soviet and East European enthusiasm for the Final Act was hardly surprising. The idea had been promoted initially by the USSR. As early as February 1954, Soviet Foreign Minister V. M. Molotov had suggested an all-European treaty of collective security, and the following November the Kremlin formally proposed the convening of a European Security Conference. Two principal motivations were then at work: preventing the emergence of West Germany as a military power, and reducing or ending the United States presence in Europe. These aims masked a crucial third one: assuring the status quo in Eastern Europe. With the emergence a decade later of Leonid Brezhnev as General Secretary of the Soviet

Communist Party, the concept of a Conference on Security and Cooperation in Europe began to take true shape. In a real sense, he is the father of
the Helsinki accord, as the Soviet press glowingly recognized on the occasion of his 75th birthday in December 1981.

At the 23rd Soviet Communist Party Congress in March-April 1966,
Brezhnev (along with Premier Aleksei Kosygin) outlined specific proposals for a CSCE. The purposes were delineated as settling the German
question, recognizing the post-war borders in Europe, developing cooperation, achieving arms reduction, and removing the presence of foreign
(i.e., non-European) troops. On April 2, Foreign Minister Andrei Gromyko explicitly challenged the "permanent status" of the "American
Army" in Europe. About this question, he insisted, "the peoples of Europe are having and will continue to have their say. . . ."[10]

The Warsaw Pact's Political Consultative Committee, meeting in July
1966 in Bucharest, endorsed the Brezhnev line by calling for a European
conference that excluded the United States and Canada and that would
recognize the borders in Europe (including those of the German Democratic Republic).[11] The Bucharest declaration, for the first time, spoke of
the need to foster greater cooperation between East and West in science,
technology, art, and culture. The following year, European communist
parties meeting in Karlovy Vary, Czechoslovakia, echoed the call for a
European Security Conference and cited the solution of the German
problem as its main task.

The appeals from the East did not fall on deaf ears in the West. The
fear of nuclear war, the growing trade relations between East and West,
and a certain easing of tensions during the mid-1960s had prompted an
emerging interest in dialogue. One critical stipulation was made by
NATO: the United States and Canada must be part of any European security conference.

The US reacted with both skepticism and coolness to the project, but
West European interest intensified. Even the Soviet invasion of Czechoslovakia in 1968 did not seriously reduce the Western interest. From the
Soviet viewpoint, the Czechoslovak experience stirred a more intense determination to move ahead on the security conference, no doubt with the
intention of improving its tarnished image as a ruthless oppressor. Willy
Brandt's *Ostpolitik* of 1969 gave the interest a solid national base. In December 1969, NATO's response paralleled, to a significant degree, the
Bucharest declaration. It proposed that the subject of environment be
added to the pan-European issues requiring a cooperative effort. More
importantly, the NATO declaration mentioned for the first time that a

European conference should deal with the subject of freer movement of people, information and ideas. During 1970, the dialogue continued through respective communiqués—the Warsaw Pact powers meeting in Budapest, the NATO members meeting in Rome. In Rome, NATO emphasized that such a conference must include the freer movement of people, ideas, and information in the cultural, economic, technical, and scientific fields, as well as in the field of human environment.

With the dialogue through communiqués beginning to reflect the détente evidenced elsewhere by the thawing relations of the United States and USSR, West European governments became increasingly intrigued at the prospect of discussing future relations with the East on a broad basis including, on the one hand, humanitarian issues, and on the other, confidence-building measures to avoid or deter surprise military attack. The dialogue had begun to gradually shape the focus of a possible Conference on Security and Cooperation in Europe. Once the German question was settled, a precondition established by the allies, the groundwork could be laid for CSCE.

The signature of the Quadripartite Agreement on Berlin by the USSR, Britain, France, and the United States came on September 3, 1971. This was crucial from the NATO viewpoint. The next year, West Germany reached renunciation-of-force agreements with Poland and the USSR. A culminating treaty between West Germany and East Germany came at the end of the year. By then, too, agreement had been reached for Mutual and Balanced Force Reduction talks (MBFR) covering Central Europe to begin in January 1973 in Vienna.

Détente in Central Europe, together with the assurance of the Western presence in Berlin, moved the dialogue to a new level. With the USSR acquiescing to the participation of the United States and Canada in European security talks, a formal Conference on Security and Cooperation in Europe could be initiated. The German problem may have been resolved and, in this way, a critical Soviet objective had been realized, but Moscow still sought NATO sanction for the post-war borders of Eastern Europe, utilizing the language of the German renunciation-of-force treaties. It was given a stronger urgency by the Chinese-Soviet border tensions that had continued after armed clashes in 1969. "Inviolability of borders" in Europe was to be the cry of Moscow as it pressed for CSCE.

Preparatory meetings on CSCE were held in Helsinki beginning in September 1972. The initial period of gestation was nine months, as the conflicting visions of détente brought out tactical compromises. What emerged was a 17-page document entitled "Final Recommendations of the Helsinki Consultations."[12] The principal recommendation was the establishment of the CSCE forum. Three stages were envisaged. The foreign ministers of the United States, Canada, and the European countries would meet in Helsinki in July 1973 to adopt formally the "Final Recommendations," and constitute themselves as the Conference on Security and Cooperation in Europe. This largely ceremonial affair would be designated as Stage One and last but a few days. Stage Two was to embrace a much longer period, as a detailed accord reflecting both détente and the dialogue of the Warsaw Pact and NATO communiqués. The CSCE discussions would be held in Geneva from September 1973 to July 1975, and culminate in Stage Three—a Final Act signed in solemn ceremony in Helsinki on August 1, 1975.

The two years of deliberations, frequently heated, at times deadlocked, and rarely expressing a common set of values, produced the extraordinary Helsinki Final Act.[13] It was the quintessential expression of détente, carefully balancing the security concerns (and trade objectives) of the East with the human rights aims of West Europe. The neat balance was reflected in ten fundamental principles—at times called the Decalogue— that were designed to regulate the relations between the Conference signatories. The major aim of the Warsaw Pact powers was realized in Principle III, "Inviolability of Frontiers." The Kremlin and its satellites saw it as legitimizing the post-war borders of Eastern Europe. The other principles in which they had a keen although not exclusive interest were Principle II—"Refraining from the Threat or Use of Force"; Principle IV—"Territorial Integrity of States"; and Principle VI—"Non-intervention in Internal Affairs."

In two respects, however, the Soviet purpose of freezing the status quo in Eastern Europe did not totally succeed. The Federal Republic of Germany, supported by the West, was insistent that "inviolability of frontiers" could not and must not mean that the reunion of the two Germanys by peaceful means was precluded. The USSR refused to have any modification introduced into Principle III itself, but did agree to a "floating sentence" that "participating states consider that their frontiers can be changed only in accordance with international law by peaceful means and by agreement."[14] The "floating sentence" was "registered" (i.e., provisionally agreed to) at the same time as the "inviolability" principle. The idea of the peaceful change of frontiers in accordance with international law was eventually incorporated into Principle I, dealing with sovereignty and equality of states. On the eve of the signing of the Helsinki Final Act, West German Foreign Minister Hans-Dietrich Genscher told the Bundestag: "The Conference has not finalized the status quo in Europe. And what the Conference did not do by texts we should not do by words."[15]

In addition, Principle VIII provided for "self-determination of peoples," which allowed "all peoples . . . to determine, when and as they wish, their internal and external political status without external interference." This principle was vigorously opposed by the USSR as a right associated with the aspiration of colonial peoples, not those of Europe. The West insisted on keeping the principle, not only to permit the possible unification of the Germanys, but also to preclude the reapplication of the Brezhnev Doctrine that had sanctioned Soviet military intervention to crush the "self-determination" of Alexander Dubcek's "communism with a human face" in Czechoslovakia.

In contrast to the East's emphasis upon Principle III, the West's basic striving was summed up in Principle VII: "Respect for human rights and fundamental freedoms, including the freedom of thought, conscience, religion or belief." It constituted a milestone in international diplomacy. For the first time in history, an international agreement formally recognized human rights as a fundamental principle in regulating relations between states. West European delegations, notably those from the United Kingdom, France, the Federal Republic of Germany, the Netherlands, Italy, and Denmark, were largely responsible for this development. They were vigorously supported by a number of neutral countries, including Austria, Sweden, and Switzerland. In contrast, the role of the United States was hardly a prominent one.

In addition to its landmark character, Principle VII incorporated three basic concepts alien to Soviet tradition and practice and which, therefore, set a major standard toward which the populace in East Europe might aspire.[16] The second paragraph of the Principle carried language specifying "the inherent dignity of the human person." It was introduced by Switzerland to express the Western concept that human rights are inherent in the human condition and not simply a privilege extended by the state, which, of course, was the basic view held by the Warsaw Pact powers.

The second concept established, albeit somewhat indirectly, the dependence of détente upon human rights. The text described human rights as "an essential factor for the peace, justice and well-being necessary to insure the development of friendly relations and cooperation. . . ." The formulation reversed the hierarchical priorities of the communist world, which made all progress and relationships dependent upon détente. Thirdly, Principle VII offered for the peoples of totalitarian and authoritarian regimes, in which the state commands the media and determines what information is appropriate, the revolutionary notion that an individual has a right "to know and act upon his rights. . . ." Once grasped in Eastern Europe, the idea could constitute a challenge to the authorities that was potentially explosive.

Equally important, in terms of human rights, was Basket III—"Cooperation in Humanitarian and Other Fields." The first "basket" (an odd term, suggested by the Netherlands, which stuck and became part of the language of Helsinki) dealt with security and, particularly, confidence-building measures to promote security (in addition to the ten principles). Basket II was concerned with the advancement of trade and the removal of obstacles to its realization. Basket III, in contrast to the other two, was exclusively a Western proposal (and, indeed, an existing standard in the West), and was aimed at fulfilling the aspiration elsewhere of "freer movement of people and ideas." The basket embraced four sections: human contacts; information; cooperation and exchanges in the field of culture; and cooperation and exchanges in the field of education.

The centerpiece of Basket III was the human contacts section, in which the key phrase was "reunion of families." It became a euphemism for emigration, at least with respect to family and kin. Final Act signatories pledged themselves to "deal in a positive and humanitarian spirit with persons who wish to be reunited with members of their family." Signatories were further obliged to "facilitate" and "expedite" the granting of visas, to charge only moderate sums for visas, and to refrain from reducing or removing the rights of those seeking to emigrate. The significant implications of this language for East European governments were self-evident.

As important as the incorporation of human rights obligations in the Final Act was the linkage of such obligations to other aspects of the accord. The Act stipulated that *all* of its ten principles were of "*primary* significance and, accordingly, they will be *equally* and unreservedly applied, each of them being interpreted *taking into account* the others" (emphasis added). Thus, human rights were formally considered under the accord as important as security, to be taken into account when dealing with the latter. Similarly, linkage meant that there would have to be a balance in treating with the three baskets. None of the baskets, whether security, trade, or human rights, was to be considered as more important than the other two. And, indeed, in acting upon any of the baskets, one would have to take account of the others.

Clearly, linkage was perceived as being at the very heart of détente. To the extent that détente was considered indivisible, reciprocation was indispensable. Accommodation in one field required a commensurate response in another. Progress in Basket I on security or in Basket II on trade necessitated a corresponding advance in Basket III on human rights. Indeed, the history of the Final Act reflected the linkage principle. The decision to create a CSCE was itself a trade-off between security and human rights. And the discussions of 1972-75 were an endless series of bargaining sessions revolving around these considerations. Clearly, the Kremlin accepted human rights as a negotiable item on the international agenda, even if only as a bargaining chip.

Yet, the Soviet acquiescence did not come easy or quickly. The Kremlin resistance to human rights provisions during 1972-75 debates within CSCE was intense and prolonged.[17] The USSR delegation consistently attempted to circumscribe or diminish or emasculate the human rights clauses. The first major threat was advanced in a discussion of the preamble to Basket III. The Soviets sought to use language of Principle I—covering sovereignty and rights inherent in sovereignty which enabled a state to determine its own "laws, regulations and customs"—and vigorously demanded that the reference go into the preamble to Basket III. The aim was patently self-evident: to the extent that Soviet "laws, regulations and customs" were not in consonance with Basket III provisions, the latter were nullified within the USSR.

The West, with the behind-the-scenes encouragement of the United States, resisted the debilitating initiative.[18] The delegation of Finland worked out a key compromise—the "Finnish compromise"—that provided for a preambular insertion that made specific reference to Principle I. Since the West, and especially the neutrals, were concerned about the possible misuse of the "compromise" by Moscow, they pressed successfully for new language (sponsored by Sweden) in Principle X, which, after granting the right to states to determine their own laws, nonetheless obligated the signatories to "pay due regard to and implement the provisions of the Final Act of the Conference on Security and Cooperation in Europe." The Soviet attempt to nullify Basket III was quashed.

The second Kremlin attempt at circumscribing the human rights provisions was made in connection with Principle VI—non-intervention in internal affairs. The Warsaw Pact negotiators made an extraordinary effort in terms of time and energy to build escape clauses into Basket III through specific references to Principle VI. Western negotiators tried to shape the principle so that it would be limited to intervention by some form of coercion. In this connection, it should be emphasized that the West was intent upon having the Final Act carry a strong statement on "non-intervention," if only to nullify the Brezhnev Doctrine from an international law standpoint. Thus, a delicate balance in the wording was essential to serve different purposes.

The text of Principle VI ended up by carrying the term "coercion" (in its third paragraph), which was perceived as clarifying what was meant by "intervention." Thus diplomatic demarches or other forms of government complaints about violations of Basket III provisions could be legitimized on grounds that they could hardly be described as "coercion." But even with this insertion, the Soviets would not hesitate to later use Principle VI to neutralize Principle VII.

The third Soviet effort focused upon the awkward title of Principle VII. The USSR deliberately supported the language of the title because it would parallel the language of Article 18 of the International Covenant on Civil and Political Rights. Paragraph 3 of the Covenant's Article 18 established sharp limitations on the exercise of freedom of religion on grounds of protecting "public safety, order, health, or morals or the fundamental rights and freedom of others." Moscow hoped to use the escape clauses of the Covenant to weaken the human rights provisions of the Final Act. The Soviet delegation first pushed for language which would stipulate that Principle VII should be "in accordance with" the Covenant. When that failed, Moscow then tried to write the escape clauses directly into the text. That, too, did not succeed. Principle VII merely carries a subsidiary reference to the Covenant only in the sense that contracting parties to it are called upon to "fulfill their obligations."

Nonetheless, later on the Kremlin would pull out the Covenant's escape clauses to justify abridgement of freedom. And this in the face of the priority language of the Final Act that required governments to act "in conformity with . . . the Universal Declaration of Human Rights," a document without escape clauses.

That the USSR, even if defeated on human rights issues during 1973-75, felt that the adopted clauses constituted no threat for the foreseeable future and that the Final Act as a whole was a major historic contribution to its strategic objectives is evidenced by the intriguing position it took on the status of the Helsinki accord under international law. A key and burning question at the CSCE meetings was whether the Helsinki Final Act would be regarded as a legally binding document. While almost all delegations thought that the Final Act clauses should be considered morally compelling, they did not initially see them as legally binding. As the negotiations proceeded, more and more enthusiasm was registered by the delegates for an emphasis upon language that at least implied the document was a legally binding instrument.

The trend was a cause of concern to the US delegation, which was keenly aware of the predisposition of Congress to question the right of the President to conclude important international agreements without its consent. Moreover, and far more significantly, the administration was at best quite indifferent to the Final Act; at worst, it considered that US strategy should be geared to damage limitation. A legally binding treaty was the last thing desired.

It was the British who initially used the phrase "Final Act" (later taken up by the Netherlands) in order to create the presumption that the document was intended to be a legally non-binding instrument. But, given the US determination to make evident the non-binding character of the Final Act, its delegation as well as the British supported a West German proposal that a clause in the act be inserted stipulating that the instrument was not a treaty susceptible to registration under Article 102 of the Charter of the United Nations.

The USSR, Switzerland and Romania resisted the initiative as unnecessarily denigrating the results of the conference. These countries proposed that the language in the accord should define only what the Final Act was, not what it was not. A compromise proposal provided for a paragraph that "requested" Finland to transmit the Final Act to the Secretary-General of the United Nations. But even this was not satisfactory to the United States, which, along with Britain and West Germany, insisted upon the drafting of a letter stating what the document "is not" and which the Finnish government would use in forwarding the document to the UN Secretary-General. The USSR opposed all such negative language. Only after many hours of difficult discussions was a satisfactory letter prepared which made the point that the Final Act was a legally non-binding document.

Nonetheless—and strikingly—the USSR chose to regard the Final Act as virtually having a juridically binding character. At Helsinki, Brezhnev declared that his assumption was that all the countries "will implement the undertakings reached;"[19] as for the USSR, "it will act precisely in this manner." The statement was repeated almost verbatim in a joint announcement issued on August 6 by the Politburo, the Supreme Soviet Presidium and the Council of Ministers. Two days later, *Izvestiia* declared that the Helsinki principles should be "made a law of international life" not to be breached by anyone.[20]

The most precise Soviet statement on the juridical character of Helsinki was made in the November 1975 issue of the Soviet journal *New Times* by well-known Soviet commentator Valentin Yaroslavtsev: "The signatures affixed to the Final Act have also a legal significance—they made it a binding international document."[21] The firmness of the Soviet legal commitment was given special emphasis in the closing communiqué of the October 1975 meeting between French President Valéry Giscard d'Estaing and Brezhnev in Moscow. They declared "their resolve to observe strictly and to implement in all fields" the principles of Helsinki. They also expressed their intention "to implement fully all the provisions of the Final Act," including those in the humanitarian fields.[22]

The emphasis on the binding character of Helsinki was in keeping with the Kremlin's determination to maintain the post-war status quo in Europe. But did it apply to the human rights clauses? Brezhnev himself appeared to have second thoughts about the question when he met on August 15, two weeks after Helsinki, with 18 US congressmen in Yalta. He was quoted as distinguishing between some provisions of Helsinki which had "a binding nature" while others would be "fulfilled according to agreements reached on the part of the [participating] states."[23] He specifically mentioned the information clause in Basket III. Only "as time goes on," he observed, would the fulfillment be realized "according to agreements."

The Brezhnev distinction was raised two days later by US presidential aspirant Terry Sanford, at the time visiting Premier Kosygin in the Kremlin.[24] Sanford reported that Kosygin rejected any distinction and "went to some length to stress that they intended to be bound by the total agreement." Brezhnev himself appeared to drop the distinction at a Polish Communist Party Congress in December 1975. He told his audience that "we stand for putting into practice the concrete points of the Final Act."[25]

Contemporary international legal scholars, interestingly, were somewhat more inclined to the early Brezhnev interpretation about the accord being legally binding than to the American and Western positions advanced during 1973-75. Thus, after an extensive survey of the existing international legal literature, the French scholar Alexandre Charles Kiss and co-worker Mary F. Dominick concluded in 1980 that the Helsinki Final Act "falls within a special category of international legal instruments not anticipated by traditional definitions of the sources of international law—that is, non-binding, but *directive* texts which produce limited legal effects."[26] Another expert, Jordan J. Paust, emphasized the notion that the Final Act was more than a "non-binding instrument." It had an "interpretative" quality that could play an important role "by furthering and perhaps reshaping patterns of legal expectation concerning human rights."[27] Such interpretations came to reflect subsequent views of US and other Western delegations at Helsinki review meetings even as they started being rejected by Warsaw Pact delegations.

During 1973-75, the Kremlin not only pressed for a legally binding interpretation of the Final Act; it sought to give the Conference on Security and Cooperation in Europe a permanent institutional form, a sort of European Security Council that would be serviced by a permanent secretariat operating from a permanent headquarters.[28] The secretariat would have numerous functions, including the issuance of regular reports on implementation of what was hoped would be legally binding obligations. As Western delegations, especially the United States, were reluctant to accept Helsinki as a juridically binding agreement, so, too, were they suspicious about any institutionalization of CSCE. From their perspective, the creation of permanent central organs would have given Moscow a toehold in Western security concerns. Moreover, many saw the institutionalization as a possible device by the USSR to exclude the US from Europe or reduce its influence, an early Kremlin objective.

Denmark proposed a compromise in the form of "review meetings" which would "continue the multilateral process" through a "thorough exchange of views" on the "implementation of the provisions of the Final Act" and on the programs for "deepening" mutual relations, "improvement" of security, and "development" of both cooperation and "the process of détente in the future." Only one review meeting was specified—that in Belgrade—but this one would "define the appropriate modalities for the holding of other meetings." What was seen as a modest device for blunting Soviet insistence upon institutionalization ultimately became a means which the West could and would use effectively and about which the USSR would become increasingly wary and even hostile.

But, "we didn't know what we were doing" at the time, according to a State Department official who had been in charge of CSCE matters in 1973-1975. No one, he recalled, understood clearly what the words of the Danish proposal meant; especially unclear was the term "review." The official later observed that "we didn't know what we were after" and, in consequence, "people were tapping around in the dark." If the West did not understand its own language, all the more did the USSR fail to comprehend at the time the significance of follow-up review meetings.

The Soviet attempt to make the Helsinki accord binding and institutionalized was part of a broader Kremlin objective to make the idea and practice of détente irreversible; indeed, the Soviets sought to incorporate into the Final Act language that would have détente formally declared so. The West resisted, determined to describe détente as a preliminary step in a *process* of improving relations between groups of states and peoples. The text of the key preamble of Basket I ultimately read: "Convinced of the need to exert efforts to make détente both a continuing and increasingly viable and comprehensive process, universal in scope, and that the implementation of the Conference on Security and Cooperation in Europe will be a major contribution to this process. . . ." The language gave the Helsinki Final Act a dynamic quality which could be reinforced and given expression by the follow-up review meetings. Such dynamism could and would have enormous ramifications.

If the US was not in the forefront of the effort to include human rights in the CSCE agreement, it would be an error to assume total American indifference, as has been implied or suggested in various commentaries on the early history of the CSCE. The basis of this latter interpretation is the then-prevailing attitude of Henry A. Kissinger, who had served first as National Security Adviser and later as Secretary of State during the shaping of the Helsinki Final Act.

In his memoir of the 1969-1972 period, *White House Years*, Kissinger does not make a single reference to human rights as part of the preliminary discussions about CSCE. He did not perceive human rights as an essential ingredient for making the discussions viable or even as a bargaining chip to be used for purposes of leverage and balance. Indeed, his view of the CSCE process was one of great skepticism. He saw the US role as damage limitation, slowing down negotiations once they had begun. In Senate testimony in 1974, Kissinger rejected the use of human rights for changing Soviet internal policy. "The issue is not whether we condone what the USSR does internally," he said, "it is whether and to what extent we can risk other objects—and especially the building of a structure of peace—for these domestic changes. . . ."[29] He went on to emphasize that détente "is not rooted in agreement on values. . . ."

The Kissinger volume carries an instructive comment on the origins of CSCE.[30] In his view, it was an outgrowth of a Soviet diplomatic strategy that placed emphasis upon perseverance: Soviet repetitiveness in pressing an objective had the effect of eroding, sooner or later, the resistance of restless democracies. Pressures build up to accept the Soviet proposal "in principle" or at least to talk about it. Once the subject is accepted as legitimate, the discussion immediately switches to specific terms. The yearning for relaxation of tensions in the West created a presumption in favor of the Soviet agenda. Clearly, Kissinger saw CSCE as largely reflecting the Soviet agenda and not as a balance in which Western values played or could play an important part.

In specifying his own role as the West Europeans began responding positively to the Warsaw Pact proposals, Kissinger observed that to turn down Soviet overtures would leave the United States isolated within NATO. He recommended to President Nixon that the United States urge upon NATO a course of action that would link progress on a security conference to progress on concrete European issues, especially with respect to Berlin, as well as with regard to mutual and balanced force reductions. NATO approved the recommendation in April 1969. Kissinger was pleased that the security conference was deliberately placed on a "slow track."

Kissinger's linkage strategy concerned security issues only, not trade, and certainly not human rights. So long as no agreement was reached over Berlin, where the United States by virtue of its occupying-power status exercised a veto, the CSCE idea could not be realized. In this way, as Kissinger noted, the United States was in a position to encourage détente and to control its pace. If West German Chancellor Willy Brandt, who pressed hard for a security conference, felt that the Soviets had made a significant concession in accepting US and Canadian participation in CSCE, Kissinger was far less impressed. The idea that Soviet approval was needed to legitimize the US role in Europe he considered "dangerous." In President Nixon's 1971 foreign policy message to Congress, he sharply noted that so long as the "main security issues" of the German question, Berlin, and mutual force reductions were not settled, a conference would not be welcome.

Kissinger was prepared to proceed once the Berlin talks were concluded, because the European security conference and West Germany's treaties with Warsaw and Moscow had become dependent upon a Berlin agreement meeting US objectives. At the same time, he pressed the hesitant Soviets to agree to simultaneous MBFR talks in Vienna. When Moscow ultimately acquiesced, CSCE could begin to take on shape. But even then Washington was barely enthusiastic. President Nixon, in his 1972 foreign policy address, spoke of the need for a "clear picture" of the issues CSCE would address, and raised questions as to "what concrete contribution to security it can make."

In contrast to Kissinger's tough line, Willy Brandt suggested two kinds of positive and meaningful results. CSCE, he speculated, was desired by most East European countries as a means of buttressing their respective autonomy. Moreover, he saw East-West trade as mutually beneficial, and for that reason opposed trade linkage to political negotiations. To the very end, Kissinger continued to express skepticism. He privately warned that the establishment of CSCE could provide the US Congress with an excuse for troop reductions; indeed, Senate Majority Leader Mike Mansfield had pushed for several years for the reduction of the number of US troops stationed in Western Europe.

Kissinger's massive second volume, *Years of Upheaval*, is almost devoid of any reference to the CSCE process, even though lengthy and intensive discussions by delegates of the 35 participating states were pursued in Geneva and Helsinki during the time frame covered by the book (1973-74). The human rights aspect of these discussions is altogether avoided. A State Department official closely involved at the time with the CSCE process recalled that when one or another American official would write a memorandum to Kissinger proposing that he be authorized to take a more positive stance, Kissinger would send back a memorandum saying, "Do nothing!" It was the judgment of the State Department official that Kissinger failed to understand that he was conducting 20th-century, not 19th-century, diplomacy, in which human problems are crucial. This failing, said the official, prevented Kissinger from realizing that CSCE was a "major victory for the West." Kissinger's only substantive comment about CSCE in his second volume focused upon the issue of a heads-of-state meeting in Helsinki that would cap the negotiating process. He revealed that the United States had assumed a strategic posture of resisting such a summit. But by the time of the Nixon-Brezhnev meeting in Moscow in June-July 1974, the United States felt compelled to acquiesce to the proposed summit gathering. According to Kissinger, US acquiescence resulted from the fact that many West European leaders had by then already agreed to a summit. It would be pointless for the United States to resist the tide.[31]

Kissinger does acknowledge, if ever so briefly, that the State Department—in contrast to the White House—perceived the CSCE forum as one which might yield positive results. Some positive consequences could emerge in the area of human rights. But the recollections of one of the US participants in the CSCE discussions suggest the controversial nature of raising the human rights issue. He recalls that among the sharp early Helsinki differences between Secretary of State Rogers and National Security Adviser Kissinger was one relating to the USSR. "Let's not agitate the Soviets" is the way the participant characterized the Kissinger posture. And human rights advocacy in the CSCE talks would have done just that. At the same time, Assistant Secretary of State for European Affairs Martin J. Hillenbrand stressed that "we have no illusions that the Conference will solve the problems of a divided Europe. Nor do we think that even modest improvements will come easily. . . ."

Nonetheless, the head of the US delegation to the preliminary talks of CSCE in Helsinki in 1972, George Vest, played a very active, if "behind-the-scenes," role in the Western discussions on Basket III.[32] Indeed, some of the meetings of the Western, neutral and non-aligned representatives on the Basket III discussions actually took place in the Helsinki head-quarters of the US delegation. The general policy line which Vest was given by the State Department was to extend as much cooperation as pos-sible on Basket III to America's European friends. During the Helsinki deliberations, Vest received no specific instructions from the State De-partment. He considered his mandate as loose, flexible and supportive. Every six weeks, Vest would visit Washington and discuss progress with State Department officials and, at the same time, touch base with Na-tional Security Council specialists on Soviet affairs. The latter apparently merely listened and, according to Vest, offered no objections.

America's publicly passive role thus had a tactical basis and did not re-flect an indifference to Western objectives (although, of course, Kissinger himself was indifferent). "We did not tactically put ourselves in front," re-called Vest, because the overriding strategic objective of US policy at the time was to avoid a Soviet-American confrontation, which surely would have taken place had the issue been one of human rights. The choice of tactics, as Vest noted, was "deliberate on our part." With Europeans in the forefront of the Basket III effort, he added, superpower tangles could be avoided.

As the CSCE Helsinki meetings moved from its preparatory stages to formal conference deliberations in 1973-75, mainly in Geneva, the United States continued the earlier pattern. According to a knowledgeable source who later served as head of the US delegation, Ambassador Al-bert Sherer, Jr., the Americans had "a small but active and influential del-egation. . . ." Sherer went on to say: "We were passive in the sense that we urged [NATO] to take the lead in public discussion."[33] He added that the US delegation was "active behind the scenes, especially in our relations with Warsaw Pact delegations." Besides concentrating on the Eastern delegates, the US officials "were helpful across the board" with the neu-tral and non-aligned delegations.

As with Vest, US delegation members to CSCE meetings in Geneva were "given a free hand," according to Sherer. He remembers that "very, very few instructions were ever sent by telegram or letter" from Wash-ington. There was but one oral instruction which was general in nature: "You know what you are supposed to do, don't screw it up!" One of the leading US negotiators at the time, Harold S. Russell, the Assistant Legal

Adviser for European Affairs in the State Department, who was especially active in connection with the drafting of the Declaration of Principles in Basket I, recalls that he and his legal associates in the American delegation were "nervous" in not having any instructions. In a memorandum of February 25, 1974, he and an associate noted that they "have been operating without substantive instructions on the drafting of the Declaration of Principles," and sought to obtain official approval of a special policy paper they had prepared so they might have "some confidence in the technical support for our posture."

A later-published work by an Italian specialist, which drew upon first-hand oral accounts of participants in the CSCE process prior to the adoption of the Final Act, testified to the limited involvement of the American delegation at both the preliminary talks in 1972 and the formal CSCE deliberations in 1973-75.[34] Russell's work on the Declaration of Principles was particularly noted, as was the work of a US colleague who developed a proposal on a key thorny problem dealing with the "peaceful modification of frontiers." The fascinating, almost day-to-day Italian account indicated that the American delegation played a generally supportive and largely passive role. Only once did the US assume a posture which diverged from its NATO allies. That dealt with the hot issue of whether the deliberations ought to be expedited so that a final summit conference could be held as early as possible. This was a major Soviet objective, which the European democracies vigorously resisted. Kissinger was not averse to the Soviet aim, as he was less than enthusiastic generally about the Helsinki negotiations; US hesitancy inevitably irritated its allies.

According to the Italian account, on several occasions, especially during 1974, Kissinger did play a positive role when key human rights issues were stalemated. A highly informed State Department official recalled that, with time, Kissinger shed his more pronounced anxieties about Helsinki. In his bilateral discussions with Gromyko, Kissinger was able to persuade his Soviet counterpart of the negative consequences of deadlock on East-West détente. Kissinger's intervention was particularly helpful during the very last stages of the Helsinki discussions.[35] During the late spring and early summer of 1974, the discussions reached a state of "stagnation" as the Soviets sought to block progress on the crucial Basket III. In meetings with Gromyko, Kissinger praised the section on human contacts and called for a serious Soviet response.

Still, the United States at the CSCE discussions scarcely exercised the leadership role warranted by its power, its significance in NATO, and its traditional commitment to human rights. Russell, one of the few Americans active behind the scenes, recalled with chagrin and embarrassment that only one or two of the literally thousands of *formal* proposals advanced at the Helsinki-Geneva talks during 1972-74 were American in origin. The Italian account of the proceedings characterized America's role as primarily one of "detachment . . . ostentatiously displayed." The account traced the detachment to the "tendency of Kissinger to consider CSCE as an exercise, at best significant for public opinion, but certainly not as an essential component of the . . . process of détente."

A somewhat more balanced view of the US role was presented by Swedish scholar Karl Birnbaum, who interviewed many of the Helsinki participants. While characterizing the US posture as being one of "low profile" and "passive," he nonetheless considered the role to be important at certain stages: at the preparatory talks in Helsinki in 1972, and at the very end of 1974. Birnbaum traced the passive role to Kissinger's preference for bilateral diplomacy and the conviction of decision makers in Washington that no primary interests were involved in the CSCE exercise.

That view would change after the 1977 inauguration of President Jimmy Carter. From a largely passive, low-profile role, the United States moved to a very active, high-profile position, especially with respect to the area of human rights. To a certain extent, the transformation resulted from the follow-up meetings, which inevitably gave the process a high visibility. In addition, "internal" factors became more and more important in the evolution of the US perspective. The US Helsinki Commission, an unprecedented feature of US diplomacy, had a great impact on public and official consciousness of the Helsinki process. The Helsinki Watch groups abroad were no less important.

▪ 2 ▪

Changing the American Perspective: The US Helsinki Commission

onventional wisdom in the United States concerning the Helsinki Final Act at its adoption, as recorded by diplomatic partisans who had been intimately involved in the drafting process itself, was highly negative. The shaping of this hostile image was affected by several sources. Ignorance was a major factor. To an astonishing degree, the media neglected to ascertain what happened in the closed diplomatic drafting process, and, therefore, failed to comprehend and report on the significance of the human rights provisions of the Helsinki accord. Downplaying of the accord by the State Department contributed enormously to the ignorance. Lack of knowledge extended to otherwise sophisticated political personages, like Jimmy Carter, who only later would learn the contents of the accord and how they could be effectively utilized.

The communication failure was in large part a consequence of Henry Kissinger's generally negative attitude to the Helsinki process from the beginning.[1] In his influence with and upon correspondents and reporters, few were his equal. If he manifested little, if any, interest in the accord's human rights provisions, the media was not very likely to be attracted by them, either.

Public attitudes in the United States overwhelmingly focused upon the "inviolability of borders" theme. For conservatives and anti-communist leaders, whether of the Democratic or Republican parties, the theme evoked negative images of another Yalta, another capitulation to Soviet imperialism. Helsinki, from this perspective, constituted a betrayal of the people of Eastern Europe: the Soviet Union had extracted Yalta-like concessions without granting the West compensation.[2] Thus, the Helsinki exercise was nothing but "a defeat for the West."[3]

It is startling to note that this view of Helsinki was similar to Moscow's perception. The USSR publicly placed virtually exclusive emphasis upon the "inviolability of borders" theme and almost totally minimized the extensive human rights elements of the Final Act. Moscow, therefore, championed Helsinki as a victory for its purpose and exulted in its status quo features, while deliberately neglecting the elements of potential dynamic change.

If conventional wisdom thus held that the Helsinki Final Act was a betrayal of the peoples of Eastern Europe, two unexpected sources would soon challenge that wisdom. Powerful currents would emerge from these separate sources. One was official, a congressionally created body—the US Helsinki Commission; the other was unofficial and almost subterranean—the Helsinki Watch Group, a dissident human rights committee in Moscow, soon joined by other activists in the Soviet Union and in other East European countries. Together, they would fundamentally alter American thinking on Helsinki.

In August 1975, after the Final Act was signed in Helsinki, an 18-member congressional delegation headed by Speaker of the House Carl Albert went on a special visit to the Soviet Union. One of its members, Congresswoman Millicent Fenwick, was profoundly moved by her meetings with Jewish activists and refuseniks (those refused exit visas for purposes of emigration to join families in Israel). The meetings had been generally prearranged by an American Jewish organization, but it was largely the refuseniks on their own who pursued the objective of visiting the congressional delegation and outlining their plight.

Fenwick, of elitist origin and regal bearing, a Republican from New Jersey, was enormously impressed by the courage of her refusenik visitors. She recalled: "We would meet them at nights at hotels in Moscow and Leningrad. I would ask them, 'How do you dare to come to see us here?'"[4] The way they responded would eventually guide her later plan of action: "Don't you understand? That's our only hope. We've seen you, now the KGB knows you've seen us." It was precisely because a refusenik had been visited by a congressman or congresswoman that they were safer. The KGB, in most cases, would have a reluctance to use brutality against those who had become known to or involved with prominent American officials. Fenwick would later remember: "I felt, my God, it's like being on a transatlantic steamer in the middle of a terrible storm, and seeing people go by in rafts, and we are trying to pick them up, but can't. But at least we have our searchlights on them."[5]

The New Jersey legislator, looking for ways to assist the dissenters and refuseniks, must have sensed that the Helsinki Final Act might prove useful. Her feelings were validated at a meeting she had with three prominent scientists and dissenters—Yuri Orlov and Valentin Turchin, who had been active with Amnesty International, and Veniamin Levich, a leading refusenik.[6] It was a discussion that would have important ramifications. For Orlov, who would a year later play the key role in organizing a Helsinki monitoring body of private Soviet citizens, the Helsinki Final Act may have been a "weak document" as compared with the Universal Declaration of Human Rights, but it was "more important."[7] His reasoning was based on the fact that the Soviet Union had signed it and had declared it to be important. What was especially vital about the Final Act, in his view, was Moscow's perception, which "gave us something to work with."

The Congresswoman was most strongly impressed by a young mother from Odessa, Lilia Roitburd, who, along with her husband, Lev, had been refused visas for Israel a year earlier.[8] Lev was fired from his engineering job, denounced in the local newspaper as "an imperialist puppet," and later arrested for allegedly striking a police officer. Fenwick was overwrought by the difference between Lilia's image on a snapshot and the "ravaged face" of the woman pleading her family's case. "I still have nightmares about it," she would tell listeners upon returning to the United States.[9]

Back in Washington, Fenwick told herself: "We've got to do something for Lilia. We've got to do something."[10] Soviet President Leonid Brezhnev had called the Congresswoman "obsessive" after she had met him in Yalta at the end of the delegation's trip and she had pressed him to deal with several humanitarian cases.[11] His comment was on target. On September 9, 1975, she introduced a bill calling for the establishment of a "Commission on Security and Cooperation in Europe," which would monitor implementation by East European governments of the Helsinki accord's human rights provisions. She contended that only by keeping a public searchlight on the struggling refuseniks could their plight be relieved.

The text of the proposed legislation did not specifically mention Eastern Europe, but the intent was clear enough. The law would require the Commission "to monitor the acts of the signatories which reflect compliance with or violation of the articles of the Final Act . . . with particular regard to the provisions relating to Cooperation in Humanitarian Fields. . . ."[12] The latter was the title of the Helsinki accord's Basket III. The Commission was also "to monitor and encourage the development of programs and activities of the United States Government and private organizations with a view of expanding East-West economic cooperation and a greater interchange of people and ideas between East and West. . . ."

To assist the Commission's work, the draft legislation required the President of the United States to provide it with a semi-annual report which surveyed the extent of compliance or non-compliance by the signatory powers. The Commission itself would report to the House and Senate on a periodic basis and provide individual congressional members with appropriate information when requested.

The Commission itself, as conceived by the legislation, would have a distinctive character, combining members of the Congress and the administration. The text originally provided that the number from Congress would total eight, four from each house (when later adopted, the number from Congress was increased to twelve, six from each house) and three from the administration, one each from the State, Defense, and Commerce departments. The legislation provided for the Speaker of the House of Representatives to name the chairman of the Commission.

On November 17, Fenwick's Republican colleague from New Jersey, Senator Clifford Case, introduced the same legislation in the upper house. He was extending a courtesy to a friend and legislative associate from the same state. But more than that, he was adding his very significant political stature, as a prominent long-time Senator, to a proposal by a very junior Congresswoman serving her first term in office. The Case-Fenwick legislation not only had the Commission monitor the human rights violations, but also required it to evaluate progress in commercial ties between East and West. In introducing the bill in the Senate, Senator Case offered a rationale which found a favorable echo among many of his colleagues already distressed with the relative indifference of the administration to human rights issues. While the United States can expect the State Department and Defense Department, he said, to "keep an eye on the degree of compliance in their immediate area of interest"—notably security issues of Basket I—"Congress should be able to play an important role in the all-important area of human rights, which all too often appear to be of only secondary concern to the executive branch."[13]

The theme reflected the irritation of many legislators with Kissinger's realpolitik, which came at the expense of human rights. The irritation was compounded by the Soviet Union's repudiation in early 1975 of the US-Soviet trade agreement of 1972. In its repudiation, Moscow specifically singled out for condemnation the Jackson-Vanik Amendment, which had been enacted by Congress to link US trade benefits for communist countries to eased emigration procedures. The condemnation scarcely endeared the Congress to the Soviet Union.

At least initially, though, Congress hardly rushed to enact the proposed legislation. While Rep. Fenwick picked up 96 co-sponsors for her bill, it remained unattended in the House Committee on International Relations. It was ethnic politics in the US that gave the bill momentum.[14] Various ethnic groups saw the Fenwick measure to be a useful device for helping their co-religionists or ethnic brethren in Eastern Europe. Especially active was the National Conference on Soviet Jewry, which was increasingly concerned by a declining emigration rate of Jews from the USSR (20,000 in 1974; 13,000 in 1975). To the Conference, a coordinating group of virtually all national and local Jewish organizations, Basket III of the Final Act offered a major frame of reference for pressing Moscow on the question. The basket called upon the signatories to "deal in a positive and humanitarian spirit" with requests for exit visas to reunite separated families.

According to one incisive account of the legislative history of the Fenwick measure, a development at the signing of the Helsinki accord pointed to a useful means for expediting emigration arrangements.[15] Behind the scenes at the ceremony, two of the signatories—the Federal Republic of Germany and Poland—reached an agreement whereby Germans living in Poland could join kin in the Federal Republic in return for large-scale credits to Warsaw. Could a similar form of leverage be used for Soviet Jews? Some in the Jewish community and in the US legislature thought so.

The Ford administration was scarcely enthusiastic about legislation that appeared to interfere with the prerogatives of the executive branch of government. On January 19, 1976, the State Department made its opposition clear in a letter from Robert J. McCloskey, Assistant Secretary of State for Congressional Relations, to the Senate Foreign Relations Committee. The letter read:

> ... We share the interest of the sponsors of these bills in effective monitoring of CSCE implementation, but do not believe the proposed Commission would add to the efforts and procedures already established. Therefore, the Department of State recommends against enactment of this legislation.[16]

The State Department explained that procedures for Helsinki monitoring could be easily handled by its own machinery; moreover, the proposed Commission "would not appear to be equipped to add significantly to the action being taken or the information being compiled."

Not made explicit was a concern of Kissinger and his Soviet affairs experts that the overt intrusion of human rights issues into the superpower relationship would complicate that relationship and jeopardize his policy of balance and equilibrium among the major powers. In addition, the Department was historically envious of others trespassing on its preemi-

nence in the foreign affairs field. Especially disturbing was the proposed
unique feature of the Commission, combining members of Congress and
the administration. This was seen as a possible subordination of department policy to Congress. The McCloskey letter singled out "the extraordinary composition" of the Commission for criticism, noting that it
"would not seem to provide an appropriate or effective means for coordination or guiding our efforts."

Kissinger's strong opposition to the Commission was not allowed to
manifest itself fully. The White House was deeply concerned about the
harsh criticism registered by Governor Ronald Reagan of California and
his supporters against Ford's signing of the Helsinki accord.[17] With Reagan already threatening the President's hope for renomination, Ford did
not want to add to his own difficulties within the party. Resistance from
the White House to a measure sponsored by two legislators who, incidentally, were active members of the Republican Party was conducted in low-
key fashion.

In fact, much more could have been made in the McCloskey letter and
elsewhere about the "extraordinary composition" of the proposed Commission. By including members of both Congress and the administration,
the draft legislation created an unprecedented hybrid in the making of
foreign policy. As the Commission's makeup gave Congress a stronger
role in an area of foreign affairs, where tradition and law favored the executive, such an institution could have raised serious questions with respect to the constitutional separation of powers.

The issue, however, surfaced only once. In a debate on the Senate floor
on May 5, James Allen, the Democratic Senator from Alabama, asked: "I
am wondering if the Senator [Hubert Humphrey of Minnesota, the floor
leader] has considered the fact that the function of this Commission could
well be an executive function as distinguished from mere congressional
oversight and congressional action."[18] Senator Humphrey, joined by Senator Case, pointed to two mixed commissions as precedents—the National Commission on Water Quality and the Commission on the
Reorganization of the Executive Branch of the Federal Government (the
so-called Hoover Commission).[19] They stressed that the function of these
bodies was limited to oversight, not acts. Case, referring to the Water
Quality Commission, commented: "Its function was to study, draw conclusions and make recommendations. It had no power. It had no authority."[20] Allen was "not persuaded," but was willing to go along because
"the sponsors are willing to take that [constitutional] risk."[21]

Senator Case's version of a Commission that would merely study and
advise hardly accorded with the thrust of earlier congressional initiatives

in the human rights field during 1973-75, especially the enactment of the Jackson-Vanik Amendment. Moreover, the challenge quickly assumed a political dimension when Congressman Dante Fascell (D.-Fla.) reshaped the Fenwick formula to give the Democrats a clear majority in the congressional representation.[22] Fenwick had conceived of the Commission being comprised of four members from each house, evenly divided between Democrats and Republicans. When four Congressional Republicans were added to three members from the administration, the White House could enjoy a 7-4 majority.

In the changed Fascell version, the Commission would be increased from 11 to 15, with six (instead of four) appointed from each house according to a formula of four from the majority party and two from the minority party. Because the Democrats enjoyed a majority in each House, they would have eight members on the Commission to the seven Republicans. (In 1985, the size of the Commission became 21, with 18 of the commissioners coming from Congress.)

The Fascell thrust had an additional personal dimension. In the Fenwick bill, the chairman of the Commission would be appointed by the Speaker of the House. The logic for this flowed from Fenwick's own sponsoring role in the House. Because the Florida Congressman was a senior member of the House of Representatives and a ranking Democrat on the Foreign Affairs Committee, he was certain to be named chairman. So prominent did the Commission become, and so central was Fascell's own role in its creation and direction, that, not surprisingly, it would often be referred to as the Fascell Commission.

By the time of the Senate debate, the power of ethnic constituencies could be felt on Congress. Not only was the Jewish community deeply interested, but Polish, Hungarian and Czechoslovak émigré organizations also endorsed the Fenwick bill.[23] So, too, did the Baltic American Committee, comprising citizens of Lithuanian, Latvian, and Estonian origin. Originally, it had vigorously opposed the Helsinki Final Act, as the latter was believed to accept the permanent incorporation of the Baltic areas into the Soviet Union. The Committee's spokesman, testifying before a House panel, pointed to the provisions of the Helsinki accord on "family reunification or visitation" as a positive element. If the State Department under Kissinger was reluctant to push for implementation of these provisions, the spokesman observed, then "we feel that the US Senate and the House, overseeing this Commission, will bring pressure to bear on the US Department of State."[24]

Congressman Stephen Solarz of Brooklyn welcomed the testimony of the Baltic Committee, for it emphasized, he said, the State Department's "historic indifference . . . to these questions of human rights in other countries."[25] What he had been reminded of was the State Department's indifference to the Nazi persecution of Jews. Solarz concluded: "I can see over the course of the years they haven't learned much or changed their attitude." A more measured comment came from Congressman Fascell. He observed that the State Department is so preoccupied with a variety of concerns, "it makes it very difficult for them . . . to do some of the things some of us think they ought to do." Soon, he would be able to demonstrate what "things" they ought to have been doing.

The House Foreign Affairs Committee approved the Fenwick-Case bill on April 23. Shortly afterward, on May 5, the Senate adopted it without opposition. And, on May 17, the full House of Representatives gave it an unchallenged endorsement. On June 3, the bill was signed into law by President Ford. A formal Commission on Security and Cooperation in Europe was established. A major new instrument for reshaping US policy on human rights generally, and specifically with respect to the Helsinki process, had now come into existence.

Just before the final vote in the House, Fenwick announced that a few days earlier the Helsinki Watch Group had been created in Moscow. Her words were simple and moving. The Moscow group, she said, was planning "to do the same thing" that her bill would do. "They and we are hoping that this international accord will not be just another empty piece of paper," she added.[26] The Moscow Helsinki Watch Group was, of course, scarcely similar in character to her *government* instrument, but this was irrelevant to her moral perspective.

The Congresswoman then moved to make her major point. She reminded her colleagues of what was central to the American tradition, the "principles that have distinguished this country for many years," most notably "respect for the dignity of the individual":

> This ought to be the basis of our international relations. These ought to be the things of which we speak to the world; a concern for our fellow human beings, knowing that we are one family regardless of distance and descent or any other kind of barrier; concern for their right to freedom of religion, for their right to travel and be unified with their family.[27]

"This is what this bill is about," were her concluding remarks. No wonder then that Secretary of State Henry Kissinger would later refer to Fenwick as his "tormentor."[28] He warned that she was setting a "dangerous precedent."

For the Secretary of State, the new institution posed serious dangers of "unwarranted invasion of the executive's constitutional prerogatives in the conduct of foreign policy."[29] He reportedly urged a veto of the legislation. But the bill's considerable support in both houses made the question of sustaining the veto highly dubious. Besides, its principal sponsors were prominent Republicans. And the White House itself was under attack for not being forceful enough on human rights.

An alternative route was pursued. The question of the potential constitutional issue of executive branch participation in what was primarily a legislative body was formally put to the Department of Justice.[30] Perhaps a challenge could be presented by judicial experts on the constitutionality of the legislation. The Department, however, dismissed the concerns on grounds that the Commission was really an intergovernmental agency with no legislative authority.[31] It could hold hearings, issue reports and make inquiries of other governmental agencies, but in fact had no direct role in the formulation of legislation.

That a clash between the Commission and the State Department was certain to unfold became clear from the beginning. At the Commission's first two sessions—July 27 and August 5—several executive branch officials informally attended but were unable to give definitive information on the required administration appointments to the Commission.[32] On August 24, Fascell, Fenwick, Case, and Senator Claiborne Pell met with Secretary Kissinger about the question of an early appointment of the three executive branch members to the Commission and about protecting "the integrity of executive branch participation in this endeavor." Kissinger was also asked about and agreed to meet with the full Commission "at an early date."[33]

A month elapsed and no appointments were made. Chairman Fascell wrote President Ford a sharply worded letter on September 27: "I am distressed by the delay in the appointment of representatives of the Executive Branch to the Commission. It was my understanding that recommendation had been made some time ago and that all legal and constitutional questions have been thoroughly examined prior to your signing of the bill."[34] The letter went on to point out that Kissinger had "assured" him on August 24 that the "appointment would be forthcoming." Finally, it complained that, despite Kissinger's promise to meet with the Commission, no date had been set and "Congress is about to adjourn."

It was common knowledge in Washington that Kissinger was engaged in a delaying action. Not only was there the constitutional question, about which the administration continued to express concern, but the Secretary of State—as noted by a prominent commentator—"did not want three administration representatives to be put in a position of getting outvoted by a dozen members of Congress or to have to sign as a minority a report critical of some Communist country's noncompliance with its humanitarian promises. . . ."[35] He also was said to be concerned that administration representatives could question Commission witnesses in ways that might prove embarrassing to his foreign policy.

Fascell was anxious to bring matters to a head. The day after his letter to the President was sent, he made the text public at a Commission session. And he augmented the release by publicly stating: "It's four months now, and we haven't resolved this thing. We will go on and hope they make their appointment right away."[36] To add to the pressure, Fascell and Senator Walter Mondale, then the Democratic candidate for Vice-President, let it be known that the latter would raise the issue in his forthcoming television debate with the Republican candidate, Robert Dole.[37]

The tactic worked. On the day of the debate, President Ford appointed the three executive branch members of the Commission. His letter to Fascell, dated October 2, conveyed "the deep commitment of the Executive Branch to full cooperation with the Commission. . . ."[38] At the same time, he wanted the Commission to know that he saw "potentially serious constitutional and policy problems" in its composition. To partly resolve these "problems," he indicated that the executive branch members would abstain from all votes, would not examine witnesses and would not assume responsibility for the Commission's findings. They would in essence be "observers" rather than full participants.

Fascell reluctantly accepted the conditions, which in the end proved inconsequential. The chairman, in any case, kept votes of the Commission to a minimum. When the Carter administration came to power, the possibility of public confrontation disappeared altogether. If Ford had won the election and kept Kissinger on as Secretary of State, confrontation was certain to follow. He surely would have made a determined effort to diminish the Commission's function, if for no other reason than that it would have constituted a major challenge to his foreign policy in Eastern Europe.

The Commission's determination to pursue a dynamic role was made evident at its early sessions in mid-1976. The commissioners agreed that they would take an active, aggressive approach toward the monitoring duties noted in the law creating the body.[39] They further agreed to pursue vigorously the compiling of information on human rights practices in Eastern Europe. They saw their objective to be facilitating compliance with Helsinki's Principle VII and Basket III provisions.

Central to this purpose would be a talented and skilled staff. In August, Fascell chose Spencer Oliver, a lawyer, as the director. A young Democratic Party activist, he had administered the American Council of Young Political Leaders. Oliver recognized that technical expertise was essential if he was to cope effectively with challenges from the foreign policy establishment. The initial choices were first-rate. Alfred Friendly, formerly head of the Moscow bureau of *Newsweek*, was named deputy staff director. Also appointed were Martin Sletzinger, a Harvard University PhD in East European studies, and Meg Donovan, who had long worked for the National Conference on Soviet Jewry. Other staffers, mostly youthful, came from academia or from congressional staffs or from non-governmental organizations.

But in order to compensate for the staff's admittedly limited experience in foreign affairs, Oliver happily hit upon the idea of requesting three career foreign service officers with experience in CSCE affairs to be assigned as staff consultants. Such appointments might also serve to allay the fears of the State Department about competition from the outside. A breakfast meeting between Fascell and Kissinger in September produced the required result. Fascell prevailed upon the Secretary that foreign service officers on the staff of the Commission would enhance the ability of the Commission to pursue its goals and also strengthen the confidence of the State Department in the Commission.[40]

Kissinger, in accepting the proposal, appointed one of his key aides, Lawrence Eagleburger, to implement the plan. Difficult negotiations between Oliver and Eagleburger followed, with Oliver seeking the service of highly trained career officers and Eagleburger reluctant to dispense with his own pool of CSCE talent.[41] On October 8, the State Department finally agreed to the assignment; especially important was the choice of Guy Coriden, who had been deeply involved with the US delegation in the Helsinki negotiations. He knew the subject as few others did.

Tensions with the State Department extended to the crucial question of its classified documentation. The Commission staff sought access to the Department's documents and cable traffic on CSCE matters and, in view of the sensitivity about such confidential material, offered assurances that its officers and document storage facilities would pass security review. Initial requests for information from the Department, however, went unanswered. Several discussions by the commissioners—key congressmen and senators—with senior Department leaders finally elicited a somewhat favorable response from Eagleburger on October 6.[42] He gave the Commission assurances that a satisfactory working arrangement would be made at the staff level.

But the assurances could not be easily fulfilled. The point of contact for the Commission was the office of Regional Political–Military Affairs in the Bureau of European Affairs (EUR-RPM), the Department's focal center for CSCE issues. The office was primarily concerned with NATO coordination, and would naturally resist any effort that would weaken, undermine or threaten NATO on policy issues. It was traditionally a preserve of enterprising and ambitious career foreign service officers whose perspective was NATO-oriented. To the extent that European NATO countries perceived their relationship with Eastern Europe less in human rights terms than in security terms, sharp disagreements quickly arose. One Commission staffer described the relationship as "frosty and unproductive" and complained of "condescending, elitist attitudes" on the part of the career officers.[43]

A climactic high point in the intense dispute with Kissinger and his bureaucracy was reached in October, when the Commission announced its intention to travel to most of the Helsinki signatory states November 5-23. What prompted the Commission's decision was its philosophy of activism. Effective fulfillment of the function to "monitor and encourage" implementation would require it to have direct contacts with the other signatory states, including East European states.[44] Only through direct contacts, it was argued, could the Commission hope to gain access to additional information and press for greater compliance.

But the Commission was not a "standing committee" of Congress, and had no travel budget. In a series of parliamentary maneuvers and expert politicking, Chairman Fascell forced through a prepared amendment to the June 3 law that created the Commission. The new legislation defined the Commission as a "standing committee," entitling it "to use funds in accordance with such sections" as provided by the Mutual Security Act of 1954.[45] Both houses approved the amendment on September 30.

Only a pocket veto by the President could negate the superbly timed political coup of the Commission head. President Ford was, indeed, extremely hesitant about signing the legislation. The State Department made clear its position about the Commission's proposed travel plans in the form of a letter from Kempton Jenkins, McCloskey's successor as Assistant Secretary of State for Congressional Relations, to the Commission in October.[46] He warned that the Commission would meet a negative response from many European governments. This reaction would be based "in part upon ignorance of the Commission's objectives and in part on what these governments might regard as interference in their domestic affairs." Jenkins went on to warn "that the trip could have an effect directly contrary to the aim of the Commission and this could affect adversely compliance with the Helsinki Final Act in the Soviet Union and Eastern Europe."

Political pressure on the White House, prompted by the Commission itself, forced the President's hand. A British correspondent reported that "after a last-minute battery of telephone calls from East European émigré groups," President Ford signed the travel-fund legislation on October 18, just hours before the bill would have died.[47] What may very well have greatly weakened the White House resistance was the incredible blunder made by President Ford during the course of his second televised debate with Jimmy Carter on October 6. A stunned viewing public heard him say that there is "no Soviet domination of Eastern Europe. . . . I don't believe that the Poles consider themselves dominated by the Soviet Union."[48] The bursting anger among East European émigré groups could hardly be mollified on the eve of the election; President Ford must have been reluctant to add to the fury by vetoing a bill that seemed to benefit US activism on East European matters.

With the journey to the Helsinki signatories now definite, the State Department entered into lengthy discussions with the Commission for purposes of establishing procedural guidelines. Commissioners were to make clear in their meetings with foreign governments that their monitoring and information-gathering function was in no way intended to replace or affect the conduct of foreign policy, which was the exclusive responsibility of the executive branch. It was also agreed that the Department and its embassies abroad would help the Commission by setting up appointments with relevant government officials, with members of NATO and the European Community, and with those private persons who had a special interest in CSCE matters.[49]

Cooperation was refused in one area. The White House, in an about-face, decided not to permit the executive branch commissioner-observers to participate in the trip beyond an initial session with NATO and a closing meeting in London. Fascell compared it to "Soviet obstruction," and charged that it signaled to the communist nations that there was "divided counsel in Washington on the importance and potential of the Helsinki accords."[50] The State Department called the Fascell statement "outrageously erroneous" and "motivated by partisan politics."[51]

Even more disturbing to the Commission was the failure to receive a response from the Warsaw Pact countries concerning its request for visas. Top staff officials of the Commission were suspicious about Kissinger's role. They contended that only a few days before the scheduled Commission departure, the Secretary of State had a private, unpublicized meeting with Soviet Ambassador Anatoly Dobrynin.[52] Soon afterward, according to these sources, Moscow informed the State Department that the requested visas would be denied because the Soviets regarded the trip as interference in internal affairs. Almost immediately, every other Warsaw Pact embassy offered the same reasoning using the same language. One staffer related that a senior Warsaw Pact diplomat later informed the Commission staff that the denial of the visas to the Commission had been at the behest of Secretary Kissinger himself.[53]

Whether true or not, the charge testified to the intense skepticism of Kissinger's actions in the ranks of the Commission. Moscow may very well have refused the Commission visas irrespective of what Kissinger may have advised. In any case, the Ford administration was a lame duck by the time of the Commission's trip—November 5; three days earlier, Jimmy Carter had been elected President. TASS, on November 4, the day prior to the Commission journey, described the monitoring body in hostile terms, accusing it of aiming "to usurp the functions of supreme interpreters of the Final Act."[54]

Once on the journey, the Commission found US diplomats uniformly cooperative. The mission proved to be far more rewarding than expected, even if it was limited to the democracies of Western Europe. The Commission learned from foreign governments and private experts that, in their judgment, the Helsinki accords had turned out to be more productive than anticipated. This reinforced the view of the Commission on the significance of Helsinki. It was also advised that the provisions of the accord had a restraining effect on some repressive behavior in the East European communist countries.

European officials told the Commission of their concern with the comparatively limited US participation in the Helsinki process, which diminished prospects for the accord's success and "undercut the important Soviet acknowledgment that the United States did have 'political business' being in Europe."[55] The Commission, in turn, counseled the Europeans to disseminate information more actively about the Helsinki process. It had found "a general lack of public information in Europe on government activity within the CSCE framework."[56] An informed public opinion, the Commission argued, would be of great value in promoting the objectives of Helsinki. No doubt it was projecting upon others what it perceived its own function to be.

Most important, the Commission established itself as a player in the CSCE process, a force to be reckoned with in respect to US policy making. Foreign governments were apprised of the strong and sustained interest of the US Congress in the CSCE process. In essence, they were put on notice that the era of a detached and passive approach by the US to the CSCE process was at an end. Fascell pronounced the Commission's report of its first study mission to be "an outstanding job well begun."[57]

Even while establishing a relationship with the governments of Western Europe, the Commission was also pursuing contacts with the major dissident group in the Soviet Union—the Helsinki Watch Group—which by a curious coincidence had come into existence at almost the same time that Congress was adopting legislation creating the Commission. On September 5, Dr. Yuri Orlov, the chairman of the Moscow Helsinki Watch Group, wrote to Congresswoman Fenwick, whom he had met the year before, advising that the Group would now send its findings to the Commission.[58] He received a reply in late November from Chairman Fascell: "We look forward very much to receiving more of [your] reports in the months to come."[59]

Even more important were the contacts established with Jimmy Carter both before and after the 1976 presidential election. His administration would embrace human rights as a major focus of US foreign policy and accord the Commission a central place in human rights policy formulation. From a mere critic of Kissinger and Ford policies, the Fascell Commission would be catapulted into the Washington political limelight.

Oddly enough, Carter during the bulk of his campaign gave little attention to either the Helsinki Final Act or to human rights. In a major foreign affairs address to the Foreign Policy Association on June 23 in New York City he referred to neither. Only in his acceptance speech three weeks later would the newly nominated Democratic candidate for President declare that "peace is the unceasing effort to preserve human rights."[60] Reference to Helsinki, however, was absent.

Indeed, the Helsinki accord became the target of a harsh political attack by the Democratic Party candidate on October 2, in Pittsburgh. Speaking before a Lithuanian-American group, Carter said that Helsinki had given Leonid Brezhnev "a tremendous diplomatic victory."[61] The Soviet leader demonstrated thereby "that he was able to induce the West to accept the Russian takeover of Eastern Europe following the Second World War." Strikingly, on the eve of the election, Carter was parroting the standard harsh allegation that Helsinki constituted not an opening for human rights, but rather a betrayal of them and of the people of Eastern Europe. If the line served a politically partisan purpose, it certainly testified to indifference or ignorance among Americans as to what the Helsinki accord was all about.

The staff of the Commission, according to a highly placed staff member, launched an "intensive effort" to "educate" Carter's advisers.[62] It paid off handsomely in the course of the presidential debate on national television during which Ford's gaffe on the Polish question made history. A question was put to the candidates about the Helsinki accord. After President Ford stumbled in defending it, Carter provided an effective commentary in rebuttal:

> It may have been a good agreement at the beginning, but we have failed to enforce the so-called Basket III part, which insures the right of migration, to join their family, to be free, to speak out.[63]

The inauguration of Jimmy Carter ushered in a new foreign policy era, with human rights a foremost item on his agenda. The Helsinki Commission was as instrumental in setting forth the new priority as it had been in educating the nominee on Helsinki. The alliance of the two would eventuate in a fundamentally new policy line concerning the Helsinki accord. From passivity, the United States would shift to a visible leadership role; from a low-priority emphasis, Helsinki would now be given an extraordinarily high-priority status.

The symbiotic relationship of the Commission and the administration emerged on the eve of the inauguration. At a meeting of President-elect Carter with his foreign-policy transition team, which included Fascell and several other members of Congress, Carter spoke about the need for a moral component in foreign policy.[64] He did not use the term "human rights." Fascell spoke up. Human rights, he said, must be a "major component" of the new administration's foreign policy. He was vigorously supported by a veteran Democratic leader, Senator Hubert Humphrey, a former Vice-President and presidential candidate. The intervention of the elder statesman was decisive. The President-elect asked Fascell for "talking points" in the preparation of his inaugural address and the Commission chairman made sure that these points underscored human rights.[65] They became the centerpiece of the address and, indeed, of the new administration.

Far more significant was the establishment of a strong and direct relationship between Fascell and the newly designated Secretary of State, Cyrus Vance. While they had met when Vance had served as Deputy Secretary of Defense, neither really knew the other. For Vance a closer relationship was important, as Fascell was chairman of a House subcommittee that authorized the State Department's budget.[66] In turn, for Fascell, a warm relationship with the Secretary of State could remove all the obstacles to an active Helsinki Commission. When Fascell was invited to a December dinner party in New York City at which—he knew—Vance would be present, he had no hesitation in flying up from Miami.[67]

The questionable wisdom of flying from Miami to New York in early December just for dinner paid off, and the relationship blossomed. Vance and Fascell held a series of meetings and exchanged letters during January and February. Fascell's "talking points" for the inaugural address were in a letter of January 4.[68] In the meetings and letters, Fascell contended that the Commission offered a useful forum through which Congress and the administration could express their mutual concerns about human rights violations in the USSR and Eastern Europe. At the same time, a cooperative bipartisan legislative-executive relationship could dramatize forcefully both at home and abroad the high-priority character of human rights.

Fascell articulated the need for adequate prior consultation by the Secretary of State with the Congress, a practice neglected by the previous administration. He urged that Congress be brought early on into the decision-making process when it concerned human rights. Especially relevant was Fascell's recommendation that the Commission be quickly integrated into decision making for the very first Helsinki follow-up meeting, scheduled for October 1977, in Belgrade, Yugoslavia. Specifically, he wanted the President or the Secretary of State to announce publicly the integration of the Commission as a full partner in the government's preparations for Belgrade.[69] And, to flesh out the relationship, Vance was advised to appoint Commission Chairman Fascell as co-chairman of the US delegation and to select as members of the delegation Commission staff along with State Department personnel.

The Secretary of State was responsive to the Fascell proposals. In a letter dated March 10, 1977, Vance made clear his strong desire "to bring about a relationship of full cooperation between the State Department and the Commission."[70] Vance proposed that the two agencies "establish a staff level Working Group on preparation for Belgrade to include the [State] Department officials directly responsible for CSCE and members of the Commission staff." More importantly, he agreed to have the Commission and its staff represented on the US delegation to the Belgrade preparatory session in June and at the regular session beginning in October. Commission staffers, it was made clear, were to take their instructions from the State Department when they acted as part of the CSCE delegation.

On an issue tangential to CSCE and Belgrade but highly pertinent to Commission concerns, Vance was equally cooperative. Fascell had urged that the State Department representative on the Commission not come from the Bureau of European Affairs, with which it had been having a running controversy, but rather from the Department's recently created human rights office.[71] In order that such an appointment be technically feasible in terms of rank, Fascell asked that the new office be upgraded so that its chief would be titled "Assistant Secretary of State." By this means, Assistant Secretary for European Affairs Arthur Hartman could be bypassed and replaced by someone more sympathetic to Commission objectives—an "ally," as a Commission staffer said.[72] Vance complied. Patt Derian, a tough human rights advocate and head of the rights office, was made Assistant Secretary of the newly named Bureau of Human Rights and Humanitarian Affairs and selected to serve on the Commission.

According to a high Commission official, the State Department's Bureau of European Affairs bitterly resented the Derian appointment and opposed the plan integrating the Commission with the State Department in preparations for Belgrade.[73] Even if the Bureau failed here, it was nonetheless scarcely surprising that high-level decisions in the Department, at least in terms of their spirit, would be thwarted or modified at the working level when daily routine matters had to be considered, especially as they related to the forthcoming meeting at Belgrade. Whether and how to raise the question of human rights violations in Eastern Europe? This was a central tactical issue.

If the issue of human rights was a matter of concern for the career officers staffing the bureau, it was, nevertheless, not dominant or all-consuming for them. It had to be weighed against the US interest in détente and in avoiding alienation of European allies. Priority had to be given to preservation of the NATO alliance system, not to splitting it with a confrontational approach on human rights issues. According to a US ambassador closely involved with NATO affairs, joint planning sessions of NATO in 1976 and 1977 operated on the assumption that if a "full, frank and balanced survey of implementation" was conducted at Belgrade, nonetheless "deep-seated differences" would be kept "under control" so that "forward-looking new proposals might prove acceptable."[74]

That assumption included the view that "détente in Europe offered the best hope for progress in human rights." From the perspective of the career officers, progress in advancing human rights in East Europe and the USSR could only advance in the slow building of more cooperative, broader East-West relations in the CSCE framework. In essence, they subscribed as had Kissinger before them to the notion of "quiet diplomacy" as the best means for making progress in the human rights field. The difference in ideological perspective from that held by Commission members was reinforced by a resentment of territorial encroachment by an outside body, one hardly experienced in foreign affairs, into what was traditionally the province of State Department specialists.

The perspective of the Commission was very different. Its priority was human rights and casting a giant spotlight upon rights violations as the only way to make progress in the field. From the Commission's viewpoint, therefore, the focus of early government preparatory operations for Belgrade and, indeed, for the Helsinki process as a whole was totally mistaken. Almost from the beginning, it called for the transfer of the center of government's nervous system on Helsinki affairs to another area of the Department. As expressed by a key staffer, "given the highly political, public nature of the Helsinki process, CSCE matters should be handled at the political level within the Department." He went on:

> In the Commission's view, the all-important issues of CSCE implementation and compliance would never get the attention due them in the Department as long as responsibility for CSCE rested in the hands of those most concerned with NATO problems and preserving alliance unity at all costs.[75]

Despite continuing efforts by the Commission to move the operational center of the State Department's CSCE program, the center remained within the Bureau of European Affairs. Friction and tensions persisted, exacerbated by the growing influence of the Commission's authority in Washington political circles.

Fascell and his associates and staff took the monitoring function inscribed in law seriously. The Commission held a series of public hearings, offering testimony of witnesses like prominent former Soviet political prisoner Vladimir Bukovsky and Anatoly Michelson, who had been trying unsuccessfully for over 20 years to get his wife out of the Soviet Union. Other witnesses were experts from the government, academia, the media, and non-governmental groups.[76]

In introducing the Commission's first hearings, Fascell gave emphasis to the panel's objective:

> We hope for a sincere effort at compliance. . . . We hope for a mutual willingness of each signatory to expose its record of implementation—its actual practices—to the comment and inquiry of the signatories. That is the dialogue—without false premises—we hope to pursue and believe important to maintain.[77]

Clearly, "quiet diplomacy" was not his purpose.

The hearings were augmented by creative research studies. The first, an especially imaginative one, was undertaken as early as mid-November

1976, and was an outgrowth of the Soviet Union's rejection of the Commission's request for a visit. As recalled by a top staffer:

> The Soviets wouldn't let us in, so we decided to go to Israel and interview the [Soviet Jewish] émigrés in the absorption centers.[78]

A long questionnaire was prepared in Russian, asking how many times the emigrant had to apply before being allowed to emigrate, how long he had to wait for approval and how long before he actually left, and what other difficulties had he experienced, such as loss of an apartment or a son drafted into the army. All the questions were, of course, linked to the Helsinki accord, especially Basket III.

Spencer Oliver took eight staffers, all fluent in Russian, who conducted the interviews in the absorption centers. What emerged from this original inquiry was a fairly clear picture of the considerable obstacles to emigration from the USSR. The statistical data, while limited and skewed, offered valuable insights.

Further documentation poured in once the Commission became known as a point of contact for ethnic groups with knowledge and experience related to human rights. By early 1977, the Commission had received hundreds of letters and phone calls from families and friends of those Soviet citizens specifically denied permission to emigrate. The Commission's case list ultimately numbered 3,500, a huge resource of fully documented items.[79]

A January 25 memo from staff assistant Meg Donovan, who was accumulating the case load, to Spencer Oliver recommended steps to give the emigration issue high priority.[80] Deputy Staff Director Friendly sent a memo to Fascell, arguing that the Final Act gave the United States a legitimate basis for inquiring into the status of emigration applications in the USSR and elsewhere in Eastern Europe, a position frowned upon in the previous administration. He urged that the matter be broached with Vance.

Raising the emigration issue posed a problem. Emigration was not specifically referred to in the Helsinki accord.[81] Basket III spoke only about reunion of families and of travel. But careful analysis of the accord by the staff demonstrated in a most cogent manner that free emigration was clearly implied by the drafters. The analysis was eventually spelled out in the Commission's 194-page study of the implementation record of the Helsinki signatories. Published on the second anniversary of the signing of the Helsinki accord, the very first implementation report of the Commission offered detailed findings and recommendations.[82] As the initial documented record of the Helsinki implementation, it served as a guide and standard for future studies, and provided policy makers with effective and cogent argumentation. Similar definitive reports would be published in 1980 and 1982.

The Commission, building upon its symbiotic relationship with the Helsinki monitoring groups in the Soviet Union and Eastern Europe, translated and published a total of five volumes of their works during 1977-78.[83] As a repository of source material on Helsinki, and especially on the implementation records of the signatories, the Commission was unequaled. The documentation was requested by many with an interest in the subject, including the foreign ministries of Helsinki signatories, none of whom had created a body remotely resembling the Commission.

Among the major recipients of the Commission studies were non-governmental organizations with special interest in human rights and Eastern Europe. Indeed, these groups had been a primary source for the documentation. The non-governmental community also served as the principal constituency of the Commission, supporter of its aims and channel for its information. The relationship was notably reciprocal. Through the Commission, the groups were able to communicate their concerns to the US government and thereby exert some influence on the formation of CSCE policy. In turn, the Commission could reach out to the grass roots of broad segments of the United States in a close and intimate way.

Solidly entrenched in key citizen and community groups, and with a reputation for expertise in the field, the Commission now moved to assure itself a position of power in the formation of CSCE policy. The forthcoming Belgrade follow-up meeting was critical, and the Commission was determined to be heavily involved.

Vance had already created a structure within the State Department that would focus upon Belgrade. Deputy Secretary of State Warren Christopher, a personal colleague of the Secretary and the second-ranking official of the Department, was placed in overall charge of CSCE policy, assuring that career bureaucrats would not preempt policy making.[84] Christopher's own deputy on CSCE was Matthew Nimetz, a member of Vance's law firm; Christopher himself directed EUR-RPM to make available to the Commission on a regular basis all essential reporting cables and other classified material.

Weekly meetings at the State Department on CSCE preparations to Belgrade were attended by Commission staffers, who urged that the US move more vigorously within NATO to counter notions that a thorough review of human rights implementation would jeopardize the success of the session.[85] The Commission feared that the hesitations and doubts in the NATO alliance would have an impact upon the State Department and prevent Belgrade from being the proper forum for criticism of human rights violations. As early as March, Nimetz met with Oliver, who outlined his perspective on policy at Belgrade. Nimetz later wrote a memo to Vance advising that "the broadest range of policy alternatives [be] considered as we prepare for the Belgrade conference."[86] More of the State Department should be involved "in the preparations," he said, in order to "ensure" this development.

The concerns of the Commission were carried to the summit of policy-making. Fascell wrote to President Carter on April 27, expressing concern about the apparent reluctance of NATO alliance partners to support the human rights dimension of the President's foreign policy.[87] He urged Carter to persuade his Western colleagues to take a more vigorous stand both bilaterally and especially at Belgrade to criticize the Soviet Union and various Warsaw Pact members for failure to comply with Helsinki commitments.

Fascell also met privately with Carter's National Security Adviser, Zbigniew Brzezinski, and zeroed in on the source of the Belgrade policy issue.[88] The Commission chairman questioned the degree to which US policy on CSCE should be linked to NATO policy. He noted that the advantages of NATO unity should be weighed against the constraints this unity could impose on the central element of American policy—human rights. While reminding Brzezinski that Carter had made human rights and Helsinki priorities of US foreign policy, Fascell pointedly complained that the State Department had not yet restructured its CSCE policy to comply with such overall guidelines. No structural change, however, took place or would take place.

If the Commission did not succeed in its efforts to alter the structure of CSCE policy formation and policy implementation in the State Department, it nonetheless contributed significantly to raising the issue of human rights to a much higher level of priority in CSCE policy planning. At the same time, it helped shape a new perspective about Helsinki, stimulating therewith a fundamental shift from a passive, indifferent and, at times, negative view that had previously characterized US policy and policy makers to an activist and positive view. Soon the administration would assume a leadership role in the Helsinki process, for which the Helsinki Commission might very well claim considerable credit.

In a major innovative study in 1979 of Congress' role on foreign policy, Professors Thomas Franck and Edward Weisband argued that a "new

Congressional oversight" over executive branch formulation and execution of policy had developed, particularly in regard to human rights.[89] In essence, this had allowed Congress to "co-determine" foreign policy without regard to constitutional traditional limitations.

Several years after their work was published, a scholar working for the House Foreign Affairs Committee, Margaret Galey, delivered a paper documenting the validity of the Franck-Weisband thesis as it applied to the Helsinki Commission.[90] While her focus was primarily on the Commission's later role in US delegations to the Helsinki follow-up conferences, the argument could very well have applied during the very first year of the Commission's life. By the time of Belgrade, the Commission could be said to be involved in the "co-determination" of American policy on CSCE.

∎ 3 ∎

Using Helsinki as a Banner

A t a May 12, 1976, press conference in Moscow called by Andrei D. Sakharov, Yuri Orlov announced the creation of the Public Group to Support Compliance with the Helsinki Accords in the USSR.[1] It was quickly dubbed the Helsinki Watch Group. Comprised of 11 hardy activists from various intellectual, national, and religious dissident movements, it would soon become the central address for human rights documentation in the USSR. Even though Sakharov called the press conference, he did not serve as a member of the group. He had repeatedly refused to become involved with any formal structure of dissent. He would later say that "because of my psychological make-up and aspirations, I am not and cannot be the leader of any movement."[2] However, Sakharov's wife, Yelena Bonner, was a founding member, along with such well-known individuals as Anatoly Shcharansky, Aleksandr Ginzburg, Ludmilla Alexeyeva, Anatoly Marchenko, Pyotr Grigorenko, and Vitaly Rubin.[3]

Even if not a formal member of the group, Sakharov was to play a major role in publicly articulating its concerns about human rights violations. As early as 1968, this distinguished scientist had demonstrated the central significance of human rights in modern society with a special memorandum he wrote entitled *Progress, Coexistence and Intellectual Freedom*. Later, in 1970, together with two other scientists, Valery Chalidze and Andrei Tverdokhlebov, he formed in Moscow a Committee on Human Rights, which gave emphasis to the need for protecting individual rights in the USSR. A towering figure in the struggle for freedom, he symbolized more than anyone else the movement of democratic dissent in the Soviet totalitarian world. Whether he participated openly in the Helsinki Group was less consequential than his commitment to its principles, which he was able to highlight in frequent public statements and letters to world leaders.

An early form of the Orlov idea for a special Helsinki advocacy group was advanced by the Jewish activist Anatoly Shcharansky, who taught

English to Orlov, Vitaly Rubin, and Andrei Amalrik.[4] Much of the class time was spent in political discussion. At the beginning of March 1976, Shcharansky delineated a complicated proposal by which members of the Soviet intelligentsia would invite their Western counterparts to form committees that would monitor compliance with the Helsinki provisions. Once this was done, then—according to Orlov's recollections—"after a while, we can create the same sort of committee at home with less risk of persecution."[5] Instead of governments examining the implementation of the Helsinki accord, non-governmental bodies would do it, giving human rights a public dimension.

Shcharansky even went to the trouble of drafting the appeal to the West, which Orlov and Amalrik then edited. The three planned to collect signatures from Soviet intellectuals to append to the appeal. At this point, Orlov developed second thoughts about the idea. Mulling over the plan for a month, he came to the conclusion that "nobody in Europe will care" about human rights, as the Western intelligentsia were totally preoccupied with disarmament issues.[6] The only way to proceed, in Orlov's view, was to have the dissenters themselves organize a formal non-governmental group in Moscow. He recalled that "if we wanted compliance with the Helsinki Final Act, it was up to us to monitor it."

Orlov, a prominent physicist and member of the Armenian Academy of Sciences, had been tangentially involved with dissenters since the 1950s. In 1975, he helped form the USSR chapter of Amnesty International. What he felt essential was "forcing the authorities into a dialogue with society." In his view, only such a dialogue could result in a liberalization of the regime and of society.[7]

The Helsinki Final Act fit neatly into his perspective. The Kremlin had, after all, signed a document endorsing human rights and expressly upholding the right of individuals to know and act upon them. Moreover, the entire text of the Helsinki accord had been published in *Izvestiia* in September 1975. If, as a chronicler of the dissident movement noted, Soviet readers of the Helsinki text in the press "were stunned by its humanitarian articles,"[8] few immediately saw its ramifications in terms of organizing quickly a monitoring group. More than ten months would elapse before such a group was created.

Why that was the case is not clear. The chronicler, Alexeyeva, suggested that Soviet activists considered the human rights provisions of Helsinki regressive in comparison with the UN's Universal Declaration of Human Rights and the International Covenant on Civil and Political Rights.[9] That assessment was correct, but not necessarily relevant.

According to Orlov's personal account, "many of us among the dissidents, including some religious activists and even a group of political prisoners in the Mordovia camps," had invoked Helsinki in appeals to the West about Soviet violations of human rights.[10] Apparently, however, no one advanced the idea of organizing in a formal way to exploit the Helsinki accord. At most, Orlov's thinking initially was oriented to encouraging Western governments to utilize the agreement. Thus, he related that when he and his two colleagues met with Congresswoman Fenwick in August 1975, they advised that "the West should use the Helsinki Accords to pressure the Soviet government to honor its human rights obligations, and monitor how well it honored them."[11]

Crucial to the thinking of the Helsinki group founder was the belief that Western governments had a "Munich"-like approach to the Soviet Union. These governments knew in advance, he recorded, that the USSR would fail to fulfill the human rights provisions of Helsinki, but they accepted this limitation because of détente. In the West's perspective, détente was an absolute value and, for its fulfillment, Western governments were "prepared to sacrifice human rights in the USSR."[12] In fact, according to Orlov, the West did not even obtain the benefits of détente; he noted that even as the Helsinki talks proceeded, the Kremlin had installed medium-range missiles in Europe and greatly increased its military presence in Latin America, Africa, and Asia.

Orlov had his own idea concerning security for the West. Only the democratization of the Soviet Union, including genuine free movement of people and ideas, could guarantee mutual security.[13] A totalitarian structure will inevitably embark upon the subversion of détente, he believed. In Orlov's opinion, few in the West understood this view and even fewer believed that democratization of the USSR was possible.

It was to be the principal function of the Moscow Helsinki Group, as explained later by its chairman, to change the approach of the West. The expert documentation of the group was oriented precisely in this direction. Not every Soviet dissident understood Orlov's logic. Malva Landa, who was asked to join the group, sharply condemned the initiative along with the group's formal name. Supporting Helsinki, the critic argued, meant "supporting the Soviet regime."[14] What was the point or the logic of support? But Orlov thought the very language of Helsinki, along with its basic concepts, offered opportunities to expose Soviet human rights practices and, at the very same time, educate public opinion in the West.

Orlov was apparently the first to note "that this is the first document in which the idea of preserving peace is directly linked to respect for human rights."[15] And he also recognized that Moscow had a far greater stake in Helsinki than it had in the key UN human rights documents. As he put it, "if the Soviet government said [Helsinki] was important, it was, in fact, important."[16] He added that "it was the Soviet government itself that gave us something to work with."

In Orlov's view, too, the humanitarian articles could be perceived as minimal international standards. True, he argued, the major goal of Helsinki was peace, but its preservation was linked to human rights. The latter was no longer a matter of internal affairs; it had assumed a general concern. Finally, the accord called upon the citizenry of the signatory powers to assist in observing the humanitarian provisions.

On April 30, 1976, Orlov broached his idea of a monitoring group to Ludmilla Alexeyeva and asked her to join. The group, he explained, would "gather information about specific cases of human rights abuses, issue documents and send them to the governments of the 35 countries that signed the agreement."[17] Documentation would extend to exit visa refusals, interruption of telephone and mail services, political prisoners or "prisoners of conscience," arbitrary incarceration in mental hospitals, and the deprivation of religious and national rights.

The Helsinki group's formation was scheduled for 11:00 P.M. on May 12. A carefully planned announcement of its function declared that "it will accept written complaints about violations of [Helsinki accord] articles directly from the citizens . . . and . . . would readdress those complaints to all the heads of governments who signed the Final Act. . . ."[18] And, to stress its peaceful intention, the group issued a declaration prepared by Shcharansky that stressed that human rights problems "are directly related to problems of international security."[19] It called upon the people of the signatory-nations to form their own national groups of support, which would then lead to "an International Committee for Support."

Orlov and his tiny group were not naïve utopian idealists. They were fully aware that the Soviet regime would act sharply to limit or halt their activities. In toasting the formal creation of Moscow's Helsinki Watch, Orlov said: "To the success of our hopeless task!"[20] Several months later, on September 5, he wrote to Fenwick that his colleagues "can be compared with people who openly throw themselves on barbed wire, hoping that there will be others who will step on their bodies to cross the wire."[21]

Three days after the formation of Helsinki Watch, on May 15, the courageous Orlov was picked up by KGB plainclothesmen and taken to KGB offices. A dispatch from the Soviet news agency TASS related that he had been warned about the "unconstitutional nature" of his activities.

What Orlov was doing, according to TASS, was engaging in "provoca-tive" actions designed "to cast doubt in the eyes of the world community about the sincerity of the Soviet efforts. . . ."[22] The KGB bluntly told Orlov that his acts were unacceptable, anti-Soviet and "punishable by law." Vitaly Rubin, a Zionist member of the Orlov group who was also a specialist on Chinese civilization, confided to his diary that the creation of the group and the hostile response of the regime "raises the dissident movement to a new level."[23] The official response, he noted, revealed "ex-treme aggravation," which for the time being merely served as "adver-tisement for the group."

Soon the Helsinki Watch Group was turning out solidly based docu-ments on various human rights violations. Friendly reporters would make them available to a mid-level US diplomat who, in turn, would have them reproduced and circulated to other CSCE embassies in Moscow.[24] Copies were also made available to the US Helsinki Commission, with which an unexpected relationship had developed. In late November 1976, Orlov obtained the warm reply from Fascell, which went on to further relate that the Commission had been refused visas so that it might meet with him. And the letter offered best wishes for the success of the group's work.[25] The KGB would later use the Fascell letter as evidence that Orlov was receiving instructions from the United States.

From the very beginning, the Helsinki Watch Group made clear that it sought to compile documentation that it hoped "would be considered at all official meetings planned under the Final Act."[26] It specified that cer-tain types of cases would warrant special attention: the taking of children away from parents who are intent upon bringing them up in their own faith; forced psychiatric treatment of individuals with the aim of changing their thoughts, conscience, or beliefs; particularly dramatic examples of separation of families; and examples of especially inhumane treatment of prisoners of conscience. Documentation of these egregious cases would be sent to heads of governments, with requests to "form international commissions for checking the information on site. . . ."

The impact of the Helsinki Watch Group on Western publics would not only be felt through the direct media contacts of group members and through the help of friendly Western embassies. Within minutes after cor-respondents in Moscow had filed their stories, the dispatches would also be carried back to large audiences within the USSR. Translators and broadcasters at Voice of America and Radio Liberty made possible a reg-ular flow of information to the Soviet Union about human rights viola-tions. Much later, Orlov would express his thanks to the foreign radio "voices."[27] Accounts in the Western media also served as a powerful means for stirring consciousness in the United States and fundamentally changing attitudes toward the Helsinki Final Act.

If it was the hope of the Moscow monitors to promote similar monitoring groups in other East European Communist regimes, they found that the first responsive groups came from within the USSR, from non-Russian Soviet republics.[28] Given the impulses flowing from radio transmissions, even if at times jammed or partially jammed, it was scarcely surprising that non-Russian national dissenters would have learned about this brand-new weapon in their striving for individuality and national autonomy. On November 9, six months after the Moscow Group started, the Ukrainian Helsinki Group was formed. On December 1, the Lithuanian Helsinki Group emerged; on January 14, 1977, came the Georgia Helsinki Group; and on April 1, the Armenian Helsinki Group.

Soon afterward, specialized human rights associations were formed. Especially important was the Working Commission to Investigate the Use of Psychiatry for Political Purposes, directly linked to the Moscow Helsinki Group.[29] Other bodies connected with various religious communities would surface, as would some linked to repressed national groups in Russia, such as Tatars. An elaborate, informal system of "messengers" was set in motion, with the Moscow monitoring group at its core. Visits to and from Moscow from the other national republic Helsinki groups and from religious and national organizations enabled the core to amass a considerable amount of valuable documentation.

The various national dissident groups were not the only ones who responded to the appeal by the Moscow Group. In September 1976, the Committee for the Defense of Workers (KOR, later called Committee for Social Defense) was formed in Poland.[30] It insisted upon adherence by the Warsaw government to the provisions of the Helsinki accord. Later, as KOR was transformed into the mass movement Solidarity, the Helsinki accord acquired a major instrument for its public promotion.

In Czechoslovakia, the human rights provisions of the Helsinki accord found a powerful echo in the monitoring group Charter 77. Founded on the first day of 1977, its "declaration" called attention to the International Covenant on Civil and Political Rights and the Helsinki Final Act as instruments to which the state had "the duty to abide."[31] The declaration noted that these instruments were listed in the government's official Collection of Laws and therefore binding. Yet, the Charter 77 document noted that freedom of expression and of religious confession were trespassed upon in violation of the state's obligation to adhere to these international agreements.

The newly created Prague monitoring group sought to highlight the rights accorded all persons in the UN covenants and in the Final Act by "drawing attention to various individual cases where human and civil rights are violated"; Yuri Orlov had articulated the same theme when he founded the Moscow Helsinki Watch Group. The declaration concluded by pointing to the "symbolic name" of the group. The date "77" signified that it was founded at the beginning of that year "in which a conference in Belgrade is due to review the implementation of the obligations assumed at Helsinki."[32]

Even in the brutally repressive regime of Romania's Nicolae Ceausescu, Helsinki found a modest echo. The prominent intellectual Paul Goma, together with several other members of the Romanian intelligentsia, sent on February 18, 1977, an "Open Letter" designed for circulation eight months later to the Belgrade review conference.[33] It complained about the trampling of civil rights in Romania, specifically those enshrined in Basket III, "the right to free movement of persons, ideas, information. . . ." The letter went on to expose the rationale of totalitarian regimes, including Ceausescu's, whereby "the principle of non-interference in internal affairs"—Helsinki's Principle VI—was used to deny the rights of the international community to concern itself with the non-observance of human rights and fundamental freedoms.

The well-known examples did not exhaust the list of those for whom Helsinki provided a banner and sanction for their beliefs and quiet struggle for personal integrity and human rights. James F. Brown, the Director of Radio Free Europe, commented in testimony to the US Helsinki Commission about "countless cases throughout Eastern Europe, totally unreported, in which the Helsinki freedoms have been invoked."[34] He added that those invoking Helsinki knew that they were "gaining publicity in the West."[35] It was the media that helped shape and interpret their distress as well as their hopes. A Swiss scholar, Ernst Kux, has emphasized the role of the "modern electronic media" in opening up "the Iron Curtain,"[36] and a Soviet analyst acknowledged that the "information revolution" acted as a powerful force to reveal "the unseemly aspects of life" in East Europe.[37] This perspective was very strongly endorsed by a US diplomat and scholar specializing in the early Helsinki process.[38]

But it was the enormous personal courage of the known and unknown monitors that gave the media an extraordinary human story to tell. The creation of the Helsinki Watch Group, triggered by the Helsinki accord, in turn stirred a strong and positive American reaction and helped alter Washington's earlier attitude toward Helsinki. There was yet another movement in the USSR that was deeply affected by the Helsinki accord and that would have strong impact upon Washington. Since November 1969, Soviet Jews had built a movement oriented to emigration to Israel. The movement was distinctive, quite unlike any other social movement in the totalitarian Soviet society. If the democratic dissenters had aspirations to liberalize Soviet society by introducing the rule of law, and if the nationalist dissenters in the various non-Russian regions of the USSR sought greater autonomy or independence from Moscow's imperial rule, the Jewish aim was oriented to the outside.

The would-be émigrés did not preach reform of the communist system; rather, they hoped to opt out of it altogether. Jewish activists took the view that anti-Semitism was so deeply rooted in the system that Jews could aspire to a future for themselves only outside of the Soviet Union, particularly in the Jewish state of Israel.[39] There was yet a second feature of the Jewish experience in Eastern Europe that lent itself to emigration. The Holocaust had severed or dispersed many Jewish families. Part of the Jewry of the USSR, and especially of the outer Western regions, ended up in Israel, where even in the mid-1970s, more than 30 years after the Holocaust, its survivors might look for family remnants to help reknit a cleft national body and soul.[40]

A cardinal rule of the Jewish national movement was to avoid any challenge to the established order of totalitarianism.[41] The activists perceived themselves to be marginal players on the Soviet scene. In their view, once recognized as marginal by Moscow, they would be permitted to emigrate. They thus consciously rejected becoming involved in the struggles of the democrats or other nationalists, lest they attract the attention of a basically anti-Semitic system and leadership.[42]

The Jewish movement took naturally to a Helsinki accord that, in Basket III, significantly focused upon "reunion of families" and the obligation of the signatories to facilitate and expedite same. "Reunion of families," while resonating with post-Holocaust reality of severed families, carried with it the right to emigrate, or, as articulated in the International Covenant on Civil and Political Rights, "the right of everyone to leave any country, including his own, and to return to his country."

It was this right that stood at the core of the Soviet Jewry movement. The significance and meaning of this right was made clear in a special study prepared by a Philippine jurist and diplomat, José D. Inglés, and published in 1963 by the United Nations, *A Study of Discrimination with Respect to the Right of Everyone to Leave Any Country, Including His Own, and to Return to His Own Country.*[43]

The landmark UN study of Article 13(b) of the Universal Declaration of Human Rights demonstrated in a most vivid way how, next to the right to life, the right to leave a country has been and remains the most important of human rights. Socrates regarded the right as an "attribute of personal liberty." And the Magna Carta of A.D. 1215 emphasized that it was part of "natural law." With the rise of political democracy in the 18th century, the right was incorporated in constitutions or in statutory law. Thus the French Constitution of 1791 included it, and the American Congress in 1868 formally declared that the right is "a natural and inherent right of all people, indispensable to the enjoyment of the rights of life, liberty and the pursuit of happiness."

Judge Inglés held this right to leave as critical to the exercise of other rights. Thus, he argued, when a person is restrained from emigrating, he may thereby be prevented from observing or practicing the tenets of his religion; he may be frustrated in efforts to marry and found a family; he may be "unable to associate with his kith and kin"; and he might not get the kind of education that he desires. The jurist concluded that disregard of the right to leave "frequently gives rise to discrimination in respect of other human rights and fundamental freedoms, resulting at times in the complete denial of these rights and freedoms."

When the Filipino jurist prepared draft principles on the right, he again stressed that limitations on the exercise of the right ought to be minimal.[44] The right to leave, he observed, "shall not be subject to any restrictions except those provided by law, which shall be only such as are reasonable and necessary. . . ." Once again, the priority of the right was underscored when, in the preamble to the draft principles, Inglés wrote that it was "an indispensable condition for the full enjoyment by all of civil, political, economic, social and cultural rights."

The significance of reunion of families and the right to leave with respect to the Helsinki process cannot be too strongly emphasized. Sakharov considered the emigration right as a veritable precondition for any kind of détente relationship between East and West. The Helsinki Watch Group, in its documentation, gave the subject heavy, at times central, attention. For the US Helsinki Commission, it was a top-priority subject, which, at the beginning, received the greatest amount of research and documentation.

In Washington, even before the Helsinki Final Act, the prominence of the right to leave had become very much part of a throbbing national concern. A leading figure in the US Senate, Henry M. Jackson, drew upon Article 13(b) to introduce the first piece of US legislation consciously and deliberately inspired by the Universal Declaration of Human Rights.[45] It was a draft that linked the grant of certain trade benefits for communist (non-market) countries to the easing of emigration restrictions. The benefits were most-favored-nation tariff treatment (MFN), subsidized (and, therefore, low-interest) government credits, and credit investment guarantees. Such guarantees were extended to US allies and major trading partners. Jackson's proposal had already been introduced in the House of Representatives by Congressman Charles Vanik of Ohio. The legislation—popularly known as the Jackson-Vanik Amendment—clearly aimed at the Soviet restriction of Jewish emigration. Its connection with the Inglés study which preceded it by a decade was evident and direct.

The amendment was hardly unique in American history. Such concern was very much a part of American history that relates to immigrants generally and Jews specifically. America's humanitarian involvement on behalf of Russian Jewry went back more than 100 years.[46] As early as 1869, President Ulysses S. Grant, upon hearing of the contemplated expulsion of 20,000 Jews from an area in southwestern Russia, intervened with the Tsarist authorities. If the banishment was halted, the chronicler of the episode notes, it was "very likely as a result of the US concern. . . ."[47] At least 13 US presidents from Grant to George Bush have intervened, directly or indirectly, on behalf of Russian Jewry during the past 120 years.

In 1891, Benjamin Harrison's Secretary of State, James Blaine, formally justified diplomatic intervention in the internal concerns of a foreign country on grounds that "the domestic policy of a State toward its own subjects" may be "at variance with the larger principles of humanity. . . ."[48] Such "humanitarian intervention" on behalf of persecuted Irish and Armenians, as well as Jews, had been a distinctive feature of the American diplomatic landscape during the 19th and early 20th century.

Frequently, the Congress has acted as a spur to administration action.[49] In 1879, for example, the House of Representatives adopted a resolution criticizing, in part, a Tsarist policy that refused Jews the right to own real estate. The measure was introduced by Samuel Cox, like Charles Vanik a Congressman from Ohio. The following year Cox inserted into the *Congressional Record* a letter from a Russian Jew who wrote: "In this hour of all but hopeless misery, groaning under the yoke of cruel and heartless despotism, we turn to the West. . . ."

In 1883, a House resolution called upon the administration to "exercise its influence with the government of Russia to stay the spirit of persecution as directed against the Jews...." A decade later, in 1892, the House refused to allocate funds for food transport to Russia on grounds that the

Tsarist regime, by its treatment of Jews, had "shocked the moral sensibilities of the Christian world."

Especially significant was the legislative effort in 1911 to abrogate an 80-year-old Russo-American commercial treaty.[50] It constituted almost a dress rehearsal for the Jackson-Vanik congressional drive. Behind that 1911 effort was a determination to relieve the desperate plight of Russian Jews, although the battle was technically fought over the more narrow issue of passport discrimination against American Jews seeking to visit Russia. A March 1910 proclamation by President William Howard Taft, extending minimum tariff rates to Russia despite reluctance by the US Tariff Board, prompted a public campaign. Toward the end of the year, New York Congressman Herbert Parsons cautioned the administration that the House might demand the termination of the 1832 commercial treaty.

The implied threat was rebuffed. The Secretary of State, Philander Knox, argued in a note to the President that "quiet and persistent endeavor" ("quiet diplomacy" in contemporary parlance) would be more effective than treaty abrogation in changing Tsarist policy. A series of State Department memoranda, in early 1911, buttressed the Knox note with arguments that found a remarkable echo later: America's commercial and investment interests would allegedly be harmed, and additional hardships would supposedly befall Russian Jewry.

Much of the American public saw the issue differently. A massive number of petitions and resolutions bombarded Congress. Public rallies were held in several cities, culminating in a mass meeting in New York City addressed by Woodrow Wilson and other luminaries on December 6, 1911, under the auspices of the National Citizens Committee.[51] One week later, speaker after speaker arose in the House of Representatives to express sympathy for Jews and to condemn barbaric practices of Tsarist Russia. The vote for abrogation was overwhelming: 301 to 1.

With the Senate certain to have a similar lopsided vote, the Secretary of State hastened to soften the impact upon the angry Tsarist regime. In language that stressed friendship between the two countries, he advised the Russian foreign ministry that the United States was terminating the commercial treaty as of January 1, 1913. Russian officials reacted with astonishment. They failed to comprehend, a historian of the event observed, "how a moralistic crusade could dictate political action."[52] That failing would also obtain in the 1970s. Senator Jackson repeatedly emphasized both publicly and privately that the United States, as a "nation of immigrants," had a vital stake in promoting the right to emigrate freely.[53]

Two developments, closely related in time, had prompted the Jackson legislation. In August 1972, the Kremlin secretly enacted an edict imposing a so-called "diploma tax" on all Soviet Jews who were granted exit visas for emigration.[54] Those with higher education would be required to pay an exorbitant sum of money, presumably compensating the state for the costs of that education. Scientists with an average annual income of 2,000 rubles were asked to pay 40,000 rubles for themselves and their family.[55]

It was clear that the "diploma tax" constituted a crude effort to halt Jewish emigration. The gates to exodus had been opened by the USSR in March 1971 to placate Western opinion at a crucial moment when détente was just beginning. Approximately 1,000 Jews left the USSR each month that year. But the limited emigration current became a flood during the first six months of 1972, when the monthly rate increased threefold and the requests from Soviet Jews for affidavits (*vizovy*) from Israeli relatives skyrocketed. To end the hemorrhaging, Soviet policy makers decided upon a tax that they probably assumed would prove an insuperable obstacle to emigration.

Jews were especially vulnerable to the diploma tax, relative to other nationalities, because they were the most highly educated segment of Soviet society.[56] According to census data, one third of Soviet Jewry had completed higher education. Jewish activists denounced the unprecedented tax as creating a "new category of human beings—the slaves of the 20th century." Many were keenly aware of the enormous financial problem which confronted them. Not unusual was the situation of art critic Igor Golomshtock, whose "freedom" was purchased by Pablo Picasso for about $20,000.[57] During the eight-month period between August 1972 and through March 1973, 1,450 Soviet Jewish emigrants paid approximately $7 million; how many others were kept from applying or leaving is not known.

An angry Jackson met with American Jewish leaders in Washington in September 1972 and assured them of his determination to respond to the challenge with appropriate legislation.[58] The character of the response was determined by a second development. In October, the United States reached an agreement with the USSR to settle the multibillion-dollar Lend-Lease debt Moscow had accumulated during World War II. The US would receive a small portion of the debt—$722 million—and in return, the administration pledged to seek Congressional approval of legislation granting MFN to Soviet Russia.[59]

The American-Soviet agreement, part of the détente process, offered Jackson-Vanik appropriate leverage. MFN would be tied to the removal of artificially imposed emigration barriers, including devices similar to the diploma tax. The amendment, indeed, specified that only "nominal" taxes be imposed on exit visas.

Of particular significance was the narrow target upon which Jackson-Vanik focused. Not a government's human rights policy generally, or even its specific violation covering a broad spectrum of rights, was at issue. Rather, it was merely one right, although a key one, the right to leave. Other human rights may be important, but for the United States to deal with all or some of them in substantive legislation would have been ineffectual or even counterproductive. If the target was of vital and critical consequence, then strong intervention involving the restriction of certain benefits was appropriate.

Andrei Sakharov, the great Soviet physicist and human rights advocate, viewed Jackson-Vanik in a similar way. He regarded the right to leave as a "minimal right," but one that nevertheless could establish "the proper direction" for an American-Soviet détente.[60] At the heart of that détente, he wrote, "mutual trust" must be rooted in the acceptance of basic international principles of conduct. Without acceptance of basic principles, Soviet policy could be "highly perilous for all mankind, for international confidence, and détente."

Sakharov gambled heavily on the United States adopting the amendment. He took the considerable risk of appealing over the head of Kremlin leaders to the US Congress in an extraordinary letter written in September 1973.[61] Putting his own personal security at stake, he told Congress that failure to enact Jackson-Vanik would constitute "a betrayal of the thousands of Jews and non-Jews who want to emigrate, of the hundreds in camps and mental hospitals, of the victims of the Berlin Wall."[62]

The amendment had enormous bipartisan political support.[63] The lower house version carried 237 co-sponsors—more than one half of the membership—and the Senate version had 75 co-sponsors—three quarters of the Senate. From its very beginning, the amendment—even before enacted into law—exerted a profound positive impact. (It was adopted as part of the Trade Reform Act by both houses in overwhelming votes in December 1974, and was signed by President Gerald Ford on January 10, 1975.) The immediate target was the diploma tax, as was made clear in a joint public statement by Senator Jackson and Congressman Vanik, who denounced the "outrageous price list on human beings that reduced trained and educated men and women to chattel."

By coincidence, a high-level Soviet trade delegation headed by Deputy Minister of Foreign Trade V. S. Alkhimov was in Washington at the time the amendment was initially submitted. A prominent Senator, Democrat Edmund Muskie of Maine, told the delegation at a meeting sponsored by the National Association of Manufacturers that the Soviet visitors "would be profoundly mistaken if they underestimated American feelings on the exit visa question. Americans properly perceive the exorbitant tax on Jewish emigrants . . . as being in violation of fundamental human rights and freedoms."[64]

Alkhimov was personally given the strong message in a meeting with a powerful Congressman, Wilbur Mills, the Arkansas Democrat who headed the key Ways and Means Committee. After the meeting, the Soviet trade official said, "I can see we are not going to get most-favored-nation out of this Congress and my job is to tell Moscow that." At approximately the same time, Treasury Secretary George Shultz traveled to Moscow, where he delivered a similar message to President Leonid Brezhnev and other government leaders. Shultz reported afterward that Soviet officials showed "both the spirit to try to solve the problems and the willingness to tackle them in very real terms."

This was made apparent almost immediately, indicating the potential effectiveness of Jackson-Vanik. Probably for the first time in Soviet history, a Soviet edict was made null and void only six months after its enactment. On March 20, 1973, the USSR publicly disclosed that 44 Soviet Jews with higher education were allowed to leave without paying the tax. The following day Soviet journalist Victor Louis, whose official connections with the KGB were well known, wrote a special article for an Israeli newspaper, *Yediot Achranot*, which announced that the "diploma tax will not be enforced any more."[65] After acknowledging that the Kremlin decision was a result of congressional pressure, Louis added that Soviet Jews seeking to emigrate "have won a victory in the six months' war against the education tax."

When the USSR repudiated in early 1975 the Soviet-American trade agreement of 1972, it neutralized for the moment the effectiveness of the Jackson-Vanik Amendment in dealing with the Soviet Union (although it was effective with other countries). The leverage of the trade agreement no longer existed. Though a later study of the refugee and emigration question by the Twentieth Century Fund called the amendment "the single most effective step the United States has ever taken against the new serfdom [of totalitarian societies],"[66] for Soviet Jews new leverage was needed. Adoption of the Helsinki Final Act in 1975 was more than timely. It provided a potential lever for political and diplomatic action.

During the balance of 1975 and continuing into 1976, more than one-third of the large number of Jewish petitions and appeals sent to the

Kremlin or abroad specifically framed their legal argument in the context of Helsinki.[67] According to activists Ilya Essas and Benjamin Fain, an unsung non-Jew played a key role initially.[68] His name was virtually unknown in the West. Vladimir Albrecht, reportedly of Polish Catholic origin, was active in the general Soviet dissident movement. A specialist on international law, he clearly comprehended how Helsinki provided a "legal framework for aliyah."[69] He volunteered to advise Jewish activists on the technical legal aspects of the Helsinki accord, and, having a "very creative" mind, he became the "Chalidze of the Jewish movement." (Valery Chalidze, although a scientist, had steeped himself in human rights law and worked with Andrei Sakharov and other prominent dissidents in the early 1970s.)

A Jewish lawyer, Yakov Eisenstadt, also advised those seeking to emigrate. When interviewed later at Hebrew University in Jerusalem, he expressed the opinion that Helsinki carried a special moral force, partly because it had been personally signed by Soviet President and Communist Party boss Leonid Brezhnev.[70] Equally important, he said, the Helsinki accord specifically referred to the Universal Declaration of Human Rights and the International Covenant on Human Rights, both of which obliged governments to assure "the right of everyone to leave any country." In Eisenstadt's view, Helsinki created an especially "useful mechanism" in the form of follow-up meetings. These forums permitted the public raising of Helsinki issues in the international arena, enabling activists to focus widespread attention upon them. It was the forums that gave meaning and emphasis to the theme of reunion of families and turned that theme into a core issue of the Helsinki process.

Not surprisingly, that issue would resonate loudly in the United States, which had for over a century been concerned with the Russian Jewish plight. American Jewry considered emigration a question of the greatest urgency. Indeed, for the Jewish community and its allies and supporters, Soviet Jewish emigration became the key issue, a virtual metaphor for Helsinki, just as several years earlier arms control had become for Henry Kissinger and many other US policy makers a metaphor for détente.

▪ 4 ▪

The Eve of Belgrade

One of the greatest achievements of the Helsinki Final Act was the concept of the follow-up meeting. For it was the follow-up meeting—where implementation of the accords was reviewed—that lent the Final Act a semi-juridical and politically binding character. Without the follow-up, the accord constituted simply a declaration, a manifesto, or a statement of principles, but nothing that compelled or required fulfillment of promises that authorities had made. Being held up to moral obloquy at review sessions conceivably could serve the purpose of a moral sanction. Governments resent being exposed to a process of "shaming," of being held up to public contempt. Prestige and image are very much factors in world politics, especially for superpowers. In their efforts to exert influence in countries, they rely not only on military or economic might. In the modern world, the moral image they cast is almost as vital upon world opinion as their military or economic strength.

Belgrade would provide a major test of the value of the Helsinki accord. It was for that reason that dissidents in Eastern Europe and their supporters in the West placed great hopes upon it. Sakharov, moral conscience of democratic and reformist tendencies in the East and a voice of integrity unchallenged in the West, sent a special message to the Belgrade conference on its opening day, October 4.[1] The message stressed that Helsinki was an "inseparable bond between international security and an open society," which he defined as the freedom of people to move across state borders, the free exchange of information, and freedom of conscience. Sakharov placed the responsibility upon the West to secure the human rights aims of the Helsinki accord. He asked:

> Is the West prepared to defend these noble and vitally important principles? Or will it, little by little, accept the interpretation of the principles of Helsinki, and of détente as a whole, that the leaders of the Soviet Union and of Eastern Europe are trying to impose?

The scientist-humanist stressed that Moscow and its satellites "have always tried to neutralize the humanitarian sections of the Helsinki accord by emphasizing the principle of non-interference. . . ." Sakharov contended that every person serving in the gulag for his beliefs, every person hospitalized in a psychiatric ward for political reasons, each person refused permission to emigrate or travel was a victim of the direct violation of the Helsinki accord. Warning that failure to support "freedom of conscience in an open society" would lead to "surrender to totalitarianism and the loss of all precious freedom," Sakharov called upon "the West, its political and moral leaders . . . not to allow this."

He specifically appealed to President Carter and the US Congress "to declare the defense of human rights in the whole world to be a fundamental moral policy of the United States." It was to the United States that the Soviet (and East European) dissidents, democratic activists and refuseniks looked for assistance in transforming Helsinki into a positive weapon for their relief. Thus, the Sakharov message, with its special appeal to the United States to assume a leadership role at Belgrade, basically echoed their views as well as those of the increasingly vigorous US Helsinki Commission. Nothing would have been more natural than for the United States to assume this new posture, as Carter had built his presidential campaign, in considerable part, upon the United States placing emphasis upon human rights in its foreign policy. It was to be the heart of US policy in dealing with international issues generally, whether with reference to Latin America and the developing world or to the totalitarian states of Eastern Europe. Human rights policy toward the Soviet Union had already been signaled in the early days of the new administration when the President responded warmly to a letter from Sakharov.[2] Later, in June 1978, Carter went out of his way and, in an unprecedented manner, formally denied that Anatoly Shcharansky had been an agent of the Central Intelligence Agency, thereby calling into question the arrest and the formal charge leveled by the Kremlin against the spokesman of Moscow's Helsinki Watch Group.[3] Shcharansky had been arrested in March for alleged espionage activities, including spying for the CIA, and was convicted in July 1978. The charges were, of course, totally baseless.

If the Soviets were encountering human rights pressure from a new source—the US executive branch—their problems with an older nemesis continued unabated. Moscow's irritation and anger with the US Congress was growing. Fascell acknowledged to an academic conference in April 1977 in Williamsburg, Virginia, that "we are producing new tensions with new emphasis on human rights, but that ought not to deter us."[4] In Fascell's mind, this was not altogether unexpected; indeed, it was welcome, because to him implementation of the Helsinki accords would achieve a reduction of tensions over the long run.

In the summer, Moscow's leading authority on US affairs, Gyorgy Arbatov, stressed that the USSR was unhappy with the US human rights policy.[5] From Moscow's point of view, according to Arbatov, US advocacy of human rights and support for Soviet dissidents were not legitimate aspects of permissible ideological struggle. Moreover, the hostile Soviet attitude on dissidents had sharpened. KGB boss Yuri Andropov, in a rare public speech on September 9, forcefully denounced dissidents as nothing more than common criminals.[6]

Even as the anti-US criticism grew, some prominent democratic activists and non-conformist artists were suddenly allowed to leave; indeed, they were encouraged to stay abroad permanently. Thus, Valentin Turchin, a top-level computer scientist who had helped found the Soviet branch of Amnesty International, was told on August 30 that his earlier visa application for a temporary leave had been granted, with the understanding that he should not return.[7] Over a dozen leading dissident figures were granted permission to leave this way. On the other hand, the heads of the Helsinki Watch Committee—Orlov, Shcharansky, Aleksandr Ginzburg—remained incarcerated. Jewish emigration was kept low. Thousands of Soviet Jews were either refused exit visas or were discouraged from making application to emigrate. This was indicated by the huge numerical difference between the size of the figure for those who requested affidavits (vizovs) from an Israeli relative between 1971 and the end of 1976 and those who actually left.[8] That difference totaled 186,419. (Initiation of the emigration process required an affidavit.) Moreover, the applicants were harassed with dismissal from jobs, threats of being brought to trial on charges of parasitism, arrests on trumped-up charges, and military conscription. Virulent anti-Semitic propaganda and newly proposed laws on religion also seriously affected Jews.

The Soviets dropped hints of a withdrawal from Belgrade should the United States continue pursuing the heightened human rights theme at the follow-up meeting. Moscow encouraged such reports to intimidate the West Europeans, who—the Soviets hoped—would in turn seek to restrain Washington. French parliamentarian Claude Marcus demonstrated this West European anxiety when he told the Williamsburg conference participants "the French were cautious on the matter of human rights" because "they were afraid there might be some damage to the positive effects of détente."[9] He was specific about his fears for the Helsinki process:

"If we interfere too much in Soviet internal affairs," he said, "we fear we may lose détente."

More specific was a member of West Germany's Bundestag, Peter Corterier. He noted that in the short two-year history of the Helsinki accord, some 60,000 East Germans had emigrated to the Federal Republic of Germany.[10] For this reason alone, Bonn was reluctant to jeopardize the program of détente by raising human rights issues in the Soviet Union.

British parliamentarian Alan Lee Williams expressed the fears of many of his countrymen about a hostile Moscow reaction, quoting a remark by David Owen, the British Foreign Secretary: ". . . any approach to the USSR must be sufficiently balanced as not to jeopardize détente."[11] Yet, Williams was not altogether reluctant to defend Western values. In his view, Moscow badly needed Western technology and, therefore, excessive Western defensiveness was unwarranted. But even Professor Richard Pipes—a hard-liner on Soviet affairs—cautioned that, unless the United States was determined to be forceful and systematic in raising human rights over the long run, it would be a mistake to push for human rights altogether.[12]

The anxieties of major West European democracies, most notably the Federal Republic of Germany, constituted a vital element in NATO decision making, and had an effect on those State Department officials whose responsibility it was to reinforce and avoid disruption of US ties with NATO and Western Europe. These were the career officials in the Department dealing with NATO affairs—the Bureau of European Affairs— the Helsinki Commission's rivals in CSCE affairs. How they would have preferred to handle Belgrade was later suggested by the Department's principal Final Act negotiator, Ambassador Albert Sherer, Jr.[13]

Sherer would not have rejected raising the human rights issue. On the contrary, "American human rights principles" required Washington to "adopt a stance" for articulating them, he said. But such a stand, in his view, must not take a form that resulted in "jeopardizing realistic hopes of practical results." This meant two crucial tactical guidelines. First, the United States "should revert to a lower profile," and should "encourage the West European countries to take the lead." In other words, Sherer would have opted for the policy that characterized the US negotiation style during the three years it took to prepare the Helsinki accord.

But it was precisely a higher profile and a leadership role by the United States that marked President Carter's thrust. This was never expressed in any concrete way, but it was inherent in the President's report about Belgrade. He wrote that the follow-up conference's "major task" was to conduct exchange of views on CSCE implementation since the Helsinki summit.[14] This would have necessitated a "higher profile" and a US leadership role, for no one else would have demanded and followed through on the question of CSCE implementation.

Secretary of State Vance was the key figure to advance the President's strategy. In June 1977, he told the Helsinki Commission that "we seek full implementation of all the commitments contained in the Helsinki Final Act" and "we must not be diverted from an assessment of how fully the specific undertakings of Helsinki have been carried out by all the signatories."[15] The emphasis upon review of implementation was precisely the view of the Commission.

How did this strategy fit in with the United States' or Carter's human rights purposes? One "basic objective," Vance said, was to improve "the lot of the individual citizen" in each signatory-state. The best way of reaching this goal, he went on, is "by concentrating . . . on the review of implementation." The problem with the Secretary's presentation was that, while he emphasized individual rights as a US goal, at the very same time, he also stressed as a "basic objective" the "improving [of] the relationship between states." Might not the review of implementation be sufficiently critical as to produce a confrontation with the Soviet Union, and would this not lead to a worsening of US-Soviet relations?

Vance did not resolve the contradiction. Whether or not the United States was to raise implementation publicly or through "quiet diplomacy" would be determined "on the spot," he said. In a speech at the University of Georgia on April 1, he had observed that no "mechanistic formula" could produce "an automatic answer" in dealing with human rights. "Informed and careful judgment" is essential in dealing with the issue in a specific setting.

The legislative co-author of the Helsinki Commission, Senator Clifford Case, worried that Vance was straddling the issue. "There is confrontation here," he told the Secretary of State, suggesting that any genuine review meant disclosure of the repressive conditions prevailing in the Soviet Union and Eastern Europe and, therefore, constituted a serious challenge to the Kremlin, to which, incidentally, Case did not object:

> The ultimate confrontation is between the system of the East and the system of the West. Unless we really treat this as involving that, I do not think we are doing what at least I believe the Congress considers ought to be done.[16]

Without "confrontation" at Belgrade, thought the Senator, "it would be to just go through an exercise and waste an awful lot of good people's time." In a stunning manner, he threw down the gauntlet to the urbane Secretary of State: "Frankly, I have not yet seen the kind of spirit to have the knock-down, drag-out real confrontation that I think is called for at this stage."

Commission militancy would not overwhelm Vance, who was on record as strongly in favor of cooperating with the Fascell Commission and who, besides, spoke for an administration that stood for human rights. After assuring the Senator that "we will make a real effort" to fulfill at Belgrade the "obligations" the US had assumed, he commented:

> Our commitment to human rights and to reviewing the implementation of the Helsinki accords on human rights is deep and abiding, and I think it is just as deep and abiding as that of the Congress.[17]

A friendlier questioner was Senator Claiborne Pell, co-chair of the Commission. A former foreign service officer and sensitive to the problems of diplomacy, he raised probing issues in two areas.[18] First, he sought to ascertain whether the emphasis on human rights was "having an adverse effect" on US détente relations with the Soviet Union, particularly with respect to the vital issue of arms control. Pell surmised that human rights ran on a separate track from arms control and, therefore, policy with respect to one need not spill over onto the other.

Vance's response was most revealing. He agreed with the two-track concept. The question of arms control, especially in the strategic area, he thought, "stands on its own two feet" so far as the "basic interest" of the USSR was concerned.[19] Thus, the Secretary argued, there was no "linkage" between the two separate tracks of arms control and human rights. It was very clear that he did not want them linked. The absence of linkage was to have profound repercussions for Belgrade as a whole.

Pell's other question dealt with the attitude of the NATO allies to a US policy that openly raised the human rights issue. Vance's response sought to play down differences. The various NATO countries would have "different public responses" to the question. In private, *all* of the allies, he added, told the US "that they are very much with us" but cannot afford to be "as outspoken." In any case, he assured Pell, the US would "coordinate very closely with our allies" in Belgrade.[20]

Vance's testimony came on June 6, some ten days before the beginning of the preparatory meeting for working out the agenda for the regular session in the fall. The US team was headed by Ambassador Sherer, an experienced foreign service officer, but included Spencer Oliver, Guy Coriden and Marty Sletzinger—three staff members of the Commission already playing vital roles in the Helsinki process.

The US delegation avoided any confrontation. Deliberately, it played all issues in what was described by a knowledgeable journalist in "low-key" fashion.[21] The objective of the delegation was purely technical and procedural, rather than substantive—to make certain that an adequate amount of time would be devoted to a thorough review of implementation. In pursuit of this aim, the US permitted the West Europeans to take the lead.[22] The United Kingdom introduced the West's principal agenda proposal on the issue of time allocated for implementation review. Still, it was evident that, unlike the earlier era when the US role was "detached," now American negotiators were very active, and openly so.

An example of the newly evident US influence was found in the Western proposal that called for far more public sessions than had been held during the 1972-75 negotiations. Almost all of the latter had been held in private, a procedure now sharply criticized by the Americans. Nevertheless, there was nothing in the preparatory meetings that would suggest, as one journalist reported, that "Carter is riding into battle waving a human rights spear."[23]

It was at the preparatory Belgrade meeting that a vital document for the entire Helsinki process was formulated and agreed to, the so-called "Yellow Book" establishing the "grid" for the follow-up meeting.[24] The specific time and place of each plenary or working group session were precisely spelled out in the grid. The document could not, of course, spell out how much or what would be accomplished. The Yellow Book also provided that the first week of the plenary sessions was open to the press. At the initial sessions, the host country and each participating state would give opening speeches. This would be followed by a closed session, lasting one week and devoted to a general discussion of the agenda. The subsequent week would be given over to speeches by the non-participating Mediterranean states.

In addition to the Yellow Book, each delegation would be provided a copy of the "Green Book" that carried the provisions of the Helsinki Final Act (green was the color of the cover of the document). The two "books" formed a kind of Bible for the sessions of the Belgrade review conference, an indispensable source of guidelines. They would later facilitate arrangements for future review conferences as well as prevent alteration of the rules.

The plenary would meet almost daily for the first three weeks, after which focus would shift to subsidiary working groups corresponding to each of the baskets. The working groups would meet every weekday up to the twelfth week. The mandate for the working groups at Belgrade was scheduled to end on December 16, and the conference was expected to be finalized with a "concluding document" on December 22.

The earlier conflict between the Commission and the State Department career officers intensified after the preparatory session. The Commission was especially anxious that it prevail at Belgrade in giving high visibility to human rights issues. From the Commission's viewpoint, there was little in the Department's conduct or its plans that had suggested a more vigorous human rights line in the fall.[25] Besides, one former top Commission staffer complained, the US career diplomats held meetings without inviting the Commission staffers and prevented the latter from receiving invitations to social functions.[26]

In contrast, what disturbed the career professionals, as indicated in an unpublished essay by one key Department officer, was the "little interest in or sympathy" on the part of the Commission "with the broader policy concerns of European governments in the CSCE process."[27] And, he added, the Commission was "largely unconcerned" about how CSCE meetings affect "East-West atmospherics." Instead, he saw the Commission as simplistically engaged in "legalist accounting" of the implementation record, which inevitably led to "systemic criticism" of the USSR. Such "narrowness" bred a skepticism of other vital CSCE topics, such as arms control. This was the big danger.

What no doubt played an important role in strengthening the hand of the Commission in its struggle with key State Department officials on the question of quiet diplomacy was the position taken by Zbigniew Brzezinski, the National Security Adviser to the President. At a meeting on August 23, 1977, of the Policy Review Committee, the top-level interagency body dealing with foreign affairs, Brzezinski, as his personal journal noted, "pushed hard . . . for a more assertive US posture in CSCE."[28] He went further. Assuming the role of devil's advocate, he "stunned everyone" at the meeting by proposing that a paper be prepared which would deliberately examine the advisability of "a confrontationist approach" to the Soviet Union.

The journal went on to record his impression that "the State Department types were horrified even by the thought."[29] The Brzezinski proposal was part of his aggressive, consciously anti-Soviet overall policy approach on East European questions. In his view, only by his pressing for the tough confrontation approach could he "stiffen . . . backs" of the State Department officials and thereby permit the United States to "take the lead in pushing" CSCE toward higher standards. The struggle against the State Department was, at least in part, a reflection of Brzezinski's political and ideological conflict with Cyrus Vance over the direction of US policy.

But the principal decision maker on US policy at Belgrade was the President himself.[30] His instrument: a totally unexpected, last-minute appointment. Chosen in September, two months after the preparatory session and but a short time before the plenary began, Arthur J. Goldberg had a reputation far exceeding that of any other US ambassador or any of the other CSCE ambassadors at the time. Initially a labor lawyer and negotiator who had occupied a high post in the AFL-CIO, he served President John F. Kennedy as Secretary of Labor, and was later appointed to the Supreme Court, where he came to be positively identified with human rights. President Lyndon Johnson enticed him to step down from the Court and become his Ambassador at the United Nations, where he played significant roles on both Middle East and human rights issues.

If Goldberg seemed like a perfect symbolic choice, in fact the appointment was almost accidental. Apparently, Carter had initially asked him to serve as a presidential envoy to mediate Middle East tensions.[31] However, resistance to this decision came from both Vance and Brzezinski, each of whom had a different perception of how the Middle East conflicts should be handled. Someone in the upper echelons of the administration evidently proposed finessing a political embarrassment—as Goldberg had already agreed to take the Middle East job—by offering him the CSCE ambassadorship.

The selection of Goldberg to head the US delegation in Belgrade was a dramatic demonstration of the US commitment to human rights, and particularly of President Carter's determination to give it the highest priority. A draft communication of the State Department dated September 2, 1977, found in the Sherer archive, highlighted the administration perspective.[32] The cable, intended for the principal US embassies in Europe and Canada, but apparently not sent, read:

> As demonstration of deep US commitment to CSCE, President Carter has appointed former Ambassador and Supreme Court Justice Arthur Goldberg as Ambassador-at-Large with responsibility for CSCE.

The various US ambassadors were to have been advised that they "should seek urgent appointment with Foreign Minister" or a "most senior" ministry official and "draw" upon the following:

> Decision to appoint Ambassador Goldberg reflects President's belief that the broad importance of CSCE to American policy in Europe justifies appointment of a single high level official who can concentrate on CSCE matters exclusively.

... Ambassador Goldberg is one of the most distinguished of American political leaders. His varied career in the fields of labor and social policy, the judiciary
and diplomacy provides him with a unique perspective for dealing with complicated issues connected with CSCE.[33]

The appointment could hardly have sat well with the State Department's career officers for whom CSCE meant a unique field that properly
was their prerogative. It was perceived, as Sherer later noted, to be a
"delicate fabric" that "should not be strained by international burdens it
was never meant to carry."[34] Sherer advocated avoiding "headline accusations" and "confrontation."[35] Instead, while human rights would be
pursued, the United States delegation should have a "lower profile," with
the West European countries encouraged "to take the lead." Yet the very
nature of the Goldberg selection meant a high profile and a definite leadership role. Not accidentally, Goldberg was given the title of "Ambassador-
at-Large," while all the other CSCE delegation heads were simply called
"Ambassador."

Later, in a speech prepared for the American Bar Association in August 1978, Sherer contrasted Geneva, where the Helsinki accord was
largely drafted, with Belgrade.[36] While he disclaimed "value judgments,"
he could not avoid indicating his preference. At Geneva, the US delegation had been devoted to working out "compromise language," for "we
operated on the assumption" that "close cooperation" was required by
the consensus rule. Instead of press conferences (which deliberately were
not held), all meetings were kept confidential. Sherer then made the crucial observation that obviously was at the heart of his irritation: "Very little attention was paid to US domestic politics." He clarified the point by
adding "nobody's 'credibility' was at stake." The reference was to Goldberg's later constant assertion that the President's "credibility" was at
stake at the Belgrade meeting. Human rights, Sherer went on, had not
been perceived at Geneva as being in "a special category." Rather, the
dominant definition of CSCE had been the "European security conference," not the "Helsinki agreement on human rights."[37] If the "Helsinki
Final Act was not on human rights," he said, there had been also no intention by anyone "to change the political or social systems of others."
Progress would be made by "patient, long-term, step-by-step improvement." Clearly, the thrust of the new US policy at Belgrade was not to his
liking.

For Sherer, who was kept on as deputy chief of mission, the new appointment was obviously most disturbing. He had, after all, directed the
US role in the CSCE negotiations for several years, including the

preparatory talks to the Belgrade plenary meeting. Goldberg told a Commission staffer that he had met with Sherer and suggested to him that he take another embassy position elsewhere. (The story was related by the staffer in an interview.[38]) Sherer was reported to have responded that he chose to stay and, since he had ambassadorial rank, could not be dismissed. The staffer surmised that Sherer was strongly encouraged to stay on by George Vest, then the Assistant Secretary of State for European Affairs.

That tensions would result was not unexpected. The coolness between the head of delegation and his deputy was apparent to all. Goldberg recognized that his appointment was resented by the State Department's career officers, and he clearly reciprocated. In Goldberg's view, career officers could not transcend the limitations of training and experience which had focused upon accommodation and not upon challenging other diplomats with respect to human rights. The unpublished memoirs of Dorothy Goldberg, the Ambassador's wife, who served as a member of the delegation, record that her husband was "impatient" with Sherer's being someone who was "completely responsive to Departmental directives."[39] At the same time, she perceptively recognized that those "who had been associated with the Helsinki agreement from the beginning virtually had a vested interest in maintaining an equable climate at Belgrade. . . ."[40] This was pursued "for the sake of détente."

An "equable climate," of course, was not Goldberg's interest, nor that of President Carter. The tensions between the new Ambassador and his deputy proved beneficial to the Helsinki Commission staffers, who could be relied upon to assist vigorously Goldberg's activism. Spencer Oliver, the Commission's staff director, was named counselor of the delegation, its third-ranking official. His relationship with Goldberg would be close.

Goldberg's prominence and high status spilled over to his relationships with the other ambassadors, especially as he was prone to reflect it in his conduct. As described by a Commission staffer who had observed Goldberg closely, he was at times officious and imperious, but this—thought the sympathetic staffer—was as much a consequence of his bearing and age as it was of an extremely successful previous career.[41]

More significant than his distinguished career in enhancing Goldberg's display of self-esteem and his attitude to State Department subordinates and ambassadorial colleagues was his personal "anointment," as it were, by the President of the United States. Sherer's wife, Carroll, recalled in an article that Goldberg "constantly reminded members, not only of his own delegation, but of others," that he was "responding to direct orders from the White House," and "several times he claimed to have been telephoned by the President himself."[42]

Mrs. Sherer's observation was probably correct, even if she was uncertain as to whether Goldberg was giving expression to "fact or fancy." Recorded in Dorothy Goldberg's memoirs is a forthright assertion by the Ambassador that he took his orders from the President of the United States and not from the State Department. The occasion was a small meeting in Washington with Secretary of State Vance, Deputy Secretary Warren Christopher, and National Security Adviser Brzezinski just prior to Goldberg's departure.[43]

What was being discussed was the preliminary draft of the maiden speech that Goldberg would deliver at the Belgrade conference. The newly appointed Ambassador had found the State Department's text of the draft inadequate. It was Goldberg's desire to state simply that Moscow and several other East European countries were not honoring the Helsinki human rights commitments. He did not intend at that stage to cite specific cases and names. But even this moderate perspective was challenged by "various quarters in the State Department, and notably by Professor Marshall Shulman, its top Kremlinologist." Finally, a determined Goldberg made it very clear that "he would not make his maiden speech in the way the State Department wants." And he reminded the group that "he represented the President of the United States, not the State Department."

The close relationship with the White House was demonstrated on November 18, 1977. Goldberg, temporarily returned from Belgrade, met with President Carter at the White House. The President was extravagant in his praise of the Ambassador, who had been "particularly effective," and emphasized how he was "very proud of what you have accomplished."[44] At a press conference afterward, Goldberg publicly noted that he had "aggressively" pursued the subject of human rights "under instructions by the President."[45]

While the appointment of Goldberg was the most stunning example of the new policy line of the administration on the Helsinki process, several minor developments pointed in the same direction. No longer would "quiet diplomacy," so characteristic of the pre-Carter epoch, prevail. Rather, "public diplomacy" was the order of the day, oriented as it was to involving the public, trumpeting the issues, openly expressing the grievances of the peoples of East Europe and the Soviet Union, and specifically planning at Belgrade for a detailed review of implementation.

Matthew Nimetz, the Counselor of the Department, a confidant of Secretary Vance and certainly not a career officer, sent several letters to non-governmental organizations, highlighting the new orientation. On July 29, he wrote to the NGOs that, even while the Belgrade preparatory meeting was still going on, he was certain that the signatories would agree to "a thorough review of what has and has not been done since Helsinki to implement all sections of the Final Act."[46] On August 25, he wrote again, inviting the NGOs to a meeting with State Department officials in order to ascertain the public's view.[47] Nimetz told the recipients that "the stage for an honest review of implementation" had been set.

One week later, September 2, Nimetz sent Christopher a memorandum.[48] It reported that in response to an invitation he extended to NGOs regarding a September 9 State Department meeting, he had received a joint letter from ten leading ethnic groups relating their concern. Copies of the memo and the letter were sent to key Department officials, including those connected with the Bureau of European Affairs. In the letter, the groups expressed anxiety about "the inadequate process of implementation of the Final Act by the Warsaw Pact signatories," and called upon the US delegation to "utilize every opportunity to raise this issue."[49] They further urged that special attention be given to the "Human Contacts" section of Basket III dealing with reunion of families and travel for personal and professional reasons.

The fact that Nimetz took the letter seriously and sent it to key Department personnel for their consideration testified to the totally new style of policy formation in the Carter administration. To a considerable extent, this was due to the impact of the Fascell Commission, which had cultivated the ethnic NGOs, urging them to become involved, and had spurred President Carter and Vance to be responsive to "public diplomacy."

An outgrowth of this style was the administration's decision to appoint to the US delegation representatives from different walks of life and of varying ethnic origins. Thus, the citizen's delegation included a representative of the labor movement, a Roman Catholic monsignor, an Eskimo, a black woman lawyer, a Polish-American political science professor, a college president and others.[50] As described by a Commission staffer, each functioned, "in effect, as both a symbol of and conduit to their respective segments of US society."[51] They may not have performed useful diplomatic roles, but they certainly underscored President Carter's commitment to human rights and citizens' involvement in that effort. To those inclined to traditional modes of foreign service, the size and character of the delegation were mind-boggling. And, it was, of course, true that no other CSCE delegation included ordinary citizens or representatives of non-governmental organizations.

Another departure from the diplomatic norm was the US decision to hold frequent press conferences in Belgrade so as to inform the media about the closed sessions. This form of public diplomacy was uncharacteristic of previous Helsinki practice. But that practice had been guided throughout by the narrow diplomatic perspective that the sessions must remain closed to realize any progress. As late as the preparatory meeting in Belgrade, it was agreed that, as in the earlier sessions in Geneva, the regular review conference would be kept closed to the public. The career professionals, not surprisingly, disdained the press conference procedure.

Especially significant as a departure from traditional diplomacy was the role the Commission staff played in Belgrade. While, symbolically, the Commission was accorded high status, with Fascell and Pell appointed vice-chairmen of the delegation, it was on the staff level that the Commission's presence became most pronounced. Nine staffers served in various capacities, enabling them to outnumber the purely State Department professional group.[52] They fulfilled every essential task from writing speeches and drafting reporting cables to lobbying with other delegations. In time, they developed an unequaled expertise: while career officers would serve on CSCE jobs for several short years and then move on to other posts, Commission staffers, in the main, stayed on. They became the "memory" of the CSCE process, and, having mastered the critical procedural matters, could effectively help guide future delegation heads, unlike most State Department members.

Goldberg, in a letter to Fascell, would later comment that the Commission staffers provided "invaluable help" to him. He was "particularly impressed" with the "caliber" of their work.[53] In public testimony, Goldberg acknowledged that there was a "great deal of skepticism" as to whether this joint executive-legislative cooperation could effectively work. He went on to respond to the skeptics:

> In fact, I very early made no distinction between those who represented the State Department and those who represented the Commission and other agencies of the government.[54]

The Ambassador's embrace of the Commission and his extending it "an important front-seat role" at Belgrade—as noted by Dorothy Goldberg in her memoirs[55]—intensified the alienation of the State Department personnel who were traditionally inclined and opposed in principle to involving congressional representation in diplomatic matters. Her memoirs record that "some of our foreign service people" regard the congressional Commission as a "dubious element whose very outspoken commitment to the Helsinki process appears unduly enthusiastic, even a bit rash. . . ."[56]

▪ 5 ▪

The Breakthrough at Belgrade

or Ambassador Goldberg, the central purpose of Belgrade, he told his wife, was to "*review* implementation of the Final Act."[1] In order to underscore his point, he would deliberately spell out the word, "R-E-V-I-E-W."

As a jurist, Goldberg looked upon the Helsinki obligations as virtually contractual even though the Final Act was not a binding treaty and even though decisions were reached by consensus. Moscow had, after all, signed the document, just as the United States had. Moreover, the very nature of the rule of consensus made implementation more compelling than would ordinarily be the case. With no state compelled to accept the text, there was no excuse whatsoever for refusal to implement the Act.

Nor could it be said that the Soviet Union was unaware that "review of implementation" meant precisely a critical examination of the conduct of Helsinki signatories in the human rights field. At the Belgrade preparatory meeting, Moscow's negotiators fought to keep the regular review sessions, opening on October 4, as short as possible, with a firm cut-off date and a work program that would limit the scope and nature of the implementation review.

A State Department report, not released until June 1978, revealed that at the preparatory meeting the USSR had strongly resisted the establishment of subsidiary work groups or committees to allow detailed examination and discussion of implementation.[2] What Moscow wanted and failed to achieve was a restriction on implementation discussion to only the large and unwieldy plenary sessions. Moscow also sought to blur the distinction between a review of implementation and a discussion of "new proposals," so as to limit evaluation of Helsinki commitments. Indeed, the USSR attempted—unsuccessfully—to insert language in the agenda designed to avoid the past and current conduct of the signatories and focus instead on future "positive" and "forward-looking" proposals.

These restrictive initiatives came to nought; a full-scale review was accepted.

It was at Goldberg's first news conference at the State Department, after he was sworn in as Ambassador to the Belgrade talks, that America's policy at Belgrade was publicly indicated.[3] The focus would be on implementation of Helsinki's provisions. Significantly, US policy was perceived in the context of a *process*, rather than of a specific point at which an agreement would be reached, a problem solved. The newly appointed Ambassador emphasized that in dealing with Eastern Europe, "progress has always been very slow," but nonetheless, "I regard Belgrade and the Helsinki Accord to be a process. . . ." Even if future followup forums were by no means certain, Goldberg was convinced that "there will be other Belgrades in other places." Central to the process, he emphasized, was "a continuing monitoring of performance by all signatories to the accord," the core of American policy.

The question was posed as to how focus could be on implementation without leading to confrontation with the Soviet Union. Goldberg sought to finesse the issue by noting that the Helsinki accord on human rights already existed, with a follow-up conference dealing with implementation at its heart. But when the question of confrontation was again raised, he decided upon a categorical statement: ". . . there would be no confrontation."

At the same time, he acknowledged that American policy would be geared to reviewing Soviet practice on free expression of ideas, on free movement of Jews and Germans, on access by Western journalists, and on removing obstacles to travel and family reunion. The review of such matters will put a "human face on détente." One of the journalists at the press conference asked Goldberg whether rejection of confrontation did not mean that he, therefore, would not put "pressure on them to comply." The Ambassador flippantly commented that he was not sending the Sixth Fleet. The US would simply "do our best through diplomatic means to accelerate and improve performance."[4]

A second feature of American policy at Belgrade was to have the record aired publicly, and Goldberg stressed that this would be done through briefing journalists on what transpired at closed meetings. As for those with a special stake in the Helsinki process—dissidents and human rights activists—the Voice of America and Radio Free Europe/Radio Liberty would carry the message to them.

The powerful Sakharov message on the opening day of the Belgrade meeting provided enormous tactical support for the Goldberg line. It refuted the argument that raising human rights issues at the Helsinki session would produce more rather than less hardship for Soviet political prisoners and, thus, "quiet diplomacy" should be pursued. At a private dinner in Belgrade hosted by the head of the West German delegation shortly after the sessions began, Goldberg made clear the inspiration he drew from the Sakharov message. As recorded by his wife, he observed that among the many provisions of the Helsinki accord,

> ... for those of us in the West who believe in human rights, there can be no question that fundamental human rights and freedoms must rank above all others. It follows, that the duty of NATO is to insist that the East must account for its failure to honor the accord's promise. If we fail to do this thing, we shall bear a heavy responsibility, not only to the dissidents . . . but to the people of our own countries, who have learned from the experience of two world wars that observance of human rights is the key to a just and lasting peace between all nations.[5]

US policy for the Belgrade session was expressed in a list of 13 proposals that Goldberg carried with him to NATO headquarters in Brussels prior to his journey to the Helsinki follow-up meeting.[6] At Brussels, he planned to meet with the CSCE ambassadors from NATO countries and their NATO permanent representative colleagues to brief them on US "thinking" concerning Helsinki. The 13 points could be summarized as follows:

1) The United States would "vigorously but not polemically" insist upon the obligation of all signatories to adhere to all provisions of the accord, including "particularly, human rights."

2) The meeting, while covering all parts of the Final Act, must nonetheless place emphasis upon the "poor implementation records of the Eastern countries," especially with respect to Principle VII and Basket III.

3) In presenting the "strong views" of the United States on these rights, the US delegation "should not seek confrontation, but should also avoid platitudes."

4) This perspective required that "specific cases and problems in the human rights area will be presented," as deemed appropriate by Ambassador Goldberg.

5) In pursuing this objective, the US delegation should "first" seek "consensus" support from US allies and, "if possible," from the neutral/non-aligned countries. At the same time, however, the United States "of necessity, must take a leadership role" both at the review conference and, generally, in efforts to obtain "better implementation" by the East of Helsinki provisions.

6) A vigorous US leadership role "is essential to preserve the President's credibility on the subject of human rights" and to assure progress in East Europe.

7) The US delegation, in asserting the American position "with frankness and candor," at the same time, must do so "in a manner compatible with customary diplomatic usage."

8) In dealing with the subject of "new proposals" scheduled to follow the implementation review, it would be appropriate to avoid use of the quoted phrase. This would limit the possibility of the USSR and its satellites using "new proposals " as means to filibuster at the expense of a complete review of implementation. Instead of "new proposals," the US delegation should more correctly use the phrase "measures to further implement the Final Act."

9) With respect to such "measures," the US delegation should strive to reach agreement with NATO on what measures should be introduced, and who should introduce them in plenary or the working groups.

10) The United States should seek to assure continuation of the CSCE process through an agreement on periodic review conferences similar to Belgrade. The next one should be held in the fall of 1979.

11) Measures proposed by the US or by its NATO allies should be substantive in character, not propagandistic.

12) While meetings of the working groups were closed, the US delegation should brief the press fully on the discussions that took place.

13) Special arrangements should be made to keep special interest, non-governmental groups fully informed of the deliberations and the conclusions reached even as the review conference progressed.

While the 13-point guidelines were aggressive and emphasized the new activist US leadership stance, they did not clearly specify whether names and incidents would be cited during the review procedure. It was precisely this point that concerned everyone—the Soviet Union and its allies, as well as the NATO partners of the United States. So far in the Helsinki process, no such specification had been demanded or applied. But the very nature of detailed review, as proposed by the US, pointed clearly in this direction. At the United Nations, it was standing operating procedure in dealing with human rights issues to deliberately avoid citing names or incidents. Allegations were made in such a way as to make it clear which country was the target of the criticism and what the nature of the criticism was about.

Mrs. Goldberg, in her memoirs, revealed that "in the beginning, there was the understanding that no names were to be mentioned of incidents that showed failure to comply with the Helsinki Pact—no persons, no countries, no particular incidents lest it sound like recrimination and jeopardize the initial good will."[7] To her, this process appeared "silly" and childish, reminding her of teenage guessing games. The absurdity was highlighted by remarks made by the French representative at an early meeting of the Basket III Working Group. Somewhat impatiently, he blurted out: "I shall not name names because the person in question is sitting right in front of me, but in his country the practice is. . . ."[8] The person sitting in front of him was a representative of East Germany.

When Goldberg, in his first speech on October 6, failed to mention any names, a reporter asked: "Did the State Department or the President tell you what you are to say and do here?"[9] Rumors had spread among the press on October 4 and 5 that the Carter administration had softened its position on human rights and the US delegation would not mention names. Indeed, Goldberg's initial speech strove to be conciliatory. He emphasized the value of détente in East-West relations.[10] At the same time, however, he contended that there existed a link "between the freedom and welfare of each of our nations, and the freedom and welfare of our individual citizens: the two are inseparable." He went on to say the pursuit of human rights would not put détente in jeopardy.

Goldberg did raise cases, but in an indirect way that shielded their specific feature and the names involved. Thus he spoke of "continuing interference" with foreign broadcasts, obviously referring to the jamming of Radio Liberty and Radio Free Europe. He noted, too, how a certain ill and aged husband—obviously in the USSR—was denied the right to leave in order to join his nearly blind wife and their daughter.[11] If the failure to mention names served diplomatic finesse, no "dialogue" was taking place, either. Moreover, no meaningful review, in the language of the Final Act (or Green Book), was occurring and no "thorough exchange of views," in the language of the Yellow Book, was being expressed.

Of course, the preparation of the Helsinki accord had tacitly operated on the assumption that anonymity would be preserved. It was clear that this resulted from the "insistence" of the Warsaw Pact group. For the signers of the Final Act, the hope was to "prevent confrontation" and maintain the "club cordiality," in the opinion of Dorothy Goldberg. The "previous" US negotiators had "consented" to the procedure "presumably to show that the Cold War was dissolved in the past." But, as her memoirs noted, if Belgrade meant "a thorough exchange of views," then, naturally, "names have to be named."[12]

At the first session of the Basket III Working Group on October 17, US delegate Guy Coriden spoke of the arbitrary refusals by "some signatory states" to permit their nationals to rejoin relatives abroad. The cases cited, without mentioning names and details, were shrouded in a certain vagueness even when the specific features of the cases were defined.

It was on the following day—October 18—that the new US policy made its debut.[13] The setting was again the Basket III Working Group. To the surprise of many, including members of the US delegation, Ambassador Goldberg suddenly appeared, seated himself next to Coriden and, when it was America's turn to speak, took the floor instead of Coriden. Goldberg first referred to a "court trial for several citizens who only wanted to talk to the government about the Final Act." What, heretofore, was always indirect, oblique, hazy, and vague was now unveiled by means of an unexpected ruse. The former justice then began reading from a United Press International dispatch of the previous day, which cited a respectable communist source, *L'Humanité*, the organ of the French Communist Party.

> The French Communist Party daily, *L'Humanité*, charged Monday Czechoslovakia has barred its reporter from covering the Prague trial of four supporters of the Charter 77 Human Rights Movement.
>
> *L'Humanité*, which has been increasingly critical of Soviet bloc political repression recently, said Czechoslovak authorities have refused to grant an entry visa to the paper's reporter, Marcel Veyrier.
>
> We regret this, *L'Humanité* said, and we sharply protest against a refusal which will deprive our readers of direct information on a trial challenging human rights for which we are fighting.

The impact of the citation was stunning. The apparent sundering of the tacit understanding about specific incidents evoked an explosive response. The Czechoslovakian representative sharply raised a point of order: "I must protest against this distorted information." What was at stake in the Prague trial was not human rights, he added, but rather the "flagrant violation of the laws of our country." Heatedly, he concluded: "I reject this absolutely."

Soviet delegate Sergei Kondrashev quickly joined the fray: "I am surprised," he told the delegates, by the action of "this distinguished representative of the United States of America." That the quoted report came from a communist source "does not make us smile here." Such reportage, from whatever source, must not be brought before the meeting. In the view of Moscow's representative, Goldberg's statement "is nothing other than an attempt to interfere in the internal affairs of a state represented here." He went on to declare categorically: "This is not the forum for such statements."

Delegates from Hungary and East Germany soon joined in the criticism, with the chairman observing, in an understatement, that "the temperature rises somewhat." By the next day—October 19—the key issue had become non-interference in the internal affairs of other countries. Does the review of specific cases constitute interference? The question was left unexplored. But the United States would not be intimidated. Once the door was opened on citing specific cases, the delegation rushed through. Coriden detailed crude Soviet practices aimed at preventing emigration, and demanded that Moscow disclose its unpublished procedures on emigration. Especially helpful, he noted, would be a definition of "state security," the device used by Soviet authorities to deny exit visas to Jews.

Several days later, Coriden ridiculed a Czechoslovakian attack on Radio Free Europe as subversive, charging that what Prague feared were RFE disclosures of the repression of Charter 77 signers. Coriden went on to offer examples of American journalists in the USSR being expelled or detained, such as George Krimsky and Robert Toth (the latter had been interrogated by the police on his contacts with the Helsinki Watch Group). Later, Coriden touched on the case of Yosef Begun, a Soviet Jewish cultural leader fired from his job because he had sought an exit visa. And he challenged the Kremlin device of incarcerating people for alleged "parasitism" when their applications for exit visas led to their being fired from their jobs.

A factor that may have played a role in promoting Goldberg's specific citing of Czechoslovakia on October 18 was a bipartisan congressional letter sent to President Carter on October 14, which arrived in Belgrade on October 17.[14] The letter was signed by 127 members of the House of Representatives, including Clement Zablocki, chairman of its foreign affairs committee, and 16 senators, including Daniel Patrick Moynihan, Robert Dole, and William Proxmire. It called attention to Moscow's repressive campaign against the Helsinki Watch Group.

The letter contained a strong demand that Soviet violations of the Helsinki agreement be vigorously raised and countered, lest "the credibility and effectiveness" of Helsinki "be undermined" along with all "other bilateral negotiations" with the USSR. This urgently required, the legislators wrote, that the US delegation "press this point in as forceful a manner as possible, in closed as well as open session." Goldberg was now keenly aware that any initiative he might take at Belgrade would have the powerful support of key congressmen on both sides of the aisle. Whether diplomats, enemy or allied, proved hostile was much less his concern than that the US Congress would be responsive.

While the USSR strongly resented the West's raising of human rights issues within Soviet borders, it had no hesitancy to doing precisely that with respect to other signatory countries when it suited Soviet purposes. Thus, Yuli Vorontsov, the Soviet Ambassador to the Belgrade talks, in addressing Basket III issues in the Working Group, raised the problem of a certain country's refusal to grant visas to Soviet trade union officials. The unnamed country, everyone recognized, was the United States. Then Vorontsov alleged provocations by Radio Liberty and Radio Free Europe that violated "mutual understandings." Finally, he sharply criticized the raising of human rights questions about the USSR in the working session. This can only be seen as "a flagrant violation of the Helsinki Pact," intended to weaken the "atmosphere of trust and lasting détente."

The perspective of America's West European allies was quite different. When Goldberg had initially outlined his proposals at NATO headquarters in Brussels before arriving at Belgrade, the proposal failed to "elicit a sympathetic reaction," according to his wife's memoirs. In Belgrade, the NATO caucus was "lukewarm in support of the United States tactics."[15] Among West Europeans, the dominant concern was preservation of détente, which they feared would be weakened by an open assault on Soviet Union human rights practices. By a curious coincidence, on the very day that Goldberg first criticized the failure of the East to comply with the provisions of Helsinki—although it was done indirectly and without citations of names and incidents—*The Times* (London) carried a long article by David Owen, the Foreign Secretary of the United Kingdom, which spelled out the West European perspective on raising human rights issues.[16]

Owen argued that human rights is "only one element in the Final Act, only one strand in the complex web of East-West relations." What followed was a line that was repeatedly featured in Moscow's propaganda campaign; "The greatest human right is, after all, the right to live, and to live in peace, without fear of nuclear or any other kind of war." Arms negotiations were at the heart of détente, not human rights.

Conflict within the alliance between the United States and the European democracies was grist for the communist propaganda mill. A long article in *Pravda* reported that at a closed NATO meeting, the West Europeans told Goldberg that "the passion for human rights propaganda can only complicate the détente process."[17] A London newspaper report of the meeting cited in *Pravda* urged him to "modify the tone of his speeches." The Communist Party organ also quoted from a dispatch in *The Washington Post*, which noted that Goldberg stood "isolated" and alone.

The Washington Post article, filed from Belgrade, had appeared on October 16, only two days before the surprise Goldberg intervention.[18] Obviously drawn from interviews with various NATO delegations and with disgruntled US delegation members anticipating Goldberg's tactics, the report noted that the Western allies stood for "a more general approach" rather than for the style of citing examples. Only if communist delegations were to "dispute their arguments or deny that problems exist"—when a "general critique" was made by NATO—would it be appropriate to cite specific cases or incidents. Thus, Goldberg was seen as a kind of "spoiler" in the Western diplomatic community.

The US Ambassador's irritation with his colleagues grew. Toward the end of the session, in February, a rumor spread that the USSR would be prepared to settle on a concluding document were it not for US high-handedness. The rumor was traced to the West German delegation, which was the most inclined to avoid any conflict with the USSR and most intent upon reaching compromises. At a NATO caucus meeting, an angry Goldberg read an "oral demarche" (cleared by the State Department) that denounced the rumor as creating "a climate which is making it impossible" to adopt a substantive concluding document. The demarche cautioned NATO members "to be very careful" lest they make statements that might "disrupt alliance unity and aid the Soviets."

Anger turned to burning rage when Goldberg learned that someone in the NATO caucus had worked out a schedule concerning discussion of final drafts with the neutral/nonaligned bloc chairman and with the Soviet delegation without consulting him. In a fury, he told his colleagues: "I have not been consulted, so I am denying consensus. . . ." He later told his wife: "They assume we're reasonable and will always go along with whatever they do." What followed was a clear indication of his thinking and of his basic outlook on multilateral diplomacy: "But the United States has to lead. We must consult, of course, but we cannot escape the responsibility of a superpower."[19]

As compared with the State Department's perspective during the Helsinki negotiation years, Goldberg's position was a 180-degree turn, from passivity to leadership. It also reflected a preoccupation with human rights, in sharp contrast to Kissinger's central concern, security. This is not to say that the State Department, at its very top echelon, was no longer concerned with security issues. Secretary Vance certainly was; he had a deep interest in promoting arms control, particularly in the strategic nuclear arms field, even while he helped guide the Department to an unprecedented focus upon human rights. But Vance's priorities ran on separate and different tracks.

More disturbing to Goldberg than the criticism of NATO allies was the opposition from within his own delegation. This opposition was no doubt responsible for leaks to the press, making possible such headlines as that which appeared in *The Washington Post* on October 16: "Goldberg and Aides Differ on Tactics at Belgrade Parley."[20] An unnamed US official was quoted that "our problem is how to preserve allied unity without sacrificing the essential goals of this conference." This "problem" had been and remained the principal concern of the Bureau of European Affairs of the State Department. While the Department had been given the task of focusing upon human rights issues, its career foreign affairs officers saw their chief function as preserving NATO solidarity. How was this to be done? Apparently only by accepting the NATO tactics of a general critique in place of specificity.

Goldberg's fury was revealed at the regular morning staff conference before the plenary session on October 21, where he put the matter bluntly: "If there is a feeling in the delegation that we are going too far, express it."[21] The air was thick with tension, not only because of the press reports of dissension, but because some were clearly unhappy with his speech three days earlier. After some moments, a young career officer, Jonathan Greenwald, spoke up. The Ambassador's speech, he said, was "too tough in substance and in fact." Goldberg's response was curt and cold: "Our instructions are to pursue human rights vigorously."

At this juncture of tension, Mrs. Goldberg sought the floor. The Ambassador refused to recognize her. When she continued to stand, seeking the floor, he told her: "Sit down." She persisted: "I have something to say." "I haven't recognized you," he shot back. Mrs. Goldberg insisted upon speaking: "I just want to say I think we should be glad to live in a free society where a young member of our delegation can differ with his superior officer." She noted that, at the other end of the building, where the Soviets were located, they could not. Greenwald asked for the floor: "I thought it was silly of the State Department to let you name your wife to the delegation, but I've changed my mind. I'm glad she's here now."

The cleavage in the delegation was naturally of keen interest to the press. *The Washington Post* correspondent had highlighted a crucial difference between Goldberg and career officials. If diplomats generally preferred to work "within narrowly defined limits," Goldberg sought "to extend those boundaries by trying to shame the Soviets with a dialogue on human rights."[22] At the same time, the reporter noted that the Helsinki Commission members and staffers were laudatory rather than critical. One of them was quoted as calling the embattled US Ambassador "a gutsy old man." (Goldberg was amused by the reference. He asked the young secretaries whether he was "gutsy." They responded with a favorable declaration signed to that effect, which was then posted on the bulletin board of the delegation office.)

Pravda picked up the theme on October 23, pointing out that "there is no unity of opinion within the US delegation itself."[23] The party organ stated the opposition came from the "more restrained and sober professional diplomats," who constituted half of the delegation. Goldberg's support, said *Pravda*, came only from the "diehard members" of the "notorious" Helsinki Commission. The Commission's report on implementation, which had been distributed at the beginning of the Belgrade session, was then denounced as "slanderous," "false" and a "libelous attempt to distort the human rights situation in Communist countries."

The anger and irritation of the US Ambassador did not detract from the focus of his attention—the Soviet Union and its allies. Could they be sufficiently stung with embarrassment that they might enter into a dialogue with the West? And from such a development, might not positive steps in the direction of human rights be undertaken? But even as he kept his eye on official Moscow, he also directed glances toward the activists and dissenters. Was their morale being assisted? Were US tactics helping or hurting them? Goldberg knew the courageous dissenters in the Soviet Union and elsewhere in East Europe were following the Belgrade proceedings with close attention. He would record later in a letter to *The Economist* that "it is ironic that many of the Helsinki Watchers in Eastern Europe have been enabled through samizdat to follow the Belgrade proceedings more closely than many Western readers."[24]

On the day the debate began on Principle VII (November 1, 1977), *The Times* (London) reported that an emergency call had come in 24 hours earlier from the wives of two of the leaders of the Helsinki Watch Group in Moscow, Orlov and Ginzburg.[25] Both had been arrested and imprisoned for monitoring Soviet human rights implementation practices. Orlov, it was widely feared, might be charged with treason. Irina Orlova warned in the telephone call that if the men were still in prison when Belgrade came to an end, "the Soviet authorities will be able to do anything they like with them." The two wives also appealed to the West to speak out publicly at Belgrade about their husbands and other arrested Helsinki Watch members. *The Times* also quoted distinguished Polish philosopher Leszek Kolakowski that Helsinki "had encouraged East Europeans to voice their human rights grievances and demands."

Goldberg saw himself as their echo. During the Belgrade session, he and his staff discoursed at length on religious intolerance, on ethnic and national discrimination, and on deprivation of the rights of speech, press association, assembly, and conscience. Examples were cited, but in a general manner. Names were named, but this took place in only seven instances (including especially the Orlov and Shcharansky cases). Yet, those instances, even if remarkably limited, set a precedent of enormous dimensions.

Moscow's reaction to America's human rights emphasis was given very early at Belgrade. At Goldberg's first private luncheon with the head of the Soviet delegation, Yuli Vorontsov, a long-time Kremlin diplomat who had served as Anatoly Dobrynin's deputy in the Soviet Embassy in Washington, the American asked: "Are you prepared to do anything on human rights?" Vorontsov's response was a dismaying negative: "No, we have done nothing wrong."[26] Two months later, after numerous US speeches documenting Soviet non-compliance in the Helsinki human rights field, Vorontsov noted the Soviet position:

> The core of Helsinki is security. Only through peace and détente can cooperation be put into effect. Here it is—the whole purpose of our meeting, to insure peace and security in Europe. I emphasize peace and security. . . . Hence, the purpose of the Belgrade meeting is to focus on reduction of arms, and avoidance of military confrontation.[27]

Not a word was said about human rights, Principle VII, Basket III, or for that matter, anything else, including Basket II, which dealt with economic and commercial issues.

Vorontsov kept driving home the theme that security, rather than human rights, was the heart of Helsinki. After one Goldberg address, he took the floor and, with a voice dripping with sarcasm, reminded the delegates that the US Ambassador had not been at Geneva when the negotiations on the accord took place. Obviously playing on the growing irritation of the Western allies with Goldberg's tactics (as well as the concern of some in the US delegation), Vorontsov observed that the "veterans of Geneva should explain to him how it took all that time to do the huge work that was done there." The centerpiece of the Geneva negotiations, he said, had been détente and economic issues, but "all this does not fit into the mind of the delegate of the United States. All he cares about is the internal happenings of other states."

Vorontsov sought to buttress his counterattack on US policy with a lengthy argument centering on Principle VI, non-intervention in the internal affairs of other countries. He and his Warsaw Pact colleagues contended that the raising of human rights issues in the USSR and its allies constituted a serious violation of Principle VI. The false thesis was repeated over and over again. From the US vantage point, it was essential to respond effectively to the argument, otherwise the thrust of Principle VII would be undermined.

To Goldberg's dismay, the State Department had not prepared a strong legal brief to counter the charge. But as a jurist of considerable experience, he chose to do his own research and inquiry, concluding that the "intervention" referred to "armed interventions or similar forms of coercion," not to "speech." Goldberg made the additional sensitive point that the Nazis after World War II had used the Nuremberg laws to reject criticism of their internal practices as "intervention." Moscow was reminded that "the Soviets themselves condemned the Nazi use of the Nuremberg laws." Its high judicial officials actively participated in the international tribunal meeting in Nuremberg in the immediate post-war period, which rejected any defense based upon adherence to those laws.

More to the point, Goldberg stressed that the Final Act made the free flow of information a legitimate subject of international concern and, therefore, appropriate for dialogue at Belgrade. All the more was this the case when persons who distributed information about their Helsinki rights were arrested and brought to trial. It followed that making speeches about human rights without providing specifics about particular incidents "would make our own deliberations here dealing with the human rights provisions of the Final Act a mockery."

Logic and legislative history regarding the non-intervention provision of Principle VI would not overcome Vorontsov's rejection of a human rights "dialogue." He decided to employ the tactic of threat rather than of accommodation. "If these attacks continue," he warned in the debate on non-intervention, "it will break up the conference. Such talk undermines and weakens the intent of the Final Act."[28]

On the following day, the Soviet shifted to another threat. Should the US continue to press the Soviets, Vorontsov said he would raise the issue of US human rights violations, such as racism, unemployment, and CIA activities in Vietnam. In finishing his speech, he chose to underscore his threat by walking out of the room. Goldberg immediately and loudly

responded: "Who is warning whom?"[29] Vorontsov charged back into the
room, and even though the chairman had already ended the session, he
blocked the chairman's exit and repeated his earlier warning: "This conference will break up if such remarks continue."

The threats carried little impact. If some West Europeans were fearful
at the beginning about the possibility of a Soviet walkout, they now took
it in stride. Besides, they found the arguments used by Moscow about
Principle VI unacceptable. On the vitally important legal question as to
whether human rights issues could be raised, they sided with the United
States, even if they objected to the manner and style used by the Carter
administration in doing so. Finally, they must have been aware, as certainly the US was, that the Kremlin had too great a stake in the Helsinki
accord to walk away from it. Leonid Brezhnev, after all, took enormous
pride in the fact that, to a large extent, it was his diplomatic achievement,
perhaps his greatest achievement.

Nor could the Kremlin deny that Brezhnev's handiwork, the Helsinki
accord, also included, if unwillingly, references to human rights.
Vorontsov, in a stunning comment made in December, said that human
rights was "at the core of the entire Soviet ideology," although he qualified his position because "it would be unrealistic to expect all sections of
the Final Act to be implemented."[30]

Vorontsov's response, in substance, supported earlier observations
Brezhnev had made to visiting US congressmen.[31] The implication was
clear: a distinction had to be made between different parts of the Final
Act. Human rights issues, such as "contacts among people" and "cultural
cooperation," had been placed on the agenda of Europe "for the first
time." As such, expecting quick implementation was not realistic, in
Vorontsov's view. The contrast with security issues was sharp. That section of the Final Act had been central to the European agenda for a long
time, and was a matter of immediate urgency. Central Europe was already, said Vorontsov, a "powerhouse of armaments."

Vorontsov made a second point about human rights implementation
that was even more crucial. In making the distinction between the different sections of the Final Act, Vorontsov clearly indicated that only over
time did the "possibility" of progress in the field of "human cooperation"
exist. However, he added with a determined firmness, the "possibility"—
not certainty, by any means—of progress is "only available on the basis
of an atmosphere of détente. . . ." In the view of the Soviet official,
progress in the human rights area had to be "calibrated" to progress
made in the area of détente.[32] The Soviet thesis of human rights progress

as conditional on security advances was made for the first time in a Helsinki context, formulated in a limited manner. Later at Madrid the linkage would be sharpened and transformed into a kind of blackmail: unless agreement was reached concerning Soviet proposals in the area of disarmament, human rights would either not be considered or would suffer.

With the United States, policy ran in the very opposite direction. Détente or peace depended less on security considerations than on human rights. For Arthur Goldberg, the essence of Principle VII was that it permanently established the interrelationship between the "universal significance of human rights" and "the prospects for international peace, justice and well-being."[33] Thus, the policy of citing violations of human rights and the naming of names, along with "the free exchange of ideas and communications do not hurt, but [rather] help détente." The implication of linkage between favorable human rights steps and a willingness to respond on security issues was inherent in the argument, although it would not be addressed until Madrid.

With the West challenging the Soviet argument of non-intervention at the same time the Soviets were giving limited credence to human rights issues, it was not altogether surprising that Moscow altered its tactic of refusing to bring up Basket III issues. The new thrust would be oriented to criticizing American practices, which the US did not find unwelcome. Of course, the challenge was mainly in the direction of social and economic rights. The Soviets charged the United States with permitting slavery and a high incidence of unemployment, and chastised the country for failure to ratify international human rights treaties, such as the Genocide Convention and the International Covenants on Human Rights.[34] Goldberg relished the opportunity which the allegations presented: "I'm glad to respond to questions like these. . . ." By following this new course, Moscow undermined its own thesis that Principle VI precluded human rights criticism. Besides, Goldberg, as a former Secretary of Labor, could provide effective documentation to counter Soviet arguments about unemployment and social inadequacies.

The failure to ratify international human rights treaties was quite another matter. Goldberg had been a strong advocate of ratification, and he was frustrated by the obstacles, both technical and political, to Senate action.[35] "The only relief," his wife commented, "was the fact that President Carter was urging ratification and had signed the International Covenant on Human Rights as a step in that direction."[36]

Significantly, however, Soviet counterthrusts in the area of human rights at Belgrade were rare. Not until the last day of the session, on

March 9, 1978, did Vorontsov offer an elaboration of charges. His points merit quoting, if only for historical purposes:

> These attempts [to challenge the socialist countries on human rights] have failed completely and it couldn't have been otherwise. Indeed only someone who has completely lost a sense of reality would question the practice of genuine socialism, where the working man is the focus of attention. And what else could be said by those who have on their hands and their conscience such problems, insoluble for capitalism . . . of infringement on the rights of women, humiliation and discrimination of national minorities . . . in employment and education, in everyday life and political activity? What else could be said by those who practice racism and uphold apartheid, who victimize champions of civil rights, not stopping short of legal persecution on false charges?[37]

Even as Vorontsov spelled out the allegations about US human rights non-compliance, he nonetheless rebuffed all efforts to permit the adoption of a "concluding document" which focused upon implementation and the failure on the part of various states to comply with the provisions of the Helsinki accord. On January 17, upon returning from a long Christmas recess in Moscow, the Soviet had tabled his own three-page draft of a "concluding document." It said nothing about human rights or Principle VII, carried no reference to the discussion on implementation and what was reported as lack of compliance, and even failed to comment on the security issue concerning confidence-building measures.

Vorontsov contended that the document ought to express only the agreements reached, however marginal or modest they were, and not the disagreements. In one respect, it did feature a positive and crucially important matter, fixing the next follow-up meeting in Madrid in 1980. Throughout the deliberations of the subsidiary working group at Belgrade dealing with the follow-up, Soviet delegates had refused to give their assent, repeatedly threatening there and in the plenary that unless the United States desisted from its verbal human rights onslaught on the USSR, Moscow would not agree to a follow-up session.

That Moscow finally agreed to a site and time for the review conference no doubt responded to a concern that Brezhnev's historic initiative would altogether collapse, jeopardizing therewith his reputation, along with whatever benefits the Soviet Union continued to derive or might in the future derive from Helsinki. In any case, the decision gave sustenance to a process that had significant implications for the future, though not for the immediate present, with respect to human rights. Helsinki could more easily have been stifled in its embryonic stage; later, it would be far more difficult to do so. Dissenters, democratic activists and refuseniks now had a much longer lease on life and hope. Goldberg called the Soviet decision "a good omen."

In every other respect, the Vorontsov text and comments with which he introduced it had a profoundly dampening effect on the Belgrade meeting. He made it clear that the Soviet text was submitted on a take-it-or-leave-it basis and that Moscow would not deviate from it. The reaction of the West and of the neutrals and non-aligned, an observer noted, was "a stunning silence."[38] What Moscow had submitted was virtually an ultimatum. And, indeed, after January 17, the persona of the Soviet Ambassador assumed a new and different character. The polished, tactful and patient—if condescending—professional diplomat became the personification of "coldness and indifference," in the opinion of one eyewitness.[39]

The Kremlin had evidently decided that Belgrade had become counterproductive; therefore, its early demise was essential to Soviet interests. Soon afterward, Sergei Kondrashev, the number two in the Soviet delegation, set the time when all plenary and working-group discussion must end—February 12. The deadline meant that by March the meeting would close, for only the language of the final text remained to be approved. (Instead of the Soviet draft, the CSCE negotiators adopted a text which, while largely inspired by Denmark, accepted some basic Soviet guidelines.)

A mid-February breakfast meeting between Goldberg and Vorontsov at the American's residence testified to both the firmness of the Soviet decision and the value the Kremlin still placed upon Helsinki.[40] Vorontsov was emphatic that Belgrade must end without Moscow having to accept Western proposals on human rights or on confidence-building measures: "Listen, Art, I've told you I have instructions. They're absolute, and we are absolutely not to go along on CBMs." Goldberg asked: "You do want to end this meeting, don't you, with some dignity, some sense of satisfied achievement?" The Vorontsov response was vigorous: "I do." Both superpower ambassadors agreed that language had to be formulated to make clear that Belgrade was not "a meaningless thing."

Could it have ended differently? The later follow-up meetings in Madrid and Vienna did conclude with substantive statements of considerable length. Belgrade was the exception. Why? The opponents of Goldberg (and of the Carter human rights policy generally), whether in the Warsaw Pact camp or among Western allies at NATO or among State Department career officials and their journalist supporters, blamed it on Goldberg's tactics, most especially the tactics of public diplomacy. An article in *Saturday Review* by Don Cook, who had spent only a short period of time in Belgrade, gave emphasis to the thesis.[41] He argued that US strategy had caused disarray in NATO and non-aligned ranks, handing the USSR a "victory." The article's headline read: "Making America Look Foolish."

In fact, public diplomacy on human rights would remain a continuous and dominant feature of US policy after 1977. The stress on public diplomacy did not preclude quiet diplomacy and behind-the-scenes negotiations. There were those who denigrated Goldberg's skills as a negotiator because he had not served as a long-time professional diplomat, but his experience in the US labor movement and as Secretary of Labor had honed his negotiation skills. More importantly they had already been tested in a diplomatic context, having very much come into play when President Johnson called on Goldberg to serve at the United Nations. At the time, he had displayed great talents in negotiating Security Council Resolution 242, which brought an end to the Middle East war of 1967.

If these skills could not be brought effectively into play during the Belgrade sessions, it had nothing to do with the tactics of public diplomacy. Quiet diplomacy would become effective, in Goldberg's view, "once negotiations are conducted in earnest."[42] The problem at Belgrade in 1977-78 was that the Soviet Union rejected any meaningful negotiations in the area of human rights that would have permitted such traditional diplomacy. In Goldberg's opinion, when one side had no intention of keeping a commitment in negotiation, the "only possible recourse is to make it public."

Significantly, Moscow's refusal to negotiate also applied to the area of security. Confidence-building measures (CBMs) in Basket I dealt with matters related to making defensive military acts more transparent so as to reduce the possibility of surprise attack. Thus, the Helsinki accord required military maneuvers or exercises of a certain size to be reported to CSCE members well in advance, and to permit the stationing of observers from other CSCE countries in the area of the maneuvers. The accord also provided that the area covered within the Soviet Union would be limited to 150 miles from its Western borders. This permitted a vast Western territory stretching to the Urals to be shielded from reportage on Soviet military maneuvers. Suggestions advanced for a greater transparency through, for example, advance reporting of smaller exercises, met with Soviet demurral. Vorontsov made clear that the USSR simply was not interested in further CBMs.

The Helsinki accord, itself, testified to the manner by which substantive progress could be made. Trade-offs between the baskets, most notably between Basket I and Basket III, and between the Principles, was the route taken in the negotiating process at Geneva and Helsinki to make forward movement possible. Afterward, too, at meetings in Madrid and Vienna, it was precisely through such trade-offs that agreement would be reached on substantive concluding documents.

The United States delegation at Belgrade was, indeed, keenly sensitive to seeking out possible areas for trade-offs. Sherer's archive contains a detailed memorandum on the subject prepared by Jonathan Greenwald on November 2, 1977, and given to Ambassador Goldberg.[43] Greenwald, perceptively, began by noting that trade-offs affecting the entire range of US relations "are . . . those most likely to affect a major movement in the Soviet position at Belgrade. . . ." He cautioned that "even if the Soviets were to agree . . . to take a more forthcoming human rights position in CSCE in return for better prospects in, say, SALT [the Strategic Arms Limitation Talks], it would be necessary for them to obtain more compensation at Belgrade."

But Vance had apparently ruled out the implied suggestion of a possible "cosmic" trade-off involving SALT and human rights in CSCE when he stressed in testimony to the Helsinki Commission that disarmament and human rights ran on totally different tracks.[44] It was a view with which Moscow seemed to agree. At Belgrade, Vorontsov constantly spoke about disarmament, especially in the nuclear arms field, and berated the United States for not giving the subject adequate attention. At the same time, he did not offer the slightest hint that Moscow would welcome a trade-off between some aspect of disarmament and human rights.

This was, indeed, the central problem. As Greenwald noted, "our leverage is distinctly less than it was in the Geneva negotiating phase that led to the summit."[45] His explanation was precisely on target:

> Then Brezhnev had put his full prestige behind CSCE and behind a summit meeting. We were able to use that commitment to obtain concessions that the Soviets probably still regret. On the other hand, the type of moderate extension of the Final Act or commitment to implement the Final Act better that we seek at Belgrade are of a lower nature than the concessions we were seeking at Geneva when the question was what the very nature of the Final Act would be.

During the Belgrade session, Moscow did put forward several security proposals, but the applicability of the two central ones as bargaining chips was precluded by NATO security considerations. On October 21, 1977, the Soviet President, in a toast to visiting Indian Prime Minister Morarji Desai, recommended a "Plan of Action" that would include a treaty among the 35 CSCE states pledging non-first use of nuclear weapons.[46] The plan also called for a commitment that neither NATO nor the Warsaw Pact would accept new members.

The non-first use pledge had been part of the Soviet propaganda arsenal for some time. It was a non-starter, because the basic military strategy of NATO rested upon nuclear weapons as a deterrent to discourage a Soviet invasion of Western Europe. The overwhelming superiority of Soviet weaponry in Central Europe, particularly with respect to tanks and artillery, made US and allied airpower, including nuclear airpower, a vital element in the strategy of deterrence. Advancing the idea of non-first use during Belgrade was a propaganda maneuver, hardly a serious proposal for negotiation.

Moscow's proposal for a commitment that neither NATO nor the Warsaw Pact accept additional new members was an outgrowth of its awareness that Spain had been engaged with NATO in discussions regarding entrance into the defensive alliance system. This concerned the USSR, as it would extend NATO power to a strategic point in the western Mediterranean. With Spain a parliamentary democracy, the decision was very much Madrid's to make. Vital security needs of both Spain and NATO made it inconceivable for the issues to be bargained away. Like the non-first use of nuclear weapons, the proposal to refuse new members whether to NATO or the Warsaw Pact (who could be willing to join it?) was a non-starter.

The "Plan of Action" was vaguely phrased, but carried earmarks of an earlier Soviet concept initially advanced at Geneva and totally unacceptable to the West. The plan also provided for a new forum composed of all CSCE states, which would "consult" on European-wide security issues in parallel with MBFR (Mutual and Balanced Force Reduction) talks that had been going on in Vienna.[47] Greenwald saw this new institutional security structure as "most far-reaching and potentially dangerous." It recalled Moscow's initial plan of a permanent security institution dealing with all kinds of European issues. Greenwald thought that Moscow might be "interested in reverting to their classical conception of a security conference without the human rights albatross in which they would be free to raise issues already being handled in other forums like MBFR, or issues such as Cyprus or the situation in the Iberian Peninsula which are the proper business of Western Europe alone." He appropriately recommended that the United States should make it clear that "we would under no circumstances be prepared to accept any new structure in the security area."

A very different perspective was articulated with respect to a fourth Brezhnev point. The Soviet leader called upon the Belgrade meeting to endorse his proposals for convening three high-level conferences of all CSCE states on energy, environment and transportation. These, of course, fell under the Basket II rubric. Greenwald recommended that the West "show a considerable degree of forthcomingness" in responding to the Basket II proposal.[48] At the same time, he added that, because "a cardinal point of CSCE theology is that a general balance must be maintained between all the baskets," it would be appropriate to "demand something tangible . . . in Principles and Basket III" for a responsive Western attitude toward some Soviet proposals.

Evidently, a trade-off between Baskets II and III became a subject of speculation during the first week of November. One reporter covering the Belgrade proceedings wrote that "some Western delegates suspect that the East Europeans may have a kind of barter in mind" with respect to Basket II proposals they were pushing.[49] But the balloon soon collapsed. The Soviet's vital concerns were in the security area, not in economic and environmental matters.

But there appeared to be nothing they sought in the security area that the US and West could favorably consider. Bargaining seemed to be out of the question. Moreover, US-Soviet tensions outside of the Belgrade conference rooms seemed to call into question détente itself. And, as the CSCE conferees clearly understood, Belgrade and the Helsinki process constituted a reflection of the outer world, a kind of barometric reading of its tensions and relaxations. The chief delegate of the host country summed up the problem by observing that "the CSCE process cannot be carried on outside the context of the existing political, military and other realities in Europe."[50]

Human rights was, in fact, at the core of the weakening of détente. The Kremlin was determined to smash the very articulation of Helsinki's human rights provisions. Not only were the major figures in the Moscow Helsinki Watch Group arrested, but the group's principal spokesman, Anatoly Shcharansky, was placed on trial for the most serious of crimes, espionage (under Article 64A of the Russian Criminal Code). Only four months after Belgrade ended—on July 14—Shcharansky was convicted and sentenced to a long term of 12 years imprisonment and forced labor.[51] This, despite unprecedented assurances from President Carter that Shcharansky had no connections with the CIA. The Soviet court decision testified to Moscow's fierce determination to put an end to what the Final Act had stirred up. If this meant putting détente into question, so be it.

For the neutral and non-aligned countries and to many in the West, Belgrade was a failure. The respected Swiss Ambassador, Rudolf Bindschiedler, summed up prevailing diplomatic opinion in a press conference on March 7: "One can say that this conference is a 1% success and a 99% failure."[52]

This perspective was far too negative. Belgrade set a unique standard for participants in future follow-up meetings. Dante Fascell noted that it broke "the silence barrier."[53] CSCE human rights violators had been put on notice that violations would not escape attention, that they would be aired, and that demand for their rectification would not be stilled. In fact, the number of names named at Belgrade was extremely modest—only seven; at Madrid and Vienna, the number would run well into the hundreds.

What Goldberg had done stirred the hopes and aspirations of dissenters, democrats and refuseniks everywhere in Eastern Europe. Their fate was by no means an isolated one. Helsinki forums would provide an opportunity for raising their plight, as would the Helsinki bilateral negotiations that took place between countries prior to review sessions. And, through foreign radio broadcasts into the Soviet Union and East European countries, notably by Radio Liberty, Radio Free Europe, Voice of America, the British Broadcasting Corporation and Deutsche Welle, the Helsinki forum discussions reached millions. A statement by Soviet activists, including Sakharov, put out in late November 1977 illustrated how closely the dissenters followed developments at Belgrade.[54] The statement commended the United States, Holland, Denmark, Norway, Sweden, and Belgium for taking a positive stance, while accusing Britain, France and West Germany of remaining "quiet."

To the extent that Helsinki was a process, Belgrade had to be viewed from the long run far more than from the narrow perspective of whether or not it had achieved a substantive concluding document. Thus, a report by President Carter would observe that "the views exchanged during the meeting, and the precedents and issues which derive from them are . . . the most important legacy of the meeting itself."[55] He was not alone in recognizing the significance of what had occurred in Belgrade. West German State Secretary Günther Van Well, in a speech at the session on March 9, commented that the Belgrade meeting "has been an attempt at a new kind of approach in international relations."[56] All had to share to some extent in an "open discussion of matters which previously had, to a large extent, been diplomatic taboos." If the United States was alone at Belgrade in naming names and citing instances, in later follow-up conferences Washington would be joined by others. Ground had been broken for a broad application of a more public diplomacy.

The centerpiece of the concluding statement may not have been earth shaking, but it vigorously reaffirmed *all* the provisions of Helsinki, which

meant Principle VII and Basket III: "The representatives of the participating states reaffirmed the resolve of their governments to implement
fully, unilaterally, bilaterally and multilaterally all the provisions of the
Final Act."[57] That, together with the agreement of a follow-up review session, assured continuance of the human rights struggle.

Belgrade did something else; the setting provided opportunity for the
West and neutrals to meet officials of East European countries for private
discourse on common issues and concerns. Over time, it became increasingly difficult for Moscow to keep its Warsaw Pact allies in line. Thus,
Romania often absented itself from the regular Warsaw Pact caucus
meetings.[58] Reportedly, the delegations of Poland and Hungary often
sought to push the Soviet Union into assuming a more moderate posture.
According to a diplomat from a neutral state: "It's these caucuses as well
as the more open debates that are enabling some of these countries to assert their independence and their own voice."[59] He was privately informed by most of the East European delegations that "they hoped this
will spill over well after everyone's left Belgrade and Helsinki is only a
memory."

American policy encouraged what came to be called "differentiation."[60] Thus, the countries most frequently targeted for US criticism both
at Belgrade and in presidential reports were the Soviet Union, Czechoslovakia, and East Germany. But two other Warsaw Pact countries—
Poland and Hungary—were only mildly rebuked, and in certain respects
were accorded special treatment. President Carter made an official visit
to Poland at the very height of the Belgrade proceedings. Also, during the
conference, the US completed negotiations with Hungary both for the return of the Crown of St. Stephen, the symbol of the state's sovereignty,
and the grant of most-favored-nation tariff status under Jackson-Vanik.

What the follow-up meeting in Belgrade provided—and this would be
replicated in later meetings as well as at Helsinki experts' forums—was
an umbrella to shield East European countries, enabling them to express
to some extent their own foreign policy interests. Soon, the modest autonomy would be reinforced by another aspect of the Helsinki process.
Prior to CSCE sessions, US officials from both the Helsinki Commission
and the State Department would journey to East European capitals for
discussion with key foreign policy aides in the various countries about the
forthcoming conference agenda. The discussions assumed a wide-ranging
character in the human rights area, which was the principal specialty of
Helsinki Commission members.

Beyond the official state-to-state talks, an informal dialogue was
conducted through the Helsinki process with the various local publics,

particularly with non-governmental groups that had a special stake in Helsinki, like Charter 77 or KOR (and later, Solidarity). Western views at follow-up meetings would be communicated through foreign radio transmissions, notably Radio Free Europe. East European NGOs would reciprocate by providing documentation on human rights matters to the Helsinki Commission. Such documentation, in turn, would reach larger local audiences as a result of the US delegation citing it in plenary speeches, which were then translated and broadcast on Radio Free Europe channels.

It was the Helsinki connection now and later that helped expedite the breakaway of East Europe from the Soviet empire in 1989, and the human rights theme gave the rupture a powerful moral impulse. The Belgrade conference helped lay the foundation for the new Europe which would ultimately spring into existence. For all the criticism of Goldberg's arrogance and his indifference to Western Europe's interests, the "gutsy old man" left a positive legacy.

▪ 6 ▪

The Road to Madrid

While Helsinki Commission Chairman Fascell welcomed in an article in *Foreign Policy* the Belgrade outcome as "a partial victory for the tenaciously-held Western view that the Final Act had made concern for fundamental human rights in any signatory country a matter of international concern,"[1] this was certainly not the perspective of the career bureaucracy in the State Department. As the second follow-up meeting, scheduled for Madrid in November 1980, approached, the principal negotiator of the Helsinki Final Act, Ambassador Albert Sherer, also published an article in *Foreign Policy,* which sharply challenged US strategy at Belgrade.[2] By a "confrontation policy," the strategy had "doomed" the "idea that a détente in Europe offered the best hope for progress in human rights. . . ." The result of Belgrade was a "détente . . . in disarray," with CSCE itself "being but one victim." Sherer called for a reversal in US strategy if CSCE was to be productive. He expressed strong doubts about change. "Nothing short of a miracle," he wrote, could return CSCE to its original track.[3]

The Fascell-Sherer exchange merely reflected an intensification of the earlier controversy and the political maneuvering between the Helsinki Commission and the career bureaucracy in the Department of State over fundamental policy considerations. What enormously complicated the conflict between 1978 and Madrid in 1980 were new and vital security considerations. For one thing, the French government had introduced in May 1978, only two months after Belgrade closed, a proposal for a two-stage Conference on Disarmament in Europe (CDE). It was circulated by a Quai d'Orsay memorandum to all CSCE member states.

Of even greater significance was the December 1979 NATO decision, taken with the strong encouragement of the United States, to introduce powerful and sophisticated Pershing II and cruise missiles in Western Europe to counter the several hundred SS-20 missiles the USSR had installed in East Europe and in the western parts of the Soviet Union in the 1970s. The Soviet missiles had upset the military balance of power in a profound manner. While the Pershing II and cruise missiles would not be introduced until December 1983, the subject was already a matter of keen debate within NATO.

The same month as the NATO decision saw a Kremlin military action in Afghanistan, which evoked great concern in Washington and in the West generally.[4] If Moscow was initially motivated to intervene in order to end internal political conflicts in Kabul and assure its own domination of the area, Western policy makers perceived the aggression as potentially directed toward altering the regional balance of power in the Persian Gulf and threatening Western oil supplies. The United States responded with vigorous support for the Afghan Moslem insurgents, as well as with strong military supplies to Pakistan. The result was a deepening of East-West tension, with negative consequences on the Kremlin's human rights practices.

The various security concerns required a great degree of US diplomatic activity on Helsinki issues that were oriented to NATO. In the case of the French proposal, the administration had to contend with a variety of options and countervailing pressures, which necessitated considerable finesse and tact.

The French-proposed disarmament conference, in its first stage, would focus on confidence-building measures, amplifying and extending those on prior notification of military maneuvers and exchange of observers already stipulated in the Helsinki Final Act.[5] The second stage would concentrate on an examination of measures for the actual limitation and reduction of conventional weapons and forces. To avoid both premature failure and the abuse of the forum for purely propaganda purposes, France emphasized that the second stage should be called only "when substantial results, regarded as satisfactory by all participants, have already been achieved."[6]

When the French plan was first introduced, the US refused to discuss it, partly out of concern about the abuse of a CSCE forum. There was also deep official anxiety that human rights would be sacrificed to security concerns, quite a reversal from the days of Henry Kissinger. President Carter, in his own Helsinki anniversary speech on July 29, 1980, emphasized that Helsinki "should not become significantly an arms control forum."[7]

The French view ultimately prevailed with NATO, although accompanied by important changes that eased the fears of the principal allies. On

December 13-14, 1979, the NATO foreign ministers, meeting in Brussels, accepted the basic features of the French proposal as "a useful concept."[8] They agreed to work at Madrid toward this objective, provided it was interrelated with the CSCE process and was "part of a balanced outcome." The key word was "balanced." It meant that approval of a two-stage disarmament conference required Soviet concessions in the human rights field. Equally important was the description of the conference mandate. A meeting on confidence-building must deal with "measures" that are "militarily significant," "verifiable," and "applicable to the entire continent of Europe." The June 1980 NATO foreign ministers' meeting in Ankara defined "the entire continent of Europe" as including "the whole of the European part of the Soviet Union," bounded by the Ural mountains.[9]

The Helsinki Final Act had envisaged Europe's eastern boundary as extending only 250 kilometers (150 miles) into the Soviet Union. The Soviet Urals lie almost ten times beyond that distance. A modification of the Final Act would therefore be required, even though the Urals as a boundary line seemed both reasonable and appropriate for a body designated as the "Conference on Security and Cooperation in *Europe*" (emphasis added).

The Kremlin viewed the French proposal with considerable interest in light of the scheduled installation of US cruise and Pershing II missiles in Western Europe. Indeed, the Soviets were prepared to shelve a more tendentious 1979 Warsaw Pact proposal for a conference on arms reduction in favor of the French one. Since the French had placed stress on confidence-building measures that would extend to the Urals, Brezhnev would later go out of his way in a major policy address to the 26th Congress of the Soviet Communist Party in February 1981 to accept publicly the new demarcation, provided the West made a geographical concession.

The NATO decision on US missile installation, initially prompted by Chancellor Helmut Schmidt of the Federal Republic of Germany, stirred great anxieties and fears among West Germans, as well as among West Europeans in general. Torment about the possibility of a nuclear conflict became a preeminent public issue and concern, which the USSR was determined to exploit to the maximum. Indeed, halting the installation of the US missiles became a top Soviet priority. The United States and various leaders in Western Europe were equally determined to see the missiles deployed to neutralize Soviet missile superiority in Europe or to compel withdrawal of the SS-20s.

Assuaging the fears and anxieties of the West Europeans was a matter of vital, high-level US policy. Ambassador Max Kampelman, the principal US negotiator at Madrid, would later explain a key American objective:

> We decided to strengthen the Western alliance by recognizing that our West
> European friends who share our values were geographically in the forefront of
> confrontation with the Soviet Union; that they were concerned about a nuclear
> catastrophe; and that they were, therefore, in no position to "ostracize" the So-
> viet Union.[10]

This disclosure, which was not made public until 1985, gave military-security considerations within the Helsinki process far greater emphasis than had ever previously been the case. Failure to comprehend the preeminent importance of the security factor in US thinking would lead to misunderstanding Washington's approach to Madrid and to how the human rights issue would be played.

The new emphasis on NATO may have prompted the career foreign service officers staffing the State Department's European bureau, and especially its NATO office, to resume the struggle for power and turf with the Helsinki Commission. If the Commission thought after a much-lauded role at Belgrade that it had secured a permanent and prominent role in Washington's CSCE planning, it was wrong. Opponents in the bureaucracy were eager to exploit allied irritation to prevent a repetition of the Belgrade experience. In view of the increased focus on the significance of allied unity, some in the European bureau who concentrated on CSCE matters began wondering about the continued advisability of maintaining full Commission integration into the US CSCE process.

Over the long run, according to a Commission staffer, many in the State Department sought a US delegation to the Madrid review conference and other CSCE meetings that would be primarily composed of career diplomats, with the Commission or private interest groups excluded or given a reduced role.[11] And, with the reduced role of the Commission, the aggressive posture of the US on human rights would also diminish. It would be the European NATO allies who would play a leading role at Madrid, and with a softer tone, as Sherer himself made explicit.

The first indication of the new thrust of the Department's European Bureau came shortly after Belgrade's conclusion. The occasion was a formal request in spring 1978 from the National Security Council to the State Department. The NSC asked the Department for an assessment of the outcome of the Belgrade conference and for policy option proposals for the future.[12] The memorandum, apparently, asked the Department to request all agencies and desks involved in the Belgrade mission to participate in the policy review, but the State Department neither informed the Helsinki Commission of the policy review request nor asked it to participate.[13]

Some time later, Commission staff director Spencer Oliver learned about the NSC memo at a White House ceremony in the Rose Garden honoring Ambassador Goldberg for his Belgrade services. An NSC staffer had innocently queried Oliver on the progress being made by the Commission on the policy review.[14] A startled Oliver learned that the policy review request had been made two months earlier. He asked and received from the staffer a copy of the request.

Furious about the maneuver, the Commission staff director had his colleagues put aside everything else to concentrate on the White House request. The State Department officials tried to head off a Commission contribution, but did not succeed. What emerged by mid-year were two separate policy reviews and two sets of recommendations.

At the heart of the differences between the two memoranda was the question of how the United States should deal with its NATO allies on the raising of human rights issues. An "executive summary" prepared by the Bureau of European Affairs and cited in an unpublished Commission staff memorandum strongly recommended that the US give primary consideration to the views of its NATO allies, who would otherwise "shrink" from an "excessively confrontational US approach or one which is designed to appease domestic US constituencies."[15]

The Commission staff memorandum took the very opposite course. It urged a quick White House decision on the issue of naming names on human rights issues so that the US could inform the allies and then "seek to enlist their assistance and support for this tactic."[16] The US, it emphasized, must assume the leadership role; if it failed to do so, "then no one will take the lead on human rights."

From the vantage point of the Commission staff, the State Department's report to the National Security Council was "slanted toward an emphasis on military security at and after Madrid, while, at the same time, only paying lip service to human rights and humanitarian concerns." In essence, the Commission charged that the Department was recommending that "the human rights issues be relegated to the quiet diplomatic bilateral channels," while reserving the "more visible multilateral forum" for military security and Basket II initiatives.

As for the French proposal on CDE, the Commission staff found it a diversion from the human rights aspects of the CSCE process. The failure of the Department to take a firm position against it—as the "summary" appeared to suggest—provided "tacit support for the proposal, which jeopardizes US leverage for the improvement of human rights issues and endangers prospects for 'balance' in the Madrid follow-up." The Commission staff further recommended that the "public member" category which was used at Belgrade be enlarged to include 25 "member-observers" who would be allowed to participate in delegation deliberations. It urged, too, that the delegation to Madrid be headed by a political appointee with strong human rights credentials and the support of the various US non-professional constituencies, both NGO and congressional.

Finally, the staff memorandum raised again the earlier objection against EUR-RPM's handling CSCE matters. It contended that the result of such policy structuring was that officers with expertise and experience in CSCE issues would be subordinated to NATO and to the interests of allied unity. In this way, the importance of CSCE itself would be diminished, together with human rights. The Commission staff pushed for prime control of CSCE policy at the political level of the Department, meaning the Warren Christopher-Matthew Nimetz team. While technically in charge of coordinating CSCE policy, a key staffer contended, they had been "increasingly diverted to other issues," with the result that the "influence of the career bureaucracy" had "unfortunately dramatically increased."[17]

Beyond the current moment, said the Commission memorandum, it was necessary to formulate a coordinated long-range CSCE policy and create appropriate consultation mechanisms to maximize executive and legislative liaison. To realize this purpose, the Commission sought the establishment of an interagency CSCE steering group, chaired by Nimetz, that would include the Commission.[18] It would replace the State-Commission working group which had met prior to Belgrade. The career bureaucracy, noted a Commission staffer, "concurred" in the formation of the interagency group, though "with much carping."

Chairman Fascell reinforced the staff memorandum to the NSC in a follow-up letter to Secretary Vance.[19] The letter warned against a shift in US CSCE strategy away from human rights, seemingly now possible as a result of NATO support for the French CDE proposal. Fascell stressed that at Madrid the review of implementation should remain the top US priority, accompanied by the tactic of criticizing violations and specifying names and cases. He reiterated his view that a "balance" between human rights and military security issues be the central concern of US negotiators at CSCE meetings.

In most respects, the White House adhered to the recommendations of the Commission report and the Fascell letter, although it once again rebuffed the Commission attempt to reduce the authority of the Bureau of European Affairs. More important was the Carter administration's willingness by the end of 1979 to consider the French CDE proposal as positive. The reasons were clear enough. The proposal had the strong support of NATO members. Secondly, it fitted in with the administration's search for a formula that would facilitate disarmament or arms control. And, thirdly, with the issue of Theater Nuclear Forces (Pershing II and cruise missiles) hanging fire and dependent upon a favorable NATO response, it would be counterproductive to reject out of hand a French proposal backed by NATO.

The Commission's status remained high despite the pressures and maneuvering of the State Department's career bureaucracy, buttressed by the strong new security interests tightly linked to NATO considerations. Commission staff played a key role in three CSCE experts' meetings mandated at Belgrade. Spencer Oliver had functioned as the co-chairman of the US delegation to a meeting held between October 31-December 11, 1978, in Montreux, Switzerland, on the "Peaceful Settlement of Disputes." Deputy Staff Director Guy Coriden headed the US delegation to the Bonn preparatory meeting of the Scientific Forum, held in 1978, and occupied a key place in a mainly scientific delegation attending the forum itself in Hamburg in 1980. Commission staffers were also heavily involved with the US delegation in a meeting in Valletta, Malta, on cooperation in the Mediterranean. At the Madrid preparatory meeting in September 1980, Staff Director Oliver was designated as deputy chairman, which gave him a role second only to the head of the US delegation. Commission staffers served as major players throughout the Madrid deliberations, which ran from November 1980 to September 1983.

A crucial reason for the Commission's continuing prominence was the power exercised by Congressman Fascell. His personal and professional relations with Secretary Vance (and, indirectly, with President Carter) enabled his voice to be heard clearly in foreign affairs. When Edmund Muskie replaced Vance in the aftermath of the Iran rescue imbroglio in the spring of 1980, Fascell continued the relationship which he had enjoyed with Vance. The Commission chairman and his co-chairman, Senator Claiborne Pell of Rhode Island, were appointed as vice-chairmen of the US delegation to Madrid.

There was yet a second factor that explained the undiminished status and visibility of the Commission. A characteristic feature of the State Department's personnel policy is rotation. As Madrid approached, most of those in the Department who had accumulated CSCE experience and skills in the pre-Belgrade era had been re-assigned to other posts. The inevitable vacuum was filled by a Commission staff whose continuity assured both institutional "memory" and invaluable expertise. With the Helsinki process distinguished by special and unique procedural features, such expertise could not easily be replicated. Beyond procedural matters, the Commission staff was also well versed on substantive issues. Technical skills, especially in Helsinki's human rights areas, were joined to the political influence of the Congress in assuring the Commission an especially viable role.

For example, Commission members now participated in the bilateral meetings with East European governments concerning the forthcoming Madrid review session and the future of CSCE. In the past, the State Department had exclusive responsibility for the bilateral meetings with East Europeans. Moreover, the meetings offered a significant, if closed, forum for raising outstanding human rights and other CSCE-related issues. Entrance into the process of the bilaterals was clearly a major step forward for the Commission.

Bilateral meetings were held in overseas capitals with Hungary, Romania, East Germany, Poland, and Bulgaria, as well as with several neutral and non-aligned countries. Though headed by State Department officials, each delegation always included at least one Commission representative, who was appropriately given the task of making the official US presentation on human rights. Integration into these crucial meetings meant, too, that the East European countries, aside from the Soviet Union, would perceive the Commission in quite a different way than previously. The East Germans and Bulgarians, for example, had earlier followed Soviet *diktat* in not recognizing or dealing with the Commission. Suddenly, the Commission had become a legitimate governmental entity.

A major aspect of the bilaterals was delivery to East European countries of lists of unresolved family-reunion problems. Persons on the list had been refused the Helsinki right to join a spouse in the United States or to travel to the US or to emigrate there in order to join kin or family. Evaluation of a country's compliance with the provisions of Basket III relied, to considerable degree, on the positive response to the lists. The Commission staff already had been engaged in developing them. Now the research function was joined to an implementing function in pressing for a solution to human-contact problems.

In another departure from previous experience, Commission representatives were invited to sit in on the NATO "consultations" which were held periodically leading up to Madrid. While the meetings were largely the domain of the State Department and remained so, the consultations permitted the Commission to be seen as "expert" on CSCE by West

European officials. The Commission's presence at CSCE meetings, at strategy sessions or in lobbying activities became quite normal.

Even as its diplomatic functions grew, the Commission continued to concentrate on human rights research and monitoring. In Eastern Europe and the USSR, the period leading up to Madrid was marked by considerable repression and by wholesale violations of rights spelled out in the Helsinki Final Act. Commission files constituted a vast repository of case studies for use by the US delegation when the sessions would begin. The files were augmented by documentation provided directly by the Moscow Watch Group and other Helsinki Watch groups, and by Charter 77. Supplemental information was obtained through several Commission hearings at which experts testified. What would emerge on the eve of Madrid was a solid implementation report, the second one the Commission issued.[20] It was undoubtedly the single most detailed source of violations about human rights in the CSCE community.

A striking Commission initiative in human rights implementation, unrelated to East Europe, attracted considerable attention. It was a study to examine US compliance with the provisions of Helsinki.[21] The research report responded to suggestions to the Commission from Congress that the United States ought to demonstrate its commitment to Helsinki by an objective and critical inquiry into its own practices. Perhaps the Soviet Union and the countries of Eastern Europe would be encouraged to engage in a similar self-examination and undertake efforts to correct gross violations. Certainly, the initiative could be utilized to rebut criticism that the United States was only interested in communist infringements and not in its own compliance.

The study took on special meaning as a response to charges by the USSR about US human rights practices made in the latter part of the Belgrade session. A directive from President Carter to all domestic government agencies enabled the Commission staff to interview appropriate officials and examine documentation in the Department of Justice, the Department of Health, Education and Welfare, and in other major governmental agencies.

In its inquiry, the Commission took account of allegations not only made at the Belgrade review meeting and at bilaterals, but also those made by human rights groups, such as Amnesty International, who were invited to testify at Commission hearings about US compliance. The intent here was clear: to demonstrate to the USSR the legitimacy for this type of activity by NGOs in the USSR. Even if unproductive in affecting Soviet attitudes, the study was a model of its kind; no CSCE country had prepared anything similar.

One particular case—the "Wilmington Ten"—which had attracted extensive coverage in the communist world and, indeed, been commented upon at Belgrade, warranted special attention. The ten blacks had been convicted in North Carolina of arson and given long prison terms.[22] The violence apparently grew out of strong racial tensions in Wilmington. Many in the US and abroad saw it as a miscarriage of justice and symptomatic of anti-black prejudice.

Spencer Oliver gave the case his personal attention.[23] He journeyed to the Orangeburg state prison in North Carolina and met with Reverend Ben Chavis, the head of the group. He worked with several lawyers in the Justice Department who had filed an *amicus curia* brief on behalf of the group. And he spoke at length two or three times with the Governor of North Carolina, James B. Hunt. The Governor commuted Chavis' sentence and called Oliver in Madrid to tell him about it. By a curious coincidence, the phone call came through just as Oliver was preparing to give a speech on the "Principles" of the Helsinki Final Act during the opening week of the Madrid session. Whether the case had any impact upon Moscow is doubtful, but it demonstrated the Commission's willingness to be fair.

It was in its impact upon White House decision making with respect to CSCE that the Commission was most effective. In its memorandum to the National Security Council, the Commission strongly urged that the "public" aspect of CSCE be reflected in the selection of the US delegation. Carter appointed some 30 public members as advisers to the delegation.[24] (Most came for short periods of a week or two, and had no diplomatic function.) They came from a variety of ethnic, economic and civil rights constituencies and, if traditionally oriented State Department personnel looked on the idea with contempt, the appointments no doubt helped sustain a strong sense of commitment to the Helsinki process.

The Commission's recommendation of a political appointment to head the delegation was similarly followed. President Carter chose his personal lawyer and former Attorney General, Griffin Bell, to head the delegation. As the second-in-command who would lead the US delegation at the earlier preparatory meeting, the President chose a leading liberal and civil rights advocate whose foreign affairs outlook was strongly anti-Soviet and anti-communist, Max Kampelman. Prominent in Washington's legal and political circles, he was a major figure in the tough-minded, defense-oriented Committee on the Present Danger. Zbigniew Brzezinski later confided that it was he who was largely responsible for the President's choice.[25]

Bell's contribution to the Madrid proceedings was very limited. He served only a few days in Madrid when the session opened. After Carter was defeated in the November 1980 elections, Bell resigned and Kampelman, who had represented the United States at the crucial preparatory session, took charge. The new President, Ronald Reagan, reappointed him as head of the delegation. No other high-level Democratic appointee was kept in his position by the Reagan administration. What it testified to was recognition of an extraordinary combination of diplomatic and political talents, a creative mind joined to an articulate tongue, and a toughness in dealing with Moscow that matched President Reagan's. Indeed, several years later Kampelman would emphasize in an interview that in 1975 he had opposed the Helsinki accord as a capitulation to Moscow.[26] He had been on the same wavelength as Reagan and Henry Jackson at the time.

Kampelman's credentials as a vigorous human rights advocate and tough negotiator certainly conformed to the guidelines of delegation leader that the Commission had proposed. He soon showed vigorous determination with no hesitancy to name names and cite cases in reviewing Moscow's non-compliance with the Helsinki accord. Nonetheless, he was far from being the Commission's "man," although it was during his CSCE ambassadorship that the Commission reached its greatest political heights. Three of Kampelman's eight staffers at the preparatory meeting were Commission professionals. At the regular Madrid session, he was directly assisted by Oliver and a sizable group from the Commission staff. Of the six subsidiary working groups dealing with the substantive issues at the Madrid session, Commission staffers were the chief US negotiators in four.[27]

No greater tribute could have been extended the Commission staff than that later given by Undersecretary of State Lawrence Eagleburger, the highest-ranking career diplomat in the State Department. He told the Commission in testimony on March 23, 1982:

> Throughout the [Madrid] conference, but especially in the recent session, the Commission staff has been a mainstay of our effort in Madrid, both through their participation on the delegation and through their back-up work here in Washington.[28]

It is ironic commentary that only six years earlier Eagleburger had served as Henry Kissinger's principal agent in opposing the creation of the Commission.

Even before the Madrid follow-up meeting, "the shadow of Afghanistan" —as the Canadian External Affairs Minister Mark MacGuigan would describe the international atmosphere[29]—had an impact upon the Helsinki process. Probably more compelling upon Western public opinion were rigged trials of two prominent Helsinki monitors in the summer of 1978 and, later, the forced internal exile, without even a trial, of the Soviet Union's leading human rights advocate, Andrei Sakharov. That sudden and arbitrarily imposed exile in January 1980 to Gorky, a "closed" city, was designed to isolate him from his colleagues within the USSR and his contacts in the West. The exile had no basis in Soviet law. It was accompanied by a vicious campaign of slander in the press. Over time, the conditions of his arrest worsened, while his jailers became more brazenly abusive. The Kremlin's hope was to silence a voice whose echoes resonated powerfully and widely in the civilized world.

These harsh events were to provide a backdrop in 1978-80 to a Helsinki experts meeting mandated by the Belgrade session. A Scientific Forum was scheduled for Hamburg, West Germany, in February 1980. Its aim was to be that of advancing Basket II purposes on scientific exchange by bringing together leading figures in the science community of each CSCE state. The agenda of the Forum was to be prepared by CSCE representatives meeting in Bonn in the summer of 1978, 18 months before the experts' meeting. That preparatory session could hardly ignore developments in the USSR affecting Helsinki monitors as the delegates were assembling in Bonn.

Orlov, the chairman of the Moscow Helsinki Watch Group, had already been sentenced to seven years in forced labor. But in July 1978, Shcharansky and Ginzburg, the two other leading figures in the group, were placed on trial.[30] Shcharansky, the Group's spokesman, was convicted of espionage and sentenced to twelve years of incarceration. Ginzburg was convicted of the standard charge of anti-Soviet propaganda and given a lesser sentence. The West was shocked. Even David Owen, the British Foreign Secretary who had earlier desperately sought to reduce confrontation with the Soviet Union and who had been critical of Arthur Goldberg's tactics, was angry enough to respond. After informing Parliament that the West expected respect for all parts of the Helsinki accord, including human rights, he provocatively raised the question as to whether it was worthwhile participating in a Helsinki meeting if one part of the accord was being violated. Owen ordered the British delegation to raise the matter at the preparatory meeting in Bonn. The US quickly joined in this initiative.

Fearful that the Hamburg Scientific Forum would prove disruptive to détente objectives, communist delegates at Bonn scrutinized Western suggestions for the Forum's agenda, anticipating that the West might transform the Forum into an ideological confrontation. They objected to the overall theme which the West proposed for the Forum—the role of science in meeting "fundamental human needs." The phrase smacked too much of fundamental human rights.

When the scientific delegation members of the CSCE states would assemble in Hamburg in February 1980, Western representatives were determined to press their concern for the great Soviet scientist—and their colleague—Andrei Sakharov, who had been exiled a month earlier.[31] In the opening statements of Western delegates at the conference plenary, his name continually reverberated. But they also went beyond his plight to elaborate on all the official restrictions imposed on Soviet scientists— to travel, to emigrate, and to host international science conferences. These restrictions were systematically applied to the thousands of Jewish refuseniks, most of whom were scientists.

The argument was repeatedly driven home that the advancement of science urgently required the removal of restrictions on scientific interchange. Many wanted it clearly understood in Moscow that unless the Soviet authorities restored the rights of scientists to work and to think, all scientific exchanges and communications with major scientific nations were in grave jeopardy.

Dr. Philip Handler, President of the National Academy of Sciences and head of the US delegation, later disclosed the details of the Hamburg meeting as it related to human rights.[32] After noting that "communication" among scientists was "a tradition of five centuries," and in fact was "the very essence of science," he stressed that "communication," whether related to monitoring the Final Act or requesting permission to travel or to emigrate was being trampled upon:

> By the time we had gathered, it was apparent that the scientists of the West were primarily concerned with what they considered to be serious infringements of the human rights and freedoms of too many of their scientific colleagues in the East.[33]

The American scientific delegation, Handler explained, was determined to establish the principle of the indivisibility of freedom. Freedom of inquiry was "indissolubly bound" to every other freedom and especially to the "freedom of one's person." Scientists, he said, could not be silent about the condition of their colleagues in the USSR.[34]

At the insistence of the Western scientists, the Scientific Forum adopted a document which carried two pointed statements on human rights that not only challenged the Kremlin's conduct, but at the same time carried an implicit warning that Soviet behavior might deleteriously affect East-West exchange programs.[35] One statement specified that "respect for human rights and fundamental freedoms by all states represents one of the foundations for significant improvement of their mutual relations and of international scientific cooperation at all levels." A second statement noted that "improvements" in "international scientific cooperation" can be achieved through "equitable opportunities . . . for wider communication and travel for professional purposes."

Highlighted in both statements was the principle of linkage between that part of Basket II dealing with scientific exchange and the human rights provisions of Baskets I and III. Progress in scientific cooperation can only be realized by upholding basic human rights standards. Handler himself would later call attention to this "statement of linkage" as reflecting the views of the Western scientific community. Of course, the Soviets had rejected the principle of linkage to human rights at Belgrade.

The report of the Scientific Forum required consensus, just as the concluding document at Belgrade had. Why then did the USSR permit the acceptance of a crucial Western idea? It would be an error to presume that Moscow responded with any enthusiasm to the linkage principle. Nor could the Soviets welcome the repeated references at the Forum to the plight of Sakharov and of Jewish scientist refuseniks. But, at the same time, the Soviet leadership was sensitive to the palpable threat of a severance of contacts between its own scientists and the Western scientific community. Had the Hamburg meeting ended in an unresolved and angry furor, such an outcome was quite plausible, a risk the USSR was scarcely anxious to run. Soviet science remained vital for the Soviet political elite attuned to the advanced technological needs of industry.

Soviet willingness at Hamburg to tolerate both an unpleasant assault on its human rights posture and an overt linkage that it had regarded with disdain carried an object lesson for the West. Even a disintegrating détente could allow for a strong human rights statement in the context of Helsinki. Under certain circumstances, Moscow would not veto a determined Western position on human rights, although that position would have to accord with at least some Soviet interests perceived by the Kremlin. Ascertaining the circumstances for a positive Soviet response to Western human rights initiatives became the central focus of Western tactics at Helsinki meetings.

Ambassador Kampelman would later say that it was essential to arraign the Soviet Union in a "world court in continuous session." From the very beginning, the Commission saw the function of follow-up meetings as precisely that of focusing world attention on Soviet violations of human rights (as well as human rights violations by other communist countries, most notably Czechoslovakia and East Germany).

The period November-December 1979 had been a demarcation point for a qualitatively stepped-up Soviet policy of repression. One critical index was the rate of arrests for all dissidents and refuseniks. It rose sharply from the last two months of 1979 through 1980, then remained at about that level until 1983. The totals for 1980-82 were respectively 268, 205 and 241, significantly exceeding the highest totals of previous years (196 in 1972 and 198 in 1969). Comparison of data on the average number of arrests during 1975-78—the waning years of détente—with the level during 1980-82 was especially illuminating. During 1975-78, the average level was 89; during 1980-82, the average escalated to 238—almost three times greater. In the pivotal year of 1979, the level reached 145.

Two factors explained the new Kremlin policy. The first was the imminence of the Olympic Games in Moscow and four other Soviet cities. The authorities were fearful that dissenters would use the Olympics for demonstrations, press conferences and the distribution of literature. A second factor was the Soviet military invasion of Afghanistan in December 1979. Aside from the violence and repression unleashed against the Afghan population, the Kremlin cracked down on any immediate or potential public opposition to the invasion.

If the Sakharovs were isolated and other prominent activists incarcerated, lesser-known dissenters were warned against publicizing their plight to visitors, lest Moscow's international prestige be damaged and its economic interests harmed.[36] Preventive arrests were indirectly acknowledged by the head of the KGB in the Ukraine, Vitaly Fedorchuk. Referring to "40 Ukrainian nationalists"—obviously the Ukrainian Helsinki Group—he publicly declared: "In order to avoid unnecessary international friction, some of them have been put away on criminal charges."[37]

Police officials had no hesitancy in privately informing the dissidents of their intent. By August 1981, an official would openly say: "Previously we brought people to trial only for their actions. But now we will try them for preparing to act and for assisting others."[38] In September, another official told a dissident: "I'm telling you straight: by the summer, there won't be a single democrat or [Jewish] nationalist left in Moscow."[39]

The intensity of suppression was climaxed by an unprecedented article in the leading party theoretical organ, *Kommunist*, in September 1981 by KGB First Deputy Chairman Semyon Tsivgun.[40] It openly acknowledged the massive crackdown, linking it to the need to neutralize imperialist "subversion." Tsivgun's exercise of Orwellian inversion could be summarized as follows: "Imperialism's special services" oriented their "subversive work" to exploiting anti-Soviet leaders in an "anti-social" confrontation with the Soviet socialist system. When the activists appealed for "revision of our political and ideological principles and institutions," they were merely doing the bidding of the "imperialist special services and anti-Soviet centers." For that reason, the "illegal activity" of so-called "defenders of rights" and "champions of democracy" had to be "exposed and rendered harmless." Tsivgun admitted that activists were "charged with criminal offenses," and that "relevant preventive work" had to be undertaken "with respect to deluded people."

Certainly, the large number of arrests and convictions constituted a frontal assault on the Helsinki principles, which had as their cornerstone the "right to know and act upon one's rights." Sometimes, admission of the repression and what it meant for Helsinki slipped out. A party official, for example, in 1980 observed in the presence of a dissenter "we signed the Helsinki accords, but morally we are against them."[41] At Madrid, Soviet officials would take another verbal stance, shielding their discomfiture with a stream of invectives hurled against dissenters. Thus, the head of the Soviet delegation, Leonid Ilyichev, at a press conference called the dissenters "people without shame or honor who choose the path of criminal deeds."[42] In short, they were nothing but "criminals" for whom incarceration was perfectly appropriate. A period of time in prison or in a labor camp would effectively intimidate many who might choose the path to exercise their rights.

Paralleling the arrests and incarcerations was a severe cutback in emigration. Jewish emigration had continued to rise during 1978-79 even as Helsinki monitors were being silenced. It rose to 28,000 in 1978 and an unprecedented 51,320 in 1979.[43] What probably explained the upsurge was Moscow's desire to have the US Senate ratify the SALT II agreement, which had been signed by the leaders of the two superpowers in the summer of 1979. But Washington's anger with the invasion of Afghanistan compelled the Carter administration to withdraw the agreement from Senate consideration. Another factor was Jackson-Vanik. Moscow hoped that the administration would use the waiver provision of the amendment to allow the Soviet Union MFN tariff treatment and subsidized government credits. Initiatives in this direction also collapsed in the face of the Afghanistan offensive.

Jewish emigration now plummeted. The decrease was already apparent by November–December 1979. In 1980, the total was cut by far more than one-half, to 21,471. The plunge then entered a veritable freefall: 9,400 in 1981, 2,700 in 1982, and a mere 1,315 in 1983.[44] The official explanation for the drastic drop was provided by a newly created Kremlin instrument for dealing with Jewish issues—the so-called "Anti-Zionist Committee," which came into existence in April 1983. Its top official, Samuil Zivs, claimed that the process of reuniting divided families had been completed.[45] Only a few still sought to leave to be reunited with kin, he insisted.

In fact, some 400,000 Soviet Jews had requested affidavits from relatives in Israel, which was the first stage in the emigration process.[46] Thousands would now enter into the category of refuseniks, subject to various forms of harassment. An existence of uncertainty and a state of limbo characterized the life of many Jews. The most frequent technique for refusing an exit visa was the charge that the applicant possessed "state secrets." Capricious refusals often carried a Kafkaesque character. Some were told that they would never be permitted to emigrate.

The severe exit-visa cutback was accompanied by a massive police assault upon Jewish cultural leaders and Hebrew culture.[47] Nine key cultural figures, including the editor of the samizdat journal *Jews in the USSR*, Viktor Brailovsky, were arrested and imprisoned. The police warned some 80 private teachers of Hebrew to stop their educational activities or face trials and incarceration.[48]

Jews were not the only ones affected by the new Soviet policy. Emigration of Soviet Germans to West Germany declined heavily (from 9,704 in 1976 to 1,447 in 1983), although the German emigration level—15 percent—was significantly greater than the Jewish emigration level, which had fallen to a mere 2.5 percent.[49] Emigration of Armenians, who, along with Jews and Germans, were the only ethnic groups permitted to emigrate and be united with kin, also dropped. Pentecostal Christians were almost totally barred from leaving. A high KGB official told one Pentecostal group in 1980: "Don't you compare yourselves with the Jews. They fetch a good price. But we get very little for you."[50] The reference appeared to mean that some Jewish emigration could result in the improvement of opportunities for obtaining American trade benefits under Jackson-Vanik legislation.

The assault on "freer movement of people" was soon accompanied by sharp thrusts at the parallel Helsinki aim—the "freer movement of ideas." First, radio jamming of the Voice of America, BBC and Deutsche Welle was resumed in the summer of 1980.[51] It had ended in 1973, no doubt to facilitate final negotiations of the Helsinki Final Act, although Radio Liberty had been jammed throughout. What certainly prompted resumption of jamming was the highly significant growth of Solidarity activity in Poland during that time frame. Such activities, from the Kremlin perspective, might stimulate somewhat similar conduct by Soviet workers and peasants. It was therefore vital to shut off any positive news about Solidarity.

Other standard means of communication were severely ruptured as well. The recently introduced system of East-West direct telephone dialing was suddenly shut down, and the number of phone circuits linked to the West was reduced by two-thirds.[52] Mail service was similarly tightened. Letters to and from dissidents' families were often confiscated, and a growing number were told orally that no further parcels would be delivered to them.[53] When Western governments appealed to the Universal Postal Union in Switzerland on legal grounds that international agreements had been strongly breached, Moscow refused to even discuss the matter.[54]

Controlling and limiting contacts were extended to travelers. Foreigners suspected of having contacts with dissidents or refuseniks were frequently denied visas to enter the Soviet Union. Foreign journalists, tourists, diplomats and academic exchange visitors were discouraged from visiting contacts by occasional detentions or expulsions and by police questioning.[55] At the same time, dissidents were warned to avoid all contacts with foreigners. The failure to observe the warning at times resulted in various forms of house arrest.

Particularly dismaying to the Western world in 1979-80 was the continuation and intensification of the government's virulent anti-Semitic propaganda campaign, which masqueraded as anti-Zionism. Much later, in July 1990 during the era of glasnost, *Pravda*, in a long article, acknowledged the anti-Semitism of the campaign:

> Considerable damage was done by a group of writers who, while pretending to fight Zionism, began to resurrect many notions of the anti-Semitic propaganda of the [Tsarist] Black Hundreds and of Fascist origin. Hiding under Marxist phraseology, they came out with coarse attacks on Jewish culture, on Judaism, and on Jews in general.[56]

Typical was an article published in the youth tabloid, *Pionerskaia pravda*, on October 10, 1980, by a notorious bigot, Lev Korneyev. He told his young readers that "most of the major monopolies producing arms are controlled by Jewish bankers" who were responsible for wars and civil wars in various parts of the world, including the resistance in Afghanistan to communist rule. For "the business made on blood" brings them "enormous profits." In addition, the readers were informed that "Zionists are trying to infiltrate into all the spheres of public life, into ideology, science and commerce." Youngsters were warned that "Levi jeans"—at the time a popular item on the black market—served to benefit the coffers of Zionism.[57]

Korneyev climaxed his career of hate-mongering in early 1982 with the publication by the state of *The Class Essence of Zionism*, which brought together all of the main themes of his writings.[58] He cited approvingly from Tsarist anti-Semitic works, and claimed the Holocaust was largely a figment of Zionist imagination. *Izvestiia* gave the work a glowing review.[59] A second leading anti-Jewish hate panderer, Yevgenii Yevseev, turned out a booklet, *Zionism in the Chain of Imperialism*, which was printed by a facility housed in the Ministry of Internal Affairs.[60] The work charged that Zionism was "more dangerous" than even Nazism or Fascism, for it was "destroying the spiritual and moral health of the working class."

According to a Jewish historical researcher in Moscow who had closely examined the numerous official anti-Semitic writings, these works virtually plagiarized the ideas of the Tsarist Black Hundreds and the Nazis. The researcher, Ruth Okuneva, wrote a study in which she assembled in three parallel columns anti-Semitic statements of recently published Soviet books and strikingly similar assertions in the works of Black Hundred and later Hitlerian writers.[61] She sent her study, "A Few Pages of Analogy," to Communist Party General Secretary Leonid Brezhnev on April 12, 1980, with a summary that stressed that "their works are full of hatred of Jews." And she emphasized that the writings were "violating the ideals of socialist internationalism that form the basis of the Communist Party's national policy." An official of the Central Committee later called her to express appreciation for her "very thorough" documentation and observed that "it will be of use to us."

The impact of the incendiary anti-Semitic propaganda was considerable in the international community. It became a subject of intense debate in the Council of Europe's deliberations in Strasbourg[62] and could hardly escape commentary at the Madrid follow-up meeting, especially because the propaganda was accompanied by discrimination against Jews in higher education,[63] by deprivation in Jewish cultural activity, and by barriers to Jewish emigration.

The official report by President Carter on Helsinki implementation covering the six-month period June 1-November 30, 1980, forcefully addressed the depressing human rights record in the Soviet Union:[64] "The Soviet human rights record continues to worsen. The relentless year-long government campaign of repression against human rights activists of all sorts remains in force." The report took note of the exile to Gorky of "one of the most forceful and eloquent spokesman for human rights." It elaborated upon "the continuing persecution" of the Moscow Watch Group, which had "severely and increasingly impaired" its activities.[65] The result had been a halt to studies for which the group had become famous. Since its founding, it had released and distributed almost 150 formal reports on Soviet compliance with Helsinki obligations. The topics had covered every area of Basket III, and had been an indispensable source for CSCE participating states.

Special attention was given to detailing the tragic plight of the Helsinki Watch Groups in the USSR.[66] Orlov was said to be serving his seven-year sentence "under harsh conditions" in the notorious Perm #2 labor camp. In September 1980, he was sentenced to six months of solitary confinement for protesting interference with his mail and for demanding improvement in camp conditions. The Ukrainian monitoring group was hit especially hard, with most of its members imprisoned or exiled. The other monitoring groups in Armenia, Georgia, and Lithuania "have also been systematically hounded and suppressed."

The report took note of "severe harassment" of those religious groups that were not officially registered—their leaders imprisoned, their activities subjected to a "wave of arrests and trials" in the past six months, and their membership virtually categorized as criminal.[67] Pentecostals were especially targeted "with interrogations and house searches." Only recently, on November 5, said the report, the group launched a five-day fast to dramatize their demand to emigrate. Other items covered in the report were the "disturbing signs of anti-Semitism" expressed in official press attacks on Zionism, the jamming of Western radios, harassment of Western newsmen, and the significant cutback of the distribution of the USIA magazine, *America Illustrated.*

The report was not the only source of documentation. Petitions from Soviet Jews seeking the right to leave continued to be forwarded to Helsinki participants, but at a much slower rate than had been the case during 1976-78.[68] The repressive atmosphere within the Soviet Union was hardly conducive to running risks with the mail. Other groups began displaying a strong interest. During the course of the Madrid session, a group of political prisoners from Czechoslovakia—the "Mirov Prisoners" —sent a letter to the Western delegations bitterly lamenting their status: "We ourselves are testimony to judicial discrimination in prisons and are an embarrassment to justice in a state that does not observe human rights in any way."[69] It called upon the CSCE conference to "demand an immediate release of political prisoners in Czechoslovakia and strict observance of civil and political rights."

An angry response to repression, when operating in an information void, can exert little impact. If, however, the response is publicly channeled through appeals, letters and petitions, it may stir public reaction. Documentation of the acts of repression was rapidly mounting. Helsinki, through a follow-up meeting in Madrid, offered a platform to arouse the conscience of Europe.

·7·

Madrid: "City of Dissidence"

L e *Monde* captured the opening of the Helsinki conference in Madrid on November 11 with the marvelously descriptive phrase "city of dissidence."[1] The Spanish capital had become a magnet for dissidents and democratic activists from every part of Eastern Europe, along with their human rights champions and advocates in the West. Spouses and relatives of Soviet "prisoners of conscience" and refuseniks mingled with representatives of Western non-governmental human rights organizations in rallies, demonstrations, press conferences and mini-review sessions. Displays and leaflets, films and posters, and books and recordings were everywhere. The corridors of the Helsinki sessions or of nearby hotels were sites for hurried press conferences by, for example, Nina Lagergren (the half-sister of Raoul Wallenberg) or Anatoly Shcharansky's wife, Avital. Especially active in arranging for public exposure of Soviet and East European activists who were present was the US Helsinki Watch, which leased office space and staffed it with a highly skilled professional. A vast array of reporters from virtually every West European country and from many East European countries had descended on Madrid.[2]

To a far greater degree than Belgrade, Madrid had become the stage for grand human rights theater. One reason was its accessibility; the city was close to most Western organizations. A second was the strong democratic character of Spanish society and of the Spanish government, in contrast to Yugoslavia, where a certain arbitrariness befitting an authoritarian regime made for caution and restraint in any public display of human rights. A third reason was the Western public reaction to Moscow's repression of the several Helsinki Watch groups. Of the 71 individuals who comprised the half-dozen Helsinki monitoring groups, 24 had been tried and found guilty, with 19 of them serving a total of 156 years in forced labor or internal exile. A further 11 were under investigative arrests, nine were serving sentences that had been imposed earlier, seven were encouraged or allowed to emigrate and two were stripped of citizenship while traveling abroad.[3] By September 1982, the devastation was so overwhelming that the Moscow Helsinki Watch Group chose to go out of business altogether.[4]

Demonstrations in Madrid in favor of the Helsinki Watch groups or against the repression were based on the assumption that Moscow was not unresponsive to public outcry. One of the most prominent Soviet dissenters, the historian and writer Andrei Amalrik, who was virtually forced out of the USSR, told an interviewer on the eve of Madrid: "The Soviet authorities do react quite sensitively to Western public opinion."[5] He, himself, was on his way from France to join a "counter-conference" in Madrid, when an automobile accident put an end to a possibly brilliant future in literature.

Spain's next-door neighbor, France, was echoing the dissidence of Madrid. During the week of the scheduled Helsinki review opening, a huge two-day gathering in Marseilles of some 1,000 participants from various countries called on the Western community to insist at Madrid on the Soviet Union granting the rights of family reunion and freer movement of people stipulated in the Final Act.[6] Alain Ravennes, co-founder and Secretary-General of the Parisian Intellectuals Committee for Freedom in Europe, publicly demanded that the West press at the very opening of the Madrid meeting for the Soviets to withdraw all their troops from Afghanistan. He asked, too, that the West demand the release of all East Europeans who had been imprisoned simply because they called for the full implementation of the Helsinki accord. In his view, the West must not participate in a masquerade that would cover up Soviet Helsinki violations.

Moscow was engaged in major initiatives concerning two procedural questions at the preparatory meeting in Madrid, which had begun in September.[7] The first would halt or limit implementation review and focus instead on new proposals and, thereby, security considerations. The second would leave up in the air the precise date for the next review conference. Both procedural initiatives would have reversed Belgrade's principal achievements. The Soviet Union's tactics at the preparatory sessions, in keeping with their initiatives, appeared to many as an attempt to scuttle the Helsinki process. From this perspective, the tactics added enormously to the drama of Madrid.

At Belgrade, the United States had won agreement on the Yellow Book, the basic series of guidelines spelling out the time to be devoted to review (as distinct from consideration of new proposals). The Yellow Book had stipulated seven weeks for review of implementation, but

Moscow now decided to challenge its validity. At a private meeting in mid-September, chief Soviet delegate (also Ambassador to Spain) Yuri Dubinin told Austrian delegate Franz Ceska (a leading figure in the neutral/non-aligned bloc and in the Helsinki process) that Moscow considered the Yellow Book prejudiced in favor of the West and therefore not consonant with Soviet interests.[8]

The Soviets were disturbed by certain procedural features with implicit substantive ramifications. Moscow objected to the fact that the guidelines provided for no cutoff date for ending discussions and no definite date for concluding the follow-up meeting itself. The Kremlin clearly feared a repetition of Belgrade, which would make the Soviet Union and its human rights practices, as well as those of some of it allies, targets for endless Western criticism.

More distressing to the Soviet Union was the book's handling of the ending of the conference. Instead of a definite date, it set various target dates, concerning which "every effort should be made" to meet. But the book specified that "in any case," the meeting "will end . . . by adopting its concluding document and by fixing the date and place of the next similar meeting." Because the Helsinki process operated on the basis of consensus, the provision meant that the conference could go on indefinitely, or until everyone was satisfied with the concluding document. What the Soviet Union wanted and initially proposed at Madrid was to limit implementation review to only two and one-half days or, at most, one or two weeks.[9]

From the US and Western viewpoint, this limitation was unacceptable. The very heart of the Helsinki follow-up meetings was review of the provisions of the Final Act, particularly those dealing with human rights. The emphasis now took on a far greater pertinence than at Belgrade, for the evidence pointed to massive repression of human rights in the USSR and several other Warsaw Pact countries, especially Czechoslovakia. Besides, the United States and the Western powers had been shocked by Soviet aggression in Afghanistan, which itself carried ramifications in the human rights field.

Indeed, the most important purpose of Madrid, from the US viewpoint, was a detailed review of implementation of all aspects of the Final Act, with special attention to human rights and the Soviet invasion of Afghanistan. This was made explicit in a report to Congress prepared by the Helsinki Commission in the summer of 1980.[10] No mention was made in the document concerning any advocacy of "new proposals." The only reference to the subject at all was that "any new measures agreed upon must be balanced," meaning that if proposals were advanced regarding security, they would have to be balanced with human rights proposals.

Following two weeks of heated negotiations, Czechoslovakia, on behalf of the Warsaw Pact countries, tabled in late September a working paper on guidelines.[11] Five and one-half weeks would be given over to opening statements, the general debate, review of implementation, new proposals and a host of other items. The follow-up meeting would run from November 11 to December 19, resuming January 6 (1981) to draft a concluding document. "It is indigestible," commented a Dutch delegate.[12] US Ambassador Kampelman considered it a mere introductory tactic of "trying out the water."[13] But the United States and the West stood firm on maintaining the Yellow Book guidelines. Speaking for the neutral/non-aligned members, Ambassador Ceska also objected to the Warsaw Pact attempt to curtail review and comment through excessively restrictive time limits.

The deadlock over Yellow Book procedures was compounded by the unresolved date and place of the next follow-up meeting. Would the Madrid review sessions have the authority to do this, as the book provided? Official Warsaw Pact reasoning made manifestly clear at the preparatory discussion that the entire question was "iffy." Whether the next follow-up meeting would be held at all, Moscow and its allies indicated, would depend on how the main Madrid session progressed. Until then, it would be premature to state formally what the time and place of the follow-up meeting should be.

Challenged herewith was the very basis of the Helsinki process. Moscow was conveying a distinct threat to the US and the West. Were Madrid utilized in the same way as Belgrade had been for sharp attacks on the Soviet Union and its allies, then further follow-up meetings would no longer be of any interest to Moscow. The threat was not communicated in any document or in any specific language. Instead, it was delivered by strong hints, together with the stonewalling tactics during procedural discussions.

The Soviets began early, stonewalling on the agenda of the conference and the very order of speakers that would follow the neutral address by the Spanish Foreign Minister, José Pedro Pérez Llorca, on its opening day, November 11.[14] The Soviet Union repeatedly rejected the proposal for drawing lots to ascertain when the various delegates would speak. Speculation spread throughout Madrid as to how the conference, based on consensus for everything, could even last for a few days without an agenda and list of speakers. As journalists and non-governmental organizations poured into the city, the question on the minds of many was whether all semblance of détente, together with its most significant expression—the Helsinki process—had come to an end.

As midnight approached with no decision on key procedural issues, the conferees finally agreed to "stop the clock" two minutes before midnight November 10. This would permit informal negotiations on the agenda and on the timetable. But the new negotiations could not end the deadlock and the Netherlands delegate chose to withdraw his approval of the clock-stopping machination. November 11 formally began with a new complication: who was to serve as chairman? The delegate of communist Hungary—Ambassador Janos Petran—had occupied the chair on November 10. With November 11 formally beginning, the chair should go to the host country, Spain. Liechtenstein so moved.

It was actually 8:00 P.M. and the scene resembled a Marx Brothers film, only with serious political ramifications.[15] The Soviet delegate rose to say that consensus was required to approve a new chairman, and that he would not acquiesce to the change. US Ambassador Max Kampelman twice intervened to tell Petran that his occupancy of the chairmanship was illegal, a claim the Soviets and Hungarians rejected. A US delegation spokesman told the media: "It is the view of my delegation that this is a usurpation on the part of the Hungarian chairman of the chairmanship and it is illegal. The Hungarian Ambassador has conducted the meeting in an artificial manner."[16]

The bizarre maneuvering came to a sudden halt just one hour before the Spanish Foreign Minister was scheduled to mount the rostrum for a two-minute greeting to the CSCE delegates. At a lengthy coffee break, the Spanish and Soviet delegations agreed that the reputation of all CSCE states would be damaged were the squabbling to prevent the conference from beginning. Petran was permitted to remain in the chair and the Spanish Foreign Minister formally opened the proceedings, but there was no agenda or order of speakers. Not until a post-midnight session was the procedural issue resolved. Lots were drawn for the order of speakers. More importantly, a compromise on the agenda was reached.[17] The neutral and non-aligned powers had drawn up documents, which they presented on a "take it or leave it" basis. They allowed a full six weeks for discussion on implementation, with the West reserving for itself the right to extend its commentary on human rights issues beyond six weeks if new violations were to occur. This would be permitted even when new proposals were discussed.

In substance, the Yellow Book guidelines were kept, although with a reduction of the time for review from seven weeks to six. Pragmatically, the reduction meant little, as the West continued to raise human rights issues when other matters, such as new proposals, were examined. As part of the compromise, a significant step was taken on the question of the conference's authority to set the time and place of the next follow-up meeting. It was agreed that the chairman of the Madrid conference would read a statement noting a "general understanding" that "appropriate modalities for the holding of other meetings includes setting the date and place of the next meeting similar to the present one."[18] Despite the opaque formulation, it was apparent that the West had prevailed in the long and confusing procedural wrangle. Detailed examination of compliance with Helsinki's human rights provisions would be conducted, and the future of the Helsinki process seemed assured.

What was the purpose, then, of the Soviet stonewalling? Clearly, Moscow did not relish being embarrassed in a major international forum by the raising of human rights issues, which tarnished its image as a leading power at the same time that it stirred discontent among Soviet citizens, particularly non-Russians, as well as the citizens of its Warsaw Pact allies. Moscow had resumed the jamming of Western radio stations precisely to keep out criticism from the West.

A telling indicator of the concern in the Kremlin about the cataloguing of individual human rights cases at a Helsinki forum was provided by a prominent Soviet Jewish prisoner of conscience, Iosif Mendelevich. When he was released from a forced labor camp in February 1981 after ten years of incarceration and then permitted to emigrate to Israel, he related an episode about the pertinence of Madrid.[19] In November 1980, Mendelevich had started a hunger strike. The labor camp administrator came, seeking to discourage him from continuing. When the prisoner wondered aloud why the sudden interest in his strike, as he was but "an unimportant person for the Soviet power," the administrator responded: "You are wrong because you are not alone. There is a Madrid conference at the present time, and many things have happened in the world which [we] have to take into account."

Significantly, Mendelevich was released one year before his 12-year sentence was served. His experience was not the only index of high-level Kremlin concern. A second example was the quick Soviet decision concerning a member of Sakharov's family. The physicist's adopted son (who had been born to Yelena Bonner when she was married to her first husband) had been forced to emigrate to the United States, where he lived in the Boston area. He sought to have his Soviet fiancée, Yelizaveta, join him. But her repeated requests for an exit visa were rebuffed. Sakharov, in November 1981, went on a protest and dramatic hunger strike lasting over two weeks to attract world attention. He sent a plea to the Madrid meeting asking that his son's plight be raised as a violation of Basket III provisions.[20] A copy was urgently forwarded to Ambassador Kampelman, but before the US envoy could raise the matter publicly, Moscow chose to allow the fiancée to emigrate. Obviously, the Kremlin wished to head off additional criticism in the Madrid setting.

Soviet authorities may have believed that their delaying tactics would exploit and widen differences both within the NATO alliance and between the neutral/non-aligned and the alliance. Everyone recalled the disarray in NATO ranks at Belgrade and the irritation with Goldberg's confrontation tactics. Moscow had benefitted significantly from these internal ruptures. Aware, too, that the various European democracies feared any threat to détente, the Soviet Union sought to exploit such fears and anxieties by focusing simply upon the seemingly modest agenda issue of the amount of time devoted to human rights.

Moscow was already using trade as a means to open rifts and widen fissures in Western ranks. During the first nine months of 1980, Soviet imports from West Germany jumped by 31 percent, to $3.3 billion, and imports from France rose 33 percent, to $1.9 billion. At Madrid, Kremlin spokesmen played on these figures, taunting the US for losing out in the foreign trade competition by "Cold War" restrictions on Soviet-American trade.[21] The tough Soviet tactics at the preparatory talks could have been designed to stimulate anxieties about the continuation of the flourishing trade.

The US strategy at the preparatory talks—and it carried over into the conference itself—had been guided by the conviction that the USSR was not prepared to dump an agreement of which Brezhnev himself had been a prime advocate.[22] Moreover, the Soviet President, in a *Pravda* interview on the fifth anniversary of the Final Act, expressed the belief that the Madrid meeting must lead to "important" results, especially regarding the convening of a conference on military détente and disarmament.[23] That Moscow would jeopardize the possibility of such an important conference because of agenda considerations must have seemed unlikely. During the deadlock, an Italian official visited Soviet Foreign Minister Gromyko in Moscow and bitterly complained about the filibuster in Madrid.[24] Gromyko told him that the Madrid conference was certain to be held. When this was reported to the NATO caucus in Madrid, tension diminished.

Indeed, the Soviet strategy was largely bluff. A top-ranking Soviet official later confided to a US delegate that "we have instructions to work closely with you."[25] Clearly, the Soviets were not going to discard dialogue prematurely, but their strategy of stonewalling and brinkmanship was based on a serious miscalculation. Yuri Dubinin privately disclosed to Warsaw Pact colleagues that the Kremlin had not expected either the US adamance or the tightness in NATO ranks. Dubinin himself was gratified by the outcome, according to East European sources. He told them that had the stonewalling pushed the follow-up meeting over the brink, he would have lost his job.

Moreover, the Soviet Union and Dubinin personally were engaged in a major effort to keep Madrid out of NATO. To torpedo a conference of which Spain was the host would only damage the Soviet initiative. It is hardly surprising that the breakthrough in the early deadlock was spearheaded by a special meeting of the Soviet and Spanish delegations. When deadlock again threatened at the end, the personal intervention of the Spanish Prime Minister, to whom the Soviet Union responded positively, similarly produced a favorable outcome.

Moscow's stonewalling, at best a dangerous gamble with a potentially disastrous outcome, aroused the anger of the Western and neutral delegations, permitting Washington to achieve a solidarity which had escaped it in Belgrade. A Western delegate commented:

> We never had too many illusions about the Soviet Union before Belgrade. Now we have none. And the way the Soviet Union and its allies behaved in the preparatory meeting destroyed any ideas that they might be prepared to be reasonable.[26]

The miscalculation meant, too, that the world's media would be drawn to the ideological confrontation. Newspapers, particularly in Western Europe, gave the clash over the agenda—and, therefore, over human rights issues—far more prominent coverage than Belgrade had ever received. The consequence was a significant "consciousness-raising" about the elements of Helsinki, especially those related to human rights. It was scarcely the consummation the Kremlin had wished, but it was certainly welcomed in Washington.

Only a few weeks earlier, Ronald Reagan had been elected President. What was striking was that American policy at Madrid would not shift at all, even though the new Chief Executive had initially opposed the signing of the Helsinki Final Act and, during the campaign in June 1980, called for a boycott of Madrid.

From the very outset of the Madrid plenary, the US pressed the human rights theme with great intensity. A line-by-line review of the Helsinki accord remained at the heart of the American strategy, together with continuing briefings to the press of what was transpiring at plenary sessions and at work groups. Throughout the balance of November and well into December, the US, joined by the Western democracies, continued the verbal assault. A cartoon in the *International Herald Tribune* on November 26 caught the mood that had seized the West.[27] A seated and bloated Leonid Brezhnev, his haunches resting heavily upon oppressed little people striving to be free, is asked by a conference spokesman of the West: "Will the Soviet delegate please rise?"

The Soviet conquest of Afghanistan was targeted specifically at Madrid. Virtually every Western and neutral delegation, 26 in all, rose to condemn the invasion as a violation of a half-dozen key principles of Helsinki. On the defensive, stocky, chain-smoking Leonid Ilyichev, Deputy Foreign Minister and a top Kremlin troubleshooter, only evoked giggling when he charged that Western criticism was intervention in the internal affairs of Afghanistan. A Western delegate sarcastically commented that Ilyichev "had flapped his wings like an angry pigeon."[28]

The confrontation ranged over a broad area. The Western system of values, with its emphasis on the individual, was contrasted with the Soviet system of collective values. Articulating the differences, Kampelman, lawyer-like, precise, at times eloquent, noted that the "collective values bring with them suppression of the individual,"[29] thereby depriving him of his freedom under the Helsinki Final Act itself. Illustrations were abundant: the internal exile of Sakharov in January 1980, the scandalous trials and dispersal of the half-dozen Helsinki monitoring committees in the USSR, the sudden arrest of refusenik physicist Viktor Brailovsky on the very eve of Madrid.

Bolstering the ideological challenge was an extraordinary critique of the Soviet conception of détente. Kampelman dropped a bombshell in closed session when he cited a Brezhnev statement made at a secret conclave of Warsaw Pact leaders held in Prague in 1973. The Soviet leader was quoted as characterizing "détente" as a device to bring about a decisive shift in the international balance of power. Said Brezhnev: "Trust us, comrades, for by 1985, as a consequence of what we are now achieving with détente . . . we will be able to extend our will wherever we need to."[30] The revelation stunned representatives of the other signatories of Helsinki, while it sent Soviet delegates scurrying to seek repudiation (or verification) from Moscow. No repudiation was forthcoming.

Kampelman did not even hesitate to challenge the legitimacy of the Soviet borders in the Baltics, which the USSR considered taboo under the Helsinki provisions. The US representative pointedly remarked:

> I am well aware that the Soviet Union calls itself a "socialist" state and that by
> definition, its definition, it can never be guilty of imperialism, regardless of what
> it may do. There is an American saying: "If it walks like a duck, talks like a
> duck, and looks like a duck—it's a duck." Some may wish to call the duck a
> goose or a chicken, Mr. Chairman. But it's still a duck. The acts of aggression
> against the three Baltic states were acts of imperialism.[31]

If a decade later the challenge had become commonplace, with even prominent segments of Soviet officialdom acknowledging that the Baltic territories were annexed as part of a secret agreement in 1939 with Adolf Hitler, the mere raising of the question in 1980 sent the Kremlin into a state of apoplexy. Soviet Foreign Minister Gromyko sharply complained to the US Ambassador in Moscow, Thomas Watson, about Kampelman's tough and confrontational style. But following a top-level State Department meeting, the tactics of the US delegate were strongly endorsed.

Special attention was given to Basket III. What Ambassador Goldberg had pursued—the naming of names, the specific citing of cases—was quickly outdistanced. Indeed, Goldberg's achievement at Belgrade paled before the non-stop documentation by Kampelman and his colleagues in the US delegation. At Belgrade, Goldberg had cited by name seven cases, and it was thought to be revolutionary. At Madrid until its December 19, 1980, adjournment, the US referred to a total of 65 persons, including many of the Helsinki Watch Group members.[32] Every item of Basket III—human contacts, reunion of families, cultural and religious rights, freedom of information—was provided maximum exposure with appropriate documentation.

Strikingly, and in sharp contrast with Belgrade, the Western allies of the United States joined in the criticism of Soviet practices and, in some instances, named names and cited cases.[33] It was a remarkable transformation from their hesitancy at Belgrade. In part, the altered posture of the West had been provoked by the Kremlin's intensified repression, which had generated great public concern. Soviet stonewalling at Madrid served only to deepen that concern and to reinforce irritation among the delegates. East-West tensions growing out of NATO's decision for missile deployment by December 1983 and Moscow's military aggression in Afghanistan further contributed to strengthening Western unity. A final factor which helps explain the transformation was the diplomatic skill of the US Ambassador.

Max Kampelman proved to be an unusually articulate spokesman, but more importantly, an extraordinarily talented negotiator. NATO caucuses were held two to three times a week, and the Americans sought to encourage others to take the initiative and even assume leadership on various issues. Kampelman avoided strong-arm and overbearing techniques. Even if the separate interests of the parties precluded uniformity of opinion, diverse perceptions were subordinated to a common approach. Kampelman would use a musical metaphor to make his point. "In an orchestra," he told his colleagues, "there is need for a drummer as well as a harpist; what is most important is that we play music together."[34]

The way in which the Soviet Jewish issue was highlighted exemplified the distinctive new trends at Madrid of specifying cases and involving other NATO and non-aligned powers in the process.[35] In this respect, the Madrid meeting marked an historic breakthrough. Never in a formal international setting had so many countries raised the issues; never in such a setting had so many individual Jewish cases been publicly noted; never in a similar milieu had so many facets of the Jewish question been aired. Nine Western countries raised aspects of the Soviet Jewish question. In addition to the United States, the United Kingdom, Ireland, Belgium, the Netherlands, Denmark, Sweden, Norway, and France all voiced concern. The presence of France in the list was especially unusual. At the Belgrade review conference, only the United States had dared raise the Jewish question.

Almost a dozen cases of refuseniks and prisoners of conscience were placed on the table, including such well-known names as Shcharansky, Brailovsky, Ida Nudel, and Aleksandr Lerner. Each was cited to illustrate specific types of violations of Helsinki Final Act provisions, whether arbitrary and capricious refusals of visa requests, or arrests and imprisonment for basically exercising the right to emigrate. At the same time as the Western delegates highlighted individual cases, they all expressed dismay about the 50 percent cutback in the Jewish emigration rate as compared with 1979. The British delegate, John Wilberforce, accused the Soviets of "apparent manipulation for political motives of the rate at which Jewish persons are permitted to leave the Soviet Union."[36] He also charged them with "discrimination" against would-be emigrants and against their families as well.

The Brailovsky case, perceived correctly as a turning point in the Kremlin's Jewish policy, was given special attention. Brailovsky was the single most prominent figure in the Jewish cultural movement. Besides being committed to emigration, he sought to raise the consciousness and self-identity of Jews through a special samizdat publication, *Jews in the USSR*, devoted to Jewish culture. The Stalinist (and post-Stalinist) suppression of Jewish cultural institutions had created a void which Brailovsky sought to fill at least in part. Kampelman called his arrest "brazen disregard" by the USSR "of its commitments" under the Helsinki Final Act. The American spoke eloquently of the hardships endured by Brailovsky and his family for eight years and of how his arrest "makes him the 12th Jew currently in prison in the Soviet Union for attempting to emigrate."[37]

At Belgrade, the subject of anti-Semitism had not been discussed. At Madrid, US delegation member Jerome Shestack noted in a detailed human rights brief that the Soviet state "restricts the right of Jews to live as members of an ethnic and religious minority."[38] He pointed to the "lack of Jewish schools for the study of Jewish culture and the Hebrew language."

More startling was the charge leveled in the Basket I working group during a discussion of Principle VII by the Belgian delegate, René Panis, against the Kremlin's "intensified anti-Semitism," which he said showed a "rising mercury level in that horrible barometer" of hate.[39] Stung by the accusation, the Soviet delegate waved a copy of the Soviet Constitution and shouted that anti-Semitism was forbidden by Soviet statute. And, as anti-Semitism was rejected by the Soviet Constitution, it "never existed and never will exist in Soviet society." The Belgian replied that he was happy to hear that the future of anti-Semitism in the USSR was uncertain. If, as the Soviets claimed, the evidence pointed in that direction, then he would certainly report it to his government in Brussels.

A powerful response to the Belgian charge came from a totally unexpected source three months later. Brezhnev, in the course of a five-hour policy address to the 26th Congress of the Soviet Communist Party, specifically denounced anti-Semitism as a "nationalist aberration" that is "alien to the nature of socialism," a condemnation unique in the annals of party history.[40] At no party congress since 1898 had the party leader singled out anti-Semitism for criticism in a policy speech. The Brezhnev condemnation was the first by a high Communist Party official since 1965, when Prime Minister Aleksei Kosygin castigated anti-Semitism in a speech published in *Pravda*.[41] Analysts found that after the Brezhnev speech some of the more vulgar and obscene forms of Soviet anti-Semitism in the Soviet media were either eliminated or modified.

How did the US evaluate the initial effect of its human rights tactics at Madrid? Undersecretary of State Eagleburger, testifying before the Helsinki Commission in early 1982, concluded that CSCE in general was "terribly valuable to the whole process of American foreign policy."[42] With reference to human rights, Eagleburger went on, Helsinki "gives us a forum that the Soviets simply cannot ignore, nor can the people of the world ignore, to remind the world of their failure to meet their commitments under the Helsinki Final Act."

Kampelman later called the tactic "ostracism," the informal mechanism of naming of cases and incidents. The process had legitimized the casting of shame, thereby ostracizing the violator of human rights from the comity of European nations. On the public level, there were the numerous speeches by Kampelman and his associates at the review sessions, which the US delegation then made available to the media.

In addition, Madrid offered a private channel of communication. Throughout the entire session, Kampelman met frequently in a private rendezvous with one or another of the top Soviet delegates at Madrid, mainly Sergei Kondrashev.[43] According to the US Ambassador, the private meetings ran to 300 hours of "off-the-record" discussions. What made these superpower sessions unique was the fact that, with the collapse of détente and its arms control talks conducted in several neutral locations, Madrid was the only site, beyond traditional diplomatic channels, of an ongoing dialogue. Not until late 1982, when talks between the superpowers on intermediate-range nuclear weapons began in Geneva, would the Madrid dialogue be supplemented.

While the dialogue was by no means restricted to human rights, it still enabled the United States to underscore that Washington saw issues of human rights compliance as particularly vital. Kampelman, in a talk to US diplomats in Europe in 1983, observed: "One of our primary purposes is to send a continuing and consistent message which clearly communicates to Soviet authorities . . . our deep and specific concerns about their behavior. . . ."[44] Private discussions were designed to supplement his speeches, which he knew were forwarded to Moscow immediately after their delivery at the Madrid sessions. To judge from memoir and archival material available, the number and length of Kampelman's private dialogues with high Soviet officials far exceeded those Goldberg held at Belgrade.

The importance of these off-the-record dialogues should not be minimized. The US could indicate a special interest in a particular dissident or an unpublicized way of resolving a foreign policy issue. Moscow, too, could use the occasion to make its concerns felt. It was Kampelman's view that the communication of a message need not produce immediate results. However, its constant repetition over a period of time could, and indeed sometimes did, prove effective.[45] Quiet diplomacy, when used in conjunction with public diplomacy in the human rights areas, reinforced the public message over the long run. For this reason, Kampelman pleaded for patience when his critics on the right criticized the Helsinki process.

The handling of the Shcharansky case was illustrative of the use made of the private channel. The imprisoned dissident was appropriately regarded in the West as a hero, a symbol of the striving for freedom and the right to emigrate. He was a centerpiece of public activity on behalf of Soviet Jews and of the Helsinki Watch Group. His wife was invited to plead his case with the highest officials in Western society. The United States had a certain special remorse about his conviction, as a key person in his trial and conviction—Dr. Sanya Lipavsky—had been accepted as a "voluntary" CIA agent by Kissinger's "Committee of 40,"[46] which had been especially created to advise the Secretary of State on especially delicate and high-level intelligence matters.

Kampelman gave the Shcharansky case high priority in his discussions with Kondrashev, who, while only the third-ranking official in the Soviet delegation, exercised great influence.[47] Kondrashev was a major general in the KGB, and had played a critical role in the Soviet foreign intelligence operation. According to revelations in *Spycatcher*, Kondrashev had served as "control officer" of the notorious British spies Kim Philby, Guy Burgess and Donald Maclean.[48] After various Kampelman-Kondrashev exchanges, Moscow agreed to release Shcharansky from the gulag, provided he write a letter to the Soviet authorities pleading a worsening personal health situation. Kampelman, in an interview, elaborated upon this plan, which was obviously intended to provide Moscow authorities with a certain moral cover.[49] In essence, they would be responding positively to a humanitarian request without undermining the supposed integrity of their intelligence and legal system.

The problem was that Shcharansky would have none of it. As he later related, his brother Leonid and his mother came to visit in July 1983. Leonid outlined the understanding and what was required:

> The Helsinki review conference is now drawing to a close in Madrid and the Americans made it clear that they won't sign the final document without a resolution of your problem. The head of the Soviet delegation has informed Max Kampelman, the head of the American delegation, and Kampelman told Avital, that if you sign a statement requesting a release for reasons of health, the request will be granted. In Moscow, the KGB told us the same thing. Kampelman thinks the Soviets are serious, and that this is a major concession. They aren't asking you to admit guilt, or to recant or to condemn anyone else. Elena Georgievna [Bonner] in the name of herself and her husband [that is, Sakharov] asked me to tell you that in their opinion, it's possible to accept this proposal.[50]

Shcharansky interrupted his brother to ask whether Avital also agreed. When told that she had registered no opinion, Shcharansky "sighed with relief," for otherwise, he said, "it would be the first time I had to disagree with Avital since my arrest, which would have been a terrible blow to our spiritual unity."

His mother was crestfallen, but Shcharansky remained firm. He had "committed no crimes." The crimes were committed by the people who arrested him and kept him in prison. Therefore, the only appeal he could make to the Soviet state presidium was a demand for his immediate release and the punishment of the "truly guilty" ones. Moreover, said Shcharansky, to ask the authorities to show humanity "means acknowledging that they represent a legitimate force that administers justice." The moral fervor Shcharansky communicated, especially given the opinion by the Sakharovs that appeared to accept the KGB offer, was heroic in his determination to clear the record publicly, but to the end of his imprisonment the KGB and the state treated him as a spy. Several years later, he would be taken from the gulag and released as part of an exchange of spies.[51]

The episode, even though the US initiative proved unsuccessful, demonstrated the effectiveness of joining public and quiet diplomacy. From the point of view of Soviet activists and dissenters, the Helsinki Final Act served as the principal banner to which they could cling, and Madrid was the sounding board for their hopes and aspirations. They directed a stream of appeals and petitions to Madrid with the thought that their conditions might ease or even, conceivably, that they might be granted their requests. Unlike Western conservatives who criticized the Helsinki process, activists did not conceive of the forum as worsening their plight; instead, they saw it in most cases as relieving more extreme forms of repression and as the indispensable means for maintaining hope and sustaining morale.

Congressman Elliott H. Levitas (D.-Ga.), after an official visit to the USSR in January 1982, reported that Soviet activists with whom he had met considered the Madrid meeting as "vital for their security and wellbeing."[52] It was a typical view given to prominent Western visitors. In January 1983, when a delegation of the US Helsinki Commission traveled to the Soviet Union, they were told by dissenters and activists, "don't abandon us in Madrid."[53]

From Kampelman's perspective, the open advocacy of human rights at Madrid had an additional, silent intent. On the one hand, the fundamental question for US policy, thought Kampelman, remained: "What can we do about Soviet behavior that can be effective?"[54] But no one could be more skeptical than he about how difficult the task, how limited the progress, how long the road before something positive emerged; still, he pursued the effort with determination. On the other hand, if the Soviet Union was to be arraigned before a "world court in continuous session" as part of a "war for the hearts and minds" of humanity, the US had to always keep an eye cocked on "the hearts and minds" of the population of Western Europe.[55] Only later, years after Madrid, did the Ambassador speak of this issue. At the time, he did not address it publicly, but referred to it in private interviews.[56]

The attitudes of the public in the Western democracies of Europe were a vital component of the struggle. If they were unaware of how Moscow threatened the fundamental values of the West, it would have been difficult, if not impossible, for Western leaders to garner public support for the primary Western security objective, Theater Nuclear Force (TNF) modernization. What was uppermost among the strategic US goals, indeed, what probably enjoyed the highest priority in the period of Madrid, was the deployment of the Pershing II and cruise missiles to neutralize or force withdrawal of the Soviet SS-20 missiles.

Timing was a vital factor. The NATO decision reached in December 1979 stipulated Pershing II and cruise deployment in December 1983. It was during the Madrid meeting that the battle for the hearts and minds of West Europeans would be waged. Disclosures in the West European media from the Madrid rostrum concerning Afghanistan, internal Soviet repression, anti-Semitism and the violations, crude and otherwise, of the Helsinki Final Act could help shape a favorable response to TNF. Kampelman, in an interview later, said that, in competition with Moscow, the United States perceived the function of the Madrid sessions as keeping "those elements who are friendly to us" and "deterring those who are against us."[57]

· 8 ·

Madrid and the Strategy of Linkage

When Undersecretary of State Lawrence Eagleburger testified before the Helsinki Commission in March 1982, he initially spoke of human rights as a central element of the US government's policy on Helsinki. This was how Helsinki was popularly understood, and more pertinently for his audience, it was the priority concern of the Commission. But Eagleburger also outlined a second reason for Helsinki being "terribly valuable" for US policy. It "gives us a place in a forum which discusses European issues," he said, and were the United States not there, "what you [would] have . . . is the Soviet Union talking to Europeans about European problems, where[as] I think it is clear that European issues are in fact American issues as well."[1]

Strategic European issues as related to Helsinki were high on the US agenda when Eagleburger spoke to the Commission. Especially pertinent was the question of a proposed conference on "confidence-building and security measures," in which the Soviet Union and France were interested. Several other European security-related issues, not directly tied to Helsinki, hovered in the background. One dealt with the Pershing II and cruise missile deployment. A second was related to the possible entrance of Spain into NATO. And a third involved developments in and near Poland which seriously challenged the status quo in Europe.

In particular, the proposed confidence-building conference enabled the United States to play the human rights card as strongly as it did without causing a Soviet withdrawal from Madrid. Washington effectively applied a strategy of linkage that was designed to win a certain amount of human rights progress in the CSCE field. (Henry Kissinger had been an early advocate of linkage, but it had nothing to do with human rights within Moscow; benefits to the USSR were extended in return for moderating its behavior in Third World areas.) How this could be and was accomplished needs special attention. Emerging from the Madrid deliberations would be a trade-off between Basket I and Basket III, between security and human rights.

From the beginning, the disarmament-conference proposal stirred controversy. President Carter was initially opposed to the idea. So, too, were the Helsinki Commission and Arthur Goldberg, the first US Ambassador to a Helsinki follow-up forum.[2] All saw the idea as burdening the Helsinki process, which should have been primarily focused on human rights, with an unnecessary and unwarranted security dimension. When the Carter administration finally agreed to the proposal, it was accompanied by a series of caveats that circumscribed the character of the conference and meticulously delineated its function.

How would the new Reagan administration relate to the question? Indeed, how would it relate to the Helsinki process itself? The new administration had come into office only a week before the Madrid conference resumed its deliberations on January 27, 1981 (the conference had been in adjournment since December 19, 1980). From Helsinki's first moments, Ronald Reagan had been no supporter of the Final Act. While governor of California, he had urged President Ford not to attend to sign the document.[3] Like other conservatives, he had seen Helsinki as a Western defeat. During his presidential campaign in 1980, he reflected no fundamental change of attitude. His view on the forthcoming Madrid meeting was articulated in a *Time* interview June 30, 1980. What he seemed to recommend, as he had to President Gerald Ford in 1975, was the notion of boycott. "Frankly," he said, "I have an uneasy feeling that going to Madrid is negating what we thought we could accomplish by boycotting the Olympics. If the athletes can't go, why should the diplomats go?"[4] Equating Madrid with the Olympics, needless to say, was rather simplistic, and failed to take account of the potential of an important international forum, particularly one that existed in an open society where journalists had easy access, if not to the sessions, then certainly to the participants.

What had no doubt prompted the initial negative Reagan reaction was the pressure from a Republican Party wing that had looked on the Helsinki Final Act as a sellout of Eastern Europe through what was thought to be the ratification of postwar Soviet conquests. The viewpoint was expressed in an article by William Safire, who called on Reagan to declare publicly that the Madrid meeting was "anathema to him" and tell the Republican Platform Committee to consider rescinding approval of the Helsinki agreement entirely.[5] Again at the end of the year, a month after Reagan had been elected, Safire urged the United States and its allies to effect "a multilateral renunciation of the treaty."[6]

The Republican Platform Committee, instead, responded to other advice. It specified that "as a party to the Helsinki Conference Final Act, a Republican Administration will insist on full Soviet compliance with the humanitarian provisions of the agreement."[7] Instead of boycott, an activist policy was advanced, involving utilization and exploitation of an international forum. Significantly, Helsinki activism became Reagan's policy on the eve of the election. He issued a statement on October 17, which, after taking note of the Madrid preparatory meetings, stressed that the Helsinki Final Act "involve[s] important commitments to basic human freedoms."[8]

The Reagan statement proceeded to call for a militant advocacy posture on human rights by the US delegation at Madrid. It criticized the Carter administration for allegedly speaking "timidly" to the USSR at the previous meeting in Belgrade. The accusation was not buttressed by documentation and hardly accorded with the facts. Nonetheless, it was consciously fitted into the general Reagan criticism of Carter's human rights policy, which was denounced as lacking consistency. At Madrid, Reagan urged, the United States needed a "vigorous" human rights policy.

It is clear that Kampelman consulted Reagan foreign policy advisors prior to and during the resumed meeting in Madrid. In a major address on November 17, Kampelman declared: "The US government under both President Carter and President-elect Reagan is ready to negotiate significant, verifiable and balanced arms control agreement once mutual determination to do so becomes evident."[9]

A visit to Madrid on November 22 by a congressional delegation that included several Helsinki Commission members offered additional opportunity for calling attention to Reagan's policy. Commission Chairman Fascell told a press conference on November 26 that the Reagan administration would be committed to the human rights issues which had been forcefully expressed at Madrid. "The nuances might vary from time to time," he added, "but there will not be a fundamental change."[10] Two Republican members of the delegation reinforced his view.[11] New York Congressman Benjamin Gilman told the press conference that "human rights is a bipartisan issue. Our incoming administration will adopt that attitude, I feel certain." Millicent Fenwick, the godmother of the Helsinki Commission, commented that "all of us share the same values."

President Reagan's general view on human rights was less important than his specific outlook on the principle of linkage as a foreign policy device. In his very first press conference after his electoral victory, he stressed that linkage would be the means by which he would conduct US relationships with the Soviet Union—very different from the Carter-Vance approach to the two separate tracks of human rights and arms control.[12]

How the Soviet Union would react to the strategy was uncertain. Besides, there were growing doubts in congressional circles and the public at large as to whether human rights or security could be advanced in a Helsinki setting. One congressman asked Undersecretary Eagleburger, for example, whether the Helsinki process should not be "chucked in."[13] He responded that the process "is an important element of our foreign policy, and one that keeps the pressure on the other side, and one that is 100% an advantage to the United States and to the West."[14]

What he certainly had very much in mind, but did not articulate, was the situation in several East European countries as a result of Helsinki.[15] The Helsinki process, after all, applied not only to the USSR. Indeed, State Department policy was oriented to "differentiating" each communist country from another and especially from the Soviet Union. The Helsinki process facilitated this policy. For several communist countries, the process provided a multilateral framework within which bilateral discussions were both tolerated and acceptable. Channels outside the Helsinki framework were quite limited, even with the presence of embassies in the respective capitals or through UN organs. Prior to review sessions, a dialogue was conducted with each of the communist governments as US delegations were sent to various capitals to take soundings on positions concerning key upcoming issues and the degree of implementation of Helsinki's provisions. During the follow-up meeting in Madrid the dialogue continued, although it was limited by the discipline maintained within the Warsaw Pact structure by Soviet authority.

The human rights provisions of the Helsinki Final Act exerted a significant liberalizing impact on a number of East European countries, a crucial fact that appeared to have gone unnoticed in the West. A report issued in June 1981 by President Reagan to the Helsinki Commission illuminated the broad range of responses in Eastern Europe, especially in the area of freer movement of people.[16] Although the general political situation in Poland had worsened, the improvements in other countries noted in that report were impressive. While Hungary for some time had permitted emigration to expedite reunion of families, the situation also improved in Bulgaria, Czechoslovakia and East Germany. Similarly, travel to these countries by Western citizens, especially for family visits, was eased. Visas for those involved in binational marriages came easier. Even Czechoslovakia, which mimicked Soviet conduct in most human rights matters, was reported to have a "good record" in resolving family reunion cases with the United States. The same applied to visitation cases.

Hungary's record was especially good, with the number of family visits to the United States running into the thousands and almost no denial of visas to Americans seeking to visit family members in Hungary, according to the President's report. Particularly noteworthy was the temporary turnabout in Poland's conduct following the Solidarity movement's success and the ouster of the Edward Gierek regime in September 1980. On the eve of the Madrid meeting, the Warsaw government, in what the United States termed "a major positive development," resolved some 550 outstanding cases of Polish citizens seeking to emigrate to the United States. Significant differences, however, prevailed with regard to travel rights for personal and professional reasons, which had been specified in the Final Act. Hungary (and Poland, for a brief time) maintained a liberal travel policy, while others followed the Soviet practice of applying tight control on tourist travel by their citizens. Visas were eased, especially for those seeking to marry a national from another country or to join a spouse who was a foreign national. Except for Romania and the USSR, most abided by the obligations in respect to binational marriages involving Americans.

Basket III emphasized, besides emigration and travel, the freer movement of ideas. In the category of dissemination of information, only Poland had taken "serious steps forward in terms of fuller implementation of the provisions of the Helsinki Final Act," the 1981 presidential report noted.[17] While much of Eastern Europe followed the Soviet pattern of jamming Western radio broadcasts, although by no means as intensively, Hungary, Romania and East Germany had not. Working conditions for journalists were quite good in Poland before martial law was imposed in December 1981, and, to a lesser extent, in Hungary and Bulgaria. Elsewhere, the restrictive Soviet model prevailed.

Visits by orchestras, artists, theatrical companies, exhibits and academic specialists, along with exchange programs involving scholars, students and scientific researchers, were widespread by-products of the Helsinki Final Act, and very much involved the Soviet Union's Warsaw Pact allies. The exchange programs, particularly, were fruitful in expanding horizons and extending the flow of ideas. According to a Ford Foundation specialist who had been involved in these exchange programs sanctioned by the Helsinki Final Act, they had "a significant impact on dissent in Eastern Europe" in that they helped "introduce alternative ideas and ways of looking at things which would not otherwise be permitted."[18]

Fellowships for study in the United States and elsewhere in the West, granted by leading academic institutions, were not without a critical

effect.[19] Among Polish winners, not surprisingly, several became prominent lecturers in the "Flying University" of the Polish renaissance associated with Solidarity, or followed other independent intellectual pursuits.
Fellowship winners and alumni of exchange programs were frequently
found among independent thinkers in Poland, Hungary, Czechoslovakia,
Romania and East Germany.[20] To what extent the exchange programs affected the initial Solidarity movement in Poland cannot, of course, be determined with any degree of accuracy. But a definite relationship existed
between the reform movement and Poland's participation in the Helsinki
process. One of the principal demands of Solidarity, as of its predecessor
KOR, had been the government's full adherence to the Helsinki Final
Act.[21]

The contrast with the Soviet Union in most instances was enormous.
Freer movement of people and ideas in that country had come close to a
dead end. While the Helsinki forum made a worsening of the situation
unlikely and, in a number of individual instances, proved beneficial, there
were no breakthroughs, however modest, in such areas as prisoners of
conscience, reunion of families, travel, cultural or religious rights and
radio jamming. Yet Moscow did not intend to convey the view that it
would not be conciliatory under some circumstances. In response to the
accusation emanating from almost a dozen Western countries concerning
the cutback in Jewish emigration, Deputy Foreign Minister Leonid
Ilyichev responded that the USSR is "prepared to consider, in a business-
like way, problems concerning the conditions for the reunification of
families."[22] The term "businesslike" cropped up over and over again in
statements made by Soviet representatives or in TASS releases.

Precisely what "businesslike" meant was not defined with precision.
But a key Soviet spokesman suggested in a closed session that it had a distinctly crass and crude character. "The more détente prospers," declared
Sergei Kondrashev, "the more Basket III prospers. Thus those circles
who do not want détente also limit the implementation of Basket III."[23] If
the assertion had the ring of blackmail, Soviet authorities had no hesitancy in ventilating such a perspective in a closed setting. Signaling the
West that, indeed, Soviet Jews were hostages to the Kremlin's détente
purposes was at least a frank, if vulgar, way of communicating in business-
like fashion. It indicated that at least some aspects of human rights were
considered negotiable items on the international agenda.

What Kondrashev was referring to when he spoke of détente was
Moscow's desire for a disarmament conference. The chief British
delegate, John Wilberforce, quickly grasped the implications: "One

would not have thought that the Conference on Security and Cooperation in Europe would witness such a crude and unprincipled attempt at
linkage."[24] The Soviet delegate, he said, had connected his government's
"willingness to deal with humanitarian cases" under the Final Act with
"progress in matters of interest to it," especially a disarmament conference. Wilberforce concluded: "The idea that individual human beings
should be held hostage to the political objectives of a certain government
is totally unacceptable."

But, if linkage could serve unprincipled ends, it could also serve principled ones. The Final Act had, after all, made explicit that détente and
peace were conditional upon human rights, and not the other way around.
To evaluate, however, the possibility of a successful trade-off—assuming
the ends were principled from a human rights viewpoint—the United
States had to weigh two crucial questions: 1) How anxious and determined was Moscow to have a security conference on confidence-building
measures? and 2) Did such a conference serve America's interest? If the
Soviet Union was anxious to have a CSCE-sponsored security conference, it would have to be flexible as to the character of the conference,
and thus would have to agree to accept trade-offs in the human rights
field. Yet, at the same time, the US could only seek a *quid pro quo* to
advance human rights if the proposed conference benefitted American
strategic interests.

What disturbed Moscow in the last year or two of the Carter administration and into the early years of the Reagan administration was US
rearmament. If the West saw this effort as an attempt to counter the massive Soviet military buildup of the 1960s and, particularly, the 1970s,
Moscow regarded it as a threatening challenge to the military parity in
which the USSR took particular pride. A leading Soviet diplomat who
often served as a spokesman for the Foreign Ministry, Vladimir Lomeiko,
explained Moscow's primary objective after Belgrade: "Unless the arms
race is stopped, it will stop all progress of détente."[25] This was the reason
he noted for Soviet insistence "on political détente measures." Lomeiko
gave particular attention to proposals advanced in Washington for a neu-
tron bomb, which he considered would certainly threaten military parity
and, therefore, détente.

The expressed fears of the former Foreign Ministry spokesman were
certainly the motivation for Brezhnev to emphasize on the virtual eve of
Madrid that he considered the outcome of that follow-up conference to
be "important."[26] No doubt it was the search for a military détente that
prompted Moscow to retreat from the very edge of stonewalling intransi-

gence which almost prevented the opening of the Madrid session on November 11; Moscow's anxiety was already high because of the December 1979 NATO decision to deploy advanced missiles in Europe. The Soviets sought an across-the-board halt in the arms race, and the means for reaching it was a Helsinki-sponsored conference on disarmament; such a project had been initially advanced by the Warsaw Pact.

For its own reasons, France had advanced in 1978 a proposal for a two-stage disarmament conference in which the first stage would cover confidence-building measures. Extensive discussion in NATO and a host of internal compromises led to its acceptance. Hesitant approval by President Carter and by an even sterner President-elect Reagan (which came in December 1980, a month after the election) meant that a modified idea could see the light of day.[27] The logic of the idea was clear enough. Mutual suspicions were too great to permit holding a conference on disarmament. From the Western point of view, and especially from the US view, such a conference would simply serve as a platform for endless Soviet diatribes about the US rearmament program. The consequence of a disarmament conference at this time would lead to a greater and deadlier confrontation, not a diminution of its likelihood. At the MBFR negotiations in Vienna, the suspicions were so great that the two sides could not even agree on a method for estimating the size of the opposing armies.[28]

Instead, if appropriate confidence-building measures were taken in the security field, it could reduce tensions and advance trust, laying the groundwork for an eventual conference on disarmament. The Helsinki accord did spell out two extremely modest confidence-building measures. The first required any CSCE member to notify in advance all of the other members if and when it planned military maneuvers involving more than 25,000 troops. A certain concession was given the USSR by the Helsinki Final Act: notification of military maneuvers was only required when they were to take place within 250 kilometers or 150 miles from the USSR's western borders. Thus, military maneuvers for much of the area stretching to the Urals—the usual demarcation point of European Russia—was not covered.

The Helsinki accord also called on CSCE members to voluntarily invite military observers from the other CSCE members to view the maneuvers. Notification and observers were considered useful devices for reducing the risk of surprise attack. The Final Act also offered recommendations, not obligations, aimed at encouraging CSCE states to take additional steps for purposes of confidence building. One recommendation was for notification of maneuvers involving less than 25,000 troops. A second suggested reporting on forms of major military movements other than maneuvers.

The recommendations of voluntary measures did not elicit a positive reaction among Warsaw Pact nations. Since 1975, the latter had given notification of only three maneuvers numbering less than 25,000 persons. In contrast, NATO countries had done so 20 times.[29] Neutral and non-aligned countries also gave notification of smaller maneuvers much more frequently than had the Warsaw Pact nations. With respect to invitations to observers, the Warsaw Pact group record was significantly lower. The group invited observers to only seven of 13 major maneuvers, while NATO invited observers to a total of 22 large and small maneuvers.[30] The asymmetry was compounded by the difference in technical assistance given the observers. NATO provided transport, binoculars, maps and detailed information to the observers, and extended opportunities for them to see actions of military significance.[31] In contrast, the Warsaw Pact provided few facilities and little information. The observers reported, too, that they sensed that the maneuvers they were watching were staged demonstrations.

These experiences prompted the West Europeans, along with the neutral and non-aligned countries, to establish effective and specific criteria for confidence-building measures. Out of preliminary discussions, agreement was reached that the new measures must be binding—not voluntary—on all signatories; that they must be of military significance; that they must be verifiable; and that they must apply to all signatories equally. The last point about equality had, as its target, the unequal provision of the Helsinki accord which allowed the Soviet Union to hold major maneuvers within European Russia more than 150 miles from its Western border without having to notify the Helsinki signatories.

Soviet martial actions related to Poland in late 1980 gave considerable pertinence, even urgency, to the issue of military maneuvers and surprise attack, and therefore of confidence-building measures. The Polish independent trade-union movement, Solidarity, was winning powerful public support against an increasingly wobbly Communist Party regime. The Kremlin hurled angry verbal thunderbolts at Solidarity in response, and the Red Army reinforced the anger with maneuvers by some of its 30 divisions within Poland. A political crisis was beginning to bubble under the surface of European society.

France, the leading advocate of a conference on confidence-building measures, immediately called attention at Madrid to the Polish problem. "Many people have recently had their attention drawn to certain military movements in the heart of our continent," said delegate Benoit d'Ab-boville on December 17, 1980.[32] He reported that "a high number of divi-sions" had been brought into play, reservists had been called up and some units had been "placed on alert." In his view, military maneuvers were taking place on a scale that was threatening, and this "proved conclu-sively the need for measures to increase confidence in Europe."

Not surprisingly, a half-dozen proposals on confidence building were on the Madrid table by December. Two came from neutral and non-aligned countries—Sweden and Yugoslavia; a third came from a Warsaw Pact maverick, Romania. Emphasis in each of them was placed on adop-tion of measures to develop trust and confidence, not on disarmament. As one neutral delegate explained, "No disarmament is possible in a cli-mate of distrust, and therefore CBMs must come first."[33] On behalf of the Warsaw Pact, Poland submitted its own two-stage proposal, which matched the French idea.[34] Eventually it would be replaced by a French proposal entitled "Conference on the Military Aspects of Security in Europe."[35]

Several of the French proposal's aspects bear noting. First, it called for a post-war meeting (Stockholm was later chosen for the site) concerning "militarily significant" measures on confidence building. To be avoided at the meeting, as one delegate explained, were "cosmetic proposals that would contribute nothing to security." A second required feature of the conference was "provisions ensuring appropriate verification of commit-ments." Thirdly, the conference would eschew "discretionary" measures and insist upon binding obligations. Fourthly, the French proposal of-fered suggestions on appropriate categories of confidence-building mea-sures, notably on pre-notification and other measures to increase stability.

A fifth point was especially important. To be meaningful, the confer-ence must deal with all of Europe, and thus all of European Russia, not merely a small part of it. Only in this way could the conference "con-tribute to increasing stability and security in Europe." To ignore portions of European Russia would hardly contribute to confidence building, es-pecially when those areas contained military forces which potentially threatened European security. Initially, the USSR strongly objected, ar-guing that the border limitations affecting it in the Final Act were the re-sult of a balance of interests at the time.

Then, in an extraordinary reversal, Brezhnev went out of his way at the 26th Congress of the Soviet Communist Party in February 1981 to ac-cept publicly the proposed line for confidence-building measures at the Ural mountain range, provided, however, that the West make a similar concession.[36] The Soviet leader's comments came in his major policy address and testified to both his desire for building upon what he regarded as his initial handiwork and his search for a means to halt Western rearmament.

What kind of concession Moscow sought was not clear. At first, the Soviets wanted the West to agree to provide notification of military maneuvers held in the eastern half of the United States and Canada.[37] When the West refused on the obvious grounds that CSCE dealt with peace in Europe, not North America, Moscow insisted that, at a minimum, the West provide notification of naval maneuvers extending deep into the Atlantic. This demand was likewise rejected. Ultimately, Moscow agreed to a compromise promoted by the non-aligned for advance notification of air, naval and military maneuvers in the seas adjoining the European continent.

Of major significance was a sixth point in the French proposal. It established a formal link between the conference on confidence-building measures and the CSCE process. The decisions reached at the conference would be referred to the Helsinki follow-up meeting. The linkage had ramifications with reference to the second or next stage, which was supposed to deal with disarmament. However, this second stage could not be introduced until the next Helsinki meeting evaluated the progress made on confidence-building measures. Thus, the United States could place severe restrictions on further steps in the arms control field if it so chose.

In a speech on February 16, Ambassador Kampelman endorsed the French proposal as providing opportunity "to explore the new and promising field of confidence-building measures."[38] He commented that, because the US was "interested in genuine arms control," it would oppose "imprecision" in language. He warned against a "cosmetic and meaningless" negotiation on confidence-building measures. Only genuine negotiations could produce measures which were "militarily significant," verifiable, binding and applicable to all of Europe.

One additional "criterion" advanced by Kampelman reflected America's special focus on human rights and had been pressed by the Helsinki Commission: maintenance of the "balance" between security and human rights needs.[39] That term was a favorite of the Commission, and Kampelman, while suggesting the theme of linkage, made clear that CSCE "cannot survive in the future solely as a security negotiation."

Still, the bulk of Kampelman's argument was given over to security considerations as they related to Europe. Washington displayed a vital interest in NATO's needs and preoccupations. European issues, as Eagleburger had maintained, were in the last analysis also American issues.

The alternative would have been Western Europe talking to the Soviet Union.

Whether and how the French proposal would have been advanced, in the absence of US approval, cannot be known. What is certain, however, is that the shape the proposal finally took was a result, in part, of US insistence on certain crucial elements, including the linkage to CSCE and, therefore, to human rights. Had the United States followed the course advocated by the Commission or by Arthur Goldberg, and initially supported by President Carter, there would probably have been no agreement on a two-stage disarmament conference. Carter had separated arms control and human rights to ensure, in particular, the viability of the former. The Commission concurred in order to maintain chief public focus on the latter. Kampelman, the Carter appointee picked up by Reagan, was one of the first successful proponents of linking the two diverse sets of concerns.

According to Kampelman's thesis, NATO concerns were not dismissed; on the contrary, they were integrated into other US priorities like human rights. That is what made Kampelman a most unusual diplomat. Even without Foreign Service or State Department credentials, he instinctively recognized the value of both West Europe's and NATO security needs and human rights; better than anyone else, he understood how to balance the baskets.

Among NATO security concerns with which Kampelman was personally concerned was the bringing of Spain into the military alliance, a matter that had been discussed in the Brussels headquarters for several years. Spain's membership in NATO would enhance the latter's naval prowess in the western Mediterranean and provide air and communications bases in a strategic corner of Europe. Moscow, recognizing the political and military implications of Spanish adherence to NATO, sought at Belgrade to win commitments from the West to freeze the size of the separate alliance systems.

Kampelman meticulously pursued a policy of cultivating Spain.[40] Its representatives were invited to sit in on NATO caucus meetings. They were encouraged to participate as an active member of the Western bloc. Throughout, the United States remained especially attentive to Spanish concerns. The results of this diplomacy proved remarkably beneficial for both NATO and CSCE. During the course of the Madrid meeting, Spain formally joined the Western alliance, much to the irritation and anger of the USSR. And the Spanish government played a key and critical role in making possible at the end of the conference a significant breakthrough in the human contacts area despite Soviet opposition.

Kampelman's skills proved he was the right man for the hour. Mid-December 1981 saw the imposition of martial law in Poland by General Wojciech Jaruzelski, plunging Europe into crisis and seriously threatening the viability of CSCE, not to mention that of the Madrid session. Civil liberties in Poland were suspended, while numerous Solidarity leaders and activists were arrested and imprisoned. The new arbitrariness and military authoritarianism stood in sharp and ironic contradiction to the Helsinki Final Act itself. Not only had Principle VII been trampled upon; Solidarity, which had demanded that the Final Act be printed and disseminated throughout the nation, was itself placed in limbo.

The moment was especially awkward for the Madrid meeting. After one year of deliberations, the follow-up meeting was approaching its final stage. The neutral/non-aligned group was circulating a draft concluding document seeking to harmonize the views of the opposing alliance systems. On December 18, five days after the declaration of martial law in Poland, the Madrid meeting was scheduled to adjourn for the holiday season. The resumption in early February, it was expected, would lead to a consensus document.

In the few hours that remained before adjournment, the West responded to the violence in Poland with outrage. Ambassador Kampelman bitterly criticized the USSR for the border military maneuvers that preceded and probably prompted the Jaruzelski takeover.[41] He called on Moscow to honor the principles of the Final Act "so that Poland, that proud country, may strive successfully to resolve its problems and decide on its destiny without further violence and bloodshed."[42] Denunciations of martial law came from the ambassadors of France, the United Kingdom, the Federal Republic of Germany, Spain and Belgium, among others.

How was the West to deal with Madrid when it resumed on February 9, in the face of the obvious assault on its integrity? Different perspectives among the allies nearly ruptured the close connections which Kampelman's diplomacy had earlier cobbled together. From the US vantage point, the imposition of martial law in Poland made a mockery of the Helsinki accord. The continuation of Madrid under such circumstances was questionable.[43] To return to a business-as-usual approach was unseemly, for it would breed utter cynicism about Helsinki and risk undermining public support.

In sharp contrast, the West German government urged that the continuation of Madrid was all the more warranted by the crisis.[44] The forum which it provided permitted the West to complain directly to Warsaw and Moscow about developments in Poland. Were Madrid ended, it would relieve Moscow of any public responsibility for compliance with the provisions of the Helsinki accord. Besides, Madrid involved other broad Western interests, such as the proposed conference on confidence-building measures. Moreover, would not human rights activities throughout East Europe be deleteriously affected if the conference shut down? These views, articulated in Bonn's policy circles, were not derived merely from the Madrid experience. From the West German perspective, East-West contacts are all the more valuable in times of crisis.

The allies hammered out an understanding for a common NATO approach that would be based on a sharp series of angry critiques of the military crackdown delivered by the foreign ministers, and then a quick adjournment; there would be no substantive decision while a CSCE member had been subjugated. At the same time, the Polish Deputy Foreign Minister, Jozef Wiejacz, warned: "We shall not take part in conferences in which Poland would be made to stand in the dock."[45] But that is precisely what the United States and the West had in mind.

US Secretary of State Alexander Haig's Madrid address on February 9 constituted a powerful indictment.[46] He considered that "we are at a critical crossroads in the postwar history of Europe," where the very principles of the Helsinki Final Act were "under attack." He targeted the communist leaders of both Poland and the USSR: "The generals of this war against the Polish people are none other than the Polish regime itself, acting under the instigation and coercion of the Soviet Union."[47] Then Haig asked: "How can these actions be reconciled with Polish and Soviet signatures on the Helsinki Accords?" The Secretary of State examined each principle of the accord's Decalogue, showing them as ravaged and subverted by the Moscow-encouraged Polish military.

Haig then demanded the release from prison of "those trade union leaders and others who seek to realize the objectives of the Helsinki Final Act for their people." And he further called for the lifting of martial law and "the resumption of the process of reform and liberalization." In concluding remarks, the Secretary of State made clear that "business as usual here in Madrid would simply condone the massive violations of the Final Act now occurring in Poland." So far as the United States was concerned, no further negotiations at Madrid on "new undertakings" were possible "while existing obligations are . . . so blatantly ignored."

Soon after the Haig speech, the Madrid forum was turned into a procedural, Kafkaesque nightmare.[48] Occupying the chair on February 9 by prearrangement made before the adjournment was Polish Ambassador Wlodzimierz Konarski. After angry speeches by Haig and the foreign ministers of Canada, Belgium, Italy, and West Germany, Konarski ruled that the session was ended for the day. However, there were still left on the list of speakers eight foreign ministers from Western countries. Indeed, the next speaker was supposed to have been French Foreign Minister Claude Cheysson. He was furious, as were the others who had been refused the floor.

Uproar followed, with Konarski banging the gavel. When Ireland proposed that all speakers on the list be given the floor, the Soviet Union and Czechoslovakia refused consensus—and all CSCE procedures were based on consensus. While the Polish chairman was determined to end the meeting, the West was equally determined to prevent any adjournment, and so the allies also fell back on the consensus rule. The argument over procedure raged for seven hours, and only when Ambassador Ceska of Austria appealed to both sides for a night adjournment was there a general willingness to comply. Cheysson was not placated. He stormed out of the plenary, telling reporters that the episode was "shameful and comic." Norwegian Foreign Minister Svenn Stray harshly declared: "If you believe that you can stop people from the free West using their right to speak, you are mistaken, sir!"[49]

The next day, with Portugal in the chair, the other Western foreign ministers could give expression to their angry views. But they all, whether Western or neutral, took the occasion to criticize the attempt to stifle speech. The Austrian Foreign Minister, for example, noted that the entire purpose of Helsinki was "to promote dialogue," yet here he found a chairman seeking to "prevent speakers from speaking." Kampelman added: "The Soviet Union is acting to undermine the Helsinki Final Act both substantively and procedurally."[50]

Once the speeches were made, the West sought to adjourn the session. The leading spokesman for such a move was neutral Switzerland, whose Foreign Minister, Pierre Aubert, contended that martial law in Poland had already done severe damage to the international atmosphere. A continuation of the meeting under such circumstances, he believed, could only damage the Helsinki process itself. Switzerland had always been a great champion of Helsinki. Its credentials in calling for an early adjournment could not easily be questioned.

On the other hand, the USSR was determined to have the session continue, arguing that the draft concluding document was already circulating. No doubt, too, Moscow did not want to see the Helsinki process end when it was so close, finally, to realizing the Brezhnev objective of a security conference leading to disarmament discussions. By virtue of the consensus rule, the USSR could keep the body in continuing session. Kampelman made clear that if the meeting continued for a "few more weeks"—which some in the neutral/non-aligned bloc sought—the United States would make those weeks as uncomfortable as possible for the Soviet Union.[51]

The key procedural issue now turned on preparing and approving the weekly work schedule of the drafting committee, which was supposed to eventually finalize the draft of a concluding document. But on March 5, NATO announced that it would not agree to preparing the work schedule for the succeeding weeks. It would only agree to a schedule for the twice-weekly plenary meetings. Further, in a plan reportedly formulated by Spencer Oliver, Kampelman's deputy and the Commission's chief staff official, the West would only use these plenaries for addressing the situation in Poland or Soviet violations of the Helsinki accord.[52] No other alternative was seen for breaking the procedural deadlock. West German Ambassador Jörg Kastl and his British colleague, John Wilberforce, approved the plan; the others from NATO agreed with the tactic.

"The night of silences" is the way Friday, March 5, would go down in Helsinki accord history.[53] When the Czechoslovak chairman asked for concrete proposals regarding the work program of the plenary, he was met by stony silence from the Western delegations. Coffee breaks would interrupt the "silences." Efforts to simply close the meeting and reassemble on the following Monday were frustrated by Soviet refusal to give assent. A neutral delegate commented: "Procedures have already been seen to have political implications, but now keeping silent has also acquired political meaning. We just sit, and look and stare! Another coffee break? Even coffee breaks are of no more use."[54]

When midnight passed, another procedural problem arose. Would the Czechoslovak give up the gavel to the next-day chairman, a Turk? The Soviet Union rejected any change on grounds that the meeting was continuing and that a coffee break did not designate a break in the meeting; it was merely an interruption. When the neutral/non-aligned bloc registered strong objection to the argument, the Czechoslovak refused to budge from the chair. An analysis of the Madrid session characterized what prevailed after 2:40 A.M., when the silence had already lasted fifty minutes: "Fifty minutes of silence in a full chamber is a long time. Some diplomats read the paper, some nodded off and some gossiped with their neighbors."[55]

The internal discipline of the West was remarkable. The British Ambassador said the "eloquent silence" spoke much louder than words: the repression of Poland would not be passed over lightly. Attendants at the coffee bar were awakened from their sleep to open the bar. This time, various caucuses at the bar came up with a formula: a coffee break would be called that would extend to Monday morning 11:00 A.M. Since the clock now struck 5:30 A.M. on Saturday, the break would last 54 and one-half hours, an episode which no textbook on diplomacy had ever contemplated.

Over the weekend, a compromise package deal was worked out by the neutral/non-aligned group. The drafting committee would meet for just three meetings in one week and the conference would then enter a recess lasting until November, when work on the draft concluding document would resume. During the three work-day sessions, the West, together with some in the neutral group, maintained silence. Principle was not abdicated.

When the Madrid conference resumed in November, the repressive situation in Poland continued. While the United States was hesitant about returning, its Western allies were anxious to resume negotiations about a concluding document.[56] From their perspective, nothing anyway could be done about Poland, while negotiations about a conference on confidence-building measures were crucial. An agreement was hammered out within NATO ranks that permitted a return to Madrid on condition that NATO would press for inclusion in the concluding document of 14 Danish-drafted human rights amendments, including recognition of trade unions and the right to strike.[57] Clearly, the latter was directed precisely at the Polish situation. Another amendment included in the 14 was an end to jamming of Western broadcasts, which had become especially intense after the military coup in Poland. An initial indifference of other NATO powers to the amendments was overcome by the awareness that only a toughened alliance posture on human rights could lead to US willingness to resume at Madrid.

With the November resumption, the follow-up meeting had entered its endgame. Moscow uncomfortably found itself on the defensive. While the Soviets continued to press for the security conference on confidence-building measures, as they had ever since the beginning of the session, they could not escape the undiminished criticism. This could scarcely endear the Helsinki process to the USSR. Kremlin leadership may not have had second thoughts about Helsinki's value, but it certainly no longer occupied the priority place that it had before Madrid.

Until November 1980, slogans of support for the Helsinki accord were included in the key list of slogans issued annually by the Communist Party on the occasion of the anniversary of the Bolshevik Revolution.

After Madrid opened, the slogans of support disappeared from the annual list.[58] Moreover, the Soviet figure most closely linked to Helsinki—Brezhnev—was ailing and would pass away in 1982. His successor, Yuri Andropov, in one of his first addresses as General Secretary, spoke about détente without specifically referring to Helsinki.[59] It did not go unnoticed, however, that Andropov's son, Igor, was assigned to the Soviet delegation at the resumed session in November.[60] Though he ranked fifth in the delegation, he was assigned the task of making several important statements.

As the endgame was played out, the West was equipped with the important lever of the proposed conference on confidence-building measures. This was the big objective which Moscow had sought from the beginning of Madrid. The idea of a conference had, of course, been greatly shorn of the original purposes which Moscow had intended, disarmament or propaganda about disarmament. The mandate for the conference, as drafted, restricted it to promoting specific technical benefits that served both sides and for which Moscow gave up a special geographical privilege extended by the Final Act.

The Soviet Union was looking beyond the first stage of the conference toward the second, which would be primarily concerned with disarmament. But even the first stage could be used for propaganda in which Moscow might claim that it was champion of disarmament. Undoubtedly, the intense advocacy of the conference was partly designed to counter NATO plans for TNF modernization. But here the timing no longer played into Soviet hands. Indeed, the contrary was the case. The conference was scheduled for January 1984 in Stockholm. But deployment of the US missiles was to begin in December 1983, and Soviet tactics at Stockholm could exert little impact.

In return, the US and the West won approval for a meeting of human rights experts which would meet for six weeks in Ottawa, Canada, beginning in May 1985. It was a modest breakthrough, because although the Helsinki process had never previously held a conference specifically devoted to human rights, it was unclear whether such a meeting would accomplish anything. But, as a "first," it certainly seemed to symbolize progress. The sponsors, besides the United States, were Canada and Spain.[61]

This was one of only three new proposals to which the US affixed its sponsoring signature. In each case, it joined several other Western delegations.[62] A distinguishing feature of US strategy throughout the Madrid session was the downplaying of new proposals. They were regarded as being of secondary importance in comparison with "review of implementation"—the naming of names and citing of incidents. Still, in these three instances Washington felt the proposals were important enough, as well as strongly enough related to US priorities, to warrant joining in their co-sponsorship.

A second new proposal was far more consequential, and met with far greater resistance from the Soviet Union. It called for a six-week meeting of experts which would deal with "reunion of families," the phrase used in the Helsinki accord that to a considerable degree covered emigration. Madrid designated the experts meeting "human contacts," rather than "human rights."[63] The proposal was co-sponsored by Canada, Denmark, Greece and the United Kingdom. Debate at Madrid on reunion of families had been quite extensive. The United States, joined by other Western countries, had severely criticized the USSR for its very restrictive policy of emigration. The heavy decline of Jewish emigration and the surge in the number of refuseniks during 1980-83 provided a key Helsinki index and attracted extensive commentary. In order to underscore the tragic character of the humanitarian problem (which also involved refusal of visas for one spouse to be reunited with the other spouse, or children with parents), the US and Canada had pressed strongly for a conference of experts.

Before the Christmas adjournment in mid-December 1982, according to an informed media account, Soviet negotiators were warned several times at private meetings "that the USSR must make a major human rights concession if it wants Western agreement to a key meeting on military security."[64] Though Western negotiators did not specify what concession they had in mind, it appeared quite likely that Soviet agreement on a reunion-of-families conference would be very much welcomed. Moscow, however, remained firmly opposed. The Soviets did not relish further European attention to what was regarded as a closed matter. Soviet resistance persuaded the neutral/non-aligned bloc to drop the proposal from the compromise draft concluding document. But the US and the West would not budge from what was considered an important issue of principle. Kondrashev's response to the reunion-of-families conference was that it was "totally unacceptable."[65] His East German colleague explained that the type of conference which was requested depends on the general situation in Europe. He recommended that it would be better to wait and see how the climate developed.[66]

The intervention of Switzerland and, especially, the personal intervention of Spanish Prime Minister Felipe Gonzàlez broke the deadlock. The

Swiss government said it was prepared to invite all the participatory states to a meeting of experts in Bern in April 1986 to explore how best to achieve the objectives of the "human contacts" provisions of Helsinki.[67] In a move unique to the Helsinki process, the Spanish Prime Minister appeared in person at the plenary on June 17 to announce that "we believe it would strengthen the Helsinki process for the Madrid meeting to accept that invitation on behalf of all the states."[68] He sought to sweeten his recommendation by urging that the West drop its demand for an end to jamming of the "free flow" of information over international radio broadcasts.

Why Prime Minister Gonàzlez assumed this personal and risky responsibility of intervention is clear. A deadlock on this issue would end the Madrid follow-up meeting without reaching any substantive decision. At stake, to some extent, was the reputation of the Spanish state. Madrid would either be remembered, for all of its intense controversies, as a contribution to the Helsinki process or forgotten as another Belgrade.

The West complied with the request to drop the anti-jamming demand. Spain was, after all, virtually a member of NATO. Besides, what existed was a "dangerous impasse," as articulated by a leading West European diplomat.[69] But would the Soviets respond favorably? Edward Killham, who, along with Spencer Oliver served as deputy chief of the US delegation, told the Soviets at a plenary session that the Spanish compromise was the "absolute rock bottom" of what the West would accept.[70] He made it clear that "we will not give up anything more," and as far as the West and the United States were concerned, "the striptease is over." The Soviets would have to deliver or face the end of the Madrid meeting without a concluding document.

The two principal Soviet delegates flew to Moscow at the end of June 1983 for a final consultation. Deputy Foreign Minister Anatoly Kovalev returned on July 1 to tell the plenary that "the Soviet delegation is ready to act within the framework of the initiative of the Spanish government."[71] But, even with this concession, Moscow still sought to diminish the significance of the human contacts experts meeting in Bern. Soviet delegates insisted that the Bern meeting be announced in the "Chairman's Statement," not in the concluding document.[72] Thus, the compromise statement would appear in an annex to the Madrid document. If, in the Soviet mind, this gave Bern a lesser status, reality pointed in a somewhat different direction. The Bern meeting would still have all the features of a Helsinki-sponsored conference.

Besides the major victory on the Bern conference, the US and the West, in the Madrid concluding document, won some modest improvements on the Helsinki accord. This was seen most notably with respect to reunion of families and travel.[73] In cases of marriages between citizens of different states, decisions on exit visas would henceforth be taken within six months. In emergency family cases, like death or illness, decisions would be reached as expeditiously as possible. Under any circumstances involving emigration requests, the applicant and his family would not be penalized by loss of job, social benefits, or housing rights, which was all too often the case when Soviet Jews sought to emigrate. (At Belgrade, when the West had tried to get these understandings through, it had been rebuffed by Moscow.) Madrid also provided for the lowering of fees for visas and passports until they reached a moderate level in relation to a person's average monthly income.

On freedom of thought, conscience and religion, the concluding document required of the signatories that they "will take the necessary action in their respective countries to effectively ensure this right." The same was demanded to "ensure" the freedom of the individual to practice alone or with others a religious belief. Minor advances were approved in making possible access to foreign missions, in easing the living and working condition of journalists, in obtaining foreign newspapers and journals, and in repudiating terrorism.

Of some limited significance was the agreement that "the participating states will ensure the right of workers freely to establish and join trade unions; the right of trade unions freely to exercise their activities; and other rights as laid down in relevant international instruments." This was aimed at according recognition to Solidarity. But the trade union rights were severely circumscribed by the first section of an added clause insisted upon by the Warsaw Pact: the rights "will be exercised in compliance with the law of the state and in conformity with the state's obligations under international law."

A number of the other 14 points in the Danish human rights proposals to which NATO had agreed were dropped as part of the negotiating process between East and West. Thus, the anti-jamming proposal, as noted, was removed at the request of the Spanish Prime Minister to win Soviet approval of the Bern experts meeting. No doubt, the Soviet Union would have resisted the anti-jamming proposal, preventing its adoption. Not only had Kondrashev declared it to be "totally unacceptable,"[74] but Soviet and Czechoslovakian spokesmen made wild allegations at Madrid that Radio Liberty and Radio Free Europe stations were manned by "war criminals."[75] The two Warsaw Pact powers had actually introduced a proposal calling for a halt to the financing and the providing of facilities for RFE/RL. Another Western proposal which met fierce Soviet opposition was the endorsement of citizens' monitoring groups for Helsinki compliance. The intent was to end the Soviet persecution of the Helsinki Watch Groups. Kondrashev and another Soviet delegate charged that the West was trying to "subvert" the Helsinki agreement by placing such emphasis on individuals.[76]

If the Madrid concluding document could hardly be viewed as a major step forward in promoting human rights, it nonetheless offered a modest and limited advance for the Helsinki process. In contrast to Belgrade, a new document was approved, carrying additional obligations for the Soviet Union and the Warsaw Pact countries. Franz Ceska, the old "Helsinki hand," emphasized that the USSR would now be held accountable in world public opinion to additional Helsinki-approved demands.[77]

This view also found expression in a formal statement made by Ronald Reagan on July 15, 1983: "Together with the Helsinki Accord, the Madrid Agreement sets forth a clear code of conduct for all 35 states—a set of standards to which we and the other Atlantic democracies will continue to hold those who will have pledged their word at Madrid."[78] On the closing day of Madrid, September 9, 1983, Secretary of State George Shultz, who had succeeded Haig the previous year, for the first time stated the long-term purpose of US policy to Helsinki, although somewhat obliquely.[79] He spoke of the "division of Europe" as being "unnatural and inhuman," implying the rejection of spheres of influence and the Brezhnev Doctrine. The division, he went on, can only be maintained by "raw power," which inevitably must be "a source of instability."

Shultz drove the point home by saying that "lasting security or cooperation" cannot be achieved so long as "one government is afraid of its own people" and its next-door neighbors. He concluded with the remarkably clairvoyant thought that "in the most profound sense, the Helsinki process represents an historic effort to erode the cruel divisions between East and West in Europe." Heretofore, the focus had been on building "cooperation." No one had used the phrase "cruel divisions" nor the activist verb "erode." If there was no perceptible policy difference on Helsinki between Haig, who had served in office for a little more than a year, and Shultz, the latter does seem to have given the process much greater thought during his initial year. Later, he would give the process, especially its human rights facets, his personal attention.

Central to the Helsinki procedures was the fixing without conditions of the time and place of the succeeding follow-up meeting. Were parties to the CSCE to raise doubts or uncertainties about holding the next follow-up conference, the Helsinki process *qua* process would be brought to a halt. That almost happened during the Madrid preparatory meeting, when Moscow sought to keep the question of the follow-up meeting up in the air. The maneuver failed, and the USSR solemnly agreed to adhere to previous "modalities" for setting the time and place of the next review conference. Still, Moscow kept intimating that agreement on a time and place of the follow-up meeting—Vienna in November 1986 had been designated—was conditioned on the simultaneous fixing of the time and place of the European conference on confidence-building measures. A Bulgarian proposal gave expression to this linkage, setting forth a paragraph in the concluding document in which the same sentence mentioned both the time and place of the disarmament conference and that of the follow-up meeting.[80]

If the process seemed assured for the immediate future, this did not necessarily mean that meaningful progress could be expected at the human rights and human contacts experts meetings in 1985 and 1986 as a *quid pro quo* for the conference on confidence-building measures. Each of the experts meetings was scheduled to last several weeks, a time frame hardly commensurate with the virtually unlimited period—some two and one-half years—for the meeting on confidence-building measures. Moreover, one could hardly be sanguine that each or both of the experts meetings would translate into genuine progress.

No less an authority on the Helsinki process than the former Ambassador to the Belgrade talks, Arthur Goldberg, even expressed doubts about the achievements of Madrid, especially of its setting up of separate meetings covering distinctly different subjects at Ottawa and Bern.[81] In his view, the separation of "the security aspects from the human rights and humanitarian provisions" of the Helsinki accord has "severely imbalanced the Final Act." Besides, Stockholm was certain to be, in Goldberg's judgment, "grist to the Soviet mill" by giving the Kremlin a "purely propaganda platform" for spouting slogans carrying "great popular appeal" in Western Europe. At the same time, he emphasized how the security meeting was given a time frame of nearly three years while the human rights meetings were scheduled to last but a few weeks. Bern, particularly, he saw as having a "low priority" because it was incorporated in the Madrid chairman's consensus statement instead of being in the main body of the concluding document.

Rebuttal came from Kampelman's State Department deputy, Edward Killham, who pointed out that the Stockholm meeting was strongly supported by all of America's NATO allies and, in addition, its mandate was "very carefully drafted to protect US interests. . . ."[82] The career officer specifically rejected the notion that Bern would have a "low priority," noting how Moscow had "fought tooth and nail" against the human contacts meeting. Yet Killham failed to address the theme of separation of security from human rights. Goldberg reacted by reminding the foreign affairs specialist that one of the "great virtues" of Helsinki was precisely the conjoining of the two aims.[83]

Once again, he sharply contended that "isolating security matters from consideration of human rights . . . would jeopardize the balance of the Final Act." Goldberg dismissed the argument that Stockholm was responsive to Western allied interests. "It is dangerous," he said, "to yield to allied timidity and to relinquish our role as a leader of the free world." Reflected here was the posture he had taken at Belgrade which had alienated both NATO and the State Department.

Eventually, it would become apparent that Goldberg's argument as it applied to the meetings of Ottawa and Bern had considerable merit. Without a security aspect to them, leverage for the West would be greatly diminished. Yet, the fact that such human rights meetings could be approved at all at Madrid was testimony to the effectiveness of the strategy of linkage. That strategy pointed to the way meaningful human rights progress might ultimately be achieved.

▪ 9 ▪

Stalemate and Crisis
in the Helsinki Process

T
he end of the Madrid meeting did not lead to an improvement either
in East-West relations or in the status of human rights which the
Madrid concluding document seemed to promise. Indeed, in both
respects the situation worsened, although the tensions were not of
the heated and threatening character that had surrounded the Polish crisis of 1981. Action by the Bundestag of the Federal Republic of Germany
in November 1983, only two months after Madrid, approving the deployment of Pershing II and cruise missiles within its borders, evoked a sharp
Soviet response. Aware that the emplacement which it had fiercely resisted for several years was now certain, Moscow broke off talks with the
United States in Geneva on strategic arms reductions (START) and on
intermediate-range nuclear forces, and angrily withdrew from the stalemated, 12-year-old negotiations in Vienna on Mutual and Balanced Force
Reductions (MBFR). For the next two years—until March 1985—key
outposts of the East-West negotiating process had ceased to function.

Fears of the resurgence of Western military power in Europe were ag-
gravated by a succession and generation crisis in the USSR, which some
compared to the "Time of Troubles," that era in Tsarist history of the late
16th and early 17th centuries that had witnessed a succession of rulers and
pretenders to the throne. The successors to Brezhnev—Yuri Andropov
and Konstantin Chernenko—were old and sickly. With death hovering
over each succeeding ruler and the system providing for no constitutional
or legitimate successor, uncertainty prevailed in the highest echelons of
power. Uncertainty and unpredictability inevitably bred graver internal
anxiety, while at the same time augmenting the power of the Soviet security services. Soviet repression during the two last years of Brezhnev rule
and the interregnum that lasted until March 1985 stirred a hostile reaction from Washington. President Reagan dubbed the USSR the "Evil

Empire" and, if the phrase carried a primitive ring, it reflected widespread public sentiment. That sentiment served to reinforce a determined policy line at Helsinki meetings. Stigmatization of Soviet practice in the context of the Helsinki accord became a high priority at the same time as Washington took steps in Europe to counter an expanded Soviet military power.

The year 1984 was marked by an intensification of internal repression in the Soviet Union. Measures were taken to prevent or "neutralize" personal contacts with foreigners suspected of friendly relations with Soviet citizens.[1] Visas were frequently denied them. Foreign journalists were warned or threatened through a variety of devices—police questioning, occasional detentions, or expulsions. At the same time, dissidents and refuseniks were openly discouraged by the authorities from having foreign contacts, sometimes by such extreme devices as house arrest.[2] As for the towering figure of Sakharov, his isolation in Gorky was made almost totally complete, while his wife was warned of her pending arrest and trial.

In January 1984, a new provision was added to the Russian Criminal Code to discourage or prevent the giving of gifts to dissidents and refuseniks by foreigners.[3] The authorities were, of course, aware that the very sustenance and survival of dissidents and refuseniks depended on such gifts, because jobs and sources of income were frequently unobtainable. The new provision stipulated that if "anti-Soviet agitation and propaganda" was conducted "with the use of money or material valuables received from foreign organizations or from persons acting in the interests of these organizations," the offender could be punished with the very stiff penalty of up to 15 years of imprisonment and exile.

Enactment of another decree during the same month was aimed at preventing information about internal developments, including repression, from getting out of the Soviet Union. The decree provided that publishing material which constituted a "work-related secret"—not a "secret" itself—could lead to imprisonment of up to eight years.[4] In May 1984, an additional decree was introduced to strike at any closeness with foreigners. It forbade Soviet citizens, under penalty of a maximum sum of 100 rubles, of having a foreigner spend the night in their home without official permission.[5] The decree also forbade a Soviet citizen from inviting a foreigner for a ride in his or her automobile.

On August 1, 1984, Moscow halted the established practice of allowing the foreign sender of a parcel to a Soviet citizen to prepay the cost of custom duties.[6] Now the recipient would have to pay the cost, which for him or her could be prohibitive. If the result was increased hardship for those dependent on foreign parcels, it served the Kremlin's interest in severing all connections with the West and in stifling the dissident or refusenik phenomenon.

The sharp new legal thrusts against the dissidents were accompanied by strong blows aimed at Jewish emigration.[7] During 1983, the number of approved exit visas amounted to a total of 1,315, half the level of 1982. The number of Jews who had been permitted to leave after Madrid was significantly less than during the follow-up meeting itself. In 1984, the total reached the lowest since the emigration process had begun in 1971— 897 emigrants for the entire year. The year 1985 saw the level rise slightly, to 1,140. (Emigration levels of Soviet Germans and Armenians were similarly very low.)

Because the Madrid concluding document actually strengthened the Basket III provision about "reunion of family" and the obligation of governments to facilitate such "reunion" when exit visas are requested, how could the USSR publicly justify the clear violation of new Helsinki obligations as they applied, for example, to Jews? A top Communist Party official, Leonid Zamyatin, said in the fall of 1984: "Almost all the families who would like to leave to the West have already left."[8] This assertion was repeated in various ways by officers of the Anti-Zionist Committee, a special Kremlin creation in April 1983 of largely handpicked Soviet Jews.[9] Soviet publications also insisted that 98.6 percent of exit-visa applications were approved, while only a tiny percentage were refused on grounds they allegedly knew "state secrets."[10]

However, a Soviet expert to a UN human rights body gave emigration figures in November 1984 that showed that the Kremlin during 1982-84 had refused exit visas to over 50 percent of those who had requested them.[11] The number of Jews who had been prevented from leaving over the years totaled 383,628 by the end of 1984. Only one-third of Jewish applicants for exit visas had received them. Besides, the West had a list of about 10,000 Soviet Jews who were refuseniks, with some 3,600 who had been waiting for five years and quite a few for over ten years.[12]

The refusenik category, in the main, was made up of persons whom Soviet authorities said possessed state secrets. In fact, the decisions were made in a grossly arbitrary and capricious manner.[13] Some refuseniks had not worked at a classified job for well over ten years. One individual might be refused, while another who had done exactly the same job was granted a visa. Besides, the legal systems of most advanced countries did not provide for the state secret restriction on exit visas.[14] International legal studies, including a major one done by the United Nations, put a maximum limit of five years for refusals based on state secrets.[15]

Soviet authorities must have been fully cognizant that their behavior with respect to emigration did not conform to international norms and standards. At times, they would disclose that their conduct was based on extralegal considerations, not on accepted norms. Sergei Kondrashev, the Soviet delegate at the Madrid conference, acknowledged that, concerning the issue of "reunion of families," it is "the level of détente" that determine the pace of Basket III implementation.[16] During 1984, refuseniks in Moscow reported that Soviet officials were telling applicants that the bad state of East-West relations prevented them from receiving exit visas.[17] A leading Soviet economic official was quoted as saying that "if good relations were restored with the US, 50,000 Jewish émigrés annually would be no problem."[18]

Clearly, Jews (and other potential emigrants) were hostages to Soviet-American relations. International law was not the governing consideration; nor was the Helsinki accord or the Madrid concluding document. What made matters worse was that applicants would find themselves punished simply for making application for an exit visa.[19] Thus, they might face loss of a job, enormous obstacles to getting another job, impoverishment, or official charges of parasitism because they failed to obtain another job. They or their children might be expelled from a university or other institutions of higher learning; their sons might be conscripted into military service. In several notorious instances, an applicant had been stripped of his advanced academic degrees. Applicants also faced loss of a telephone, social ostracism, surveillance, and physical attack.

Worse complications for refuseniks occurred when they chose to embark on efforts to study and teach Hebrew or to actually foster Jewish culture.[20] Police crackdowns by the state became the predominant mode of response, even if this clashed with Helsinki's rule justifying the right to know and act on one's rights. After June 1984, arrests intensified. By the end of December 1984, at least 19 Jews were serving terms of imprisonment or awaiting trial for one or another form of Jewish activism.[21] The allegations, in most instances, charged violations of Article 190-1 of the Russian Criminal Code (which referred to the "Circulation of Fabrications Known to be False Which Defame the Soviet State and Social System").

The essence of the Soviet Jewish tragedy in the mid-1980s was that at a time when anti-Semitism prompted a drive for exodus, the Kremlin imposed rigid obstacles that made emigration extremely difficult, almost impossible. No wonder, then, that the Jewish plight captured the concern of Helsinki advocates.

While the scheduled Helsinki human rights experts meeting was to be held in Ottawa in mid-1985, there had already opened in January 1984 a

Helsinki-sponsored session in Stockholm on confidence-building measures concerning the security area. But was it appropriate to raise human rights questions at a conference (which would run for nearly three years) explicitly devoted to reducing the possibility of surprise attack? The United States recognized the distinctive character of the Stockholm conference; indeed, it had played a major role in precisely defining the guidelines for the sessions. But the US also recognized that Stockholm was intimately linked to the Helsinki process and, therefore, in some way to human rights.

As early as September 16, 1980, long before Stockholm, this set of connections was made apparent. On that date, Department of State Counselor Rozanne Ridgway appeared as a witness before the House Subcommittee on International Organizations. When asked about the proposal of France for a post-Madrid security meeting, she offered instructive comments. While the proposal presented "potential difficulties for us," she said, nonetheless it was patently clear that if security issues were "broken out of the CSCE framework into a separate forum," it would be harmful.[22]

Ridgway went on to explain that a totally separate forum would disrupt "the balance among human rights, economic and security measures which we believe necessary to the health of the Final Act." Not only would it be disruptive to the balance, the contemplated conference would "distract attention from human rights and shift the focus we believe must be maintained." She further informed the congressional body that NATO was fully informed of the US view that "we cannot consider any post-Madrid meeting which is not firmly and explicitly part of the CSCE process." She concluded by reporting that within NATO "there is an emerging consensus . . . in favor of our position."

The linkage issue became crucial as the opening sessions of the Stockholm conference on CBMs coincided with a life-threatening hunger strike by Andrei Sakharov, his second, to protest the total isolation and humiliation to which the Soviets had subjected him. The US Congress and the Helsinki Commission were determined to use the CSCE security meeting to raise the plight of the great Soviet scientist and humanist.

In May 1984, Congress adopted a resolution demanding, in the case of Sakharov, Soviet adherence to the provisions of the Final Act.[23] On May 22, Ambassador James Goodby, head of the US delegation to the Stockholm deliberations, sent a letter to each delegation leader calling attention to the congressional resolution (the text of which was attached to the letter).[24] Goodby was careful to avoid raising the Sakharov matter at the formal Stockholm sessions. But on June 15 the Soviet delegation circulated a paper accusing the US of "attempting to inject extraneous matters into the Stockholm meeting with the intention of sabotaging the negotiations."[25]

By the fall, the Sakharov question had become too burning an issue to be left to indirect formulations. He had been forcibly confined to a hospital in Gorky and no one knew precisely about his condition or his whereabouts. Anxiety about his life and health had deepened, and desperate efforts were made by his family and by human rights organizations to ascertain minimum information. The US Helsinki Commission had already held public hearings on the subject, and Chairman Fascell wrote to the President of the National Academy of Sciences, Dr. Frank Press, urging a strong stand by the US scientific community on behalf of Sakharov.[26] The National Academy, under its previous president, Dr. Philip Handler, had earlier set a precedent for vigorously inquiring into the status of the Soviet scientist.

Ambassador Goodby brought human rights openly to the Stockholm floor on September 18, saying that the United States "holds that human rights, peace and security are inseparable and that it is only on this basis that the spirit of the Helsinki accords truly can be realized."[27]

The US Ambassador then went on to make reference to a recent special visit made to Stockholm and other European capitals by Ambassador Max Kampelman on behalf of President Reagan. What that visit gave "expression" to, according to Goodby, was the "truth" that "confidence can be undermined and tension can rise from failures" in the human rights sphere.[28]

If some delegations feared that the tough human rights stance could lead to a punitive Soviet response that might place the Stockholm conference in jeopardy, the reality was otherwise. The Commission reported that the Soviet response was "muted" and "did not go beyond" veiled threats.[29] Indeed, it was hardly likely that Moscow would want to jeopardize the major gain that it had won at Madrid. Stockholm, after all, offered a platform to sound the alarm about the Pershing II and cruise missiles, as well to promote other favorite international Soviet disarmament themes. According to Pierre Lellouche, a knowledgeable authority writing in *Newsweek* in July 1984: "The Soviets are quietly turning the Stockholm forum into a deadly machinery to alter to its advantage the postwar political and strategic order in Europe."[30]

Lellouche closely examined the Soviet political and propaganda campaign for this vital objective. The Soviets tried to influence Western public opinion through "empty but nice sounding declarations" that would result in a "pan-European security order from which the United States would ultimately be expelled." Moscow's sweeping proposals, repeatedly sounded at Stockholm, focused on a treaty concerning the non-use of force, a pledge by both sides not to be the first to use nuclear weapons, the establishment of nuclear-free zones in Europe, a freeze and reduction of military budgets, and a ban on chemical weapons.

But by the end of 1984, Ambassador Goodby reported that Soviet propaganda had failed to produce any "groundswell of support" for its overall program or its individual proposals.[31] The neutral and non-aligned CSCE members introduced their own confidence-building measures, which in no way resembled Moscow's. Goodby concluded that "no one can credibly contend that the Soviets have succeeded in turning Stockholm into a propaganda platform which has deceived public opinion." The Soviet failure, in part, was due to the fact that the installation by the West of the Pershing II and cruise missiles was fast becoming a *fait accompli*, thus preventing an effective Soviet propaganda initiative. Equally important was the Western determination to shape the agenda in a manner that would preclude propaganda pronouncements.

The United States and the West had sought from the beginning to avoid propaganda initiatives and to concentrate on practical issues of extending advance notification to much smaller military maneuvers as well as to alerts, amphibious operations and mobilization. The NATO allies further urged longer advance notice and annual forecasts of maneuvers. A Norwegian specialist on military strategy, Johan Holst, suggested that "we should look at confidence-building measures as management instruments designed to reduce the pressure from arms on the process of politics during peacetime and on decision-making in crisis and war."[32] This framework, thought Goodby, fitted exactly into the West's perspective, which aimed at promoting stability through measures aimed at avoiding miscalculation, achieving a greater degree of openness, and what the Belgian Ambassador called "de-mystification" of military activities.[33]

While agreement on confidence-building measures had not been reached by the end of 1985, a major concession from each of the alliance systems offered hope for positive developments in 1986. On the one hand, the Soviet Union during the Madrid meeting had agreed that Stockholm would deal with the whole of Europe from the Atlantic to the Urals, and not merely the 150 miles of western Russia provided in the Helsinki Final Act.[34] And earlier, on June 4, 1984, President Reagan, in a speech in Dublin, offered an unexpected concession aimed at encouraging the Soviets to respond more directly on confidence-building measures. He said that the US would be willing to discuss the Soviet proposal for an agreement on the non-use of force if Moscow would negotiate on concrete measures dealing with advance notification on military maneuvers.[35]

On December 3, 1984, a major procedural step forward was taken when both sides and the neutral/non-aligned group agreed on a "working structure" for further detailed discussions. It seemed to provide what President Reagan called a "flexible give-and-take negotiation process."[36] The absence, however, of concrete security agreements upon which the USSR could look favorably meant that leverage was not available to further human rights progress in the immediate future. This became all too apparent at Ottawa.

The Ottawa experts meeting, which ran from May 7 to June 17, 1985, was the first Helsinki conference devoted entirely to human rights. Inevitably, it became a source book of what was feasible and not feasible in the human rights field, and whether positive consequences could emerge from these Helsinki experts meetings. In the end, Ottawa, like Belgrade, did not result in a concluding document—a "missed opportunity," as one leading Western diplomat called it.[37]

Yet, it was distinguished by a profoundly new ideological and tactical approach undertaken by the Soviet Union, which, in turn, produced a new US and Western debating orientation with rather effective consequences. At previous CSCE conferences, Moscow had sought to counter Western recriminations about human rights violations in the USSR by charging that they constituted illegitimate interference in the internal affairs of other countries. Only when the US persisted in raising human rights issues would the USSR respond to the challenge, usually by making allegations about the human rights record of the United States (or the United Kingdom or West Germany). But the response had a hit-and-run character. The intent was not dialogue, but rather to demonstrate that Moscow could also play the human rights game. Even so, the Soviet diplomats displayed a remarkably shallow and limited debating style. They probably knew quite well that their response was inadequate, for they continued to emphasize that Washington had no right to raise the issue at all.

At the very beginning of the Ottawa session, Moscow stood firm on this defensive line. The Soviet CSCE Committee, a Kremlin-created public body that was supposed to resemble somewhat the US Helsinki Commission, put it bluntly: "Participants in the Helsinki Conference agreed to cooperate in humanitarian fields on specific conditions. They agreed that such cooperation is *possible only* if general principles of relations between states are observed, *primarily non-intervention in internal affairs*[38] (emphasis added). How then would human rights or, as the Soviet preferred to say, the "humanitarian" issues of Basket III, be dealt with? The Soviet delegation, headed by Vsevolod Sofinsky (ably assisted by the ubiquitous KGB general, Sergei Kondrashev), said that in the review process each delegation would speak only about the record of its own country.

Interestingly, the Soviet delegation justified this approach by referring to the language of the Madrid concluding document. Sofinsky, in citing from the document, used a Russian phrase—*v svoikh stranakh*—which meant "in their own countries."[39] In fact, however, this language did not appear in the Madrid text. Rather, the language of the text when referring to a review of human rights was *v ikh gosudarstvakh*, which meant "in their states." This implied the right of delegates to address human rights in all states and not merely in their own specific country. The quick verbal sleight of hand of the Soviet diplomat was rather easily discovered, and the Soviets did not choose to rebut this language clarification made by the US delegation.

The proposal would in any case have fallen on deaf ears. From the opening session, the West provided detailed documentation of the growing instances of human rights violations in the USSR as related to dissenters and refuseniks and to the severe cutback in the size of Soviet emigration. The United States, the United Kingdom, and Canada were particularly outspoken.

After a week of such a barrage, the Soviet delegation switched to a new style in debating tactics, trying to turn the table on the US and the West by demonstrating that the West had committed "horrific violations."[40] Sofinsky charged that the West violated the "right to life," as well as a host of economic, social and cultural rights. The USSR delegation went to great lengths in citing how mass unemployment in the West presumably violated the "right to work" provision of the Universal Declaration of Human Rights and the Covenant on Economic, Social and Cultural Rights. Its spokesmen further claimed that the absence of free health care, free education, maternity benefits—alleged to be characteristic of the West's capitalist societies—constituted assaults on human rights. Criticized, too, was racism in the United States and deprivation of the rights of minorities. An example of the racism to which Moscow referred was anti-Semitism in both the United States and the United Kingdom. The charge reflected a remarkable degree of gall in the face of the official anti-Semitism in the USSR.

In general, the Soviet Union avoided all reference to the standard and classic human rights incorporated in the Universal Declaration of Human Rights and the Covenant on Civil and Political Rights. Freedom of speech, press, assembly, conscience and movement—all stressed by the West—were simply not on Moscow's human rights agenda. For the USSR, only economic, social and cultural rights counted. A prominent commentator, writing in the West German press, observed that "the difference in the systems came to the fore in Ottawa with such force that one is bound to ask the question whether all participants really signed the same text of the Final Act ten years ago."[41] The West, nonetheless, very much welcomed the Soviet change of style. It was a significant departure from both Belgrade and Madrid.[42] As the British delegate, Sir Anthony Williams, noted in his closing speech on June 17: "Even if few satisfactory answers were secured, we have at least established in practice that it is possible to discuss each other's records."[43] Pertinently, he added that "we have finally exploded the groundless contention that such discussion constitutes interference in the internal affairs of others." His assessment was quite correct. The Soviet Union and its allies would, in the future, hesitate to raise an objection about discussion of domestic matters. The development was, indeed, extraordinary.

Of special interest was the focus on the "right to life." The right to life, indeed, had been given priority in the Universal Declaration of Human Rights and the Covenant on Civil and Political Rights, the twin pillars on which the Helsinki accord rested. But the Soviet delegation, most notably Kondrashev, added the words "in peace" to the phrase, which altered its fundamental meaning.[44] Kondrashev argued that the previous phrase now meant the right to be free from the threat of war, especially nuclear conflict, which in turn meant disarmament. The linguistic maneuver was justified on grounds that, in a nuclear age, the "right to live in peace" is the fundamental prerequisite for the fulfillment of all other human rights.

According to Western legal scholars, however, the "right to life" meant a person's right to be free from the arbitrary deprivation of life. This was the specific intent of Article 6 of the International Covenant on Civil and Political Rights. It did not mean disarmament, and the West found the new definition "totally unacceptable."[45] What the Soviets were doing was creating confusion between a government's obligation to keep the peace and its obligation to protect an individual's human rights.

In addition to the artificial formulation of a new "right to live in peace," Moscow sought to link human rights improvement to the reduction of international tensions. Sofinsky established the linkage at the very beginning of Ottawa.[46] The head of the US delegation, Richard Schifter, a long-time specialist on human rights and the head of the State Department's Bureau of Human Rights and Humanitarian Affairs, demonstrated that the Soviet logic here had the effect of transforming Soviet citizens into hostages of international relationships. "Does it stand to reason," he asked, "that if foreign countries establish friendly relations with a particular government, that government, in turn, will—so to speak—reward the foreign countries by dealing kindly with its own citizens?" This would mean that "a government holds its own people hostage" to how "other countries treat it in international affairs."[47]

Schifter pointed out that Principle VII of the Final Act established the correct relationship between détente or peace and human rights. The former was dependent on the fulfillment of an individual's rights and, in fact, "disrespect for human rights contributes to the deterioration of international relations." Historical examples abound, he pointed out. The "thaw" in the Soviet Union had preceded "the significant relaxation of international tensions." Similarly, the Kremlin's internal repression in 1979 had "cast an ominous shadow" over the SALT II agreement, one reason why the accord was not ratified by the Senate.

Far broader and more consequential was the US response to the Soviet allegations about economic, social and cultural rights. Ambassador Schifter joined the argument directly, and confronted Moscow on the latter's favorite ground.[48] What emerged proved devastating for the Soviet Union. Schifter had mastered a vast amount of documentation, not ordinarily exploited, which enabled him to offer a thoroughgoing rebuff to Soviet pretensions.

Rights of the individual were not swept under the rug. Stress, significantly, was given over to just those civil rights that "would not require systemic changes in the Soviet Union to effect correction." They included incarceration of persons guilty only of giving expression to their thoughts, the persecution of religious believers, the commitment of dissenters to mental institutions, cultural repression and discrimination against persons "because of their ancestry"—which was understood to mean anti-Semitism.

The charge of unemployment in the United States was met with a detailed examination of the data and with no glossing over the facts. The problem was related to market conditions, although attention was given to the government's determination to lower the unemployment rate and to provide a valuable safety net for those facing the greatest hardships. At the same time, Schifter took the occasion to stress the rights of free and independent trade unions that are denied by "certain states which profess to have been founded for the benefit of the working people. . . ."

Homelessness was fully acknowledged and sensitively treated. Schifter elaborated on how the government and voluntary groups were dealing with this "complex and difficult problem." Even if the solutions were not entirely satisfactory and although housing remained inadequate, Schifter did not flinch from a description of the nature of the problem. He dealt with racial discrimination in the same sensitive and concerned way, and included the problem of Native Americans on reservations (with which Schifter had been professionally involved). While acknowledging the problems, he stressed how much progress had been achieved. Schifter similarly analyzed the charge of discrimination against women, with the conclusion that, though "actual equality" had not been obtained, "we are clearly on the way toward that goal."

Especially instructive and fascinating was the documentation on what was correctly called "the quality of life" for Soviet citizens. This was something concerning which Soviet diplomats took special pride. Dorothy Goldberg in her memoirs described a friendly breakfast meeting in February 1978 at which Ambassador Vorontsov was their guest. When the US Ambassador raised the human rights issue, Vorontsov, with great earnestness, responded: "We will not change." At this point, Mrs. Goldberg interrupted: "No. Maybe now you cannot, but your grandchildren will understand more." Vorontsov reacted in a tone described as "confidential": "Actually, we have a very good system. It is. What's wrong with a system that takes care of everybody?"[49]

Whether, after the collapse of the Soviet economy and disclosures in the Soviet media about gross inadequacies in the "quality of life," Vorontsov still felt the same way is not known. What is known is that a half-decade earlier, Ambassador Schifter had provided powerful documentation of the subject. Using comparative statistical data, Schifter found that the standard of living of the average Soviet citizen was about one-third of the US average; in fact, he "lives less well than someone living at the official US poverty line." He further demonstrated that Soviet growth rates had plummeted and that the productivity gap between Moscow and the West can "be expected to widen in the future."

The Soviet planning system had created, analysis revealed, "an economy of bottlenecks." The result was "pervasive shortages of consumer goods and the widespread corruption these shortages generate." Aggravating the problem was the heavy Soviet expenditure on defense (twice the rate of US expenditures in terms of Gross National Product). The

dismal picture was filled in with rather sad data on conditions in agricul-
ture, on a profound and massive housing shortage, and on the distressingly
low status of Soviet women. Adding to the portrait were descriptive data
on extreme medical-care inadequacies and on vast problems of health,
including stunningly high infant-mortality rates and low male life-
expectancy rates. What complicated and worsened the documentation,
noted Schifter, was a social stratification that, notwithstanding Soviet socialist ideology, gave unusual material benefits to the *nomenklatura*. He
was reminded of Orwell's *Animal Farm*: "All animals are equal, but some
are more equal than others."

After the broad Schifter survey, Soviet diplomats should have been discouraged from raising the issue of economic, social and cultural rights in
debating human rights. But, without another more meaningful fallback
position, the Soviet delegation at later Helsinki meetings returned to the
same theme. It would, however, be played at a much lower level.

There was yet a third human rights point which the Warsaw Pact
sought to explore to counter the West's criticisms—the failure of the
United States and several other Western countries to ratify the international covenants on human rights.[50] Poland took the lead on this point,
and sought to place the United States in an embarrassing position by advancing a proposal that called on all governments which had not ratified
the covenants to do so.

After explaining the fundamental role played by the Senate in the US
treaty ratification process, Schifter posed an imaginary exchange between
a senator and himself.[51] The senator, reading from the text of the covenant
on trade-union rights, would ask whether those rights and the Polish ratification itself had not been subverted by the Polish government's conduct
toward Solidarity. The senator also asked questions regarding other
covenant rights, such as freedom of movement and freedom of religion.
The imaginary senator then asked Schifter: ". . . if all these provisions are
being violated by the countries that signed them . . . can you tell this Committee what useful purpose is served by our recommending that the Senate ratify these documents?"

The Jewish problem in the USSR received considerable attention at
Ottawa, which was not surprising, given the severe cutback in emigration
and the continuing anti-Semitism in that country. The United States, the
United Kingdom, and Canada took the lead on the question, followed by
Sweden, Norway, West Germany and even Liechtenstein.[52] Schifter focused heavily on the question in a long speech on May 28, in which he
called the Soviet policy toward Jews "schizophrenic" because, on the one

hand, it makes "life miserable for them" while, on the other, it was "not letting them out of the country."[53] His Canadian colleague spelled out the escalating number of trials of Jews.[54]

Kondrashev was obliged to provide a full-scale defense of Soviet policy. It had an "Alice in Wonderland" quality. The problem of family reunion, he said, had already been solved, although individual cases still required settlement.[55] The arrest and trials of numerous Jewish teachers and activists resulted not from their teaching of Hebrew, but from other underground "crimes." Kondrashev especially singled out Yosef Begun, an organizer of Hebrew education who had been repeatedly arrested and accused of anti-state activities.

Sofinsky entered into a harsh dialogue with Sir Anthony Williams after the latter raised the Jewish question. Sofinsky, apparently without tongue in cheek, accused the UK of suppressing the language of the Welsh and Scottish minorities. At the same time, he tried to show that the US was a fountainhead of anti-Semitism, not the USSR.[56] He ironically used the annual statistical report of anti-Semitic incidents put out by the Anti-Defamation League of B'nai B'rith as the source for the obviously absurd allegation.

In the end, Ottawa would not have a concluding document. Instead, the meeting marked a retreat to the "Belgrade syndrome." The Soviet delegation did not appear to be in any compromising mood. Among their 18 proposals incorporated into Moscow's single document draft was one that held that "the main human right was the right to be permitted to live under conditions of peace and freedom [and] the prevention of nuclear war. . . ."[57] The proposed document again stressed "non-intervention in internal affairs" and demanded the exclusion at future meetings of "questions of human rights and fundamental freedom as a weapon for inciting enmity and hatred between peoples, [and] for exacerbating international tensions." The Soviet document, of course, was unacceptable to the West.

The West had submitted 15 proposals, which were summarized in one draft.[58] It made explicit that the "frank discussion" at Ottawa concerning the "serious violations of human rights in some participating states . . . was not to be considered to be contrary to the principle of non-intervention in the internal affairs of any State." Significantly, the Western draft avoided the standard and previously used formulation for emigration, "reunion of families." Instead, it established a precedent for specific reference to freedom of movement. A second precedent which the draft established was a call to CSCE participating states to safeguard the "national and cultural identity" of national minorities. Finally, the draft proposed "regular meetings" of human rights experts for the future.

Moscow reacted negatively, and the inevitable deadlock prompted Sir Anthony Williams to comment sorrowfully: "We have been prevented from fulfilling our mandate."[59] Interestingly, the USSR blamed the failure on the Western refusal to face up to human rights violations. Sofinsky wrote in *Izvestiia* on July 12 that "the USA and its close NATO partners did not intend any serious business-like discussion, even less in the form of a dialogue" at Ottawa.[60] They wanted no concluding document because it "would have reflected all or even some of the violations of human rights which take place in Western countries." Sofinsky's catalogue of the violations had already been set forth: mass unemployment, raging racism and discrimination against women, "widespread anti-Semitism," and a "policy of genocide" against Native Americans.

Moscow, clearly, had reversed its previous public relations policy. Instead of avoiding the human rights issues by referring to non-intervention, it now claimed to champion human rights, with the West accused of human rights violations and seeking to avoid public disclosure. As with Orwellian inversion, truth was turned on its head. To underscore the new approach, Vladimir Lomeiko, Chief of the Foreign Ministry's Press Department, told a press conference in Moscow on July 19 that it was the West that undermined "constructive discussions" and engaged in "pointless rhetoric."[61] At the same press conference, Sofinsky cited "900 acts of vandalism of an anti-Semitic nature" in the US to demonstrate Western indifference to human rights. According to *The Economist* correspondent at the press meeting, Lomeiko "even tried to argue that Soviet Jews could go abroad more easily than American ones."[62] One was reminded of Humpty-Dumpty's scornful comment to Alice in *Alice Through the Looking-Glass*: "When I use a word it means what I choose it to mean, neither more nor less."

The hostile charges about conditions in the United States were made not only in the CSCE sessions; they were pointedly delivered by Sofinsky to visiting US congressmen from the Helsinki Commission.[63] Congressman Sandor Levin of Michigan found the Soviet Ambassador's comments "appalling and frightening." Referring to his discussions with various members of the Soviet delegation on American policies toward minorities and women, Levin observed: "They went into wild flights of fiction about what is happening in the United States, and showed an ignorance that was truly shocking."[64]

If Ottawa failed to produce a concluding document which offered a higher standard of human rights or more specific guidelines than those provided by Helsinki and Madrid, it also failed to have any impact at all on performance. Soviet human rights conduct was no different after the conference ended than when it had begun. Some seasoned CSCE specialists found the principal reason for these failures in the "splitting" of human rights issues from security issues.[65] The separation of the two, in totally disparate settings and sessions, meant that no linkage could be utilized to effect change, and therefore, no leverage could be exerted. From the sidelines, Arthur Goldberg bitterly complained to his wife about the separation.[66] A well-known figure in the Helsinki process, Swiss diplomat Edouard Brunner, later put the issue clearly and succinctly. Noting that the linkage between security and human rights issues stood at the center of the Helsinki process, Brunner observed in the *Neue Zürcher Zeitung* that "whoever does not understand this, has understood nothing of the Helsinki process."[67]

But equally important was the unresolved tension between East and West in the outside world. Helsinki, in the last analysis, was a barometer of East-West relationships. Positive movement, whether in the form of agreements or in actual performance, was a reflection of the state of relationships between the opposing alliance systems. One new factor had entered the equation in March 1985 when Mikhail Gorbachev was chosen General Secretary of the Soviet Communist Party, but his policy of glasnost and perestroika had not yet been introduced. Moreover, his close Politburo colleague, Eduard Shevardnadze, had not yet been appointed to the Foreign Ministry, where he would apply new thinking to foreign affairs issues. A Reagan-Gorbachev summit would not be held until November 1985. Whether tensions would diminish depended in part on the summit. In the meantime, the Helsinki process appeared to be treading water.

US officials thought the new power situation in the USSR warranted an appropriate signaling of America's perspective. It boiled down to linkage, which emerged in a discussion between the half-dozen Helsinki Commission members who showed up in Ottawa and held a 90-minute meeting with Sofinsky. They gave him a list of 30 human rights cases that they said required immediate attention. No response was forthcoming. They then sought to hand over a letter addressed to Gorbachev. Sofinsky rejected the letter, saying he was no postman.[68] At a press conference led by Senator Alfonse D'Amato of New York, who had become Commission Chairman at the beginning of 1985, the congressmen registered "dismay" with the Soviet attitude. They sought to impress upon the Soviet delegation that the attitude of Congress toward future cooperation with the Soviet Union in any field—economic, trade, or mutual security—

would be guided by how the Soviets lived up to their human rights undertakings in the Helsinki accord. Senator D'Amato summarized their perspective: "If they can't live up to these accords on freedom of expression, on freedom of religion, on basic human rights, then they cannot blame us if we are very skeptical about other promises they make."[69]

Ambassador Schifter was in a position to deliver a similar message on behalf of the Reagan administration. If General Secretary Gorbachev wanted better relations with the US in any field, he told Sofinsky, the Soviet leader would have to improve Moscow's human rights record.[70] Schifter cautioned that this record would be used increasingly as a standard to measure the bilateral relationship. He noted that were an arms control agreement reached with the USSR in Geneva, Senate ratification would depend on satisfactory answers to human rights issues. In this context, he stressed as a kind of model the linkage established by Jackson-Vanik between trade relations and Jewish emigration.

At a meeting with the press, the US delegation chief said, "The message we are trying to send is that if the Soviet Union wants better relations, it must be ready to pay a price by honoring its human rights commitments."[71] The naming of names and specific cases at Helsinki meetings, he added, had as its purpose the "drawing [of] a map for the Soviet Union and its allies . . . [as to] what they have to do."

Western uncertainty about the future of Helsinki became apparent the month after Ottawa concluded. On July 30, 1985, Helsinki was the site where the 35 CSCE foreign ministers gathered to commemorate the tenth anniversary of the Final Act. It should have been a landmark occasion, but the Finnish capital was scarcely distinguished by a mood of celebration and joy. The contrary was the case. Somber reassessment of the value of the Helsinki accord had become the order of the day. The two years that had elapsed since the end of the lengthy Madrid review session offered few indications to show significant human rights progress.

Professor Richard Pipes of Harvard University's Russian Research Center, who had served on the National Security Council staff under President Ronald Reagan, reflected the mood of skepticism and uncertainty in conservative US quarters in an essay for *The New York Times* on the occasion of the anniversary. He questioned the value of the original Helsinki trade-off, noting that when the West accepted the "confidence-building measures" and, particularly, the human rights provisions of the Decalogue and Basket III, it handed Moscow "important psychological and moral victories." Pipes was not referring to the assurances granted on inviolability of borders and other security concerns. Instead, he was contending that the West, in approving the accord, was crediting the USSR with a willingness to abide by human rights commitments. The West thereby "effectively implied that at bottom there is no difference between democracy and communism."[72]

Earlier in 1985 variations of Pipes' thesis were making their appearance in key opinion-molding journals. Conservative political pundit George Will commented: "As the Western public becomes used to the sight of Western and Communist diplomats deliberating about freedom of expression, travel, trade unions and other matters, the public concludes that the people talking so earnestly, for so long, share a political vocabulary and frame of reference, so the Helsinki process spreads a fog of false but soothing assumptions."[73]

A prominent writer and columnist in West European publications, Leopold Unger, criticized the Madrid agreement for failing even to mention Poland.[74] He noted, too, that the Stockholm conference so ardently sought by the Soviet Union was already taking place, thereby enabling Moscow to promote its various "peace" initiatives. In contrast, the Madrid-directed human rights conferences for Ottawa and Bern were scheduled for later and short periods.

Encounter, a leading publication in London, carried the views of George Urban, an official of Radio Free Europe, who argued that Madrid and its concluding document, like détente, rested on false assumptions about the thinking of Soviet leaders. In his view, these false assumptions were that Soviet leaders appeared to be like Western leaders and that, therefore, they did not aspire to world revolution. For him, the key question is whether the Helsinki negotiating process significantly contributed to undermining "our public perception of what the Soviet [Union] is about and how it proposes to achieve its objective?"[75]

Conservative intellectual opinion was strongly reinforced by several prominent exiled dissidents, such as Vladimir Bukovsky, Aleksandr Ginzburg, and Leonid Plyushch. They urged in letters, public statements, and guest editorials in various organs that the West withdraw from the Helsinki process because of Soviet violations of the accord's human rights provisions.[76] Echoes of this perspective found expression in US congressional circles, even including the Helsinki Commission itself. This viewpoint would grow and intensify during 1986, and threaten by then the Commission's earlier positive perspective toward Helsinki.

In contrast to the widespread and deepening criticism in the West of the Helsinki process, the official mood in the USSR was "celebratory."[77] (Only in the Soviet Union was the Helsinki anniversary meeting called a "celebration.") The Kremlin-run Soviet Committee for European Security and Cooperation released on the occasion of the anniversary a 10,000-word report which extolled the Helsinki accord as a "European Peace Charter." The Committee pronounced the accord to be "a unique law document" which "imposed definite international commitments of a political and moral nature." Significantly, nothing was mentioned about human rights; rather, détente, peace, and security were the key words.

Strikingly, however, the anniversary was also welcomed by a spokesperson of the former Moscow Helsinki Watch Group, now defunct. Ludmilla Alexeyeva, living then in the United States, emphasized that "no one at all" among the Soviet human rights activists in the USSR "wants the West to abandon Helsinki because, through these accords, human rights has ceased to be a purely internal affair for the Soviet leadership."[78] Her posture on human rights fulfillment was completely different from that of the Kremlin, yet from its different vantage point the article viewed Helsinki as significant in the same way as did the Soviet leadership. Alexeyeva was as critical of Bukovsky and his associates on the subject's significance as the Soviet government's organs might have been.

Nor were Western governments prepared to discard Helsinki as no longer useful. A detailed 250-page report of the US Helsinki Commission, completed in March 1985, concluded that

> Nevertheless, with all its shortcomings, what began in Helsinki in 1975 is still perceived by most participating Western States and many non-governmental sources as worth continued support.[79]

West European governments contended that the CSCE process had to be evaluated over the long term. The process could not be expected to bring about immediate and far-reaching improvements in human rights. Nor could it heal the ideological rift between East and West.

From the Western perspective, the study noted, "the mere existence of the CSCE process . . . has had a beneficial effect on life in all of Europe." It has helped the West maintain a "fabric of relations" with the East, however thin. And it has provided a "fixed point of reference for public opinion" with respect to human rights, whether in Eastern or Western Europe. The CSCE process was also seen as creating a framework to cope with East-West problems and tensions, thereby facilitating multilateral contacts. For the non-Soviet communist regimes in East Europe, CSCE offered a certain, if limited, maneuvering space. In sum, the study found that CSCE was both a symbol of the unity of Europe and of what remained of détente.

If, then, there was disappointment at Helsinki about what had transpired or not transpired in the human rights field, a certain hope remained. Indeed, according to one informed source, the "atmosphere" at the actual anniversary meeting in Helsinki "was better than expected."[80] The speeches may have been tough, but the private meetings and bilateral discussions were less belligerent than usual. The French Foreign Minister appropriately called it "a loosened atmosphere, but not yet détente."[81]

▪10▪

The Early Gorbachev and the Helsinki Process

I n his first few months in power, Mikhail Gorbachev hardly revealed any significant policy change. As with his predecessors, he considered the strained international climate to be the result of Washington's aggressive rearmament policy, particularly with respect to the introduction into Europe of Pershing II and cruise missiles, as well as the US decision to embark on the elaborate Strategic Defense Initiative (SDI). Perceiving arms control as the key to US-Soviet relations, he insisted that there could be no improvement in this relationship until Washington had abandoned SDI.[1] His first few months of office were marked by no notable inclinations toward a summit. Indeed, even when he accepted a proposal from President Ronald Reagan for a summit meeting, he remained fairly lukewarm about its outcome.

Nonetheless, a certain dynamism and flexibility had entered into the making of Soviet foreign policy. Highlighting this aspect of a generational change was the replacement in July of perennial Foreign Minister Andrei Gromyko by the relatively youthful Eduard Shevardnadze. The absence of the rigid *"nyet"*-saying Gromyko at the Foreign Ministry suggested that a new orientation was possible, one in which Gorbachev could display his own special approach. Yet, no new initiatives were immediately apparent. On the contrary, Gorbachev initially revived Soviet "peace initiatives" previously advanced by his predecessors.[2]

Certainly, there was little evidence at the Ottawa meeting that indicated what later came to be called "new thinking." Richard Schifter would recall in 1989 that the head of the Hungarian delegation to Ottawa "would tell us that the spirit of Gorbachev was hovering over the hall in which we were meeting and would soon be in evidence."[3] Schifter commented, "most of us were unable to detect even a whiff of it."

Nor was there any indication at the tenth-anniversary meeting of CSCE foreign ministers in Helsinki, six weeks after Ottawa, of a more enlightened Soviet foreign policy. While Shevardnadze referred in his speech to the Helsinki accord as a "document of truly historic significance," he avoided any reference to its human rights provisions. Instead, he found its significance in the requirement that "states . . . live in peace . . . cooperate fruitfully and not . . . foist one's own views and rules upon others."[4] Secretary of State George Shultz, at the anniversary ceremonies, expected little from the new Soviet leader. If the lesson of the first decade pointed to the fact that "greater security and a more stable peace . . . depend on greater freedom for the people of Europe," nonetheless, observed Shultz, "our expectations" need not be placed too high.[5] They would have to be tempered by an awareness "that progress might come slowly."

The Budapest Cultural Forum, which had also been called for at Madrid, convened on October 15, ran for some six weeks and ended on November 25, coinciding with the Geneva summit meeting. Attended by "leading personalities in the field of culture" from each of the participating states, the Forum focused on the problems of cultural creation, dissemination and cooperation in an East-West context.[6] The problems had their roots in such human rights issues as cultural opportunities for minorities, censorship and jamming.

The US delegation, including 25 luminaries from a variety of cultural fields, was headed by Walter Stoessel, Jr., a former prominent diplomat who had been brought out of retirement for this conference. He had held a number of top ambassadorial posts (including Poland, the FRG and the USSR) and eventually served as Deputy Secretary of State, a rare appointment for a career foreign service officer. The US posture, as it related to human rights, was tough. Typical was a presentation made by Professor Nathan Glazer of Harvard University, a distinguished sociologist who had written extensively on ethnic minority issues. He raised questions about the condition of Jews in Soviet society, and inquired as to how the authorities would protect the cultural rights of Jews when they were "transgressed." Those rights were spelled out: "to preserve their religion, their culture, to study their historic language and their history. . . ."[7]

Glazer later reported in a personal letter that the "huge" Russian delegation became "very excited" by his formal raising of the Soviet Jewish question.[8] The response made by Academician Julian Bromley, an ethnographer, was that Soviet Jews had full cultural freedom. To prove his point, he gave Glazer four pamphlets, all written in English. They constituted "fierce denunciations"—said Glazer—of Zionism and Israel. Bromley then assumed the offensive, a standard feature of Soviet debating tactics, by charging the United States with tolerating a "massive extent of anti-Semitism."

In testimony to the Helsinki Commission on December 11, 1985, Stoessel reported that US interventions similar to Glazer's covered cultural repression of other ethnic minorities in the USSR, as well as in Poland, Czechoslovakia and Romania.[9] Special attention was given over to the last country, especially its treatment of Hungarians in Transylvania. The main theme of these interventions was the right of minorities "to preserve and develop their particular cultures, including language instruction, and the preservation of cultural and historical monuments."[10]

But the US preoccupation, which would continue to mark its Helsinki outlook, was with the rights of the individual. On November 8, US delegation deputy head Sol Polansky urged the removal of all barriers to artistic expression. The central theme was put in the form of a question: "What is creativity without freedom?"[11] He commented that "to speak of the creative process is surely to speak of freedom." One of the delegates, William Least Heat-Moon, an American author of partly Indian origin, gave particular attention to the incarceration of authors in the USSR.[12] During the meeting, the US representatives provided the Soviet delegation a list of some 20 writers who were in prison.

The Soviet perspective, to say the least, was the very opposite. Nikolai T. Fedorenko, the editor-in-chief of the principal Soviet foreign literature review, *Inostrannaia literatura*, who also served as Secretary of the Soviet Writers' Union, had a rather limited view of artistic freedom. In his speech, he said that it was the writer's duty to work for peace. He put it in this way: "Nothing else is worth writing about except peace."[13] The theme was extended especially to nuclear war, which he believed to be a "rising threat." For him, "the role of the writer is to tell the truth about war and the rising threat of nuclear disaster."

Moscow sought at the Forum to have the participants focus only on detailed technical proposals for cultural cooperation and to ignore the larger issue of cultural freedom. The Soviets and their allies advanced proposals for "organized" cultural exchanges between orchestras, choirs and other cultural groups, as well as exhibitions.[14] "Organized" meant, of course, that on the Soviet side the state would be the organizer, with all the ramifications with respect to artistic freedom that flowed from this bureaucratic structure.

Other Soviet proposals had a distinctly political or ideological character. Culture and the arts were called on "to shape peaceful attitudes and behavior." Culture was to be subject to "democratization" to ensure that the masses have access to it. In the end, culture would be protected by penalizing "the spreading of lies and of hatred against other countries." Ultimately, Moscow rejected any assertion that respect for human rights and freedoms was a prerequisite for cultural development.[15] And it rejected, too, language that the individual and non-governmental cultural institutions had important roles to play in advancing culture. Moscow even refused to accept principles already contained in the Final Act for inclusion in a Budapest concluding document.

In view of the sharply clashing perspectives of East and West on the very meaning of artistic freedom, agreement on a final document would not be easy. According to a Helsinki Commission report, the Soviets "had decided early on against" any kind of substantive concluding document, even one that might simply list the 200 proposals put forward by cultural personalities and delegation officials from the CSCE parties.[16] Nor would the United States support a document that did not entertain a modicum of substantive points. Between "a bad document and no document," as Stoessel reported, the US would opt for no document.[17] This was the position it had taken in Ottawa.

There was one major difference at Budapest, however. According to Stoessel, "the demand and efforts for a written result ran high among most delegates."[18] But, from the US perspective, the major need of CSCE was not more documents, but rather more compliance with the existing documents that had already been adopted at Helsinki and Madrid. The absence of a document would reflect "the gap between East and West on matters concerning human rights and fundamental freedoms," the US delegation chief commented.

The United States was, however, prepared to accept a fallback position advanced by Hungary. The latter urged adoption of a short statement that the 35 CSCE states had met to discuss problems of the cultural mandate delineated at Madrid, and had expressed different and at times contradictory views.[19] This was somewhat similar to the Belgrade concluding document, but it emphasized the additional point that contradictory views had been expressed, which might prompt examination of these contradictions between East and West. Even this alternative failed to pass muster with the Romanians, who, by blocking consensus, killed any plan for a concluding document.[20] Why the Romanians took this action was not clear. Perhaps they were retaliating against Budapest's growing agitation on behalf of its compatriots in Romania, where repression of Magyar culture was marked.

If the absence of a concluding document was disappointing, so too was the inability of the United States to change Helsinki procedures in order to facilitate discourse among the participants. The US hoped for a give-and-take discussion among important cultural figures, which might have led to the kind of impact that made human rights and Western programming more valuable. Soviet insistence, in almost all instances, on adherence to standard rules prevented a more flexible and relaxed atmosphere and, therefore, an easier exchange.[21] Moscow insisted on the maintenance of speakers' lists and no limitation on the length of speeches. This precluded far-ranging open discussion on the plenary floor, although off the floor there was considerable interaction between the cultural specialists.

Washington looked on the Budapest meeting as a test of whether a Warsaw Pact country could provide the proper conditions for international non-governmental groups to meet and interact with private groups. The US perceived Helsinki meetings as an experience for stimulating or reinforcing basic ideas of democracy. The Cultural Forum was the first Helsinki meeting held in a Warsaw Pact country and, therefore, what would be permitted in Budapest relative to the Helsinki conference might provide precedents for CSCE meetings held in other communist countries. The problem, of course, was that Hungary was almost unique among Warsaw Pact countries in providing a certain degree of openness.

Yet, even here a mixed picture resulted. On the one hand, the government of Hungary refused a request from the International Helsinki Federation, an important NGO drawn from national and private Helsinki groups, to hold a symposium in hotel rooms during the first week of the Forum;[22] US Helsinki Watch had played a central role in the international group's effort. The last-minute refusal violated an earlier commitment made by Budapest, the host city, to follow the example laid down at the Madrid meeting concerning NGOs. Washington, no doubt due to the influence and orientation of the Helsinki Commission and Helsinki Watch, placed great emphasis on NGO organizations and their relationship with the CSCE process. Ambassador Stoessel strongly protested, both publicly and privately, the Hungarian government's decision.[23] On the other hand, and perhaps spurred by the Stoessel protest, the Federation was allowed to hold its seminars and meetings in private apartments provided by interested Budapest residents. If there was some concern in the US delegation that the authorities might take punitive action against Hungarians participating in the private seminars, none occurred. Stoessel, of course, chose to preempt by cautioning the Budapest authorities about "how seriously" the United States would view further misinterpretations of the Madrid precedent.[24] Both on formal and informal levels, the American delegation went out of its way to participate as observers in NGO meetings and to share copies of manuscripts delivered there with other interested delegates at the Forum.

Janet Fleischman, a US Helsinki Watch official who helped organize the seminars, which dealt with such topics as "Writers and Their Integrity" and "The Future of European Culture," described in testimony to the Helsinki Commission the uniqueness of the experience and its impact.[25] After noting that "this was the first time that private citizens from both East and West had met openly in a Warsaw Pact country," she pointed out that the Forum and seminar gave the "Hungarian opposition" the encouragement "to continue with their activities." International attention, her testimony noted, can be quite productive. Significantly, just prior to the opening of the Forum, the Hungarian government lifted the house arrest of one writer and informed two others that they could have the passports they sought.

From the vantage point of the organizer, the CSCE meeting in Hungary stirred unprecedented discussions among citizens about censorship and the persecution of the Hungarian minority in Romania. Such discussion, she observed, "is rarely permitted." Even more significantly, the Forum had an impact on democratic and dissident movements abroad. Solidarity in Poland prepared a special report that was forwarded to Budapest. Charter 77 in Czechoslovakia addressed an appeal to the Forum and compiled a book on culture in Prague. And Hungarian activists produced similar materials. For all these groups, she noted, "Helsinki is a framework for hope."[26]

Still, the absence of a concluding document raised questions about the sincerity of Gorbachev. Budapest was the second post-Madrid conference to end in deadlock. If this challenged the very future of Helsinki in the human rights field, it also gave special focus to Gorbachev's commitment to Basket III, because Budapest ended at roughly the same time that the Soviet leader had joined President Reagan in a summit statement that articulated the basket's purpose. At the Geneva summit in November 1985, Gorbachev appeared ready to accept Western language and Western concepts about the Helsinki process previously regarded as taboo. He joined President Reagan in a statement that drew directly from the formulations in Basket III of the Helsinki accord. They pledged the resolution of "humanitarian cases in the spirit of cooperation."[27] The words "humanitarian" and "cooperation" were the key words in the title of the Basket III opening section, which covered such "human contacts" as "reunion of families" and travel.

The new conceptual orientation to Helsinki's Basket III and its relationship to security and, therefore, to Basket I was part of a larger new conceptual orientation to détente, nuclear weapons, arms control and relations with the United States. At the November summit, Gorbachev quite unexpectedly had signaled a more flexible stance by seeming to waive the Kremlin's previous condition for progress in limiting nuclear arsenals. That condition had required the US to forgo Reagan's "Star Wars" program. Instead, the Soviet leader agreed to move forward in areas where there was "common ground."[28]

He made his thoughts clearer in a statement on January 15, 1986. In view of the emergence from the summit of "preconditions for a healthier international situation," the Soviet leader said he was prepared to move toward resolving the problems surrounding intermediate nuclear forces (INF) in Europe (i.e., the Soviet SS-20s and newly emplaced US Pershing II and cruise missiles).[29] Although the Soviet leader again criticized the "Star Wars" program, he carefully delinked it from the INF question. Even more significantly, he welcomed US insistence on verification with respect to removal of nuclear weaponry. "Sweeping and exact verification," Gorbachev said, is the "most important element of the disarmament process."[30] The perspective was vital for both an agreement on intermediate missiles and for the crucial Helsinki discussions on reducing surprise attack being held at the time in Stockholm.

But it was at the 27th Communist Party congress that the language and concepts articulated at the November summit truly became Gorbachev's very own. In his major policy address to the congress on February 25, the General Secretary formally declared that a fundamental principle of "an all-embracing system of international security" would be the "resolution in a humanitarian and positive spirit of questions related to the reuniting of families, marriage, and the promotion of contacts between people and between organizations."[31] It was an altogether remarkable statement. None of his predecessors had ever made reference to any provisions of the Helsinki accord other than those dealing with military security. And certainly, none ever spoke aloud about "humanitarian" aspects of Helsinki, including "reuniting of families" (which, of course, meant emigration).

Moreover, consideration of the resolution of humanitarian cases as integral to "international security" was even more striking. In writing or speeches, the Kremlin had never predicated, either before or after the Helsinki Final Act, international security on humanitarian considerations as formulated in Basket III. This was a characteristically Western notion, of which the US had become a champion. Beginning with President

Carter, the interweaving of human rights and security was presented as a critical index of modern and effective foreign policy.

Significantly, Gorbachev carefully avoided, in the beginning, using the words "human rights," which was very much implied in the Basket III formulation of "humanitarian." (Previous Soviet leaders had hewed to a narrow and rigid conception of human rights strictly grounded in economic terms.[32] Gorbachev's immediate predecessor, Konstantin Chernenko, had even published in 1981 a book entitled *Human Rights and Soviet Society*, which typified this Orwellian interpretation.)

Still, the emphasis given the word "humanitarian" constituted a milestone in Soviet ideological history. The word was simply alien to Bolshevik political literature. Some Soviet writers had earlier used the term "humanism," but only in order to chastise its advocates.[33] What had now brought about a linguistic revolution in Soviet society was a Helsinki accord formulation which Gorbachev embraced. The English word "humanitarian" was officially translated into Russian in Helsinki documents as *gumanitarnyi*. It is this latter Helsinki term which appeared in the speeches of Gorbachev and his foreign policy associates.

In July 1986, Gorbachev formally made the words "human rights" and "humanitarian" interchangeable. The occasion was special: François Mitterrand, the President of the country which made famous the "Declaration of the Rights of Man and Citizen," was paying the Soviet Union his first official visit. In greeting him at the Kremlin, Gorbachev said that the USSR was committed to "international cooperation on humanitarian problems and these are not mere words."[34] He then added that "the theme of human rights becomes even more acute on the threshold of the 21st century." For that reason, civilization would no longer "tolerate arbitrariness and lawlessness" within countries and in international affairs. Gorbachev concluded with the observation that "human rights" was "one of the components of the all-embracing system of security."

Increasingly during the latter part of 1986, Gorbachev's foreign policy views were described as "new political thinking." Two sources broadly characterize its outline. The first was the Gorbachev address to the 27th Communist Party Congress; the second was a theoretical analysis of foreign policy in the June 1986 issue of party journal *Kommunist* by a top Gorbachev aide, Anatoly Dobrynin, former Soviet Ambassador to the United States, then serving as head of the Party Central Committee's International Department.[35] Several key theses emerged from these sources: 1) the existence of "global problems" that can only be resolved through "cooperation on a world-wide scale"; 2) a "growing tendency towards interdependence of the states of the world community"; and 3) were the nuclear arms race to persist, "even parity will cease to be a factor of military-political restraint."

Additionally, tactical flexibility, a willingness to compromise, and an all-out repudiation of Brezhnev's foreign policy provided an encouraging frame of reference for reshaping Soviet foreign policy aims, including those toward Helsinki. Gorbachev summed up the new perspective in his congress address. After repudiating the Brezhnev policy line, he called for "restraint," "tactical flexibility" and "a readiness for mutually acceptable compromises . . . the aim being not confrontation, but dialogue and mutual understanding."[36]

The US administration recognized that the Moscow perspective had changed, at least to a degree. Assistant Secretary of State Schifter later recalled that, at the Geneva summit, "all" the US participants "came away with the impression that a significant change had taken place in the Soviet leadership."[37] He reported that President Reagan had introduced human rights concerns into the dialogue. Gorbachev's response, Schifter remembered, was "not hostile," but, at the same time, "we did not receive any clear assurances, either." For reasons that were not made clear, the US participants had hoped that some positive movement would occur with respect to Jewish emigration. But, "as the months passed," he added, "we saw no change in the Soviet Union's policies of repression."

The treatment of Andrei Sakharov, regarded everywhere as a symbol of Helsinki's essence, was indicative of the uncertainty of Soviet human rights policy during Gorbachev's first year. The Nobel laureate, profoundly anxious about his wife's urgent need for heart bypass surgery, had continued from his internal exile in Gorky to press the authorities for an exit visa. (Neither had trust in Soviet medical specialists performing such operations on them in the USSR.) Hunger strikes, interspersed with forced feedings, characterized his lonely and terrible isolation until the summer of 1985. Desperate, Sakharov wrote to Gorbachev pleading for his wife and stating his intent to "cease completely my public activities, except, of course, in exceptional cases."[38]

In October 1985, Yelena Bonner was finally issued a visa for travel abroad; in December, she went to Boston and underwent sextuple bypass heart surgery. After a six-month stay in the United States, during which she addressed a gathering at the House of Representatives on the occasion of Sakharov's 65th birthday, she rejoined her husband in June 1986. He had remained cut off from links to the outside world but had, nonetheless, displayed extraordinary personal courage in a letter dated

February 18 requesting that Gorbachev release all Soviet prisoners of conscience, 13 of whom he specifically cited by name. Not until early September 1986 did a copy of the letter become available to the Western press.[39]

For a moment in October 1985, Gorbachev seemed to be inclined to a more humane approach toward Sakharov. While traveling in Paris, the Soviet leader responded to a journalist's question on Sakharov by mentioning "reunification of families . . . and other matters of a humanitarian nature."[40] This was Basket III language. But on February 7, 1986, the General Secretary shot down the burst of optimism and hope. "Sakharov," he said, "remains the possessor of state secrets of particular importance and therefore is not able to leave the country."[41]

Nor was there much indication of leniency by a glasnost-oriented Kremlin. A detailed 235-page report to the US Congress by the Helsinki Commission published in November 1986 catalogued the continuing abuse of large numbers of political prisoners in the gulag, the total dismantling of the non-governmental structure of Helsinki monitors, the repression of national and ethnic groups, the crackdown of religion, and the misuse of psychiatry for punishment purposes.[42] Several exceptions to the depressing picture, nonetheless, suggested that a certain, if very limited, flexibility prevailed. Shcharansky had been released in February 1986, in exchange for a US-held Czech spy. It was a significant concession by Moscow to Washington's demands for the release of a powerful symbol in the West of freedom and of what Helsinki was supposed to represent.

The Commission report, which drew heavily upon reports of major human rights NGOs, also gave extensive attention to the other Warsaw Pact countries. Among the worst offenders in the report was Czechoslovakia, whose regime, said the report, "continues to exile, imprison and harass" citizens expressing criticism of the ruling group. After the late 1985 crackdown on the Jazz Section of the Czechoslovak Musicians' Union, Western cultural circles expressed consternation and dismay. Also singled out was Romania, which had "kept up harassment and arrests of Romanian citizens who have sought to act upon the rights guaranteed in the Helsinki Final Act." Helsinki Commission criticism extended as well to Bulgaria (mainly for suppression of its Turkish population), Poland and East Germany. Only Hungary received commendation because of its positive handling of emigration and travel requests and the absence of crude repressive techniques.

Soviet Jewry, not surprisingly, constituted a prime focus of the report. In the last analysis, the treatment of Soviet Jews, especially concerning reunion of families, provided a kind of barometric reading as to how the Final Act's Basket III was being implemented. Jewish emigration remained at an unusually low level—1,100 in 1985 and some 900 in 1986, probably the lowest two-year figure since Moscow first authorized the granting of fairly reasonable amounts of exit visas for Jews in 1971. Restriction on granting the visas, of course, meant an increasing number of refuseniks. By the end of 1986, the number was estimated at 20,000, although the precise amount in terms of known persons on refuseniks lists was 11,000.[43]

Enormously complicating the problem was Moscow's stepped-up practice of confiscating mail from abroad sent to Soviet Jews, especially refuseniks. Often that mail included new *vizov* (affidavits), which applicants for exit visas required before submitting a formal request for a visa. The practice was extensive, as disclosed in a study conducted by Congressman Benjamin A. Gilman for the House of Representatives Committee on Post Office and Civil Service in July 1985. The detailed report was entitled *A History of the Soviet Union's Deliberate Interference With the Flow of Mail.*[44] The confiscation or non-delivery of mail limited the number of Jewish applicants for exit visas, thereby enabling the Soviet authorities to argue that the number of Jews seeking to emigrate had declined. *The Times* (London) on November 28, 1985, amusingly commented that a new term, "waitniks," had arisen to describe Soviet Jews waiting to receive *vizov* from relatives in Israel but which the Soviet post office had failed to deliver.[45]

In a separate analysis published in September 1985, *Mailing to the Soviet Union*, the US Postal Service reported that a very sizable amount of mail sent by Americans to Soviet citizens appeared to have been "subject to arbitrary and unpredictable treatment."[46] Similar problems were found to exist for mail to the USSR from Canada, Western Europe and Israel. Complaints of Soviet interference, according to the Postal Service, included mail that should have been delivered but was returned to sender; mail which senders claimed violated no postal prohibition but was arbitrarily seized; and mail that Soviet authorities said had been delivered but had, in fact, not been.

Vizov were not the only form of mail lost or confiscated or returned. Interference with the privacy of letters, including registered letters, was not an infrequent phenomenon.

The assertions made by Congressman Gilman, a member of the Helsinki Commission, and by US government authorities called attention to Principle X of the Helsinki accord, which required fulfillment from the signatories of "obligations from treaties or other agreements, in conformity with international law to which they are parties." The specific treaty to which the USSR was a contracting party was the Universal Postal Convention. It forbade any interference with mail. In fact, the Soviet Constitution Article 56 guaranteed privacy of the mails and Russian Criminal Code Article 135 (replicated in the criminal codes of other union republics) proscribed violation of private correspondence.[47]

Nor did glasnost and the new thinking bring about, as yet, a change in the prevailing attitude to either Jewish culture or anti-Semitism. The teaching of Hebrew and Jewish history was strongly frowned upon, and those who engaged in such activity were subjected to harsh punishment. By mid-1986, according to a report of the Helsinki Commission, there were at least 18 Jewish activists serving prison or forced labor terms as a result of teaching or cultural work.[48] Two-thirds of them had been sentenced from mid-1984 to mid-1986, the period of Gorbachev's ascendancy and early rule.

The contradiction between principle and practice with respect to Jewry was especially highlighted in February 1986. Gorbachev, in an interview with the French communist newspaper *L'Humanité*, said that anti-Semitism was "impossible in the USSR" because it was "prohibited by law and constitutes a crime."[49] Technically, the Soviet leader was correct. Article 36 of the Soviet Constitution prohibited discrimination against ethnic minorities, and Article 74 of the Russian Criminal Code made the stirring up of enmity between racial or ethnic groups a crime. The trouble with Article 74 of the Russian Criminal Code was its application to anti-Semitism. No one had ever been known to have been arrested in the USSR, let alone convicted and sentenced, because of anti-Semitic incitement since the 1920s.

Indeed, in February, at just about the time of the *L'Humanité* interview, the USSR published in Leningrad a new work, *On the Class Essence of Zionism* by Aleksandr Romanenko, whose views were decidedly bigoted.[50] It was published in an edition of 50,000 copies—no small amount. Romanenko repeated the traditional anti-Semitic canard that Zionism was striving for "world supremacy," and that its philosophy was rooted in the belief that "the Jews are superior to other peoples and their vocation is to rule over the whole of mankind." Romanenko claimed that the Zionists had perceived the post-Nazi era as a "unique historical opportunity" to achieve the aim of world domination. In January 1987, the party academic journal, *Questions of CPSU History*, severely criticized the Romanenko book as replete with "factual inaccuracies, distortions and errors" including the "manipulation" of quotations from the classics of Marxism and Leninism.[51] Nonetheless, TASS extolled the work in a Russian-language broadcast of May 22, 1987, which alleged that "the Zionists have as their goal domination over countries and peoples."[52]

The results of the Geneva summit, the Budapest forum, and the 27th Party Congress made for many questions as human rights experts gathered for the third and final human rights experts meeting, scheduled for Bern, Switzerland, April 15 to May 27, 1986. (Technically, the subject of Bern was "human contacts," but, like the Budapest Cultural Forum, it was intimately related to human rights.) How would Moscow's diplomats handle human rights issues at Bern? Would there be any indication of a policy modifying the icily negative posture of Ottawa and Budapest? With a dynamic new personality in the Kremlin beginning to use the human rights language of Helsinki, how would it be reflected at Bern? The meeting was critically important in demonstrating how far Moscow was prepared to go.

If the Soviets acquiesced at all to holding an experts' meeting on the topic of human contacts, a subject which Moscow and its Warsaw Pact allies had fiercely resisted at Madrid, it was because of the personal intervention of the Spanish Prime Minister. Besides, Soviet procedures with regard to emigration and travel had reached such restrictive levels as to invite universal disapproval.

How Moscow would react to the question of emigration was of keen interest to Soviet Jewry and world Jewry. Gorbachev was on record as of February favoring the treatment of requests for exit visas in a "positive and humanitarian" manner. Earlier, he told a French interviewer that refuseniks should receive exit visas after a maximum five- to ten-year waiting period. These statements offered a certain encouragement.[53] In February 1986, a Soviet scholar on the nationality question, Ye. Tadevosyan, estimated that between 10-15 percent of Soviet Jews, if given the opportunity, would choose to emigrate. This would mean a range stretching from 180,000 to 270,000, if the baseline were the census data of 1979 (1,811,000 Jews); 370,000 had already requested and received a *vizov* from a relative in Israel, the initial step in the emigration process.

In practical terms, the emigration situation for Soviet Jews at the beginning of 1986 had worsened. During the first five months of the year, the exodus rate had plunged to its lowest level in nearly a quarter-century. The total was 331 persons, 25 percent below the 1985 rate.[54] The lowest monthly figure—less than 50—came in April, on the eve of Bern, and the same figure was reached again in May.

The Committee of Concerned Scientists—a highly respected American scientific group—provided especially poignant documentation to delegations in Bern.[55] It listed 782 Soviet Jewish scientists, including physicians and engineers, who had been denied the right to be reunited with their kin in Israel. Some of the refuseniks had been waiting for more than the five- to ten-year period Gorbachev had said was the outer limit for those presumed to have "possessed state secrets;" 93 on the list had been waiting for more than ten years; 513 had been waiting from five to ten years. Details on the 606 specialists waiting more than five years were included.

The Committee study rejected the argument that the refuseniks knew state secrets. "Exhaustive documentation" demonstrated, according to the Committee, that the supposed state secrets "have been openly published" and, besides, other "colleagues who engaged in the very same work" were allowed to emigrate. The Committee presented a detailed picture of great distress affecting the scientist-refusenik community. Its study showed: "Many have been demoted or dismissed outright from their jobs, denounced by co-workers at open meetings, barred from attending professional meetings, shunned by neighbors and vilified in the media." In addition "their mail has been intercepted and their telephones have been disconnected."

Appeals from Soviet Jews bombarded the delegations to Bern. One was signed by 47 of the most prominent refuseniks: "We appeal to you with the request to help us in realization of our right to leave the USSR, the right that has been guaranteed, in particular, by the Helsinki accords."[56] They argued that "if no solution of so simple and easy a problem as Jewish emigration . . . is soon found, then other parts of the Helsinki accords, more difficult to resolve and control, may be indefinitely suspended."

In essence, they were posing the question of trust. Were a country to refuse to adhere to one part of an agreement, how could it be trusted to fulfill other parts of the agreement?

Advocacy came not only from and for Soviet Jews. West Germany's International Society for Human Rights distributed from its temporary office in Bern a 122-page dossier containing details of 1,677 divided families in East Germany, Poland, Romania, and the Soviet Union.[57] The World Federation of Free Latvians distributed a 48-page dossier on alleged Soviet violations of Helsinki human contact provisions.[58] The Turkish Association of Immigrants from Bulgaria sent a delegation to Bern to protest Bulgarian restrictions on emigration of its ethnic Turkish community.[59]

Individuals and groups came to the Swiss city to protest personally, often in front of the hotel where the Soviet delegation resided or in front of the conference center.[60] Simon Levin, who carried a banner "Release My Wife and Child," had emigrated in 1978. Just before leaving, he married his long-time girlfriend, Tamara Tretyakova. Both expected that she would be able to follow him within months. But her 14 applications had been refused. Their child, now eight years old, could only communicate with her father by phone. Other demonstrating petitioners were immediate relatives of famous refuseniks—the sister of Ida Nudel, the sister-in-law of Vladimir Slepak, the son of Lev Blitshtein.

Pentecostals, too, were among the demonstrators. Stanislav and Nadezhda Zherdev and their six children offered an illustration. The night before this Pentecostal family left Moscow in August 1980, their seventh child, Sergei, was taken away by a family member. Since then, the family had been pleading for the Soviet Union to allow Sergei to leave to join his brothers and sisters living in Sweden.

In his very opening statement, chief Soviet delegate Yuri Kashlev denied that a problem existed or that emigration was a viable question for the USSR. "In the Soviet Union," he said, "there are neither social nor national causes for emigration. We have no unemployment and the Constitution of the USSR guarantees equal social, political and cultural rights to all of its citizens of every nationality."[61] The statement was less than accurate, but even if true, hardly pertinent, as the Universal Declaration of Human Rights and the International Covenant on Civil and Political Rights—to both of which the Helsinki Final Act referred—regarded emigration as a *right*, totally unrelated to whether or not an applicant had a good reason or personal need to emigrate.

Far more significant was a Soviet proposal to seek to turn the clock back, not merely to 1975, prior to the Helsinki Final Act, but to a pre-1970 epoch, when Jewish emigration had been virtually non-existent. Jewish emigration would be brought to an end. Not only was the intent startling, so too was the tactical maneuver. It was not openly announced; rather it was initially hidden in deceptive, almost innocent, language. The granting of visas for family visits and reunion of families, according to the Soviet proposal, was to be limited to "participating states," that is to the 35 CSCE signatories; Israel—the indicated destination of the overwhelming majority of Jewish emigrants—was patently excluded.

The maneuver was a remarkable act of gall.[62] By stealth, an emigration process that had lasted over a decade and was very much integral to Helsinki would be halted. Helsinki specialists could not recall a similar maneuver that had struck as deeply at the heart of the Helsinki process. The deception was rather quickly uncovered by several Western delegations, notably Canada, the United Kingdom and the United States. When pressed, the Soviet delegation acknowledged that they sought to prevent "reunion of families" in Israel. The rationale had a political twist; Moscow simply would not allow the sending of Jews to the "war danger zone" of Israel or to "occupied Palestine." Ultimately, the maneuver failed.

The Soviet delegation's attempt testified to the limitations of the Gorbachev commitment. When challenged on the refusenik issue, Soviet officials disclosed that only a single refusenik family—Veniamin Gulko, a chess grandmaster, and his immediate kin—would be allowed out. At the same time, the Soviet delegation made clear in private talks that Moscow now considered Basket III a dead issue. What warranted further talk, the delegation observed, were the trade and technical-exchange provisions of Basket II.

The primary US goal at Bern was better compliance with already existing commitments. Thus, the focus was upon implementation of the travel and reunion-of-family provisions of Basket III. Numerous moving cases filled the pages of Helsinki Commission and State Department documentation. Russian wives unable to join their American husbands were among a variety of binational-marriage separation cases involving several East European countries. Some cases involved American citizens from birth who were taken while young to the Soviet Union by their parents and who were seeking to reclaim their US birthright through emigration. A host of other refusal cases related to travel requests for visiting a dying relative in another country or attending such intimate family ceremonies as births or funerals. An added human dimension to the agenda came as a result of the Chernobyl nuclear explosion which occurred just as Bern was beginning. Canadian and American relatives of Soviet citizens in the damaged Ukrainian area found it difficult to reach their kin by mail or phone. This was an aspect of the general problem of postal and telephonic communication Westerners seeking to reach their families in the USSR had recently encountered.

The head of the US delegation was Dr. Michael Novak, a well-known conservative scholar on philosophy and theology at the American Enterprise Institute. While not a professional diplomat, he had served for several years as the US representative on the United Nations Commission of Human Rights. A week prior to the Bern meeting, he traveled to Moscow to outline to Soviet Foreign Ministry officials what the US sought. His emphasis in these "consultations" was upon "concrete results" with respect to individual cases of divided spouses and with respect to large numbers of families seeking reunification.[63]

In an interview with the Radio Free Europe correspondent in Bern, Novak outlined the major issues he would be raising.[64] These included an inquiry into what rules or regulations guide decision making of those Soviet officials who made determinations in the emigration field. All too often, he made clear, the determinations appeared to be totally arbitrary and capricious. He would also inquire into extensive reports about deprivations, including job losses, for those seeking to emigrate. "We consider this," he said, "a very severe breach of the [Helsinki] agreement. . . ." Noting that he had a large list of these reported instances of "victimization," Novak said that he was determined to air the problem and seek redress.

The US Ambassador to the Bern talks made clear that he intended to present a list of individual cases to appropriate delegations. He also planned to raise the question of the right of an émigré to return to his homeland for a visit. And he expressed special and strong interest in contacts between persons from the same religious community but living in different countries. What was the extent of restriction on these contacts, and might it be eased? Beyond the question of contacts, he indicated deep concern about religious deprivation generally in East Europe.

In Novak's opening address on April 17, he movingly described America's family links with Eastern Europe.[65] About one in ten Americans, 23 million in all, Novak said, have "at least one family root in Central and Eastern Europe." But it is precisely these Americans who "find it most difficult to exercise freely the rights of human contact with their families abroad." He reported "pleas" from relatives (of Americans) in the Baltic states, Ukraine and the various countries of Eastern Europe who sought either to visit or to move abroad.

Novak pointed out that Americans are "a family people" and, as such, "our hearts are drawn to the divided spouses, separated from each other's arms for so many years." He added that "we are [also] touched by family members, seeking to join that portion of their family tree they freely choose." The attention to the personal heritage and roots of Americans was reinforced by the list of cases of binational marriages and separated families that Novak had personally given the Russians when he visited Moscow on the eve of Bern.

But the emotionally effective speech covered a far broader spectrum than cases involving Americans. Novak went back to the very first and founding CSCE meeting, in July 1973 in Helsinki, and cited Sir Alec Douglas-Home, then Britain's Foreign Secretary, about how Helsinki was about "ordinary people." Novak continued: "Ordinary people. If we do not improve the life of ordinary people, words are empty." The removal of obstacles, impediments, barbed-wire walls, and legal administrative tangles was essential to fulfill the "dream" of "ordinary people" for direct contact.

The generalizations made evident that the US delegation's perspective would not be restricted simply to Americans. Indeed, Novak went out of his way to pay homage to the Helsinki "citizen monitors," whether in the Soviet Union or in other communist countries, who took the words of the Helsinki accord with "dreadful seriousness."

Precisely because the Bern conference was geared to the needs of people and would also serve as a test of Moscow's new orientation, it was important to give the meeting maximum public exposure. Prior to the opening of the Bern conference, the United States and its NATO allies made a determined effort to end the closed-session character of Helsinki meetings.[66] If the US initiative had succeeded, certain sessions, at least for the first and last weeks and at intervals in between, would be open to the press and to the non-governmental organization representatives. The rationale for this radical departure from Helsinki precedent was that "human contacts" had a great relevance to the public. No doubt, too, Western Helsinki specialists thought the public airing of violations of Basket III provisions would help prevent future inroads.

The West had undertaken a similar initiative in Ottawa, fiercely resisted by the USSR. The bitter dispute had been finally resolved through an agreement that permitted the last day of Ottawa to be open to the public for the concluding speeches. In return for granting the West a one-day public session, the Soviet Union had won observance by the conference of a full day to commemorate the end of World War II on the occasion of its anniversary.

The USSR even more strongly resisted the proposal for open sessions at Bern. Ambassador Yuri Kashlev initially rejected out of hand any open session at all, as there was nothing, he said, to trade off (in contrast to the commemorative-anniversary trade-off).[67] He charged that the West wanted the open sessions as an exercise to bring anti-Soviet agitators into the conference. According to Kashlev, diplomacy could not be conducted publicly, and Soviet policies should not be held up to criticism before a Western public that did not understand them. He even objected to a Western proposal that three weeks be devoted to examining violations of the present agreements.

The dispute over openness had raged for almost a week in preparatory talks before Bern formally started. British delegate Sir Anthony Williams sought to interpret Soviet adamancy as a consequence "of a system inca-pable of trusting its own people or believing that they will want to come home."[68] April 14 marked a climactic moment. The debate ran for the en-tire day, most of the night, and into the morning of the opening day of the conference. Finally, a compromise was reached permitting the starting session to be open. The West also won agreement that three weeks would be given over to examining violations of Helsinki provisions.

Soviet refusal to allow open sessions made little difference in the end. The US and several of its allies gave the media, as they had at previous Helsinki meetings, detailed accounts of what transpired at closed plenary and working group sessions.

Moscow's negativism with respect to Jewish emigration and openness, a throwback to Soviet tactics at earlier Helsinki meetings, was mitigated by two redeeming features, no doubt the product of Gorbachev's new thinking. First, from the opening session on (in contrast to the heated preparatory discussions), the Soviet delegation avoided a hostile and con-frontational posture, except in rare instances. As described in a Helsinki Commission report, the "direct" human rights charges by the United States and the West "did not evoke responses from the East as confronta-tional as those at meetings in Ottawa and Budapest."[69] Kashlev con-ducted himself in the courteous and attentive style of the traditional diplomat, not the ideologue. While this could not be said of all his col-leagues, his own non-confrontational stance was seen as a reflection of the new Minister of Foreign Affairs, Eduard Shevardnadze.

But style could not hide unchanged fundamental policy. And, when that policy was challenged in a major way, the previous traditionally crude manner came roaring back. Novak chose to accompany his April 17 speech with a list of long-term refuseniks (appended to the printed ad-dress), which was distributed to each delegation.[70] The bulk of the names—47—were Soviet Jews seeking to emigrate to Israel. Only some 23 were asking to emigrate to the United States and the West. One of the Soviet delegation angrily called the list "libelous" and denounced it as "McCarthyism." Why the list was referred to as "libelous" and how it was supposed to have resembled "McCarthyism" were not explained. The abusive terms, upon analysis, made little sense.

The US delegation did not have a "one-note" approach to the Soviet Union. Novak went out of his way in his April 17 address to welcome Gorbachev's willingness to join in the November summit statement con-cerning reunion of families and his February 25, 1986, speech on the same subject to the Soviet Communist Party Congress.[71] He also praised

Moscow's willingness since Geneva to resolve 15 percent of the cases on America's "divided-family" list.

But what about the larger issue of granting exit visas in accordance with international standards of the Universal Declaration of Human Rights? The West pressed strongly on this; indeed, the French went so far as to urge the abolition of all exit visas. The USSR did show a certain flexibility on the Western proposals, agreeing to a US proposal requiring the publication of all laws and regulations governing travel and exit visas. It also accepted a British proposal calling for the removal of obstacles to postal and telephone communications. While important, acceptance of these two standards was insufficient from a US viewpoint. The spokesman of the US delegation, Ed Alexander, told the Associated Press: "If that's all a final document would consist of, we would not accept it."[72]

The major problem in the human contacts area remained the granting of exit visas without imposing excessive or irrational impediments and obstacles. During the meeting's last three days of intensely acrimonious debate, the Soviets resisted agreeing to an unofficial text circulated by the neutral/non-aligned bloc. Sir Anthony Williams, angered by the stonewalling tactics of the Soviets, announced that the West would table its own document setting forth the West's position on every agenda item.[73] It was 4:00 A.M. on May 26—the last day of the meetings—and, by then, 19 hours of continuous debate had led to frayed nerves and tempers. The Soviets walked out.

At 9:30 A.M. the delegates re-assembled to discuss a final neutral/non-aligned document now presented on a "take-it-or-leave-it" basis. In seeking to satisfy Moscow, the new document incorporated elements which evoked deep concern among various Western delegations, including the United States. The addition of the phrase "when personal and professional circumstances permit" to a statement that governments would "favorably" consider applications for travel "for family visits" was especially disturbing.[74] Novak saw it as a "loophole" that "cynical governments" would use "massively" to prevent travel. Another compromise formulation provided that, while a government should grant on a priority basis a travel visa for the applicant to receive medical treatment abroad, the final decision can be made only on the basis of a medical certificate issued by the medical authority in the country of residence. The potential for abuse of this provision was great, and in fact the Soviets had frequently used such a dodge to prevent Sakharov's wife, Yelena Bonner, from traveling abroad for medical treatment.

A third compromise formulation placed conditions on a number of positive travel provisions. It stipulated that the new liberalized travel privileges could be made invalid if "a change of essential significance occurs in the circumstances of the applicant." The possibilities for abuse in the interpretation of this condition were also endless. Finally, concerning travel for religious purposes, the right was restricted to "representatives" of religious institutions rather than to individual believers. In the same way, importation of religious publications and religious objects was not for distribution to congregations, but rather only to institutions.

Notwithstanding these serious and disturbing limitations, the Soviet delegation had agreed, it was clear, to some modest steps toward acceptable human rights standards in the human contacts field. Sir Anthony Williams put it succinctly when he commented that the non-aligned draft carried "pointers towards more humane arrangement for human contacts . . . and . . . the potentialities of these pointers . . . outweighed the document's obvious weaknesses."[75] Flexibility made possible a document that offered what some thought was a certain amount of progress even though the draft carried loopholes and potential for abuse.

The key question was whether the display of a limited flexibility warranted that the United States and the West accept the proposed concluding document prepared by the neutral/non-aligned bloc. The issue led to the single biggest Helsinki diplomatic brouhaha involving the United States since the process was launched.

Suggested guidelines for dealing with the problem of a concluding document were outlined in an April 24 letter to Ambassador Novak from Helsinki Commission Chairman D'Amato and his co-chairman, Congressman Steny Hoyer.[76] After commending him on various addresses he had delivered in Bern, they reminded him that, to the Commission, "a realistic appraisal of compliance should remain the principal focus of the [Bern] meeting—not the formulation of new commitments or of a final document." That theme had been emphasized in an earlier Commission letter to Novak; now it was repeated, but with additional clarification and elaboration.

Only under one of three separate sets of circumstances, the Commission letter added, would a concluding document be "desirable." First, significant progress would have to take place on specific Soviet and Eastern European reunion-of-family cases, including forward movement in the area of Soviet Jewish emigration. The stress upon Soviet Jewish emigration was crucial in appreciating the Western response to the Soviet initiative in trying to end the Helsinki connection with "non-participating states." A second set of circumstances would take account of "only minimal" or inconsequential progress on individual cases, but which at the same time offered a "realistic expectation that new promises would lead to such progress." The final set was one under which significant progress on cases was not taking place and there was no "realistic hope" for future progress. Under these circumstances, "a short statement of failure" as a concluding document would be acceptable.

The D'Amato-Hoyer letter went on to provide the overarching rationale for the highly cautionary line that the Commission took. Were an upbeat concluding document accepted in the absence of either of the two positive sets of circumstances, then the result would be "further disillusionment with the CSCE process and additional loss of public credibility." This was a key assertion, an outgrowth of the Commission's evaluation of the increasing public suspicions about, if not overt hostility to, the Helsinki process.

The tough guidelines could not easily be bypassed. The Commission's status remained strong with Congress and with the non-governmental organization community. The Commission's staff director, Sam Wise, highly experienced in foreign affairs—he had previously worked for the State Department—was now serving as a principal deputy to Novak. Prior to the Bern session, the Commission had insisted that Wise be named as an ambassador. Resistance to the title from the State Department was hardly unexpected but, in the end, the Department felt obliged to capitulate. A crucial factor in the enhancement of the Commission's status was selection of Congressman Dante Fascell, its founding chairman, as the Chairman of the House Foreign Affairs Committee. In his new role, he could exert considerable influence on the administration and the State Department, besides exercising broad leverage on the Commission staff itself.

When Fascell moved to the Committee chairmanship, he took with him Spencer Oliver as top staffer. Oliver continued his previous strong interest in the Helsinki Commission and was formally accorded the status of "consultant" to it. At a critical moment, he would bring his own considerable political weight to bear upon the US delegation at Bern.

The caution exhibited in the Commission's missive of April 24 to Ambassador Novak was indirectly reinforced by testimony to the Commission by Anatoly Shcharansky three weeks later (see Chapter 11). He expressed very strong disappointment with the US decision to approve the Madrid concluding document at a time when he and other prisoners of conscience were still suffering in the gulag.[77] Shcharansky appeared to imply that the United States should not have agreed to the document until at least some prisoners had been released. The testimony tended to uphold and strengthen the conservative and hesitant policy line toward concluding documents at Helsinki meetings.

How would the United States react to the proposed concluding document? Throughout the final exhausting and exhaustive hours of debate and negotiation, there was no clear, definitive signal from Ambassador Novak that he would reject the neutral/non-aligned document or refuse consensus. Not that he had registered any great enthusiasm or even partial support for it. Everyone recognized that he was not too happy with the document, but no one got the impression that he felt strongly enough to reject it. He sought delay of a decision until he consulted with Washington. But circumstances produced an unforeseen hurdle. The last negotiating session fell on Memorial Day, part of a long weekend, and reaching anyone in authority in Washington posed severe problems. Consultation was not easy, but by the afternoon of May 26, a decision had been reached.

Novak did talk to Rozanne Ridgway, by then Assistant Secretary of State for European Affairs, which included Helsinki matters. As she related in an interview later, she told Novak that the decision was his to make and that the Department would back him up on whatever conclusion he reached.[78] It is apparent, too, that he received advice from Assistant Secretary Schifter, the Department's principal officer on human rights. Schifter considered the draft document wholly negative; his office's subsequent analysis demonstrated to his satisfaction that, in virtually every respect, the document constituted a significant retreat from the Helsinki and Madrid accords.[79]

There was a third person whose advice had to be factored into Novak's decision-making process. Spencer Oliver had shown up in Bern over the weekend with a congressional delegation. Oliver reportedly advised Novak strongly against approval.[80] The correspondent for *The Los Angeles Times* reported that various members of the congressional group told newsmen that the US delegation to Bern had "goofed" and had "given away" too much in the negotiating process.[81] What apparently was meant by those congressmen interviewed was that Novak should have unhesitatingly opposed the proposed draft.

At about 9:30 P.M. on Monday night, May 26, Ambassador Novak finally told the other delegations that, "after very careful review, my government cannot give its consent."[82] The arguments he advanced were consistent with, and indeed seemed to echo, the language of the D'Amato-Hoyer letter of April 24. After noting how "compliance" with the demands of Helsinki "has declined" in recent years, Novak went on to talk eloquently about the importance of "the credibility of words" as the "strength" of the Helsinki process, and then made a crucial point. Given the "demonstrated decline in compliance in recent years," the United States considered it essential for the Bern document "to set a high standard." If not, then "the public would lose confidence."

What was missing, in his view, was the required "high standard" to compensate for the inadequate level of compliance. Instead of a high standard, the proposed concluding document had "loopholes," Novak said, which "cumulatively . . . eat like moths into our founding documents." Later, in an article for the European edition of *The Wall Street Journal*, he added the adjective "dangerous" to "loopholes," thereby challenging what many thought were "modest steps" forward.[83]

The decision to veto the consensus was actually communicated to CSCE members earlier, but West German Ambassador Ekkehard Eickhoff, totally stunned by the American decision, desperately sought a delay of the plenary in the hope of changing the US view. The West Germans had a special stake in the Helsinki process, probably benefitting more from it than any other CSCE member.[84] Through the expected deepening of contacts with East Germans as well as with Germans throughout Eastern Europe, Eickhoff saw the Bern document as a valuable stepping-stone for advancing détente. He had played a major role in the NATO caucus at Bern, and in the negotiating process generally, to win support for the compromises that went into the draft.

According to an oral account by Ed Alexander, press officer of the delegation, Eickhoff had met Novak at about 5:30 P.M. on May 26 on the steps of the hotel where the Bern conference was being held.[85] In desperation, he pleaded with Novak to permit a three-hour delay of the plenary so that he could reach Foreign Minister Hans-Dietrich Genscher, at the moment on an official visit to Turkey, with the thought that Genscher might call Secretary of State Shultz. As Alexander recalled the encounter, Eickhoff said: "I am pleading with you not only on behalf of Germany but on behalf of European humanity." The rhetorical excess availed him little. Shultz rebuffed the diplomatic last-minute personal, frantic and public intervention of Genscher.

The repercussions, not surprisingly, were disconcerting. *The Times* (London) reported: "US goes out on a limb spoiling consensus at East-West meeting."[86] Rudolf Torovsky, the top Austrian diplomat at Bern and a key figure in the neutral/non-aligned bloc who had played a crucial role in negotiating the compromise, called the US veto "incomprehensible."[87] His Swiss colleague in the negotiating process told Alexander that the act was "outrageous."[88] What angered the Swiss delegate was his perception of Novak as being favorably disposed to the compromise concluding document throughout the discussions and then suddenly reversing himself. The respected *Neue Zürcher Zeitung* reported that "for days on end" the US delegate "raised no objections" to what he later said were unacceptable proposals.[89] Instead, the American response had been a "vast silence."

Some Western commentators pointed out that the veto played into Moscow's hands. *The Los Angeles Times* dispatch from Bern began: "If an aim of Soviet diplomacy is to separate America from Europe, then the Reagan administration's performance here . . . must look to the Kremlin like the beginning of a dream come true."[90] British columnist Neal Ascherson wrote a sharply critical essay in *The Observer*, which was headlined: "An American Veto Delights a Russian."[91] He referred to the Soviet Ambassador as "Happy, happy Mr. Kashlev." Kashlev himself was pointed in his comments. Calling the US act "the philosophy of a world policeman," he commented:

> This decision was probably planned a long time ago. We believe that the United States is trying to kill off the whole Helsinki process. Following the successive failures at Ottawa, Budapest and Bern . . . they want to prevent any closer co-operation between Eastern and Western Europe. . . .[92]

The blistering assault not only served to exploit the American-West European split; it expressed Moscow's irritation with Washington's decision. According to Alexander, Viktor Shikalov, Kashlev's deputy, took him aside at a Soviet press conference on May 27 and told him: "Give Max [Kampelman] and Novak this message: 'This is the last time the US is going to cheat the Soviet Union.'"[93] He added that the United States had made the Soviets "look like fools."

Especially harsh was the criticism directed at the US decision by a leading anti-communist voice in the non-governmental community, Leonard Sussman, Executive Director of Freedom House. In testimony given at formal Helsinki Commission hearings, Sussman argued: "For us to veto against the judgement of all our friends and neutrals lets the Soviets completely off the hook. Indeed, we give them the clear advantage to portray the US as the sole villain of the meeting."[94] In Sussman's opinion, the neutral/non-aligned draft was "an improvement over both the Helsinki Final Act (1975) and the Madrid Concluding Document (1983)." If the "improvement" was rather limited and weak, it was hardly advisable to enable the Soviets to be given "an ill-deserved victory" in a forum where they were always on the defensive. Sussman saw the US action as a virtual withdrawal from the Helsinki process.

Not all the public comments were hostile; conservative press organs praised Novak. *The Wall Street Journal*, in an editorial entitled "Breakthrough in Bern," called Novak's decision "courageous" and predicted that it would signal CSCE members at the follow-up meeting in Vienna that "Americans are serious enough about negotiation to reject language that doesn't represent progress."[95] Norman Podhoretz, editor of *Commentary*, in a column appearing in a number of major publications, also hailed the decision as displaying "courage."[96] Novak's willingness to stand alone was compared to President Reagan's act to repudiate SALT II. Warm endorsement was also extended by *The Economist*, which wondered aloud about the value of Helsinki if its provisions were not fulfilled.[97]

The US rupture of NATO unity was at the center of the storm. The question of whether the proposed compromise agreement on a concluding document was an advance, however small, or a retreat in the Helsinki process may have been quite pertinent, but tended to diminish as a focus of concern. Disagreement in the evaluation of this question was, of course, important to determining the justness or correctness of the US decision. Outsiders, however, and even well-informed specialists found it difficult to reach a definitive judgment on what sports enthusiasts might have referred to as a "close call."

The report in *The Los Angeles Times* by Don Cook underscored his perception of the central element by stating that this was "the first time in any international forum since World War II, the United States voted alone, against all the nations of Europe...."[98] Whether the sharp, unqualified assessment was accurate would be difficult to verify with certainty. What did seem to be certain was that within the Helsinki forum, and within the full view of the European and American publics, the United States chose for the first time to split openly from its European allies. Even when Ambassador Arthur Goldberg had strong differences with NATO allies at the Belgrade meeting, it had been deliberately kept from public view. Certainly, matters at the time had not been permitted to come to a head over a major substantive Helsinki issue.

The perspective of Ambassador Max Kampelman, the architect of the Madrid concluding document, was especially pertinent; it was largely because of his strong determination that a Bern conference on human contacts had been approved at Madrid. By the time of Bern, Kampelman was President Reagan's chief arms negotiator, and was deeply preoccupied with the Soviets at Geneva. But even though heavily involved in this top-priority task, he did not neglect the Helsinki process. On one occasion during the Bern meeting, he showed up in the Swiss capital for a full day of discussions, speeches and a press conference.[99] It was apparent that he was following Helsinki developments closely. Two months after Bern ended, on July 23, Kampelman told an interviewer in his office at the State Department that he was puzzled and disturbed by the veto at Bern. This should "never" have occurred, he emphasized.[100] It is absolutely essential that the unity of NATO be maintained, he mused. A concluding document whether at Bern or Madrid he said, was not "essential," but "the unity of the allies is." How the veto came about was mystifying to him.

Oddly enough, the US decision was not unwelcome in some NATO quarters. Canadian Ambassador William Bauer, in his lengthy address to the closing session, said "it would be a mistake . . . to concentrate too much of our disappointment on our inability to produce a document."[101] The "more serious causes for disappointment" were to be found, in his view, in the failure of the Soviets to "signal some relaxation of their restrictive practices and policies concerning human contacts." The hope spurred by Gorbachev's address to the 27th Party Congress had been undermined by Moscow's actual policies. Throughout the session, Bauer had made clear his deep disappointment with Soviet human rights performance, including Moscow's total unresponsiveness to Canada's list of persons who sought to emigrate there. Nor was he pleased with the neutral/ nonaligned text, which he thought had been too greatly compromised.

Several smaller NATO partners communicated in private interviews their dissatisfaction with the text and with Soviet conduct.[102] Their misgivings were quite pronounced. Assistant Secretary Ridgway, in later testimony to the Helsinki Commission, also noted this point by observing that "other governments" were "happy" that the document was not adopted at Bern.[103] Even Sir Anthony Williams, who was a key player in moving for the endorsement of the neutral/non-aligned document, was sympathetic. He revealed in his final speech that the United Kingdom's decision to support the document was reached "a little reluctantly."[104] He said he recognized its "obvious weakness," but thought that it was "outweighed" by positive "potentialities." Yet, he concluded that "we can only respect their [the American] views."

What seems apparent is that, if the United States had taken a clear and strong line from the very beginning of the negotiating process on the concluding document, it could have decisively swayed a significant number of NATO allies. A top Commission staffer who had been at Bern most of the time related in a detailed interview that Ambassador Novak had signaled to all concerned that he was disposed to accept a concluding document if it was not "too bad" and if the United States received "solid evidence" with respect to divided families.[105] Significantly, the solid evidence of the divided-family cases, whereby 117 persons were approved for reunification, did not arrive in Bern until three hours *after* the US announced its veto. But even if the resolution of these cases were factored in, the stunning and public US decision of itself would have made its reversal an embarrassing prestige consideration.

The staffer went on to explain that the West's negotiating team was comprised of the United Kingdom, the Netherlands, and the United States. It was understood that the United States would abide by the results of the negotiations. In the early morning hours of May 26, Austrian Ambassador Torovsky told the staffer that none of the Western negotiators had raised any objections to the text, although it was understood that Novak had to "clear it" with Washington. "At that point," the staffer, citing Torovsky, said that it was understood that Novak had agreed to accept the concluding document.

In view of these largely implied understandings, said the Commission staffer, all hell broke loose when Ambassador Novak finally communicated his negative decision at a meeting of the NATO caucus. Everyone, NATO members and the neutrals, he said, felt they had been totally misled. They expressed shock, anger and dismay, which may explain why one delegate was quoted in the *Neue Zürcher Zeitung* of May 28 as characterizing the development as "dangerous amateurism."[106]

Yet the imbroglio did not seem to have any lasting impact. The State Department diplomat selected to head the US delegation to the Vienna follow-up meeting scheduled for November 1986, Ambassador Warren Zimmermann, learned this when he made a tour of NATO capitals during the summer of 1986. In an interview, Zimmermann reported that not a single allied foreign ministry official raised the Bern veto with him.[107] In Zimmermann's view, the issue and the irritation were dead.

Indeed, casting the veto may have very well turned out to be beneficial to the CSCE process with respect to human rights. If, at the Vienna conference, Moscow and the Warsaw Pact countries wished to demonstrate progress, they could not use the limited and inadequate Bern document as a point of departure or as a reference point. An entirely new set of guidelines would be required. Whether this was possible would depend upon whether Gorbachev could agree to transcend the very considerable shortcomings of the Bern document.

The ramifications of the Bern document's inadequacy would soon become apparent. Seeking to quickly exploit the unprecedented and embarrassing cleavage in the ranks of the allies, the Soviets announced that they would respect the provisions of the Bern document even though it had not been formally approved. One of these provisions required Helsinki signatory states to publish "within a reasonable time" all regulations relating to travel. Shortly after the opening of Vienna, Moscow announced new exit-visa regulations that would go into effect as of January 1, 1987. They were retrogressive rather than progressive. According to the new regulations, applicants for exit visas would now have to obtain an affidavit from a first-degree or blood relative living in the country to which they were seeking to immigrate.

Since, prior to the new regulation, exit visas were available to anyone having any relative, not necessarily a blood relative, the new Soviet regulation made for a far greater restrictiveness. If the intent of Helsinki was to liberalize emigration and travel, the new regulation placed severe constraints on the fundamental right to leave a country. Almost immediately, the US objected to the November announcement, and made it clear that "the free movement of people" was not served by the newly published regulations. Washington emphasized that performance was far more important than documents in measuring human rights progress.

If the Bern document had become a key Helsinki document, it would have provided a sanction and legitimization for restrictive legislation. But such sanction did not occur, facilitating a campaign against the restrictive and counterproductive new Soviet rules. In the end, then, the US veto, even if based upon uncertain judgments, was positive. It would have been helpful to register opposition to the compromise document much earlier, which would have prevented the issue from being cast as the United States versus everyone else. This was patently a diplomatic blunder that may have resulted from an unusual set of circumstances (including the vote taking place on the occasion of an important American holiday) and, in any case, was not very likely to ever be repeated.

Bern's ultimate significance, however, lay in its concrete results, not in the public conduct of Soviet diplomats or the controversial US veto. Despite the confrontational nature of the conference, many individual human rights cases were favorably handled. Incidentally, most were dealt with in the corridors rather than in official sessions. Approximately 1,000 cases from Warsaw Pact countries involving binational marriages or family reunion that had been repeatedly rejected by communist governments in the past were now handled with dispatch.[108] The total included the 117 Soviet cases which had been the concern of Washington. Soon after Bern ended, this total was supplemented by an additional 29 Soviet families seeking to join kin in the United States. (These cases, too, had been brought to Moscow's attention at Bern.) In all, the Soviet cases released to the US affected 200 persons, one-quarter of the total Soviet family caseload with which Washington was concerned and which it had raised with the USSR. The Romanian delegation told the United States that it had resolved about half the cases which Washington had presented to Bucharest. The Bulgarian government resolved 12 out of 18 cases that the US had presented to it.

The resolution of individual cases marked a tangible development of very modest consequence. Still, it was the most sizable response by the Soviet side concerning human contacts cases since 1975. No earlier Helsinki meeting had proved as productive; Gorbachev's commitment at the 27th Party Congress, made four months earlier, was at least partially fulfilled. However, the big categories and major issues of emigration, involving tens of thousands of people, remained unfulfilled. Did Moscow think that Washington could be assuaged by resolution of individual cases that involved strictly Americans? And did it expect that Washington would then accept the sharp limitation on the Helsinki process as applicable only to "participating states"? If so, Moscow made a gross error.

·11·

Uncertainty on the Eve of Vienna

By the summer of 1986, it was clear that Mikhail Gorbachev's "new thinking"—which overtly incorporated some human rights language and concepts of the Helsinki accord—had found very little reflection in Moscow's internal policy or in its policy at Helsinki process meetings. Ottawa and Bern—the two human rights experts meetings that the United States had fought for at the Madrid review conference —together with Budapest, had produced no significant human rights progress. Even those who thought the ill-fated Bern document had contained some positive elements recognized that these were very much circumscribed. Assistant Secretary of State Rozanne Ridgway had been quite correct in pointing out, while testifying to the Helsinki Commission, that "no Western government has defended the [Bern] document as more than a potentially modest step forward."[1]

A few months remained before Vienna, the next major CSCE meeting, was scheduled to open. What should be the US perspective for Vienna and the Helsinki process generally? Not surprisingly, critics of the process generally were beginning to make stronger inroads on public opinion. If specialized experts human rights meetings could accomplish so little, of what value was the process? And, if Gorbachev's pronouncements concerning Helsinki and human rights were without substantive intent, how seriously could the process be taken at all?

Yet, running parallel to the growing skepticism and disillusionment was a profound awareness among knowledgeable people both in the Commission and in policy-making positions of the State Department that the Helsinki process still exerted a positive impact. "Shaming" the regimes of Eastern Europe for violations of human rights at Helsinki forums could and did embarrass those governments at the same time as it generated hope among the violated. The problem was how or when would "shaming" or diplomatic embarrassment lead to a change of practice? How and in what way could changes be wrought? What circumstances would encourage the human rights violators to be responsive to a strategy of change? A certain degree of patience was essential in waiting for the opportune moment, and then toughness and finesse would be needed to exploit effectively the crucial moment.

So strongly had disillusionment with the Helsinki process crept into various congressional and public circles that the US Helsinki Commission, in its lengthy report to Congress in the fall of 1986, gave extraordinary attention to the question of the US renouncing the Final Act.[2] The report noted that the argument for renunciation rested on the thesis that the Helsinki accord had constituted a trade-off between the Soviet desire for ratification of the post-World War II borders and Western insistence upon adherence to certain human rights fundamentals. Consequently, the argument ran: "Since . . . the Soviets and most of its allies in Eastern Europe have shown continuing and contemptuous disregard for the human rights commitments under the Final Act . . . therefore, the United States need no longer be bound by its commitments under the Act." Indeed, the argument held, "continued US involvement in CSCE serves to hide these violations and perpetuates the illusion that the Soviets have respectable humanitarian concerns."

To end the charade, the United States—according to this view—should move to renounce the Helsinki accord. If this could be done jointly with other NATO allies, so much the better. But, if not, unilateral action would be appropriate. Advocates of the argument assumed that renunciation or the threat of renunciation might move the Soviet Union and its East European allies to reconsider their human rights practices to preserve that which they had gained in the 1975 trade-off. Even if they made no human rights changes, "they would at least get the message that there is a high price to pay for their poor human rights performance."

Inquiry made by the Commission of legal experts from the State Department and the Library of Congress indicated that, technically, renunciation could take place by the simple act of "a stroke of the pen."[3] As the Helsinki accord was a non-binding declaration and not a treaty, the President could renounce it unilaterally. Toward whom would the renunciation be directed? From an international legal point of view, it would make no difference whether the renunciation was directed toward all the signatories or toward one of them. However, from a practical perspective that flowed from the consensus character of the accord, renunciation vis-à-vis an individual state "would appear to be difficult or politically impossible." It would more appropriately have to assume a general character aimed at all the signatories.

Even as the Commission researched and weighed the question of renunciation, it was not yet prepared to acquiesce in this procedure. First, the Commission challenged the assumption that the Final Act froze the borders of Europe. Expert legal opinion, the Commission stated, indicated that "contrary to a widespread and continuing public belief, fostered by the Soviets and the Western press at the time of the Helsinki signing," the Final Act made no difference with regard to boundaries, and its language "is substantially less than what the Soviets sought at the outset of the negotiations."[4] Thus, any argument would be "specious" which held that US renunciation of the Final Act would thereby end its so-called "ratification" of East European borders.

Second, instead of ending the Helsinki process, renunciation would play into the hands of the USSR, which from the beginning had sought to exclude the United States from the CSCE. The Commission report concluded that the Soviets "might not be displeased to see the United States as the outsider" and to see themselves as the dominant force in CSCE.[5] Third, renunciation would produce a "strong negative effect" upon US allies and upon the neutral and non-aligned. They would interpret the act "as a sign of decreased US interest and influence in Europe."[6] Finally, given the fact that the US had played the leading role at Belgrade and Madrid in pressing for human rights, its withdrawal would very well produce "silence" at Helsinki meetings, diminishing even further the possibility of bringing about human rights change in Eastern Europe.[7]

From the Commission's perspective, US involvement in CSCE remained essential. The success of the Helsinki process, it contended, would depend on "persistent efforts" by the US to bring the "promise" of the Final Act to "fruition." Testimony which Anatoly Shcharansky gave the Commission during the height of the Bern session played a key role in shaping this positive perspective. (Two months earlier, the hero of the human rights struggle had been released from the gulag.) But at the beginning of his May 14 appearance, Shcharansky seemed to give moral support to those who had become or had always been extremely critical of the Helsinki process. Commenting upon the formation of the Moscow Helsinki Watch Group, Shcharansky said that the committee, in its documentation, "demonstrated very quickly" that "the real intentions of the Soviet Union in connection with the Helsinki accords" were "all hypocrisy . . . only lip service."[8]

Congressman Steny Hoyer, Co-chairman of the Commission, seized upon the statement to note, "you have been quoted as saying that shortly after the execution of the Helsinki accords that human rights violations became worse in the Soviet Union."[9] He asked for further comments and an explanation of "why you think it happened." The implication of the query was clear. If, in fact, human rights in the USSR worsened following adoption of the Helsinki Final Act, it placed in question the value of the agreement itself.

The witness went into a long monologue which was not too helpful in rebutting the challenge posed by Helsinki's critics. He said that "it is almost a tradition of Soviet policy that each time when they have to do something on the international stage demonstrating liberalization or good intentions . . . they are afraid that such a step can encourage people inside the country, and they immediately, almost immediately, start repressions against those who are encouraged." In fact, the Kremlin did not launch a repressive drive until months after the Final Act was signed, and that drive was no doubt prompted, in part, by the creation and activism of the Helsinki monitoring groups.

Equally in error was Shcharansky's next assertion: "As you know, emigration was diminishing all the time, except in 1979. . . ." This diminution, he clearly implied, was also due to Soviet signing of the accord. The facts are otherwise: the Jewish emigration rate rose annually from 1975 (when it was 13,221); 1976—14,261; 1977—16,736; and 1978—28,864.[10] That he was not familiar with the data was hardly surprising. To a more questioning panel, it would have raised serious doubts about his generalizations.

Accuracy became more pronounced when Shcharansky turned to the subject of imprisonment and forced labor. Relying on his own experiences and observations, he told the Commission that "practically every year, especially during the last three or four years," the "policy of the authorities" became "more and more tough, and the tortures ever stronger."

A powerful critique of Western and US policy with respect to the Helsinki process followed. It would exert a profound impact upon future Commission deliberations. Shcharansky suddenly turned to his own experience and blurted out:

> I can tell you, frankly, that one of the points of the bitter disappointment among the political prisoners of the Soviet Union, was when we found out that the Madrid ended not only without any improvement, but at the moment when the situation for us in the camps was becoming even worse.[11]

Whether objective evidence would or could validate the evidence of a worsening situation for political prisoners is beside the point. Mendelevich's experience, as earlier reported, was quite different. Assuming the validity of Shcharansky's point, could the situation of prisoners have improved if the West had refused to agree to the Madrid concluding document? No one raised the question. Hoyer simply responded that Shcharansky's "observation is very interesting as we move toward [the] Vienna [review conference] in the latter part of this year."[12]

The Co-chairman seemed to be signaling that the US delegation should be guided by a policy line at the Vienna meeting which required either the release of Soviet prisoners of conscience or the significant easing of their conditions before a concluding document could be accepted. In fact, the complete release of some 700 prisoners of conscience became a central theme of the United States at the Vienna deliberations.

Hoyer raised one final question, the answer to which gave emphasis to the vulnerability of even the best experts: "What is your thought and perhaps the opinion in the Soviet Union, to the extent that you know it, with respect to any improvements that rise on the horizon as a result of having a new General Secretary, Mr. Gorbachev?" Shcharansky had no hesitancy in expressing his doubts: ". . . I am not very optimistic about the possibilities of fulfilling human rights demands in the Soviet Union."[13]

Senator Malcolm Wallop, the Republican from Wyoming who was one of the Commission's most pessimistic members concerning the effectiveness of the Helsinki accord, was given the floor next. It was clear that Shcharansky's testimony had reinforced his perspective. He lauded the observations about the Soviet authorities' "cynical abuse of their own citizens." He added: "I thank God that you are here to tell us what we do not care to hear."[14] Pressing ahead with some hot-tempered, if hardly diplomatic, views on Soviet-US relations, the Senator urged that Yelena Bonner be invited to address a joint session of Congress and perhaps Gorbachev, "should he be here." It required the Commission's principal organizer and first chairman, Congressman Dante Fascell, to pose the key question that got the hearings back on track. In a crucial prefatory comment of considerable bluntness, Congressman Fascell declared:

> So, let's set the record straight . . . and say that it was your group . . . who really shook the world, especially the skeptics who thought that the Helsinki accords was a mistake for the United States and for the West. . . .

What the Helsinki group had done was to demonstrate that "the signature of the Soviet Union" to the Helsinki accord should be taken "very seriously with respect to the rights of their own people," and "that maybe [the] Helsinki accords was a good idea, especially Basket III. . . ."

Having set the tone and context of his questioning, Fascell bluntly asked: ". . . should the United States repudiate the Helsinki accords?"

Shcharansky responded with a clear and ringing clarification: "I think the important thing is to insist on its fulfillment and to make no progress, no progress in any branch before there will be progress in the third basket."[15] The Congressman sought to elicit an even more concrete endorsement of Helsinki. "In other words," Fascell asked, "our policy should be that we would not do anything with respect to Basket II, Basket I, or other matters unless we have equivalent progress in Basket III?" Shcharansky's response was "exactly."

What both Fascell and Shcharansky were setting forth was the political strategy line of linkage. Progress in any basket required progress in Basket III. It would be at the heart of US policy at Vienna. Later on in his testimony, Shcharansky elaborated on his concept of linkage. He considered it not only appropriate for the baskets of the Helsinki accord, but appropriate as well for military negotiations. Emphasizing that any military agreement involves "an atmosphere of trust," he urged that the US press on a *quid pro quo* basis for those human rights that would make the Soviet Union a more open society. In his view, human rights "have a very practical meaning."

Fascell quickly followed up with two more significant questions. Noting that the witness displayed "disappointment after Madrid" because no "visible progress" had been evident with respect to Basket III, he asked: "Now, what should we expect as a minimum, not the maximum, but as a minimum out of the review conference in Vienna this year?" Shcharansky's response was precise: "The reunion of families by means of Jewish emigration," as spelled out in the Helsinki accord, "must take place," and "all prisoners of conscience must be released." All signatories of the Helsinki agreement "have a full right to demand that," he went on. Without these two minimum preconditions the US should sign no concluding document. That recommendation, too, would find its way into America's linkage strategy at Vienna.

Fascell's next question dealt with philosophy. It carried a special urgency, as critics continued to challenge certain key assumptions that underlay the Helsinki process. Should the US employ both "public diplomacy" and "quiet diplomacy" to achieve human rights objectives? Some commentators, as well as various State Department officials, had stressed the use of "quiet diplomacy" and discouraged "public diplomacy." Shcharansky's answer was a model of succinctness:

> Well, my position is that quiet diplomacy can help only if it is the final point of strong public pressure, strong public diplomacy. Exactly as it was in my case, the final exchange, my final release was reached in quiet diplomacy in exchanging of

spies, but as you all understand, it would never take place if there wasn't such a strong campaign in which the Congress of the United States and the President of the United States and many other people in different levels took part.[16]

Senator Dennis DeConcini posed another important question carrying philosophical overtones. After referring to visits he and other members of Congress had made to Soviet Jews, the Senator asked:

These visits have always bothered me. I have asked this question before, and I want to ask it to you. Do these personal contacts within the Soviet Union jeopardize the safety and security of those that we contact or those that we put on a list and give to Soviet officials, asking them to release them and expedite their visas?[17]

Shcharansky quickly retorted: "I will say the moment you will stop trying to contact them, or stop displaying interest in your contact with the authorities, they will be doomed to much worse." When a variation of the same question was put to him by Congressman Jack Kemp, he offered a more upbeat response, saying strong US support emanating from the highest political levels in Washington for the oppressed in the USSR made the situation "better for these people."

Explicitly indicated in the important Shcharansky testimony was the value for the oppressed in the USSR of public diplomacy and of pressure exercised by the United States. Even the signing of a concluding document at follow-up meetings or at experts meetings should not be agreed to unless and until major human rights issues were resolved. The Commission, too, identified with the Shcharansky perspective of continuing application of public diplomacy and pressure to achieve Helsinki's human rights objectives. Both rejected—and did so in no uncertain terms—the advisability of repudiation or renunciation of Helsinki even when little or no progress was realized.

Critical analytic questions were left unanswered in the Commission report and the Shcharansky testimony. How and at what point should any genuine Kremlin progress in human rights performance or standards be recognized in new concluding documents? Experience since Madrid, particularly during and following the human rights experts meetings of Ottawa, Budapest and Bern, was hardly heartening or encouraging. Even with Gorbachev's new thinking and his favorable approach to Helsinki language and ideas, progress was limited and optimism was at best reined in, even by those who viewed Helsinki in the most positive way.

Still, Gorbachev's incorporation of the conceptual language of Helsinki and Basket III could not be dismissed outright, as Assistant Secretary

Ridgway had emphasized in her testimony to the Commission in June. The fact that Gorbachev used the "same language" as that of the Final Act, even if his initial purpose may have been cynical, had testified to the impact of Helsinki concepts.

Even more striking than Gorbachev's use of Helsinki language was the creation of an unprecedented governmental agency aimed at institutionalizing the Basket III language on "humanitarianism." In July 1986, the Ministry of Foreign Affairs, heretofore organized generally on the basis of geographical divisions, established a new office on humanitarian and cultural affairs (technically, the office was termed an *upravlenie*, or "administration," which has a status slightly below an *otdel*, or "department").[18] The new office, (apparently seen as the equivalent of the State Department's Bureau of Human Rights and Humanitarian Affairs) was headed by Yuri Kashlev, who had led the Soviet delegation at the Bern conference on human contacts in April-May and who would soon serve as the chief Soviet representative at Vienna. A smooth and polished career diplomat, Kashlev had served in a variety of posts, including a very short stay in London in 1971, where he and over 100 other Soviet representatives had been rounded up by the British government and expelled for alleged espionage activities.[19]

Moscow also announced that in the fall of 1987 there would be established a new human rights commission to be composed of intellectuals, workers, and journalists. Presumably, its function would parallel that of the US Helsinki Commission. But the official announcement of the new body indicated that its principal task would be "correcting" Western "distorted opinion" about human rights in the Soviet Union.[20] Soviet officials further revealed that the government would issue reports on the human rights conditions of Helsinki signatories, a practice similar to that conducted by both the US Helsinki Commission and the State Department. Moscow, under Gorbachev, was clearly prepared to drop its earlier defensiveness on human rights and move to the offensive. At Ottawa in May–June 1985, and especially at Bern in April-May 1986, features of the new Soviet offensive were clearly displayed, with the West, especially the United States, denounced for such alleged human rights abuses as unemployment, homelessness, racism, anti-Semitism, and genocide.

The Soviet leader was even prepared to have Helsinki extended beyond its European geographical parameters. At the very same time that the new "humanitarian" department was being created within the Foreign Ministry, Gorbachev traveled to Vladivostok on the Pacific to make his first major statement on Soviet policy toward Asia and the Pacific. In it, he recommended that a Helsinki-type process be introduced in Asia.[21] This was the very first time that any leader, European or otherwise, proposed replication of the process in other broad geographical areas.

No doubt, the Soviet leader had a special national purpose in mind. In his recommendation of a Helsinki-type process, he offered as justification for his suggestion the fact that Helsinki "had brought about a certain stability and reduced the probability of armed conflict." Gorbachev may very well have been thinking about freezing the Soviet-Chinese border area, as well making permanent the Soviet military conquest of the Kurile island chain, a major source of Soviet-Japanese tension. Neither China nor Japan offered any response to the unprecedented Soviet proposal; nor was it likely that either would wax enthusiastic about territorial arrangements that challenged their territorial aspirations. But even if Gorbachev's perspective in his Vladivostok speech was on the security aspects of Helsinki, his recommendation of the Final Act for Asia meant that he would also find acceptable and applicable—or, at least, that he would have to tolerate—the accord's human rights provisions.

Moving Moscow to *act* in accordance with Helsinki was, of course, another matter. Clearly, the strategy of pressure of public diplomacy was not adequate to the task. US diplomats at Ottawa, Budapest, and Bern did apply public diplomacy in a major way, as did the Helsinki Commission, but comparatively little was accomplished beyond the release at the end of Bern of several hundreds from divided families. The hundreds of prisoners of conscience, thousands of refuseniks, and tens of thousands prevented from emigrating starkly illuminated the limits which had been reached. A highly experienced British diplomat at Bern, who had been involved with Helsinki issues for quite a few years, privately acknowledged in an interview that the very nature of the experts' meetings made human rights progress virtually impossible.[22] To the extent that these meetings were exclusively devoted to human rights, they offered no trade-offs to the Soviets. Only when Moscow was able to obtain some concession in the security or military field would it be willing to extend concessions in the human rights area, he said. The trade-off of Basket I for Basket III, in his view, stood at the very heart of the Helsinki process.

The Briton's point was crucial. Only by offering Moscow something in the security or military area which it badly wanted could a bargaining process begin that might lead to a trade-off. Recognition of this linkage was central to Ridgway's testimony in June. If one would be less skeptical and more optimistic about the outcome at the forthcoming review conference in Vienna, she suggested, it was because such a trade-off was possible: "It may prove easier to achieve real progress on humanitarian issues" at Vienna because "all the baskets . . . will be under consideration."[23]

The Conference on Disarmament in Europe (CDE) in Stockholm was central to the post-Madrid Helsinki process, even if it rarely attracted public attention. It had opened in January 1984, with discussion focused on the kind of confidence- and security-building measures (CSBMs or CBMs) necessary to reduce the risk of surprise attack. Stalemate had characterized most of the deliberations until June-July 1986, largely because of Moscow's stonewalling in the 12 rounds of negotiations.

It would not be altogether incorrect to surmise that the immobilism on the human rights front at Ottawa, Budapest, and Bern was a coefficient of the absence of movement in the security talks at Stockholm. "Balanced progress" was a core formula that expressed the linkage of the two subjects, and the absence of movement with respect to one was certain to have an impact on the other. Nonetheless, even in its stalemate, Stockholm remained important as the only locus of talks between East and West from September 1983—the end of Madrid—until March 1985, when the interrupted negotiations on strategic and intermediate missiles and on MBFR were resumed in Geneva and Vienna, respectively. (They had been halted by a Soviet walk-out in November 1983.)

Hints of a possible greater degree of flexibility at Stockholm appeared in mid-April. As noted by *The Times* (London), a Gorbachev address to the East Germans on April 18 implied "a readiness to move forward on conventional arms control generally."[24] In the Swedish capital, Soviet negotiators had begun to query Western delegates as to the kind of confidence-building measures the Western powers had in mind. With the Soviets dropping most of their earlier demands (e.g., "no first use" of nuclear weapons) except for a declaration on the non-use of force (which the West had indicated it was willing to accept), this suggested a newfound seriousness of purpose. Moscow's listening to Western ideas on CBMs meant that the Soviets no longer held to the view that such proposals were really sly NATO attempts to spy on the Warsaw Pact's military structure.

A fundamental change in the Soviet attitude at Stockholm came in July, when flexibility on Moscow's part emerged on the crucial issue of verification procedures concerning compliance. The head of the American delegation to the Stockholm talks, Ambassador Robert L. Barry (who had replaced James Goodby in November 1985), surmised that a Politburo decision the previous month had overruled the strong objections of the Soviet military on verification issues.[25] In Barry's opinion, the

Gorbachev-led Politburo was eager for both a second stage of the CDE and a bold public relations move concerning arms control compliance.

Moscow had always pressed for the second stage of CDE discussions on disarmament. But it was keenly aware that movement in that direction could not be achieved before progress was made at the first stage, on confidence-building measures aimed at reducing the possibility of surprise attack. Since these measures, as proposed by the West, entailed on-site inspection, it was hardly surprising that the Soviet military establishment would have tried to delay them. Yet, with Vienna now only a few months away and Gorbachev anxious to win its sanction for a second stage of CDE, the obstinacy of the military resistance had to be overcome at the political level.

The expected July arrival in Moscow of French President Mitterrand no doubt helped expedite the decision. Gorbachev sought to impress the French leader with Moscow's strong new commitment to Helsinki and, therefore, to human rights generally and to Basket III provisions specifically. During his visit, according to Barry, the Soviet decision to accept on-site inspection was communicated privately to the West. Marshal Sergei Akhromeyev, Chief of the Soviet General Staff, formally communicated the decision to the Stockholm meeting two months later.[26]

Negotiations were stepped up in earnest during the summer, as September 19 was the required closing date of the Stockholm talks. After that, only six weeks would remain before the opening of the Vienna review conference. As the negotiations were very close to an agreement when the target date arrived, the negotiators applied what had become almost a standard Helsinki device. The clock was stopped (as it had been several times at the Madrid deliberations). The negotiations were finally completed on September 21, but the clock at Stockholm still read September 19.

Stockholm constituted a milestone in the Helsinki process. The agreement that was reached, a result of extensive compromises and trade-offs, set in motion major developments with respect to security issues and human rights matters, although this was not immediately apparent. Vienna, the next follow-up meeting, took on totally new significance. But the impact extended well beyond the Helsinki process. The entire East-West military negotiating process, covering strategic and intermediate missiles and possibly extending to conventional arms as well, assumed a new and unexpected dimension. If verification, including inspection, was possible with one type of security matters, why not with others?

The Stockholm agreement provided that both NATO and the Warsaw Pact notify one another with advance information about all land military exercises and troop concentrations involving 13,000 or more soldiers or 300 tanks.[27] In the original Helsinki Basket I provision, the threshold was nearly twice as high (25,000 troops), and its eastern perimeter extended only 150 miles into the western part of the USSR (instead of the entire territory stretching to the Urals). Further, under the Stockholm agreement, military maneuvers exceeding 75,000 troops would need be reported two years in advance, and those of 40,000 or more troops one year in advance.

Far more significant than its notification requirements were the newly established inspection and verification procedures. When the maneuvers exceeded 17,000 troops, all Helsinki signatories would be invited to observe the exercise and given facilities to do so by the country on whose territory they were conducted. In the event any signatory suspected that another was engaged in military activity about which it should have been notified in advance, it could carry out a snap inspection on land or from the air, with the inspected country providing the aircraft. (A total of three such inspections could be claimed.) The inspectors could bring their own observation and camera equipment and control the flight path of the plane. Initially, the US had wanted the inspectors to use neutral planes, as proposed by Switzerland and Sweden, but it had to settle for the compromise after the Soviet Union refused further concessions and Britain and West Germany persuaded President Reagan to accept it lest the entire Stockholm agreement be placed in jeopardy.[28]

Ambassador Barry, while not totally enthusiastic about the agreement—"no one can get everything he wants," he said—at the same time saw it as "a first step" which showed East and West "can say yes to each other for a change."[29] The European NATO allies, especially West Germany (which awaited national elections) and Great Britain, were more exultant. Gorbachev was particularly laudatory in welcoming the agreement. In a formal statement on September 24, he called Stockholm "a major step" for reducing international tension and a "victory for common sense."[30] He added that "the Soviet Union sees in this agreement upshoots of new thinking in world politics that are germinating on European soil." The comment may have indirectly served to accentuate inevitable differences between the US and Western Europe on security matters.

Even as the East was exultant about forward movement in the security area, it was being cautioned that a reciprocal move was expected in the human rights area. Ambassador Barry put it somewhat obliquely. Noting that the Stockholm outcome "will weigh on the positive side of the balance" in the Helsinki process, he pointed to the fact that "there will be much on the negative side," referring to the absence of compliance with the human rights provisions.[31] Barry's reference to balance hinted that the US and the West would now press for its restoration. His British colleague, Michael Edes, made the point explicitly as Stockholm came to an end: "We must have balanced progress in the humanitarian field."[32]

A further development in the summer of 1986 gave additional attention to the potential value and validity of Rozanne Ridgway's focus on linkage. Gorbachev had publicly indicated in June that dramatic new initiatives should be taken by NATO and the Warsaw Pact to reduce conventional arms.[33] What was in the back of his mind was made clear shortly afterward in the Warsaw Pact "Budapest Appeal." The appeal proposed that the deadlocked MBFR discussions, which had been taking place in Vienna between NATO and the Warsaw Pact for some 14 years, be ended and that new conventional arms talks brought under the Helsinki umbrella.

The proposal was certain to attract support from President Mitterrand. From the beginning of MBFR, France had absented itself from its deliberations, in keeping with the Gaullist notions then prevailing. France would certainly welcome the burial of a forum from which it had excluded itself. If the deliberations came under the Helsinki umbrella (i.e., within CSCE, in which France was an active participant), it would be all the more responsive. Gorbachev's timing for this arms reduction strategy was telling.

The fact that the security basket of Helsinki was suddenly enlarged carried potent ramifications for the West. On the one hand, there were those who were already disconcerted and disturbed by the failure of Ottawa, Budapest, and Bern, and the lack of compliance with Basket III. Blame would be laid in such thinking upon the existing "imbalance" in the Helsinki process, which had been made possible by the West's acceptance in 1979 of the French proposal for a two-stage conference on disarmament (CDE).

Just as the US Helsinki Commission had been unsympathetically disposed to earlier US policy on CDE, so, too, did it find a distinct threat to the notion of balance within Helsinki by the addition of new security burdens and responsibilities.[34] The delicate balance could be decisively tipped against human rights, thereby transforming Helsinki into what Moscow had initially wanted it to be—purely an instrument for advancing and protecting security interests, and not one for promoting and assuring human rights. A highly circumspect Commission attitude toward the Gorbachev proposal was inevitable.

On the other hand, might not the enlarged Helsinki umbrella enable the process to become more effective in the human rights field? Would not additional security functions for Helsinki permit the West to exert greater leverage for human rights on grounds that balanced progress must be sought? Of course, the emphasis must be placed upon balance; otherwise, the Soviet thrust could diminish human rights in the process to a veritable nullity. It was perhaps not accidental that, when Soviet officials met privately with leading congressmen from the Helsinki Commission, they began by seeking clarification of the US position with respect to Stockholm and the Budapest Appeal.[35] Such manifest anxiety and concern could be allayed, Moscow would recognize, by concessions in the human rights field. Gestures had to be geared to restoration of the balance between security and human rights.

The new dynamics in the security and arms control field were given an additional impetus a few weeks after Stockholm and just before the opening of Vienna. At the superpower summit in Reykjavik, Iceland, on October 11-12, new horizons in disarmament were glimpsed in what President Reagan called "historic advances." Gorbachev sought to tie radical disarmament progress, including the "zero option" in intermediate missiles in Europe, to a halt in SDI. It was a bold maneuver. President Reagan had been an advocate of the zero option, and Gorbachev's predecessors had unhesitatingly rebuffed the proposal. The new Soviet leader had the courage and foresight to reject their views and the support for them in powerful Soviet military circles. While the Reykjavik package was ultimately unacceptable to the United States, Gorbachev refused to be pessimistic about the eventual outcome: "I think that the discussion with Reagan can be continued. . . . I don't think we have to plunge into despair."

The summit was not without a human rights dimension even if the subject was not on the agenda. Just prior to the meeting, Professor Yuri Orlov, the organizer and head of the Helsinki Watch Group in Moscow, was released from a forced labor camp after eight years of incarceration. As it directly pertained to the Helsinki process, the gesture was of considerable significance. Other prominent prisoners of conscience were also freed and allowed to emigrate. (Orlov came to the United States and, soon thereafter, was invited to sit with the US delegation to the Vienna follow-up meeting at the opening plenary session.) At the Icelandic capital, Soviet officials for the first time agreed to meet with important former Soviet dissenters and protesters now living abroad.[36] Affability and courteousness marked the conduct of Soviet officials and extended to discussion on the flight back to Washington.

The distinctly new Soviet style—what might be termed diplomatic glasnost—was continued to the opening week of the Vienna meeting, which began on November 4. No longer would inquiring reporters, NGO representatives, divided spouses, and even aggrieved family members of human rights victims be brushed aside or avoided, as had been the case at the previous review conferences.

The Western (and other) media were especially courted. A total of six press conferences were held during the very first week of the Vienna meeting. The contrast with previous follow-up meetings, when such press conferences were very rarely held, was glaring. Moreover, Western reporters were deliberately sought out and advised: "You know, things are changing since the bad old days." Only one press conference turned out to be awkward. In keeping with the prevailing Kremlin line on emigration that not only do Soviet Jews no longer wish to leave, but rather, many who had emigrated presumably seek to return, the Soviet Embassy in Vienna staged an event for the media with four former emigrants. Three had been living in Israel and the other one, an actor, had worked in Austria. All related that they had made a monumental error in emigrating, and they desperately pleaded that they be allowed to return. The obsequiousness of the pleaders and the seemingly forced and artificial character of the proceedings alienated the reporters. In addition, the Embassy translator was so inadequate that the Russian-speaking journalists demanded her replacement, which was done.[37]

Besides the press contacts, Soviet delegates responded to almost every request for a meeting with private persons and representatives of voluntary organizations (only Andrei Sakharov's stepson, Aleksei Semyenov, was refused); courteously, even sympathetically, they listened to pleas about emigration restrictions and refuseniks. Promises to look into individual cases were made and assurances were given to either arranging meetings with top Soviet officials or reporting back to the inquirer. But the promises were rarely, if ever, kept. In one meeting with a Jewish representative, anti-Semitism of the subtle type reared its head. During the course of a friendly discussion, Soviet officials drew upon the traditional misinterpretation of the "chosen people" concept as racism to explain their perspective on the so-called "Zionism-racism" equation and on the presumed power of Jews.

As to whether the Soviet Union would change its emigration policy, Kremlin officials repeatedly pointed to the forthcoming publication of rules and regulations covering exit visas after January 1, 1987. While this stirred hope in some quarters, concern was registered that talk about the rules remained vague. Later, when the regulations became available, much of the optimism was dissipated. The only significant change offered was that an applicant for an exit visa would be given an answer within a month. The low monthly Jewish emigration figures continued.

According to Shcharansky, who carefully studied the new rules, they served only to narrow the basis for emigration by specifically limiting the definition of family (with whom one can be reunited) to blood relatives.[38] Moreover, the new official reasons for denying an exit visa were presented in a vague way, thereby reinforcing the arbitrariness of bureaucrats in making decisions. Shcharansky, interviewed December 9 while on a visit to Washington, expressed concern that the regulations would fool people into thinking that emigration procedures, by being regularized, were being eased. "It shows us the success of all this new public relations work of Gorbachev," he concluded.[39]

For a fitting climax to the new Kremlin style, Soviet Foreign Minister Eduard Shevardnadze dropped a public relations bombshell, immediately attracting worldwide attention. After contending that the USSR "attaches paramount significance" to the Helsinki principle on "human rights and fundamental freedoms"—it was in fact the first time that a Soviet official had ever directly referred in a positive manner to this Helsinki principle—he then proposed holding in Moscow "a representative conference" of the Helsinki signatories to discuss a whole range of humanitarian problems.[40] Shevardnadze, of course, said nothing about whether jailed Helsinki monitors would be permitted to attend, or about whether ordinary Soviet citizens (including activists and dissidents) and representatives of international non-governmental human rights organizations would have access to delegates. Soviet public relations officials in Vienna were extraordinarily vague in responding to reporters' normal queries on the proposal.

On December 10—Human Rights Day—Soviet First Deputy Foreign Minister Anatoly Kovalev arrived for a special address to the Vienna meeting on the proposed conference. He spoke at length about how the USSR was "guided by good intentions" in advancing its plan and about his expectations that the Vienna participants would treat it "in an interested, unbiased, and well-intentioned manner."[41] Kovalev sought to assure everyone that "we wish to create most propitious conditions for [the Helsinki conference's] future work and to organize the [humanitarian] conference in keeping with international standards." But, again, he avoided specifics about the role of international non-governmental representatives, about Helsinki monitors both within and without the USSR, and about the press. Instead, he focused on the participants, that is, the official delegates of governments, whom "Moscow will welcome and accord hospitality." Kovalev spoke as if the Kremlin were a great human rights advocate and the Soviet Union a model to emulate. "We do not fear voices of criticism," and "we also have [something] to say to many countries about human rights," the Soviet official commented. Participants, he emphasized, "will be able to see with their own eyes how Soviet people live and . . . get a feel of the moral and political climate in our country."[42]

The fabulous public relations show in the Austrian capital stunned both participants and observers with its brazenness and gall. But whether the Gorbachev style would prove convincing was questionable. An editorial in the independent Austrian newspaper *Die Presse* reflected the mood of the West as well as the neutrals: "Even its allies were surprised when the Soviet Union . . . called for a human rights meeting in Moscow, of all places. This would be, so to speak, a debate in the fox-den about raising chickens."[43] Particularly instructive for the Helsinki participants was the character of the dialogue with Soviet delegates within the closed sessions of the Vienna conference and away from the media. In fact, no genuine dialogue took place. Instead, Soviet officials reacted angrily whenever the issue of human rights violations was brought up. Charges were sharply and quickly dismissed, and Soviet representatives would then unleash a broadside of repeated allegations concerning the West.

A rather dramatic example of the technique came on November 14. Ambassador Warren Zimmermann of the United States addressed himself to the subjects of labor camps and internal exile, and then spoke of the ordinary individuals who "have spoken out for their own rights and for the rights of others."[44] The detailed description of life in the gulag which Zimmermann drew from reports of Orlov, Shcharansky and others struck the listeners with horror. The Ambassador then spoke about the brutalized condition of Anatoly Marchenko. (This was just a few weeks before Marchenko's death was reported. An extraordinarily courageous advocate of freedom, Marchenko had spent much of his adult life in the gulag; he had described the system in a samizdat work smuggled out of prison.) A description of the harsh treatment accorded other Helsinki monitors, especially that meted out to distinguished psychiatrist Anatoly Koryagin, followed. The tragic condition of Andrei Sakharov and Yelena Bonner in Gorky, as well as the plight of individual Jews arrested for their cultural and religious activities, were outlined. The Ambassador concluded with a list of case studies of divided spouses, long-time refuseniks, and cancer victims who wished to emigrate for medical treatment abroad.

Zimmermann's intent was "to put a human face" on various categories of human rights problems in the USSR. But mere characterization was stronger than the simple prose in which it was delivered. The delegate of Liechtenstein, Count Mario Ledebur, was so moved that he asked for a moment of silence during which the delegations would rise in recognition of the plight of the victims.[45] As consensus was required, Soviet delegate Vladimir Morozov rejected the Liechtenstein proposal, countering that the US diplomat's evidence was drawn exclusively from "rumors" and "slander" provided by "criminals." He followed up with a long string of statistics that was supposed to show massive violations of human rights in the United States.

The detailed statistics, clearly drawn from US newspapers and journals, were the basis of repeated assaults on the United States whenever a US delegate charged the Soviet Union with violating the Helsinki accord. It was a practice followed by Soviet delegates at the United Nations and other international meetings. In the afternoon of November 14, Kashlev took the floor with a recitation of the following data: 30 million Americans underfed, 15 million unemployed, and 2 million homeless. The argument had clearly been shifted from individual rights and specific cases to economic-social rights and broad categories. It was repeated over and over again, together with counterattacks used in other international fora, that peace is a form of human rights, indeed, the most important of human rights, as it assured the right to life.[46]

Kashlev and his colleagues also frequently noted that the United States had failed to ratify the International Covenants on Human Rights (sometimes, they would call attention to other international conventions that the US had not ratified, like the Convention on Racial Discrimination). They would further argue that the US incited hatred of the USSR through such films as *Rambo* and *Rocky IV*. This would be linked to harassment experienced by some Soviet dancers and singers when performing in the United States.

Not only would the stream of accusations flow in the plenary and in working-group discussions whenever Soviet human rights violations were raised, the same tactics were followed when congressional delegations arrived to meet with Soviet officials. Thus, after Helsinki Commission heads Hoyer and DeConcini privately raised various individual human rights cases with Soviet officials in Vienna, the latter chose not to respond to the specific cases, but rather to generalize about Soviet policy, taking particular note of the new regulations on emigration, and then to assume the offensive by accusing the United States of suppressing the novels of

Charles Dickens (in some Missouri school district), along with economic-social rights charges accompanied by statistical data.[47]

Clearly, genuine dialogue on human rights was marked by its very absence in Vienna. Indeed, as the session approached the Christmas-New Year adjournment, the atmosphere deteriorated. With the United States, supported mainly by Britain and Canada, continuing to raise specific human rights issues, the Soviet abusiveness deepened. When Ambassador Zimmermann asked on December 12 for a moment of silence following the announcement of Anatoly Marchenko's death in the gulag, the Soviets, joined by Bulgarian delegates, deliberately walked out.[48]

It was apparent that the attention given by Gorbachev and his colleagues to the language of Helsinki's Basket III, to human rights formulations generally, and to a new style of conduct by Soviet diplomats had not altered in any substantive way Soviet performance with respect to dissidents and would-be emigrants. However, as the opening session of Vienna was approaching adjournment, Gorbachev set in motion a series of positive, if limited, developments with a direct relationship to the Helsinki process.

On December 14, a team of technicians suddenly appeared at the Sakharov apartment in Gorky and installed a telephone.[49] On the following day, the police guards around his home were removed. The most startling development came on December 16, when the scientist received a personal call from Gorbachev informing him that his exile was over, and that Yelena had been pardoned. Two days later, Dr. Yuri Marchuk, the President of the Soviet Academy of Sciences, arrived in Gorky to discuss with Sakharov his return to work in Moscow's scientific community. On December 23, the Nobel laureate arrived at the Yaroslavsky train station in Moscow, and was greeted by more than 200 correspondents.

There is little doubt that the Soviet ruler had been contemplating this landmark decision for some time. He had come to recognize that the political price the Kremlin was paying for Sakharov's internal exile was too high and was no longer justifiable. On the one hand, the prestigious Soviet Academy of Sciences was virtually boycotted and isolated by all the most important American and West European scientific associations. If Gorbachev hoped to attract Western support for his policy of glasnost and his new thinking, the most prominent individual object of Soviet repression had to be released. On the other hand, Sakharov's critical stance on the invasion of Afghanistan, which had prompted the exile, was no longer a matter of public concern. Indeed, Gorbachev was already moving to withdraw Soviet troops from that country and end an occupation that had become a terrible burden on the Kremlin. Besides, in the context of Gorbachev's new arms control policy toward the West, Sakharov's own critique of Reagan's SDI program could offer valuable public relations assistance.

Soviet historian Roy Medvedev believes the actual timing of the move was influenced by the unexpected death of Anatoly Marchenko in Chistopol prison on December 9.[50] (The popular dissident had been a "prisoner of conscience" in forced-labor camps for many years. His early demise was very likely due to the deprivations that he had suffered in the gulag and the reported cruel violence of his KGB interrogators in early 1986). It was only five days after Marchenko's death that Gorbachev chose to act. Medvedev noted that Sakharov and his wife were not in very good health at the time and, "if anything happened to them while they were still in exile, the reputation of the new Soviet leader would be irreparably tarnished." Besides, the Sakharovs were known to be close friends of Marchenko and his wife, Larisa Bogoraz, and connections might very well have been drawn in the public mind if their physical conditions worsened.

The principal forum for world concern about the tragedy of Marchenko was the Helsinki meeting in Vienna, which Gorbachev had embraced with the most vigorous endorsement. If anything untoward happened to Sakharov or his wife, the whole new Soviet thrust would have collapsed with powerful repercussions. United States Ambassador Zimmermann had already used the Vienna forum to highlight repeatedly the plight of the Sakharovs. Significantly, one of the early private letters (January 25, 1987) written by the Soviet scientist after release from his Gorky exile was to Zimmermann, expressing his "deepest thanks for the support which my wife and I consistently received from the American delegation at the Vienna conference and from you personally."[51] Sakharov credited the support as being "one of the factors which made possible our return to Moscow."

Concrete evidence of direct benefits flowing from the Helsinki process is always difficult to come by as, all too often, a number of factors come into play. The Sakharov letter was rare testimony to the positive impact of Helsinki. Moreover, it reinforced those still committed to the Helsinki process in the face of a growing skepticism about its value and significance.

·12·

Linkage and Leverage

At a glittering assemblage in the Kremlin in February 1987, over 1,000 international celebrities from 80 countries heard Mikhail Gorbachev pronounce himself the champion of Helsinki's Basket III.[1] He told the audience that his approach "to the third Helsinki basket is there for all to see." Gorbachev was alluding to recent releases of political prisoners and a renewed exodus of Soviet Jews. The Soviet ruler's public embrace of Helsinki's human rights section was tied to the central theme of his address, which claimed that new thinking had led to the humanizing of international relations.

The reference to the "third Helsinki basket" was unprecedented. If Gorbachev had used the language and concepts of Basket III in his historic 27th Party Congress policy address in February 1986, he had meticulously avoided relating it to a specific basket, instead pointing to the entire Helsinki accord as the source. The Final Act had, of course, been widely and authoritatively sanctioned in the USSR since 1975; in contrast, a taboo had hung over Basket III. Gorbachev's willingness to become an open champion of the human rights basket revealed a certain courage at the same time that it indicated how his public relations instincts were attuned to an international audience. Not accidentally, he made sure that the recently released Sakharov was present at the occasion, so that Western intellectuals might glimpse the Soviet leader in his supposedly real element.

In January 1987, the Kremlin announced the first large-scale release of political prisoners, startling the West.[2] In the course of three months, some two hundred prisoners were set free. In addition, a number of long-term refuseniks began receiving exit visas. By March, Jewish emigration had jumped from a mere 32 persons in January to 138.[3] In March 1986, the emigration figure had been only 47. As significant was a decision Soviet authorities took either in late 1986 or early 1987 to halt the prosecution of dissidents and religious activists under what had been notorious Articles of the Russian Criminal Code—70, 190-1, 142 and 227. The first two articles made felonies of such acts as "anti-Soviet agitation and pro-paganda" or "defamation of the Soviet system." The latter two branded illegal the participation in an organization of unauthorized religious groups. As no public announcement of this decision was made, analysts in the West did not become aware of these important developments and could not comprehend, as yet, their ramifications. Yet, a high Soviet legal official, Aleksandr Sukharev, came to Vienna and claimed that a planned reform of the penal code "would affect two-thirds of the articles."[4]

On yet another Basket III level, Foreign Ministry spokesman Gennadi Gerasimov announced in January that the jamming of BBC and other major Western stations would end.[5] He made a critical exception, how-ever, in the case of the "most anti-Soviet and subversive" stations, such as Radio Liberty and Radio Free Europe.

A Communist Party Central Committee plenum at the end of January 1987 marked a turning point for Gorbachev's internal policy.[6] He won its support, after a marathon lobbying effort, for his proposal to have multi-ple candidates and secret ballots in local party elections. The plenum also agreed in principle that non-party members could hold top positions in public life. (But other Gorbachev proposals for reform, including in-creased power for elective bodies, were rejected.) In the General Secre-tary's effort to shake up the party, if only to reconstruct the economy—the term "perestroika" had just come into popular use—he insisted that "we need democracy like air." His concluding remarks to the plenum were:

> If we fail to realize this or if we realize this but make no really serious steps to broaden it, promote it, and draw the country's working people extensively into the perestroika process, our policy will get choked and perestroika will fail.[7]

Of particular significance was a Gorbachev maneuver to bypass further obstacles and hasten the reform process by having the Central Commit-tee call a special party conference for the summer of 1988. Party confer-ences were exceedingly rare in Soviet history, the last one having been held in 1941. Participants in the conference would be elected from the grass roots, instead of being appointed by local party bureaucrats. Gor-bachev was counting on the specially chosen conference, acting under emergency circumstances, to move his program of perestroika forward.

Several weeks after the Central Committee plenum, to the dismay of party conservatives, who remained dominant in the Politburo, Gor-bachev called for a vast public reexamination of the Stalinist epoch, the "rampage of evil." "There should be no forgotten names or blank spaces, either in history or in literature," he stressed.[8] It was a revolutionary step that would lead to the uncovering of a mountain of lies, distortions and deceptions.

Running parallel to Gorbachev's domestic initiatives was a major step taken with respect to international affairs. In March, he untied the famous-but-rejected "Reykjavik Package" and offered to reach a separate agreement with the United States on intermediate-range missiles (opening the path for elimination of all medium-range nuclear weapons in Europe—the SS-20s of the Soviet Union and the Pershing II and cruise missiles of the United States—using an elaborate on-site verification system, inspired by the Stockholm agreement).[9]

No doubt, Moscow's military conservatives viewed the concession untying the Reykjavik package with grave suspicion. President Reagan's zero option had been acceded to, which meant junking the huge SS-20 arsenal deployed in Europe during the 1970s. At the same time, no US concession on the feared SDI program seemed required.

As domestic Gorbachev initiatives challenged the power of national and local party bureaucrats and aroused concern in security circles, especially the KGB, it was hardly surprising that the General Secretary would shift to a marking-time approach. Conservative forces including the military were beginning to exert countervailing influences, especially in the Politburo. Maverick Moscow party leader Boris Yeltsin reported that Yegor Ligachev, the seconding-ranking CPSU leader, and KGB boss Viktor Chebrikov sharply disapproved the liberalizing glasnost trends. By the end of 1987, the reform had slowed considerably.

The sputtering reformist trend within the USSR, after the initial dynamism in early 1987, had an impact at the Vienna follow-up. To the extent that the United States and the West placed emphasis upon compliance with Helsinki rather than upon a concluding document, there was growing disappointment with Soviet performance. Even if emigration rates shot up—a 700 percent increase in Jewish emigration as compared with the beginning of the year, and even higher percentage increases for German and Armenian emigration—the absolute figures still remained limited. For Jews, it was a mere 8,000 for the year.[10] Moreover, Moscow was strictly applying the new January 1987 regulations, which required an affidavit only from a first-degree relative. The requirement was a powerful constraint, especially when other devices to refuse visas were guided by caprice and arbitrariness.

Nor was there much significant progress in the negotiating process for a concluding document.[11] The USSR and the Warsaw Pact powers stonewalled major initiatives for breakthroughs in freer movement of people and ideas. Resistance, too, marked their attitudes with respect to the broadening of religious and ethnic rights. Soviet delegates would respond to every public exposure at Vienna of non-compliance or of poor performance with the usual invectives about homelessness or unemployment or racism in the United States (or repression of Irish Catholics in Ulster, should Britain raise compliance issues). Nonetheless, while Vienna could not be compared with either Madrid or Belgrade in terms of tension, the atmosphere had not significantly improved. Ambassador Zimmermann, who had served for a time as Max Kampelman's deputy at Madrid, continued the policy of naming names and citing cases. Before Vienna, he publicly stated that the US delegation "will insist on compliance with [Helsinki] commitments" and that he would "rigorously draw the balance between promises made and promises kept."[12] Where appropriate, he took cognizance of positive Soviet developments, but was uncompromising about inadequate performance or noncompliance.

Zimmermann was aware that a mix of praise and criticism would not significantly advance progress. Like Assistant Secretary of State Ridgway, he counted on effective leverage in the security field to force a positive response. In December 1986, Zimmermann's boss, Secretary of State Shultz, at a meeting of NATO foreign ministers prevailed on his colleagues, some of whom were hesitant, to pursue a linkage and leverage strategy.[13] Even earlier, Shultz had warned Moscow that advances in the arms control and related security fields would be "constrained" until "there is substantial Soviet progress in the vital area of human rights. . . ."[14]

The linkage strategy initially grew out of two important military-security objectives of the USSR. The first focused on a second stage of the Stockholm conference on confidence-building measures. The initial stage, with its agreement on extensive notification arrangements and unprecedented verification procedures, had won unusual enthusiastic support from Moscow. Indeed, the results of the agreement validated the hopes of both sides.

The deputy US ambassador at the Vienna talks, Robert Frowick, elaborated on the remarkable success of the Stockholm experience in an address to a closed security working group at the Vienna follow-up on September 1, 1988.[15] After detailing the experience of a US military team inspecting a Soviet-Polish military training operation in Poland in June 1988, Frowick praised the Soviet and the Polish army officers, who had extended broad cooperation. He noted that this had been the eleventh inspection carried out under the provisions of Stockholm, and observed that all the Helsinki signatories which had conducted inspections found them "a valuable tool." Frowick added that the inspection mechanism provided "an opportunity to further advance openness and the confidence-building process."

At Vienna, Soviet Foreign Minister Shevardnadze and chief delegate Kashlev demanded that the conference embrace the agreement on confidence-building measures and quickly set an early timetable for Stockholm II. There was little doubt at Vienna that it was the prospect of Stockholm II, with its eventual focus on disarmament, that had particularly attracted the Soviets in the first place and compelled them to make the significant concessions on verification at Stockholm I. The early convening of Stockholm II would fit neatly into key aspects of Soviet strategy. First, it would enable the Kremlin to use an appropriate international forum for the propagation of Soviet views on disarmament, particularly the establishment of nuclear-free zones and pledges on no-first-use of nuclear weapons. (Possibly, too, it might be used for Soviet views on "Star Wars.") Second, this type of forum, with its potential appeal over the heads of government to various publics, could help facilitate the long-term Moscow objective of lulling Western public opinion, splitting NATO, and isolating the United States.

The second Stockholm conference would serve two other Soviet military purposes, as indicated by a high Soviet military official at the Vienna meeting. General Viktor Tatarnikov declared that the USSR would seek advance notification of NATO air and naval exercises which were independent of military exercises taking place on land.[16] It also would want to have the zone covered under Stockholm I for notification and verification extended beyond the Atlantic coast toward the United States. Both proposals had been advanced by Soviet delegates at Stockholm without success.

At Stockholm, the West had insisted that, within the Helsinki accord, the focus of confidence-building measures in the security area must be exclusively on Europe, from the Atlantic to the Urals. Only those air and naval maneuvers beyond the European borders specifically connected to particular land maneuvers in Europe would be subject to the new notification and verification procedures.

Of an even higher priority, in the mind of Moscow, was the aim of incorporating under the Helsinki umbrella the proposed NATO-Warsaw Pact Conventional Arms Stability (CST) talks. In this way, Moscow hoped to move the talks out of their deadlock in MBFR and, with the support of France, into a more dynamic setting. Gorbachev was pressing for the removal of military tensions in Central Europe, and CST negotiations, possibly running parallel to the reduction of intermediate-range missiles, would greatly serve his domestic and foreign interests.

Some strong Helsinki advocates, including senior officials and staff of the Helsinki Commission, were hardly enthusiastic about the idea of bringing conventional arms talks within the Helsinki framework. In the late 1970s, they had raised strong objections to Helsinki sponsoring the Conference on Disarmament (later held in Stockholm) on grounds that it might imbalance the relationship between Basket I and Basket III.

With the Stockholm meeting alone posing such concern, all the more would the anxiety deepen when conventional arms stability issues were joined to confidence-building. Diplomats with long memories would recall that the thrust of Soviet policy in the 1950s and 1960s had been a European security conference, one with no human rights dimension. The ghost of Kremlin past hovered over the Vienna deliberations; Western ambassadors' frequent reiteration of the need for "balance" never quite exorcised it. Not surprisingly, in the spring of 1988, when considerable progress had already been reached on security issues (including a mandate for CST) but human rights progress was stymied by Soviet stonewalling, an unidentified Western diplomat expressed fear that Moscow was seeking to break the linkage between security and human rights.[17] "It would mean the end of the whole Helsinki process," he added.

But if some stressed the possibility of security issues overwhelming human rights issues, others saw the additional Helsinki security responsibilities as opportunities for greater leverage on the Soviet Union in advancing human rights. Secretary of State Shultz was of the latter school.

As noted earlier, Rozanne Ridgway's June 1986 testimony to the Commission indicated that the Vienna meeting offered special opportunities to extract human rights progress by linking it to security issues. Shultz had to sell the linkage idea to his NATO colleagues. At the same NATO ministerial in Brussels in December 1986, the NATO foreign ministers accepted that a new forum within Helsinki would focus on conventional arms, although MBFR was not completely dropped.[18] And NATO also made it clear that the negotiations for the mandate for CST, as well as CST itself, would be restricted only to the 23 members of the NATO and Warsaw Pact powers. The neutral/non-aligned CSCE powers would be kept out, although they would be kept informed after decisions were taken.

What intimately tied human rights to security issues at Vienna was a very crucial time factor that involved the peculiar and complex relationship between CSCE and the CST mandate talks. The 35 Helsinki signatories comprising CSCE met regularly in one part of Vienna. A different group, mainly specialists on military affairs from only the NATO and Warsaw Pact powers—23 instead of 35—met elsewhere in Vienna to formulate the mandate for the CST talks which would be adopted by the Vienna CSCE.[19] As CST had come under the CSCE umbrella, any decisions reached by the mandate negotiators could not be finalized unless and until the Vienna CSCE meeting, with its human rights component, had also reached agreement.

Thus, the adoption of the arms control mandate was totally dependent on consummation of CSCE negotiations relating to all the baskets. As the United States and the West had placed a high priority on reaching a significant agreement on human rights issues, it was clear that those from the Soviet bloc especially interested in getting the mandate completed and the CST talks started had to be generally responsive to Western human rights demands. Otherwise, the US, for example, could sit endlessly at the Vienna CSCE awaiting such responsiveness.

How the strategy would operate was explained in a candid letter from Ambassador Zimmermann to Helsinki Commission Chairman Hoyer on April 9, 1987:

> The Soviets are in a hurry to finish the Vienna meeting because it must end before they can move from the mandate negotiation to the actual negotiations on conventional arms reductions. *This gives us considerable leverage on human rights.*[20] [Emphasis added.]

Zimmermann went on to note that "we will not end the Vienna meeting without an adequate human rights result" and that this "condition also applies to the concurrent mandate discussions." Performance and deeds were stressed, although "a substantive and balanced final document" was also desirable.

Among the steps urged on the Soviet Union were "the full release of political prisoners, resolution of the family reunification cases, a steep increase in emigration and an end to jamming." Equally important, for Zimmermann, were requests dealing with the institutionalization of the process:

> We are asking the Soviets to provide credible assurances that compliance will continue to improve beyond the Vienna meeting. Examples would be: abolition of Articles 70 and 190 of the Criminal Code, abolition of the psychiatric hospitals run by the Interior Ministry . . . a mechanism to ensure higher levels of emigration and unambiguous commitments in the Vienna final document.

But questions remained as late as a year after. Morris B. Abram, then the chairman of the National Conference on Soviet Jewry, in a letter to

Zimmermann dated March 30, 1988, had queried about apparent US support for proposals advanced by the selected coordinator for a Basket III draft, the Swedish Ambassador to the Vienna talks.[21] What disturbed Abram was that the coordinator's draft did not carry "definitive language on significant performance" and, therefore, the Soviet Union would "see this as an easy way" out of Helsinki obligations. Performance might be sacrificed, Abram warned, as he speculated about the tactical direction of the US delegation at Vienna.

The Zimmermann response, dated April 21, did not neglect the issue of performance:

> The primary US objective at Vienna has been and remains significantly stronger performance by the Eastern countries in implementing the obligations of the Helsinki and Madrid documents. For us, performance is more important than additional texts, because the Soviets and their allies in the past have ignored textual commitments when it suited them to do so.[22]

It was an unflinching statement, but at the same time it made clear to the NGO leader that the emphasis on performance did not preclude the US pressing also for "a strong final document."

Zimmermann's explanation provided three reasons for the attention to the concluding document. First, a good document could add greater specificity to more general and less concrete provisions of Helsinki and Madrid. Second, a good document could provide an additional standard for holding the human rights conduct of East European countries up to public scrutiny.

The third reason was especially important. Ambassador Zimmermann pointed out that new texts are "critically important" for US allies. In an instructive and revealing comment, he noted that only the United States could effectively press the Soviet Union on performance; NATO allies "lack the weight" to do so. It is, therefore, not surprising that the allies would consider obtaining a specific and meaningful concluding document as "a primary arena of activity." In the interest of maintaining a unified NATO strategy at Helsinki meetings, Zimmermann observed, the United States took allied concerns very seriously. At Madrid, as at Belgrade, it was apparent that the State Department's career diplomats were more sensitive to NATO interests and perspectives than were the largely congressional Helsinki Commission or non-governmental organizations.

In any case, howsoever the question of priorities in US objectives was defined, much US diplomatic activity at Vienna—as at previous follow-up meetings—focused on preparation of a concluding document. The other

Helsinki participating states were similarly absorbed in the drafting process. The bulk of the lobbying, the contact meetings, the smaller group sessions, and the reports to and from capitals revolved around the process of preparing the concluding document. What emerged as a document from Vienna, in the US perspective, would simply have to go "significantly further" than previous concluding documents, whether accepted, as at Helsinki and Madrid, or rejected, as at Bern.

Linkage was thus tied to both performance and a meaningful and effective concluding document. Zimmermann hammered on the theme over and over again at press conferences, in plenary speeches, and in private meetings with various delegations, including the Soviet delegation. The United States would simply refuse to permit the ending of the Vienna meeting and, therefore, the onset of a Stockholm II session or of talks on conventional arms stability until it was satisfied on both compliance with prevailing standards and a document that improved on them.

The consensus feature of the Helsinki process—which had often stymied progress—also made possible the application of a tough leverage strategy, because trade-offs between Basket I and Basket III had always been a built-in component of Final Act diplomacy. In an interview, Zimmermann demonstrated his thinking on the strategy of leverage: "Tensions between the military and human rights aspects of the Helsinki process have provided the dynamic by which that process has developed and has established itself as a major phenomenon in East-West relations."[23] Elaboration of the strategy came from Ambassador Frowick, who served as Zimmermann's deputy, principally specializing on security issues. He explained in an interview that "Warren's strategy" was to keep the security discussions, which ran on a separate track, a step ahead of human rights.[24] Progress on the security track could be used as a trade-off for accompanying movement in human rights.

Clearly, the incorporation of conventional arms stability into the Helsinki process proved not the feared albatross but rather a powerful lever of change. When handled tactfully—as was the case in Vienna—the results could be enormously impressive.

Additional, if unexpected, leverage was provided by yet another factor—the Soviet desire for holding a Helsinki-sponsored human rights conference in Moscow, as proposed by Foreign Minister Shevardnadze at the very opening of the Vienna review meeting. Most Soviet delegates were taken aback by the proposal, and Kashlev privately acknowledged to the other diplomats later that he had not been consulted on the matter.[25] No one in Shevardnadze's entourage was prepared to respond to reporters' inquiries about how the Moscow conference would function and whether it would allow the traditional rights enjoyed by non-governmental representatives and journalists at other Helsinki-sponsored meetings. All indications suggested that the proposal had not been thought through and that the decision to advance it was limited to a few. (The Foreign Minister later revealed in his memoirs that the idea had been strongly opposed in the Politburo.[26])

For the United States and several of its Western allies, especially the United Kingdom and Canada, the proposed conference was an anomaly. How could a conference on human rights be held in a country whose record was less than adequate? At one point, Shultz explained that the host country must have an "exemplary" record in the field. The wording was later fundamentally changed. Countries were requested to show "significant improvements" in the human rights field.[27] But the US initially chose to emphasize a very different consideration—access to the proposed conference.

On July 28, 1987, Ambassador Zimmermann sought to obtain concrete assurance about the proposed Moscow conference by setting forth in a plenary speech ten conditions to be addressed before the United States would even consider the Moscow proposal.[28] The first required any Helsinki host government to guarantee entry and exit visas to all those who wished to attend. His statement made clear that such prospective attendees included both human rights activists and Soviet émigrés, who had traditionally attended Helsinki meetings. The host government would also be required to allow these groups to organize meetings, demonstrations, book fairs and press conferences; it would also be obligated to permit its own citizens to have access to the public meetings, to all delegations and non-governmental organizations, and to foreign journalists. Finally, all foreign journalists and broadcasters were to be given unhindered access.

Soviet diplomats in Vienna rejected the Zimmermann speech and its conditions. They said that it constituted interference in internal Soviet affairs, a charge that the United States denied on grounds that the conditions are the same for any country seeking to host a Helsinki meeting.[29] A few days before the Zimmermann speech—on July 24—Ambassador Kashlev had said that access to the Moscow meeting would follow the procedure of other Helsinki functions.[30] Nonetheless, details about the organization of the conference remained uncertain. During the first few months after the Shevardnadze speech, unofficial reports floated by the Soviet delegation spoke of sharp differences between the Soviet Foreign Ministry and hard-line Communist Party and KGB officials, who allegedly had not been consulted and who were strongly opposed to the idea.[31]

In an effort to obtain greater clarity about Moscow's intentions, the Vienna-based International Helsinki Federation for Human Rights sponsored on September 17 a special panel, comprising several governmental delegates to the Vienna follow-up meeting. The key figure was Professor Yuri Kolosov, who, in addition to serving on the USSR delegation, was also deputy head of the Department for Humanitarian and Cultural Affairs at the Soviet Foreign Affairs Ministry.

Responding to a query about access, Kolosov observed:

> Every state has its own rules on issuing visas. We also have our rules. Every state has a list of unwanted people. The list is computerized. If any person in the computer is persona non grata with respect to entering our country, such a person will not be admitted.[32]

The implication was clear. Those barred from entering Moscow under ordinary circumstances would not be permitted a visa to attend the human rights meeting. Kolosov also expressed doubt as to whether reporters from Radio Free Europe and Radio Liberty would be permitted in to cover the conference.

The Canadian panelist, Ambassador William Bauer, was particularly angry about Kolosov's reference to exclusion-by-computer. He commented: "When you start saying certain people are not acceptable, you ultimately wind up with a situation in which none are acceptable."[33] Even the representative of neutral Sweden, Nils Eliasson, expressed doubts. While his country, he said, had an "open" attitude to the Moscow meeting, it was "up to the Soviet Union to convince us." There were, he added, many questions about a Moscow meeting that required clarification.

Whether Kolosov was speaking for the Kremlin is not clear. On November 1, *The Sunday Times* (London) carried an interview with him by Nicholas Bethell, who had represented the European Parliament at the Vienna conference. It revealed Kolosov to be a "Mr. *Nyet*," with a hostility toward the West as intense as his hatred of Soviet dissidents, one of whom, Yuri Orlov, he called "not quite sane."[34] Bethell, noting that Gorbachev had criticized those Soviet diplomats who had acquired the reputation of a "Mr. *Nyet*," surmised that "perhaps he had Kolosov in mind."

For the balance of 1987 and for the first eight months of 1988, nothing further was heard about a Moscow conference. During the early summer, Western diplomats were saying that the Soviet Union seemed to have lost interest in the proposal. They told reporters that Moscow appeared to have reached the conclusion that the opposition of the United States, Britain, Canada, and France to a Moscow conference was too great and, therefore, there was little point in the Soviet Union pressing for a favorable outcome.[35]

But there were some Western diplomats in Vienna who expressed doubts that Moscow had totally abandoned the idea. An unidentified senior Western diplomat was quoted by a Radio Liberty reporter in Vienna in early June that the Soviet Union never forgets about any meeting it has proposed. The diplomat explained:

> It seems likely that the USSR recognizes that the time is not yet ripe. The West has set too many conditions that would be difficult to fulfill at this time. But I am sure they will return to it eventually. So long as some senior Soviet officials believe it would be a propaganda coup to have such a conference in Moscow, the idea is not likely to go away.[36]

Two technical considerations ultimately required some kind of decision, positive or negative, on a Moscow conference. First, the Vienna discussions had already concluded that, as part of a proposed implementing mechanism dealing with the "Human Dimension," three one-month-long experts meetings on human rights would be held sequentially in the years 1989, 1990, and 1991. Paris and Copenhagen had been provisionally nominated for the first two; some city had to be selected for the third. If it was not to be Moscow, Switzerland put in a claim for Geneva. More importantly, the Vienna conference could not end without a decision on the third human rights meeting. That choice inevitably became a compelling concern.

By the end of summer 1988, keen Soviet interest in a human rights conference in the Soviet capital surged. Shevardnadze on his various travels and Kashlev in Vienna intimated that, indeed, Moscow remained keenly interested in hosting the third meeting of the so-called "Conference on the Human Dimension."

What very likely helped propel a shift in the Kremlin's public posture on the Moscow conference was Gorbachev's defeat of powerful conservative forces in the spring and late summer.[37] The Nina Andreyeva affair in late March demonstrated the conservative attempt to halt the anti-Stalinist drive and limit the liberalizing trends. Andreyeva, a Leningrad teacher of strong Stalinist and anti-Semitic views, had written a long letter published in the conservative Communist Party organ, *Sovetskaia Rossiia*, on March 13, which sharply attacked reformist trends in the USSR and the assault on Stalin's heritage. Gorbachev was out of the country at the time, and his absence was exploited by supporters of his conservative opponent, Ligachev, to publish the letter. The published letter was given maximum exposure in various provincial Communist Party organs by the same forces. Momentum was building for an ideological attack on Gorbachev's glasnost policy.

Upon his return to Moscow, Gorbachev made the Andreyeva letter a vital political issue for the Politburo. He won needed support for a rollback of the Ligachev maneuver. An editorial was authorized for *Pravda* on April 5, apparently written by Gorbachev's close colleague, Aleksandr Yakovlev, harshly condemning the Andreyeva letter as benighted.

The potent reactionary offensive against glasnost and perestroika was brought to a halt. At the subsequent Central Committee meeting, a major personnel decision was taken; 110 committee members resigned. They were described as "dead souls" who represented "old thinking."

Gorbachev crowned his successful initiatives against the right wing at the historic 19th All-Union Communist Party Conference in late June. Democratization of the party and a "rule-of-law state" were his clarion calls. If earlier Gorbachev was too uncertain about his power base to press for a Helsinki human rights conference, which the right wing may very well have opposed, by the end of the summer the powerful conservative resistance had been dispersed, at least for the time being.

Shevardnadze outlined a fascinating argument for the value and pertinence of the USSR holding a human rights meeting when he visited Paris on October 9-12.[38] He said that it would assist the Gorbachev regime to correct internal human rights abuses, resolve questions of political prisoners, and alter its penal code. He acknowledged Moscow had "problems in this area" of human rights, and said the Helsinki process could be useful in solving them. He implied that Gorbachev needed continuing international support to help maintain his victory over conservative domestic forces.

The target of Shevardnadze's campaign was vital. France had been one of the strongest opponents of a human rights conference in the USSR. Meetings with French Foreign Minister Roland Dumas and President Mitterrand brought about a remarkable turnaround. Besides agreeing in a discussion over future CST deliberations, pinpointing the precise areas where confronting conventional armed forces could be reduced, they also reached an understanding on a human rights meeting in Moscow. France would support it. In return, the USSR would permit the establishment of a French cultural center in Moscow, the first such center in that city by a Western nation.[39]

Foreign Minister Dumas commented that "our goal was to bring relations to a higher level and give a new beginning to diplomatic activity

between the two countries."[40] Indeed, a host of controversial issues between the two was set forth on the agenda for discussion and resolution.
As for human rights, Shevardnadze appeared accommodating. The question of political prisoners in the USSR had "developed over the years and
cannot be resolved overnight," he said. Once a new penal code was enacted, this situation would change.

In sharp contrast to France, the United States viewed acquiescence to a
Moscow human rights meeting not in terms of a traditional diplomatic exchange of benefits, but rather as a means of extracting significant improvement in Soviet human rights performance. This perception was
initially quite different from that held by British Prime Minister Margaret
Thatcher. As she later explained in an interview, Moscow's maneuvers for
the conference were nothing more than "a political ploy" and "human
rights are not a political ploy." She movingly added:

> My worry is . . . that the hopes, the dreams, the faith of hundreds of thousands
> of people beyond the Iron Curtain, with names we do not know, who put their
> belief in us, if we did anything to make them think we have been hoodwinked.[41]

The State Department, however, was guided by advice Sakharov had
tendered in September that a Moscow human rights session could prove
beneficial for those seeking to reform Soviet society. If the Department,
then, did not object in principle to a Moscow conference, it nonetheless
could not agree to support the proposal unless the USSR took meaningful steps demonstrating good faith with respect to human rights. As early
as October 1987, Zimmermann had given the Soviet delegation a list of
conditions that would have to be fulfilled: the freeing of all political prisoners, including all Helsinki monitors; a significant increase in emigration; progress in the ending of jamming; and, assurances about the
institutionalization of these changes.[42]

A year later and after the French decision, the United States chose
once again to reemphasize the required conditions. On October 13, the
State Department said publicly:

> The United States will only consider this [Moscow conference] proposal in light
> of significant steps by the Soviets to improve their human rights performance
> and of credible guarantees of access and openness by the Soviets to anyone who
> wishes to participate in this meeting.[43]

It ought not to be assumed that this line was accepted by every key
agency in the US government. The National Security Council staff, according to Ambassador Zimmermann, held to a "negative" view of the

proposed conference, not dissimilar from the one advocated by Mrs. Thatcher.[44] Its conflict with the State Department on this issue lasted for over a year. Precisely what motivated the NSC staff is not known. Mrs. Thatcher believed that further human rights concessions by Moscow were essential. Whether this was held by the NSC staff is not apparent. In any case, the staff was clearly a participant in the decision-making process on this issue, which did not seem to apply on other Helsinki-related questions. In the end, Shultz's view prevailed but not without strong resistance in various quarters. The differences over the strategy of how to affect Soviet human rights practices were of considerable importance and require close examination.

Vigorous concern about when to conclude the Vienna session was expressed in Congress. On August 19, Representative Fascell publicly warned that the US delegation in Vienna seemed "to be backing away from . . . performance requirements due to pressure from other delegations, including some of our key NATO allies, to end the Vienna meeting as soon as possible in order that the CST may begin this fall."[45] The performance requirements to which he specifically referred were the release of *all* political prisoners, the resolution of *all* bilateral family reunification cases, a "substantial" increase in emigration and the end to the jamming of "several Western radios."

Fascell offered general data to buttress his comments. There were, he said, "at least 200 political prisoners" in the USSR, "several dozen divided family cases" and "thousands of human beings in the Soviet Union and Eastern Europe who have been struggling to emigrate."

This key congressman considered it vital that the United States "not bow to pressures" for an end to the Vienna meeting "until the human rights objectives" of the US delegation "have been achieved." Were the Vienna conference to be concluded and the Conventional Stability Talks begun without fulfillment of the performance aims of the US, it "would be a permanent blemish on our record." How long must the United States remain in Vienna? He offered no time limit in the letter; rather, he advised patience and perseverance "when fundamental principles of human rights" were involved.

For good measure, Fascell took an indirect swipe at the inclusion of the CST mandate within CSCE, referring to it as another "arms control forum" linked to Gorbachev's proposal of an "all-European summit." His previous concern that the Helsinki process might be weighed down by preoccupation with security matters quickly surfaced. Fascell recalled that, in an earlier letter to Secretary Shultz, he had complained that the

US and its allies had previously "agreed to expand the security dimension of the Helsinki process to an unprecedented degree" by encompassing the conventional arms stability talks. Now, it appeared to him, the "expansion of the military security aspects" of CSCE was taking place "at the expense of the human rights and human contacts provisions" of Helsinki.

In Fascell's opinion, the movement toward an ending of Vienna without "comprehensive and concrete improvements" in the human rights performance testified to the serious imbalance which had emerged between security and human rights interests. If the balance was not quickly restored, Fascell saw the successful fulfillment of the "long-term Soviet efforts to pervert the CSCE process with an all-European security forum devoid of all human rights components." Only by insisting at Vienna on the Soviet fulfillment of all Western performance objectives could the delicate balance between human rights and security with CSCE be maintained.

Support for the Fascell position, not unexpectedly, came from the Helsinki Commission; Chairman Steny Hoyer took the occasion of the State Department briefing for representatives of NGOs on September 8 to question whether an additional document emerging from Vienna was essential.[46] "We just want the promises of Helsinki fulfilled," he said. Failure to fulfill Helsinki obligations, he went on, should not be "papered over" with new documents. Challenging the administration's intention to fulfill its commitment for "staying in Vienna until we get the performance we're looking for," Hoyer put the matter bluntly: the United States "should be prepared to stay in Vienna until next year to get the [required] performance, including [performance from] the Romanians."

The special reference to the Romanians was an outgrowth of the briefing provided to the NGOs by Rozanne Ridgway.[47] In her evaluation of the Vienna talks, the West had made considerable progress with the USSR and most of its allies in advancing human rights aims in the draft concluding document. Only Romania was an exception. The Ceausescu regime was "intently marching backward," she said, which might require all other CSCE signatories to leave Romania "isolated in the end."

Hoyer was not in a compromising mood. Even if the French and West German governments were impatient and pressing for an early end to Vienna in order to move to the conventional arms stability talks, the Commission head insisted that the United States "needs to take the strongest possible stand on human rights."[48] In his view, Moscow was especially anxious to advance to the military-security negotiating process; all the more reason, then, for "our negotiations to stay until we have accomplished what we need to accomplish."

Ridgway chose to avoid a direct confrontation with the Helsinki Commission. After all, the audience was composed of public groups, with whom the Commission had an especially close working relationship. She studiously evaded any timeframe focus and, instead, seemed to borrow the Hoyer line. During the question period, for example, she observed, "There are moments when you try to extract all you can get—and the US is doing just that." It remained for Paula Dobriansky, a State Department deputy assistant secretary for human rights and former aide in the Reagan National Security Council, to provide a logical rationale to bring Vienna to a halt without satisfying all the delineated major objectives of the United States. She pointed out that "Helsinki is only one vehicle—there are other ways."

What the other ways were was not clear. But she was probably referring to the direct diplomatic negotiations on human rights between the USSR and the United States, a distinctive feature of the Reagan-Gorbachev era. Human rights was among four subjects that were handled in separate sub-groups at all high-level contacts between the two superpowers.[49] If considerable progress was made in the areas of emigration, political prisoners, family reunions and religious tolerance, it was due in some degree to these bilateral talks. A central figure in these talks would later disclose the wide range of human rights issues covered, but it would be difficult to estimate precisely how a specific discussion led to a specific forward step. As long as Gorbachev placed a high priority on his deepening relationship with Washington, these bilateral talks could be expected to continue and take on added significance. Dobriansky's superior, Assistant Secretary Schifter, explained in some detail the special significance of this channel.[50] He noted that while the other NATO powers, especially the smaller ones, needed Helsinki as a forum to negotiate on human rights with the USSR, the United States could and would do this directly. And, indeed, he indicated, the USSR was pleased with this vehicle.

Furthermore, the adoption at Vienna of a newly proposed mechanism for dealing with the human dimension offered an additional means for resolving human rights questions over the long run. The series of CSCE human rights meetings over the period 1989-91, under the rubric of the Conference on the Human Dimension, provided a forum for dealing publicly or privately with pertinent concerns. Helsinki, Dobriansky observed at the briefing, was becoming "an endless process."

Several weeks after the Hoyer critique at the State Department briefing, Co-chairman Dennis DeConcini joined his colleagues in indirectly questioning the Vienna policy line of the US delegation. He released a strongly worded congressional statement which expressed concern that military-security and trade issues were being permitted "to dwarf the human rights dimension of CSCE."[51] The emphasis on these issues at Vienna, he cautioned "could endanger the Helsinki process."

Officially, the US administration appeared to be holding firm to a non-endorsement of the Moscow conference. President Ronald Reagan, in a letter to a non-governmental group on October 20, declared that the US will "stand fast for acceptable performance [by the Soviet Union] for as long as necessary."[52] Speculation centered on the Soviets' reaction in the event they did not fulfill the conditions and the US formal response to a Moscow conference was negative.

Threatening gestures quickly emerged in the bargaining process. Soviet officials in Vienna warned Ambassador Zimmermann that if the US persisted in its attitude, they would reject all the other proposed human rights meetings (in Paris and Copenhagen), together with the entire projected human rights mechanism.[53] The United States warned, in turn, that it would not sit still on issues already adopted in which Moscow had an interest, clearly a reference to security and military matters.[54] The overt Soviet threats diminished, but the outcome was still far from certain. How would the Soviet Union respond to a US rejection? Would the Kremlin reject the concluding document? "I don't think that they will," Ambassador Zimmermann said in a private interview on October 16.[55] They had too much to gain in terms of the mandate on CST, he added.

When threats failed to work, Moscow sought to explore another avenue; how could the Soviets be certain that compliance with the conditions would lead to US agreement and participation in the Moscow conference? The operative word in the formal State Department position of October 13 was "consider," which did not connote a definitive and positive response. If Moscow took clear-cut steps of compliance with the US demands, could it be certain of a definite "yes"? And, if the yes were forthcoming, would not a "no" from the United Kingdom—as Mrs. Thatcher seemed to make clear—negate the understanding?

As the State Department strategy was primarily geared to extracting meaningful Soviet *performance* in the human rights field, it was unseemly to adhere to an uncertain or indefinite view concerning the Moscow conference. Thus, the term "consider" could be dropped. Given compliance, the US would approve (not "consider" approval).[56] But the other question posed about the British position was far more difficult. What would bring about a change in the attitude of Mrs. Thatcher? Communication between President Reagan and Prime Minister Thatcher followed, along with discussions between Shultz and Foreign Secretary Geoffrey Howe.

While details of these exchanges are unavailable, enough is known to indicate that Mrs. Thatcher was prepared to modify her uncompromising opposition to a Moscow conference if US conditions included two crucial points: the release of long-term refuseniks, and assurances that Soviet legal statutes would be enacted that would make recent human rights measures permanent. In an interview with *The Washington Post*, she said Britain agreed to approve a Moscow conference if several conditions were fulfilled by Moscow, including steps that "indicate an irreversible resolve" to provide a firm legal basis for recent Soviet human rights measures.[57]

On November 9, Shultz sent Shevardnadze a letter spelling out conditions for US (and British) approval of the Moscow conference.[58] The letter reportedly contained two separate sets of conditions. The first set listed steps that the Soviet Union was to take before the end of the Vienna meeting: the release of political prisoners from prisons, labor camps and psychiatric institutions; a significant increase in emigration; an end to jamming; and the granting of visas to long-term refuseniks. The second set listed measures the USSR would have to guarantee to undertake before the end of 1989 in the area of legal reform to institutionalize human rights progress. Britain had made it clear, in this connection, that it expected to see the abolition of laws which had been used to harass and jail human rights activists.

Nor did US diplomats neglect at Vienna the question of access to a Moscow conference for NGOs and journalists. They drew up a detailed list of requirements for all forthcoming and future conferences.[59] Every host country would be obligated to fulfill specified requirements which maximized access. The Soviets and their allies objected to commitments on openness as they applied to their own citizens, but Zimmermann threatened to veto the whole concluding document if these commitments were not included. In the end they were; a far-reaching openness text was ultimately accepted by consensus and became part of the concluding document of the Vienna review conference.

Progress during the next few weeks was impressive, indeed, extraordinary.[60] *All* political prisoners sentenced under the traditional repressive political and religious clauses of the Russian criminal code—Articles 70, 190-1, 142 and 227—were released, including the remaining two incarcerated Helsinki monitors. Ultimately, more than 600 prisoners were released since the opening of the Vienna meeting.

In mid-December, informed sources indicated that there remained approximately 140 political cases of persons either convicted under other criminal code articles or placed in psychiatric institutions. The Soviet

Union repeatedly denied that they were *political* cases. To resolve the conflict, the United States pressed for a mechanism to be created in its Moscow embassy that would examine, with the cooperation of Soviet judicial officials, the court records of the person involved. The Soviets also agreed to allow well-known Western psychiatrists to examine those persons incarcerated in psychiatric institutions whose incarceration the US was able to demonstrate was politically motivated.

Concerning emigration, the record was impressive.[61] During the last two months of 1988, the rate of Jewish emigration escalated to the highest level since 1979—2,300 in November, 3,600 in December. Emigration of Germans and Armenians also reached fairly high levels. For the year 1988, the emigration total was a remarkable 77,000. In addition, most of the bilateral cases of divided families, blocked marriages, and dual nationals were satisfactorily resolved. Only seven of some 55 cases remained in limbo.

However, progress with respect to long-term refuseniks was quite limited. Part of the problem lay in the definition of "long-term." The United States seemed to have accepted a ten-year definition for this category.[62] Human rights groups which monitored the refusenik problem would have preferred a five-year definition. The reason for their view was the fact that most refuseniks were rejected on grounds of state security, and the most recent United Nations study had urged a limit of five years for the application of this negative device.[63] A responsible scientific monitoring group reported that there were nearly 500 Soviet Jewish scientists who had been refuseniks for over five years.[64]

In early December, the Soviets announced that the state-secrets ban had been lifted for 120 refuseniks. According to an informed source, only 65 of the 120 cases had become known and, of this group, only 15 had been actually granted exit visas.[65] Clearly, the refusenik issue was far from resolved.

If the record on the prisoner and emigration questions was less than perfect, the same could not be said on the jamming issue; all the jamming devices hindering foreign radio broadcasts were turned off. (In his closing Vienna speech, Shultz urged that the jamming instruments be dismantled and scrapped.) That the Soviet Union was responding to determined US pressure at CSCE was apparent. Soviet chief delegate Kashlev put it gently when questioned in Vienna about the cessation: "If one of our priorities coincides with the situation at the CSCE meeting here, then it is good for the CSCE and good for us."[66]

In cultivating the positive new image aimed at winning support for the Moscow human rights conference, the Kremlin invited for the first time the US Helsinki Commission. In mid-November, 14 congressmen and senators from that body, which had often been sharply critical of Soviet human rights policies, arrived to meet for a four-day seminar with Soviet parliamentarians, and were treated with considerable deference. The Kremlin resolved some 150 emigration cases that the Commission raised, and agreed to examine several hundred other cases. Chairman Hoyer found the meetings "very worthwhile."[67] Later, on December 9, as Soviet emigration practices continued to improve, he appeared to be optimistic about a Moscow human rights conference. He said it was being given "very serious consideration" by the West.

While considerable progress had been made by the USSR in fulfilling the conditions of the November 9 letter, stumbling blocks persisted with respect to certain prisoners, long-term refuseniks, and assurances of insti-tutionalization of Soviet reforms. Moreover, President Reagan had not yet reached a firm decision on the question of a human rights meeting in Moscow and, as noted earlier, the National Security Council staff attitude was scarcely enthusiastic.

To preclude the possibility of an unfavorable response from the United States, Gorbachev told President Mitterrand that if the West could not then accept the proposal of a Moscow conference, "we can wait." He was certain that its "time will come."[68] The Gorbachev view was conveyed to Mrs. Thatcher by President Mitterrand on December 1 at their meeting in Mont-St.-Michel.[69] Two days later, *Le Monde* carried an interview (con-ducted on December 1) with Vadim Zagladin, a top Soviet ideologist and adviser to Gorbachev, in which he said, "if the West is unwilling, it is not a tragedy."[70] The USSR, he said, no longer regarded agreement on the Moscow conference as a precondition for concluding the Vienna meeting and, therefore, for beginning the conventional arms negotiations.

The reason for the new Soviet position was not clear. The Kremlin may have concluded that a harsher and threatening public line would have been counterproductive. It may also have been hedging against a possible rejection. At Vienna, Kashlev spoke in gentle terms about the Kremlin's willingness to withdraw the proposal for a human rights conference in Moscow. He added: "The ball is now in NATO's court. One should tell us what one wants us to do. We have shown good will and want to sign the final document as soon as possible."[71]

In fact, Shultz seems to have reached a decision in early December to support the Moscow conference, and hinted as much in a meeting with American Jewish leaders in the first week of December.[72] On December 9, while at a meeting of NATO foreign ministers in Brussels, he reportedly instructed Zimmermann to press for a conclusion of the Vienna meeting if it could be on Western terms.[73] There was, however, no formal statement of approval by the administration.

Several reasons were offered for Shultz's positive view.[74] He felt that the West had attained most of its human rights objectives, and additional pressure might prove counterproductive. With the new Bush administration coming into office on January 20, an inevitable delay in policy decisions and personnel appointments with respect to Vienna could seriously interrupt the positive momentum in the human rights field, possibly even causing a reversal. On the other hand, however, a new administration would not be saddled with decisions its predecessor had reached, and it might even wish to choose its own course.

Of critical significance, though, was growing pressure in Congress and among arms control specialists that further delay in Vienna would prevent or postpone vitally important negotiations on arms reductions. The INF treaty, it was thought in important quarters, had revealed great Western vulnerability vis-à-vis Soviet military power in Central Europe. This perspective was strongly embraced by various West European countries, most notably West Germany.

There was also the personal equation. Shultz had taken a keen interest in all aspects of the Helsinki process and strongly wished to have it consummated "on his watch"—as he was quoted as saying.[75] Finally and tellingly, he was fearful that a vital opportunity, if not seized now, might be forever lost. He privately told an observer later that if the Moscow conference had been delayed indefinitely, then "nine months down the road," human rights groups would have been energetically complaining about a missed opportunity.[76]

Some Western delegates felt that the clear signals of US willingness to sanction the Moscow human rights conference would weaken Western leverage. If stronger language on certain human rights was required in the concluding document, such as on the state-secrets issue or on use of the term "monitors," and if additional positive performance was sought in the area of political prisoners and refuseniks, would not such objectives be jeopardized by premature indication of a willingness to settle?[77] Such attitudes were especially dominant in the British and Canadian delegations.

But for how long in the endgame does one wait for additional concessions, and at what point does continuing pressure produce either a diminishing positive consequence or, worse, a counterproductive result? The dilemma for Secretary of State Shultz was not as stark as the questions seemed to suggest. He saw in the Helsinki accord a continuing process made ever more dynamic and interactive by the Vienna concluding document's requiring a number of follow-up meetings in security and human rights. On January 4, the White House formally endorsed the Moscow conference. Clearly Shultz's perspective on the question was decisive. In the official White House briefing, it was noted that "the President recognizes that there is much yet to be done in the Soviet Union before that nation meets acceptable and universal standards."[78] The statement, nonetheless, indicated that the decision was not permanently fixed. US approval was itself seen as a useful form of leverage, "a means of encouraging continuation of the significant progress in human rights that has taken place in the Soviet Union over the past three years," as the White House briefing noted. Leverage remained as the centerpiece of US strategy.

In his major address to the Vienna meeting on January 17, Shultz stressed the process itself and emphasized that CSCE stood now at a new "beginning" stage.[79] The process, especially in its new stage, provided for the continued application of leverage. At a press conference immediately afterward, Shultz warned that if there was "lack of real progress" on human rights performance by the Soviet Union, then "no doubt, the American government won't send a delegation" to the Moscow conference.[80] He need not have added that other Western democracies would be similarly guided. In any case, pressure would remain on the Soviets to perform, especially with respect to commitments on basic legal reforms that would institutionalize the changes that conformed with Helsinki. And, as Shultz made evident at Vienna, it was projected into the future as well.

·13·

Vienna: A Landmark

During the third week of the New Year, Vienna was aglow with festivities marking the end of the follow-up meeting. Even as the foreign ministers assembled to give their final speeches—the concluding document having been signed on January 15—and to hold press conferences before a huge media corps, elaborate balls and fine dinners were scheduled. It was, after all, time to celebrate a 26-month-long marathon of plenary sessions, subsidiary working groups, and private sessions that had finally come to an end. It was the longest review conference since Helsinki started. While Madrid ran several months longer, much of its nearly three-year session was actually passed in lengthy periods of adjournment.

Nearly 175 years earlier, in 1815, the historic Congress of Vienna had come to an end in order, in the words of its principal architect, Britain's Viscount Castlereagh, "to bring back the world to peaceful habits."[1] The Congress formally concluded the era of Napoleonic wars and ushered in a new era focused upon the security of the status quo. Somewhat similarly, the new Vienna document could be understood as laying the groundwork for a new security structure that would end the Cold War in the not too distant future.

A curious formulation—the "Final Act"—was adopted on June 9, 1815, constituting the concluding document of the Congress. That phrase, of course, would be replicated in the formal title of the Helsinki accord. As understood in 1815, it had simply meant the end of the Congress. In contrast, the Vienna concluding document of January 1989 was understood to mean, as George Shultz noted, only a "beginning." If the old Congress was oriented to preserving, even freezing, the established order, the new Vienna assemblage was underwriting change, notably in the human rights field. Dynamism was its essence. The Congress of Vienna had had only one human rights dimension—the slave trade. Castlereagh had been as determined to end that gross human rights violation as he was to end the Napoleonic epoch, and he had succeeded in both.

The British statesman stressed in his memoirs that his aim at Vienna was "not to collect trophies."[2] In contrast, the leading figure for the West at Vienna, George Shultz, did collect a "trophy" in the form of a major concluding human rights document. In only a few days, he would cease being Secretary of State, as the new Bush administration would be inaugurated in Washington on January 20. No one had a greater claim on the concluding document. It was Shultz who dominated the decision-making process in Washington and with allies in the endgame that made possible the breakthrough. A report of the US Helsinki Commission grasped the centrality of his role:

> The Vienna Meeting came to an end when it did primarily because US Secretary of State George Shultz decided, in consultation with Soviet Foreign Minister Eduard Shevardnadze, to try to have it conclude before he was to leave office in January 1989. As a result of this decision, the US delegation made a major effort, beginning in December 1988, to persuade other delegations to join the United States in meeting the Shultz deadline.[3]

The Helsinki process had operated for so long on the fringes of international affairs that few observers immediately caught the landmark significance of what was transpiring in Vienna in January 1989. The very length of the Vienna meeting may have anesthetized many; others had concluded long before that Helsinki was primarily an exercise in oral disputation. Nonetheless, foreign ministries in Europe and North America during the fall and winter of 1988 had become extraordinarily preoccupied with the Helsinki process. According to one diplomatic insider, fully 50 percent of NATO officials' deliberations in Brussels were devoted to that process during late 1988.[4] It can be assumed that a similar preoccupation seized the Warsaw Pact participants. US Ambassador Warren Zimmermann commented in an interview that Helsinki had become "a growth industry."[5]

What emerged from the deliberations in CSCE capitals, at NATO and Warsaw Pact headquarters, and especially at Vienna was a human rights agreement unprecedented in Helsinki history. Canadian Ambassador William Bauer, an experienced Helsinki hand, observed that the earlier Madrid document paled before the Vienna agreement. The former, he said, was so full of ambiguities that it could now be "chucked in the wastebasket." Ambassador Zimmermann said the Vienna concluding document was "light years better" than any Helsinki accord, including the Final Act itself.[6] Four substantive human rights sections of the adopted document illuminated the progress reached at Vienna: the right to leave a country; religious rights; ethnic rights; and the right to information as it related to foreign broadcasting. Other rights were also improved. The concreteness and specificity in each instance were extraordinarily impressive.[7]

Undoubtedly, of all the areas in which substantive progress was made, Alec Douglas-Homes's July 1973 vision of freer movement of people came closest to full realization at Vienna.

Heretofore, Helsinki documents had avoided specific references to the right to leave a country, which is the language of both the Universal Declaration of Human Rights (Article 13[2]) and the International Covenant on Civil and Political Rights (Article 12). Instead, the focus of Basket III's "Human Contacts" section had been on "reunion of families." At most, the Helsinki accord required participating states to "facilitate" *freer* movement—not *free* movement—and to extend "favorable treatment in a humanitarian spirit" to expedite visas for reunification of family or for joining spouses together. Madrid had added little to this formula. Now for the first time in the Helsinki process, "the right of everyone to leave any country, including his own, and to return to his country" was clearly and explicitly stipulated (in this form: "everyone shall be free to leave any country"). The new language marked a "sea change," according to a legal expert on the subject.[8] Precisely because of the revolutionary character of the change, the various facets of the new agreement on freer movement of people, together with the remaining limitations, require noting.

In keeping with the humanitarian objectives of Basket III, Vienna specified time frames for emergency travel purposes. Applications for visas to visit a sick or dying family member abroad would be processed within three days, for ordinary visits within a month, and for exit visas to be reunited with family or spouse within three months (instead of six months as provided in Madrid). Since at the time of the Vienna document signing, there was a huge backlog of "outstanding cases"—mainly refuseniks—the new document specified that solutions to these cases would be determined within six months after the conclusion of the conference.

Other provisions were also substantial. CSCE signatories agreed "to respect the wishes of the applicants on the country of destination," totally repudiating the Soviet initiative at Bern to limit travel and emigration rights to only the Helsinki countries. Vienna also stipulated that particular attention be paid to cases involving reunification of minors with their parents. Further, applicants refused exit visas were to be informed in writing of the reasons for the refusal and of the administrative and judicial remedies available to them to seek redress.

Especially important was a new stipulation that the right to leave "shall not be subject to any restrictions," except those "provided by law" and

"consistent . . . with obligations under international law." Far more significant was the specification that any restrictions in documents of international law (like those in the Covenant on Civil and Political Rights) would
be clearly understood as "exceptions." The document stressed that the
"participating states will ensure that these restrictions are not abused and
are not applied in an arbitrary manner. . . ." All too often, Moscow had
utilized the restrictive language of the Covenant concerning "national security" (i.e., "state secrets") or "the rights of others" to capriciously deny
exit visas, creating a vast category of refuseniks and stifling the desire to
emigrate generally.

Stress on the word "exceptions" placed sharp, though undefined, limits
on bureaucratic arbitrariness. Within this context, Vienna also sought to
tackle the capricious, erratic and controversial technique Moscow had
used to deny visas to Jewish applicants on grounds that they allegedly
possessed state secrets. The new document asserted the participating
states would ensure that the refusal for "reasons of national security"
would have "strictly warranted time limits," as short as possible and not
applied in "an arbitrary manner." For further clarification, Vienna required that an applicant could have his refusal reviewed within six
months and at regular intervals thereafter, with account taken of the
"time elapsed since the applicant was last engaged in work or duties involving national security. . . ."

While the entire thrust of the right-to-leave sections of the Vienna document emphasized the right itself and the removal of obstacles to the exercise of this right, it still failed to come to grips in a concrete and specific
way with the crucial problem of state secrets or national security. The
United States had sought to cope with the issue in the NATO caucus by
suggesting a five-year limit; after five years away from classified material,
the US proposal implied, a person would not likely be in possession of secrets.[9] This view, based upon the assumption made explicitly in a mid-
1980s United Nations study of the right to leave, held that scientific
advances in the contemporary world moved at such a fast pace that even
the most secret information was outdated in a short time, certainly within
five years. The UN study, conducted by Zambian legal specialist C.L.C.
Mubanga-Dipoya, held that a visa should never be denied except when
there is "a clear, imminent and serious danger to the State."[10]

A five-year limit in the Vienna document might very well have won
Moscow's acquiescence. Gorbachev had himself, during an interview on
French television in October 1985, used the figure of five to ten years as
an outside limit on the state-secrets refusal device, although in a Decem-

ber 1987 interview on American television he failed to set a limit; he simply noted that "we have only those who have not been given permission
to leave because of state security reasons . . . and we will continue to act in
that way."[11] But a year later, his remarkable December 7, 1988, address to
the UN General Assembly offered a specified humane approach, even
using the language of the Vienna document, then still in draft form:

> The problem of exit from and entry to our country, including the question of
> leaving it for family reunification, is being dealt with in a humane spirit. As the
> Assembly will know, one of the reasons for refusal of permission to leave is a
> person's knowledge of secrets. Strictly warranted time limitations on the se-
> crecy rule will now be applied.[12]

That address—particularly the quoted part of it—was designed to signal
to the West Moscow's positive intentions concerning the Vienna document.

The day after the UN address, Fyodor Burlatsky, an early Gorbachev
adviser and Chairman of the Public Commission on Humanitarian Problems and Human Rights of the Soviet Committee for Security and Cooperation in Europe, revealed that a new law being drafted by the Supreme
Soviet would probably set seven years as a maximum limit for the possession of state secrets; his own committee had requested that the limit be
placed at five years on grounds of the speed of technological progress.[13]
One month later, before the Vienna document was signed, Soviet legal
specialist Professor Vladimir Kartashkin told an interviewer from a leading Soviet journal that a limit of "seven years in our country would be a
very important positive step which would sharply limit opportunities for
[bureaucratic] department arbitrariness."[14] When asked whether seven
years was not an excessively long period in view of scientific progress,
Kartashkin conceded that perhaps it was, and that five years would be
sufficient. During the following month, a prominent member of
Burlatsky's commission, Semyon Mariev, wrote in a major Soviet ideological journal that the maximum time limit for state secrets should be
five years, adding that this view enjoyed wide support in the Soviet public
as well as among jurists and the party leadership.[15]

The American five-year-limit proposal ran up against an unexpected,
and ultimately insuperable, obstacle in the NATO caucus: Bonn strongly
objected. Its agreement with East Germany permitted East Berlin to
refuse visas for travel to West Germany on grounds of state secrets, but
that refusal had a specific one-year limitation. The FRG delegates feared
that a five-year maximum would sanction an East German initiative to
raise the level beyond the prevailing one-year limit. NATO felt obliged to

accept a Bonn substitute draft which committed all states to "refrain from any abuse of restrictions" based on national security and to establish a maximum limit which "will in no case exceed one year from the time the individual last had access to national security information." The one-year formula needed consensus from the Soviet bloc, and, of course, it failed to obtain such. Vienna's language specifying "strictly warranted time limits" constituted a not-too-satisfying compromise.[16]

Yet, during the following several years, the USSR appeared to abide generally to a fairly flexible application of the Vienna formula. Almost all of the long-time refuseniks on the 1989 lists were permitted to leave during the subsequent two years, although new refusenik names would be entered on the lists. The problem persisted until mid-1991, when the Supreme Soviet finally approved the promised emigration law, which provided for a five-year maximum limit on state-security cases. If the Vienna document's extensive right-to-leave provision had a significant impact on the Soviet Union even before its adoption (as evidenced by Gorbachev's UN General Assembly speech), as well as afterward, it also exerted an enormous influence on post-Vienna developments in Eastern Europe. (See Chapter 15.)

With respect to religious rights, Vienna also marked a giant step forward. In contrast to the very limited and greatly circumscribed comments about the exercise of religion made in the Helsinki accord and only slightly broadened at Madrid, the Vienna document offered in elaborate detail specific rights both on the religious-community level and on an individual basis. While these rights were recognized in other international agreements, such as the Covenant on Civil and Political Rights and the UN Declaration on the Elimination of All Forms of Religious Intolerance, for CSCE they were altogether new. Religious communities would be allowed "to establish and maintain . . . places of worship and assembly," as well as organize themselves "according to their own hierarchical and institutional structure." In the Soviet Union, only the Russian Orthodox Church had been accorded this status in full. Now, it would apply as well to smaller recognized religious communities, including the Jewish one.

More significant were new rights guaranteed to religious communities to "select, support and replace their own personnel." They would also be permitted to engage in fund raising and the training of religious personnel. They were now authorized to acquire, possess and use religious articles and manuals (including sacred books), along with religious publications "in the language of their choice." And religious communities would also be permitted to import and disseminate religious publications and materials. Such rights were completely absent in the USSR prior to Vienna.

On the individual level, the rights accepted and granted were unprecedented for communist societies. The text relating to religious education for the individual was particularly impressive: Vienna provided for "the right of everyone to give and receive religious education in the language of his choice, whether individually or in association with others." And parents were granted the previously unheard-of "liberty" to "ensure the religious and moral education of their children in conformity with their own convictions." This liberty was not restricted merely to education given by parents; religious education could be given either individually or on a group level by teachers.

Religious rights, whether on an individual or on a group basis, were also given a transnational dimension. Religious communities would be allowed "to establish and maintain contact and communication with each other, in their own and other countries." Contact would also mean "participation in assemblies and other religious events" within or outside the borders of a country. In contrast, traditional communist practice had aimed at restricting contacts of a native religious community with the same religious community in Western societies. Moscow had even prevented formal religious contacts among a single religious community on a national level within the USSR.

Major advances were also made in the parallel area of rights of national minorities. This subject had been given little attention in the Helsinki accord and Madrid's concluding document. In these earlier documents, participating states of a multinational or pluralistic character had been simply called upon to facilitate the contributions of their respective national minorities to culture, and they were further required to assure minorities full human rights without discrimination. Now, at Vienna, a broad consensus emerged for greater attention to the subject and more detailed specificity concerning rights.[17] (Hungary's strong advocacy of national minority rights, no doubt prompted by its concern over the repressive treatment by the Ceausescu regime of the Hungarian minority in Transylvania, was a crucial factor in raising the level of CSCE interest in the subject.)

Helsinki signatories were now required to adopt domestic legislation that assured human rights for their respective national minorities, and were called upon to "protect and create conditions for the promotion of the ethnic, cultural, linguistic and religious identity of national minorities on their territory." Clearly, Helsinki held that national minorities were positive entities, not neutral ones, and cultivation of their culture and language was a significant value for society as a whole. In fact, their value was so great that governments were required to "create conditions" for their benefit, not merely to exercise the negative function of protecting them.

Minorities were guaranteed the right to "maintain and develop their own culture in all its aspects, including language, literature and religion" and to "preserve their cultural and historical monuments and objects." Minorities were to have the right to "disseminate, have access to, and exchange information in their mother tongue." And they were to be assured the right to "give and receive instruction on their own culture, including instruction through parental transmission of language, religion and cultural identity to their children." The specified right had far-reaching implications for the multinational Soviet society, which had in the past practiced discrimination against many of its ethnic components, especially dispersed groups such as Jews.

Minorities' transnational contacts were also protected. All too often, the Warsaw Pact countries, most notably the USSR, had sought to sever such links between its various national minorities and their brethren abroad, seeing them as subversive. Vienna, in contrast, stipulated that national minorities "can establish and maintain . . . contact through travel and other means of communication, *including contacts with citizens of other states* with whom they share a common national origin *or cultural heritage*" (emphasis added).

The Vienna document contained a fourth innovative feature that was almost revolutionary in the Helsinki process, relating to the right of individuals to choose freely their sources of information. Jamming of foreign radio frequencies, a traditional feature of communist societies in Eastern Europe, was specifically banned.

If the Helsinki Final Act had required unhindered imparting of knowledge through all forms of communication, this obligation had been simply observed in the breach through jamming. Two key radio stations had been the principal targets of the jamming by the Soviet Union and several of its Warsaw Pact allies, Radio Free Europe and Radio Liberty. They were seen as the very embodiment of capitalist and imperialist evil, whose presumed aim was the subversion of communist society. Other foreign radio stations that had been jammed on the eve of the Vienna decision were Deutsche Welle and the Voice of Israel; earlier, the Voice of America and the British Broadcasting Corporation (BBC) had been jammed.

Interference with foreign radio broadcasting had been rationalized, despite the intent of Helsinki, through a 1936 treaty of the defunct

League of Nations.[18] The agreement had permitted states to prohibit broadcasts which were considered either detrimental to international understanding or were of a character likely to incite populations to act against the security of their own states. What the drafters at the time had in mind was the Nazi propaganda endeavors to stir up ethnic German minorities in Eastern Europe against the established governments.

Moscow had given no attention to the League of Nations treaty during the post-war period even though it had begun jamming the two radio stations (Radio Free Europe and Radio Liberty—RFE/RL) in the early 1950s.[19] During the 1982 Madrid discussions on freedom of media expression, which the West had been stressing, Soviet researchers must have come upon the League treaty. Suddenly, almost 50 years after its adoption, Moscow brought it to the Supreme Soviet for quick action. The ratification was completed in 1982, in time to respond to a proposed Swiss-Austrian draft of a concluding document. If the draft obliged Helsinki signatories to "permit direct and normal reception of foreign radio broadcasts," the Soviet delegates could insist upon an additional clause: "which are in accordance with the regulations of the International Telecommunications Union and other international instruments." The phrase "other international instruments" was intended to cover the unearthed League of Nations treaty and its sanction of jamming.

That sanction especially focused upon Radio Free Europe and Radio Liberty. Even when jamming was lifted early in 1987 against BBC and the Voice of America, RFE/RL remained the targets of almost apoplectic verbal assaults by Soviet delegates in Vienna. In September 1988, Ambassador Zimmermann led the fight against the radio interference with the demand that "jamming must cease across all frequencies, and institutional changes must be introduced to ensure that jamming does not begin again."[20] But Soviet delegate Vladimir Morozov denounced the US initiative as a means to help stations whose only purpose was allegedly to promote propaganda fomenting unrest in East European countries.[21] Firmly and repeatedly, he declared that Moscow would never agree to end jamming. An especially uncompromising line was taken by the head of the Soviet delegation, Yuri Kashlev. Soon after the Morozov statements, he emphasized: "The time has come for the West to abandon attempts to protect the fossil remnants of the Cold War that the propaganda establishments [had] designed to foment political, nationalist and religious fervor in other states through their broadcasts."[22]

The Kashlev statement came two months before Vienna reached its climactic stage. No one expected the Soviet delegation to reverse itself.

Some were certain that Moscow would reject any text that explicitly banned jamming. Others, basing themselves on several hints by high-level Soviet officials, speculated that a text banning jamming might be approved if its formulation was sufficiently ambiguous as to permit a resumption of jamming when deemed appropriate. Even Shultz's November note to Shevardnadze did not provide language of the zero option type. A certain ambiguity was used to make the Western demand more palatable.

Gorbachev himself put an end to ambiguity and uncertainty. In his historic address to the United Nations General Assembly in December, he said, "We see an end to the jamming of broadcasts by all foreign radio stations that transmit programs to the Soviet Union, also within the context of the Helsinki process."[23] The concluding reference to the Helsinki process revealed a determination to adhere to the international human rights standards which, with respect to radio broadcasting, would be made explicit in the Vienna document. The Gorbachev announcement was followed nine days later by a similar decision of the Czechoslovakian government. The formal disclosure of the action was made at the Vienna plenary, where the Prague delegation sought to demonstrate how its government no longer engaged in repressive acts, but rather now conducted itself in conformity with Helsinki accord provisions.[24] The last of the jammers in East Europe—Bulgaria—made the new orientation unanimous. On December 23, it halted interference with Radio Free Europe broadcasting.[25]

Vienna provided numerous other examples of positive advances. US government human rights specialists did a close analysis of the text at a fairly early drafting stage, and found that of 71 articles covering the Basket III section on "humanitarian and other fields," more than one-half—43—constituted a "step forward."[26] Some were even "significant."

Of special interest to the United States was the section on international communications, which had been the subject of a bitter struggle over a period of several years. Until 1988, international postal and telephonic communications with Soviet citizens was uncertain at best; at worst it was less than minimal, reflecting an authoritarian and nationalist determination to cut communications with the West and to break normal bonds of family and friends. The Vienna document required the participating states to "ensure the rapid and unhindered delivery of correspondence, including personal mail and parcels." The privacy and integrity of postal and telephonic communication were guaranteed, along with "conditions necessary for rapid and uninterrupted telephone calls."

Several other advances merit noting. The signatories were required to bring their laws, regulations, and policies into harmony with CSCE, an aim which the USSR and some of its allies had initially opposed at Vienna. The participating states were also required to publish and make accessible all laws, regulations and procedures relating to human rights and fundamental freedoms. Specific remedies were spelled out for those who claimed violation of their rights, including the right of appeal to governmental organs, and provisions for a fair and public hearing with the legal counsel of one's own choice. It also provided for the appellant to be promptly and officially informed, as a rule in writing, of the decision on the appeal so that further available remedies could be pursued.

The governments of participating states assumed greater commitments regarding the monitoring of their citizens' rights as related to Helsinki, a particular aim of the United States since the time of the Belgrade meeting. If the US delegation could not prevail upon the Warsaw Pact powers to accept the specific term "monitors,"[27] they did win agreement on comparable substantive language. Signatories were to "respect the right of their citizens to contribute actively, individually or in association with others, to the promotion and protection of human rights and fundamental freedoms." Another Vienna clause obligated governments to "respect the right of persons to observe and promote the implementation of CSCE provisions, and to associate with others for this purpose." Vindicated here were the voluntary non-government monitoring structures that had been created in the USSR, Poland and Czechoslovakia soon after the Helsinki accord had been signed, and which had been afterward crushed by repressive governments.

Of considerable significance, too, was the creation of a mechanism—strongly pushed by the Netherlands—for implementation of the Helsinki accord and of specified new rights. While by no means considered truly enforceable compliance machinery, the new mechanism for the first time legitimized the right to make complaints—although the word used was "representations"—and the right to have the complaints seriously considered. First, the mechanism provision called upon the signatories to "exchange information and respond to requests for information and to representations made to them by other Participating States on questions relating to the human dimension of the CSCE." Second, the mechanism enabled any Helsinki participating state to make representation to any other that the former considered was violating human rights provisions of CSCE documents. The Vienna document required the accused member to meet with the complaining state to discuss and possibly resolve the issue. Given the Warsaw Pact countries' traditional reaction to charges about human rights violations, it was apparent that a giant step forward had been taken.

Third, to encourage a positive outcome to the bilateral negotiations, a complaining participating state was permitted to circulate information about specific situations involving human rights violations to the other CSCE states. Through this means, pressure could be exerted upon alleged violators to offer remedial action. As a final element in the compliance mechanism, the Vienna follow-up meeting scheduled three one-month-long human rights experts meetings in each succeeding year: 1989 in Paris, 1990 in Copenhagen, and 1991 in Moscow, under the title "Conference on the Human Dimension." Each meeting would evaluate the current status of rights fulfillment, as well as the effectiveness of the compliance mechanism, giving added impetus to enforcement. The notion of annual sessions almost lent Helsinki a character of permanent and continuing process with respect to implementation. Human rights would now appear center stage in the international public arena. The next follow-up meeting was scheduled for March 1992 in Helsinki itself, where the process had begun 20 years earlier.

The new emphasis given to a mechanism of implementation meant that the Helsinki signatory powers had accepted a fundamental policy position that performance was as important, if not more so, than written commitments on human rights. At Belgrade, this policy line became evident, at least for the United States. By the time of Vienna, the policy was central to British and Canadian CSCE thinking, and had moved beyond them to most of NATO and even some of the neutral/non-aligned countries. The concluding document made the policy official for CSCE as a whole. As one perceptive commentator noted, "the states have now moved towards the notion of effective human rights."[28] Gorbachev explicitly gave it the support of the Soviet Union and its allies. In his December UN speech, he said: "We intend to expand the Soviet Union's participation in the human rights monitoring arrangements in the United Nations and the Conference on Security and Cooperation in Europe."[29]

Two crucial points in the initial Western draft for the human dimension proposal did not obtain consensus. One would have allowed any member to request a special meeting of CSCE "to discuss and resolve specific situations and cases."[30] This limitation, however, was overtaken by the scheduled conference on the human dimension, at least during 1989-91. The second early-draft provision required that governments respond also to requests for "information and representations" from private persons or groups, as well as from other governments. Rejection of this proposal meant, in essence, that individuals and groups were denied formal standing in the Helsinki process.[31]

Still, individuals and groups could continue to use the "good offices" of friendly powers to take up their case. Moreover, Vienna took a major step forward in assuring individuals and groups their right to be heard through a special annex (XI) in the concluding document. The annex carried a chairman's statement—which had been formally agreed to earlier—concerning "practices of openness and access to CSCE meetings," including meetings of the Conference on the Human Dimension. The unprecedented requirement, supported by the United States, guaranteed:

> ... access to the host State, to the venue and to open sessions of CSCE meetings for representatives of the media, representatives of non-governmental organizations or religious groups and private individuals, both nationals and foreigners; unimpeded contacts between delegates or visitors and citizens of the host State; respect for CSCE-related activities, including the holding of peaceful gatherings, and for the freedom of journalists to report without hindrance, as well as to pursue their professional activity in conformity with CSCE commitments.[32]

The human dimension chapter of the Vienna concluding document, with its references to new monitoring procedures and specialized conferences, thereby facilitating compliance and encouraging performance, added to the vocabulary of CSCE. "Human dimension" now became a generic phrase for "human rights and fundamental freedoms" as well as for "human contacts and other issues of a related humanitarian character." The phrase "human dimension" summed up the aims of Principle VII, Basket III and the related provisions of the Vienna document.[33]

It should be emphasized that the concept and the implementation provisions, including the Conference on the Human Dimension, were largely conceived and pressed by the smaller NATO powers of the European Community. The United States was not a strong advocate of the kind of machinery created at Vienna, although it supported the European initiative (the "Proposal on the Human Dimension of the Helsinki Final Act") when Belgium and 16 other countries originally submitted it on February 4, 1987.[34] Washington was, of course, a vigorous advocate of compliance, but thought that it could be more effectively achieved through direct (i.e., summit) negotiations during the period of the growing détente with Moscow (1987-89). Indeed, human rights was established as a regular topic with specified personnel in a work group at every bilateral summit or foreign ministers' meeting. US leverage was greatest in this relationship, rather than through the use of the mechanism.[35] At the same time, Washington recognized that the new mechanism would be most useful for the West European countries, especially the smaller ones.

Vienna constituted a milestone on several other levels beyond the concluding document itself. If Madrid was important in creating a kind of implementation machinery by citing names and cases—all for "shaming" purposes—Vienna surpassed this achievement. According to a Helsinki Commission staff report on Vienna, "More individual cases were cited and more issues were raised by a larger number of delegations than at any time in CSCE history."[36] Literally hundreds of individuals in the Soviet Union and Eastern Europe whose rights had been violated were mentioned in the course of speeches by Ambassador Zimmermann or his staff and his European colleagues. In addition, specific minorities and religious denominations that had felt the lash of repression were openly discussed. What Arthur Goldberg had opened up in Belgrade in a most modest fashion and to great opposition had become a normal, large-scale phenomenon at Helsinki conference rooms, as well as in the media which covered the meetings.

The Vienna progress is perhaps most marked by a comparison of the US position at the end of the meeting—as recorded by the Helsinki Commission staff—with Secretary of State Shultz's speech over two years earlier, on the second day of the Vienna plenary, November 5, 1986. Noting the "tragic human rights situation within the nations of the East," he had cited particular human rights violations in the Soviet Union, Bulgaria, Czechoslovakia and Poland. In Shultz's 1986 view, the United States was obligated to raise these cases and pursue "full implementation of the Final Act" in order to "achieve a more stable peace."

Among the names mentioned and incidents cited, one stood out. The case of Raoul Wallenberg, the great Swedish hero of the Holocaust who had helped rescue tens of thousands of Hungarian Jews, had been enveloped in silence by Moscow ever since the Soviet secret police had seized him in Budapest in January 1945. America's interest in the subject was special. Wallenberg was the only foreigner, except for Winston Churchill, to be made an "Honorary Citizen" through unusual legislative statute. As early as 1945, Secretary of State Edward Stettinius showed a strong interest in the condition of the Swedish diplomat. At first, the Soviet Union denied that he had been apprehended. Later, in 1957, it acknowledged that he had been a Soviet prisoner but that he had died of a heart attack in July 1947. Few believed the official story and Wallenberg became a *cause célèbre*. The Soviets maintained a cover-up for more than 40 years. The authorities denied knowing the circumstances of Wallenberg's arrest, his incarceration, and his supposed death of a heart attack at the age of 35 years. At the Madrid review conference, his name was raised by both the Swedish and US ambassadors.[37] It had evoked no reaction then.

In September 1988, during the Vienna review conference, the United States sought to end the silence that surrounded the Swedish hero. At a plenary that month, Ambassador Zimmermann called for "a full and open accounting of that part of Soviet history affecting a man who stood for so many of the [Helsinki] ideals to which we are dedicated."[38] The British and Canadian delegation chiefs quickly joined in, urging a Soviet investigation and disclosure. Of far greater significance was the fact that the Hungarian delegation chief, André Erdös, also rose to plead with Moscow: "We would welcome with great emotion any new information which would shed light on his [Wallenberg's] fate or [that would] complete our knowledge." It was the first time that a Hungarian ambassador dared to challenge Moscow in a European public plenary meeting.

The head of the Soviet delegation, Yuri Kashlev, responded by warmly endorsing Wallenberg as having engaged in "noble activities." It was the first time that a Soviet official had praised him. Kashlev promised any new documentation Soviet authorities uncovered concerning Wallenberg (as they pursued the task of removing the stains on past Soviet history) would be published.

Several months later, optimism soared when the Soviet Ambassador to Belgium, Petr Bogdanov, showed up for a special ceremony honoring the Swedish hero at Brussels' Egmont Palace.[39] The sponsoring group was the Belgian Committee for Raoul Wallenberg. Never before had a Soviet official participated in a Wallenberg ceremony. The event, held on January 19, 1989—the day that the Helsinki accord talks came to an end in Vienna—could not and did not go unnoticed. Wallenberg's half-brother, Guy von Dardel, told the Brussels gathering that "the presence of the Soviet ambassador is a significant gesture that . . . gives us hope for a change in the Soviet attitude toward the Wallenberg case." (Whether it would, in fact, remained uncertain.)

Non-governmental organizations from the West played a larger role in raising cases than ever before, mainly in the early stages of Vienna (over 50 groups from the United States alone came). Their activities were quite varied: demonstrations, press conferences, seminars, and the presentation of appeals to delegations. Significantly, the NGO lobbying activity no longer met with contempt from the Soviets and their allies. Glasnost and the new Soviet style permitted Western NGO representatives to meet openly and freely with the Soviet delegation, often resulting in frank discussions.

A host of traditional petitions by individual Soviet and European citizens was brought to the attention of the delegates. Two examples were unusually impressive. One was signed by 438 citizens from the Soviet

Union and several East European countries, including Yugoslavia.[40] It appealed for the release of those imprisoned for objecting on grounds of conscience to serving in the armed forces. Especially startling was a petition from seven former political leaders of Romania, still living there, who called upon Western delegations to encourage reform and greater respect for civil and political rights in the Ceausescu regime.[41]

On a third level, a remarkable degree of "differentiation" unfolded among the East European communist countries. No longer were the East European countries acting as a single unit under Soviet aegis. Genuine and open differences now manifested themselves within the bloc for the first time in Helsinki history. Bulgaria, Czechoslovakia and the German Democratic Republic each objected vehemently to many of the strongly worded commitments made in the new document; in contrast, Hungary and Poland expressed a general willingness to accept them. Hungary, in an unprecedented act, joined as a co-sponsor of a Western initiative to assure the rights of national minorities. The Soviet Union occupied a middle ground. Differentiation also found expression in Western targeting of violators. As the Vienna conference proceeded and Gorbachev's influence within the USSR blossomed, Western criticism of Moscow diminished to an extent, and was balanced with sharper verbal assaults upon Czechoslovakia, Bulgaria and East Germany.[42]

But the leading target of Western criticism was Romania, the odd man out. A barrage of denunciations against Ceausescu's ruthless policies against religion, ethnic minorities (especially Hungarians), and democratic dissenters emanated from almost every Western country. And they were joined by communist Hungary, while the Soviet Union and the other Warsaw Pact members stood aside. The Romanian delegation, in turn, made it clear that it would not accept either the new and higher human rights standards or the newly created mechanism for achieving compliance. It issued a statement saying "Romania assumed no commitment to implement those among the provisions of the concluding document regarding which it has presented observations and reservations that have not been accepted—provisions that it considers to be inadequate."[43]

Interestingly, the Ceausescu dictatorship chose not to offend the Soviet Union and its other Warsaw allies by openly denying consensus. However, its decision to allow consensus but simultaneously reject the application of the document to itself was a contradiction in terms. Citing the CSCE rules of procedure, the Canadian Ambassador underscored the fact that "all provisions of the document are equally binding on all participating states."[44] He was supported by Austria and, indirectly, by Bulgaria. From all three CSCE groupings, Romania found no support for its hostile and negative views.

An authoritative work on the Vienna conference calls the sessions "a turning point in East-West relations."[45] Certainly, the evidence of its achievements is overwhelming. The NATO strategy of leverage and linkage which enabled the allies to obtain a milestone concluding document was also definitive. What remains uncertain is why the West, and especially the US, sought a much higher level of human rights commitment than ever before in Helsinki history, and why it was prepared to apply such an adamant strategy to reach this goal.

Two basic reasons can be offered. The first revolves around the strong sense of pessimism about the Helsinki process which had prevailed in the United States on the eve of Vienna. The growing disenchantment with the process after Ottawa and Bern, and the increasing pessimism that a real breakthrough on human rights in the Soviet Union and Eastern Europe was possible, had led some to urge that the process be altogether renounced. This situation, according to a US Helsinki commission staff report issued after Vienna had ended, "prompted the West to undertake a very thorough implementation review" and to give "teeth" through new provisions with "greater specificity."[46] Only by pushing for a high level of standards and of implementation could credibility be restored to the process and the disenchantment be punctured.

The second reason related to the unfolding reformism in the Soviet Union and, to a greater extent, in Poland and Hungary. The changes could not fail to stir a higher level of expectation. For the Helsinki purposes to be credible, it was essential to establish more ambitious goals.[47] At several intervals, the Austro-Swiss "non-paper" of a draft concluding document was introduced and each time it subconsciously reflected changing and higher expectations by raising the new Helsinki standards to a more ambitious level.

The first non-paper of the two key neutrals came on July 31, 1987, the last day before the summer recess, offering partial solutions in a variety of areas such as emigration, religion and ethnic rights. Largely favorable to Western views, it set a standard for human rights that was already unique for the Helsinki process.[48] When the Soviet Union and its allies agreed to the non-paper's provisions as a "point of departure" for Basket III negotiations, the West could then move to raising the level to an even higher standard of aspiration. But in accepting the non-paper as a basis for negotiation, Moscow did not immediately end its resistance to higher standards. Together with its allies, it proposed some 200 amendments to the

Austrian-Swiss paper in order to weaken its provisions, especially with respect to already accepted texts on religious freedom, freedom of movement and on monitoring and implementation.[49] The West, together with
Poland and Hungary, held firm in the negotiating process.

As Gorbachev's hand in promoting reform strengthened internally, the
Austrian and Swiss delegations, with the support of the neutral/non-
aligned group, introduced a formal draft concluding document on May
13, 1988. The draft moved the religious and ethnic rights goals to very significant levels. A further upward revision was introduced on January 3,
1989, which—following Gorbachev's remarkable reform-oriented speech
at the United Nations a month earlier—permitted the Austrians and
Swiss to strengthen the draft's earlier text on jamming and limiting state
secrets.[50] The revision even permitted adding to or strengthening the
human rights aspects of Basket II, which until then had largely focused on
trade and cultural-exchange matters.[51] A third and final revision was introduced on January 14, just prior to the adoption of the Vienna draft on
the following day.

This third revision dealt in part with a critical date factor related to the
proposed Moscow meeting of the Conference on the Human Dimension.
Moscow's anxious determination to host a Helsinki human rights meeting,
it will be recalled, was a major factor in the effective leverage that the United
States and the West could utilize to achieve significantly more meaningful
performance from the Soviet Union on human rights and its greater responsiveness to higher standards in the Vienna concluding document.

In pressing for higher Helsinki standards, the United States and the
West had consistently exploited Moscow's desire for an early meeting of a
Stockholm II conference on confidence-building measures and disarma-
ment and, more importantly, of the proposed conference on conventional
arms reductions, now operating under a Helsinki rubric. A chronological
indication of the linkage was provided in July 1987. Not until then did
NATO in Brussels reach decisions on its position concerning post-Vienna
military security negotiations.[52] The approved policy position enabled its
Vienna CSCE negotiators preparing the mandate for the Conference on
Stability Talks (CST)—now to be called Conventional Armed Forces in
Europe (CFE)—to move ahead.

Two weeks after the NATO decision had been reached, the Austro-
Swiss "non-paper" was formally tabled and the Warsaw Pact powers
agreed to use the document as a "point of departure" on human rights
issues. Throughout the later stage of the Vienna follow-up meeting,
the lever of CFE took on a powerful dimension: Certainly, the higher

performance level of the Soviet Union and the far more meaningful and effective Vienna concluding document seemed to argue convincingly for incorporation of greater military-security elements within Helsinki. The levers related to military-security desiderata of the Soviet Union permitted the US to press for extraordinarily significant progress by the USSR in compliance with Helsinki standards. And it enabled the United States and the West to win acceptance of a remarkably higher standard of human rights commitments. Only *after* NATO had finally approved firm decisions related to Basket I, especially with respect to the conventional arms stability talks which the USSR anxiously sought, did landmark developments take place in the Soviet posture at Vienna.

But doubt, warranted or otherwise, remained about the drift in the Helsinki process, while at the same time there also emerged a certain miscalculation about the CSCE future.[53] The Vienna document came to be seen as the final word on the Helsinki process. A staff report of the US Helsinki Commission put it this way:

> If there is one thing that can be said with any degree of certainty after the Vienna meeting, it is that *there will be no need* for another long human rights document coming from the next review meeting in Helsinki in 1992. Either the precise, detailed, specific Vienna document works or it doesn't. Either way, time for many more words is over.[54] [Emphasis added.]

The fact is that the Vienna document embraced but a small part of human rights. It may have been seen as all-encompassing for the period up to 1989, but, with a new world aborning soon after Vienna, far larger dimensions of human rights would appear on the agenda of the Helsinki process. The time, in fact, would soon arrive for "many more words."

▪14▪

A Europe "Whole and Free"

Vienna constituted a watershed in US human rights policy concerning CSCE. Most Western objectives, summed up in the Helsinki formula "freer movement of people and ideas," had been realized both in fact and in the new language of the Helsinki process. The Soviet Union, the leader of the Warsaw bloc, had acquiesced in a new perspective. Gorbachev could now say that "world politics, too, should be guided by the primacy of universal human values."[1] His UN speech incorporated many of the West's Helsinki values. It was a perspective his predecessors had repeatedly rejected.

With the reaching of a new level in the Helsinki process, Washington policy makers were faced by the question of whether and how to transcend the heretofore prevailing language and concepts of Helsinki. The new Bush administration in Washington took office on January 20, 1989, and found it convenient to move toward such enlargement, if only to place its own distinctive stamp on the process. Former Secretary of State Shultz had been the principal shaper of strategy during the long Vienna negotiations, and he had insisted upon their completion during his "watch." The just-appointed Secretary of State, James A. Baker III, in Senate confirmation hearings, already indicated a lack of enthusiasm about his predecessor's acceptance of Moscow as a site for a human dimension meeting.[2] That Baker might follow his own Helsinki course would not be surprising.

Besides, Mikhail Gorbachev, always the imaginative phrase-maker, had projected the image of a "common European house" as summing up Helsinki progress and embracing the CSCE value system.[3] But had the Soviet Union, in fact, embraced the Western value system? Did there now really exist a common European house? Not if the Western value system meant political democracy in all of its varied aspects. The Bush administration, indeed, would move to establish new goals for the Helsinki process in which political freedom, not merely "freer movement" covering specific limited areas, became the principal target. In this way, the Gorbachev formula could be effectively challenged, and the ideological issue joined. Human rights was something much more than what been focused upon since 1975.

Baker very tentatively advanced the new human rights guidelines in Vienna in early March 1989, at a ministerial meeting which signaled the opening of two new security negotiations, both operating within the CSCE framework. The first dealt with confidence- and security-building measures (CSBMs) to further reduce the risks of surprise attack; the second superseded the moribund MBFR talks and concentrated on ways to reduce conventional arms and armed forces in Europe. The latter, while operating under the umbrella of CSCE, was conducted only by the two military blocs in direct dialogue; the other CSCE members would be informed of the process at a later stage.

Even before addressing the subject of reducing the threat of war, Secretary Baker spoke of "creating a new Europe" that would be based on four specific "freedoms."[4] The first was for Europeans "to have a say in decisions which affect their lives, including freedom of the workplace." Clearly, the role of Solidarity was in Baker's mind, for he specifically referred to it as an organization whose legitimacy should be "the norm and not the subject of negotiations." The second freedom was defined as the "freedom to express . . . political differences." He seemed to be referring to the essentials of a pluralistic society, and the one example used was instructive. "Monitors of the Helsinki agreement," he said, "should be honored and not hunted by their governments." The third was drawn from the traditional Helsinki aspiration: freedom to exchange ideas and information and freedom of movement. The latter was illustrated by reference to the Berlin Wall and "barbed wire fences." The fourth echoed one of Franklin Roosevelt's famous themes: "The freedom of all Europeans to be safe from military intimidation or attack." Targeted here were the "massive forces" of the Soviet military and the Brezhnev Doctrine.

As articulated by Baker, "These four freedoms are inseparable. They are the principles for a new Europe; they are the keys that open the door to the European house of the future." Moreover, he staked out new philosophic ground for CSCE:

> Let me emphasize once more, however, that change in the military balance is only one part of the process. Only when the causes of the division of Europe have been removed, when we have achieved the free flow of people and information, *when citizens everywhere enjoy free expression*, only then will it be possible to eliminate totally the military confrontation. In other words, we cannot remove the symptoms, unless we deal fundamentally with the causes.[5] [Emphasis added.]

"Freer movement of people and ideas" was not enough for Baker; it had to be accompanied by, at a minimum, pluralistic expression of opinion (along with the reduction, of course, of military insecurity). Did this mean that real peace required the spread of democracy to East Europe? If not precisely clear, the new US thrust appeared to point in this direction.

There was little doubt that the Baker speech constituted a major statement on Helsinki and human rights. It was his first on the subject after the new administration was installed. He returned briefly to the Vienna themes in a speech the following month to American newspaper editors.[6] He recalled that a decade earlier "the Soviet Union was on the march" and "democracy seemed to be in retreat." All that had ended, and perestroika testified to the reality that "the Western vision of freedom, peace and democracy had prevailed." If there is "a new sense of realism in the Kremlin"—which Gorbachev's new thinking was all about—it merely confirmed "the success of our efforts."

Baker continued to elaborate upon the elements of the new US thrust in a third important address, given at the Center for Strategic and International Studies in Washington in early May.[7] Challenged once more was the Gorbachev vision of a common European house. Baker emphasized that for the "house" to be meaningful "the Soviets must no longer prevent the residents from moving from room to room." But the existence of the Berlin Wall and the Brezhnev Doctrine still put the commonality into question. Was Baker hinting that advocacy of democracy and self-determination were to become the core of US policy?

Evolution of the post-Vienna policy on Helsinki human rights reached a decisive turning point on May 31. Just as the Paris human dimension meeting—the first of three such conference meetings—was beginning, President George Bush delivered one of his most important foreign affairs speeches, in Mainz in the Federal Republic of Germany.[8] Europe had entered into a new era, he said, in which the Cold War of 40 years was coming to an end. US policy with respect to the USSR was "to move beyond containment." The new aim was to help shape a Europe "that is whole and free."[9] In his view, "the time is ripe" to realize this aspiration. Only when consummated, only when Europe was whole and free, would the Cold War completely end.

The President saw democracy as a single powerful idea sweeping across all of Eurasia. From Budapest to Beijing, the communist world was "in ferment." In Poland, free elections were finally on the agenda. In Hungary, a multiparty system at the ballot box was contemplated. The President openly linked democracy, or freedom, to self-determination.

"We seek self-determination for all of Germany and all of Eastern Europe," he declared. Gorbachev's "freedom of choice" had been turned on its head.[10] If the Soviets viewed his formula as guaranteeing non-intervention into communist-dominated societies, Bush considered freedom of choice or, in his language, "self-determination," as ending communist rule, as installing democracy. In pursuit of this purpose, "we will not relax, and we must not waver."

The President challenged Gorbachev's basic design. Echoing a phrase Secretary Baker had initially advanced, Bush observed that the Gorbachev concept was inconceivable "until all within it [the house] are free to move from room to room." Beyond the conception was even a larger house where East and West meet, "the commonwealth of free nations."

The Helsinki process was central to the President's vision: "I propose we strengthen and broaden the Helsinki process to promote free elections and political pluralism in Eastern Europe." Freedom, democracy, self-determination were all part of this new US ideological framework. Priority in Helsinki matters meant a strategy which focused upon free elections and political pluralism. The US goal, now fully articulated, was to "heal Europe's tragic division, to help Europe become whole and free." The President ended his vision with the reiteration of the long-held American theme at Helsinki meetings that peace rests upon human rights: "The foundation of lasting security comes not from tanks, troops or barbed wire. It is built on shared values and agreements that link free people."

In view of the new US vision for the Helsinki process, it is altogether puzzling, indeed inexplicable, that the Secretary of State chose not to attend the first and historic Paris meeting of the Conference on the Human Dimension, where he could have given direct expression to the US thrust. Concern was first expressed by the Helsinki Commission, always the watchdog of "correct" human rights postures by the US government. A letter to Secretary Baker from Commission Chairman DeConcini and Co-chairman Hoyer on May 3, 1989, almost a month before the Paris opening, had urged him to participate and "deliver the keynote United States address."[11]

The Commission letter pointed out that Baker had recently joined other foreign ministers in opening two separate CSCE military-security conferences held in Vienna. Were he not to attend a Helsinki human rights meeting, they wrote, it would "convey a very unfortunate signal. . . ." Human rights, they emphasized, "has been the primary concern of both the executive and legislative branches of the United States government since the inception of the CSCE process."

The response from the Assistant Secretary of State for Legislative Affairs, Janet Mullins, was somewhat disconcerting. First, she noted that the Secretary of State "will be traveling with the President at the time the Conference will be opening and thus will not be able to attend."[12] (The President's trip at the time was to West Germany, only a short distance from Paris.) What followed was far more significant: "Apart from that, however, we and several of our allies believe that CSCE implementation reviews should be held at experts level only." In addition, the letter explained that "ministerial level attendance in Paris could create an unhelpful precedent for attendance at the Moscow Conference in 1991." As clarification, attention was drawn to the fact that the United States had agreed in Vienna to the latter conference on condition that Moscow continue to improve its human rights performance. Ministerial-level attendance in Paris might be seen "as prejudicing our . . . decision on whether and at what level to attend the Moscow Conference." How attendance would have prejudiced the decision on Moscow was not demonstrated in any clear fashion. The Department's reasoning scarcely displayed a firm commitment to the human rights aspects of the Helsinki process.

The irritation of the Commission was certain to deepen when several prominent foreign ministers showed up at the Paris meeting. No doubt, the Commission's chagrin was later and privately made palpably evident to the administration; in a 1990 report, the Commission emphasized that it had pressed Baker to attend subsequent human dimension meetings.[13]

If the speeches of President Bush and Secretary Baker served as a framework for US policy at the Paris meeting, specific strategy was inevitably dictated by the agenda of the meeting as predetermined in the Vienna concluding document. That agenda called for review of current human rights practices, evaluation of the new mechanism, and consideration of the new proposals. President François Mitterrand, in opening the conference, used language that became a most effective formula for crystallizing Western purposes. Referring to the significant documents of Helsinki, Madrid and Vienna, he held that the current task was to call "rhetoric to account."[14] It was a pithy phrase that Morris B. Abram, who headed the US delegation, would cite often.

Ambassador Abram was an articulate lawyer who had represented the US at the United Nations Commission on Human Rights. More recently, he had been active in the Jewish community, serving as chairman of both the National Conference on Soviet Jewry and the Conference of Presidents of Major American Jewish Organizations. Speaking for the United States on May 31, he said that "the principal goal of the US delegation . . . will be to engage in a thorough and open review of how human rights commitments are being implemented by the signatory states."[15]

The review was designed to cover the traditional areas of Helsinki—free movement, religious rights and national rights. The end of jamming and the progress attained in the communication field had already diminished the significance of the freer-movement-of-ideas topic for Paris. Besides, the subject had been the concern of the Helsinki-sponsored Information Forum held in London one month earlier.[16] Even as Ambassador Abram and his staff dug into the older topics with well-organized and effective presentations, he did not neglect the new thrust Baker and Bush had outlined. The subject acquired a special role in an Abram speech entitled "Towards a Civil Society."[17]

Preparing for a detailed review of progress in traditional Helsinki areas, the US delegation could not fail to take account of the changed atmosphere in East-West relationships which found reflection in the Paris deliberations. On June 5, one week after the session opened, Abram told his colleagues: "The atmosphere in this room—focused on the advancement of human norms—is more generally favorable than I have experienced in 25 years."[18] Six weeks later, in testimony about Paris to the Helsinki Commission, he again recalled how "I noticed a profound change in the atmosphere . . . as compared with that prevailing at other international meetings on human rights. . . ."[19]

No longer was Moscow the principal target of US and Western criticism. Already at Vienna, several East European countries were targeted with strong criticism. At Paris, the new thrust in Western criticism came into clearer focus.[20] The role of chief villain was now played by Romania, followed by Bulgaria for its treatment of its Turkish minority. Next came Czechoslovakia and East Germany. In contrast, Poland and Hungary were praised for progress made in all the main areas of the Helsinki documents. The USSR found itself somewhere in the middle between the almost Western-like achievements of Poland and Hungary and the others who languished beyond. Abram would later observe, after noting the Soviet internal changes: "These have been important changes in the USSR. There was a workman-like nonconfrontation spirit between our delegations."[21]

Freedom of movement came first in Abram's holding of rhetoric to account. Restrictions on travel and emigration, Abram demonstrated, breed resentments, impede human development, impoverish human personality and augment bureaucratic tyranny. For these reasons, he congratulated the Soviet Union for various reforms that permitted a considerable escalation of emigration. In the first six months of 1989, over

50,000 persons, mainly Jews, Germans, Armenians and Pentecostalists, emigrated, as compared with less than 2,000 a mere four years earlier.[22] In addition, thousands more were allowed to travel to the West, including 10,000 to the United States during the first half of the year. During the mid-1980s, the average annual figure for travel to the US was only 1,500.

In Poland and Hungary, virtually unfettered freedom to leave prevailed. Some meaningful progress had also taken place in Bulgaria and East Germany. Yet, except for Poland and Hungary, everywhere else in the Soviet bloc, freedom of movement was "still regarded as a privilege, and not a right. . . ." The Berlin Wall stood out as an especially outrageous violation of the right to leave. Abram documented the numerous tragic episodes of those seeking to hurdle the Wall and failing. It represented a stark contradiction to the "very positive progress" which East Germany had made with respect to permitting a greater degree of travel and emigration to West Germany, though, of course, considerable and extensive barriers remained.

If the Soviet Union had demonstrated marked progress toward freer movement of people, it nonetheless continued to utilize a capricious system of state secrets and parental authorization ("poor relatives") to arbitrarily limit the granting of exit visas. Illustrative of the irrationality of state secrets in creating several hundred refuseniks were the Vladimir Raiz and Emmanuel Lurie cases.[23] Both had left their classified positions, one in chemistry, the other in molecular biology, a quarter of a century earlier. The Vienna concluding document had specified that national security could only be employed "within strictly warranted time limits" and if restrictions were imposed, they should be "as short as possible and not to be applied in an arbitrary manner." "Surely," Abram observed, "25 years cannot possibly be construed to be a short amount of time."

As Commission Chairman DeConcini was to participate at the very opening of the Paris session (and Co-chairman Hoyer at the end) and Commission staffers were serving in key positions in the US delegation, it was predictable that the refusenik issue (and the related prisoner-of-conscience issue) would be handled directly. It turned out that the makeup of the Soviet delegation helped move the discussions to effective results. It was comprised of several officials, notably Yuri Reshetov, head of the Foreign Ministry's human rights bureau, and Rudolf Kuznetsov, chief of OVIR (the Visa and Registration Office), who were thoroughly familiar with the subjects.

Four bilaterals—as the private discussions were dubbed—with the principal Soviet officials were held in unofficial settings during the month-long session—almost one a week. Central to the discussion were two key refusenik lists.[24] The first list comprised names of some 50 persons who had been on an earlier list of several hundred persons submitted by the Commission in November. (It should be noted that the refusenik lists were based on continuously updated information provided by the National Conference on Soviet Jewry). While most cases from that list had been favorably resolved, a hard core of some 50 families remained. In addition, a newly created *consolidated* list comprising names from the State Department's own documentation and from the Commission's files had been prepared. It contained approximately 680 names, including the 50 hard-core cases. Baker had initially presented the list to Soviet authorities when he visited Moscow in April 1989. The same list was submitted again to Soviet officials in Paris on June 2. Of the 680 cases, about 20 percent were in the "poor relatives" category. Approximately 75 percent of the listings were refuseniks for more than five years.[25] On the quite separate issue of remaining prisoners who were thought to be "political," the important US-based NGO, the International League for Human Rights, at the specific request of Andrei Sakharov, provided Abram with appropriate documentation used in the bilaterals.

The critical consideration in these talks was the very important provision of the Vienna document which specified that the participating states "will take the necessary steps to find solutions as expeditiously as possible, but in any case within six months, to all applications based on the human contacts provisions of the Final Act and the Madrid Concluding Document, outstanding at the conclusion of the Vienna Follow-Up Meeting."[26] This was understood to mean that by July 19—six months after the conclusion of Vienna (January 19)—"solutions" could be found for the cases unresolved—"outstanding"—at the time.

According to the Commission, approximately 500 names fit into the unresolved "outstanding" category. And, of that number, 50 were hard-core cases, like Lurie and Raiz, who had been repeatedly turned down for unknown reasons. Throughout the formal session, US officials in plenary made it plain that they expected movement on these cases by July 19. Ambassador Abram, in his closing speech to the plenary on June 23, reminded the assembled diplomats "that the participating states agreed in Vienna to resolve all outstanding human contacts cases by mid-July."[27]

Especially important was the bilateral of June 7. The Soviet side of four was headed by Reshetov and Kuznetsov; the US group of four was headed by the Commission's Jane Fisher and the State Department's John Evans.[28] The meeting was business-like, with each side working from the same hard-core list. The Soviets offered comments on the prevailing situation on each of the cases. In some very prominent cases, they offered encouragement that the Ministry of Foreign Affairs was trying to obtain special high-priority attention for resolution. They also promised to quickly begin working on the joint consolidated list, and offered assurances that difficulties would be overcome in the less complicated cases.

Reshetov seemed especially accommodating, while Kuznetsov appeared more rigid. When Fisher indicated that "unpleasant situations" regarding the various cases could be rectified by liberalization of existing Soviet emigration law, Reshetov responded that the Soviet Union would soon be institutionalizing liberalized practices. Several days earlier, he had told Jewish NGO representatives with whom he met privately that on July 1 a new liberalized draft law on emigration would be introduced into the Supreme Soviet.[29] His information and general optimism were quite off the mark. It was not until late May 1991 that the Supreme Soviet adopted the new legislation.

In general, the bilaterals did not prove to be very productive. At times, Soviet officials promised action on certain cases or offered assurances about solutions to a significant number of names, but often the resolution of cases was modest compared to what had been promised. Fisher, in one instance, angrily warned her Soviet interlocutors that promises accompanied by tiny results were no longer tolerable or acceptable.[30] She reminded them of the July 19 cutoff date, and warned that action or lack of action by that date would have a profound impact upon whether the Soviet Union would be granted most-favored-nation tariff treatment through the waiver provision of the Jackson-Vanik amendment.

The final press conference of Ambassador Kashlev was not too encouraging with respect to the July 19 deadline on the refuseniks. His comment had an indirect character. Moscow, he said, would meet its obligations under the Vienna agreement, but would do so in accordance with its own procedures; he added that these procedures would necessitate a number of refusals.[31] Indeed, July 19 came and went without the Soviet response. How would the United States respond to the USSR when the latter appeared to violate a clear injunction of the Helsinki process reached by consensus?

At the same time as the US delegation pursued the priority objective of reviewing practices in the traditional area of emigration, delegation head Abram was also beginning to develop the new thrust proposed by President Bush and Secretary of State Baker. Abram's opening speech on May 31 took note of the Bush proposal made that same week to the effect that CSCE ought to embark upon developing standards for truly free elections "to ensure that all governments enjoy the consent of the governed."[32] Abram sought to set forth "two universal principles of real democracy." First, he argued, "the rights of the state are derived from the consent of the governed."[33] Second, free competitive elections among multiple contending parties "are the only reliable means of testing that consent." In other words, the people give power to the state; the state is not the source of the basic rights of man.

US emphasis on free elections was also intended as a response to Shevardnadze's speech made the previous day. The Soviet Foreign Minister had contended that no state should impose its notions of democracy on others. Abram observed that while no democratic system can be judged a perfect model, nevertheless all democratic systems included the two principles of free elections and a pluralistic party system. He went on to add that free elections, if conjoined with the non-intervention Principle VI of the Final Act, could heal Europe's "spiritual and historical scars, including . . . the illegal incorporation of the Baltic states fifty years ago."[34] The reference to the Baltics was surprisingly sharp.

Focus on democracy was affected, too, by developments in China. The extraordinary mass demonstrations for democracy by Chinese students in Beijing and other urban centers had captured the interest and imagination of many. And when the Chinese democratic movement was smashed by Beijing guns and tanks shortly afterward, the two critical issues of democratic institutions and miliary intervention became interlinked with the Paris discussions. Abram, in opening remarks of his speech on June 5 (which was to deal with freedom of movement), emphasized the great "tragedy not only for the Chinese people . . . [but] for the cause of human rights which we are here discussing."[35]

The contrast with how Moscow responded to events in China could not have been sharper. Only short dispatches were allowed in the Soviet press, and these only on the back pages of the major newspapers. At the same time, the Kremlin's leadership hastily pushed through the Congress of People's Deputies a resolution which declared that "the events happening in China are an internal affair of the country."[36] Public statements of outrage and dismay were rejected. When queried by the press, President Gorbachev said: "Let Bush speak for himself. I do not think we shall tell America what to do."[37] Three days later, Morris Abram called attention to the Kremlin line and underscored what the chief of the Soviet delegation, Yuri Kashlev, had said earlier in *Moscow News*: "Human rights . . . will now be the subject for legitimate discussions in international relations." The Kashlev statement only served to embarrass the Soviet position on China.

On June 9, Abram delivered an especially eloquent address—"Towards a Civil Society?"—oriented to setting a foundation for a full elaboration of the Bush-Baker policy thrust. The point of departure was the phrase of the Final Act requiring signatories to honor "the right of the individual to know and act upon his rights."[38] For Abram, this was a crucial provision around which revolved a host of governmental obligations.

To be meaningful and effective, the right to know and act upon one's rights required protection of free speech, a free press, freedom of peaceable assembly, and the right to petition government. In essence, a particular right provided by the Helsinki accord necessitated the transition to a free society. Here was one building block. Another was the toleration and encouragement of diversity.

Central to the exercise was freedom of association, the "key to the growth of a genuine civil society." In a word, pluralism flowed logically from the Helsinki accord and stood at the core of creative society. For that reason, Abram welcomed the 60,000 "informal" groups that had emerged in the Soviet Union, as a "most encouraging sign of the development of a civil society."

Congressman Steny Hoyer elaborated upon the new US thrust. On June 19, after a quick review of the continuing violations of the Helsinki accord and the Vienna document and an urgent appeal to bring about a "zero solution" to all human rights cases, Hoyer turned to "look beyond the confines of our diplomatic endeavors."[39] Instead, he would "look to the future and set the stage for what needs to be done to perfect the fulfillment of our promises."

Hoyer set out the details of a free election system: periodic, genuine and contested balloting, conducted secretly with universal and equal suffrage; the establishment by individuals of their own political parties and other political organizations, as well as of their own political programs; recognition of the right of individuals to seek (through equal access to the media) election to positions of public service; and allowing observance of election proceedings by institutions or organizations, whether foreign or domestic.

The elements of free election and political pluralism were incorporated into a formal proposal submitted by the United States to the Paris meeting on June 20. Hoyer had justified the proposal in his speech of June 19 on the basis of the Universal Declaration of Human Rights, specifically its Article 21, which stipulated that "the will of the people shall be the basis for authority of government." The expectation was that the proposal would not be immediately acted upon, as only a few days remained in the session; instead, along with other proposals, it would be forwarded to the Copenhagen human dimension meeting in June 1990.

On the last day of the Paris meeting, Ambassador Abram returned to the free elections theme.[40] Initially, he praised the USSR for permitting "very significant changes" in the human rights field, which even extended to what he called "a rudimentary election, albeit within a one-party state." But "the Soviet Union clearly has not gone far enough." He reminded his audience that toward the beginning of the Paris forum, a Soviet delegate declared the USSR is "not ready for the creation of alternative political parties." In the American's view, such a view could not be justified by "the country of glasnost and perestroika." Abram called attention to the language of the Helsinki Final Act to explain his argument. The accord recognized the "right of all people in full freedom to determine when and as they wish their internal and external political status."

While Abram ventured into one of the broad guidelines set out by President Bush and Secretary of State Baker, another crucial guideline which interrelated democracy with national rights and even used the term "self-determination" was left to his deputy, Paula Dobriansky, Deputy Assistant Secretary of State for Human Rights and Humanitarian Affairs, who was especially knowledgeable on nationality questions.

Her "National Minorities" address was delivered on June 16.[41] It took as its sources the Helsinki accord's vague endorsement of the right of national minorities to equality before the law and, more importantly, the Vienna document's call upon the Helsinki signatories to "create conditions for the promotion" of ethnic, cultural, linguistic and religious identity of national minorities. Dobriansky began by severely criticizing Bulgaria and Romania for "trying to homogenize their societies and the rich cultural heritage of their diverse populations"; she detailed the Bulgarian treatment of its Turkish minority and Romania's repression of Hungarians living within its borders.

But far larger in scope was Dobriansky's analysis of the complex Soviet national picture. After welcoming Gorbachev's rejection of the former official Soviet doctrine of the "merging of nationalities" in favor of the toleration and encouragement of a certain diversity, she turned to major "problems" in the national area. First, there were the three national minorities still suffering from the "aftermath of Stalinism"—Crimean Tatars, Germans and Meshketians. All of them had been ordered deported on false charges of Nazi collaboration and were still required to live in Central Asia.

Then there were the Jews, whose cultural organizations "are forced to work on the edges of legality since they are not registered." Besides, Jews faced the lack of legal status for modern Hebrew and the limited opportunity to import, publish and distribute Jewish literature. More serious were the threatening activities of anti-Semitic organizations.

Traditionally, Soviet minorities had had their plight discussed at the Helsinki meetings. Dobriansky went beyond these groups to refer to major nationalities. She spoke about Byelorussian and Moldavian national groups, as well as various Soviet Central Asian peoples who were striving to preserve and extend their linguistic and cultural traditions. Turning to the Caucasus, she openly complained about how "peaceful protest" led to government "violence" as "it did in the still unexplained events in Tbilisi." (On April 9, 1989, a mass demonstration of Georgians in the republic's capital city on behalf of national rights was forcefully smashed by Soviet military units using tanks and chemical agents. At least 20 persons were killed. The military violence generated shock within and without the Soviet Union, and seriously embarrassed Gorbachev's glasnost policy.)

She spoke at length of the continued Russification of Ukrainian culture and of how Ukrainian activists were harassed for promoting pluralism. The Baltic states received almost as much attention, and she hailed a statement adopted by the Popular Fronts of the Baltic countries, which endorsed "the right to self-determination" and proceeded to conclude:

> My delegation believes that genuine democracy—whether by popular referendum or competitive multi-candidate elections—provides the only guarantee for the peaceful evolution of societies.

It was a provocative challenge to a regime whose multinational structure had rested on coercion, not free expression. The fear—in Moscow, but also as far away as Washington—was that centrifugal forces would rock and undermine the centralized authority. Indeed, Dobriansky's frankness especially in regard to Ukraine and even the Baltics, would not be repeated at future Helsinki meetings. Caution had been the administration's watchword on self-determination issues and would remain so. (Indeed, as late as August 1991, when President Bush paid an official visit to Ukraine and addressed its parliament, he pointedly criticized "suicidal nationalism," which evoked anger among Ukrainians.)

For Moscow, the mere raising of the self-determination issue and its linkage with the dissatisfaction of many nationalities in the USSR was dangerous, perhaps bordering on the incendiary. Many perceived the nationalities issue as the Achilles' heel of Soviet rule. If the various critiques of the human rights situation in the Soviet Union by Ambassador Abram and various members of his staff rarely elicited a hostile reply, the Dobriansky speech evoked a sharp reaction. The task was assigned to Viktor Shikalov, Kashlev's hard-line deputy.

Shikalov, his face grim and radiating anger, let loose a barrage of charges, mixed with biting sarcasm, embracing a variety of subjects.[42] The standard targets were again raised: the US failure to ratify the human rights covenants; "political" prisoners in the United States such as Kathy Boudin; alleged deprivation of women's rights; discrimination against blacks and against Native American languages; and anti-Semitism. What was given special emphasis by Shikalov and, in fact, made the subject of a formal Moscow complaint under the new mechanism was the refusal of the United States to admit into the country, under the provisions of the McCarran-Walter Act, Soviet Communist Party members and members of affiliated organizations, including Soviet trade union officials. Did this not contravene the Helsinki Final Act and the Vienna document? How could the United States explain the fact that McCarran-Walter was still in force? And how to explain the discriminatory exclusion of Soviet trade unionists?

On the entry-visa issue for Soviet trade unionists, Abram decided to forgo a response, as it had been dealt with by delegation member John Evans during a discussion of the new mechanism (see below). The Abram failure to respond here, nonetheless, suggested that the Soviets were making a telling point that was not too easily rebutted. Significantly, during the Helsinki Commission hearings a month later, on July 18, after a brief questioning of Ambassador Abram on the subject, Co-chairman Hoyer intervened with pertinent comments.[43] The refusal to grant entry visas to official Soviet trade unionists, Hoyer said, constituted one of the few instances that "we are in violation of the Helsinki Final Act, and we should do something about it." In Hoyer's opinion, the McCarran-Walter Act was not consistent with current US advocacy of human rights. Official Soviet trade unionists, he said, ought to be admitted even if they do not speak for Soviet labor. Abram offered no response to this strong liberal view.

The most significant departure from previous US strategy at Helsinki meetings was the clear emphasis given to free elections and political pluralism. It was not only incorporated in speeches by the delegation head, but also in formal US proposals tabled in Paris. While the idea for the new thrust was projected in several speeches of Secretary Baker and, especially, the Mainz speech of President Bush, it nonetheless had to have some rooting in Helsinki documents or related sources. Otherwise, it could be perceived as alien to the Helsinki process and deliberately dragged in to serve merely political or even Cold War purposes.

A staff memorandum prepared by the Helsinki Commission offered both documentary sources and rationale.[44] In the Decalogue, the Final Act itself contained crucial language which could be utilized as a seminal source, even though its initial purpose was to protect state sovereignty. Principle VIII, entitled "Equal Rights and Self-Determination of Peoples," stipulated that "all people always have the right, in full freedom, to determine when, and as they wish, their internal and external political status, without external interference, and to pursue as they wish their political, economic, social and cultural development."

The subject was no longer alien and inappropriate. Free election processes, even if circumscribed and partially distorted, had already found expression in Poland and the USSR, and were also scheduled for Hungary; thus, the subject was no longer beyond the realm of Western or Eastern public expectations. Moreover, independent voluntary organizations were springing up throughout the Soviet Union and, to some extent, even in Eastern Europe. Since many of these groups had the making of political parties, pluralism had become a phenomenon almost intrinsic to the broad glasnost process.

Finally, the Vienna concluding document, to a remarkable extent, had incorporated the hopes of the process's past. Surely, there was no need to simply repeat the achievements of Vienna. If there were to be further documents in the Helsinki process, they had to constitute a meaningful— and specific—advance beyond Vienna. Free elections and political pluralism provided such a purpose.

The context within which the United States moved the proposal for free elections and political pluralism was an agenda item crucial to the new aspect of the Helsinki process dealing with the human dimension. At Paris, and later at Copenhagen and Moscow, CSCE members were invited to submit proposals "aimed at improving implementation of commitments and cooperation in the human dimension" and "aimed at enhancing the effectiveness" of the new mechanism.

Whether and how the proposals would become accepted by consensus were not made clear. For the moment, the Paris plenary simply accepted informally the notion that proposals would be forwarded to Copenhagen for further deliberations. Interest in the agenda item was rather widespread, with a total of 36 proposals introduced, covering a broad range of topics.[45] Keen interest was shown by some communist countries in certain proposals from the West and the neutrals, reflecting a broader base for support for Western human rights objectives within CSCE. The converse was not the case: there was little support from the West for proposals emanating from the East.

US policy on proposals was largely an extension of its earliest Helsinki aims except, of course, for the new emphasis on free elections emanating from the President himself. From the beginning of Helsinki, the United States had advocated freer movement of people, and it was scarcely surprising that the US delegation at Paris would propose the logical expression of freer movement—the elimination of requirements for exit visas to travel or emigrate. High priority was attached to such a proposal. As neutral Austria chose to take the lead on this idea and, more significantly, succeeded in winning Hungary's co-sponsorship to the proposal, the United States wisely decided to relinquish its preeminent role.[46] Hungary's co-sponsorship was testimony to Budapest's new policy on free movement and, more importantly, to its continued willingness to break through bloc patterns in the Helsinki process; the Hungarians had begun doing so at Vienna, co-sponsoring a Canadian proposal on national culture. It was, however, the US language on abolition of exit-visa requirements which prevailed in the final draft of the proposal.

Another area of US priority interest related to non-governmental organizations and their access to the process, especially to the Conference on the Human Dimension. The issue was especially relevant because Moscow was to be the 1991 site of the conference's third meeting. At Vienna, the United States had conditioned its approval of the Soviet site on Moscow's assuring full access to both national and international NGOs, as well as to its own citizens. In consequence, the US joined in co-sponsoring a Canadian proposal to facilitate access to future human dimension meetings.

Regrettably, the Kléber Center in Paris (where most of the deliberations took place) was not conducive to maximum access by NGOs.[47] The main hall was fairly small, which prevented seating of NGOs at public sessions. Besides, security anxiety by French officials hindered easy NGO access; requests for entry into the conference center were treated as burdensome. Lest the French experience be perceived as a model by Moscow for its 1991 conference, much emphasis was placed by the United States and other Western powers upon official advice given to Danish officials to ensure that Copenhagen in 1990 would provide maximum NGO access and, therefore, a precedent for Moscow in the following year. Such informal diplomacy was accompanied by pressing for the formal Canadian proposal.

The United States also joined as a co-sponsor of a Swiss proposal which would commit all participating states to allow foreign observers to attend trials.[48] In one other instance, the US extended support, though without joining as co-sponsor. This was a strongly worded British proposal on the rule of law, which detailed legal measures for establishment of an independent and impartial judicial system. The proposal committed all Helsinki signatories to accept such standard fundamental Western judicial principles as the presumption of innocence until proven guilty and toleration of all activities not expressly prohibited by law.

Review of Helsinki implementation and consideration of new proposals had been traditional features of Helsinki follow-up meetings or of human rights experts meetings. These processes were central to the Paris meeting as well. But Paris was also characterized by a new and distinctive feature: evaluation of the mechanism, newly created at Vienna, designed to achieve a greater degree of compliance with the provisions of Helsinki and, especially, with the significant obligations undertaken at Vienna.

Any of the 35 participants was now permitted to bring a "representation" or complaint about a human rights "situation" in another participating state. For the first time in the history of the Helsinki process, a mechanism existed in the human rights field to facilitate "the implementation of their [the signatories'] CSCE commitments." The aim was to make Basket III have some resemblance to Basket I. Under the latter, as achieved at the 1984-86 Stockholm conference on confidence-building measures, a device was established for one party to seek information and to check information about military maneuvers conducted by other parties.

No one at Vienna had expected that significant progress could be achieved by the first human dimension meeting. Only five months would have elapsed since the Vienna follow-up meeting, and governments were hardly attuned to swing into operation that quickly. In the case of the United States, a transition to the new Bush administration severely delayed most foreign policy activity. The State Department, headed by a new Secretary of State, was far from being adequately staffed at the policy level during its initial transition months to make crucial CSCE decisions.

Nonetheless, and remarkably enough, the mechanism did test out positively by the time of the Paris meeting. Two cases, both critically important, were brought under its provisions and were successfully resolved. As early as February 1989, just a couple of weeks after Vienna ended, Britain formally made representation to Moscow about Georgy Samoilovich, a 67-year-old Jewish mathematician, who had been repeatedly refused an exit visa for over ten years.[49] His case was seriously complicated by lymphatic cancer. Highly specialized treatment, he learned, was available to him from London's Royal Marsden Hospital, and he had made appropriate application with Soviet authorities to leave.

Early in February, London formally set in motion a "representation" about Samoilovich. For two months nothing happened with respect to the case. But on April 3, diplomats from the Foreign Office, including CSCE specialists, were visiting counterparts in the Soviet Foreign Ministry in Moscow to discuss matters of mutual interest on the eve of Gorbachev's visit to England to meet Prime Minister Thatcher.

The British specialists took the occasion to raise the Samoilovich matter. Soviet officials reacted with some embarrassment to the sudden posing of the issue within the context of the Helsinki process. The question was quickly raised at a high level at the Kremlin. Gorbachev could hardly countenance the weakening of his very friendly relationship with the British Prime Minister on the eve of his visit. That afternoon, Samoilovich was granted permission to go to London for medical treatment. Later, his family was allowed to join him. Clearly, the effectiveness of the new Helsinki mechanism could be greatly facilitated when high-level political considerations were at stake.

The second case involved the distinguished Czechoslovak dramatist Vaclav Havel, who had been sentenced on February 21 to one-year imprisonment for honoring the martyred Jan Palach in a January 16 demonstration, which had been forbidden by Prague authorities (shortly afterward, the sentence was reduced to eight months). On January 31, less than two weeks after Vienna concluded, the Netherlands government moved to apply the mechanism, with its ambassador in Prague delivering a formal note to the authorities expressing dismay about the police crackdown and demanding an explanation. Similar action was taken by France on February 7 and by the United States on February 16.[50] The impact of the representations was ultimately felt, although not without considerable difficulty; Havel was released in early May, four months before the end of his sentence. The early release was to have unexpected consequences.

These distinctive successes were, however, exceptional. Had Gorbachev not made an official visit to London, which could be lubricated, as it were, by a Soviet human rights concession, it is by no means certain that the mechanism could have been validated with the Samoilovich case. As for the Havel case, the international prominence of the playwright could not but assure that his incarceration would attract universal opprobrium. As Czechoslovakia desperately sought to diminish external criticism, release of a heroic symbol was scarcely an insuperable response. Still, Havel was technically released under "protective supervision," a sort of probationary status. He was not wholly free, and the charges and sentences had not been revoked. Moreover, others arrested with Havel remained in prison.

A limited number of cases, estimated at 24, were raised under the mechanism.[51] Of this total, quite a few were directed at Romania, which had declared at Vienna that it would not be bound by the mechanism on grounds that it constituted interference in state sovereignty. Thus, Bucharest rejected complaints about ill-treatment of Hungarians in Transylvania and about assaults upon religious freedom. Nor would the Romanians countenance representations about a half-dozen individuals whose rights had been jeopardized or trampled upon. The Swiss delegate to the Paris talks sarcastically commented that once Romania had signed the Vienna concluding document, it was not free to choose human rights "á la carte."[52]

Even with the very limited number of cases that the Helsinki signatories brought under the rubric of the mechanism, it was still clear that the West saw it as a valuable new tool to facilitate compliance. But if successful in two instances, the mechanism had yet to prove its overall usefulness. Only a few months had elapsed since the Vienna concluding document had been signed, and it was too early to reach judgments on its potential or real effectiveness. This was the broad consensus perception of the participants. They looked to the one-year time frame from the Paris conclave to the Copenhagen meeting for obtaining a better reading of what the mechanism might accomplish. Nonetheless, at Paris the Helsinki signatories entered into extensive discussions on how the mechanism could be improved, even if the body of testing experience was limited. The discussion clearly demonstrated the widespread and keen interest in the mechanism. US participation in the discussions was notably vigorous.

The United States had already used the mechanism on four separate occasions prior to Paris. The first dealt with the Vaclav Havel case. US intervention, according to delegation staff member Jane Fisher, was based upon the view that individuals "have the right to gather in a public place to engage in the non-violent expression of their views."[53] Paragraph 13d of the Vienna concluding document was the source of the opinion, as it was "a reasonable understanding of the provision guaranteeing individuals the right to know and act upon their rights."[54]

Washington also applied the mechanism to Bulgaria, which had repressed the Independent Association for the Protection of Human Rights in Bulgaria. Its members were arrested in January, their property confiscated, and their activities subjected to "administrative control." The United States called upon the government of Bulgaria to "cease its campaign of media vilification, detention and other forms of harassment . . . and to permit the Association to operate freely."[55] The Vienna concluding document, in Paragraph 13e, legitimized the right of persons to observe and promote the implementation of CSCE provisions.

A variety of concerns prompted US application of the mechanism to Romania: a) incarceration of three Romanian journalists; b) the frequently delayed completion of the expansion of a prominent church; c) refusal of a passport; and d) the psychiatric internment of a certain dissident.[56] If the representatives of Czechoslovakia and Bulgaria accepted the US complaints, Romania refused to accept even the paper on which the representation was printed. Such refusal, declared a US delegate in Paris, "can in no way relieve [Romania] of its obligations to resolve these cases."[57] As for the principal Romanian thesis charging domestic intervention, the delegate emphasized that "the mechanism is not meant to intrude or condemn; it is meant to be a constructive avenue for finding solutions to problems."

The final use of the mechanism related to the Soviet Union. The circumstances prompting the mechanism application had occurred in February, even though the decision to use it did not come until May, three months later. Seven Americans of Lithuanian ancestry had been denied visas by Moscow that would have allowed them to travel to Vilnius in order to attend an officially permitted celebration of Lithuanian Independence Day.[58] US officials believed that the visa requests had been initially approved by the Vilnius visa office, but were subsequently denied in the Soviet capital.

In raising the complaint with Moscow, Washington relied on very clear language of the Vienna concluding document. It specified in Paragraph 31 that "persons belonging to national minorities or regional cultures on their territories . . . can establish and maintain [human contacts] with citizens of other States with whom they share a common national origin or cultural heritage." In justifying the use of the mechanism, the US delegation in Paris noted that "at a time when we are calling for increased contact between the citizens of our states, and when progress in the field of human contacts is generally noteworthy, such denials are to be deeply regretted."

The Lithuanian case inevitably raised questions. Why did it take several months after the occurrence of the discriminatory act before the matter was officially raised? Why was only one case raised with the USSR, when the files of both the State Department and the Helsinki Commission bulged with a considerable number of gross human rights violations by Soviet authorities? In the case of Romania, four separate items were brought into the formal complaint. Finally, why this case and not other, more striking and dramatic examples of gross discrimination?

Attitudes on the importance of the mechanism are highly relevant in suggesting possible answers to the queries. A key State Department official, Assistant Secretary Schifter, considered the mechanism not particularly appropriate for the United States in dealing with the Soviet Union.[59] There already existed, he noted, a standing bilateral structure outside of Helsinki for dealing with human rights issues. Created during the second Reagan term after the first summit with Gorbachev, the structure permitted the United States to raise crucial human contacts problems. Long before the Paris meeting, Schifter had expressed the view that the mechanism was not of vital interest to the United States, in contrast to its potential appeal to West European powers. Later, after the Paris meeting, he said that the use of the mechanism could interfere with and possibly undermine US initiatives in the continuing bilateral sphere.[60] In his view, the mechanism was simply not consequential in dealing with the USSR.

The perspective of the US Helsinki Commission was quite different. Almost from the beginning of the Bush administration, Commission officials began pressing for the use of the mechanism by the State Department.[61] The fact that key positions in the Department, including those dealing with Helsinki, remained unfilled for a long period of time in the initial months of the new administration meant that such demands would fall on deaf ears. In this early period, Baker's leadership of the State Department was characterized by extremely slow decision making, especially with respect to the Soviet Union.

Whatever the early internal differences between the State Department and the Commission, at Paris the US delegation took a strong public position in favor of the mechanism. In Ambassador Abram's opening speech, he declared that one of three principal objectives of the United States at Paris was "to evaluate our experience to date with the Vienna human rights mechanism," a constructive new tool for the conduct of human rights diplomacy by governments. He went on:

> As we see it, the Helsinki process can only profit from measures, like this mechanism, that increase openness and transparency. Effective confidence-building measures are just as important in the human dimension as they are in the military security sphere.[62]

The comparison of the mechanism with confidence-building measures in the security area was startling. But as Ambassador Abram's perspective was not conditioned by years in the departmental bureaucracy, he may have seen in the use of the mechanism a potential value in the public relations arena that State Department officials might have discounted. One of his principal aides, Commission staffer Fisher, told a Paris working group meeting on June 7 that "although my government cannot call the mechanism truly successful in these cases [raised by the US], we remain hopeful that this avenue can evolve into an effective procedure for redressing these violations."[63]

The difference in perception between the State Department and the Helsinki Commission was not insurmountable. Erika Schlager, a Commission staffer who was especially knowledgeable about the mechanism, argued that the United States had initially pressed for the mechanism so that it could be seen as a parallel instrument to security procedures of Basket I. Dropping it now would upset the balance worked out at Vienna. Moreover, she pointed out, the mechanism could prove most useful with the other East European countries, as the bilateral structure in which Schifter took special pride applied only to the USSR. Finally, in her opinion, the bilateral negotiations were not failure-proof, and thus the mechanism could be available as a fallback device.

Indeed, the US delegation played a useful role in advancing suggestions for improving the mechanism. The mechanism specialist especially stressed two points at working group meetings.[64] First, she emphasized flexibility. Though some insisted that the mechanism follow the rigid procedure noted in the Vienna document, starting from lodging the formal complaint and ending in specified stages with the human dimension conference, she strongly recommended that no sequential order of the Vienna paragraphs be required. Flexibility might allow, for example, moving directly to bilateral negotiations. Rigid adherence to a sequential order could enable the targeted state to block further progress after the first step. Flexibility would also satisfy two alternative perspectives on the procedure. Some wanted it used for specific cases; others would have it applied to broader issues.

Sometimes, problems arose. Representations by Turkey against Bulgaria were met by "counterclaims" submitted by Bulgaria against Turkey. Several delegations saw this as a means for avoiding claims altogether; Italy, Denmark, Britain, and West Germany were of this view. The Bulgarians, not surprisingly, considered that counterclaims were equally legitimate and must be dealt with in the same process as the original representation.

In Belgium's formal recommendation, bilateral meetings should not be the occasion for introducing cases which were not the subject of the initial complaint that had led to the meeting. It was the strong opinion of the United States, registered in the speech by Jane Fisher on June 6, that counterclaims were intolerable if used to "deflect attention from requests for information," i.e., complaints.[65] "This attitude will get us nowhere," she added. She asked that all delegates look on the mechanism as "a constructive tool by which we can understand each other better and by which we can more concretely solve the problems which divide us."

Illustrative of the US view was its response to Soviet use of the mechanism. The USSR had formally complained that Washington had denied visas to two Soviet official trade union representatives. State Department official John Evans told the Paris meeting that the US respected the specified use of the mechanism to raise the issue and it "welcome[d] the commitment to the mechanism which this particular representation appears to demonstrate."[66] He added that "in this instance, we believe the Soviet use of mechanism is serious and well-intentioned."

While the formal response would be made in Moscow (where the initial complaint was lodged), Evans chose to utilize the Paris meeting to discuss substantive aspects of the complaint. His comments were instructive in showing how the US could respond to this and similar complaints which might be expected from Eastern Europe. The response took two forms.[67] First, he did not challenge the charge, but rather attempted to justify or explain the US action. He noted that the Soviet Union had repeatedly refused exit visas to anyone invited by the AFL-CIO to attend its labor convention. In November 1988, Andrei Sakharov was the first invitee to receive a Soviet exit visa to attend the AFL-CIO convention at the American organization's request.

Moreover, from the US perspective, Evans noted, Soviet trade union officials "do not truly represent the workers." This view was even given indirect credence by Mikhail Gorbachev, who had publicly acknowledged that official labor organizations in the USSR failed to represent the interests of workers and should therefore be restructured. At the same time, representatives of independent labor organizations in the USSR found it very difficult to obtain exit visas for travel to the United States.

At this point, Evans took the extraordinary step of indicating how, under certain circumstances, the Soviet complaint could be satisfactorily resolved. He said:

> To the degree to which the USSR is prepared to permit unofficial trade-unionists to visit the United States and to take other steps aimed at opening up and liberalizing its system of worker representation, we are prepared to show flexibility in applying the relevant legislation.[68]

It was a most unusual commitment, no doubt based upon consultations with the Department of Justice.

The critical point in the Evans thesis was that Helsinki had a clear relevance to US legislation and conduct. He openly observed that "we are continually reviewing our own adherence" to principles in the Helsinki Final Act and in concluding documents, including the Vienna one. Specifically being reviewed, he added, was that section of the Final Act that required the signatory powers to "facilitate the convening of meetings, as well as travel by delegations, groups, and individuals." Evans' concluding remark was especially intriguing in displaying a rather impressive responsiveness to a Soviet challenge:

> Mr. Chairman, we wish to say that we take this use of the mechanism seriously. Moreover, we wish to assure our Soviet colleagues that we welcome a continuation of the dialogue which they have initiated.

While the United States took a keen interest in the new mechanism and how it could be made more effective, it offered nothing precise about how CSCE was supposed to deal with Romania, which denied the validity of the new mechanism. The US mechanism specialist simply told the delegates that it was impermissible "to agree to a set of [Helsinki] standards in one breath and then cut the heart of those standards in another."[69] She added that Romania's "reservations" about the Vienna document "are incompatible with the object and purpose of the very document to which Romania has given consensus." Such reservations, therefore, "can have no meaning here."

Bucharest remained in virtual isolation at the Paris talks. A striking demonstration of that isolation came near the beginning of the meeting.[70] The head of every single Helsinki delegation except the Romanian was showered with applause by his colleagues after finishing an opening speech. In contrast, a deafening silence engulfed the delegation of Romania following the opening address of its ambassador. Even the Warsaw Pact members sat on their hands. For a moment, only the East German chief delegate seemed about to clap his hands. But he quickly stopped after his eye caught the passivity of his communist colleagues. A test of how to proceed in the face of continuing Romanian intransigence lay in the future. At Paris, the Romanians made it evident that they would veto any concluding document. No doubt, Bucharest would have done so at Copenhagen, and at Moscow as well, but for the overthrow of the Ceausescu regime in December 1989. (The Paris meeting lacked, in any case, widespread desire for a concluding document; the United States, at any rate, opposed the idea of one.) Implementation of Vienna's "rights" was more important than new documents.

While most of the discussions on the mechanism at Paris centered on procedure, the Swiss came up with an idea that had strong substantive content. Prompted by the confidence-building measures adopted at Stockholm, particularly as they related to verification of military maneuvers, the Swiss proposed that signatories have the right to send in inspectors to check on human rights in countries suspected of violating the provisions of Helsinki or Vienna.[71]

Ambassador Abram went out of his way in his concluding address on June 23 to laud the Swiss proposal.[72] In later testimony to the Helsinki Commission, he again endorsed the imaginative idea.[73] But a number of Western diplomats feared that, if eventually adopted, the proposed procedure could be used by Moscow or other communist countries to "inspect" more than merely the human rights situation in major Western urban centers. Bern, faced with this resistance, dropped the inspection theme. As a fallback, Switzerland then proposed that legal observers from foreign countries be permitted to attend, upon request or challenge, trials held in any of the signatory countries.

What was most striking throughout much of the Paris deliberations, whether on the proposals advanced on the new mechanism for compliance or even when implementation review took place, was the conciliatory and cooperative stance of the Soviet delegation. Only the US comments on self-determination and the Soviet nationality question had stirred a harsh and bitter Soviet reaction. This may not have been too surprising from the Soviet perspective, as what was being challenged was the very survival of its multinational polity. In the main, however, delegations were impressed by the apparent cooperative spirit of Moscow.

Indeed, the Kremlin had mounted an impressive public relations campaign in Paris. The delegation it sent to the talks was twice the size of anyone else's—a unique development in the Helsinki process—and included human rights and emigration officials who were available to talk with all non-governmental lobbyists and individual activists. At the start of the talks, the Soviet delegation held an open press conference and answered every kind of question.

Just as projecting a spirit of affability and conciliation was the tack the Soviet delegation took in public, the speeches it made in the plenary sessions emphasized the new trends in the USSR and sought to assure everyone that the complaints raised about specific Soviet policies would be satisfactorily handled in time. Greater efforts were promised in the areas of legal revision—50 new laws were projected—and in humanitarianism. In addition, the Kremlin eventually permitted several prominent Soviet Jewish activists to fly under its auspices to Paris for meetings with Western Jewish organizations and the Western press.

It was hardly accidental that the USSR's public posture in Paris assumed a remarkable air of warmth and cooperation. The human dimension meeting scheduled to take place in Moscow two years hence had a highly important symbolic value for the Soviet Union, and the Kremlin wanted to convince Western nations that their lingering fears and doubts about the location were unwarranted. Moreover, easing international anxieties about Soviet goals was one of the main objectives of Gorbachev's new thinking.

Nonetheless, the West was not about to drop its guard even if the Soviet Union was no longer the principal target of human rights criticism, and even if, as Abram put it, "the Iron Curtain is melting at the edges." Delegates from the United States and the West pointed out with dismay that while the notorious Criminal Code Articles 70 and 190-1 were eliminated, the laws replacing them were not a major improvement. The old articles had made illegal "anti-Soviet propaganda," while the new ones prohibited the "discrediting" of public institutions. They were potential threats to free expression.[74]

The caution of the West received powerful support from the towering authority of Andrei Sakharov. As the Paris meeting entered its final week, he seriously challenged the "new thinking" in relation to human rights. In a speech at the Royal Institute for International Affairs in London, Sakharov asserted that "the only real political change that has taken place in the [USSR] was that we got a man standing at the head of the government who enjoys practically unlimited power."[75] He expressed dismay at the "Gorby fever" that had seized West Germany (calling it "unjustified and dangerous"), and appeared to be warning that much of what had been reconstructed in the Soviet Union remained a kind of "Potemkin village."

Exemplifying Sakharov's doubts about glasnost was an episode at Paris involving the Wallenberg case. At Vienna, the Soviet delegation, in response to Western pressures, had shown for the first time some sympathy with Wallenberg and indicated that the matter was being investigated by researchers.

Perhaps not surprisingly, the Soviet delegation at Paris included a high official of Moscow's Procurator-General's office, Vladimir Andreyev, who was identified as having led an official investigation of the Wallenberg affair. At the big press conference run by the USSR on June 1, Andreyev was called upon to respond to a question about the Swedish hero.[76] He went significantly beyond the favorable comments about Wallenberg that Kashlev had uttered at Vienna. The arrest and disappearance of Wallenberg constituted "a somber page in our history," said the Soviet legal official. He added that "we profoundly regret [his] death." The tone, rich in sorrowful and sympathetic expressions, was aimed at assuring Western representatives that Moscow stood as one with the democracies in the outpouring of humanitarian concern for the Swedish diplomat. To reinforce the sense of identical humanitarian interests, Andreyev commented: "Our attitude towards him is positive, [and] we understand the importance of the cause which he had served."

If the Soviet official was categorical about Wallenberg's death, he had nothing new to offer about the circumstances surrounding either it or his arrest. "We know nothing new" about such matters, he commented. His associate, Ambassador Kashlev, took the floor to explain that the ones who were responsible for "destroying such persons as Wallenberg, also destroyed the documents."[77] As if to close the book on the investigation, Kashlev added that of course Moscow would make public disclosure "if, by magic, we were to obtain new information."

Magic, of course, was not easily available to judicial investigators. Andreyev sought to play down the uniqueness of the Wallenberg case and, thereby, make it appear logical and reasonable that all the evidence could disappear. "Unfortunately, he was not alone," observed Andreyev, "millions of others" similarly represented somber pages in Soviet history. But the Wallenberg case was unique, and it was mystifying that a careful investigation cast absolutely no light on his plight during the two full years that he was in the hands of his jailers—January 1945-July 1947. Available documented evidence suggested that there were considerable sources that could be tapped for information on what happened to Wallenberg and why.

Andreyev's Paris apologia was consistent with the Kremlin cover-up on Wallenberg ever since his apprehension in January 1945. Despite the explicit promises of the Soviet delegation at Vienna, and the implicit promises of Gorbachev's glasnost policy, no serious inroad was made in disclosure of the truth about Wallenberg's disappearance and presumed death. It was clear that the security apparatus in Moscow was fearful of opening up a Pandora's box about its practices.

Just a half-year after Paris, Soviet authorities suddenly "discovered" and made available to the leadership of the Swedish Wallenberg Committee newly retrieved documents—Wallenberg's prison identity card, his passport, some of his money—and this, after Andreyev had vigorously insisted that his own inquiry had located no further evidence at all. Sakharov's memoirs, published posthumously in 1990, spoke eloquently about the character of Andreyev. He was revealed to be hostile and deceitful in his interrogation of the great Soviet humanist.[78]

Still, notwithstanding such doubts about the certainties and adequacy of Gorbachev's reforms, there could be little doubt that basic changes in the domestic structure of the Soviet Union had taken place. And these pointed to a more democratic structure and the rule of law. Thus, Assistant Secretary of State Schifter, as tough an anti-communist as might be found in official US circles, could point to the following developments after March 1989 which he found truly "astonishing": 1) creation of a genuine legislative body, some of whose members had a valid mandate from the local electorate; 2) provision for democratic elections at the local and republic levels, as well as for the all-Union level in the future; 3) introduction of a considerable degree of freedom of speech, press, association, assembly and religion; and 4) the removal of the Communist Party apparatus from its monopoly of control both in government and society as whole.[79]

Schifter, looking at the developments from a historical perspective, concluded that the Soviet Union had reached a level of democracy and freedom of expression which Russia had enjoyed only in the short period from February to October 1917. What had happened throughout 1989, he said, was that "basic steps were taken which dismantled the system of government created by Lenin, elaborated on by Stalin, and maintained by Stalin's successors." It was this progress that provided a framework for Washington to pose a great challenge to the Helsinki process. The new horizon that was projected for CSCE was nothing less than a democratic order for all of Europe. The implications were revolutionary.

▪15▪

Copenhagen: A "Constitution" for Europe

The vision of a Europe "whole and free" had stirred the imagination at the Paris human dimension meeting, and sparks were soon lighting up the political and social sky in Eastern Europe. The Vienna concluding document's focus upon the right to leave a country was of special pertinence to those East Germans who, while on vacation, sought to use Hungary (and Czechoslovakia) as a halfway house in order to emigrate to West Germany. A telling and decisive historic moment came when the Honecker regime in East Berlin demanded that Hungary adhere to a bilateral treaty that required the return home of all westbound East Germans without official exit visas.

The Hungarian Foreign Ministry rejected the protest on grounds that the treaty was superseded by obligations of international law and agreements. Clearly, Helsinki and the specifics of the Vienna document now offered a sanction that legitimized emigration rights.[1] Vigorous and angry objections made by the East German government were simply rebuffed. Hungarian Foreign Minister Gyüla Horn on September 12, 1989, told Berlin that international obligations "related . . . to human rights" were more important than agreements reached with allies in the past. Two days later, his deputy, Ferenc Somogyi, stressed that Budapest now placed "absolute primacy on universal humanitarian values." Vienna's concluding document on the right to leave had taken firm root in Central Europe. Its implications—rhetorical or operational—for the Germanys were enormous. Western diplomats in Bonn in August had estimated that 1.5 million East Germans had officially applied for permanent exit visas. A West German official had put it closer to 2 million and speculated that, were emigration made completely free, about 5 million of East Germany's 16.6 million persons would leave. (Since the Berlin Wall was built in 1961, some 672,000 East Germans had been permitted to settle in West Germany; more than 200,000 had done so since 1984 alone.)

This Helsinki-legitimized development was an explosive force that would rock the seemingly invulnerable Berlin Wall and, ultimately, the communist regime of East Germany.[2] With the Wall no longer able to hold back East Germans, emigrants flooded to the West, undermining the very foundations of Honecker rule. Eventually, on November 9, the communist regime itself collapsed.

The unexpected political (and ultimately territorial) consequence of Vienna's sanction of the right to leave was accompanied by more predictable consequences as well. Jewish emigration from the USSR during 1989 was to reach 71,000, the highest annual figure since the October Revolution. In 1990, that total almost tripled, reaching 183,000. Only a few years earlier, the annual total had been but 1,000, and the Kremlin explained that Soviet Jews were no longer interested in emigrating. The Soviet German emigration pattern was almost similar. In 1989, the total jumped to 98,000, and in 1990 to 148,000. During 1991, the figures of both Jewish and German emigration remained high—167,000 and 149,000, respectively. Together with the smaller Armenian emigration figures, the overall emigration total by the end of 1992 had exceeded one million persons. Vienna's impact on what had been the ultimate centerpiece of the Helsinki process—" freer movement of people"—proved momentous.

As for "freer movement of ideas," the moral bases of the Czechoslovak revolt in November were similarly derived from the Helsinki process. It was not only that Charter 77 had been a prime advocate of Helsinki standards; the new revolutionary leaders, whether Havel or Foreign Minister Jiri Dienstbier or spokesperson (later Ambassador to the United States) Rita Klimova, were all deeply involved with the local Helsinki monitoring group. Havel's activism was facilitated by his early release from prison, which was a direct consequence of Helsinki's new human dimension mechanism (see Chapter 14). Dienstbier would claim at Copenhagen that for him and his associates in Charter 77, "Helsinki 1975 was a turning point in the struggle for the restoration of democracy."[3] They were following in the footsteps of the Solidarity movement in Poland (which had become the dominant political force in Warsaw).

The impact of Vienna was especially direct upon the Bulgarian uprising in October 1989. On October 16, the Helsinki signatories had assembled in Sofia for an environment conference, which had been agreed upon at the Vienna follow-up meeting. The Bulgarians had desperately sought the conference, and the site was finally, although hesitantly, approved by the West as part of a complicated series of trade-offs. The Todor Zhivkov regime would come to regret its plea for a Helsinki meeting. As with almost every Helsinki-sponsored conference, non-governmental organizations used the occasion to press their aims and dramatize their concerns. One of the more active NGOs in Bulgaria, Ecoglasnost, chose the event to demonstrate its demands.[4] The Sofia authorities, not accustomed to unorganized public assemblages, brutally applied police pressure to disperse the demonstrators. Helsinki delegates from the Western and neutral/non-aligned countries were shocked by the crackdown. In meetings with Sofia officials, they threatened a walkout. The repression quickly ceased. Soon the inspiration of Ecoglasnost had affected others, and a chain of events was set in motion that brought down the regime.

Even Romania could not remain immune to Vienna's democratic "virus." Nicolae Ceausescu's government was determined to quarantine the country from the Vienna decisions, publicly declaring in January 1989 that it would not be bound by the new implementing mechanism. When human rights complaints were formally lodged under the mechanism by the US, UK, and the European Community, Bucharest rebuffed the accusations. Still a total quarantine could not be effected. In March, a half-dozen very prominent former Romanian officials circulated a letter demanding both a cessation of human rights abuses and strict adherence to the Helsinki accord.[5] Distributed widely in samizdat fashion, the letter was given even more extensive public coverage by Radio Free Europe broadcasts.

An international authority on East Europe and the Soviet Union, Professor Ernst Kux of Switzerland, in analyzing the 1989 revolutions, concluded that "the Helsinki process . . . has had a greater influence on developments in Eastern Europe than Gorbachev's *perestroika*. . . ." Kux noted that the process had inspired the young generation as well as the new middle classes and "encouraged their self-confidence and the expression of their political interest." What was critically important to the spread of Helsinki ideas, he emphasized, was the "modern electronic media" which compelled "the East European societies, long isolated behind the iron curtain . . . to open up."[6]

The revolutions of 1989 had profound repercussions on the elaborate post-war security system the Kremlin had erected in Eastern Europe. Soon the new democratic regimes of Hungary and Czechoslovakia would be demanding the removal of Soviet troops, as would Poland. Far more troubling to the Soviet Union was the overthrow of communist rule in East Germany. That rump state with its 400,000 Soviet troops was the linchpin of the entire Soviet security system. With Bonn now acting as a powerful magnet on the East German public and popular demands for union of the Germanys becoming an overwhelming political reality, Kremlin anxieties assumed a fever-pitch dimension.

Ever since the late 1940s, Moscow's primary security objective was the permanent division of the two Germanys. Leonid Brezhnev's foreign policy, particularly its Helsinki aspects, were rooted in the "inviolability of borders." The preservation of communist East Germany was the centerpiece of the policy. Now the inviolable borders were suddenly disintegrating, and with them the foundation of the Soviet security system.

It was at this point that an anxious Mikhail Gorbachev called for a Helsinki II summit preserving the separate Germanys while ratifying the revolutionary changes in Eastern Europe. More than a year earlier, he had suggested an incipient form of the idea; in summer 1988, he had expressed the view that a summit be held to discuss issues dealing with security, economic cooperation, and environment. Now, on November 30, 1989, while on a trip to Rome, Gorbachev floated the idea of a Helsinki II summit to be held in 1990, a full two years before the next Helsinki follow-up meeting, scheduled for the Finnish capital itself.[7] The previous day, Soviet Foreign Minister Shevardnadze had sternly rebuked West German Chancellor Helmut Kohl for advancing the idea of German confederation that would link together the two Germanys.[8] Shevardnadze vigorously underscored the Soviet perspective that the existence of two separate Germanys was a reality that had to be accepted in order to advance East-West understanding.

The Soviet President's anxieties strongly resonated in Prague, Warsaw and, not surprisingly, in Paris.[9] One week after the Rome address, Mitterrand hastily journeyed to Kiev to meet Gorbachev. A day of intense discussions followed. The press was informed by a senior Soviet Communist Party official, Andrei Grachev, that "the development of the German question played no small role in our decision to call for a new Helsinki conference."[10] Mitterrand advised against any talk about "changing borders," and cautioned that no country could act "without taking account of the European equilibrium" and the results of World War II.[11] He joined in calling for a Helsinki II and declared that "it would be good . . . if this happened in 1990."

But the stubborn fact of a powerful surge among the East German public for reunion with ethnic brethren in the West shortly made Helsinki II's contemplated purpose obsolete. The German question was resolved pretty much on the ground, with the post-war occupying powers in time agreeing to the inevitable. The Soviet Union had little alternative but to accept the reunion, especially as the Helsinki Final Act had extended a sanction to a change of borders if it was agreed to by the countries concerned, accepted by the international community, and accomplished peacefully. Moreover, under Gorbachev, Moscow had ruled out force to maintain communist rule.[12] The transition to a unified state was to be achieved by a "two plus four" formula, which meant intensive negotiations conducted by the two Germanys, with the original occupying powers —the United States, Britain, France, and the USSR—finalizing arrangements. (Agreement was reached in September 1990.) Soviet unhappiness was assuaged by a huge loan from the Federal Republic of Germany.

By late spring 1990, Moscow chose an alternative means to cope with the awesome threat it saw to its security. Gorbachev and Shevardnadze made clear that a unified Germany could not be part of NATO. At the same time, they recommended that both alliances, NATO and the Warsaw Pact, dissolve and that CSCE, which embraced the members of both alliances, assume responsibility for maintaining the peace. The latter found an echo in public statements made by West German Foreign Minister Genscher and by the new leadership of democratic Czechoslovakia and Poland.[13] Both proposals were unacceptable to Washington, and for good reasons of interest, reality and international law. No sovereign power can be or should be prevented from choosing whether to belong or not to belong to any alliance system.

Insistence upon the neutrality of a unified Germany was at variance with the principle of self-determination and the principle of state sovereignty. As for the assumption by CSCE of the security functions of NATO, Washington stressed that CSCE, operating on a consensus or unanimity principle, could not conceivably deter the threat of aggression when deterrence often required immediate and urgent action. Secretary of State Baker did call CSCE "the conscience of the continent," but conscience could hardly prevent military conflict.[14]

Whether and how these fundamental differences between Moscow and Washington would be resolved was of vital and critical concern to the Helsinki process. On June 5, CSCE would be holding in Copenhagen its second meeting of the Conference on the Human Dimension, the first since the revolutionary wave swept over East Europe. A backdrop of tension or of sharp differences on vital issues between the superpowers could not but affect the possibly historic meeting. At this crucial point on the eve of Copenhagen, Gorbachev arrived in Washington (June 3) for a summit meeting with President Bush.

The Bush administration made a determined effort to demonstrate that it understood the Soviets' profound security concerns (and Gorbachev's own related internal problems with hard-liners), and that it was making a serious attempt to deal with them.[15] A variety of rather tasty carrots was offered the Soviet leader in the hope that he would be encouraged to accept what, in any case, could not easily be avoided—the unification of the two Germanys and their inclusion in NATO. The inducements were also designed to make these unfolding developments more palatable to a Soviet public and, especially, to military and nationalist elements, whose fears and suspicions about Germany were deep, intense and real.

Among the concessions tendered the USSR were: 1) a united Germany would pledge not to develop nuclear, chemical or biological weapons; 2) the size of united Germany's armed forces would be reduced to a modest size, with the limits worked out in treaty form with NATO; 3) NATO troops, including German units, would not be assigned to the area formerly embracing East Germany; and 4) Soviet troops occupying the same area would be allowed to remain there pending agreement on a timetable for their redeployment (which would in essence be subsidized by Germany with a multibillion-mark payment presumably covering the costs of new housing in the USSR for the 400,000 Soviet troops who would be redeployed on a staggered basis).

For the Soviet leader, the assurances provided a modicum of significant concessions that rationalized thereby the absence of satisfying alternatives. Moreover, he was still accorded in Washington the status of a respected superpower leader, not that of the head of a diplomatically defeated country. Still, the seismic changes in Eastern Europe, climaxed by the unification of Germany, had nullified the basic thrust of Moscow's policy since World War II—the freezing of the post-war borders in Central and East Europe—which had found expression in the Helsinki Final Act. If the balance of power had now radically altered, the Bush administration went out of its way to cement the cordially established relationship of some five years' standing with the other superpower in the Helsinki process. That relationship was of critical importance as the process moved to a new level of human rights concern. This new level would be illuminated at the Copenhagen meeting on the human dimension, which began two days after the Washington summit.

In view of the remarkable transformation of Eastern Europe, it was unlikely that the United States would fail to give the Copenhagen assemblage a high priority. Washington's choice to head the US delegation provided a clear signal of its focus. Ambassador Max Kampelman, the US representative at Madrid who later served as the negotiator on arms reduction with the Soviets in Geneva, was brought out of virtual retirement to represent the US at Copenhagen. Moreover, Secretary of State

Baker planned to attend and address the meeting, in marked contrast to his absence at Paris the year before.

Kampelman later spelled out what his policy instructions for Copenhagen were in view of the historic transformation that had occurred in East Europe. As a top priority, the delegation was to seek consensus approval of the US proposal on free and fair elections, which Congressman Hoyer had originally tabled in Paris in June 1989. The second priority was to support and advance proposals that would help "build democratic institutions and guarantee human rights and individual freedoms, in particular by strengthening the rule of law."[16]

Two other items in the State Department's instructions were also mentioned: to review the working of the new human dimension mechanism and consider how it might be improved, and to ensure that the Copenhagen meeting would be held in the kind of "open atmosphere" that would set "the right precedents for the Moscow meeting" scheduled for September 1991. But it was the critical elements of a democratic structure—free elections, political pluralism, and the rule of law—that were the dominant considerations.

Ambassador Kampelman quickly recognized the significance of his task, the enviable, if difficult, responsibility of offering a kind of "blueprint" for the future of East European society. Clearly rejected, although in an implicit manner, was the notion that prevailed at the end of Vienna, that the Helsinki process required no further concluding documents. At Paris, the United States had not pressed for a document, even when the host country, France, sought determinedly from the beginning to have one accepted. What would emerge from Copenhagen, in sharp contrast, as later Kampelman related in testimony to the US Helsinki Commission, was the "first formal proclamation . . . of a Europe both whole and free."[17] The document would represent "an historic new consensus" of the CSCE, "the most significant step forward since the Helsinki Final Act."

To help accomplish this task, Kampelman brought three American legal and human rights scholars to Copenhagen as public members of the US delegation. An especially important role would be played by Professor Thomas Buergenthal of George Washington University Law School, who was also a judge in the Inter-American Court of Human Rights. The other two scholars were Associate Professor Hurst Hannum of the Fletcher School of Law and Diplomacy of Tufts University and Professor Theodor Meron of New York University Law School. Tapping the expertise of highly respected legal specialists from academia was a brilliant stroke, even if it meant bypassing traditional sources from the State

Department and the Helsinki Commission.[18] But Kampelman was intent upon creating a model document and "selling" the model formulations to other members of CSCE.

It was an unusual use of the "public members" category. In the past, their main function was as a channel of the US delegation to important domestic constituencies. Sometimes, individual public members would be used to draft speeches for the ambassador or to offer suggestions concerning speeches. Sometimes, their reactions would be sought regarding proposals on the CSCE agenda. On rare occasions, some might even be pressed into lobbying functions. But at Copenhagen the task was of a totally different nature, a kind of institution building for which considerable expertise was needed. Within the course of only three and one-half weeks, an extraordinary blueprint would have to be drafted and accepted. One major European journal dubbed it a "constitution" for the new governments of East Europe.[19] Significantly, the chief Soviet delegate, Yuri Reshetov, also called the Copenhagen document "Europe's new constitution."[20]

The effort was enormously taxing. Hours were spent in lengthy meetings with the legal experts and some staff, chaired by Kampelman, no slouch himself in legal knowledge and US constitutional history.[21] He had already rejected a State Department draft proposal as mere "pablum."[22] What especially concerned him was an Anglo-French draft on the rule of law that he felt would fail to set an adequately high standard. The principal work in the US delegation was done by Professor Buergenthal, who did much of the drafting of the American proposals. He also arranged to meet with key officials in other Western delegations to emphasize the points from his perspective.

What emerged from the Kampelman initiative on the two priority objectives was remarkably impressive. The proposal on free elections, in which Canada and the UK joined as co-sponsors, won unanimous agreement. Not even the most optimistic observer could have imagined at any earlier point in the Helsinki process, even as late as the Vienna meeting, that the Soviet Union and its allies would agree to the central premise of the Copenhagen document: ". . . pluralistic democracy and the rule of law are essential for ensuring respect for all human rights and fundamental freedoms."[23] From this premise flowed the commitment of all CSCE states "to build democratic societies based on free elections and the rule of law."

That the Copenhagen document would be lengthy and detailed was hardly surprising. It reflected Kampelman's desire to be as specific and precise as possible in spelling out what constituted free elections and the rule of law.[24] CSCE formally declared the revolutionary—in East European terms, anyway—doctrine that the will of the people, expressed through periodic and genuine elections, was the basis of the authority and legitimacy of government. Helsinki signatories were enjoined to guarantee universal and equal suffrage to adult citizens, and to assure the rights of citizens to form political parties and seek public office either as individuals or as representatives of those political parties. And foreign as well as domestic observers of national elections would be invited by the participating states. These observers could come from either government or non-governmental organizations.

The section on democracy and the rule of law was even more significant in that it elaborated principles that gave substance, context and meaning to a system of free elections. Originally drafted by the British and French, it was greatly augmented by the United States. The section began by specifying that "democracy is an inherent element of the rule of law," controlling all governmental activity and, therefore, enjoining public authorities to comply with their constitutions and act in a manner consistent with law. The document established that an independent and impartial judiciary is inherent in the rule of law, providing for effective remedies to challenge administrative decisions.

In distinguishing democracies from totalitarian structures, the Copenhagen document stipulated that a "clear separation" be drawn between the state and the ruling political party and that the merger of the two be prohibited. (Significantly, this reference was also made in the section on free elections.) A second distinction was drawn, designating that a state's military forces and police are to be placed under the control of and accountable to the civil authorities.

Basic judicial due-process provisions, at the heart of a democratic system, were delineated: all persons are to have the right to a fair hearing and the right to counsel; and the presumption of innocence is explicit—if charged, an individual is to be brought promptly before a judge, who will determine the legality of the arrest. Further, equal protection of the laws and non-discrimination are to be assured to all. And, in a sharp rejection of totalitarian ways, the document provided that no one can be tried or convicted of any criminal offense not spelled out with precision and clarity in a specific law.

Traditional human rights and fundamental freedoms, as detailed in international covenants and in earlier CSCE documents (notably the Vienna concluding document), were once again reproduced here, sometimes with greater precision. The document enshrined such personal freedoms as the rights of expression, assembly, association, conscience and religion (including, for the first time, the right to change one's religion), and of travel and emigration. The right to form trade unions and to strike was also noted.

Unusually significant in Copenhagen's catalogue of rights was the way in which the subject of restrictions upon rights was handled. Absolute rights, of course, do not exist in international treaties and instruments; rather, rights are subject to certain permissible restrictions, such as those that protect national security, public order, public health or morals, or the rights and freedoms of others. Totalitarianism and authoritarian regimes, all too often, have used such restrictions to virtually nullify the exercise of rights. Copenhagen imposed severe "restrictions on the restrictions."[25] It stipulated that the restrictions have the character of "exceptions," in that they "must not be abused or applied in an arbitrary manner." If they are applied, it must be done in such a way that the effective exercise of the rights is insured. This strongly civil libertarian formulation had no precedent in any of the UN and Council of Europe human rights instruments or in previous CSCE documents.

The restriction upon restrictions was made the sharpest in respect to the right to leave a country and to return to it. It was this right that stood at the very heart of the Helsinki process from the beginning, and one which the totalitarian *nomenklatura* had consistently restricted in grossly arbitrary fashion. Copenhagen provided that restrictions on the right to leave and return "will have the character of *very rare exceptions*, and will be considered necessary only if they respond *to specific public need*, pursue a legitimate aim, and are proportionate to that aim and will not be abused or applied in an arbitrary manner"[26] (emphasis added). Copenhagen gave formulaic substance to the destruction of the Berlin Wall.

It also gave special attention to that which had been a core element of the Helsinki's Principle VII—"the right to know and act upon one's rights." In this context, governments were to provide effective remedies for violations of human rights and fundamental freedoms. Among such remedies are "the right of the individual to seek and receive assistance from others in defending human rights . . . and to assist others in defending human rights."

Of particular interest was the acceptance by all CSCE members of a right not mentioned by Helsinki documents before 1990, indeed, not even mentioned in the International Covenants on Human Rights (largely because of determined opposition from the Soviet Union). The new provision affirmed that "everyone has the right to enjoy his property either as his own or in common with others" and that "no one may be deprived of his property except in the public interest and subject to the conditions provided by law. . . ."[27]

The ground had been laid for this radical departure from the past by decisions taken at the CSCE Bonn Conference on Economic Cooperation in Europe, mandated by the Vienna concluding document and held in March-April 1990.[28] The Bonn document contained several provisions that dealt with the protection and utilization of private property. CSCE consensual acceptance of the right of property testified to how far Moscow had moved since Vienna. What had been rejected in the past as totally alien to communist tradition and to the very nature of Soviet society was now given recognition and special safeguards. As the Soviet Union moved toward privatization and a market society, property was to be accorded the kind of respect which had been more appropriately given by Adam Smith than Karl Marx.

With a profound sensitivity to the fairly recent abuses of totalitarianism, CSCE adopted strong clauses prohibiting torture and other forms of degrading treatment, including psychiatric abuse. It also approved provisions sharply limiting the power of government to suspend human rights during a public emergency. Any suspension had to be made publicly and in accordance with specific legal statute.

With respect to institutional means for strengthening the rule of law, the United States would have liked to have gone much further. Strong specific measures elaborated upon by Professor Buergenthal and pressed by the US delegation in private lobbying sessions with its principal allies were advanced for judicial review, the separation of powers, legislation regarding freedom of information, for civilian control over intelligence agencies, and precise *habeas corpus* remedies.

The resistance to the US "constitutional" thrust did not come from the Soviet Union or from the former totalitarian states of Eastern and Central Europe. Buergenthal related later in testimony to the Helsinki Commission that "our NATO allies" had rejected these US proposals: "The institutional reforms we proposed or wanted to propose would have posed real or imagined legal and constitutional problems for them."[29] Thus, "at the very moment when the East no longer objects to substantive rule of law and human rights proposals, we are beginning to touch sensitive Western nerves." And the converse was also true: "Our allies in turn are coming up with proposals that are unacceptable to us for similar reasons."

Indeed, it was the weakness and inadequacy of the initial Anglo-French proposal on the rule of law that had prompted Ambassador Kampelman from the very beginning to involve top specialists from academia in both the drafting and lobbying initiatives at Copenhagen. Given the political and constitutional vacuum that had now so obviously presented itself in Eastern Europe, the US viewed the opportunity as uniquely important and of historic proportions. Here was an opportunity to shape the East in the Western image, or rather, in the American image (since, in fact, institutional safeguards in the US system are greater than in other Western democracies).

On the one hand, the US interest in the Helsinki process was "to help reform the political systems and strengthen the democratic institutions of countries that have only now freed themselves from communism."[30] That interest, of course, did not extend to changing the constitutional systems of Britain, France or West Germany. On the other hand, Buergenthal noted, "it is going to get increasingly more difficult to . . . help the East establish effective democratic institutions . . . if we and our allies cannot agree on what those institutions should be."

Still, the US effort, according to Kampelman, had "greatly and significantly" improved the initial Anglo-French draft and "enabled us to meet . . . [the] objective" which Washington had set forth in its priority requirement of advancing proposals that would strengthen the rule of law. That, plus "the virtually wholesale incorporation [into the Copenhagen document] of our proposal on free and fair elections," as the US delegation chief further testified, could not fail to please policy makers in Washington. Helsinki Commission Chairman DeConcini commented in a hearing on July 18 that "Copenhagen achieved in four short weeks what we have been pressing for in the Helsinki process for the past 15 years. . . ."[31] He was referring to the central theme in the free-elections section that governments derive their authority and legitimacy from the will of the people, expressed through genuine elections.

That the Copenhagen section on free elections and rule of law were "historic" and "extraordinary" could scarcely be disputed. Commission Co-chairman Hoyer recalled that nobody at the Paris human dimension meeting one year earlier had expected that at Copenhagen free elections and the rule of law would be inscribed in a formal Helsinki document. As he himself had tabled in Paris the proposal on free elections, it was a startling admission of how events had simply outrun the most optimistic expectations of those in the Helsinki process. Professor Buergenthal commented that 1989-90 constituted a "milestone" in the political history of Europe in which Europe became "freer . . . than it has been since World War II . . . [and] probably freer than at any time in its history."[32]

Even though Copenhagen's consensual agreements on free elections and rule of law had a ground-breaking character, two limitations were immediately apparent. One flowed from the status of the Copenhagen session. It was not a major Helsinki "follow-up meeting" or conference; rather, it had more of an "experts" character, mandated to function for a very short three and one-half weeks. For its decisions to assume a more binding character, logic—rather than any sort of constitutional or bylaw provision—suggested they be formally approved at the Paris summit of Helsinki heads of state scheduled for November.[33] Such a positive outcome, however, was more than likely, as no opposition was registered at Copenhagen to the text on free elections and rule of law.

The second limitation would be much more significant. Democracy is not a system that can easily be imposed from above, by fiat, as it were. Rather, it is a process—what Buergenthal called "a political culture . . . a way of life"—which "must be learned and . . . lived."[34] The "political culture" in virtually all of Eastern Europe, except Czechoslovakia, lacked a deep-rooted tradition and "way of life" that was "democratic" in the broad sense. Poland and Hungary might have had a certain democratic historical experience, but Romania, Bulgaria, Yugoslavia and Albania were almost totally lacking in it. As for the USSR, the democratic experience of 1917 was short-lived. Only since 1988 had important strides been taken in the direction of democracy.

To assist in the difficult and time-consuming processes of education and institution building for democratic political culture, Copenhagen recommended that the Council of Europe, headquartered in Strasbourg, be called upon to provide the expertise in human rights and fundamental freedoms for the benefit of Eastern Europe.[35] But, how the Council could accomplish this task was not made clear, especially as its membership rolls excluded the United States and Canada, the prime movers of the democracy proposal. Besides, the likelihood of the Soviet Union joining this institution was more than questionable.

While the United States placed high priority on free elections and the rule of law, and played the central role in incorporating effective language on these subjects in the Copenhagen document, this was not the case with respect to minority rights. Kampelman, in outlining the priorities Washington had assigned him, noticeably avoided reference to them. Yet, this subject had assumed an explosive character in the months prior to Copenhagen and, unavoidably, became a major source of commentary and analysis at the meeting.

West European governments could hardly ignore the enormous up-surge of nationalism among minorities everywhere in Eastern Europe. Previously, the communist regimes had simply repressed nationalist fer-vor, but their overthrow let loose the accumulated bitterness and anger of the past and threatened to rip asunder the civic order in the multinational societies of the Soviet Union and Yugoslavia. Romania, Bulgaria and the Czech and Slovak Federal Republic (whose very renaming reflected na-tionalist tension in the eastern part of the country) also had sizable na-tional minority populations. The deepening nationalistic tensions and the powerful centrifugal forces in multinational state structures evoked fears of anarchy and chaos challenging the new democratic order. Social uncer-tainties carried other threatening ramifications. Might they not incite mass emigration, with which West European countries, already burdened with unemployment and their own ethnic tensions, would find difficult to cope?

Copenhagen wrestled with the issue in a significant, though not deci-sive, way. More than a dozen lengthy provisions on minority rights were adopted, making the treatment in the concluding document, according to Buergenthal, "the most far reaching international statement on the sub-ject to date."[36] The United Nations, except for Article 27 of the Interna-tional Covenant on Civil and Political Rights, carried nothing on the subject. The Helsinki accord carried but one brief paragraph on the "right of persons belonging to . . . minorities to equality before the law. . . ." Madrid added to it by stressing the need to protect the "legitimate inter-ests" of minorities. Vienna, to be sure, had offered two paragraphs, one of which required CSCE states to "protect" and "create conditions for promotion" of the identity and culture of national minorities.

In its initial venture into the national minorities question, Copenhagen, not surprisingly, linked the issue with freedom and the rule of law. This re-quired a distinctive focus upon the individual member of the group, rather than upon the group itself. Thus, what was stressed was the theme that "to belong to a national minority is a matter of a person's individual choice," in turn bolstered by non-discrimination rules imposed or enacted by the authorities.[37] More pertinently, "questions relating to national mi-norities can only be satisfactorily resolved in a democratic political frame-work, based on the rule of law with a functioning independent judiciary."

At this point, the Copenhagen document shifted slightly to focus upon the group. Persons of national minorities were assured the right to ex-press and develop "their ethnic, cultural, linguistic or religious identity" and to "develop their culture in all its aspects." The right to use one's mother tongue in public, to establish educational, cultural and religious institutions, and to maintain contact with other group members both within and without the country were spelled out. In elaborating the basic right of the group, the drafters formulated a somewhat workable definition of the elusive phrase "national minority." A series of shared ethnic, cultural, linguistic and/or religious features presumably distinguished a group that required protection, preservation and enhancement.

If, on the one hand, Copenhagen emphasized free choice for the individual of a national minority against forcible assimilation, it also recommended that governments support both the cultural values of ethnic groups and respect for those values on the part of others. CSCE states agreed "to take account of the history and culture of national minorities" in the general educational system, and to "promote a climate of mutual respect, understanding, cooperation and solidarity. . . ."[38]

The drafting process on the national minorities provisions was not easy. Sharp splits emerged over whether CSCE should be dealing with national minorities in multinational states or with any religious, cultural, ethnic or linguistic minorities in either national or multinational states.[39] A firm definition of national minorities was not reached. Nor did the participants reach a clear decision as to whether states should take an active role in promoting minority identity and consciousness, in contradistinction to states refraining from hindering the efforts of minorities to promote and protect themselves. Contentiousness in dealing with these questions was considerable, but the Austrian coordinator of the discussion successfully finessed the differences and reached a satisfactory result which all could accept.

The most significant part of the section on national minorities was a condemnation of a burgeoning racism, especially anti-Semitism, in Eastern as well as Western Europe. Indeed, it was one of the most important segments—if not the most important segment—of the entire document. The key paragraph read:

> The participating states clearly and unequivocally condemn totalitarianism, racial and ethnic hatred, anti-Semitism, xenophobia and discrimination against anyone, as well as persecution on religious and ideological grounds. In this context, they also recognize the particular problems of Roma [Gypsies]. They declare their firm intention to intensify the efforts to combat these phenomena in all their forms. . . .[40]

What made the paragraph (as well as the paragraphs which followed it) unprecedented and unique was the explicit reference to anti-Semitism in an international instrument. No UN treaty, no international or regional covenant, no declaration had ever specifically referred to anti-Semitism. Nor had any previous Helsinki document. Only twice before had an effort been made—both times by the United States—to include in a draft UN treaty a specific condemnation of anti-Semitism. On both occasions, the Soviet Union assumed the principal initiative in killing the reference.

During the drafting of the UN's International Convention on the Elimination of All Forms of Racial Discrimination in the early 1960s, the US had moved for incorporation in the treaty of a specific condemnation of anti-Semitism.[41] The motion was quite logical, as plans for the drafting of the treaty were prompted by the "swastika epidemic" of 1959-60 that had swept the Western world. In an effort to wreck the US initiative, Soviet delegates moved an amendment adding the word "Zionism," along with several other "isms," to the US proposal.[42] Because equating Zionism with anti-Semitism would be worse than self-defeating, the United States ultimately accepted a compromise that omitted reference to either.

A similar effort to add the term "anti-Semitism" was made when the UN was preparing in 1966 a draft of the International Convention on Religious Intolerance, a treaty yet to be completed.[43] However, in the following year, the reference was deleted by the Third Committee of the UN General Assembly.

In view of the past failures to include references to anti-Semitism in international instruments, the achievement at Copenhagen stands out as extraordinary. How did it happen? For one thing, both glasnost and the revolutions of 1989 had stirred a popular and populist anti-Semitism in Eastern Europe as a coefficient of rising nationalism. If in the Soviet Union Gorbachev's positive reform had brought an end to the official anti-Semitic propaganda that had masqueraded as anti-Zionism, the 20 years or so of the media hate drive had nonetheless left in its wake anti-Jewish bigotry. The bigotry had fed on ancient prejudices against Jewry that ran deep into Russian history. Pamyat (meaning "memory"), a strongly nationalist and anti-Semitic group, and a host of similar chauvinistic organizations had sprung into existence with the opening provided by glasnost.

Backed by powerful conservative elements in the Communist Party apparatus and bureaucracy, and by strong nationalist forces in the literary, military and security worlds, Pamyat terrorized the Soviet Jewish community with its marches, demonstrations, mailings, posters and propaganda.[44] Open threats of pogroms, which the Kremlin seemed unable or unwilling to stop, evoked among Jews fears that often bordered on panic and spurred an escalating pattern of emigration.[45]

Elsewhere in Eastern Europe, the new freedom at times produced intense nationalist fervor, which in turn stimulated or reinforced older anti-Semitic attitudes and actions.[46] Anti-Jewish bigotry was successfully exploited in elections in Hungary by conservative, nationalist and rural elements. In Romania, where anti-Semitism had a deep-rooted tradition, nationalists and anti-communists used it as a political weapon. In Slovakia, nationalists urged a memorial to Father Jozef Tiso, the head of an anti-Semitic rump state created by the Nazis during World War II. In Poland, where there were few Jews, anti-Semitism was exploited by anti-intellectual elements in the intense intramural political struggles within Solidarity. Croatian nationalism within Yugoslavia produced similar tendencies. In newly freed East Germany, soon to be unified with the Federal Republic, the absence of the positive educational programs that had influenced West German youth was not without consequence. Hate-mongering among "skinheads" and similar marginal elements surfaced, especially among young people.

Even Western Europe was not immune to the outbursts of anti-Semitism. The Jean-Marie Le Pen fascist movement in France prompted a growing public concern and, when a massive desecration of the Jewish cemeteries in a suburb of Paris took place in the spring of 1990, anxiety could not fail to emerge among Jews, intellectuals and those committed to the preservation of the democratic social order.

A leading scholar of international affairs, Dominique Moïsi, referred to the phenomenon of anti-Semitism as a specter of the past which now haunted Europe.[47] He expressed fears that people might be "fatally attracted by the dark temptations of xenophobia, racism and jingoism." A prominent Solidarity intellectual, Adam Michnik, provocatively observed that post-totalitarian societies can breed the dangers of racism, anti-Semitism and xenophobia.[48]

The subject informed the Copenhagen deliberations from the beginning. On the opening day of the session, June 4, Czechoslovak Foreign Minister Jiri Dienstbier warned that racism, anti-Semitism and chauvinism constituted serious threats that could "jeopardize European security."[49] At the end of his speech, he urged that "as long as Jewish cemeteries are vandalized anywhere," and violent threats are directed against other minorities, the CSCE focus upon human rights "should not relent."

Equally forthright was East German Foreign Minister Markus Meckel, whose speech was read by his Ambassador to the CSCE talks, Johannes Langhoff.[50] He recalled the "historic responsibility" of the Germans for the "murder of minorities," and he contended that "nationalism, anti-Semitism and xenophobia" must find "no fertile ground" in the new German society emerging. His FRG counterpart, Hans-Dietrich Genscher, if somewhat indirect in his comments, nonetheless recalled the past in a most striking manner. He reminded his audience that while November 9 was the date when the Berlin Wall fell to usher in a new era of freedom, it was also the date of Kristallnacht, which in 1938 had portended the fate of German Jews.[51]

None of the other foreign ministers made specific reference to anti-Semitism in their opening remarks. However, Max Kampelman addressed himself to the subject on June 11, in his first formal speech.[52] He warned that "anti-Semitism and racial, religious and ethnic hatreds" constituted "a symbol of this [new] danger . . . intolerance." A pointed appeal to cope with the problem followed immediately:

> The time calls for a vigorous, systematic and public condemnation of such prejudices by the highest authorities of government. There is no substitute for vigorous moral leadership.

Sir John Robson of the United Kingdom joined in, specifically referring to anti-Semitism in the Soviet Union.[53]

The Canadian delegation submitted a proposal on "Elimination of Hate Propaganda" that called for strong legislative and educational measures against racism, although it carried no specific reference to anti-Semitism.[54] A rather dramatic indication of the remarkable change in the Soviet posture at Helsinki meetings came early in the session. The head of the Soviet delegation, Yuri Reshetov, who also served as chief of the Foreign Ministry's humanitarian affairs department, announced that his first act upon arriving in Copenhagen was to ask to be permitted to co-sponsor the Canadian proposal.[55]

After the Canadian proposal was introduced (with the co-sponsorship of the USSR and Italy) on June 5, West Germany and East Germany joined on June 7 in sponsoring a resolution against racism, with specific reference to anti-Semitism.[56] France, supported by the EC, also tabled a draft, but with no reference to anti-Semitism.

The Canadian delegation was responsive to the urgings of Jewish representatives, with whom it met on June 12.[57] Two days later, a Canadian draft including references to anti-Semitism became the focus of the initiative. The other drafts were eventually withdrawn. A number of delegations later gave strong backing to the Canadian proposal, which culminated in a final text also condemning racist hostility to Gypsies. This, too, was unprecedented in an international instrument.

Besides condemnation, the Copenhagen document offered two major devices for combatting racism and anti-Semitism. One was law, the other education. With respect to the first, the document called upon the participating states to

> take effective measures, including the adoption . . . of such laws as may be necessary to provide protection against any acts that constitute incitement to violence against persons or groups based on national, racial, ethnic or religious discrimination, hostility or hatred, including anti-Semitism.[58]

The document also urged adoption of appropriate measures to protect individuals or groups "who may be subject to threats or acts of discrimination, hostility or violence as a result of their racial, ethnic, cultural, linguistic or religious identity. . . ." With respect to education, the text asked CSCE states to "take effective measures . . . to promote understanding and tolerance" and "endeavor to ensure that the objectives of education include special attention to the problem of racial prejudice and hatred and to the development of respect for different civilizations and cultures."

There were two problems. One related to the ironic question of free speech and free expression, critical elements of democracy and the rule of law to which the West, especially the United States, had given high priority at Copenhagen. Restrictions on speech and expression for purposes of combatting racism and anti-Semitism would subvert civil libertarian features of the rule of law. The West, no doubt strongly pressed by the US, sought to cope with the problem through the phrase "inciting to violence," reckoning that speech or expression inciting violence cross the boundary of freedom into the category of a "clear and present danger" to the democratic order itself.

Some would have wanted language that would have made it easier to prosecute racism.[59] Thus, they would have preferred the language of the UN Convention on the Elimination of All Forms of Racial Discrimination, which bans "incitement to racial discrimination, as well as acts of violence or incitement to such acts. . . ." For the civil libertarian, the language was much less acceptable than "incitement to violence." (The United States had registered concern about the convention's language when it was adopted in 1965. Incitement to discrimination rather than violence was perceived as inconsistent with the US Constitution's First Amendment.)

The second problem had to do with implementation. Of what value is a law against racism if it is not implemented? A blatant example was provided by Article 74 of the Russian Criminal Code—replicated in the criminal codes of other Soviet republics—which barred incitement of ethnic discord. It was this law to which Soviet authorities referred when they contended that anti-Semitism was legally forbidden in the USSR. However, prior to 1990, no one had ever been charged with, let alone convicted and sentenced for violation of, Article 74 on grounds of anti-Semitic incitement.[60] Reshetov, in an address to the University of Copenhagen Law School Symposium, noted that recently the Soviet law against incitement of national hatred had been strengthened, and that Soviet prosecutors intended to use the statute against Pamyat.[61]

(In fact, just a few weeks after Copenhagen ended, Moscow prosecutors placed on trial one Konstantin Smirnov-Ostashvili, the head of an extremist Pamyat group, for anti-Semitic incitement of violence against an assemblage of liberal writers meeting in January 1990. This unprecedented case led in October to Smirnov-Ostashvili's conviction and a judicial sentence of two years' imprisonment.[62])

Counteracting racism and anti-Semitism in Eastern Europe through education would require an entirely new pedagogical perspective for the region. The subject of racism was simply not taught, nor was the meaning and significance of the Holocaust. In the Soviet Union, which was the only country in the area with a Jewish population of over 100,000—its estimated total was 2.25 million persons—Jewish history had been simply plunged down an Orwellian memory hole. Textbooks in the elementary and secondary schools made no reference to Jews. More disturbingly, they blotted out any reference to the Holocaust: Hitler's specific genocidal program against Jews—a subject that could have been effectively raised to combat anti-Semitism—was completely suppressed.[63]

But, for the moment, a vigorous government public posture, as suggested in the Copenhagen document, would appear to be the most effective means. The document stipulated that CSCE states "clearly and unequivocally condemn" racism and anti-Semitism. Kampelman, more than anyone else at Copenhagen, appeared to recognize what would be required. No one else there addressed the subject. He urged "vigorous moral leadership" by the "highest authorities of government" to combat anti-Semitism and racism. Kampelman continued:

> If governments . . . stand by and do nothing as hatred consumes their society, then they are part of the problem. If, in contrast . . . they make a firm public stance against prejudice, then they are part of the answer.[64]

The US representative, as extensively trained and experienced in political science as he was in law, recommended the use of high political office as a "bully pulpit," in the words of Theodore Roosevelt, to set the moral tone of a nation with respect to bigotry.

Such leadership was sorely lacking in the USSR. President Gorbachev had offered few comments in the past about the deepening anti-Semitism and what he had to say was scarcely helpful. In February 1986, he publicly declared that anti-Semitism was "impossible in the USSR" because it was "prohibited by law and constitutes a crime."[65] In 1987, he openly linked anti-Semitism with Zionism, a formula similar to the notorious 1975 UN resolution which had defined Zionism "as a form of racism. . . ."[66]

In 1989, with anti-Jewish hate-mongering spreading, intellectuals and liberals petitioned and pleaded with Gorbachev to denounce it in ringing terms. The petitions were buried, the pleas rejected.[67] With fear of pogroms growing in 1990, the Soviet President finally got around to briefly extending a critical comment: "I believe that we ought not to allow the raging of nationalism, chauvinism, anti-Semitism or any other 'isms' to occur."[68] Awkward and indirect, the comment hardly compared to Lenin's sharp, pointed, and harsh repudiation of anti-Semitism during 1918-19.[69] Nor did it fit the guideline that Ambassador Kampelman set forth at Copenhagen.

Still, the Kampelman recommendation and the Copenhagen document may very well have exerted some impact upon the Kremlin. On July 22, a month after Copenhagen, the Communist Party organ *Pravda* featured a lengthy and powerful indictment of anti-Semitism in the Soviet Union, giving specific attention to the activities of Pamyat and the vituperative publications of nationalists.[70] The timing of the *Pravda* article was surely not completely accidental.

If the Copenhagen document thus constituted a historic breakthrough for international instruments in condemning anti-Semitism, it is instructive to note that the leadership on this issue was exercised by the Canadian, German, Czechoslovakian, British and French delegations, in approximately that order. The US was not in the forefront of the effort to include specific reference to anti-Semitism in the Copenhagen document, although it played a mayor role in having the subject raised in plenary deliberations. Indeed, when Shoshana Cardin, the chairperson of the National Conference on Soviet Jewry, met with Kampelman for lunch on June 14, she was astonished—as she later reported—that he was not responsive to inclusion in the document of a specific condemnation of anti-Semitism.[71] Nor did he believe that the references to anti-Semitism would win the support of others. According to a staffer from the National Conference on Soviet Jewry, it required intensive lobbying by both the Helsinki Commission and Jewish NGOs to bring about change in the State Department position.[72]

In fact, Kampelman's priorities were free elections, pluralism and the rule of law. In contrast with the speeches of at least several foreign ministers on the opening day of Copenhagen, Secretary of State Baker said nothing on the subjects of racism and anti-Semitism. This did not mean that Kampelman himself was reluctant to tackle the issue openly. As indicated, he was firm on the role and responsibility of governments to discourage hate and prejudice. But, he did not view the minorities question as something about which a "constitutional" document could propose detailed provisions. Free elections, human rights and the rule of law could be delineated with precision. The promotion of tolerance and understanding was far less susceptible to legally binding formulations.

In the end, Kampelman welcomed the decision on incorporation of the reference to anti-Semitism in the Copenhagen concluding document. He told the Helsinki Commission at its hearings on July 18:

> We achieved what I believe is the first internationally agreed condemnation of anti-Semitism and . . . explicit mention of the problems experienced by Gypsies in Europe.[73]

He went on to comment that the preparation of a "major new document . . . was . . . much more positive than ever before in my CSCE experience." It was quite a commentary from one of Helsinki's veterans.

With a new "constitutional" structure of free elections, political pluralism, minority rights and the rule of law being erected, it seemed all the more appropriate to concentrate attention on implementation mechanisms, that is, on how to ensure that human rights and the rich variety of new civil and political rights were observed. Vaclav Havel, Czechoslovakia's president partly by virtue of the newly created mechanism adopted in Vienna 18 months earlier, not surprisingly offered a comment. And, brilliant ironist that the playwright politician was, his comment had an oblique character. In the only letter from a head of state sent to the Copenhagen conference, he raised questions about how to confront nonfulfillment of norms and standards. "Continuous, regular and purposeful exchange of information"—this is what is essential to compel governments to live up to their "international commitments."[74] In any case, public challenge was required. "Persistent silence" in the face of willful repression must be rejected, Havel warned. Copenhagen, by openly addressing these issues, would become "a truly new chapter" in the Helsinki process.

One of Vienna's signal achievements was the creation of a rather modest mechanism designed to facilitate compliance by institutionalizing government-to-government human rights complaints. Within a few months of Vienna's conclusion, the mechanism was already being used effectively. Extensive discussion on its merits and inadequacies at Paris suggested that the mechanism would be widely used after June 1989, but with the surging waves of revolt sweeping throughout Eastern Europe and glasnost deepening in the USSR, it was simply bypassed, superseded by revolution. According to Danish Foreign Minister Uffe Ellemann-Jensen in the opening host address to the Copenhagen meeting, only one or two examples of the use of the mechanism to that point could be ascertained.[75]

The report to the Helsinki Commission on the Copenhagen meeting later noted that "the human dimension mechanism did not fully keep pace with those [revolutionary] events."[76] Time was a factor in its non-use. Revolutionary events in Eastern Europe continued to the end of 1989. Thus, since the end of those events, only six months had elapsed before the Copenhagen conference began. After the eventful fall of 1989, observed the Commission, "few countries" made any "representations" based on the mechanism. As a result, the delegates at Copenhagen found themselves with "a record which was difficult to assess." Nonetheless, many delegations felt that the mechanism, according to the Commission report, "has greater potential to be used constructively than ever before."[77]

The United States chose to apply the mechanism, formally complaining to the new Romanian government about its brutal use of miners, brought into Bucharest on government trucks, to smash demonstrations by students and other dissidents in the city's University Square. At the same time as it invoked the mechanism, the United States cautioned that "good faith" had to be the guideline of the complaining government, not political purposes. Pointing to the post-revolutionary "trans-Atlantic relationship that is less marked by polemics and more closely identified with cooperation," the US hopefully expected that "the mechanism is a vehicle through which we can communicate our concerns over the issues which trouble us."[78]

Without the accumulation of much mechanism experience, the CSCE found if difficult to offer more than the most modest of recommendations. An Italian proposal devoted to enhancing the effectiveness of previous procedures through greater clarification and precision emerged. The Copenhagen document stipulated that the recipient government must respond in "as short a time as possible" after a complaint, but no later than four weeks.[79] If a bilateral meeting were requested, it should take place "as soon as possible" or "as a rule" within three weeks of the request.

A third and final clarification was an outgrowth of the problem that arose after Turkey complained to Bulgaria, prior to the Paris meeting, about the repression and expulsion of Bulgarian Turks. At the bilateral session, Bulgaria, instead of responding to the allegation, chose to raise the issue of Turkish treatment of its minorities. The tit-for-tat device tended to politicize the mechanism and threatened to undermine its usefulness. The Copenhagen document obliged the government receiving the complaint "to refrain" at a bilateral meeting "from raising situations and cases" not connected with the subject of the meeting, unless both sides agreed.[80]

A number of governments would have strongly welcomed more substantive recommendations. Prague's Foreign Minister Dienstbier, following up on the Havel letter, said the mechanism should be "further developed" by adding to it "control elements."[81] The mechanism should be open to the public and therefore for use by non-governmental organizations. This, he suggested, would put pressure on participating states to correct human rights abuses. Dienstbier called for an independent institution with intrusive authority, based upon "clearly defined rules . . . [to] ascertain in an operative manner . . . the true state of affairs in cases of suspected human rights violations." After its assessment of the situation, his proposed "European humanitarian inspection" institution might then propose for the concerned governments steps that could be taken to resolve problems.

Switzerland, Canada, Denmark and the Netherlands supported Dienstbier's vision, variously proposing either specifically appointed observers or rapporteurs or a formal Committee on the Human Dimension.[82] Advocates of these proposals were seeking to apply implementation machinery like that set up by the Stockholm security meeting on confidence-building measures.

The effort to create implementation machinery failed largely because of strong resistance by a number of participating states simply unprepared to accept forms of institutionalization. In their view, such crucial decisions should be left to the heads of states at their forthcoming summit scheduled for later in the year, which prompted Ambassador Kampelman to later tell the Helsinki Commission that "in the end we fell short of achieving a major step forward" with respect to the mechanism.[83] It was, however, apparent that the Helsinki signatories at Copenhagen were already thinking of some institutional form to be added to the Vienna mechanism. In the concluding document, they spoke of the need for measures to "enhance conflict prevention and confidence-building in the field of the human dimension. . . ."[84]

Judging from Secretary of State Baker's remarks at Copenhagen, the United States was prepared to support greater involvement of non-governmental organizations in the mechanism. After lauding the extraordinary contribution made to the CSCE process and the revolutions of 1989 by the Helsinki monitors in the Soviet Union and in other East European countries (among whom Jiri Hajek, the head of the Czechoslovakia delegation, was singled out), Baker suggested that their type of principled courage must be applied to the emerging European structure. The "same strengths," channeled through CSCE, "can become the conscience of the continent."[85]

At earlier Helsinki review conferences and experts human rights meetings, the United States had placed emphasis upon the regular review of implementation. As Ambassador Kampelman had once explained, the review constituted a kind of substitute mechanism for achieving compliance through the mobilization of shame. But at Copenhagen, the US virtually discarded the review technique. Kampelman acknowledged in testimony to the Commission that the review was "less thorough than in the past."[86] In an interview, he pointed to the change of atmosphere in CSCE, where confrontation was no longer the principal mode. If nonconfrontation was now dominant, it was buttressed, he said, by a new (Moscow-included) consensus that made democracy the frame of reference for all discussion.

In his first speech on June 11, one week after the session began, Kampelman commented very favorably on Reshetov's June 7 presentation regarding "the monumental reforms" in the USSR.[87] The US representative vigorously commended perestroika and enthusiastically praised Gorbachev for advocating "an open, human, law-ruled democratic society." Kampelman's catalogue of human rights developments in the USSR stood in marked contrast with speeches he had been accustomed to making at Madrid. The new competitive elections, the repeal of obnoxious laws, the release of political and psychiatric prisoners, the rapid development of various freedoms, the dramatic increase in emigration and travel, and the unfolding process of institutionalization of reform—were all noted and greatly welcomed.

Not that Utopia could be said to have arrived in Moscow. As Kampelman himself observed, the promised legal reforms were not yet completed; some prisoners remained incarcerated for what the US suspected were political considerations; about two dozen prisoners continued to be held in the notorious Perm Camp #35 under sentences that reflected old thinking; the expected exit and entry legislation institutionalizing liberalized practices had not been adopted; and 60 unresolved refusenik cases persisted, along with the cases of ten persons on the US bilateral list (mostly separated spouses). But Kampelman placed the negative features in an overall picture that diminished their prominence.

Kampelman did raise the question of the Baltic states, which he linked to "the tragic legacy of the Hitler-Stalin Pact." As the pact had been declared "null and void" by the Soviet Congress of People's Deputies, the incorporation of the three states into the Soviet Union was logically also null and void, a position that the US had held from the beginning. In posing the problem, however, Kampelman carefully avoided a confrontational approach. He did not call for the immediate liberation of the Baltic states. Rather, he said, the US "looks to the day"—clearly sometime in the future—when the three states "will be widely recognized as independent and sovereign," able to join CSCE. In the meantime, he urged "continuing and patient negotiations," not economic embargoes, the movement of tanks through the streets, the forcible entry of troops into media offices and installations, and "other threatening actions." The appeal to Moscow was framed in mild terms, as if uttered by a sympathetic associate: "Let there not be a scar on a steadily improving record of compliance with the Helsinki Final Act."[88]

Significantly, when the three Baltic republics requested observer status at the Copenhagen meeting, the United States carefully avoided pressing the issue, though its delegation arranged for a press conference by the foreign ministers of the three states. Prior to Copenhagen, observer status—a category allowed by the Helsinki rules—had not arisen as a CSCE issue. It was suddenly posed at the beginning of the session when Albania, which in the early 1970s had refused becoming a participating state, now sought observer status. The Danish Foreign Minister, as host chairman of the opening session, chose to grant the Albanian request after formally inquiring as to whether there were any objections to such a decision. While no objection was registered to the sudden Danish maneuver, Kampelman was more than a little piqued by Denmark's failure to raise the question at the prior NATO caucus.

Serious diplomatic reasons were at the root of the American Ambassador's pique. If observer status was extended to Albania, why not the same status for the Balts? The very posing of that question publicly would have raised the hackles of the USSR and, at the same time, impaled the US and the leading West European democracies on the horns of a most uncomfortable and insoluble dilemma. No one wanted to embarrass Gorbachev while he was being challenged by rightist and Russian nationalist forces. Fortunately, for all concerned (especially the Danish Foreign Minister), the USSR made in advance its veto position extremely clear.

Those observers at Copenhagen who were less than convinced of Moscow's progress on human rights issues could also turn to a report given in that city on June 6 by the International Helsinki Federation for Human Rights (IHF), an umbrella body of various national Helsinki Watch groups, of which Yuri Orlov was Honorary Chairman.[89] At least a dozen different examples of negative phenomena in the Soviet Union were highlighted. The IHF report was based upon testimony taken by the group in Moscow just prior to Copenhagen. At the end, the IHF remained very much uncertain as to whether Moscow should be accepted as the host of the human dimension conference scheduled for 1991.

Given the warming US-Soviet relationship during the previous half-year, including the especially friendly superpower summits in Malta in December 1989 (where the Cold War was declared ended) and in Washington the following June (just prior to Copenhagen), as well as the deepening Baker-Shevardnadze rapport, "the less thorough" review of implementation was what Kampelman later in the Helsinki hearings called "appropriate to the occasion."[90] This rather delicate comment by the official head of delegation was followed up with the observation that, given the Helsinki Commission's formal presence at Copenhagen (through DeConcini and Hoyer), it could hold private discussions with Soviet delegates about human rights violations. Kampelman himself participated in some of these discussions. And if sharp criticism of Soviet practices was made, the Commission was a more appropriate finger-pointer.

Not that the US posture neglected assuming a much tougher public character when it was so inclined. For the very first time in Helsinki history, Kampelman openly criticized Yugoslavia for its repressive human rights abuses against Albanians in the Kosovo region.[91] US diplomats might have heretofore chastised Belgrade's policy on human rights in individual instances, but they had done so privately, through quiet rather than public diplomacy. Fear of an accelerating disintegration of the multinational state of Yugoslavia, together with the growing world outcry about repression in Kosovo, undoubtedly prompted the "historic departure"—the phrase was Kampelman's—in US policy toward Belgrade.

Still, the Yugoslav case was an uncharacteristic example of US interest in implementation machinery; the only other example of formal US application of the mechanism was the one involving Romania. If there was considerable talk behind the scenes about how the Helsinki process would now be institutionalized, little of a precise nature was placed on the table about institutionalizing its human rights facets. Secretary Baker's speech did outline several steps that were projected for regularizing and reinforcing the CSCE structure, but the only new mechanisms that he included had to do with military or security matters.

It was nonetheless clear that, for Baker, free elections were important. He devoted more paragraphs and time to this subject in his speech than to any others. And, as he did so, the Secretary of State slipped in a piece of weighty, if inchoate, advice:

> And when the 35 consider proposals to institutionalize CSCE, I urge all to start with mechanisms to ensure that governments are freely chosen by the people.[92]

He did not elucidate how such mechanisms would operate, but here, in embryonic fashion, was the one CSCE institution—an organ on free elections—which the United States would welcome. Presumably, once free elections were successfully taking place in Eastern Europe, other human rights problems would diminish in scope and intensity. That, at least, appeared to be the thinking of the Bush administration.

At the same time, the US had been inclined to pair free elections with the rule of law, and this pairing inevitably had to address the difficult subject of "political culture." Could the rule of law be somehow imposed? Baker related that President Bush had told President Gorbachev at the recent Washington summit "how highly we value Soviet efforts to institutionalize the rule of law, glasnost and democratization in the USSR." Did "institutionalize" here mean more than the adoption of laws? And was this sufficient to cope with civil liberties and civil rights problems? Baker acknowledged that the consolidation of democracy through free elections did not guarantee all aspects of individual liberty. "We must continue," he said, "to press until CSCE's high standard of human rights prevails throughout Europe. . . ."[93] But he did not explain how this could be done and whether new institutions were needed to achieve it. His Danish host had wanted to go further, proposing creation of a Committee on the Human Dimension.[94] Interestingly, Soviet Foreign Minister Shevardnadze endorsed the proposal in his address to the meeting.[95] But it failed to win a consensus.

Institutionalization of the Helsinki process was very much in the air at Copenhagen, but it was left for the Paris summit to work out. Basic ideas advanced by the leaders of Britain, France, the Federal Republic of Germany, Poland, the Czech and Slovak Federal Republic, and the USSR found their way, in summary fashion, into Shevardnadze's address. He referred to biennial summit meetings, annual foreign ministers' meetings, regular consultative meetings of senior officials from the 35 CSCE members, a center for the resolution of conflicts, and a permanent CSCE secretariat. Baker, in his address, spoke in favor of the first three proposals. He avoided endorsement of the last two permanent-type institutions. At the same time, he recommended that CSCE follow-up meetings be held more frequently, perhaps every two years, but with a fixed duration of about three months.

The idea of a fixed time of short duration for CSCE review sessions testified to a degree of change in US tactics regarding the Helsinki process. Until then and, especially at Vienna, US Helsinki policy was geared to open-ended review sessions to compel Moscow to agree to some human rights progress before the United States would allow the meeting to end. But accepting time limits was one thing; US acceptance of a permanent secretariat and permanent Helsinki institutions was quite another. This had been the initial aim of the USSR in the early 1970s, and, at the time, Washington had categorically rejected the proposal. By Copenhagen, the US had not yet altered its former position, although Baker did not explicitly attack the advocacy of a permanent CSCE secretariat and institutions. He simply avoided addressing the issue.

But although the Secretary of State did not commit himself on permanent institutions, he extended strong support to proposed mechanisms for enhancing security. The shift in the balance of the Helsinki process had begun. Perhaps this was not too surprising, as the revolutions of 1989 and glasnost had radically changed the former political architecture of Europe. With free elections and the rule of law universally accepted, a new structure had started to emerge. And, largely in consequence of US initiatives, the structure would now have a distinctive "constitution."

▪16▪

The "Anti-Congress of Vienna"

Even as the Copenhagen meeting began its deliberations, plans were being laid for the Helsinki II summit to be held in Paris but five months later, on November 19-21, 1990. Indeed, the French delegate to the Copenhagen talks formally announced the schedule during its opening session.[1] For the assembled representatives at Copenhagen, the announcement of the Paris summit suggested that their own deliberations and concluding document carried an air of tentativeness. The revolutionary proposals concerning free elections and the rule of law incorporated in the document would take on finality when formally sanctioned by the heads of state, meeting at the Paris summit.

In fact, as one legal specialist noted, "there is no rule which limits the authority of intersessional meetings vis-à-vis full-scale review meetings."[2] Yet, the closeness of the time frame to the summit may have spurred such a perspective. Had there been no sanction, the Copenhagen resolutions would have had to await the next scheduled review session, planned for Helsinki itself in 1992. Now the formalization would be handled at an even higher level, by the heads of the CSCE states. But the standard number of states for the CSCE—35 since 1973—would be different by November. East Germany (the German Democratic Republic) would be absorbed into the Federal Republic Germany and therefore cease to exist as a Helsinki "participating state."

Ironically, the very purpose of Helsinki II, as initially projected by its leading advocates—the USSR, France, Poland and Czechoslovakia—had been to preserve intact the borders of East Germany. But the forces unleashed by the revolution of 1989 undermined their best intentions, making necessary a wholly different agenda for the Paris summit. If initially conceived (like Helsinki I) as freezing the status quo with perhaps some modest adjustments, the new summit was obliged to assume a very different character, one that legitimized the revolutionary forces of democracy and, therefore, of self-determination.

In his host address, President François Mitterrand appropriately dubbed the stellar Helsinki occasion, the first in 15 years, the "anti-Congress of Vienna."[3] The session would not resemble, Mitterrand made clear, the historic reactionary achievement of Prince Klemens Metternich in freezing the status quo and repressing revolutions. Rather, the summit would legitimize the revolutionary forces of 1989, as well as their consequences. And, it would sanction in a new charter the continuation of those very forces.

The "Charter for a New Europe," a grandiloquent statement of purpose which British Prime Minister Margaret Thatcher compared to the Magna Carta itself,[4] called for the establishment throughout Europe of "democratic government . . . based on the will of the people, expressed regularly through free and fair elections. . . ."[5] It was a new trumpet, one that sounded no uncertainty. Human rights and fundamental freedoms, together with democracy, were the Charter's main themes. And to provide these themes with a sense of continuing dynamism, as well as with a set of assurances to provide for security, the meeting summoned into existence unprecedented and unique institutions.[6] Helsinki would no longer be a constantly changing address without headquarters or offices or staff. It would soon have distinctive, fixed and formalized structures, together with a permanent, if small, bureaucracy.

How Paris reached this extraordinary historic and landmark stage was not happenstance. A pre-planned and rationally organized series of steps were taken to move from Copenhagen to the summit in Paris, with Washington playing a decisive role at the same time as Bonn and Moscow performed extremely significant parts. In the end, the incorporation of a unified Germany into an undivided and free Europe was to formally bring to a completion the post-war occupation of Germany and technically close the book on World War II itself. Paris, not Yalta, would be the substitute peace treaty.

Events in the months following Copenhagen helped define the dynamic and revolutionary character of the summit. Four stand out: 1) a unique NATO conclave in July; 2) a Kohl-Gorbachev meeting shortly afterward; 3) the drafting during the summer of an extraordinary and massive arms reduction agreement—CFE; and 4) a special CSCE Foreign Ministers meeting in New York in October. Together, these developments determined the basic features of the Paris conference in November.

Two weeks after Copenhagen concluded, the heads of state of NATO assembled in London. The extraordinary NATO assemblage, with President Bush playing a leading role, issued a communiqué on July 6 that was remarkably uncharacteristic of the military alliance.[7] Formally proposing to the Warsaw Pact member states that the two rival groups solemnly state that "we are no longer adversaries," the London Declaration paralleled Bush's assertion that the Cold War had ended.

But it went beyond the call for a joint announcement. In an unprecedented initiative, the declaration read: "We today invite President Gorbachev . . . and the representatives of the other Central and Eastern European countries to establish regular diplomatic liaison with NATO. This will make it possible to share with them our thinking and deliberations in this historic period of change." Moscow promptly responded favorably. A positive response was certain from the other Warsaw Pact invitees, as that military alliance was already ceasing to exist and its political structure was nearing demise.

The London Declaration placed "the highest priority" on completing the Treaty on Conventional Arms in Europe (CFE) and on a CBMs agreement, thus setting the stage for discussions for reducing short-range nuclear forces, which could then be extended to nuclear weapons generally.

NATO concluded that the Paris summit "should become more prominent in Europe's future . . . [and] . . . set new standards for the establishment and preservation of free societies." The very unusual declaration specified such distinctly human rights purposes as free elections and the rule of law—as worked out in Copenhagen—and the Bonn CSCE decisions on free and competitive markets. Finally, the NATO statement proposed that the Helsinki summit institutionalize the CSCE process with the following: a program of "regular consultations" involving at least annual meetings by the heads of state or their foreign ministers; the holding of review conferences every two years; the establishment of a small CSCE secretariat; a mechanism for monitoring free elections; a Center for the Prevention of Conflict, which would seek the "conciliation of disputes" involving CSCE member states; and a CSCE parliamentary body.

If the absence of saber-rattling and the attention to human rights were strongly welcomed in various CSCE quarters, the NATO declaration evoked a horror-filled response from those holding to traditional power concerns. Former Secretary of State Henry Kissinger delivered a blistering attack on the statement as portending the denuclearization of Europe and consequent "decoupling of the United States from Europe. . . ."[8] Denouncing the "failure to define a serious political role for NATO," he expressed contempt for the "unsettling" enhancement of CSCE. He saw this as playing into the hands of the Soviet Union, because "it is at the CSCE that the Soviets will be present and the opportunity for publicity will be greatest." In fact, it was the publicity by the United States and the West generally at CSCE meetings that had unleashed the revolutions in Eastern Europe of 1989 and ended Soviet domination. It is altogether striking, but not in the least surprising, that Kissinger said not a word about the declaration's unprecedented human rights statements.

The second crucial step to Helsinki II was taken only days after the NATO meeting. Helmut Kohl traveled to the Caucasus and met at length with Gorbachev for discussions on the issue of a unified Germany within NATO, which still troubled the Soviet Union.[9] On July 16 at Zhelez-novodsk, they reached agreement that a united Germany would remain part of the Western alliance, that German troop strength would be reduced from 600,000 to 370,000, and that 350,000 Soviet troops would be withdrawn from the former East Germany over a four-year period (to 1994). Bonn promised to allocate a total of 12 billion marks until 1994 for the upkeep of the Soviet troops in East Germany and for their ultimate pullout and transportation to the Soviet Union, as well as the cost of building homes for them in the USSR.

And this was only the beginning. In essence, Germany would become a veritable economic ally of the Soviet Union. By mid-1991, Germany would provide the USSR some $31 billion in grants and credits. Within the councils of major industrial powers, Bonn became the principal advocate for loans to and investments in the USSR.

The Soviet military, along with nationalist and conservative elements in the Communist Party, may have viewed the agreement as a blow to Soviet power, but from a rational perspective other options did not exist. Only a week earlier, reactionary hard-liners at the 28th Congress of the Communist Party were brutally asking: "Who lost Eastern Europe?"[10] Now their clamor would be reinforced. Shevardnadze would become the immediate target of their anger and in December he felt compelled to resign. Ultimately, Gorbachev himself would be targeted by the hard-liners. The eventual culmination of their efforts in the form of a military coup in August 1991 was rationalized, in part, as aimed at restoring the Soviet Union's image and power abroad.

Yet, the withdrawal of Soviet troops from Germany and Eastern Europe was certain to produce a corresponding benefit for Moscow. By August 1990, the French government decided that all of its 48,000 troops stationed in Germany would be withdrawn by the end of 1991. Richard Ullman, a scholarly observer of security issues, predicted that by 1995 the number of US soldiers on the continent would be down to 50,000, with Britain's total down to 25,000.[11]

Linked to the Soviet-German agreement were the "two plus four" discussions that took place during the summer months. Comprising the governments of the two Germanys and the four occupying powers (the United States, the United Kingdom, France, and the USSR), the "two plus four" formally signed on September 12, 1990, the Treaty on the Final Settlement with Respect to Germany. The occupation of Germany and of Berlin was formally ended. Several weeks later, the foreign ministers of the CSCE greeted the Treaty on the Final Settlement as "a historic step" toward a Europe "whole and free."[12]

The third vital stage toward Helsinki II were the negotiations on the CFE agreement. As early as March 1990, NATO Secretary-General Manfred Wörner called CFE "an essential cornerstone" of the CSCE and "the basis for opening the way to a new European order, politically and geographically."[13] The treaty was aimed at greatly reducing the preponderance of Soviet conventional military power in Central Europe, thereby strengthening the fabric of democracy in Eastern Europe at the same time as it diminished the threat of war. It would be the first post-WWII arms agreement whose purpose was not the placing of a ceiling on heavy weapons but, rather, upon destroying many of them.

In 21 months of talks in Vienna that had been mandated by the CSCE Vienna follow-up meeting, the conferees reached agreement on a 200-page document which was signed on the day that Helsinki II opened in Paris, November 19.[14] NATO and the Warsaw Pact agreed to massive cuts. At the heart of the agreement were great reductions in military force levels, especially for the Soviets. Each alliance was limited to 20,000 tanks, 30,000 armored cars, 20,000 artillery pieces and 6,800 combat planes spread between four European zones. An indication of the military significance of the draft agreement was that some 19,000 Soviet tanks would be taken out of service. (Earlier, in May 1989, Washington and Moscow established limits of troop strength in Europe to 195,000 each.) Hundreds of inspections of military installations on both sides over a 40-month period were scheduled for verification of the cuts. Paralleling the negotiations on the CFE treaty were the CSCE discussions, also conducted in Vienna since March 1989, on additional confidence-building measures designed to reduce the risk of surprise attack or of an accidental outbreak of war. The 50-page accord provided for new measures for increased sharing of military information, including establishment of a communications network and a consultation mechanism that would handle questions of "unusual military activity."[15] A Center for the Prevention of Conflict would be created immediately after the Paris summit to serve as the headquarters for both the new network and the new mechanism. In addition, the accord permitted visits to air bases previously considered off-limits.

After November 26, further negotiations on each of the military-security agreements were to resume in Vienna. They would continue in this fashion until the next CSCE follow-up meeting in Helsinki in March 1992. After that, the two security processes would merge into one.

Nearly two years of security deliberations (one conducted under the CSCE umbrella, the other by CSCE directly) since the precedent-shattering Vienna conference had produced remarkable results. The accord on conventional arms was especially promising for ending the post-World War II tensions in Europe and improving the atmosphere for far-reaching human rights commitments. The sequence would recall the argument, advanced by Soviet officials at earlier CSCE meetings (most notably by Sergei Kondrashev at Madrid), that human rights progress was dependent upon prior progress in diminishing tensions. In the context of the Helsinki Final Act, it had meant that any advance in Basket III must be preceded by an advance in Basket I.

In fact, however, the monumental human rights developments agreed to at Vienna in January 1989, which in turn helped unleash eight months later the landmark democratic revolutions throughout Eastern Europe, provided the stimulus for the staggering security and military agreements. With Germany "whole and free," and two key Warsaw Pact countries— Hungary and Czechoslovakia—to be emptied of Soviet troops in consequence of democratic revolutions, security for each and all was greatly facilitated. Reuters quoted a senior Western diplomat in Vienna as saying in November 1990:

> One of the main Western objectives at the start of the talks [on CFE] was to squeeze Soviet forces out of Eastern Europe. The changes in the region have done that for us.[16]

Another Western envoy told the correspondent that the CFE was "in many ways" the first arms treaty in history "to be implemented before it is signed."

Hans-Dietrich Genscher made a point of applying the relationship between human rights and security to the unification process in Germany. The task from the beginning, he said, was "to create a basis for change in Europe." This had been accomplished through CSCE and, he clearly implied, its human rights provisions. "If there hadn't been a CSCE, we would have to invent it now," he quipped on the eve of the Paris summit.[17]

Because "we are now living in a fundamentally changed Europe," Genscher stated, "our expectations have been fulfilled."

The culmination of the transitional steps came at the beginning of October at a special meeting of CSCE foreign ministers held in New York City. For the first time since the founding of CSCE in July 1973, the foreign ministers of the participating states were meeting in a separate and substantive session. (They did meet for a commemorative event on August 1, 1985.) Their function was to review the progress on agenda preparations for the Paris summit, which had been proceeding in Vienna since July 10. The technical work on the summit was in the hands of a preparatory committee made up of senior foreign ministry officials. As many of these officials had heretofore worked on CSBM matters, their new responsibilities (to be continued in a new form after the Paris summit), pointed to the future thrust of CSCE. Security issues rather than human rights issues would eventually predominate.

The chosen site for the foreign ministers meeting was of considerable symbolic significance. It was the first meeting of CSCE on US soil. Initially the country with the least interest in CSCE, the United States now served as host. Moreover, the United States stood at the very center of the Helsinki process, staking out the human rights direction, guiding the negotiations leading to German unification (and bringing a formal end to the occupation of that country), and setting the crucial and indispensable condition for a summit meeting—a Treaty on Conventional Armed Forces in Europe.

US world leadership status at the moment—October 1990—was illuminated by its efforts to guide events in the Middle East. The New York meeting coincided with Washington's initiative to mobilize, through the UN Security Council, a military and diplomatic coalition of varied powers to compel an Iraqi withdrawal from occupied Kuwait. Testifying to the extraordinary influence of America's leadership role in CSCE was its successful endeavor in winning a resolution from the CSCE foreign ministers on the Middle East question. The opening paragraph of the approved CSCE "statement" pointed to its uniqueness:

> Consistent with the principles contained in the Helsinki Final Act, which guide our mutual relations, we, the Foreign Ministers of the Participating States of the Conference on the Security and Cooperation in Europe (CSCE) . . . join the United Nations in condemning Iraq's invasion and occupation of Kuwait.[18]

The statement went on to "call upon the Government of Iraq to withdraw from Kuwait immediately and without conditions." Even if there was no precedent for this action in CSCE history, reference was made to the principles of the Helsinki Final Act as "guide" to "our mutual relations."

Of course, no statement on Iraq would have been possible without the acquiescence of the Soviet Union. In addition, Ceausescu was no longer around to offer any resistance. But whether the new conceptual vision for CSCE was appropriate and logically rooted in Helsinki's history and tradition is open to question. Regrettably, neither the State Department nor the National Security Council provided any explanation for the radically new departure.

President Bush's New York speech to the foreign ministers effectively captured the newfound US pride in its nearly preeminent role in CSCE. He began by noting that the CSCE meeting—"the first ever on American soil—comes at this time of momentous change."[19] And, he added: "For just as Europe enters a new and promising era, so, too, do America's relations with Europe." As the United States was bound to Europe "by a shared heritage and history and common bonds of culture," now that Europe was "whole and free," the CSCE community could "forge a new transatlantic partnership . . . a commonwealth of free nations. . . ."

Bush said the entire European continent had been "transformed," and that "the cause and catalyst" of the "transformation" had been the Helsinki Final Act. Helsinki was both witness to and participant in "this monumental triumph of the human spirit," the President noted. In his view, the purpose of the forthcoming Paris summit was to "consolidate these great gains for freedom. . . ." For the first time, Bush addressed himself to the subject of institutionalizing the Helsinki process by creating permanent bureaucratic structures. He had never done this before, although at Copenhagen in June, Baker had intimated that Washington was willing to break with the past posture and support a certain limited institutionalization.

The President mentioned the Center for the Prevention of Conflict, which had its origin in the confidence- and security-building measures taken at Stockholm, which had "done so much to reduce" the risk of war by accident or miscalculation. Bush then proposed a "small permanent secretariat" to service "accelerated schedules of . . . consultations and review conferences." The third proposal was for a free elections office fostering "the fundamental democratic principle from which all other follow." The last institution was an "Assembly of Europe," comprised of representatives of parliaments.

The sequence was revealing. A security focus, rather than human rights instrumentalities, would consolidate the gains of 1989: the only serious threat to the new democratic order Bush contemplated was military con-flict or the possibility of it. Thus, at the very end of a speech which had waxed rhapsodic about the immense political and human rights transfor-mation of Europe, he emphasized that the reduction of conventional armed forces in Europe "remains *the cornerstone* of a new security archi-tecture for Europe" (emphasis added). Completion of the conventional arms accord continued as the "essential prerequisite to a CSCE Summit." Even with the scheduled Helsinki II only six weeks away, Bush still in-sisted that it would not be held unless the negotiators in Vienna "redou-ble their efforts" and finalize the treaty draft.

With the fundamental security issues of Europe resolved, the CSCE could proclaim in the French capital a "new Europe." An end of an entire era had been reached. Paris would signal the beginning of a new era and a new century.[20] The participants acknowledged and acclaimed the pivotal events of the Helsinki epoch. Totalitarianism and its accompanying one-party system, arbitrariness and absence of human rights were tossed into history's dustbin. Living proof of the revolutionary transformation occu-pied a number of chairs at the table, specifically those of Poland, Czecho-slovakia and Hungary.[21] Previously, they had been the political prisoners of the now discarded totalitarianism.

For all the security emphasis Bush expressed, the Paris summit carried a human rights focus. Rehearsed again and in detail were the rights ini-tially elaborated five months earlier at Copenhagen. Free elections, polit-ical pluralism and the rule of law, together with the familiar catalogue of human rights covering conscience, religious expression, association and movement were all spelled out.[22] Various minority rights, along with the sharp denunciation of racism and anti-Semitism—as they had been at Copenhagen—were noted. The Charter of Paris only added a certain lus-ter and authoritativeness to the Copenhagen concluding document. It was, after all, being approved by the CSCE heads of state, including those who were the living embodiment of CSCE's human rights values.

The Charter, as Mrs. Thatcher implied, was a modern-day version of the Magna Carta. Recalling the historic document of A.D. 1215, she would have the new document "enshrine for every European citizen, including those in the Soviet Union," the basic human rights.[23] Mikhail Gorbachev virtually echoed the theme:

> We are entering into a world of new dimensions, in which universal human val-ues are shared by all the people, in which human freedom . . . and the unique value of human life must become the foundation of universal security and a supreme criterion of progress.

In glowing terms, he boasted of the "historic shift" in the USSR

> ... away from the totalitarian to freedom and democracy, from the bureaucratic command system to a state anchored in the rule of law and political pluralism. . . .[24]

The bulk of the Charter's language, borrowed as it was from Copenhagen, dealt with freedom and human rights. In that sense, it came close to reversing the relative space given to the subject in the Helsinki Final Act. If the latter constituted a fairly careful balance between security issues and human rights matters, the Charter was overwhelmingly a human rights- *and* democracy-oriented document. References to security were almost accidental in character. The participating states pledged "to refrain from the threat or use of force against the territorial integrity or political independence of any state." And they promised to undertake additional "common efforts in the field of military security." Of course, the Treaty on Conventional Armed Forces in Europe, which the United States had insisted upon as a precondition of the summit and which had been approved on November 19, fairly well summed up most of the security aspirations of CSCE. However, confidence-building measures and disarmament remained for the future.

Europe's Magna Carta, with its elaboration of election procedures and the rule of law, resonated almost instantaneously in the last outpost of totalitarianism on the continent. On December 9, just a few weeks after the summit, students at Tirana University in Albania launched large-scale demonstrations that quickly spread to several other cities.[25] Of even greater significance was the formation on December 11 of Albania's first independent political party, the Democratic Party, which claimed its lineage in the Helsinki process. Later, its chairman, Dr. Sali Berisha, would tell the Helsinki Commission how its parliamentary group "prepared a package of 13 laws, all taken from the Helsinki agreements on human rights, the rule of law and market economy."

In fact, Albania's communist rulers themselves had earlier begun to respond to Helsinki in order to end their country's self-imposed 40-year isolation from Europe and the world. In April 1990, President Ramiz Alia gave a speech opening the door to the reestablishment of diplomatic relations with the United States, Britain, the USSR, and the European Community, and expressed an interest in joining CSCE. The next month, he welcomed UN Secretary-General Javier Pérez de Cuellar as his guest. To cap these initiatives, President Alia sent his representative to the Copenhagen meeting in June 1990 to formally request admission to the Helsinki process. Nearly 17 years earlier, Albania had refused an invitation to become part of CSCE.

Now, Alia was desperately trying to enter the club of Helsinki signatories. Between May and December of 1989, students and young workers had mounted demonstrations protesting living and working conditions. According to Ismail Kadare, Albania's best known intellectual, the Helsinki process played a major role "in the reawakening of Albania."[26]

The regime responded by a series of reforms, including one that rescinded the law making unauthorized emigration from Albania a crime. Fleeing the country became the most pronounced gesture of freedom and free expression. Some 5,000 took refuge in a handful of foreign embassies during July 1990, the first major challenge to the regime. Human rights reform proposals suddenly were pouring out of government offices while political prisoners, in parallel fashion, were exiting from state prisons. On December 18, the regime authorized multiparty elections for the first time. The Communist Party, which went by the name of the Labor Party, would no longer be able to hold a monopoly of power. On the last day of the year, a new draft constitution including the basic human rights—freedom of religion, press, conscience and association, the presumption of innocence, the right to travel abroad and move about the country—was promulgated.

The key test of Albania's commitment to the Charter of Paris was the multiparty elections on March 31, 1991. Nearly 2 million voters, or nearly 97 percent of those eligible to vote, cast ballots—the highest turnout for any multiparty system in Eastern Europe. The (Communist) Labor Party won some two-thirds of the vote, overwhelmingly in rural areas. The Democratic Party captured nearly one-third of the votes, mainly from the urban areas. A Helsinki Commission staff team carefully observed the election process, concluding that "the voting and counting of ballots . . . were, in general, orderly and correct, although there were numerous complaints of irregularities and disturbing reports of intimidation of voters in the countryside."[27]

Whether a significant difference in the voting pattern would have resulted absent manipulation or intimidation in the countryside was by no means certain. What was certain to the Helsinki Commission observers was that "the holding of elections was an advance for democracy," even if the process "in many respects, fell short of international standards for free and fair elections," prescribed in the Copenhagen concluding document. Even before the elections, the communist regime, in its anxious determination to conform to Helsinki standards, met with a delegation of officials of the International Helsinki Federation for Human Rights. The government promised to "abide by international human rights standards," including the Final Act and "subsequent human rights documents adopted by the CSCE."[28]

From the perspective of Democratic Party leader Berisha, the various reforms adopted by the communist regime, including the elections of March 31, were prompted in part by "foreign democratic opinion," including the "spirit of Helsinki."[29] In testimony before the Helsinki Commission on May 22, Berisha and Kadare strongly recommended that Albania be granted full membership in CSCE.[30] It was their opinion that full membership would help "increase pressure for democratization" in Albania.

Shortly afterward, a huge strike of 350,000 workers clamoring for higher wages and freedom forced the communists to relinquish power. On June 12, a new coalition government was formed in which representatives from all political parties participated. In view of this major step toward a multiparty system, CSCE could scarcely refuse admission to Albania. At the first regular Helsinki foreign ministers meeting, held in Berlin on June 19, 1991, under the new institutionalized CSCE system, Tirana was formally accepted.

The new institutional structures for CSCE, elaborated in a lengthy annex of the Paris Charter,[31] were as important as the extensive human rights and democratic standards which it had enshrined. Helsinki's institutionalization was manifested in both the regularization of the process itself and the creation of various permanent structures, each with a small bureaucratic apparatus. On the first level, no longer would future Helsinki meetings be determined largely on an ad hoc basis, usually at review sessions or, as Helsinki II itself had emerged, through pressures exerted by various CSCE leaders. Instead, meetings would be fixed on a permanent basis.

The core of the process, until now, had been the follow-up meetings. In the future, beginning with the already scheduled follow-up meeting in Helsinki in March 1992, sessions would be held once every two years. Instead of the previous open-ended character of these meetings, they would carry a fixed time frame of three months, unless otherwise determined by the participating states. Each follow-up meeting would, significantly, be accompanied by a summit of heads of state, although it was not specified whether the summit sessions, presumably of two or three days, would take place at the beginning or end of the review conferences.

In any case, summits would become integral to the future process. Heretofore, only two summits of the state leaders had taken place, one at the Helsinki Final Act signing in August 1975, and the other at Paris in

November 1990. Thus, the process was now raised to a higher level of authority and linked the heads of state more closely to decision making. The greater frequency of these meetings could enable CSCE problems to be more quickly resolved or at least addressed.

Of far greater consequence was the creation of a Council of Foreign Ministers of CSCE, which would meet at least once a year. On earlier occasions, the CSCE foreign ministers assembled quite irregularly, usually at the time of review sessions. At Belgrade, they did not participate; at Madrid, they gathered at a period of profound crisis in February 1982 (after the imposition of martial law in Poland) and again in September 1983; and at Vienna, they appeared at both the beginning and the end of the sessions—November 1986 and January 1989. Most foreign ministers also appeared at the beginning of the Paris meeting of the Conference on the Human Dimension in May 1989 (Baker was a notable exception) and at the Copenhagen meeting in June 1990.

The primary reason for the ministers' appearance at CSCE meetings was symbolic, for speech-making purposes, not for negotiating objectives. Of course, the presence of foreign ministers offered opportunities for off-the-record meetings, as was frequently the case at annual opening sessions of the UN General Assembly in the fall. The one time that the Helsinki foreign ministers met for business purposes was in New York on October 1-2, 1990. There they prepared the agenda for the Paris summit the following month and formally sanctioned the unification of Germany (and technically ended the rights of the occupying powers).

CSCE foreign ministers were now placed at the heart of the Helsinki process. Their annual meetings would not be limited in terms of either time or frequency. If agreed by consensus, they could be held as often as necessary. Their function was defined in the Charter as overseeing the progress of the CSCE process, the preparation of summit sessions, and the planning of the future agenda of CSCE. Location of the meetings would be rotated, with the first to be held in Berlin in June 1991. Symbolically, the decision, reflecting the establishment of the newly unified German state, was of considerable importance. Meetings of the council were to be chaired by the foreign minister of the host country.

Especially important was the creation of a Committee of Senior Officials, just below the foreign ministers' level. As a rule, the Committee would meet for two-day sessions, but the Charter stipulated that it might meet as often as deemed necessary by its members or their respective foreign ministers. Were the Committee to become preoccupied with a pressing problem, its sessions could become almost continuous. The sessions of the Committee would be led by the representative of the state whose foreign minister chaired the preceding Council meeting.

The Committee's responsibilities would be quite extensive, suggesting thereby the possibility of a permanent, executive body. It was to prepare the meetings as well as the agenda of the Council of Foreign Ministers, review current problems, and implement the Council's decisions. Arising from this authority was the embryo of a permanent administrative apparatus, but rooted in national power—not in the independent organization itself.

The locus, however, of the regular meetings of the Committee did point to the permanent bureaucratization of CSCE. Only when a Committee meeting immediately preceded a Council meeting would it take place in the country whose foreign minister chaired the Council session. Otherwise, all Committee meetings were slated for Prague, where a permanent secretariat was created, reflecting the new institutionalization of the process.

Another development pointed to the probability of an escalating authority for the Committee. Various drafts submitted at Paris focused on holding emergency meetings of the Council of Foreign Ministers.[32] Emergency or "snap" sessions would be called under threatening circumstances, a reasonable expectation which, in fact, had been discussed at earlier Helsinki meetings. Some drafts at Paris, for example, proposed a procedure for convening a two-day emergency meeting of the Council should a crisis emerge which the concerned states were unable to resolve within 48 hours. The crisis might result from either a violation of any of the ten principles of the Helsinki accord (the Decalogue) or from a civil disturbance.

At Paris, consensus was reached on an approach to the problem of emergency. The Council of Foreign Ministers, it was decided, "will discuss the possibility of establishing a mechanism for convening meetings of the Committee of Senior Officials in emergency situations."[33] Clearly, various parties felt the Committee could only function as an operating arm of CSCE for dealing with emergencies after the foreign ministers could come up with appropriate language that would not do violence to state interests.

Fear that the procedure could lead to abuse, and that emergency sessions might be arbitrarily called without regard for the interests of all states (notably those of the major powers) was an ever-present concern, particularly of the USSR. What weighed on Moscow's thinking, for example, was the kind of initiative later undertaken by Austria. In January

1991, during an ad hoc meeting of experts, Austria proposed an emergency CSCE meeting to deal with Moscow's sudden and brutal crackdown at that time in the Baltic republics.[34] The proposal was killed by a Soviet veto.

Besides the regularization of the Helsinki process, with its own great potential spillover toward a permanent operating apparatus, the Paris Charter spelled out specific new institutions for Helsinki, where they would be located, and how they would be staffed. The first envisioned was a permanent secretariat for the maintenance and circulation of CSCE documents to the participating states. The secretariat would also extend appropriate and requested information on CSCE to the press, interested individuals, to non-governmental organizations, various international organizations and non-CSCE states. Finally, the secretariat would provide support to those serving as executive officers from host countries of summit conferences, follow-up meetings and various experts sessions.

Prague was selected as the headquarters of the secretariat, which comprised a director, three officers, and lesser administrative personnel. The choice of the Czechoslovak capital was not unexpected, for it had been among the first to clamor for institutionalization of the Helsinki process. Moreover, inter-war Czechoslovakia had been the region's most progressive democracy, and it was strategically located, almost in the center of Europe. Besides, President Havel, a hero of the Helsinki process, had been intensely lobbying for its placement in Prague.

A second new institution was the Conflict Prevention Center. Perceived in a number of speeches at Copenhagen and later at Paris as a major breakthrough in the area of peacekeeping, its principal function was to "assist the Council [of Foreign Ministers] in reducing the risk of conflict." However, the focus of the Center was not on intra-state ethnic and racial tensions, but rather on potential inter-state conflicts as related to notification of military maneuvers. The specified point of departure for the Center was the agreement reached at Vienna just prior to the summit concerning confidence- and security-building measures. Under that agreement, each country's information was to be shared with other CSCE members, with such exchanges supervised by the Center.

The Center would hold an annual review of CSBM implementation, thereby filling a gap in the review process of Basket I. It was further to serve as host for seminars on military doctrine, a vital new element in confidence building. Should a CSCE participating state request clarification of unusual military activities by another participating state, the Center would arrange for a meeting between the two. Finally, the Center functioned as the critical exchange point for compilation and publication of data on military budgets and deployment of weapons, forces, structures and equipment in a CSCE military yearbook. As an exchange point, the Center, staffed by a director and two officers along with administrative and technical personnel, would be given the task of overall responsibility for a communication network among CSCE states to explain and resolve potentially hazardous military incidents.

The Paris Charter anticipated that the mandate of the Conflict Prevention Center might be extended to the conciliation of disputes between states. CSCE had, in fact, established a mechanism for the peaceful settlement of disputes at a meeting in Valletta, Malta, in January 1991. Several months later, on May 27, the newly created Committee of Senior Officials asked the Council of Foreign Ministers to approve placing the new mechanism at the Center. The broadening of the Center's mandate constituted a major step forward.

Logic dictated that the site of the Conflict Prevention Center should be Vienna, as that city had been and would continue to be the venue of CSBMs negotiations, and so much of the Center's functions would be related to these negotiations. CSBMs negotiations had been launched in March 1989 at exactly the same time as the CFE negotiations had begun. As a neutral, Austria was ideally suited to supervise the various security purposes of CSCE. The Paris Charter linked the Conflict Prevention Center and the CSBMs negotiation. And the Charter had mandated the creation of a new CSCE Consultative Committee to supervise the Center's work. The makeup of the Consultative Committee illuminated both its character and its priorities. It would be comprised of the heads of CSCE delegations to the ongoing CSBMs negotiations and it was to operate in its role "according to CSCE procedures."

Yet the potential of the Center contrasted heavily with its actual early "deployment." In mid-June 1991, a half-year after the adoption of the Charter, a reporter found the $1 million operation almost empty of meaning and significance.[35] A four-room suite (located in a drab Vienna office building) with but one occupant—the director himself—hardly suggested a humming operation. Yet the Director, Bent Rosenthal, was not altogether pessimistic. "The real question is," he asked, "can we live up to this impressive name?"

The international circumstances at the time of the reporter's visit certainly suggested that the Center could become a possible focus of future public and diplomatic attention. At that moment, national tensions in Yugoslavia between independence-oriented Slovenia and Croatia, on one side, and a Serbia-dominated federal state on the other, strongly pointed to military conflict. Was not the threat of conflict and violence related to the Center's function? Yet, as Rosenthal noted: "It's not clear if the provisions setting up the Center apply to internal use of force."[36] The Yugoslav crisis was an outgrowth of internal tensions, not external threats of violence. In any case, the military maneuvers in either Yugoslavia or somewhat earlier in the Baltics had not immediately led to any appeal to the Center for help.

The chief US representative to the CSCE security negotiations in Vienna, Ambassador John Maresca, acknowledged that the Center had "a very loosely worded mandate."[37] He said it was originally designed to make it "more difficult for nations to prepare hostile actions," and the initial intent of the drafters was to "focus the light of public opinion on the problem." But no one apparently perceived the internal Yugoslav crisis as an immediately appropriate subject for the Conflict Prevention Center of CSCE.

The third and last new institution established by the Charter was an Office for Free Elections. Pertinently, it was to be located in Warsaw, Poland, which had been the first of the East European communist countries to hold free elections.

The functions of the new Office were initially rather modest. It was supposed to facilitate the implementation of the extensive commitments on free elections made in the Copenhagen concluding document. Though this general role seemed quite broad, even extensive, the Office's only specified direction involved compilation and transmission of information regarding elections in the participating states and about observers from governments and non-governmental organizations to those elections. Basically, the Office had the character of a resource point rather than the kind of operating and administrative role assigned to the Conflict Prevention Center. Its staff, too, would be commensurately smaller—a director, one officer, and some clerical personnel. And its budget would be but one-half that of the Center.

Aside from the narrowly defined resource role, the Charter mandate implied that, with time, the Office might take on added responsibility. In the words of the mandate, the Office "will carry out other tasks assigned to it by the Council." Clearly, there were those among the Charter drafters who wanted to see the new institution, the only one oriented to specific human rights purposes, take on further burdens related to democratic institution building. But its early described function was distinctly limited.

Besides creating three totally new bureaucratic offices, the Paris Charter mandated the establishment of a CSCE Parliamentary Assembly. Heretofore, only the US Congress, through the Helsinki Commission, had been actively involved in the CSCE process; other parliaments had no such connection. The new institution had a strong link to the democratic aspirations that the Charter had spelled out, and, therefore, had human rights implications. Still, no special institutional office was provided the Assembly. Indeed, President Bush, addressing the CSCE foreign ministers meeting in early October, spoke of a parliamentary assembly as a body drawn from a "growing family of democracies which can chart a common course towards this new Europe, whole and free." He called on the parliaments to pursue contacts with each other and reach agreement on "the field of activities, working methods and rules of procedure . . . [for a] . . . CSCE parliamentary structure."

Baker had advanced the idea of a parliamentary assembly in late 1989 and early 1990 in several speeches which addressed the "architecture" of a new Europe. And, no doubt, officials at the Council of Europe in Strasbourg saw an opportunity in the collapse of communism in East Europe to extend the Council's sway and link the new institutional apparatus to its own Parliamentary Assembly. NATO's ground-breaking London Declaration of July 1990 appeared to sanction a thesis which made the Council of Europe in Strasbourg the core of a projected parliamentary assembly. The declaration referred to a CSCE parliamentary body, "the Assembly of Europe," as based on the Parliamentary Assembly of the Council of Europe.[38]

Helsinki Commission leadership in the United States had been infuriated.[39] How could the Brussels military-political structure, comprised exclusively of executive officials from the various countries' bureaucracies, presume to speak for or to recommend parliamentary bodies? To the Commission and the Congress, the diplomats involved in the London NATO meeting had clearly exceeded their authority. By October, President Bush, in a speech at a CSCE meeting dropped any linkage between the "Assembly of Europe" with the Council of Europe.

The Paris Charter helped correct the embarrassment. The decision on what was needed and wanted was left to the parliaments themselves. Still, the Council of Europe pushed for greater authority and responsibility; its Secretary-General, Catherine Lalumiére, told the Paris summit that the Council was rapidly becoming an important organ for "pan-European cooperation," and that the Parliamentary Assembly could become the "basis" of the future pan-European parliament.[40] Lalumière stressed that

Hungary had become a member of the Council two weeks earlier, and that Poland and the CSFR were scheduled to become full members in 1991. In addition, the Soviet Union, Bulgaria, and Yugoslavia already held observer status with the Council (such status permitted a country to participate in the Assembly debates but without a vote).

Given political reality however, the Council of Europe was most unlikely to ever serve as anything more than a model or consultant to CSCE, even if Lalumiére did call her organization "the safest reference point for realizing the Helsinki human rights process." The US Congress was keenly jealous of its prerogatives, and was hardly inclined to join a regional legislative structure in which it had not played a key role in shaping. Nor was the US about to become a member of the Council of Europe and adhere to its binding human rights treaty—the European Convention on Human Rights—and be bound by decisions of its Court of Human Rights, its own European Commission or Committee of Ministers. Canada, too, was not a member.

For the two North American parliamentary bodies, the Strasbourg-based assembly could not be the core of a CSCE legislature. Although Lalumiére told a Paris-based correspondent that she had "reason to believe that our US and Canadian friends" could be persuaded to agree with her plans, the correspondent found that the North American parliamentarians expressed fears that they would be "swallowed up" by the proposed structure.[41]

Moreover, while the former communist states of Eastern Europe were taking fairly rapid steps to embrace the Council of Europe, the USSR had demonstrated no such decisive movement. Observer status was not the same as a contractual acceptance of a rather rigorous human rights treaty and of adherence to decisions of a higher foreign judicial tribunal. With the two superpowers not expected to be part of the Council of Europe for the foreseeable future, it was inconceivable that the CSCE would permit the Council to play a decisive or dominant parliamentary role. The superpowers, after all, were the key players in CSCE.

On April 2-3, 1991, parliamentarians from the 34 CSCE states gathered by pre-arrangement in Madrid to establish formally the CSCE Parliamentary Assembly.[42] Top Helsinki Commission members, not surprisingly, were actively involved in the deliberations, which avoided subordination of the new structure to the CSCE Secretariat or other CSCE bureaucratic institutions. Instead, the Assembly established its own "small permanent secretariat."[43] The headquarters, budget and resources of the secretariat would be decided by a "Committee of Heads" of each parliamentary delegation.

Population and power determined the size of each delegation. As worked out at Madrid, the Assembly comprised 245 delegates, with the USSR and the United States each having 17. Germany, France, Italy and Britain had 13 each, and Canada and Spain had ten each. Other CSCE states had between two and eight delegates.

The conclusions reached at Madrid hardly suggested that the parliamentarians would be a major power in the new CSCE structure.[44] The planned assembly would meet only once a year (in July) for five days in a capital of a CSCE member, with the first meeting scheduled for Budapest in July 1992. The purposes of the annual meeting were necessarily modest: 1) assess the implementation of the objectives of CSCE; 2) discuss subjects addressed by the Council of Foreign Minsters and by the heads of state; and 3) "initiate and promote whatever measures may further co-operation and security in Europe." Only the last offered a substantive opportunity, but with 245 parliamentarians in attendance during a time frame of less than a week, it was hardly possible to expect a serious outcome. And the very modest character of the parliamentary function meant, too, that the legislators would scarcely be able to enhance the human rights process. Yet, this was by no means disappointing to the Helsinki Commission, which had opposed in any case significant institutionalization of the process.[45]

Washington's acceptance of the need to institutionalize the Helsinki process came rather surprisingly and suddenly. It had resisted all pressures for creating permanent CSCE bureaucratic institutions during the Final Act negotiations of 1973-75. Ambassador Kampelman, at a Washington meeting of the American Society of International Law held in April 1990, firmly rejected any thought of institutionalizing the Helsinki process:

> . . . I believe that one of the strengths of the Helsinki process was the fact that it was not institutionalized. It does not have a staff; there is no building, there is a kind of informality about it that is not bureaucratized. I now hear discussions suggesting that should be changed. I look at institutions like UNESCO, and the idea of institutionalizing the Helsinki process becomes frightening. I doubt it can fulfill its goals in that format.[46]

While Ambassador Kampelman was extremely dubious about institutionalization, a colleague who had been involved in negotiations on CSBMs and would later serve on the Committee of Senior Officials, John Maresca, hinted to the international lawyers that some sort of institutionalization of the Helsinki process was essential:

> The Helsinki process is based on a loose amalgam of meetings. To grow and take on real importance, it needs to be more concrete and relevant to the everyday problems of Europeans. This does not necessarily mean creation of a huge bureaucracy.[47]

Maresca had no objection to a modest, rather than huge, bureaucracy. He talked about "many ideas . . . being tossed about" in connection with forthcoming CSCE meetings, adding "certainly one focus will be on institutionalization issues—ways of strengthening the process."

Maresca's comments, and the flat assertions with which he conveyed them, showed that some thought had been given at the State Department to institutionalization. Maresca himself had advanced several proposals in the past that he now underscored as relevant to the institutionalization process.[48] In 1986, he had written an article proposing Helsinki observers for purposes of observing free elections. In 1989, another article of his—"The People Have a Right to Choose"—concentrated on the question of self-determination, which he had called Helsinki's "Basket IV." And in his speech to the international lawyers, he established a tight link between observers and self-determination.

In Maresca's perception, observers clearly were part of a functioning bureaucratic apparatus. He placed considerable emphasis upon CSCE undertaking initiatives to stabilize Eastern Europe "as it evolves toward pluralistic democracy and also re-Balkanizes." Stabilizing a territorial situation involving various nationalities strongly suggested the need for regional bureaucratic personnel. One example that he urged was "to prevent persecution of ethnic minorities in East Europe," a purpose he believed worthwhile. This, too, implied bureaucratic efforts.

Yet, Maresca's views were clearly not those of US policy makers. It was the Kampelman perspective which predominated before and even during the Copenhagen meeting, although Secretary Baker did articulate an attitude which appeared to point the way to some institutionalization.

How then explain the fundamental shift in the US position from opposition to institutionalization of the Helsinki process to support for it? A major factor was the attitude of two key new East European democracies—Poland and the Czech and Slovak Federal Republic. As early as January 1, 1990, Polish Prime Minister Mazowiecki, in an address to his parliament, proposed the creation of a "permanent council of European cooperation."[49] Later, the Polish government proposed that the Paris summit meeting offer "a signal to start a step-by-step, pragmatic process of institutionalization of the CSCE. . . ."[50] It sought in this process to create ultimately a "European Confederation," a vision which French President Mitterrand had also sketched.

The Polish document hinted at the need to end Soviet isolation. It repeatedly referred to a "more united Europe" in which "mechanisms of European cooperation" regarding ecology, science and education would be strengthened and extended to more political matters. Mazowiecki, speaking later on the occasion of the Paris summit, stressed that "while NATO plays an enormously positive role" with respect to "European stability," nonetheless, "CSCE represents the broadest platform for agreement among European nations and with the United States and Canada."[51] He also said it provided "an important institutional framework for the Soviet Union in the life of our continent."

Mazowiecki was clearly preoccupied with security concerns and with preventing another Soviet military takeover. Extension of human rights, already largely achieved, was no longer the principal aim of Solidarity-governed Poland. But Poland's geographic location next to the USSR inevitably posed a possible security threat. He certainly welcomed NATO as a factor offsetting Soviet power. His positive comments about the Western military organization clearly testified to that. But for Poland to join NATO, as opposed to joining the European Community or Council of Europe, was more than a mere hazardous step. Moscow could hardly countenance a NATO partner on its borders. Nor would NATO have been inclined to accept Poland as a member, for such an act would have assured a great increase in East-West tensions.

All the more, then, from Warsaw's perspective did CSCE take on enormous significance. The Helsinki framework included the United States and the Western powers, thereby providing a counterbalance to Soviet military might. And it also embraced the USSR, thus preventing its isolation and reducing the psychological problems which might burden an isolated power. If the Helsinki structure was valuable for the security of Poland, it would be even more so if it had the framework to shoulder the burdens of confronting and preventing potential conflicts. A CSCE that was institutionalized with full-time professional officers coping with tension and conflict would go some distance as a substitute for NATO.

Prague vigorously pushed in the same direction. In April 1990, its government called for a European Security Commission of the Helsinki states which "would provide an until-now-missing permanent all-European platform for the consideration of questions related to security on the continent, and for seeking their solution."[52] The Prague memorandum spelled out nine functions for the Commission, all of which dealt with security matters, arms control and disarmament. Nothing remotely resembling human rights came within its purview.

At the Paris session, President Havel drove home the point that it is "very important . . . to institutionalize" the Helsinki process.[53] NATO might be praised as "a guarantee of freedom and democracy" but, in itself, it could not effectively assure the security of East Europe. At the same time, Havel condemned the Warsaw Pact as an "outdated remnant of the past . . . a typical product of Stalinist expansion. . . ." If he welcomed over the long run the creation of an all-European confederation, initially Mitterrand's suggestion, the earliest he could expect it becoming a "reality" was "at the beginning of the next millennium."

A certain irony characterized the aspirations of former communist countries in Eastern Europe. It was the Mazowieckis and Havels who had initially clamored almost exclusively for filling Helsinki baskets with human rights aims; now, having triumphed over their former overseers, their preeminent concern was security. Of course, this change made sense. In their view, a resurgent nationalist or Stalinist Soviet state might once again send troops to uproot their new freedoms.

In contrast, the British perspective for a future CSCE focused on human rights. In March 1990, Prime Minister Thatcher had stressed that CSCE in no way "take on a defense role," which would remain NATO's task.[54] What CSCE "can and should do is to strengthen democracy, the rule of law and human rights." In one important respect, however, she did advocate an important security function for CSCE. It should have a "conciliation role" whereby "its good offices" would be made available "in any dispute between two or more of its members. . . ." As an example, she pointed quite presciently to "matters concerning minority rights." The Paris summit did not act upon the idea. Had it done so, the growing nationality conflicts that tore at the fabric of Yugoslav society might have been nipped early on.

The United States could not easily dismiss the views of the new democracies in Eastern Europe concerning institutionalization. After all, they were the products, in part, of Washington's Helsinki policy, and their concerns carried weight. Nor were they alone in pressuring the US. Germany, perhaps the most direct beneficiary of Helsinki, saw in institutionalization a means for placating the USSR, whose security fears had escalated with the collapse of the Warsaw Pact. A leading advocate of institutionalization since the beginning of Helsinki, the Soviets saw it as the means by which the military alliance systems—especially NATO—could be replaced. Those who sought to maintain NATO, and this included all of Western Europe, urged a special sensitivity to Moscow's anxieties. Washington, at first hesitant, fell into line once it was agreed generally that the bureaucratization would be limited.

Even as the summit leaders were glorying in historic democratic and human rights achievements and in elaborating machinery for extending these achievements into the future and reducing the military means for threatening the security concerns, they also expressed deep anxieties about burgeoning economic problems and escalating racial and ethnic tensions. Prime Minister Mazowiecki pointed to the economic distress in East Europe. "Our common future may be darkened by the sinister conflicts of bygone days," he warned, "unless the split into a rich and a poor Europe, an 'A' class and a 'B' class in Europe, is overcome." Hungarian Prime Minister Jozsef Antall cautioned that "a new welfare wall may arise in place of the Iron Curtain, which has now been removed."[55]

Both Eastern European leaders were referring to the consequences of the collapse of the communist command economies. The establishment of a market system and the privatization of broad segments of the economy had engendered profound social problems, including great levels of unemployment. The social contract that had undergirded the communist system was ruptured and, in the absence of a new one, impoverishment deepened while class conflict threatened. Especially in multiethnic states, these new socio-economic tensions helped stir the embers of renascent intercommunal animosity. The likelihood of chaos loomed.

Another feared consequence of the emergent economic distress was the prospect of vast waves of migrants from Eastern Europe hammering at the gates of West European countries. Refugee affairs specialists predicted a range of 5-20 million persons moving westward. For the European Community, the potential influx posed grave problems. Italian Foreign Minister Gianni de Michelis commented that "this would be a kind of invasion that could create dreadful conditions of destabilization."[56]

There was, of course, a certain irony in the fear of an "invasion." A fundamental aim of the Helsinki process from its very beginning had been acceptance of the right to leave a country, a "freer movement of people." Now there was talk in the West of border controls and other devices to prevent the expected flood. Such a negative perspective was certain to prove counterproductive.

But it was the exploding ethnic and nationality tensions throughout Eastern Europe that stirred the greatest concern at Paris. Antall told his colleagues that "despite the changes that have taken place in the direction of democracy, we now see ethnic or nationality problems emerging in Europe, sometimes with greater intensity than in the past."[57] Chancellor Kohl stressed that the great human rights advances of the year past "must not be undermined by new discord between neighbors or nationalities."[58]

At least on the surface, a new determination to cope with the problem appeared. The Paris Charter committed the heads of state "to combat all forms of racial and ethnic hatred, anti-Semitism, xenophobia and discrimination against anyone, as well as persecution on religious and ideological grounds."[59] The assertion was close to the one adopted at Copenhagen, but it lacked the specifics on law and education the latter had carried. Nonetheless, the Paris Charter had the clear intent of incorporating Copenhagen's basic perspectives, and in fact, made special reference to the Copenhagen concluding document.

Ramifications of the nationalist tensions in multinational societies of Eastern Europe were not lost on the conferees. Yugoslav President Borislav Jovic drove home the point by observing that in situations of "national bigotry, democracy falls as the first victim."[60] Yet, easy solutions were not quickly available. The preeminent recommendations at Copenhagen had been free elections, political pluralism and the rule of law. But if the national enmities within Yugoslavia or the Soviet Union, as examples, were simply irreconcilable for broad historical and cultural reasons, then free elections could scarcely provide an effective answer to the problem. Or, if they did, and the outcome of the balloting was self-determination, might that not generate the equally disturbing consequence of instability? President Gorbachev posed the contradiction rather sharply at Paris when he said that "unbridled nationalism and mindless separation" constituted a serious challenge to the new European security order.[61]

What plagued the Soviet ruler especially was the Baltic states' insistent clamor for independence. The fact that only a year earlier the Soviet authorities finally acknowledged how the incorporation took place could only cast doubt on Moscow's authority over them. (The inclusion of Lithuania, Latvia and Estonia in the USSR in 1940 was the result of a secret treaty with Nazi Germany in the fall of 1939, and not the consequence of voluntary choice, as the Communist Party myth had held.) The three republics continued to demand observer status at the CSCE meetings. President Mitterrand initially extended their leaders special status as guests of the host country at the summit, but under pressure from Moscow the invitation was withdrawn.[62]

Sympathy for the Balts within CSCE was growing. Favorable speeches on their behalf were given at Paris by Norway, Sweden, Denmark, Iceland, the Vatican, Poland, and the CSFR.[63] Needless to say, the support could not but reinforce their determination to speak out. A statement from the Supreme Council of Lithuania the day after the Paris summit warned all CSCE members that Moscow was threatening the Baltic republic with "destabilization and massive misfortune" through a rupture of economic relations and the imposition of violence by Soviet military units.[64] The Lithuanian statement demanded "the immediate inclusion of the question of the independence of the Baltic countries on the agenda of . . . the CSCE."

For the United States, the Baltic issue posed a profound dilemma. Although Washington had never recognized the incorporation of the three republics into the USSR in 1940, it was still reluctant to press Gorbachev on the issue other than to warn against the use of violence. Some observers saw Western pressure as playing into the hands of right-wing Communist Party, military and nationalist forces, thereby undermining Gorbachev. With stability in Eastern Europe now a priority objective of the United States and the West, strong support for self-determination in multinational societies in East Europe could unravel the carefully constructed architecture of the new Europe.

Nationality and minority issues were sore thumbs, unresolved throbbing concerns to CSCE, especially for those whom the Charter marked a moment of apotheosis in the history of Helsinki. The summit recommended that a special CSCE seminar be held in Geneva in July 1991 to deal with the problem.[65] But at the end of the Paris meeting, everyone recognized that, despite the extraordinary victory of democracy and human rights, enormous difficulties had suddenly surfaced within CSCE that threatened grave consequences. President Mitterrand eloquently summed it up: "We Europeans have ten years in which to win our race against history."[66]

·17·

Racism and Nationalism: Helsinki's Unsolved Problems

Europe's "premier post-cold war political forum"—such was the characterization of CSCE by a leading Washington foreign affairs columnist soon after the Paris summit.[1] And, indeed, that is what it seemed to be for the moment. The heads of all CSCE states had committed themselves for the first time to democracy "as the only system of government of our nations." Progress in advancing fundamental freedoms was clearly marked, as a Helsinki implementation report by the President indicated. The report, covering the period April 1, 1990, to March 31, 1991, and published in July 1991, noted continuing improvements in Eastern Europe and the Soviet Union.[2]

The CSCE role in the transformation of Europe seemed hardly challengeable. President Vaclav Havel of Czechoslovakia, speaking at the Paris summit, gave the thesis high visibility and pronounced credibility when he directly linked CSCE to the Velvet Revolution.[3] Only five years earlier, in 1985-86, many seemed to despair of the Helsinki process as fatally ineffective in changing a Europe bisected by an impregnable wall. Now CSCE was called upon at the highest level of the US government "to forge a new transatlantic partnership" at the same time that it constructed a free and secure Europe.[4]

The third meeting of the Conference on the Human Dimension, scheduled for Moscow on September 10-October 4, 1991, was projected as the consummation of the Helsinki process, its final landmark in resolving outstanding human rights problems. Moscow was to be the last of the three meetings that had been envisaged and planned in the Vienna document for fulfilling significant compliance with Helsinki human rights obligations. The initial Paris human dimension session in June 1989 took meaningful strides forward. At Copenhagen, the following year, momentous changes in the character and structure of the process were approved to correspond with the vast transformation of Eastern Europe. If there had been controversy over Moscow as the site of the third and last human dimension meeting, there was little doubt about the expectation of significant progress.

In a thoughtful lecture at Georgetown University in March, Helsinki Commission Co-chairman Steny Hoyer wondered aloud whether the enthusiasm about CSCE did not reflect "wishful thinking," a kind of euphoria.[5] He cautioned against a "tide of rising expectation" that could be as problematic as the credibility question of 1985-86. He pointed to ethnic strife and "the threat of a tidal wave of immigrants" from the East fleeing from "economic dislocation and ethnic violence" as posing serious challenges to the achievements of CSCE. At Copenhagen, and later at the Paris summit, minority rights problems, including racism and anti-Semitism, were placed at the heart of Helsinki's immediate concerns. Hoyer specifically added the self-determination issue, reflected in developments in Yugoslavia and the Soviet Union, as warranting urgent attention. The central problem for CSCE in the future, he surmised, was "to manage conflicts within the states themselves."[6]

Sir Isaiah Berlin, the distinguished philosopher of history, would call attention in the fall of 1991 to the reality that not democracy, but rather racism and nationalism "are the most powerful movements in the world today."[7] Some may have thought that racism and nationalism had only recently become "resurgent." In fact, he wrote, they had "never died."

Clearly, the "end of history" had not been reached, even if communism appeared to be in its death throes. Indeed, the victory of democracy may very well have provided the opportunity and setting for vibrant racism and nationalism. A special experts' meeting on minority rights problems had been scheduled by the Paris summit for Geneva in July. And it was expected that the Moscow session would later proceed to cope with the recommendations from Geneva. In dealing with what seemed to be the last obstacle to a Europe "whole and free," would CSCE then reach its apotheosis? Or would the problems associated with minority issues prove so intractable as to place in grave doubt the value of Helsinki now that human rights aspirations had been realized to a considerable extent?

It was hardly unexpected that movement toward regularization and institutionalization of the Helsinki process would proceed apace. Europe had in fact become the "common house" imagined by Gorbachev, with the major barrier removed and a standard type of political system accepted. To make permanent the new structure and tackle the emerging and threatening problems, ad hoc procedures were no longer appropriate.

No sooner did the Paris summit conclude then consultations quickly moved forward on building the new Helsinki framework. The first meeting of the Committee of Senior Officials, the core group, was held in Vienna in January 1991. The directors of the new CSCE institutions were selected and their budgets approved.[8]

Left undecided was the crucial question of how to set in motion the emergency mechanism for calling future urgent meetings of the Committee. The Paris Charter had referred to the new mechanism, but did not indicate how the triggering device would operate. Not until the first post-charter meeting of the Council of Foreign Ministers held in June was this gap filled in.[9] By then, the threat of civil war in Yugoslavia drove the Council to an early decision. Two steps were defined. First, any participating state, if it considers the situation in another state as having an emergency character, may request clarification from the latter, which is obligated to respond.

If the "serious emergency situation" remains unresolved, a request can then be made to the chairman of the Committee of Senior Officials. The stipulated time frame for the emergency session would be two days. However, before the session can be called, 12 or more CSCE states must officially support the request. The Committee chairman would then advise all CSCE states of the forthcoming meeting, which would be held within two to three days after the decision is reached.

The action of the Council of Foreign Ministers meant a breach with the fundamental Helsinki principle of consensus. No longer was consensus required for CSCE to act. Thirteen states—roughly one-third of the membership—can call for a special emergency meeting of the process's new executive organ.

Almost immediately after the Council's decision, the first test of the emergency provision was put into effect. The nine European countries belonging to the Western European Union (WEU), along with the United States, Austria, and Hungary, formally asked the Committee to hold an emergency meeting to deal with the Yugoslav Army's military action in Slovenia. The Committee of Senior Officials met in Prague on July 3-4, 1991, and took several actions: 1) it issued an urgent appeal for a cease-fire; 2) it offered to send a "good offices" mission to facilitate dialogue between Yugoslavia and the breakaway state of Slovenia; and 3) it endorsed an initiative of the European Community for the dispatch of a team to Slovenia that would observe the implementation of a cease-fire.[10]

The initial intervention by the EC, which had been vigorously backed by CSCE, led to a cease-fire agreement. Fighting subsided in Slovenia.

But shortly afterward, fierce battles erupted in Croatia, where Serbs in that republic (totaling 12 percent of the population), joined by the Yugoslav Army, sought to prevent the establishment of an independent Croatia. The Prague meeting of the Committee, which had dealt with Slovenia, was now called back into session by its chairman (from Germany) on August 8-9. At the new session, the Committee again offered a "good offices" mission.[11] It also agreed to the extension of the scope of the observers' mission to Croatia, as well as to the inclusion of additional personnel from other CSCE states.

What had become clear was that CSCE, even with its institutionalization, did not have the means to supervise a cease-fire. CSCE's function was aimed at providing sanction for the role of the European Community.[12] But EC itself was sharply split on how to respond to heightened conflicts between Croatia and Serbian-dominated Yugoslavia.

With civil war growing, policy divergences among members of the European Community deepened. Germany and non-EC Austria, responding to the pressures of their respective and powerful Christian democratic parties and to their large Catholic constituencies, urged the recognition of independent Slovenia and Croatia. This was vigorously rejected by the others of the European Community as opening the way to endless demands for national self-determination (not only within Yugoslavia and the USSR, but within major West European countries themselves—France, Spain, Belgium, and others).

Military intervention was scarcely a meaningful option. The British could remind their colleagues of the example of Northern Ireland. An armed German presence would trigger memories of Hitler's invasion of the area. Already, the Serb authorities in Belgrade were beating the propaganda drums about alleged German expansionism. Instead, the EC opted for economic sanctions as a method for halting the violence. But the effectiveness of sanctions could only be realized through the UN, as much of the imports came from outside the EC area (e.g., the critical commodity of oil was largely imported from Libya). Reluctantly, the EC had to turn to the UN Security Council to make effective and meaningful economic sanctions.

The United States was initially a strong advocate of Yugoslav unity in dealing with the unfolding crises.[13] If earlier its emphasis was exclusively on democracy, it now made unity a major objective because it believed that "unity offered the best prospects for democracy and stability throughout Yugoslavia."[14] Given the country's heated ethnic disputes, the State Department concluded that "the only alternative to some form of democratic unity was violence, suffering and long-term instability."

As the year progressed, however, Washington no longer talked about unity, because "the deterioration of the situation has made other goals more immediate."[15] The other goals were a cease-fire and dialogue between the parties that might lead to some form of confederation.

In pursuing these goals, Washington opted for supporting the efforts of the European Community rather than taking the lead itself. For one thing, a key State Department official explained, Europe had a greater stake in resolving the crisis and, more importantly, Europe had a greater leverage in the area.[16] The United States accounted for only 5 percent of Yugoslav foreign trade, Europe for nearly 80 percent; while the United States provided Yugoslavia with $5 million in assistance, mainly technical, the EC had given the country $935 million.

It could hardly be said that the new emergency mechanism was working very effectively, or that the regularization of the Helsinki process through more frequent meetings of the Committee of Senior Officials showed great promise in promoting security and preventing conflict. But, then, these devices did provide a sanction for a modest intervention of the European Community (and later of the United Nations). Besides, when conflict had assumed a military form in the past, the Helsinki process had never exercised more than a marginal role. Thus, the Soviet invasion of Afghanistan in December 1979 might be universally condemned by the West and the neutrals at the subsequent Madrid follow-up meeting, but Moscow's withdrawal was not forthcoming. Nor did the Madrid meeting halt Soviet military maneuvers to intimidate Solidarity and democratic forces in Poland during 1981 or prevent the subsequent imposition of martial law there. Only in the long run had the Helsinki process been able to act upon world opinion to help spur an end to war and military rule.

The Committee of Senior Officials, as a kind of executive organ of CSCE in its post-Paris institutionalized structure, merits special attention. It was largely a security-oriented body, comprised of many of the same ambassadorial personnel who served as delegation heads of the Consultative Committee based in Vienna which dealt with CSBMs (confidence- and security-building measures). When circumstances warranted, the members flew to Prague, the headquarters of the CSCE Secretariat, changed hats—as it were—and operated not as the Consultative Committee, but as the Committee of Senior Officials.[17]

During 1991, it met ten times, six based upon the "emergency" mechanism and the balance in regular session approximately every three months.[18] The meetings of the Committee of Senior Officials were closed and produced no documents. The CSO's agenda, like the call for the meetings themselves, was determined in a very informal way. A key figure in the proceedings was the person serving as chairman, who represented the country in which the Council of Foreign Ministers last met. The US representative at the beginning was Ambassador Jack Maresca, a highly experienced CSCE diplomat, whose work *To Helsinki: The Conference on Security and Cooperation in Europe 1973-1975* is an authoritative account on the shaping of the Final Act. Obviously, his role in both Vienna and Prague, to the extent that it reflected US interest and concern, was important, though by no means dominant.

Interwoven into the enhanced institutionalization of CSCE was substantial attention, for the first time in the Helsinki process, to the notion of the "peaceful settlement of disputes," one of ten principles in the Final Act (Principle V). The issue here was a dispute *between* states, not within a state. Two earlier special CSCE meetings on the subject—in Montreux (1978) and Athens (1984)—achieved little progress for the obvious reason that the polarization in power and ideology had made it difficult to agree on formulations that would be both neutral and effective.[19] Now that the East-West polarization had ended, a rational approach to the subject could at least begin, even if national security interests of the separate European states still generated differences.

The Paris Charter specifically referred to the forthcoming third Helsinki conference on the peaceful settlement of disputes, scheduled for Valletta, Malta, between January 15 and February 8, 1991, as a special "opportunity" of which "full use should be made." The summit then went on to mandate the new and powerful Council of Foreign Ministers, whose first meeting was to take place on June 18-19 in Berlin, "to take into account" the results of Valletta.[20]

The timing of Valletta proved to be unfortunate. Just hours before it opened, Soviet military forces in Lithuania, mainly from the Ministry of Interior, killed over a dozen unarmed civilians. The action, at least in spirit, seemed to contradict Principle V of the Helsinki Final Act. A total of 18 individual CSCE delegations protested the Soviet action in their opening statements. In addition, Luxembourg, speaking on behalf of the European Community, denounced the killings. Especially bitter were the comments of each of the former Warsaw Pact members. The Czechoslovak representative summed up their concern by calling the events in Vilnius "tragic and sinister."[21] Throughout the meeting, numerous countries, including the United States, invoked the CSCE human dimension mechanism. Additionally, the Committee of Senior Officials, meeting in Vienna, also heard similar strong protests.

Notwithstanding the tensions over the Lithuanian incident, the major powers avoided an open clash. President Gorbachev personally denied responsibility for the killings, which could not but reflect poorly on either his integrity or authority. The US and the West, at the very same time, however, were determined to maintain a solid front at the United Nations where the deadline for Iraq's withdrawal from occupied Kuwait had expired (on January 15). Washington considered Moscow's agreement to US military action under UN auspices vital.

Out of the Valletta deliberations there emerged a CSCE Dispute Resolution Mechanism (later called "the Mechanism"), which eventually would have certain ramifications for a new human dimension mechanism to be established in Moscow.[22] Should CSCE participating states be unable to resolve peacefully a dispute between them, they are to seek the assistance of a third party, the awkwardly called Mechanism. The Mechanism established in Valletta is comprised of one or more persons selected by common agreement of the disputing parties from a "register of qualified candidates." The register would ultimately be kept in the Conflict Prevention Center in Vienna. Names on the register would be nominated by CSCE states, with each entitled to select up to a maximum of four persons.

The function of the Valletta Mechanism was limited to facilitating the resolution of a dispute by the parties themselves, and not to propose on its own a specific resolution. Reflected here is the view that externally imposed solutions are often unsuccessful in the long run. An exceptions clause further restricted the Mechanism. If either party to a dispute considers that the matter may relate to "territorial integrity or national defense, [or] title to sovereignty over land territory," it can prohibit the Mechanism from being used.[23] This self-judging clause, in effect, would preclude the Mechanism from being used in the most pressing issues between states.

Even with this severe limitation, a beginning was made in advancing the long-stalled issue of the peaceful settlement of disputes. CSCE veteran James Goodby warned in December 1990, just prior to Valletta, that if "satisfactory answers" cannot be found for "procedures for peaceful settlements of disputes" and "for the role of the Council of Ministers," then "the future of the CSCE is bleak."[24] But whether "satisfactory answers" could be obtained was extremely difficult to predict. National interests, reinforced by the operational requirements of consensus, were serious obstacles to be hurdled.

To a significant extent, the US played a key role at Valletta in creating and defining the Mechanism.[25] The Swiss had originally broached the idea as early as 1972, and had pushed it vigorously since the 1978 Montreux meeting. The initial Swiss formulation had been highly legalistic and not consensus-oriented, which made it virtually incompatible with CSCE, particularly in a context of East-West tensions. With the end of the Cold War, however, Washington considered the opportunity appropriate for addressing more meaningfully the subject of peaceful settlement of disputes.

The United States introduced the Mechanism proposal with strong emphasis on flexibility, and successfully pressed for its adoption. Opposition came mainly from the delegations of the United Kingdom, France and Turkey, who insisted upon the crippling exceptions clause. Concern that the Mechanism might apply to Gibraltar and Northern Ireland no doubt shaped Whitehall's thinking, which was extremely critical to the Valletta deliberations.

For the moment, the challenge to stability in Europe was less the matter of disputes between states as within states. It was the inter-ethnic or nationality disputes within Yugoslavia and elsewhere in Eastern Europe that tormented policy makers. The US and Western delegates confusingly tended to refer to the dispute as involving minorities. Slovenes are hardly a minority in Slovenia, or Croats in Croatia, or Macedonians in Macedonia, or Montenegrins in Montenegro. To refer to Slovenes in Slovenia or Croats in Croatia as a minority made for confusion. The issues in most instances were nationality issues, not minority issues. To the extent that nationalism and minority rights had become the priority issues in the post-Cold War world, Woodrow Wilson's self-determination became the axis around which Helsinki revolved.

In 1918, President Wilson informed Congress that "self-determination is not a mere phrase. It is an imperative principle of action which statesmen will henceforth ignore at their peril."[26] The "imperative principle" had been seized upon by activists throughout Yugoslavia, the Soviet empire, and Eastern Europe. Where Lenin had ultimately failed, Wilson had eventually succeeded. His central vision held: "Every people has a right to choose the sovereignty under which they shall live."[27]

Wilson's Secretary of State, Robert Lansing, recognized that self-determination was "simply loaded with dynamite." In a confidential memorandum in December 1918, he pointedly queried: "Will it not breed discontent, disorder and rebellion?"[28] Lansing was convinced that self-determination would prove "utterly destructive of the political fabric of society and would result in constant turmoil. . . ." Always the realist, he spurned the Wilsonian version as "the dream of an idealist who failed to realize the danger until too late." He then added: "What a calamity that the phrase was ever uttered!"

The Lansing critique was not without its effect. President Wilson acknowledged to the British Ambassador in Washington that, were self-determination "pushed to its extreme," the result would be "the disruption of existing governments to an undefinable degree."[29] Western Europe, in the recent period, has been certainly sensitive as to the potential impact of self-determination upon each country. If Slovenes in Yugoslavia or Georgians in the USSR (or South Ossetians within Georgia) could insist upon independence, then why not the Basques in Spain, the Corsicans in France, the Scots in Britain or even the Quebecois in far-off Canada? Belgium has had its tense internal nationality problem of Flemings demanding independence and Britain has had to contend with a burning Irish Catholic problem in Ulster for decades.

At the United Nations, whether in the Universal Declaration of Human Rights or the two International Covenants on Human Rights, self-determination was treated as a basic right. In 1970, a kind of qualification was introduced by the General Assembly in a declaration stipulating how the right might be exercised.[30] It stated that the right ought not be applied if it jeopardizes the territorial integrity of multinational states *provided* those states are based upon democratic principles and human rights, and allow for the exercise of these rights.

In the Helsinki Final Act, self-determination was treated as almost an absolute right. Principle VIII in the Decalogue stipulated that "all people always have the right, in full freedom, to determine, when and as they wish, their internal and external political status. . . ." The West did not urge the insertion of some type of qualification when the subject was brought up during the deliberations of 1973-75. The reason was fairly obvious. What concerned Western diplomats at the time was the Brezhnev Doctrine, which legitimized the crushing of the Dubček regime in Prague and rationalized Soviet domination of Eastern Europe. An unpublished Helsinki Commission study in 1991 highlighted this background and concluded that "Western efforts to include Principle VIII in the Final Act was primarily to counter complete Soviet control in Eastern Europe, not to lend support to national movements within participating states."[31]

The Final Act implies, as the study indicated, a certain limitation. Even as Principle VIII speaks of self-determination, at the very same time and in the very same sentence, it speaks of "equal rights" of "peoples." From the perspective of the study, the section means that "the self-determination of one people is inextricably linked to the self-determination of other peoples, and that a balance therefore must be struck between the goals and aspirations of all peoples." More significantly—and this point is not mentioned in the study—Principle III of the Final Act makes the borders of a state inviolable. If self-determination of one people leads to the alteration of state borders, it could violate the central Helsinki principle. The exception that was specified did permit the changing of borders when it is agreed to by the parties concerned, approved by a democratic vote, and has satisfied the requirements of international law. The exception permitted the unification of East and West Germany in October 1990.

The Commission study noted that the Final Act made a distinction between minority rights and self-determination. The former was covered in Principle VII, which spoke of "persons belonging" to minorities. Thus, its focus was the individual ("persons"). Self-determination, in contrast, is a collective right, as it applies specifically to "peoples." In the opinion of the study, self-determination may be the only collective right, although it suggested, too, that the establishment of bilingual schools could also be seen as satisfying a collective right.

That Eastern Europe would constitute the primary source of inter-ethnic disputes and tension was hardly surprising. A noted German specialist, after a careful study of the nationalities within the area, concluded that "the reservoir of conflicts in Eastern Europe is immense."[32] (Excluded here were the nationalities of the Soviet Union.) About a dozen take on a distinctly "politico-territorial aspect" in which a strong "psycho-political component" is to be found. Thus, the author noted that the various ethnic groups make repeated references to "unjust borders" in the schools, universities and presses which are under their control. The potential for revisionism and open conflict is inherent in such situations.

Adaptation, or rather the lack of same, reinforces the revisionism. Most of the borders of Eastern Europe were not demarcated until the 20th century. The different populations have not had a long time span to adapt to existing territorial arrangements. Besides, collective memory and collective myths in the area act as sources for identifying the enemy and projecting a utopian past onto the future. Finally, economic modernization in the era has been limited, thereby reinforcing attitudes and patterns of the traditional society. In traditional societies, collective myths and memories exert a powerful role. Tackling inter-ethnic tensions at the July 1991 CSCE Geneva meeting would have to cope with these enormously burdensome realities.

The problem would be compounded later as nationalist fervor seized the numerous ethnic groups within the USSR. Border disputes surfaced, with potential consequences of mass chaos. Researchers at the Institute of Geography of the Soviet Academy of Sciences calculated that of the 23 borders of the union republics (as of August 1991, prior to the independence of the Baltic republics), only three were not contested.[33] The total number of territorial conflicts in the Soviet Union (embracing the numerous nationalities of Russia proper, as well as of other republics that include several nationality groups) was estimated at 75, a staggering figure.[34]

Geneva would also seek to respond to the escalating evidence of anti-Semitism, anti-Gypsy attitudes and acts, and hatred of foreigners. Significantly, one month prior to the Geneva session, a major, if unexpected, step to educate against racism and anti-Semitism was taken by CSCE. This was achieved at the Helsinki "Symposium on Cultural Heritage" held in Cracow, Poland, from May 28 to June 7.[35] Its primary focus was to have been on the preservation and protection of cultural monuments, hardly a subject that would fit in with or be related to the intensifying nationalism. Insistence by the French delegate on a special subject concerned with the Nazi Holocaust transformed the debate, inter-relating it with the issue of racism and how to confront it effectively.

The Paris representative set on the table, almost from the beginning, a proposal to preserve and protect extermination sites together with related archival material, along with cultural monuments.[36] The reference was clearly to the Nazi epoch and its program of genocide. In introducing the subject, he explained that the proposal had been promoted with intense fervor by several French non-governmental organizations that would not or could not be persuaded that the subject was inappropriate. His comments certainly gave emphasis to the significance and value for the Helsinki process of national NGOs.

Prevailing upon his colleagues was not an easy matter. The US delegate was not too sympathetic with the French proposal because it seemed to have a unilinear focus—the Nazi epoch and Jewish martyrdom. Were there not other forms of genocide, like the famine in the Ukraine, the earlier Turkish destruction of Armenians, the large-scale killings of Poles by the Nazis and the massacre of the Cambodians by the Pol Pot regime? The Canadians intervened with a compromise in language that removed the unilinear focus and, therefore, the US concern and enabled the latter to become a supporter of the proposal. American support was important as the German delegation was, initially, hardly enthusiastic about that which would inevitably target Germans. And strong opposition for a long period came from the Polish delegate. His resistance might have been prompted by Polish circles resenting the worldwide pressure from Jews for the removal of a nuns' institution erected on the outskirts of Auschwitz.

The concluding document adopted at Cracow was a milestone in the recognition, on an international authoritative level, of teaching about the Holocaust. The key paragraph read:

> The participating states will strive to preserve and protect those monuments and *sites of remembrance, including most notably extermination camps,* and the related archives, which are themselves testimonials to tragic experiences in their common past. [Emphasis added.]

What followed was a vitally critical thesis:

> Such steps need to be taken in order that those [extermination] experiences may be remembered, may help to teach present and future generations of these events, and thus ensure that they are never repeated.[37]

Intent upon underscoring this thesis, the CSCE drafters apprised educational leaders as well as public-opinion molders that "the interpretation of sensitive sites of remembrance can serve as a valuable means of promoting tolerance and understanding among people. . . ."

Relevance of the Cracow thesis to the USSR was immediately apparent. The Holocaust itself had been virtually expunged from the historical record since the end of World War II. The great work of historical documentation of the Holocaust, *The Black Book,* assembled and edited by the distinguished writers Ilya Ehrenburg and Vasily Grossman, was suppressed in 1946, all its copies destroyed, and even its type-mold smashed. At the first All-Union Congress of Jewish Organizations held in Moscow in December 1989, the participants bitterly concluded: "There are no historical studies and publications in the USSR devoted to the genocide of Soviet Jews; in the schoolbooks, the tragedy of the Jewish people is not mentioned."[38] Close scholarly examination of Soviet textbooks, used in elementary and high schools, validates the Congress' lament.[39]

Blotting out the Jewish trauma meant, too, the total neglect or indifference to the "sites of extermination" on Soviet soil. No memorials or monuments were erected to commemorate specifically the Jewish tragedy. Yevgeny Yevtushenko, the eloquent poet, captured in 1961 the torment of the Jewish trauma when he began his famous poem: "There are no monuments over Babi Yar."[40] Overtly, Yevtushenko linked the failure to erect a memorial to traditional Russian anti-Semitism, which violated the internationalist dream of Communism.

Moscow's outlook on the Holocaust was not unique in Eastern Europe. The Romanian parliament's honoring of Marshal Ion Antonescu, a practitioner of genocide against Jewry, was an indication of Bucharest's perspective on the subject.[41] An especially blatant example of contempt for the Holocaust, joined to a crude anti-Semitism, can be found in a book by the President of Croatia, Franjo Tudjman, *Wastelands—Historical Truth*, published in 1988 and republished in 1989 and 1990. He wrote: "The estimated loss of up to 6 million dead is founded too much on both emotional, biased testimonies and on exaggerated data. . . ."[42]

The Cracow symposium served as a modest, if limited, curtain raiser for the Geneva CSCE experts' meeting on minorities mandated by the Paris summit for July 1991. The racism issue was, however, a minor facet of Cracow. The broader concern about escalating racism and nationalism warranted more detailed attention. Initially, the United States had objected to the Geneva meeting because of the hectic schedule that CSCE would be burdened with prior to the next follow-up meeting in Helsinki in March 1992.[43] But, as the urgency of the problem became increasingly apparent, the objection was withdrawn. The Charter itself noted the "urgent need for increased cooperation on, as well as better protection of, national minorities."

The timing was especially appropriate. In late June, the breakup of Yugoslavia had begun with announcements of independence from two key republics—Slovenia and Croatia. In the USSR, nationalist fervor was spreading beyond the Baltics to the Caucasus and in various other directions as well. In response, right-wing forces in the Communist Party, joined by the strong nationalist elements in and out of the military, were threatening Gorbachev and the program of glasnost.

The overall focus of Geneva was underscored in the opening address by the top Swiss official dealing with foreign affairs, René Felber.[44] He noted that the CSCE process "has enabled a decisive turning point to be reached by defining the problem of minorities as being henceforth a question of human rights." Certainly, until Copenhagen, little attention had been given the subject of minorities. Now, it was suddenly a top priority. But whether it fitted entirely into the human rights category was not too clear. Uncertainty and confusion about the subject made for a reluctance to deal with it meaningfully. Besides, the "experts" were hardly experts at all. Rather, in most instances, they were the CSCE functionaries of foreign ministries.

Weakness and inadequacy in grasping the nettlesome problem were soon apparent. Central to the agenda, as with other CSCE agendas, was a thorough and specific review of implementation of the existing commitments on minority rights. Yet a "great and unfortunate reluctance" to engage in a meaningful and traditional type of Helsinki review was characteristic of the Geneva proceedings.[45] A staff report of the Helsinki Commission illuminated the reluctance.[46] The US and Hungary were exceptions in their willingness to participate in a detailed review; the bulk of the participants largely avoided the issue. Most felt that a frank exchange of views on implementation would be perceived as confrontational.[47] And confrontation was seen as a relic of the bygone Cold War era.

The serious US attention to review of implementation was consistent with Washington's commitment to the Helsinki process ever since the Belgrade conference, when Ambassador Goldberg had given the term "review" the definition of a detailed examination of the record. For Ambassador Kampelman, review had become a kind of mechanism for achieving compliance. An honest evaluation of one's own conduct and that of others in the field of minority rights, through dialogue, was seen as a means for exposing inadequacies, which could then lead to commitments for progress.

Hungary's special devotion to review when it came to minority rights flowed from its anxious concern for the condition of the Hungarian diaspora populations, especially in Romania, but extending now to Slovakia and Yugoslavia, where rising nationalism could have serious negative impact upon sizable local diaspora minorities. As early as the Vienna follow-up, the Hungarian delegation—even if communist in character—had been willing to join in Western-sponsored resolutions on minority rights which had as their target the repressive policy of the Ceausescu regime.

America's strong interest in having the minorities issue given special attention was evidenced by its selection of Ambassador Max Kampelman to once again head its delegation, even if the meeting was supposed to have a lesser, "experts" status. Other delegations were not led by such an experienced and high-profile diplomat. Kampelman, in his opening remarks, put his finger on the pressing new problems that threatened the Helsinki process: ". . . strong ethnic and national minority tensions cast a kind of evil spell . . . somewhat like a cloud interfering with the sun's rays as we look to the new dawn."[48]

The US Ambassador was forthright in denouncing anti-Semitism, discrimination against Gypsies, and other ethnic hatreds. But the single greatest concern in his speech was given over to warning against the "threatened disintegration" of Yugoslavia, which he called "particularly dangerous." This had been wrought, he believed, by nationalist tensions that were also endemic to other East European states. His partial solution for the Yugoslav problem was a new federal structure that would include greater autonomy for the republics. If a unified state still remained the ultimate US objective, his emphasis was that it should be achieved "through peaceful means, by negotiation."

With racism and national hatreds the principal target, Kampelman tried his hand at proffering solutions. One was "leadership," a thesis he had propounded well and effectively at Copenhagen. Governments, he reiterated at Geneva, must openly condemn "intolerance and discrimination and hatred" and "must actively promote, encourage and reward attitudes of tolerance."[49] At the same time, anti-discrimination laws "must be enacted and enforced." The themes were the guidelines of human rights agencies, a result of years of experience with which Kampelman was quite familiar.

It was when he ventured forth to offer solutions for nationalist contempt in multinational societies that he appeared to flounder. Here is the way he put the appropriate response:

> The United States is fully convinced that democracy and the principles of human liberty and freedom and the rule of law are fundamental if we are to act constructively in the face of these challenges.[50]

At the core of this perspective was the individual of a minority and his or her basic rights. A somewhat startling observation followed:

> Indeed, if all CSCE states were firmly established as democracies, ethnic and related concerns would be lessened considerably, if not essentially eliminated.

The fact is that the democracy of Havel's Czechoslovakia did not reduce the national hostility of the Slovaks, just as the democracy of Thomas Masaryk and Edward Beneš, his predecessors of an earlier era, had not diminished the national animosity of the Slovaks and especially the hatred of the Sudeten Germans. Indeed, democracy may very well have brought such hostilities to the surface. As for Yugoslavia, it was only when democracy started to make inroads in the structure of society that the drive for self-determination and secession deepened. Demands for independence in Slovenia and Croatia were an outgrowth of free elections to which the US was so strongly committed. And the nationalist intransigence of Slobodan Milosevic in Serbia was assisted by strong public support, as expressed in the elections of that republic.

Much too much may have been made by the United States about free elections prior to Copenhagen. It had almost been equated with democracy itself. At Copenhagen, far greater attention had been paid by Washington to pluralism and the rule of law. Yet, the one institutional apparatus dealing with human rights that had emerged at the Paris summit was an Office on Free Elections. Not until mid-June 1991, just a few weeks prior to Geneva, did Secretary of State Baker begin to speak preliminarily about replacing this office with an Office on Democratic Institutions.[51] The irony of what a free election might lead to was the subject of pertinent comment by a perceptive long-time observer of the scene, David Shipler.[52] His focus was Zviad Gamsakhurdia, President of the Soviet republic of Georgia.

Noting Gamsakhurdia's landslide victory for president in May 1991, Shipler pointed out that this earlier "fiery Georgian nationalist" had become the very embodiment of an authoritarian ruler. Once in office, he had imprisoned political opponents, silenced the press, and brutalized ethnic minorities. In Georgia, as in many places in Eastern Europe, elected rulers might very well turn out to be tyrants. It was Shipler's conclusion that "elections alone do not make democracy."

Equally troublesome, the focus on individual rights led to the virtual dismissal of group or collective rights. When Kampelman examined minority rights at Geneva, it was always in the context of the rights of an individual belonging to a minority, not of the rights of the group as a whole.[53] Later, he would reject the notion of group rights as almost antithetical to democracy.[54]

Part of the problem resulted from the legal difficulty of defining a minority in terms of a group in a precise and exact manner. A 1985 United Nations study did, however, offer a useful approach. After a survey of the history of the definitions of the minority problem before and after the establishment of the UN, the author concluded that an effective working definition would be the following:

> ...a group of citizens of a State, constituting a numerical minority and in a non-dominant position in that State, endowed with ethnic, religious or linguistic characteristics which differ from those of the majority of the population, *having a sense of solidarity with one another, motivated, if only implicitly, by a collective will to survive* and whose aim is to achieve equality with the majority in fact and in law.[55] [Emphasis added.]

A "collective will to survive" strongly suggests a consciousness that applies to the group that, indeed, transcends the consciousness of the individual that belongs to the group. The individual may seek to have all the characteristics of the group—ethnic, linguistic or religious—disappear. In contrast, suggests the author, the group, as a whole, has a collective will to survive. Thus, groups would seek all the educational and communal-institutional means for maintaining survival.

The International Covenant on Civil and Political Rights adopted in 1966, in Article 27, would appear to have given a certain recognition to collective rights, even if on balance, its emphasis is upon the individual:

> In those states in which ethnic, religious or linguistic minorities exist, *persons* belonging to such minorities shall not be denied the right, *in community with other members of their group*, to enjoy their own culture, to profess and practice their own religion, or to use their own language.[56] [Emphasis added.]

Implied here is a right enjoyed by a "community."

A 1991 report by the UN Commission on Human Rights, reflecting the views of its members, accepted both individual and collective rights. In the view of some, the author emphasized, "The groups as such must be protected in order to accomplish the effective protection of their individual members."[57] This perspective inverts the traditional relationship between the individual and the group: the individual can be meaningfully protected only if the group as group is. The language of Article 27 of the Covenant on Civil and Political Rights—"in community with other members of their group"—is seen as a "bridge" between individual and collective rights.

Rejection of collective rights affected the thinking of the United States and the West in dealing with the various multinational societies in Eastern Europe. One serious reflection of this perspective was a lack of responsiveness to the demand for self-determination by a national group or national minority. This was apparent from the very origins of CSCE. The preparatory work of the Final Act showed that many of the participating states "feared that an unqualified proclamation of the right of self-determination might kindle separatist aspirations to the detriment of national unity."[58] In consequence, the participating states avoided any linkage between national minorities and the right of self-determination. Only "peoples"—an undefined term—were given the privilege of enjoying this right.

If, then, the US perspective on the nationality issue was limited, on the related question of racism, however, the Kampelman view could not be challenged. His staff followed his leadership and, in several speeches, pushed vigorously for government activism. In the end, they were disappointed with the unwillingness of most delegations to give the subject careful consideration as part of the review process.[59] On July 4,

Ambassador Samuel Wise discussed the positive steps taken in Bulgaria with respect to the aggrieved Turkish minority.[60] On Romania, he was critical of the leading nationalist publication, *Romania Mare*, and the group Vatra Romaneasca, both of which peddled bigotry with impunity against Jews, Gypsies, and Hungarians. He also briefly surveyed anti-Semitism in the USSR, anti-Gypsy attitudes in Hungary and anti-Albanian repression by the Serbs in Yugoslavia's Kosovo province.

Five days later, on July 9, Wise turned specifically to the subject of anti-Semitism, attacking the rehabilitation by Romania's parliament of Marshal Antonescu, who had "supervised anti-Jewish pogroms and massacres."[61] Sharply attacked, too, were the non-official anti-Semitic groups and publications in the USSR, as well as the official Ministry of Defense organ, *Military-Historical Journal*, which had published sections of Hitler's *Mein Kampf* in 1990 and was scheduled to print the infamous *Protocols of the Elders of Zion* in 1991. Wise observed: "The Soviet leadership somehow appears reluctant to condemn anti-Semitism unequivocally and publicly."

Another US staff member, David Evans, on July 12 gave special and lengthy attention to the Gypsy problem in Europe where, in a number of CSCE countries, "prejudice has taken a violent turn."[62] He noted a recent opinion survey by Freedom House in Czechoslovakia, Poland and Hungary, which showed that nearly 80 percent of the respondents admitted that they "would prefer not to have any Roma move into their neighborhoods." He also cited examples of anti-Gypsy discrimination and violence in Bulgaria and Romania. Evans contended that the stereotyping of Gypsies as criminal elements "threatens to undermine the basic concept of law enforcement." It was the task of governmental leadership, he said, to provide a "bold and consistent demonstration" of beliefs and acts against anti-Gypsy hate-mongering and violence.

Kampelman, in closing remarks on July 19, took particular pride in the initiative of the US delegation to have "the distasteful and shameful issues of discrimination and prejudice against Roma and Jews taken out of the dark closet of silence and into the daylight of recognition so that they can receive constructive attention by all of our states."[63]

The document which emerged from the Geneva meeting addressed the problem of hate in a stronger way than had the classic work of Copenhagen.[64] The Geneva document expressed deep concern about "the proliferation of acts of racial, ethnic and religious hatred, [and] anti-Semitism. . . ." Significant was the term "proliferation." It had not appeared earlier in the Copenhagen document. The intent, clearly, was to emphasize the spreading and growing nature of hate.

As at Copenhagen, the Geneva participants placed initial emphasis on public condemnation of hate or anti-Semitism by the state authorities. The signatories "stress their determination to condemn on a continuing basis such acts [of hate] against anyone." The new and key word here is "stress." It implied a particularly strong commitment. And the newly added phrase "on a continuing basis" gave public indication that the condemnation of hate should not be a one-shot affair, but rather required continued moral denunciation until the problem is resolved.

To a somewhat greater degree than at Copenhagen, the Geneva participants appeared to agree on a greater variety of measures to combat hate. For example, after condemning racism and anti-Semitism, the participants promised to "take effective measures to promote tolerance, understanding, equality and good relations between individuals of different origins within their country." The emphasis here was on the positive rather than merely on condemnation. The promotion of tolerance and understanding implies a variety of educational means for countering or rejecting negative stereotypes.

Violence and incitement to violence were central concerns of the Geneva document, just as they had been in Copenhagen. Law was seen as the principal means for dealing with these matters. The participating states were called on to "take effective measures including the adoption . . . of laws that would prohibit acts that constitute incitement to violence based on national, racial, ethnic or religious . . . hatred, including anti-Semitism. . . ." As earlier, the US civil libertarian theme of the protection of free speech was clearly understood or accepted. Only acts or incitement to acts are to be punished. Washington continued to jealously guard the First Amendment at the Helsinki talks. Indeed, the Geneva document made emphatic that the adoption of laws to deal with hate must be in conformity with a country's constitutional law.

In another important respect, the Geneva document's comments on the use of the law constituted a certain, if modest, advance over Copenhagen. Effective measures for dealing with violence or incitement of violence must also include, according to the Geneva document, "policies to enforce . . . laws" that prohibit these evils. The language specifying the enforcement of laws was not used in Copenhagen. All too often, even when effective statutory laws obtained in a given country, the practice of the authorities to wink at legal transgressions in essence nullified the law. Thus, as previously noted, the article in the Russian Criminal Code which made the stirring up of ethnic hatred or enmity a crime—Article 74—was, until 1990, observed in the breach. And, when finally applied, it was carefully circumscribed.

The Geneva document also added a significant step deliberately designed "to heighten public awareness of prejudice and hatred" as well as "to improve enforcement of laws against hate-related crime." Participating states committed themselves "to collect, publish on a regular basis and make available to the public, data about crimes on their respective territories that are based on prejudices as to race, ethnic identity or religion. . . ." This imaginative concept, based on an American proposal and drawing on US experience in large urban areas, could contribute to the enlightenment of the citizenry as to the seriousness of the problem of hate.[65] If Copenhagen did not address itself to the raising of public awareness of the dangerous consequences of racism, Geneva certainly did.

While the United States had offered substantive suggestions with respect to racism and hate which then found expression in decisions taken by the participating states in the concluding document of Geneva, far greater confusion reigned regarding the issue of inter-ethnic disputes. It was a priority objective of the US to create CSCE machinery for resolving inter-ethnic disputes, but a variety of obstacles intervened, requiring its postponement.

The American purpose was to build upon the human dimension mechanism already approved at Vienna and extend it to national minority problems, as well as to inter-ethnic disputes. Kampelman, a veteran and expert negotiator, suggested that a "good offices" device could be useful for facilitating dialogue and resolving differences among interested and affected parties. The US proposed at Geneva that a resource list of experts be established from which a three-person panel would be chosen.[66] The panel's function would be to observe, collect relevant information, and make its "good offices" available to all concerned.

Switzerland and Austria also advanced proposals for the use of such panels. But these proposals differed considerably one from another concerning modalities on how the group would be established, how its members would be selected, and the limits of its mandate.[67] Significantly, the Soviet Union supported the US proposal, and its delegate in Geneva indicated that Moscow was prepared to accept CSCE good offices in inter-ethnic disputes in the Caucasus.[68] But the French posed strong objections, arguing that adoption of any type of new machinery by CSCE must be decided at the ministerial level, not by an experts meeting.[69]

Since the US proposal commanded wide support and was especially relevant, the opposition of the French made for more than disappointment.

Kampelman suggested US irritation when, in his speech on the last day, he said:

> We regrettably did not fulfill our task to forge a procedure which will permit CSCE to implement the plans and hopes we have set forth in words. We intend to do so in Moscow at our September meeting. Our delegation intends to introduce its good offices proposal which was so well received here.[70]

The Geneva document took account of the commitment and the strong support the idea had received. The participating states, it read, "recommend that the Third Meeting of the Conference on the Human Dimension of the CSCE consider expanding the Human Dimension Mechanism." It was to function in respect of both the protection of the rights of individuals as well as "rights of persons belonging to national minorities."

Adoption of the Geneva document as a whole was not easily achieved. Sharp differences of opinion surfaced over the definition of the phrase "national minority" (e.g., France made it clear that Corsicans or Bretons did not fall into that category) and over "group rights" (as distinct from individual rights).[71] Inter-related with this conflict was the issue of how far government must go to protect a group's ethnic identity. The US was in the forefront of those opposing group rights, while Hungary steadfastly advocated such rights, a response to the problems facing Hungarian minorities in Romania, Czechoslovakia and Yugoslavia.[72]

The Swiss coordinator, Jean Pierre Ritter, sought to incorporate a variety of contradictory proposals, but his draft was quickly riddled with amendments and counter-amendments.[73] Confusion followed, which the US delegation feared might lead to a document which jeopardized the precise and significant commitments adopted at Copenhagen and for which the United States had assumed the principal responsibility. As a result, the US delegation supported an initiative of NATO states to draft a compromise document based upon an American draft. The new text, shorn of much substance on minority issues other than that related to racism, was ultimately accepted.

If Copenhagen was safeguarded, stress was placed on reviewing implementation, which had remained always a constant theme of Washington with reference to the Helsinki process. In one respect, Geneva offered a major breakthrough in the process:

> Issues concerning national minorities, as well as compliance with international obligations and commitments concerning the rights of persons belonging to them, are matters of legitimate international concern and consequently do not constitute exclusively an internal affair of the respective State.[74]

This was the first time in a Helsinki document that human rights, or more specifically, a certain type of human rights—minority rights—were declared to be a "legitimate international concern." Clearly implied was that intervention by outside powers was justified, for minority rights were no longer "exclusively an internal affair." The Moscow meeting would build on this foundation.

Aside from this radical formulation, there was little to which the US could point as warranting further lengthy concluding documents at future Helsinki meetings, as was the case at Copenhagen or at the Paris summit. A Helsinki Commission report commenting on the new trend in the Helsinki process concluded that "in rhetorical terms, the improvements in CSCE implementation have shifted the focus back to words over deeds."[75] Instead of "energy and interest" being devoted to "implementation review exercise," meetings have come to focus excessively on proposals, negotiations and documents.

But concern about excessive verbiage was secondary to Kampelman's concern with self-determination as it unfolded in intense national drives for independence. Yugoslavia and, to a lesser extent, the Soviet Union were very much in delegates' minds at Geneva. What Kampelman saw in both was a destabilizing process which he felt ran counter to Helsinki. At the very end of his concluding speech at Geneva, he embarked on an exploratory intellectual effort to distinguish between "self-determination" and "secession":

> ... the right of self-determination does not include within it the right of secession for minority groups. ... They are separate issues. The framers of the concept within the Helsinki Final Act had no intent of legitimizing actions which could lead to the destabilization of Europe. Indeed, the Helsinki Final Act emphasized the stability that comes from respect of existing boundaries.[76]

The argument had a certain artificial quality. What did self-determination mean if not the right to secede and form a separate state? True, self-determination, if carried to its logical conclusion, could be destabilizing and contrary to the Helsinki principle of maintaining established borders. But re-defining the term could hardly help. What Kampelman desired, as his speech made clear, was the need for dialogue and negotiation. If self-determination leads to secession, at least it ought to be done through dialogue and not civil war. What is needed, he said, is "rational discourse and the constructive, cooperative search for solutions." But the world of Eastern Europe was not conforming to rationalistic purposes. Nationalist striving was moving in the direction of explosive violence.

Kampelman was not alone in seeking a rational and prudential solution. Two days after he spoke, the prominent international lawyer Lloyd Cutler wrote an article for *The Washington Post* which recognized that "the world seems to be moving in . . . [the] direction" of accepting "unilateral secession from a federation" as a right.[77] At the same time, he emphasized that while the United Nations had accorded recognition to self-determination, it "has never supported a secession movement." Recalling the secession effort of Biafra from Nigeria in the late 1960s, Cutler quoted Secretary-General U Thant as saying "the United Nations has never accepted and does not accept the principle of a secession of a part of a member state."

Cutler approached the problem in prudential terms. Granted that secession is a right, it still should not be applied except through a peaceful solution. In that respect, he welcomed Gorbachev's view on the Baltics that a transition period of five years should be required before the option of secession is pursued. Given the growing civil war in Yugoslavia, he thought that the United Nations or the European Community should hold that civil war was "a threat to world peace." This would lead, he said, to ordering a cease-fire, followed by application of a mediating role for the UN.

Supposing, however, that despite cease-fire declarations—in Yugoslavia more than a dozen had been announced—and despite repeated mediation offers, the violence continued and even worsened; what then? Rational discourse had given way to impulses which had an emotional, non-rational basis. These elements were at the very core of an unbound nationalism. Even if immediately or eventually nationalism proved destructive, it was of little concern for those who were seized by it. President Bush, at the end of July 1991, chose to address the Ukrainian parliament in Kiev and warn against "suicidal nationalism."[78] The warning met with no sympathetic response.

If Yugoslavia seemed totally incapable of resolving internal nationalist tensions through creation of a fairly loose but still unified confederation, President Gorbachev, with the active support of Russian President Yeltsin, was making considerable headway along precisely those lines in the Soviet Union. A conference of the heads of nine republics (minus Moldavia, Georgia, and Armenia and the three Baltic republics) had reached agreement in April under Gorbachev's leadership on a new constitutional structure, a loose confederation with broad autonomous powers inhering in the republics. Details were to be approved and the new structure ratified at a meeting on August 20.

A powerful coalition of conservative forces from the top leadership of the Army, the KGB, the party apparatus, and the military-industrial bureaucracy struck the day before the scheduled formal sanction of the new constitutional system. Conspirators arranged for Gorbachev's detention in his Crimean vacation home. Power was seized in Moscow by the *nomenklatura* chieftains—an eight-member body awkwardly called the State Committee for the State of Emergency—who issued an appeal that focused heavily upon what they feared would be "dismembering the Soviet Union" and its very "liquidation."[79] At the heart of the State Committee's appeal was a Russian nationalist theme calling for the preservation of the Soviet Union as a great power. The conspirators sought the stability and security of the traditional Union of Soviet Socialist Republics.

Two other themes characterized the appeal—the economic failures of perestroika and the social demoralization of Soviet society. But it was the great-power focus that was dominant. While largely oriented to rejecting the various republic demands for authority vis-à-vis the center, the perspective of the coup leaders reflected the anger of Russian nationalists—including important sectors of the military—that the former Soviet authority over Eastern Europe had been lost by Gorbachev's policies.

The coup had been in the making for some time. Shevardnadze had angrily warned that "dictatorship is coming" at a Supreme Soviet meeting as early as December 1990, when he suddenly announced his resignation.[80] The principal organ of the anti-perestroika forces, *Sovetskaia Rossiia*, called on December 22 for a state of emergency to stem the tide of "disintegration" engulfing the Soviet state.[81] On January 10, 1991, the organ of the chauvinist and anti-Semitic Russian Writers Union advocated military intervention to ensure "national salvation."[82]

By the summer of 1991, rightist and nationalist signaling became more shrill. In May a particularly strong Russian nationalist and rightist publication, *Den*, carried a roundtable discussion among four top military officials with the journal's chief editor, Aleksandr Prokhanov, which clearly hinted at the inevitability of a military dictatorship.[83] On June 17, Prime Minister Valentin Pavlov, a spokesman of the military-industrial clique (and later one of the putschists), asked the Supreme Soviet to grant him emergency powers to deal with the disintegrating economy. It obviously was intended as a political maneuver to undercut Gorbachev's authority.[84] Strikingly, and not accidentally, Minister of Defense Dmitri Yazov, KGB head Vladimir Kryuchkov, and Interior Minister Boriss Pugo backed the Pavlov proposal with considerable vigor. They were to be the principal leaders of the coup.

The climactic warning of the anti-perestroika threat came on July 23, with the publication of an extraordinary special appeal entitled "A Word to the People" in the flagship party organ of hard-line nationalists, *Sovetskaia Rossiia*.[85] Chauvinism of a most blatant type characterized the article. Holy Russia is "sinking into nonexistence" and facing "subjection to our all-powerful neighbors," it declared. The article said: "Our home is already burning to the ground, the bones of the people are being ground up and the backbone of Russia is broken in two." Even as the article condemned "frivolous and clumsy parliamentarians," it denounced the effort that would "divide the tormented body of the country into portions." What was urgently needed was a "national movement . . . to halt the catastrophic collapse of the state. . . ."

Of particular significance were the 12 signers of the article. All were prominent military personages and nationalist writers. Included were General Valentin Varennikov, Commander-in-Chief of the Army Ground Forces, and General Boris Gromov, the Deputy Minister of Internal Affairs. The challenge to Gorbachev could not have been more flagrant. At the end of the month, the head of the Liberal Democratic Party, Vladimir Zhironovsky, a right-wing favorite of the KGB, announced his support of the appeal and openly spoke of "a military coup" as "the last step to save the state."[86]

Yet, Gorbachev blindly neglected all the signals and warnings. Later, he acknowledged that he should have recognized the signs.[87] It may be that he was fearful about mobilizing resistance of the masses and, therefore, he had to continue to rely on the establishment forces—his chosen allies—who would later betray him. These establishment forces were, in fact, the glue that held together the communist regime. Gorbachev had never intended to abolish those forces and remove the glue. Rather, he had hoped, through glasnost and perestroika, to modernize them, end their irrational and corrupting features, and make them more efficient.[88] From the perspective of intellectual critics, however, the Soviet leader had grossly underestimated the democratic aspirations of the urban masses. Aleksandr Gelman, a leading dramatist, communicated this view and gave it considerable emphasis during a personal interview conducted at the time of the Helsinki meeting in Moscow.[89]

The coup of August 19 threatened to reverse glasnost, perestroika and democratization, and return the USSR to a totalitarian era. And if totalitarian rule were to return to Moscow with a determined military and nationalist dimension, might it not in time mean a reversal of the monumental achievements of the Helsinki process throughout East Europe? It was scarcely surprising that the governments which expressed at the time, and later, the greatest concern (as communicated to NATO) were Poland, Czechoslovakia and Hungary. Anxiety reigned, too, in Germany, which wondered what might be the coup's impact upon the hundreds of thousands of Soviet troops still in East Germany. The extraordinary CSCE progress since 1989, culminating in the Paris Charter, was suddenly being threatened.

As the Western democracies nervously awaited developments, they meticulously avoided recognizing the coup. Most were severe in their condemnation and spoke of suspending economic aid. Yeltsin dispatched Russian Foreign Minister Andrei Kozyrev to Paris on August 20 to lobby for international resistance to the coup.[90] Kozyrev won French agreement to accept a Russian government-in-exile he would head should the need arise. The Russian Foreign Minister was planning to travel from Paris to Washington and UN Headquarters when the coup ended.

The forces unleashed by Helsinki principles and Gorbachev's democratic reforms helped save the day, along with the ineptness of the putschists. In Moscow and Leningrad, broad segments of the population which had benefitted from democratization and glasnost solidly backed Boris Yeltsin's opposition to the coup. Tens of thousands of Muscovites gathered in the streets to protect the Yeltsin White House. They were supported by crucially placed younger officers in the military, who had been radicalized by glasnost and who refused to back the coup leaders.

Nonetheless, it would be an error to assume that the resistance was massive. Outside of the large-scale demonstrations and rallies in Moscow, in Leningrad and in a couple of other cities, a uniform passivity prevailed in the population. If that passivity disappointed the putschists, at the same time, it revealed that enthusiasm for the return of Gorbachev—the cry of the Yeltsin White House—was hardly overwhelming. The potential for a long-term democratic future in the Soviet Union was by no means a certainty. Nor was the potential for the very survival of the Union itself. What had held it together, in the absence of commonly recognized traditions and legitimacy, was the Communist Party ideology imposed and maintained by the party apparatus, the KGB and military leadership. But when this institutional cement of the regime was discredited and the keystone itself—the Communist Party—declared illegal, the entire structure would sag and give way to burgeoning, separatist nationalisms.

Yet, for the moment, the popular resistance in Moscow, unquestionably rooted in the new democratic thinking, won the day. On August 21, the coup suddenly collapsed. Gorbachev returned to Moscow (though with much of his power shorn), the putschists were arrested, and Yeltsin had become a national hero. Democracy was the winner, as was the Helsinki process.

▪18▪

Moscow: "Democracy's Season"

f locating the third and final meeting of the Conference on the Human Dimension in the Soviet capital had been consistently challenged ever since the initial proposal five years earlier, after the city's resistance to the rightist coup it seemed like a perfect choice. Moscow, after all, now represented what CSCE, especially following the Paris summit, was all about—the triumph of human rights over the forces of totalitarianism. August 19-21 became a turning point in the evolution of glasnost. What the conspirators succeeded in accomplishing, ironically, was the intensified acceleration of the very processes which they had been determined to halt—the dissolution of the Communist Party, the evisceration of the KGB, and the removal of the leadership of the armed forces. Aleksandr Yakovlev later commented that they should be awarded medals for achieving in days what would have taken the new democratic forces 15 years to realize.[1]

The events of August were also central to Western aims regarding a CSCE assemblage in Moscow. Had the coup succeeded, it would have meant a total Western boycott of the human dimension session in the Soviet capital. The European Community made that explicit in a public statement issued on August 20.[2] President Bush, in a press conference that day, unhesitatingly endorsed this perspective.[3] The reasoning was clear enough. The coup's purposes constituted the very negation of the Helsinki process, especially its new human rights and democratic provisions.

Everyone involved in the Helsinki process could breathe a sigh of relief on August 21, although critical questions remained open: who would represent the Soviet Union, and how would Yeltsin's newfound power find reflection in the proceedings? Rumors flew of a likely postponement of the Moscow conference; the United States and the West strongly pressed against any delay.[4] Tough personnel decisions on the Moscow delegation were finally consummated; the go-ahead decision was announced just days before the scheduled conference.

The Soviet delegation would be headed by two persons with equal authority, a rather unprecedented development at Helsinki meetings, but one reflecting the new power reality in Moscow. Selected as the Soviet Foreign Ministry representative was Yuri Deriabin, a competent Western-oriented functionary who had been for several years supervising the CSCE operation. The co-chairman, representing the powerful Yeltsin interests and the Russian Republic, was a stunning surprise—Sergei Kovalev. A long-time human rights advocate and Helsinki activist who had been a close associate of Andrei Sakharov, Kovalev had spent years in Soviet forced labor camps as a prisoner of conscience. A deputy to the Russian Supreme Soviet, he headed the legislative body's special human rights commission. His role at the Moscow meeting would prove somewhat unusual.

Kovalev's appointment was not the only remarkable Foreign Ministry phenomenon. How key officials responded to the coup would quickly affect their careers. The Foreign Minister, himself, Aleksandr Bessmertnykh, who had conveniently taken "sick" instead of joining the Yeltsin resistance, was replaced by the Soviet Ambassador to Czechoslovakia, Boris Pankin, who from Prague had publicly rejected the coup leaders. Six high-level Soviet ambassadors were soon afterward fired for hesitancy in rejecting the coup.[5] Two of them had played a prominent role in Helsinki affairs—Yuri Dubinin and Yuri Kashlev. The former had served in the Madrid follow-up meeting opposite Kampelman and later held ambassadorial posts in Washington and Paris. Kashlev had played a glasnost-reform type of role at CSCE meetings in Bern, Vienna and Paris (1989). Ending up in the critically important Warsaw post, he reportedly had removed Gorbachev's picture from his embassy walls soon after the coup. The conduct of the former Soviet Helsinki ambassadors highlighted their bureaucratic opportunism as well as the fragility of their commitment to the Helsinki process.

A cold autumn chill engulfed Moscow when the conference opened, and for several days delegates had to put up with intermittent rain, drizzle, blustery winds, and only the rare appearance of the sun. Yet, within the chamber where the sessions were held—the Hall of Columns in the House of Unions, near Red Square—the atmosphere was warm, intimate, almost embracing. Delegates from the West, from the neutrals and from the new democratic regimes in Eastern Europe identified with the historic popular resistance to the totalitarian aspirations of the coup leaders. For them the Hall of Columns, itself bathed in a glowing whiteness from some two dozen huge hanging chandeliers, appeared to symbolize the

Helsinki spirit. Only historians of the early Soviet period might have dampened the atmosphere of democratic exaltation by recalling that the brightly lit chamber had provided the setting for the infamous purge trials of the 1930s conducted by Andrei Vyshinsky.

President Gorbachev set the tone for the opening session of the Moscow meeting with a welcoming address that found in the Helsinki process a source of the collapse of the coup.[6] He greeted the delegates as "representatives of the international community which supported us at a critical junction, helped to stop reaction and *thus demonstrated in practice that the Helsinki Final Act and the Charter of Paris are more than just well written [documents]*" (emphasis added).

The Soviet President was of course referring to the reluctance of the West to accord early recognition to the coup leaders. His appreciation of the Western response was made explicit: "The coup failed . . . because the outside world condemned the putsch and supported our democracy, regarding it as part of the entire democratic world." For Gorbachev, the key Helsinki documents testified to a "new reality" of a "world sharing common human values" that stands "on the threshold of a new historical era."

More important than Western support for the success of the resistance movement, the President recognized, was the demonstration of the opposition by the masses of Muscovites to the putsch. If its leaders counted on the supposition that the "people's commitment to democracy had not yet solidified," Gorbachev went on, nonetheless, the circumstances clearly indicated that "the changes brought about by the democratization and glasnost have proved irreversible." Indeed, while "our democracy" was "still very immature," he said, perestroika had raised the level of public consciousness to a point where it recognized that it "confronted . . . a deadly peril."

Reflecting this new and democratic consciousness was the historic Declaration of Human Rights and Freedoms, adopted by the Congress of People's Deputies on September 5, which Gorbachev called the "moral and legal foundation of our union." In sharp contrast to the earlier ideological view, which stressed collective rights, the new document placed emphasis on individual dignity and freedom as "the supreme values of our society."

The Declaration displayed a remarkable degree of similarity to the Copenhagen document. In a private interview, Ambassador Kampelman recognized the parallels in language and thought.[7] Gorbachev chose not to specifically refer to the Copenhagen document, but rather to the Charter of Paris, which drew its inspiration and much of its language from the

Copenhagen document. For the Soviet President, the Helsinki process had helped lay the groundwork for a new consciousness among Soviet citizens.[8]

Opening speeches by various foreign ministers echoed the Gorbachev themes concerning the significance of the Moscow meeting and the special relationship between the Helsinki process and the defeat of the coup. Danish Foreign Minister Uffe Ellemann-Jensen said: "A momentous chapter in world history is being written these days; the victory of the people over subjugation and tyranny." After heaping a flow of encomiums on the "courageous peoples" who flocked to the side of Yeltsin, he proceeded to establish the connection with the Helsinki process:

> The actions of these men and not the least the thousands of anonymous people who—against all odds—took their fate in their own hands, were in fact an implementation by the people of our CSCE commitments.[9]

In the Dane's view, "what the world has witnessed during the latest weeks testified to the strength of the CSCE process and to the importance of the meeting of the Human Dimension." At the same time, he warned against "the sinister forces, which still want to turn the clock back to darker ages. . . ." British Foreign Secretary Douglas Hurd, rarely given to hyperbole, observed that the failure of the coup "showed how deeply the principles which the CSCE process embodies have taken root throughout Europe."[10] The massive street demonstrations in Moscow, he believed, validated this thesis: "The way in which people turned out onto the streets of Moscow so recently showed that these [CSCE] principles of freedom have indeed taken root."

Of all the speeches, none was more poetic and lyrical than Secretary of State Baker's.[11] Indeed, it reflected a literary quality which observers had not detected in him earlier. A strikingly evocative phrase, "Democracy's Season," was the title given the text. After noting that the people of the Soviet Union were "moving forward . . . vigorously," Baker observed: "For the peoples of this land, this is truly democracy's season. Here in Moscow, we breathe the warm wind of new-won freedoms. But we know that difficult winter months are ahead and spring is distant."

The conceptual theme here was to be found in the writing of Russia's greatest poet, Aleksandr Pushkin. The lyricist's favorite season, which ran throughout his poetry of nature, was autumn. Even when uncomfortably cold—as it was in September 1991—the Russian autumn could stir creativity and vitality. The difficulties would come later with winter, while spring was far away. Baker was referring to the great difficulties in expected food and oil distribution during the coming winter months. For the moment, however, the celebration of autumn was in order. He reminded his audience, both in and out of the meeting site, that what happened but a few weeks earlier was symbolic of CSCE:

> CSCE has no divisions of tanks. It has instead the moral authority that flows from [Paris Charter] principles. But as we saw on the streets of this city three weeks ago, at critical moments people armed with principles have overwhelmed tanks.

For Baker, the key principles of democratic processes, human rights and the rule of law were not only acted upon in the street, they became the basis of the Declaration on Human Rights and Freedoms which, he said, was "the first such declaration in the history of the Soviet Union." In his view, the Declaration's early adoption demonstrated how deeply the Paris Charter principles were understood by the Soviet public.

Still, the Secretary of State sought to discourage euphoria. "Noble words on parchment . . . do not a democracy make," he observed, with a nice turn of oratorical phrasing. It is the translation into practice of "fine intentions" and of powerful language that is decisive. For that reason, he demanded that the Moscow conference begin with "a thorough review of implementation." He urged that the strengthening of the human rights mechanism be given the highest priority.

Yet, even as Baker sought to set key goals for the Moscow meeting, he was determined that the past in all its ugliness and horror not be painted over. The statesman took as his theme here once again the lyricism of a poet, one of Russia's greatest modern writers—Anna Akhmatova. What she had depicted in an especially moving poem ("Poem Without a Hero") was "a century of upheaval and human tragedy." Akhmatova was brutally repressed by Stalin in the late 1940s. For the US Secretary of State, she was the symbol of courageous resistance to totalitarianism and of those who did not live to see democracy's season. Even the stoic Texan had to halt his reading for a split second so as to clear a dry and seemingly full throat:

> It came too late for the eleven Helsinki monitors who perished in Soviet prison camps, or in foreign exile. . . . It came too late as well for Sakharov, and for the three young men who gave their lives just last month defending the people's democratic principles against tanks.

It was a rare moment in the Helsinki process when human rights activism of the past could be summoned to bear witness for a more hopeful future.

One other foreign minister's speech, that of Boris Pankin, displayed a certain literary quality. It shone especially when he took cognizance of the doubts that had prevailed in the West about scheduling a human rights meeting for Moscow:

> The doubts about how sound was our choice of Moscow as the venue for the fi- nale of the all-European symphony on the theme of the human dimension in modern politics continued to haunt our offer to convene this meeting in the So- viet Union since the time when that offer was made five years ago, in November 1986.[12]

No other foreign minister dared publicly to recall the doubts and uncer- tainties. But Pankin could make the point in order to take special pride in how the special "finale" was performed:

> And we today have every reason to feel gratified that the holding of the meet- ing [in Moscow] at this junction of transition has justified our confidence in the powerful democratic potential of our people. . . .

Pankin cited Goethe to illustrate his point: "Only he who fights for life and freedom every day deserves them." And to document the Soviet commitment to Goethe's injunction, Pankin pointed to the co-chairman of the Soviet delegation, Kovalev, the "uncompromising" opponent of to- talitarianism. The latter, he said, exemplified the spirit of the thousands who took to the streets to defeat the threat of totalitarianism posed by the coup leaders.

In a moving section which followed, the Soviet Foreign Minister quickly ran down a list of dates and events which the world associated with Soviet totalitarianism and imperialism—Berlin 1953, Budapest 1956, and Prague 1968. If Moscow was to join the ranks of those who sponsored previous humanitarian conferences of CSCE, Pankin said, it "had to re- visit the experiences" of the listed dates and events. It was at these points "where people fearlessly confronted the tanks with their bare hands and unreserved commitment to ideas of democracy." After this remarkable salute by a high Soviet official to the resistance movement in Eastern Eu- rope, Pankin took note of how Russians had earned the right to hold a human rights meeting in Moscow. For they, too, "had to fight their own tanks, not foreign."

Mea culpas for what Moscow had perpetrated on the European body politic were not the only extraordinary feature of Pankin's address. He expressed regrets about current failings in Soviet law and administra- tion to catch up with Western standards. If he could take pride in the

Declaration of Human Rights and Freedoms of September 5 and of the package of human rights laws recently adopted to advance democracy, political pluralism and "a law-based state," he remained critical of various human rights shortcomings in the USSR. The new emigration law, he said, should be brought into force sooner than the stipulated January 1993 target date; individual humanitarian refusenik cases should be resolved; and limitations of the right to leave should be guided only by national security considerations.

Pankin further expressed agreement with "justifiable" criticism of Soviet prison and forced-labor conditions, and he promised amnesty for persons sentenced for political reasons. At the same time, he offered assurances that "reliable barriers" would be erected to guard against violations of the rights of the individual. New legislation and improved administrative practices will be aimed at introducing "common human and CSCE values and the very best of the vast experience that Europe, the United States and Canada have accumulated." It constituted an astonishing rejection of what Soviet governance had until now stood for and an even more astonishing commitment to abide by Western values and practices.

Pankin took note of recent impressive Soviet decisions to open itself up to international scrutiny in the human rights area. The USSR had recently adhered to the Optional Protocol of the International Covenant on Civil and Political Rights, permitting individuals to complain to UN human rights machinery about alleged rights violations. (The United States, along with several leading Western democracies, has thus far avoided ratifying the Optional Protocol.) The USSR also withdrew its reservations with respect to two important UN treaties—the Convention on the Elimination of All Forms of Racial Discrimination and the Convention Against Torture and Other Cruel, Inhuman or Degrading Treatment or Punishment. With these actions, said Pankin, "we have unconditionally recognized the entire system of universal control mechanisms in the sphere of human rights in our territory."

But, said the Foreign Minister, it is time to "proceed further" and to introduce in the humanitarian field an elaborate *intrusive* system of "inspections and checks" that Helsinki had already set in motion in the military sphere. Taking note of the fact that national minorities issues have become "urgent items on the international agenda" and that "interethnic conflicts" have escalated, he posed the question: "What is it that we in the Soviet Union expect the Moscow humanitarian forum mostly to achieve?" The answer was to be found in the lessons obtained at the

Vienna, Paris and Copenhagen meetings. While agreement on "correct principles" are important, far more consequential are reliable guarantees for their practical implementation.

Unveiled at this point was Pankin's central and startling thesis. The guarantees for effective compliance must rest upon "international footing" and, therefore, "no matter how important non-interference in internal matters is, the supremacy of human rights and fundamental freedoms must be made absolutely indisputable." This was a complete reversal of Moscow's previous position. As recently as three months earlier, Moscow had been expressing concern that the European Community was moving toward interference in Yugoslavia's inter-ethnic dispute.[13] This attitude had fundamentally shifted. Pankin's formulation of the right of interference would probably not even have been acceptable to most Western countries.

How "the supremacy of human rights" was to be achieved was not made clear other than to reject explicitly the standard argument that "non-interference in internal affairs" must be viewed as preeminent. Pankin did offer two suggestions: 1) improve the CSCE human dimension mechanism; and 2) transform the Human Dimension Conference, which was reaching a culmination in Moscow, into "a permanent structure of the Helsinki process."

The openness of the Moscow session was reflected in the very first plenary session after the formal speeches were completed. The United Kingdom delegate, for example, posed sharp questions to Bulgaria for its refusal to allow an ethnic Turkish group to register as a political party.[14] He then turned to inter-ethnic problems in the USSR, challenging the "punitive actions" taken by the Soviet army and Azerbaijani forces in the Nagorno-Karabakh region, and the brutal treatment of the Ossetian minority in Soviet Georgia by President Gamsakhurdia. Soon a dozen countries joined in the discussion, raising one or another human rights problem. The session had assumed a distinctly spontaneous character, which was confirmed the next day at a staff meeting of the US delegation.[15] Ambassador Kampelman told the group that, at the NATO caucus on the morning of the previous day, not one country had indicated that it planned to take the floor. The spontaneity of the first review meeting and the willingness to raise human rights issues, in his view, showed CSCE at its very best.

A similar openness applied to the non-governmental community. Fears in the West that NGOs would have limited access proved to be totally unwarranted. Various interest groups circulated their individual criticisms through the Secretariat. Thus, a group representing the Greek community in Albania complained of anti-Greek repression there. A paper by an Ossetian group delineated the plight of this ethnic group in the Caucasus. Helsinki Watch distributed highly informed and well-researched studies on a number of human rights issues. Some dealt with ethnic minorities: Turks, Macedonians, and Gypsies in Bulgaria; Hungarians and Gypsies in Romania; Kurds in Turkey; and Albanians in Yugoslavia. One dealt with the use of excessive force by Soviet troops in Kazakhstan, Lithuania, Latvia, Tajikistan, Uzbekistan, Azerbaijan, and Georgia. Another spelled out the plight of a dozen ethnic groups that had been singled out by Stalin for special punishment.

The long-standing problem of refuseniks and the Jewish emigration issue continued to attract attention even though Moscow had been permitting vast numbers of Jews to leave since 1990. The remaining obstacles—sections in the new emigration law and in its administration regarding alleged state secrets, draft service in the army, and supposed financial obligations—were held to be irrational and unnecessary even as they continued to generate a limited number of refuseniks. The World Conference on Soviet Jewry circulated a paper on the subject and the British delegation took the lead, especially on September 16, to spell out how "freedom of movement . . . as one of the most basic of human rights" was being abridged in the USSR.[16] The British view was supported by the Canadians, while US Ambassador Sam Wise made a special plea to the Soviets on October 2 to allow long-term refuseniks to emigrate.[17]

What was strikingly different about the Moscow meeting, as compared with previous Helsinki sessions, was the quick willingness of the Soviet delegation to agree with the criticism. Kovalev, the distinguished humanist and former activist now serving as a principal representative, acknowledged the validity of the charges on emigration, remaining political prisoners, and holdover psychiatric cases (which had been strongly raised by the World Psychiatric Association). He nowhere challenged the accusations but, rather, on the contrary agreed with them and assured the delegations that initiatives had already been undertaken or would be undertaken to resolve the problems.[18]

The central issues at Moscow were no longer those that had agitated Europe in the past, even if not all of them were resolved. There was now fundamental agreement upon and common understanding about which human rights and freedoms had to be assured. A fairly elaborate "constitutional" structure had been worked out at Copenhagen and given a formal stamp of authority in the Paris Charter for a New Europe. Not all the *i*'s had been dotted nor all the *t*'s crossed. Delegations noticed the absence of reference to women's rights or to the rights of the disabled, both attracting increasing attention in the West. There was also a burgeoning problem of the hostile treatment of migratory workers. Besides, civil libertarian lawyers could point to inadequate assurances of judicial redress and of guarantees against military coups. With the August 19-21 near-successful coup still very much on everyone's mind, the question of how to prevent such acts was certain to evoke concern.

Filling in the constitutional gaps and crevices preoccupied, to some extent, the US delegation. But far more important was the issue of a rising and, at times, explosive nationalism. It had been given preliminary attention in Geneva in July, but it was at Moscow that the problem was expected to be dealt with in some detail. And, in attending to the question, the critical point was the establishment of machinery for reducing tensions and either moderating conflict or ending it. "How to?" became the central question. Copenhagen certainly had elaborated on the rights of minorities. But it had not offered a mechanism for dealing with inter-ethnic problems. A related question could quickly surface insofar as Copenhagen had left open the question of "how to" with respect to assuring fulfillment of all other democratic rights. Could new machinery be created to serve multiple purposes?

One earlier problem required immediate attention, as circumstances had already provided a solution; only the formal CSCE sanction was required. The issue of the observer status for the Baltic states had been on the Helsinki agenda since the Copenhagen session. If it had been enveloped in a virtual silence as Moscow repeatedly and quickly cast an unchallenged veto, the reason had very much to do with US policy and, to some extent, with the policy of major West European states. Neither the United States nor the leading European powers had wanted to embarrass or weaken Gorbachev, whose "new thinking" had contributed so heavily to the "new world order."

Of course, policy makers understood clearly that the Baltic states were in a totally separate category from other self-determination issues. They had been independent since 1918, but were absorbed into the USSR in 1940 by virtue of an agreement with Nazi Germany. Even Moscow had recognized the legitimacy of their aspiration. Gorbachev, nonetheless, insisted that their formal secession and independence could be realized only through Soviet legal procedures which would entail a five-year minimum waiting period, procedures that would hardly satisfy the Balts. In the meantime, Soviet interior ministry troops in January 1991 took action in Vilnius and Riga designed to smash the independence drives.[19] It was apparent that right-wing forces in the military and the party were determined to prevent independence.

President Bush might publicly condemn the brutality of the military in the Baltic area and urge negotiations leading to independence, but the US still avoided calling for independence and refrained at Helsinki meetings from proposing observer or membership status for the three republics. At the same time, the US delegation, faced by a delicate public relations problem, treated the three Baltic foreign ministers, who regularly showed up at Helsinki meetings, with the utmost courtesy.[20] They would be formally greeted and briefed by the head of the US delegation. But sponsorship for formal Helsinki participation—which, of course, was the key aim of the Baltic republics—was always lacking.

If the Bush administration chose to avoid irritating or embarrassing Gorbachev, no such reluctance marked the approach of the Helsinki Commission. Its leaders, Senator DeConcini and Congressman Hoyer, were in the forefront of those clamoring for the United States to grant the Baltic states formal recognition and to sponsor their membership in CSCE.[21] The Baltic leaders were given public platforms for airing their views through Commission hearings.[22] Vigorously active Americans of Balt origin, with whom the Commission enjoyed warm relations, served as an additional force to press for a change in US policy.

The effect of the August coup ended the US policy dilemma. The rightist forces were severely discredited and humiliated. Gorbachev returned to Moscow in a very much weakened political condition. The ascendancy of Boris Yeltsin, who had publicly associated himself with the striving of the Balts for independence, meant that statehood for the three republics was a foregone conclusion. The new leadership in the KGB, the army and interior ministry, either chosen or approved by Yeltsin, pointed to an eventual withdrawal of Russian occupying forces. When German Foreign Minister Genscher announced that Berlin would shortly grant the Baltic republics formal recognition, the signal to Washington could not have been more clear. Recognition by the Bush administration came shortly afterward. Gorbachev acquiesced to the inevitable a little later.

At the Helsinki meeting in Moscow on September 10, the issue was no longer observer status; full membership was what the Baltic republics sought. German Foreign Minister Genscher proposed membership at the foreign ministers' opening session. No objection was raised. Indeed, Gorbachev, in his initial address, and Pankin later, welcomed the new members with some enthusiasm.[23]

The extremely warm reception granted by the Helsinki signatories to the Baltic foreign ministers, each of whom was given an opportunity to speak, was evidence of the decision's popularity. The address by the Lithuanian Foreign Minister, Algirdis Saudargas, was especially pertinent in placing the new status in the context of the Helsinki process. He called attention to the fact that the people of Lithuania had become "actively involved in the Helsinki process" almost from the beginning. The reference here was to "the members of the Helsinki Group in Lithuania" formed in 1976 following Yuri Orlov's establishment of the Helsinki Watch Committee in Moscow. Saudargas noted that the Helsinki group in Vilnius "went through many trials in defending the principles of the Helsinki process."[24] He added that the Helsinki tradition was "taken over" by the Lithuanian parliament, which had earlier that week adopted the Decalogue of the Helsinki Final Act and committed itself to adherence to all of the Helsinki documents.

Appropriately, the first official visitors to the newly established republics was a 13-member delegation from the US Helsinki Commission, strong supporters of their independence drive. Symbolic of the special relationship was a ceremony in front of KGB headquarters in Vilnius. Hoyer and DeConcini presented an American flag to Baylis Cajauskas, who had spent 37 years in Soviet prisons and was now placed in charge of dismantling the Lithuanian KGB.[25]

The broad enthusiasm which greeted the seating of Lithuania, Latvia, and Estonia at the Moscow meeting may have been a bit premature. The increase in the membership of CSCE from 35 to 38 made the body a little more unwieldy. But where does it stop? Was not a precedent established? Suppose a half-dozen or ten new Soviet republics were to seek to join CSCE. Would they all be admitted? And, if so, would this not change the character of CSCE? Kampelman had raised the problem at his private briefing of Helsinki Watch in New York on the eve of the Moscow meeting. Now, in Moscow, in this opening speech on September 16, he gave it a sharper focus:

> Could a CSCE consisting of 40 or 45 or more states avoid being different from a CSCE of 35 states? Would further additions produce a change of chemistry, a change of approach, a possible change of spirit and perhaps of dedication? We will have to think seriously about the implications of those possible challenges.[26]

Ukraine and Armenia had already applied for membership. Might not the other Soviet republics do so? And, if that happened, who would provide assurances about their human rights obligations? When the US

Helsinki Commission members arrived in Moscow just before the CSCE meeting, they were told by Russian Foreign Minister Andrei Kozyrev that all Soviet republics must be held responsible for human rights within their own respective territories.[27] Kozyrev speculated that what might be needed in the new Soviet Union to guarantee human rights in the various republics is an "internal CSCE."[28]

Symptomatic of the problem was the decision of the Lithuanian government to release prisoners sentenced by Soviet courts after World War II without regard as to whether the convicted had engaged in genocidal acts. The Simon Wiesenthal Center of Los Angeles documented at least a dozen cases in which the released prisoners had participated in the massacre of Jews in Lithuania.[29] The Helsinki Commission delegation in its visit to Vilnius raised the matter with President Vytautas Landsbergis, who promised that no proven war criminals would be rehabilitated.[30] But serious damage to recognized post-war judicial principles had already been done.

Kampelman, in his opening address at Moscow, pointed to other examples:[31] 1) in the presidential election campaign in Azerbaijan, only one candidate was on the ballot; 2) in Uzbekistan, repressive measures were taken against democratic forces; 3) in Byelorussia, repression was undertaken against political activists; 4) in Georgia, killings of Ossetians, along with restrictions on the local Georgian population, characterized the rule of President Gamsakhurdia (who had himself once been active in the Georgia Helsinki monitoring group, but whose public statements had increasingly taken on a maliciously racist tone); and 5) in the Nagorno-Karabakh region of Azerbaijan, continued violence and persecution were directed against Armenians.

A certain irony now crept into the Ambassador's comments. On the one hand, he took account of the dramatic democratic progress reported and commitments undertaken by Soviet representatives at the Moscow meeting. Thus, Kampelman joined in enthusiastically greeting "the extraordinary turn of history" which had ushered in the meeting. "This country and this city," he went on, "today symbolize the relentless drive to end human oppression and realize the strength and vitality and stubborn perseverance of democracy and human dignity." On the other hand, he wondered aloud about the ultimate consequences of self-determination in the USSR: "We know that the tradition of human rights does not have deep roots in a number of the republics."[32]

The US Ambassador expressed special concern about a central and, indeed, historic achievement of the Helsinki process—the right to emigrate:

"We wonder whether emigration policy will be national or will devolve down to the republic level." He then drove home his point with a crucial question: "Can we expect the republics to respect these and other principles and values of the Helsinki process?"[33] In his mind at the time was the "seriously growing problem of internal refugees and the discrimination they frequently suffer." How would the republics deal with them and how would they treat the 25 million Russians who reside in the non-Russian republics? Uncertainty and anxiety marked Kampelman's vision of the human rights future in a disintegrating Soviet Union.

The ramifications of Eastern Europe's volcanic nationalism had become apparent since the Copenhagen meeting, and had to some extent been addressed in Geneva. By the Moscow meeting, it seemed to be reaching a crescendo-like level. The contradictions in the crumbling of communism were widely apparent as Kampelman pointed them up: First, Europe "is today more open and democratic" with the result that "freedom and human rights have become universally accepted as indispensable for the achievement of security and stability." Second, however, the changes in Europe "have released or rekindled passions . . . that are destructive and threatening. . . ."[34]

Some of the nationalist passions had the indirect effect of triggering what Kampelman referred to as "prejudice" and "hatreds." He called attention to the "strong evidence of anti-Semitism and of intolerance against Gypsies."[35] In the Soviet Union, manipulation of anti-Jewish prejudices by the Communist Party had intensified during the recent period.[36] This became apparent following the collapse of the August coup. According to a well-informed report in London's *The Daily Telegraph* of August 31, 1991, fleeing party officials in Moscow and Leningrad sought to destroy papers indicating the existence of close links between the party and both extremist Russian nationalists and anti-Semitic groups. At Leningrad party headquarters in Smolny, representatives of the city prosecutor found numbered packets of anti-Semitic leaflets that had been used against non-Communist candidates with non-Russian names during the parliamentary elections in 1990.[37]

Especially troubling was the pre-coup relationship between the military leadership and extremist nationalist groups and publications. Thus the army arranged for the placing in military post libraries and reading rooms such well-known nationalist and rightist publications as *Nash sovremennik* [Our Contemporary] and *Molodaia gvardiia* [Young Guard].[38] Both frequently carried anti-Semitic articles. Disturbing, too, was the official Ministry of Defense publication, *Military-Historical Journal*, with a quarter-million readers, which had already published parts of *Mein Kampf* and planned to publish the *Protocols of the Elders of Zion.*[39]

The collapse of the coup diminished for the moment the immediate danger to Soviet Jews even as it greatly weakened the threat to democracy. Still, Soviet Jews remained deeply anxious. According to a high official of the US delegation, Kenneth Blackwell:

> In talking to many Jews in the Soviet Union, our delegation has sensed a substantial fear of the return of pogroms, as Jews here witnessed daily expressions of irrational hate, and opponents of reform have not hesitated to attempt to tar individuals, groups or programs by labeling them as Zionist, Jewish or pro-Jewish.[40]

Blackwell found that "the tragic legacy of anti-Semitism" had also surfaced in Romania, Poland, and elsewhere in the Helsinki participating states. In his view, the legacy emerged as a result of the removal of the "restraints on freedom of expression."

Kampelman had already spelled out in Copenhagen how authorities can cope with the problem of anti-Semitism by assuming a strong public leadership role in condemning expressions and acts of bigotry. It was a leadership role that Gorbachev had carefully avoided. Toward the end of the Moscow meeting, on October 2, the Soviet leader received Shoshana Cardin, Chairperson of the National Conference on Soviet Jewry and a public member of the US delegation, who pleaded with him to denounce anti-Semitism.[41] Gorbachev indicated that he did not regard the matter as a high priority. He was quoted as saying: "But, personally, I don't think it represents a disease that is deeply rooted in our society."[42] Moreover, he held that "it would be a mistake to single out one problem when we have so many here." Yet, the Soviet leader appeared to be giving thought as to how he might respond. He was profoundly aware that American Jewry was very much concerned with the problem. If he offered no strong commitments, he nonetheless appeared to suggest that he intended to take some positive stance.

What was especially encouraging was that Gorbachev voluntarily advised the Jewish leader that he was sending Aleksandr Yakovlev, once again a confidant of his following the collapse of the coup, to represent him at Babi Yar commemoration ceremonies on October 6 marking the fiftieth anniversary of the Nazi massacre of Jews.[43] It was the first time that the Kremlin accorded recognition to a supreme manifestation of anti-Semitism. Gorbachev certainly must have known that President Bush had gone out of his way on August 1, only two months earlier, to visit Babi Yar and pay his respects to the martyred victims of hate. The President's address had trumpeted the view that civilized society must combat anti-Semitism before it results in violence and ultimately carnage.[44]

Besides, the Helsinki process in Cracow during May had already established a link between preserving sites of extermination—of which Babi Yar was a particularly poignant example—and public education against bigotry. The Moscow conference concluding document, adopted on October 4, two days before the Babi Yar commemoration ceremonies, stipulated that the signatories "will implement their commitments" laid down at the Cracow symposium.[45] Specific emphasis in the Moscow document was given over to effective human rights education, which, it was argued, would contribute "to combating intolerance, religious, racial and ethnic prejudice and hatred, including . . . anti-Semitism."[46]

Clearly, the Helsinki process was instrumental in the struggle against anti-Jewish bigotry. The other specific target of prejudice delineated in the Helsinki process were Gypsies, or Roma. Several delegates at the Moscow meeting addressed the subject, none more forcefully than the US representatives. On September 27, Blackwell went into some detail, noting that in many CSCE states the Roma are stereotyped in the media or in public discussion as "deviant members" of society or as members of a "criminal class."[47] When individual Gypsies committed a crime, it had sparked mob violence against entire Gypsy villages. The US delegate called attention to this phenomenon occurring in the Soviet Union and Poland during the summer of 1991. Western press reports had recorded similar outbursts of anti-Roma violence in Spain, Germany, Hungary, and Austria.

The former communist countries were not the only societies dealing with group prejudices; xenophobia had also targeted migrants and refugees in the West.[48] Mob violence had been directed against Turks, North Africans, black Africans and Asians residing in Germany, France, and the United Kingdom. Germany, which had benefited most from the Helsinki purpose of "freer movement of peoples," now ironically led a new initiative to restrict the movement.

At the end of October, German Minister of Interior Wolfgang Schaeuble brought together in Berlin his counterparts in the European Community, Switzerland, Austria and 13 East European governments, including the Baltics and Ukraine, for two days of deliberations. Tougher border controls were adopted. Schaeuble rejected charges that the curbs ran counter to Helsinki purposes. He added, "We do want freedom of movement and travel in the future, but that cannot mean the right of residence for everybody."[49] The United Kingdom quickly joined in imposing a number of border restrictions.

More disturbing and dangerous were the direct manifestations of bursting nationalism. In the crazy-quilt pattern of national groups that characterizes much of Eastern Europe, fervid nationalism threatened the very stability of state authority, let alone border demarcations. The Czech and Slovak Federal Republic was a rather mild example of the pattern. The Slovaks, constituting one-third of the total population of a state artificially created in 1918 from ruins of the Austro-Hungarian Empire, suddenly began clamoring for greater autonomy, with the more radical elements demanding independence.[50] No violence, however, was threatened. The emotional nationalist drive of the Slovaks was fed by a post-communist economic discontent that was far greater in their part of the state.[51]

Still, independence was certain to generate other national problems to which the Slovaks would respond negatively. Among the 5 million Slovaks there lived more than one-half million Hungarians scarcely enamored of Slovak sovereignty. If Slovakia became independent, the Hungarians would want autonomy. Miroslav Kusy, Havel's representative in the Slovak capital of Bratislava, summarized the essentials of the problem:

> To draw boundaries along ethnic principles is practically impossible. To change the reality in one case is to provoke reactions on several sides.[52]

Yet, the problem of Czechoslovakia paled before that of Yugoslavia, another artificial post-World War I creation, but comprising a greater number of nationalities. The declarations of independence by the republics of Slovenia and Croatia in late June 1991 led to open and brutal civil war. It was the first armed conflict to manifest itself in continental Europe since the end of World War II.

With the dead and wounded already running into the thousands, and the dispossessed reaching into the hundreds of thousands, the civil war was the preeminent focus of all in attendance at the Moscow conference. Kampelman sensed it from the moment of his arrival, communicating the same to his staff at their first meeting.[53] In his opening plenary address, he reiterated his perception that violence in Yugoslavia "has already had a profoundly important impact on the CSCE process and on the deliberations here."[54]

There was little question in Kampelman's thinking as to who was primarily responsible—the Serbia of President Slobodan Milosevic—but the

US Ambassador masked it somewhat in his initial and very tough speech in Moscow on September 16:

> We cannot tolerate the archaic, narrow-minded violent nationalism in Yugoslavia to threaten the now rapidly evolving order. . . . The Yugoslavia experience serves as early warning sign that violence within our CSCE family is unacceptable and must not be permitted or condoned.[55]

The implied threat was followed by a strongly worded refrain:

> This meeting, I am confident, will express its determination to proceed forward into the 21st century and not return backward into the dark ages.

Despite Kampelman's strongly worded opinion, US policy on Yugoslavia was deliberately and consciously subordinated to the leadership exercised by the European Community. Beginning in September, prior to the Moscow meeting, the EC initiated a special peace conference on Yugoslavia, which was to be held at The Hague and chaired by Lord Peter Carrington, the former British Foreign Secretary who had been specially designated by the Community to function as mediator. It was the EC that threatened economic sanctions, considered and rejected the advisability of deploying peacekeeping units, and eventually turned to the UN for more decisive action. A key State Department official made clear in Congressional hearings that the United States had abdicated any policy leadership function on the Yugoslav crisis to the EC. Still, the Washington perspective, as outlined by Kampelman, was very consistent with that of the EC. Within CSCE, the US played a direct and active role in supporting EC's leadership function.

It was not only civil war in Yugoslavia that occupied Kampelman's mind. He was deeply concerned about the disintegration of the USSR, with all that might connote for American and European security interests. If he avoided mentioning civil war in that great land mass, it was not because he was not alert to the possibility of nuclear missiles and weaponry being utilized by several sides. He made it clear that he stood on the side of those opting for some central authority and the maintenance of a union, however loosely structured. With a rhetorical flourish, he advised the individual Soviet republics to reject independence and, instead, "contribute the vivid colors of their own cultures to a bright rainbow of colors stretching in a coordinated way across this vast land, lighting the skies."[56] The various nationalities of the USSR, he went on, can enjoy "a better future if they can free themselves from the shackles of ancient hates and narrow bigotry."

But Yugoslavia, not the USSR, posed the immediate threat and challenge to CSCE. As the violence continued to escalate during the Moscow meeting, Kampelman returned to the subject. On September 23, the tone had sharpened, reflecting the depth of his concern and that of the US.[57] The escalating violence was seen as so "profoundly serious" as to threaten "to undermine the essence" of what CSCE has accomplished since 1975. In his opening remarks, Kampelman went out of his way to stress that the US government had asked him "to express this afternoon" its anxiety about "the violence, chaos and sheer irresponsibility" that prevails in Yugoslavia.

Singled out for the primary responsibility was the leadership of the Serbian republic, together with the Yugoslav military, which had neglected to serve as the required "impartial guarantor" of the cease-fire. But even as Serbia received the brunt of the criticism, other nationalities were not immune. Kampelman decided to "also call on the authorities of Croatia and other republics to maintain and implement their duty to ensure the human rights of all citizens, including Serbs. . . ."[58]

Kampelman prescribed specific steps for a CSCE response: 1) call for immediate implementation of an unconditional cease-fire; 2) expansion of monitoring by the European Community; 3) condemnation of the use of force designed to change internal or external borders (making it clear that the CSCE will not accept any outcome based on the use of force); and 4) demand fulfillment by Yugoslavia and all its republics of CSCE human rights commitments, especially those pertaining "to the rights of persons belonging to minorities." (It will be noted that the formulation was *not* "rights of minorities" but rather rights of persons.)

Kampelman also took the occasion to denounce Georgian President Gamsakhurdia for repression of anti-government demonstrators and the arrest of political opponents, which "totally contravenes both the letter and spirit of the Helsinki Final Act." Deplored, too, was the violence used against the Ossetians.

The context within which Kampelman and ultimately CSCE dealt with the Yugoslav issue and similar problems in the USSR was as "ethnic disputes," with which Geneva had been seized. Such disputes, he said, "are reaching new levels of rhetoric, which feeds—on itself."[59] He saw them as being a "throwback to the history of 70 or 80 years ago." It was the eve of World War I that came into view as he contemplated the urgent problems of the moment.

At Geneva, the CSCE signatories had wrestled with the proposal of creating a special mechanism for dealing with national minority problems.

At Moscow, the new mechanism proposal was refined and shaped as a potential tool for resolving ethnic disputes. To some extent, the mechanism emerging from the CSCE debates was a product of Kampelman's creative thinking and personal experience as a negotiator in labor disputes.[60] Addressing his staff for the first time in the Soviet capital, he took note of and dismissed talk advanced in some quarters of an outside military solution to the Yugoslav problem.[61] Such a solution would do violence to the Helsinki process itself, based as it is on the notion of consensus. At the same time, he criticized West European proposals that exclusively focused on the device of rapporteurs and fact-finding. He indicated that the solution *at an early stage* of an ethnic dispute must be based on "mediation," an intrinsic respect for the views and interests of both parties. Mediation was precisely the path followed initially in US labor negotiations.[62] Kampelman asked his staff to develop his view into a full proposal.

On September 18, Ken Pitterle of the US delegation formally submitted the proposal.[63] He gave emphasis as to why mediation (or good-offices procedures) was preferable to mandatory fact finding by rapporteur-observers within the context of the Human Dimension Mechanism, which was the prevailing choice of the West Europeans. From the point of view of the US delegation, fact finding and observation were "judgmental." In a potential dispute with which CSCE would be seized, the likelihood is that sharp differences of opinion would quickly surface as to the facts themselves. Did the dispute begin with a shot fired by one side or a rock thrown by the other? Inevitably, the fact finder will tilt to one side, even if inadvertently. The result could well be judgments that disappoint or anger one or both sides. In any case, resolving the problem becomes more rather then less difficult.

In contrast, an impartial mediator would seek to encourage the parties themselves to address the issues voluntarily. Skilled mediators are trained and experienced to pursue this type of procedure. Moreover, mediation as a tool is strengthened to the extent that the parties to a dispute are aware that should good offices fail, the CSCE community is certain to take additional steps that have a judgmental and possibly interventionist character that would limit the independence of either one side or both sides in resolving the problem. Thus, mediation provides an added incentive for the parties themselves to deal meaningfully with the issue.

A compromise formally known as the "Moscow Mechanism" was worked out conjoining the Kampelman voluntarist thesis with an elaborate fact-finding procedure. It constituted the centerpiece of the document agreed to in the Soviet capital on October 3 and, indeed, was described in detail immediately after the document's introductory statements.[64] More importantly, the mechanism marked a historic departure for the Helsinki process as a whole.

Two preliminary points should be made for purposes of clarification. First, the Moscow Mechanism is an addition to the Human Dimension Mechanism established in the Vienna concluding document in January 1989. That statement was the initial and pioneering effort to create compliance machinery for the Helsinki process. Its character was restricted, modest, and largely voluntary. Minority-rights questions generally did not come within its purview, although at the Paris CHD meeting the Bulgarian expulsion of Turks was vigorously raised. Having achieved certain limited successes, the mechanism was now viewed as capable, after structural modification, of a major implementing role embracing cases of both individual human rights and minority-group rights.

Second, unlike the Vienna instrument, the Moscow Mechanism incorporates an independent institutional structure in the form of a resource list comprising up to three experts appointed by each participating state. Criteria for selection were specified in the Moscow document:[65] "The experts will be eminent persons, preferably experienced in the field of the human dimension, from whom an impartial performance of their functions may be expected." They would be appointed for a period of three to six years at the discretion of the appointing state. The resource list was to be kept in the new Helsinki institutional structure established by the Paris Charter.

A logical progression of steps distinguished the application of the mechanism.[66] In the first step, a state *voluntarily* invited a mission of up to three experts from the list to visit its territory and assist in resolving a pressing human dimension problem. The assumption was that the experts' assistance would be requested at an early stage, before the problem became intractable. The experts would have considerable flexibility in using their good offices to promote dialogue or otherwise mediate among interested parties.

The second step would come into play should a state be reluctant or hesitant to invite the mission of experts in order to deal with a burgeoning inter-ethnic or human rights problem. "Friendly persuasion" could then be introduced through efforts of other CSCE states, who would formally inquire of the reluctant state as to whether it would be willing to invite a mission of experts.

It was Kampelman's hope that either of these two steps would be taken by states facing difficult or threatening minority concerns. Confrontation could be avoided and the "emerging problem"—as he put it later—could be addressed "in a non-judgmental manner and in an atmosphere that is not tinged with an aura of condemnation."[67] However, if a state refuses to seek expert mediation and rejects "friendly persuasion," the new mechanism permits the setting in motion of a third step which carries a mandatory character. That step, it should be emphasized, can be taken only after the first two initiatives have been tried.

A concerned CSCE state, having the support of at least five other CSCE states, may request that a delegation of up to three rapporteurs from the resource list be sent on a fact-finding mission to a state considered to have a serious human dimension problem. The targeted state is obliged to accept the mission. And the mission is required to prepare a fact-finding report for the Committee of Senior Officials. That a minimum of six states must urge and support the purpose of the specific mission was thought to be essential in order to discourage any frivolous use of the mandatory step. Moreover, given the genuinely revolutionary feature of this step in a Helsinki context, support by a sizable group of states was viewed as indispensable to justify intervention.

An alternative mandatory step can be invoked in exceptional cases. If a particularly serious and threatening human dimension problem exists within one state, another concerned state, with the support of nine other CSCE states, can invoke the mechanism without utilizing or exhausting the preliminary and voluntary first two steps. This alternative was held to be appropriate in circumstances where the situation was sufficiently desperate and critical as to justify bypassing the first two stages.

Sharp opposition to the emergency intrusive step arose from the United Kingdom delegation, motivated, obviously, by concern about its possible utilization in the event religious tensions in Northern Ireland were to reach serious levels of violence. This could have resulted in a British veto of the entire mechanism. Not until the last week of the meeting did the British acquiesce, apparently on the basis of instructions from London. Policy makers must have realized that Britain, as other CSCE states, could exercise under the mechanism's provision such sovereign rights as the rejection of a particular rapporteur. Besides, it would have appeared unseemly to continue to register opposition in the face of an otherwise unified European Community stance. The United States did not have to provide any special coaxing.

Both mandatory steps were designed, in Kampelman's phrase, "to mobilize the moral force of Europe in support of human rights. . . ." But he and his colleagues also assumed that the very intrusive character of the mandatory steps served as a powerful incentive to encourage states to use, at a very early stage in a dispute, the voluntary aspect of the mechanism. The Americans were careful to avoid claims about the certain or likely success of mediation. They were keenly aware of how intractable inter-ethnic problems could be. But by supporting tough mandatory steps, they hoped to stimulate use of good offices and mediation and to have a fallback position in the event of failure of the first two steps.

The Moscow Mechanism, in its mandatory provision, constituted a revolutionary departure in the Helsinki process. Intrusiveness and intervention by outside factors—rapporteurs from a resource list engaged in fact finding and rendering judgments—were unashamedly introduced and accepted by all the CSCE powers. Matters falling within the human dimension context of Helsinki were no longer to be considered by any European as purely domestic concerns immune from international intervention. The Moscow concluding document, in a revolutionary preambular paragraph to a description of the mechanism, baldly repudiated earlier arguments that had emanated from Moscow and its allies:

> The participating States emphasize that issues relating to human rights, fundamental rights, democracy and the rule of law are of international concern, as respect for these rights and freedoms constitutes one of the foundations of the international order. *They categorically and irrevocably declare* that the commitments undertaken in the field of the human dimension of the CSCE are matters of direct and legitimate concern to all participating States and *do not belong exclusively to the internal affairs of the state concerned.*[68] [Emphasis added.]

For the first time in CSCE history, the Helsinki process was equipped with the tough political means to apply its resources directly to resolving a human rights problem within a member state. Kampelman, in his closing plenary speech on October 4, declared:

> We have agreed to unshackle CSCE from the argument that somehow the principle of "non-intervention in internal affairs" prevents us from effectively meeting challenges to the CSCE process that arises from violence being done to our shared values.[69]

The radical transformation of the Helsinki process could not, of course, have occurred without a basic change in the Soviet Union's attitude. Even as late as June, the USSR was vigorously objecting to proposals advanced by various Western states for some form of intervention in the Yugoslav crisis.[70] Earlier in the year, the Soviets had killed an Austrian proposal for a special Helsinki "emergency" meeting to deal with the Soviet military actions in Lithuania.

Moscow's new perspective was disclosed the day before the opening session. On September 9, Soviet Deputy Foreign Minister Vladimir Petrovsky, in a meeting with a delegation from the US Helsinki Commission headed by Chairman Steny Hoyer, declared—as reported the next day in the *Financial Times* of London—that "the Soviet Union no longer considers foreign concern over human rights issues to be interference in its domestic affairs." Congressman Hoyer hailed Petrovsky's declaration as evidence of the "radical change [occurring] in this country. . . . If our delegation had heard no other assertion, that alone would have made our visit a success."[71]

A second factor also played a role in triggering the fundamental change in the Helsinki process. The onward rush of unbridled nationalism in Eastern Europe, especially in Yugoslavia, called into question the very stability of the new Europe that the Charter of Paris had envisioned. That challenge had to be met. Kampelman, in his final speech, emphasized that "the framers of the Final Act clearly did not intend to legitimize actions which could lead to the destabilization of Europe."[72] On the contrary, CSCE perceived existing boundaries as essential to stability, although it accepted and, indeed, envisaged future border changes, *but only* when accomplished peacefully and consummated with the agreement of all parties concerned.

But whether the new mechanism was immediately applicable to the Yugoslavia situation or to inter-ethnic problems in other multinational societies was open to question. Had it been in existence and applied at a very early stage in the inter-ethnic conflict, it is conceivable that the mechanism might have been helpful in placing the resources of CSCE members' skills—and moral authority—at the disposal of a conflict-resolution effort. Now, with nationalist tensions exacerbated and violence a way of life, the mechanism's applicability and efficacy seemed limited. Perhaps over the long run and in other cases, it could be effectively utilized. Certainly, the mechanism could be highly relevant in dealing with standard minority issues, with anti-Semitism or discrimination against Gypsies, or with violence against refugees and migrants.

In addition to establishing the complex human dimension mechanism, the Moscow conference agreed to take an important step with respect to broadening that one aspect of Helsinki's new institutional structure that deals with human rights. The Office for Free Elections was assigned at the Paris summit the very limited function of providing information, guidelines, and monitoring help. But Secretary of State Baker, at an Aspen Institute meeting in Berlin in June, gave a very high priority to the concept of broadening the scope and function of the Office of Free Elections. He wanted it to assume responsibility for helping strengthen democratic institutions in general.

At Moscow, Baker again referred to the subject, but left it to Kampelman to persuade his Helsinki colleagues to adopt the proposal. The assignment was fulfilled. The concluding document called upon the Council of Foreign Ministers or the Committee of Senior Officials "to consider expanding the functions of the Office for Free Elections to enable it to assist in strengthening democratic institutions within the participating States."[73] (Eventually, the Council, at its January 1992 meeting in Prague, rechristened it the Office for Democratic Institutions and Human Rights.)

Baker must have assumed that the Office could become a more free-wheeling technical operation to respond to the lack of democratic experience in Eastern Europe and in the vast Soviet landmass. While precision in describing the concept was missing, the US Secretary of State nonetheless thought that the adoption of the proposal warranted his warmest commendation to Kampelman. This was communicated in a private letter dated October 12 to the latter.[74] Several days later, a top State Department official told Kampelman that in the "uphill battle" for achieving approval of the Baker proposal, "Mr. CSCE" had distinguished himself.[75] The Secretary of State was said to have been "pleased with your deft handling" of the issue, which was expected to transform the "Office of Free Elections into the Office for Democratic Institutions."

The Moscow concluding document was much more than a description of how the mechanism was supposed to function or a recommendation for extending the Office for Free Elections. It built upon Copenhagen to strengthen and deepen the "constitutional" structure for the new Europe.[76] Especially important were articles spelling out the concept of an independent judiciary, which is critical to the integrity of the democratic process. To reinforce the rule of law, provisions were added to fortify the liberties of the individual in his or her relationship to the police, courts and government administrative agencies. The individual was further protected from state intrusion through assurances provided for personal communication via post and telephone. Restrictions on travel and residence were also significantly reduced.

In response to the attempted coup in the USSR, the CSCE document placed severe limitations on the imposition of states of emergency and, at the same time, assured protection of human rights during any state of emergency. This section was based on proposals advanced by Moscow and its former East European allies. Freedom of expression, even during the state of emergency, was further augmented through guarantees of unhindered operation of independent media. (The conferees must have recalled how Gorbachev reported that after being cut off from normal channels of media information while detained in the Crimea during August 19-20, his personal guards were able to establish access to BBC and Radio Liberty.)

For the first time in the Helsinki process, commitments were adopted to provide equal and non-discriminatory treatment to women. The rights of the disabled were also spelled out. And determined efforts were elaborated to offer protection for migratory workers who were facing serious and growing threats from potent xenophobia and nationalism. Innovative, too, was the recognition extended to non-governmental organizations. Taking account of the important role played by these groups in advancing the Helsinki process, the document set forth uniform standards of access and openness to all CSCE meetings. For the United States, these provisions were especially welcome, as it had served over the years as the principal advocate and protector of NGOs both at Helsinki review meetings and in countries that sought to repress them.

How significant were these improvements? Kampelman, in his concluding speech, admitted that the US delegation at the beginning of the Moscow meeting, "frankly did not contemplate" much improvement over the Copenhagen document, as the latter had been "so detailed and complete."[77] Still, he would find by the end of the meeting that several gaps were filled and various principles were reinforced. Professor Buergenthal, who at Copenhagen had played a vital role in the drafting process, wrote to Kampelman on October 15 commenting that "I would not have thought that Moscow could advance much beyond Copenhagen, but it clearly did."[78] He went on to say that he believed the Moscow document to be "revolutionary . . . as far as its substantive rights were concerned and as well as the procedures it establishes."

Whether the additional substantive rights which comprised at least sixty percent of a fairly sizable concluding document were essential for what is not a legally binding statement is open to question. One key member of the delegation sarcastically commented in an interview that the document contained an "awful lot of words."[79] It was a view which Kampelman may have shared, at least to some degree, perhaps to a great degree. In his closing speech at Moscow, he said:

> . . . I strongly sense it is time for us to stop wordsmithing at the conclusion of our meetings together. We are running out of words. We should stop debating adjectives. . . .[80]

The use of the term "wordsmithing" was the Ambassador's way—it would appear—of denigrating the excessive emphasis given to the preparation of the Moscow document, even with the elaboration of additional rights. Why his view so clearly diverged from that of Buergenthal, with whom he closely worked on the classic Copenhagen statement, is understandable when their different perspectives are taken into account. Buergenthal, primarily an international law specialist, served as a teacher as well as a jurist. Legal precision and specificity, from this perspective, are to be greatly valued. For Kampelman, a major policy figure in the State Department establishment, Copenhagen represented the core of a new democratic society in Europe. The critical need of the moment, from the perspective of one oriented to policy and politics, was less a refinement of law as much as its implementation.

Kampelman vigorously cautioned against any new concluding documents at future Helsinki meetings:

> . . . we should push ourselves away from the eating table and address how best to digest that which we have consumed.[81]

Those October 4 comments were his valedictory address. It was clear that "Mr. CSCE" wanted to use the occasion to warn his colleagues and their governments about the future. Too much "wordsmithing," he believed, could only harm the Helsinki process. The focus for the future must be "to review implementation," to put into practice the principles "we have agreed upon," and to help one another "resolve disputes," not to add more words.

If the United States found the Moscow document excessively "wordsmithing," some human rights activists, including the co-chairman of the Russian delegation, Sergei Kovalev, expressed a certain degree of frustration and regret that more intrusive measures were not approved in the event of serious threats to democratic regimes. In his closing speech on October 3, he observed that "we were ready to go much further" with respect to intervention. An article by Kovalev in *New Times* shortly afterward indicated that he would have strongly welcomed authority for CSCE states "to take any measures, including economic sanctions, against the perpetrator" of "systematic and human rights abuses."[82] In essence—and he implied as much—this would have totally eliminated the consensus principle rather than merely modify it.

Reflected here was the traditional attitude of the earlier Soviet dissent movement, which had often sought a more intrusive posture by the West on human rights issues. That attitude was no doubt reinforced by the terrifying experience of the August coup that nearly halted the unfolding of democracy in Russia. From this perspective, Kampelman and the US delegation were seen as excessively cautious. But Kovalev did not make clear how the proposed major intervention could be legitimized without undermining the balance between the state sovereignty principle and the human rights principle of the Helsinki Final Act. All that he would acknowledge in his speech was that the proposal would have created "serious difficulties." Strikingly, the view which Kovalev articulated, to a considerable extent, would come to prevail nine months later when CSCE and the United Nations were seized with the Bosnian tragedy.

The Helsinki process seemed to be moving away from its historic aspiration and achievement—a "Europe whole and free." Only two years after the extraordinary and unexpected consummation of the dreams of the courageous human rights advocates—from the Helsinki Watch Group, the Soviet Jewish emigration movement, Charter 77, and Solidarity—hatred, xenophobia and separatism had come to have a serious and disturbing impact on European political life. CSCE, noted Kampelman, had answered the "compelling call to conscience" of the human rights dreamers and activists, even as it had given voice to the "silent multitude" which helped "light the way to freedom and democracy."[83] Now there could be heard a babble of voices preaching hostility and chauvinism.

Self-determination, in his view, had been distorted or transformed into a dangerous challenge. Once again, Kampelman insisted that it "does not incorporate within it the right of secession," but his cry was falling on deaf ears. "If we permit ourselves to engage in a sterile and dangerous cycle of nationality recrimination and vengeance," he cautioned, "that folly can drag much of Europe back into the shadows from which [it] has so recently emerged. . . ."[84] The ultimate consequences of the splintering process, even if benign, were clear to him: instability and a multiplicity of independent states. Instability generates conflict and violence. As for the greater number of states, what then happens to the character of CSCE?

And as CSCE becomes swollen in numbers, how would decisions be reached? Still by consensus? Kampelman had never treated consensus with disdain, even when it denied solutions and progress. For it preserved the process, gave each state a stake in the outcome, and ineluctably required both compromise and a determined effort to reach it. The fissuring process made compromise ever more difficult to achieve as impatience mounted at the very time that violence or the threat of violence escalated.

At the Moscow meeting, a number of states raised the question of changing the Helsinki rule on consensus under extraordinary situations.

Kampelman recognized that in the unfolding circumstances involving Yugoslavia, the procedural rule of consensus might have to go. But he urged extreme caution: CSCE should search for a method initially established by consensus "under which serious breaches of behavior and commitment can be met by the CSCE community without fear of a veto by the state responsible for the severe breach of CSCE standards."[85]

Even with the machinery of mediation and/or fact finding—the crowning Moscow achievement of the Helsinki process—now in place, Kampelman acknowledged that some European states would prefer to reach further, to add a forceful "human rights monitor" to "the arsenal of Europe's ability." There was little, if any, enthusiasm in his thinking for this course of action.

It was not only the distortion of self-determination that stirred concern. At the heart of the new self-determination drive was the agreement that group rights deserved attention. But a fundamental thesis of Kampelman had been—and remained so—that human rights and fundamental freedoms were vested in the individual, not the group. He saw group rights to be "exclusionary," leading to "a preoccupation with differences in a society" rather than to "freely shared values" which bind the community. Pluralistic democracy was perceived as rooted in the differences of individuals, not of groups. Certainly, this reflected the "melting-pot" concept of American democracy as well as the views of an administration that strongly rejected "quota" systems. Advocacy of group rights can only produce, Kampelman believed, "confusions, conflict and division." Whether this perception was true or not, it hardly accorded with the trend in multinational European societies. Wholesale rejection of the concept of group rights could lead to a United States isolated in respect to Helsinki's future.

In general, the Moscow document failed to grapple with the minority rights issue in any profound sense. Lack of understanding of the problem and how to cope with it was apparent. Instead, the intensifying national hostilities were approached by major European democracies as but an extension of their respective concerns and perceptions of minorities' problems. Preoccupation with stability and border inviolability seemed to paralyze effective action. Simply absent was US leadership that advocated seizing the transitional moment in order to advance creative new approaches for dealing with the unfolding ethnic aspirations and related violence. Policy remained tied to a very recent past where freedom and the right of the individual was transcendent. The rush of events triggered by nationalist drives was yet to be comprehended, let alone acted upon.

Even with all the negatives on Europe's horizon, the Helsinki process in a significant way had helped achieve monumental results in the human rights field. An entire totalitarian structure had crumbled and, in its place, a remarkable "constitutional" set of standards was elaborated, offering a democratic infrastructure for a promising future. Besides, machinery was now installed that had as its purpose coping with tense situations or difficult human rights problems. If the machinery was ultimately intrusive, at least at its initial stage, it sought voluntary compliance rooted in compromise.

The United States had played a prominent role in guiding the process to the culminating point. Its "Mr. CSCE" was very much the architect of the new standards and of the voluntary compliance mechanism. A decade earlier, at Madrid, he had helped transform the Helsinki review conference into a kind of embryonic compliance machinery. He won plaudits from Secretary of State George Shultz, as well as from prominent foreign statesmen. The Norwegian Ambassador to CSCE talks in the Spanish capital, Leif Mevik, in his own autobiography, remembers Kampelman as "the most formidable chief negotiator I ever met," one who "had no peer in Madrid."[86] Especially impressive was the compliment the American received for his work at Madrid from Andrei Sakharov: "You remembered us when others were ready to forget."[87]

Now, after Moscow, Kampelman, together with his government and the Helsinki Commission, could take enormous pride in a historic accomplishment in the human rights field. But whether progress in the CSCE human dimension would continue to be made was quite another matter. Kampelman's retirement coincided with the appearance on the horizon of new nationalist forces, unleashed by the democratic revolutions, which constituted a challenge to a Europe "whole and free." Even as these forces pointed to the possible future splintering of states, and to conflicts among them, they also evoked memories of a bygone era of darkness, posing real threats of racism and bigotry. In the meantime, "democracy's season" still defined the European political climate. And an elaborate Helsinki institutional framework had been erected to protect and extend that season. Could winter be warded off? Or would the social-historical cycle merely replicate the weather?

■ POSTSCRIPT ■

An Uncertain Future

The first flush of reaction to the heady CSCE years of 1990-91, with the Paris Charter as their centerpiece and the Moscow meeting as their denouement, was not geographically restricted to the area "from Vancouver to Vladivostok." The vision of the future "new world order," with peace, democracy and human rights at its core, was extended in various important circles to other giant continental areas—the Middle East, Africa, Asia, and the Pacific—thereby virtually encircling the entire globe.

But euphoria about the potential worldwide significance of CSCE did not last long. Indeed, CSCE itself was confronting profound challenges to its effectiveness as an agent of security (and stability) and human rights. Social forces unleashed by the collapse of totalitarianism, notwithstanding efforts to cope with them at Geneva and Moscow in the summer and fall of 1991, were threatening European stability in the very area where democracy had proved triumphant.

Toward the end of 1991, the distinguished philosopher and political analyst Sir Isaiah Berlin pointedly stressed in an interview in *The New York Review of Books* that nationalism and racism "are the most powerful movements in the world today, cutting across many social systems." The notion of a Europe "whole and free" found itself lacking at least the unity implied in the word "whole." At the same time as nationalistic forces in the West slowed the European Community's planned integration, the remnants of former unified state structures in Yugoslavia and the USSR further disintegrated and crumbled under the impact of aggressive nationalism. Worse, the crumbling was accompanied in various areas by the violence of war, the first widespread examples of overt belligerency in Europe since World War II. More disturbing still, CSCE seemed to be unable to cope effectively with the unfolding violence; nor was the European Community, to which CSCE had mandated responsibility for action, more successful. And the United Nations itself was seriously frustrated in its humanitarian and peacekeeping initiatives as well as in its program of imposed economic sanctions.

Even in its less malign manifestations, nationalism did not have to assume a bellicose character to demonstrate a clear xenophobic striving that could rend an established fabric of unity. Czechoslovakia, or even in its later form, the Czech and Slovak Federal Republic, offered an example of the impact of the new force and how it could literally reverse the Helsinki process. By July 1992, following elections during the prior month in Slovakia, it had become clear that the dominant political forces in the area were pressing for their own sovereignty. President Vaclav Havel may have been the hero of the Velvet Revolution and the symbol of Czechoslovak freedom, but Slovak nationalists could not have cared less. Their ultimate objective was an independent Slovak state. "Crushed Velvet" was the apt description of the new situation in an August analysis by the Helsinki Commission.

The Bratislava move toward independence, in and of itself, may not have unduly threatened core CSCE principles, but the dominant political leadership was, at best, indifferent to the rights of minorities within its truncated borders; at worst, it was downright hostile to them. The Hungarian minority in the region was more than 500,000; its own leadership was fearful of Slovak domination and had already been suggesting that Hungarians seek "autonomy" as a form of self-protection. For the Bratislava regime, the human rights of minorities was not considered "essential to its own credibility," as a Helsinki Commission report in April noted. The report further observed that "high profile condemnations of anti-Semitism" were largely absent, in contrast to other areas of East Europe.

CSCE was not, however, immediately seized with the Slovak national issue; violence, after all, had not occurred. In contrast, a brutal war was being waged in Bosnia-Herzegovina, an outgrowth of aggressive Serb nationalism, which seemed totally unresponsive to a variety of pressures. With Yugoslavia unraveling—Croatia and Slovenia had already declared themselves independent—the Moslem Slavs and Croatians in Bosnia sought to join the bandwagon despite clear warnings that Serbia and Bosnian Serbs would not tolerate the development.

Playing the nationalist trump card admirably served Serbian President Slobodan Milosevic's expansionist purposes. "Ethnic cleansing" was the racist formula, echoing a Hitlerian philosophy which accompanied the violence. By mid-1992, Serb irregulars controlled almost two-thirds of the land mass of Bosnia-Herzegovina (holding only one-third of Serbs). Not to be outdone, Croatian irregulars gobbled up much of the balance except for the capital itself—Sarajevo. The human costs, mainly measured in the lives of Moslem Slavs, were staggering. Reportedly 50,000 persons had been killed and 1.2 million made homeless.

Bosnia was only the most pronounced expression of aggressive nationalism, rooted in ethnic hatred and carried to its most extreme form. But the inflammable material that had once made the Balkans the "tinderbox of Europe" could easily be found throughout the area. The situation was also threatening in Kosovo, inhabited largely by Albanians—approximately 90 percent of the population—who had been ruthlessly repressed by the Serbs and deprived of meaningful rights of political and cultural autonomy. Smoldering animosities could easily explode, particularly if the state of Albania were to throw its weight behind grievances of its brethren in Kosovo.

The Macedonian republic now claimed independence, but Greece considered the choice of the republic name an overt assault on the dignity of its own Macedonian province, the historic birthplace of Alexander the Great and Aristotle. Besides, Athens surmised that Skopje, the Macedonian capital, had the aim of annexing the northern Greek province. Greece's influence in the European Community and with Washington kept the new republic from formal recognition by CSCE and other regional and international bodies.

Moving beyond the deep tensions involving minorities, or rather nationalities, in the Balkans (which could, of course, apply to Romania, especially as related to the profound Hungarian grievances in Transylvania), the growing ethnic conflicts in the former USSR began taking on the character of cruel belligerency. The violence in the Nagorno-Karabakh region of Azerbaijan continued to flare up, while the Trans-Dniester region of Moldova, inhabited mainly by Russians and Ukrainians (who resented the domination of Romanian-speaking Moldavians), was the scene of raging military skirmishes. Related to the latter development was the emergence of a potential military nightmare, namely the Russian republic coming to the assistance of Russian nationals, a minority in several recently established republics. Approximately 25 million Russians resided in these states, a not inconsequential number. In various places like Latvia, Estonia, and Kazakhstan, the Russian minority was extraordinarily large. Sizable concentrations of Russian army units continued to occupy the Baltic states; only in early September was agreement finally reached with Lithuania for the removal of Russian troops in 1993. In Ukraine, the Russians constituted 20 percent of the population, which could hardly be overlooked, especially in the context of maneuvers concerning vital security issues like control over the Black Sea fleet.

Symptomatic of Russian nationalist public opinion concerning tension areas where a Russian minority existed was the comment of Yevgeny Ambartsumov, the chairman of the Russian Supreme Soviet Committee for International Affairs, on Russian television on June 22, 1992. A strongly committed democrat, he nevertheless told the viewing audience that he "essentially agreed" with the chauvinist remarks made about Moldova and Georgia by the tough nationalist vice-president, Aleksandr Rutskoi. Ambartsumov asserted that "the Dniester area was never part of Moldova." Referring to the Trans-Dniester region, he said that "if any national-territorial community wants to become part of the Russian Federation, it should not be denied this right. . . . We sometimes overrate the principle of the inviolability of borders." The comment stood on its head the traditional Helsinki policy of Russia. For Moscow, inviolability of borders had been considered central to its vital foreign policy interests.

Other "liberal" voices echoed Ambartsumov's sentiments, a disconcerting and ominously disturbing indication of the potentiality for aggression. Presidential Counselor Sergei Stankevich accused Moldova, Georgia, Estonia, and Latvia of oppressing Russian minorities. He threatened to use force to protect "a thousand-year history [of Russia's] legitimate interests." In Stankevich's view, the Russian government should have been more vigorous in defending the rights of Russians in the other former Soviet republics. Clearly, dangerous collisions of competing states or of ethnic minorities within states driven by aggressive nationalism and possibly involving the giant power of Russia were not excluded. On the contrary, they appeared very much on the East European agenda.

CSCE, meeting in the Finnish capital since March 24, could hardly avoid coming to grips with the violence, as the latter clearly mocked Helsinki's very character and structure. The body's membership had been enlarged since the Moscow session the previous September. Croatia, Slovenia and Georgia were added prior to the Helsinki sessions and, in April, Bosnia-Herzegovina was admitted as the fifty-second participating state. If CSCE appeared bloated and unwieldy, the membership was nonetheless determined to shape itself into an efficient and effective functioning organization; otherwise the "premier" forum of the post-Cold War era would be helpless in the face of violent nationalism and a deepening sense of insecurity.

Machinery for "crisis management" and "conflict prevention"—the new phrases would become the buzz words of the Helsinki professionals, almost as important as the words "human rights" or "balance" in CSCE's previous life—was sought. The three-month session in Helsinki was largely preoccupied with the creation of an elaborate bureaucratic institutional structure, far more intricate and detailed than had been envisaged in the recent past. (Ironically, the new emergencies growing out of the continuing nightmarish Serb assault upon Sarajevo required the interruption of the formal discussions by the Committee of Senior Officials meeting here, rather than in Vienna or Prague. It assembled eight times during the relatively short 90-day Helsinki meeting.)

That the murderous events in Bosnia would prompt CSCE to become preoccupied, almost obsessively, with institution building was not altogether accidental. Ever since aggressive nationalism began threatening the status quo in post-totalitarian East Europe after 1990, institutionalization had become the principal goal. But this aim inevitably came at the expense of focusing upon human rights or minority rights problems. All too often, the assumption of the Europeans, at times made explicitly, was that human rights issues had been largely already solved. In fact, however, the very crises and conflicts which now required a focus on institutionalization resulted from unsolved minority rights problems. To the extent that institution-building and security concerns predominated over human rights concerns, the very sources of tension remained neglected.

At the core of the new institutionalization was the proposed role of the "Chairman-in-Office." The authority of this office was enhanced for purposes of facilitating coordination and consultation objectives. The chairman would also draw to his or her side both the previous Chairman-in-Office and the succeeding one who, operating together as a "troika," might expedite decisions. He or she could, after consulting with the other participating states, create ad hoc steering groups on a case-by-case basis. And he or she could designate a personal representative with "a clear and precise mandate" to extend appropriate assistance.

A new office, the High Commissioner on National Minorities, initially advanced by the Netherlands, was specifically created for the purposes of providing the Council and CSO with "early warning" about national minority problems that might develop into conflicts potentially threatening peace, stability or relationships between CSCE states. It was an imaginative proposal that could signal "early action" by "an eminent international personality with long-standing relevant experience. . . ." As NGOs might also provide early evidence of potential dangers, the status of the new office and its closeness with the Chairman-in-Office suggested that warning signals would be acted upon, not treated perfunctorily.

If the institution of a High Commissioner was new to the process, Helsinki also strengthened aspects of the mechanism that had been delineated at the Moscow meeting—fact-finding and rapporteur missions. The target, however, was not the area of the human dimension generally. Instead, these aspects were now designated as key instruments for conflict prevention and crisis management in dealing with minorities issues. The guiding factor here would be the Committee of Senior Officials, which was given virtual carte blanche to apply a variety of means for responding to disputes at levels beyond "early warning." Its focus was to be on ascertaining "root causes" of tensions with the assistance of the Conflict Prevention Center and the Office for Democratic Institutions and Human Rights. The fact-finding and rapporteur missions could contribute significantly to this task. Beyond that, the missions were seen as vital to the process of preventing crisis and conflict. By the end of summer 1992, long-term monitor missions were projected for Kosovo, Vojvodina, and Sanjak, areas in Yugoslavia of ethnic tension and potential violence. A similar mission for Macedonia was also under discussion.

A range of additional options was also considered at Helsinki for the peaceful settlement of disputes. While this aim was seen as "a cornerstone of the CSCE process," some options clearly would carry CSCE beyond its fundamental voluntary and political character and institutional structures. One proposal clearly fell within the CSCE framework. The breakthrough Valletta mechanism, discussed in an earlier chapter, was reexamined with the thought of strengthening it. Another proposal constituted a modest extension of the Valletta device. It would create a CSCE procedure for "conciliation, including directed conciliation." Such direction clearly implied a certain degree of coercion to be exercised by the CSO or Council of Foreign Ministers.

The third proposal was significantly more controversial. It involved establishing a Court of Conciliation and Arbitration. Advanced and pressed quite strongly by the French, the idea appeared to entail the drafting of a formal treaty which would establish a judicial tribunal having a legally binding character. The United States would certainly resist such a proposal. From the very beginning of the Helsinki process, Washington strongly rejected any idea that the Final Act or subsequent agreements take the form of a treaty with juridical obligations. Even if desirable, constitutionally required treaty ratification by the United States would prove enormously difficult to achieve, particularly if foreign courts appeared to usurp the jurisdiction of US tribunals. CSCE deferred action, instead agreeing to a special meeting in Geneva on October 12-23, 1992, "to continue to develop a comprehensive set of measures to expand the options. . . ."

With the crisis deepening in the Balkans, CSCE embarked for the first time on a new course, nominally accepting a role for peacekeeping as "an important operational element of the overall capability . . . for conflict prevention and crisis management intended to complement the political process of dispute resolution." But in Bosnia, the UN had already assumed the peacekeeping function with some 14,000 troops in use.

One limitation on the CSCE role was made patently evident: CSCE peacekeeping "will not entail enforcement action." Nor would it embrace peacemaking, although the envisaged operation was rather extensive and bordered on traditional military areas. CSCE could use civilian and/or military personnel to supervise and help maintain cease-fires, monitor troop withdrawals, support law and order, provide humanitarian and medical assistance, and extend aid to refugees. The extensive responsibility, however, was circumscribed by the explicit requirements that the chosen specified form of peacekeeping necessitated approval by all the concerned parties and had to be initiated by a consensus decision. Furthermore, a crucial precondition was essential: "an effective and durable cease-fire."

CSCE could request NATO, as well as WEU (the Western European Union) and EC to make "their resources available" along with their expertise and experience so that a trained peacekeeping operation could be mounted. In addition, the special peacekeeping mechanism of the Commonwealth of Independent States (CIS—i.e., the former Soviet republics except the Baltic states and Georgia) could also be called upon for assistance.

What was particularly significant about the decision to legitimize the request of assistance from NATO was the fact that only five weeks earlier, during the first week of June, NATO itself explicitly indicated for the first time that its forces could be made available to CSCE upon request. NATO's offer had constituted a milestone for both the military alliance and CSCE. It had, of course, Washington's strong support, and President Bush went out of his way in a speech at Helsinki on July 9 to call attention to the NATO proposal, suggesting that the military alliance could serve as the security force of CSCE.

Far more significant was the willingness of Russia to acquiesce in its premise. Following the visit of President Boris Yeltsin to Washington, the White House announced a "Charter for American-Russian Partnership and Friendship" on June 17, pointing precisely in that direction. It specifically endorsed "the creation of a credible Euro-Atlantic peacekeeping capability, based on CSCE political authority, which allows for the use of the capacities" of NATO and of the NATO-established North Atlantic Cooperation Council (of which Russia and its former Warsaw Pact allies are members). For Moscow to agree to an enhanced role for NATO in Europe was startling and unprecedented.

The idea of NATO as a vital, if not indispensable, component of CSCE peacekeeping did not evoke universal support. The French, who had decades before absented themselves from the integrated military structure of NATO (though not from the alliance itself), were hostile to the idea. Viewing the United States as the dominant element of NATO, France was determined to limit any significant role for the alliance in Europe. It would opt instead for WEU or EC, neither of which, in fact, could demonstrate adequate security muscle for peacekeeping in East Europe. Behind the scene, whether in Helsinki or Brussels or in national capitals, Paris was engaged in efforts to limit the NATO role and the American presence.

The extent to which CSCE by itself might serve as a peacekeeping force, given the absence of any military command structure, experience or expertise, is open to serious doubt. Besides, as a draft letter of mid-August 1992 from the Chairman of the CSCE Council of Ministers to the UN Secretary-General makes clear, the ability of the CSCE to conduct peacekeeping activities "is dependent upon contributions from participating states, individually or collectively." On the other hand, NATO, with its critical US component, could offer effective peacekeeping power. It would not have to depend upon "contributions." But while government leaders in the major CSCE countries agreed that the Bosnian horrors perpetrated largely by Serbia were outrageous, they initially also expressed hesitancy about the advisability of military intervention since the area was perceived as a hopeless quagmire, with the potential of producing dangerous consequences.

The "doctrinal" change in the historical character of CSCE that emerged from the deliberations of the Council and the CSO was as important as the structural and institutional modifications spelled out in a formal agreement at the end of the Helsinki session. "Consensus minus one"—a formula reached at the January Council of Ministers meeting in Prague—provided that appropriate action could be taken by the Council or CSO "if necessary in the absence of the consent of the state concerned in cases of clear, gross and uncorrected violations of relevant CSCE commitments." It added that the "actions would consist of political declarations or other political steps to apply outside the territory of the state concerned."

Various initiatives taken by CSCE during 1990-1991 had already eroded the consensus principle with respect to holding meetings or sending fact-finding missions, but the Prague decision went to the vital matter of political steps. The erosion had moved from the largely procedural issue to that of substance. Significantly, the new principle of consensus minus one did not initially meet with any resistance when posed in the abstract; even Russian Foreign Minister Andrei Kozyrev offered Moscow's unambiguous endorsement.

But when the question moved from the abstract to the concrete, opposition arose. Outside events forced the application of the principle. With the Bosnian crisis worsening, Washington took the initiative in moving the Prague decision to its logical conclusion. Ambassador John Kornblum, in an especially tough speech on April 15, raised the possibility of suspending Yugoslavia's participation in CSCE because of violations of CSCE commitments. Suspension had never been formally proposed before in the Helsinki process. The clear intent was punishment, the imposition of the sanction of exclusion. Yet, exclusion was the ultimate consequence of the consensus minus one principle. That it would evoke anxiety and concern among some CSCE states was inevitable. Moscow was hardly enthusiastic and France was not sympathetic at all. Resistance stiffened.

Kornblum continued his stern, uncompromising line. On May 6, he urged immediate suspension of Yugoslavia, its representatives to be excluded from all CSCE activities until "we reach consensus that they should be readmitted." The speech carried Washington's most pointed warning ever to CSCE. If the CSO failed to suspend Belgrade, it could hardly demonstrate that CSCE will "become the body for management of change which we wish it to be." His remarks then turned sharply caustic: "If we fail to accept the challenge today, no fancy web of new structures and mechanisms . . . can make up for our political timidity."

On May 12, six days after Kornblum's angry challenge, CSO responded, setting a date of June 29, when it would again meet to reach a final decision "in light of information provided by the European Community. . . ." The delay was designed to ascertain whether EC diplomatic efforts would halt the continuing Serbian offensive.

No meaningful progress could be reported by the late June date. On July 8, the last day of the Helsinki meeting, CSCE reached an historic decision. For the first time since its founding on July 3, 1973—almost 19 years to the day—a participating state was suspended. The decision, however, was for a three-month period, not a permanent exclusion.

Suspension rather than exclusion would serve as a test of the effectiveness of UN economic sanctions and the generally tougher CSCE line. At the end of three months, CSO would meet again to decide on any further steps. The language of the resolution read: "No representative of Yugoslavia will be present at the summit of Helsinki (July 9-10) or at any subsequent meetings of the CSCE until 14 October 1992." Once again, the CSCE action explicitly indicated that its new authority was derived from the Prague document and the principle of consensus minus one.

Security issues dominated the proceedings at Helsinki, its concluding heads-of-state summit, and the documents which they produced. No formal concluding document was adopted; instead, the conference approved "Helsinki Decisions," a 73-page summary (twice the length of the concluding document adopted at Vienna or at the human dimension meetings in Copenhagen and Moscow). Max Kampelman's caveat that a surfeit of "wordsmithing" had taken hold of the Helsinki process was ignored. In his view, the CSCE verbiage had become indigestible.

But Kampelman had been referring to a past era. CSCE was now seized by security issues. The bulk of Helsinki Decisions, precisely 40 pages, was devoted to security and the institutions, described in considerable detail, that were to be established to cope with it. In contrast, only 14 pages were devoted to the human dimension, a reversal of the previous relationship between the two major components of the Helsinki process. It would be totally unwarranted, however, to assume that the initial Soviet vision of a CSCE exclusively or mainly concerned with security issues at the expense of human rights matters has ironically triumphed. What, in fact, the Helsinki document implicitly recognized (and the summit declaration made explicit) was that human rights are essential for meaningful security and that the relationship or balance between the two remains at the core of CSCE. Nonetheless, it is also clear that the institutionalization has failed to translate that relationship into structures which carry a distinctive and explicit human rights component.

What stands out in the new Helsinki agreement is a vast and intricate institutionalization. The early trend, initiated at Vienna and accelerated at the Paris summit, had now achieved unprecedented levels. The qualitative change from the time of the Helsinki Final Act constituted a dramatic 180-degree turn. If Helsinki had originally been a process marked by flexibility and by the responsibility of individual governments, it was now being transformed into a significant international bureaucratic enterprise with uncertain flexibility. The process itself was being institutionalized. Even some CSCE proponents could become anxious. One long-time Commission staffer with considerable expertise in a variety of CSCE areas, Robert Hand, in an address to a leading educational body, expressed profound "concern that the [CSCE] institutions will become a convenient vent for action that should be taken by the participating states themselves."

Institutionalization inevitably meant a level of "professionalization" that was certain to distance CSCE from that which had been a major source of inspiration to the process—the non-governmental community. The Helsinki Watch groups and their allies among civil libertarian organizations in the West, especially the United States, had raised many challenging issues (often through the Helsinki Commission) and had sensitized governments to vital human rights concerns. With the multiplication of new professional bureaucracies whose relationship to the non-governmental community was tenuous at best, the latter's earlier interest in CSCE could be expected to diminish. In particular, alienation would deepen as the Committee of Senior Officials acquired increasing authority and power. With its regular headquarters far removed from American and US-based NGOs, its agenda virtually unknown to these groups, and its operational procedures almost closed, estrangement could be expected to grow. US participants at the Helsinki meeting could not fail to note how only a handful of NGOs made an appearance at the session.

The US delegation vigorously pressed for CSCE decisions that would involve more directly the NGO community in the proceedings at follow-up and inter-sessional meetings. Some NGOs had considerable expertise on the burning minorities issues; certainly, this was the case with respect to racism. Yet, with the attention given to security considerations and problems, and with the focus placed on institution building to enable CSCE to cope with them, it was hardly unexpected that human rights and the human dimension would receive diminishing commentary. Had not the central human rights questions been resolved with the collapse of totalitarianism? And had not the new "constitutional" structure of freedom and the rule of law, elaborated in the Paris Charter, formalized a democracy now triumphant? Therefore, was not stability and, therefore, security, the fundamental issue, rather than the assault on human rights? Various delegations at Helsinki made the point, either explicitly or implicitly through the emphasis given in their presentations.

The US delegation took note of this escalating challenge to the very foundation of the Helsinki process, and expressed a growing concern. Ambassador Kornblum objected to numerous suggestions that the human dimension is already "the finished work of the [Helsinki] conference." Ambassador Sam Wise contended that the "barometer" of the Helsinki meeting would be the degree to which human rights and security concerns were linked.

Even before the sessions began, many participating states signaled that the agenda should give preeminence to military security and to institution building. At the insistence of the US and several others, however, human rights and economic and environmental cooperation were given equal priority. The organization of four separate and equal working groups on the specified subjects reflected the agreement.

Implementation review provided a telling example of the fundamentally changed atmosphere. In the review framework of previous CSCE meetings, the "shaming" device had pressured offenders to change. But at the 1992 Helsinki meeting, virtually all participating states except the United States were, in the language of a Helsinki Commission commentary, "timid in raising specific problems and naming specific countries."

US delegates addressed concrete problems and the lack of adherence to Helsinki standards even if they proved embarrassing to new friends. Delegate J. Sherwood McGinnis sharply challenged legislation and other initiatives in former communist countries that limited the right of political participation for those who had served previous communist regimes. The imposition of *ex post facto* laws based on collective guilt, he stressed, mocked the democratic process and could only lead to "a new cycle of revenge and hatred. . . ." On the other hand, Kazakhstan and Russia were criticized for keeping imprisoned those convicted of economic crimes under previous regimes; Lithuania was reminded of how it subverted justice by releasing prisoners convicted of war crimes.

US delegate David Evans, basing himself on Commission findings, noted that in Kazakhstan, Uzbekistan, and Tajikistan, the political opposition was either hampered or punished in various ways, most importantly through denial of access to the media. Tajikistan additionally posed the special problem of doing little to counteract public harassment of Jews— an implicit rejection of the value of official responses to racism as raised during the human dimension meetings.

Yet, Evans was hopeful. Encouraged by the establishment in some Central Asian republics of Helsinki monitoring groups, the US delegate proposed to "bring the CSCE to the new states" through what the Helsinki Decisions ultimately termed a "program of coordinated support." (An important reason for this action was the surprisingly low attendance record of new states at Helsinki.) According to the agreement, the Office of Democratic Institutions and Human Rights (ODIHR) would arrange for new participating states a series of special seminars on legal, diplomatic and security CSCE questions and on the democratic process. Whether a seminar on the democratic process can significantly contribute to urgently changing the political culture of countries whose traditions of freedom, civil liberties and civil rights are limited is somewhat doubtful. Still, the proposed initiative could prove useful and, in some individual cases, might have meaningful positive consequences.

Although the Prague meeting of the Council of Foreign Ministers called attention to the surging trend of intolerance, nationalism, xenophobia and racism, the Helsinki sessions contributed little to documenting its extent and character, let alone providing solutions. The United States, once again, was in the forefront of highlighting the significance of the racist challenge, time and again urging that education was the key to combating it. Yet, even the strong US efforts failed to elicit a document that underscored the rejection of intolerance enshrined in the Copenhagen document.

In dealing with racism and intolerance, a multiplicity of approaches that reinforce each other is needed. The Copenhagen document illustrates the point. The latter's forceful denunciation of racism and anti-Semitism called on governments to undertake three separate responsibilities: 1) issue public condemnation statements; 2) enact laws, and (where enacted) implement statutes against discrimination and that type of bigotry that leads to violence; and 3) promote educational programs (presumably both within and outside of schools) to combat all forms of racism.

But no attempt was made in the review of implementation at the follow-up Helsinki session to inquire as to how each government was complying with the Copenhagen obligations in combating hate and intolerance. It is through such a review that the potential of Helsinki's historic "shaming" process was traditionally brought into play.

Such a review would have been consonant with the aims of the Helsinki meeting, as combating racism had, of course, a direct bearing on the broad security concern with which CSCE had been seized. Bigotry was often the force that powered aggressive nationalist drives in the Balkans and in the former Soviet republics. The "us against them" primitive tribal psychology still retained an extraordinary resonance. The "ethnic cleansing" formula practiced by the Serbian forces in Bosnia constituted a vivid expression of that psychology. For the achievement of security and the maintenance of stability, racism and ethnic bigotry will have to be vigorously addressed.

Not everyone recognized the linkage, but the US did and incessantly pressed the connection. The Helsinki summit Declaration of July 10 provided explicit recognition of the intimate relationship between "instability" or "insecurity" and "intolerance." It is racism and xenophobia that "threaten stability," while gross violations of human rights—including those related to national minorities—"pose a special threat" to the peaceful development of society, "in particular in new democracies."

The answer to violence, read the Declaration, is the building of "democratic and pluralistic societies, where diversity is fully protected. . . ." Racial, ethnic, and religious discrimination must be rejected and "freedom and tolerance must be taught and practiced." The problem was that the newly formed freedom in East Europe after the overthrow of communism, in the words of President Havel on July 9, had brought ancient "animosities back to life and back to mind." How to maintain the hard-won freedom and incorporate within it a toleration of diversity and pluralism had become central to the security and stability of European community. It is a new Helsinki promise that urgently requires keeping.

The Declaration was hardly trailblazing. It acknowledged that its concept was derived from the Helsinki Final Act, where peace and human rights had been originally joined. Certainly, the linkage between security and fundamental freedoms has stood at the heart of the Helsinki process as it has unfolded since the Final Act was signed. What was significant about the Declaration was the fact that, in the face of a considerably diminished emphasis on human rights at Helsinki, the linkage theme was still maintained.

Whether the reinforced CSCE security structure, together with its newly assumed responsibilities for the promotion of tolerance, will successfully contain the spreading virus of nationalist violence driven by hate and bigotry is by no means certain. In the last analysis, the continued effectiveness of the CSCE will rest on the political will of the participating states to fulfill the new commitments they have undertaken.

In 1975, the promises were clear enough: freer movement of people and ideas within a stable Europe. Fifteen years later, at Copenhagen and in the Charter of Paris for a New Europe, the earlier commitment had been superseded by the promise to create a new "architecture" of free elections, political pluralism, and the rule of law. Incorporated in that promise, particularly as it related to political pluralism, were the newly established goals of assuring the rights of ethnic minorities, protecting them from racism, anti-Semitism, xenophobic nationalism, and all forms of discrimination, and, at the same time, actively encouraging tolerance and understanding. It was especially during 1991 that these promised goals were set forth, still in the context of a stable Europe.

Powerful national forces, long suppressed by totalitarian regimes, swept across multinational states in East Europe, tearing at the fabric of the new world order and challenging the commitments of 1990-91. A host of new national state structures emerged in what were formerly Yugoslavia, the USSR and Czechoslovakia. In many of them, the emerging elite, dominated by a single nationality, threatened minorities in an often geographically crazy-quilt pattern where ethnic hostility became the norm. Instability deepened, exploited by aggressive nationalism.

The result bordered on the Hobbesian nightmares of violence and chaos "nasty and brutish." Suddenly, Europe was confronted by a scenario thought long since buried—concentration camps, mass expulsions, torture.

The promise of minority rights remains to be kept and, together with it, an end to the "state of nature" of war, violence and repression. The means for fulfilling the commitment are the newly created institutional structures, a complex of bureaucratic instruments and sanctions. Yet, the new institutions cannot be said, as yet, to be very effective. The violence in Bosnia, for example, has all but shattered the infrastructure of society in its major cities and violation of human rights had become almost endemic. Particularly dismaying and shocking is the evidence that seemed to point to the potential of genocide.

Complex and meticulously delineated structures for the precise management of crises or their prevention are, indeed, useful, but can contribute little if the political will to utilize them is absent. For too long a period the Bosnian tragedy had gestated, becoming by the conclusion of the Helsinki summit an endlessly tormenting agony and anguish that called into question the meaning of the Helsinki process itself. The cry of the President of Bosnia-Herzegovina, Alija Izetbegovic, at the summit capsulated the sense of desperate hopelessness: "Is the world powerless to put an end to this evil?" The rhetorical question, in different formulations, was being put by many others who caught the images of indescribable horrors on television.

The United States and the West, in fulfilling the promise of upholding minority rights, are obliged to insist on international accountability for criminal actions. The Committee of Senior Officials in October 1991 did assert that "those responsible for the unprecedented violence against people in Yugoslavia, with its ever-increasing loss of life, should be held personally accountable under international law for their actions." An equally tough and more authoritative directive was handed down by the CSCE's Council of Foreign Ministers meeting in Prague on January 31, 1992:

> . . . all those responsible for acts of violence and for violations of ceasefire agreements . . . under international law . . . are personally accountable for their actions that are in contravention of the relevant norms of international humanitarian law.

Later, the UN Security Council, in Resolution 771 dealing with war crimes committed in Bosnia, specified that it will hold Serbian leaders personally responsible for their behavior. On August 13-14, CSO vigorously endorsed this theme and singled out the detention camps for special warning. All those who breach the Geneva Conventions on war prisoners will "bear individual responsibility for such breaches."

But it is not enough to have these resolutions published in the UN or CSCE journals; they must be given maximum public exposure in every media. No ruler or official or agent of authority should be able to claim that he is not responsible because he knew nothing about his personal accountability. A systematic effort to dramatize the theme should be determinedly pursued by CSCE.

The issue of Bosnia's integrity and survivability is not the only thing at stake. What should have been painfully evident was that the conduct of President Milosevic, if successful, would provide any aggressive nationalist ruler bent on extending his power and territory with a model to emulate. The virtually unhindered advances of Serbian militias, with their ethnic cleansing ideology, could very well resonate throughout East Europe, where national hostilities run deep and where conflict over turf is ever present. Thus, the head of a Russian activist group in Estonia, Mikhail Lysenko, in a magazine interview, evoked the language and imagery of the Serbs in Bosnia. He called for Russian intervention in the newly independent Baltic state to "cleanse" the "trash" of Estonian domination of local Russians.

Finally, there is the core issue of what Helsinki represents. One of its central principles since 1975 has been the inviolability of state borders. Even after Germany was unified and East Germany disappeared in consequence of an international agreement sanctioning a peaceful electoral vote for unification, and even after the emergence of new states following the collapse of the USSR and Yugoslavia, the principle of border inviolability remained at the heart of the CSCE. The devolution of authority in each new state extended to the specific area embraced by previously established borders. If they are to be changed at all or modified, it must be accomplished peacefully, with the agreement of all sides and approved by the CSCE community. If changes of Bosnia's territory and borders are wrought by force and violence, they could serve as a magnet pulling at all pluralistic societies. The result would be the burial of CSCE.

And yet, some advocates of self-determination would have no objection were the inviolability-of-borders principle to be discarded as a critical guideline of peaceful interstate relations. In their view, the principle of self-determination transcends any other limiting principle of international law, and, thus, force can be used to achieve national aspirations, whatever the consequences. That is the path to unrestrained violence in the global community.

It was precisely an unspoken premise of the Helsinki process that the principle of border inviolability balance that of self-determination. Central to the balance of the competing principles was the idea that border changes in the interest of self-determination could only be realized in a peaceful manner and thorough mutual agreement. Monitoring the fulfillment of the balance inevitably falls on the shoulders of the new Helsinki institutions, which, in turn, rest on the willingness of Helsinki's participating states to accept and be responsive to those institutions.

What was absent at the Helsinki summit as the CSCE heads of state grappled with the stresses of nationality and ethnic conflicts and of minority rights was evidence of a determination to prevail over challenges to the very integrity of the process. Creation of elaborate institutional structures is no substitute for the necessary exercise of political will to make the institutions operable. No mechanism, however finely constructed, can do anything when its driving force is missing.

(Illuminating the character of the human tragedy in Bosnia was a special report to the UN Commission on Human Rights by former Polish Prime Minister Tadeusz Mazowiecki. Released on August 31, it called for more UN forces to be sent to the region with a mandate to "react directly" concerning human rights violations. Specifically demanded were UN actions that would bring about the reversal of the "ethnic cleansing" process.)

Certainly, there was little political will emanating from the European Community that one could find particularly impressive. Former British Prime Minister Margaret Thatcher would scornfully characterize it as simply "paralysis." The Community had assumed, with America's encouragement, the key role in dealing with the minority rights problems of the Balkans. Repeated settlements negotiated by Lord Carrington on behalf of the EC collapsed before the ink was dry on each agreement. The one major political solution which he had advanced, a division of Bosnia into ethnic "cantons," was ridiculed and denounced by Lady Thatcher and human rights advocates as a capitulation to Serbian aggression. As for the use of military force, whether through EC or NATO or the UN, the dominant attitude was one that was largely negative.

But then the European Community, since 1975, has not had much of a record of the exercise of strong political will to which it can point. Its members, of course, had been responsible for the human rights provisions of the Final Act as the United States, under Kissinger, had abdicated any significant interest in CSCE. Pride by West Europeans in that accord is fully deserved. But once the accord was framed and signed, West Europeans displayed hesitancy, vacillation and worse in pressing for human rights implementation. Yuri Orlov's principal aide, Ludmilla Alexeyeva, told the annual meeting of the American Society of International Law in May 1990 that, at the first CSCE follow-up meeting in Belgrade, the attitude of most European diplomats was summed up in the comment: ". . . this is a diplomatic conference, not a boxing ring." She recalled that the US initiative on human rights questions at the time "was blocked almost completely."

When Washington primed the struggle, first for human rights and later for free elections, pluralism, and the rule of law within the Helsinki process, things got done. Indeed, the US role in advancing human rights issues began much earlier than is commonly credited.* Until 1977 and the advent of Jimmy Carter, though, Washington took no consistent lead on human rights issues. From then on, it became clear that Washington's leadership was critical; when it was not exercised or was lacking in clarity—as at Bern—confusion followed and little or no progress was made.

At the Helsinki summit in July 1992, the United States could once again hardly be described as determined and forceful. When President Bush addressed the crucial session, he demanded that relief supplies authorized by the UN Security Council must reach the besieged people of Bosnia "no matter what it takes." He used the same phrase in insisting

---

*In a carefully nuanced unpublished study written in 1992, *Human Rights: Challenge to the Bipolar Order*, James Goodby argues that State Department—as opposed to National Security Council—advocacy of "freer movement" was quite vigorous as early as 1969, and was instrumental in its inclusion in the NATO foreign ministerial communique of December of that year.

that the UN-imposed economic sanctions on Belgrade must be respected. But the words were scarcely of the kind that reflected a firm determination to halt the aggressors and force them out of their occupied territory and the detention camps which they had established. Tougher and significantly more adamant had been President Bush's historic statement on Kuwait: "This will not stand."

Far more important than the language was the hesitancy of the administration to back up President Bush's commitment with clear, strong and vigorous diplomatic signaling and other implementation steps. Failure to do so inevitably raised questions with both friends and enemies about the administration's credibility. An American expert on Eastern Europe, Professor Charles Gati, pointed out in *Foreign Affairs* that America had been derelict in mobilizing international action on the unfolding Yugoslav crisis from the beginning. Determined preventive diplomacy by the US, he effectively argued, might have deterred the Serbs in Belgrade and in Bosnia-Herzegovina from "proceeding as they have." Even when President Bush appeared finally to pose for the first time the use of ground troops to ensure the delivery of relief aid, only a few days later—on August 10—he undercut the new forceful posture by signaling that the US would avoid military actions that might lead to it being "bogged down in some guerrilla warfare."

Nor could it be said that the United States was required to be circumspect because of possible resistance from Moscow. On the contrary, the Kremlin rarely expressed a more supportive tone than it articulated at Helsinki. President Yeltsin, referring to the "bloody conflict" in former Yugoslav republics, called for the creation of a rapid response force. "What is needed," said the Russian President, "is action and persistence." He went on in remarkably martial terms: "Above all, these forces must be brought into action at the right time, that is, not when blood is already being spilled, but when conflicts are in their nascent stage. . . . CSCE peacekeeping operations must be quick and effective."

A knowledgeable State Department official, George Kenney, the acting chief of the Yugoslav desk, bitterly complained that "high levels in the State Department and White House" do not "really want to get involved." Upon resigning from the Foreign Service on August 25, he warned that no progress in Bosnia could be made without "very strong pressures, including military pressures, against Serbia to stop its campaign of genocide. . . ." Policy makers were apparently paralyzed by military arguments that held Bosnia to be a quagmire for interventionist forces, similar to the Vietnam tragedy or the Lebanon experience in the early 1980s (where a US Marine detachment had become an easy target for terrorists). Not until Democratic Party presidential candidate Bill Clinton in early August urged a more vigorous UN military response to assure humanitarian aid, did the wheels begin spinning at the White House.

Much more significantly, a critical article by Margaret Thatcher appeared in *The New York Times* on August 6. Lady Thatcher once again appeared in her "Iron Lady" mode. Warning of the negative repercussions flowing from a Serbian victory and the collapse of Bosnia, she ridiculed the notion that "nothing can be done unless we are prepared to risk permanent involvement in a Vietnam—or Lebanon-style conflict. . . ." In her view, this thesis "is partly alarmism [and] partly an excuse for inertia." She then spelled out a series of tough steps together with a strong and forceful overall recommendation: "A clear threat of military action would force Serbia into contemplating an end to its aggression."

What was needed in the face of the inadequacy of the European Community, Thatcher said, is "American leadership." The exercise of that leadership is "indispensable." At the same time, Washington cannot act alone; NATO, "the most practical instrument," must be brought in to "deal with the crisis." The aim would be the restoration of a Bosnian state backed by international guarantees, with those guarantees extending to the rights of the three ethnic groups—Serbs, Croats, and Moslem Slavs. She would have CSCE, not the UN, supervise the guarantees.

Thatcher's prescription for a marriage of US leadership to CSCE potential is a recognition of the relationship that more than anything else has helped the Helsinki process gain its successes over the nearly 20 years of its history. Political will has been and continues to be as necessary, if not more so, in securing human rights in Europe as any set of procedures, mechanisms or institutions that the participating states can devise. Time and again, and very often reluctantly, the United States has had to inspire that will. For whatever reason, geopolitical or economic strength, the constitutional makeup of the American polity, the particular place human rights issues occupy in the American psyche, the United States has a responsibility it must continue to acknowledge.

The former Prime Minister in essence repeated the call Foreign Secretary George Canning had made more than 160 years before, charging "the New World . . . to redress the balance of the Old." Closer in time, and just as pertinently, she reminded policy makers the world over—and particularly in the United States—what President Ford had so clearly stated almost 17 years to the day earlier, that promises are only as good as their keeping.

Appendix

SELECT CHRONOLOGY OF THE CSCE

Date	Location	Meeting
November 1972-July 1973	Helsinki	Multilateral Preparatory Talks and CSCE Stage I
September 1973-July 1975	Geneva	CSCE Stage II
July 1975-August 1975	Helsinki	CSCE Stage III and signature of Final Act
October 1977-March 1978	Belgrade	Follow-up Meeting I
October 1978-December 1978	Montreux	Experts Meeting on Peaceful Settlement of Disputes
February 1979-March 1979	Valletta	Experts Meeting on the Mediterranean
February 1980-March 1980	Hamburg	Scientific Forum
November 1980-September 1983	Madrid	Follow-up Meeting II
January 1984-September 1986	Stockholm	Conference on Confidence- and Security-Building Measures in Europe
March 1984-April 1984	Athens	Experts Meeting on Peaceful Settlement of Disputes
May 1985-June 1985	Ottawa	Experts Meeting on Human Rights and Fundamental Freedoms
October 1985-November 1985	Budapest	Cultural Forum
April 1986-May 1986	Bern	Experts Meeting on Human Contacts
November 1986-January 1989	Vienna	Follow-up Meeting III

March 1989	Vienna	Opening of negotiations on Confidence and Security- Building Measures (CSBM) and Conventional Armed Forces in Europe (CFE); (CFE concluded November 1990)
April 1989-May 1989	London	Information Forum
May 1989-June 1989	Paris	First Meeting of the Conference on the Human Dimension
October 1989-November 1989	Sofia	Meeting on the Protection of the Environment
March 1990-April 1990	Bonn	Conference on Economic Cooperation
June 1990	Copenhagen	Second Meeting of the Conference on the Human Dimension
October 1990	New York	Meeting of CSCE Foreign Ministers
November 1990	Paris	CSCE Summit II
January 1991-February 1991	Valletta	Experts Meeting on Peaceful Settlement of Disputes
May 1991-June 1991	Cracow	Symposium on Cultural Heritage
June 1991	Berlin	Council of Foreign Ministers
July 1991	Geneva	Experts Meeting on National Minorities
September 1991	Moscow	Council of Foreign Ministers (extraordinary meeting on admission of the Baltic states)
September 1991-October 1991	Moscow	Third Meeting of the Conference on the Human Dimension
November 1991	Oslo	Seminar on Democratic Institutions
January 1992	Prague	Council of Foreign Ministers
March 1992-July 1992	Helsinki	Follow-up Meeting IV and CSCE Summit III

Notes

NOTES TO PROLOGUE

1. For contemporary accounts, see *Time*, July 9, 1973, pp. 22-3; *Time*, July 16, 1973, p. 27; *The New York Times* (hereafter *NYT*), July 6, 1973.

2. Cited in John J. Maresca, *To Helsinki: The Conference on Security and Cooperation in Europe 1973-1975* (Durham: Duke University Press, 1985), p. 11. Even Nixon's reference to CSCE carried no comment about human rights. See US Department of State, Office of the Historian, *The Conference on Security and Cooperation in Europe; Public Statements and Documents, 1954-1986* (Washington, DC, 1986), p. 72.

3. Maresca, *To Helsinki*, p. 11.

4. *Ibid.*, p. 10.

5. Arkady N. Shevchenko, *Breaking with Moscow* (New York: Alfred A. Knopf, 1985), pp. 355-56.

6. Andrei Zagorsky and Yuri Kashlev, "The Human Dimension of Politics," *International Affairs* (Moscow), No. 3, March 1990, pp. 62-75. Zagorsky was a leading academic at the Moscow State Institute of International Relations, while Kashlev was a high Soviet Foreign Ministry official dealing with CSCE and human rights.

7. Luigi Vittorio Ferraris, ed., *Report on a Negotiation, Helsinki-Geneva-Helsinki 1972-75* (Alphen ann den Rijn: Sijthoff & Noordhof, 1979), pp. 66, 302, 404.

8. United States Department of State, Office of the Historian, *The Conference on Security and Cooperation in Europe: Public Statements and Documents*, p. 136.

9. See Henry A. Kissinger, *The White House Years* (Boston: Little, Brown & Co., 1979); and Henry A. Kissinger, *Years of Upheaval* (Boston: Little, Brown & Co., 1982).

10. See Harold S. Russell, "The Helsinki Declaration: Brobdingnag or Lilliput?" *American Journal of International Law*, Vol. 70, April 1976, pp. 242-72. Also, see Robert T. Hartmann, *Palace Politics: An Inside Account of the Ford Years* (New York: McGraw-Hill, 1980), pp. 339-45.

11. Hartmann, *Palace Politics*, p. 339.

12. *The Wall Street Journal* (hereafter *WSJ*), July 23, 1975. For other examples, see *The Chicago Tribune*, July 31, 1975 and *The Chicago Sun-Times*, August 1, 1975. The top diplomatic pundit George Ball called Helsinki "a defeat for the West." See *Newsweek* (International Edition), August 11, 1975, p. 12.

13. On the eve of his departure to Helsinki from Andrews Air Force Base, President Ford put out a statement explicitly denying the allegation: "The United States has never recognized the Soviet incorporation of Lithuania, Latvia and Estonia and is not going to do so in Helsinki." Kissinger, fearing that the statement would offend Moscow, persuaded Ford to drop it from his oral remarks. However, the text had already been distributed to the media. See Hartmann, *Palace Politics*, p. 342.

14. "The Euro-Atlantic Architecture: From East to West," address by Secretary of State James A. Baker III to the Aspen Institute-Berlin, June 18, 1991.

15. William Safire, "Bring on CSCE," *NYT*, October 15, 1990: "My 18-year battle against the Conference on Security and Cooperation in Europe is over."

16. Cited in William Korey, "A New Chapter for Helsinki," *The New Leader*, August 6-20, 1990, p. 11.

17. Interview with Ambassador Warren Zimmermann, December 14, 1988. The interview was held in Vienna with the US chief of delegation to the CSCE talks.

18. "CSCE Delegation Visits Independent Baltics, Georgia, Armenia and Moscow," *CSCE Digest*, Vol. 14, No. 6, Summer 1991, p. 2.

19. Interview with Spencer Oliver, conducted by Jonathan Dorosin on February 26, 1988, in Washington, DC. Oliver had been the staff director of the Commission on Security and Cooperation in Europe. Later, he became staff director of the Committee on Foreign Affairs of the House of Representatives. For detailed background, see Commission on Security and Cooperation in Europe (hereafter Commission), *Fulfilling Our Promises: The United States and the Helsinki Final Act, A Status Report*, (Washington, DC, November 1979), pp. 55-9.

20. See *ibid.*, pp. 168-74. The Commission was earlier concerned with the failure to ratify the Genocide Treaty. On this subject, see William Korey, "Sin of Omission," *Foreign Policy*, No. 39, Summer 1980, pp. 172-75.

21. "Chairman Hoyer Testifies on the McCarran-Walter Act," *CSCE Digest*, June-July 1987, pp. 1-2. It carries the full text of Congressman Steny Hoyer's testimony to the House Subcommittee on Immigration, Refugees and Law on June 23, calling for repeal of sections of the McCarran-Walter which contradicted the spirit of the Final Act. Hoyer also wrote a special article for *The Washington Post* (hereafter *WP*) on September 2, 1987, called "A National Embarrassment."

22. Max M. Kampelman, *Entering New Worlds: The Memoirs of a Private Man in Public Life* (New York: HarperCollins, 1991), p. 221.

23. This is related in the unpublished memoirs of Ambassador Goldberg's wife, Dorothy Kurgans Goldberg. The memoirs, which run to 756 typewritten pages, are entitled *A Personal Journal of International Negotiations About Human Rights*.

24. *Ibid.* Thus, on February 18, 1978, Vorontsov told the Goldbergs at a friendly breakfast: "Actually, we have a very good system. What's wrong with a system that takes care of everybody?" He forcefully emphasized that "we will not change."

25. Ambassador Kampelman made the point rather strongly in his lecture at the Institute for East-West Security Studies (New York) on February 13, 1991. He made the same point in an interview with the author on September 13, 1991, during the Moscow meeting of the Human Dimension Conference.

26. Interview with Ambassador Max Kampelman, September 13, 1991.

27. The episode is related in Kampelman's memoirs. See Kampelman, *Entering New Worlds*, pp. 275-76.

28. *Ibid.*, p. 218.

29. *Ibid.*, p. 222. Zbigniew Brzezinski communicated to the author his role in Kampelman's appointment in an interview in Washington, DC, in the spring of 1983.

30. Commission, *Hearings*, (Washington, DC), March 18, 1982, p. 8.

31. Interview with Ambassador Warren Zimmermann. The talk was held in Vienna on December 12, 1988. Zimmermann characterized Shultz's role in CSCE strategy as of central importance.

32. Roy Medvedev and Giulietto Chiesa, *Time of Change; An Insider's View of Russia's Transformation*, (New York: Pantheon, 1989), pp. 254-86; Dusko Doder and Louise Branson, *Gorbachev, Heretic in the Kremlin*, (New York: Viking, 1990), pp. 325-54.

33. Commission, *Hearings*, March 18, 1982, p. 8.

34. Commission, *The Moscow Meeting of the Conference on the Human Dimension of the Conference on Security and Cooperation in Europe: 10 September-4 October 1991*, (Washington, DC, 1991), p. 22.

NOTES TO CHAPTER 1

1. This chapter, with some modification and updating, was originally prepared as a paper by the author for the Woodrow Wilson International Center for Scholars, where he served as Guest Scholar during January-March 1983. Aside from the standard sources, the author interviewed at length, and mainly by telephone, persons heavily involved in the Helsinki process during 1972-75—Ambassador Albert Sherer, Jr., Ambassador George Vest, Harold S. Russell, and Guy Coriden.

2. Russell, "The Helsinki Declaration," pp. 242-72.

3. *Time*, August 4, 1975, p. 18.

4. Hartmann, *Palace Politics*, p. 339.

5. *Newsweek*, August 11, 1975, p. 12. The same view was held by Governor Ronald Reagan, Senator Henry Jackson and noted Russian author Aleksandr Solzhenitsyn.

6. Maresca, *To Helsinki*, p. 198.

7. See the text of his address at the Helsinki Tenth Anniversary during July 30-August 1, 1985. For a summary, see Commission, *Basket I—Implementation of the Final Act of the Conference on Security and Cooperation in Europe: Findings Eleven Years After Helsinki* (Washington, DC, November 1986), p. 13.

8. *Izvestiia*, August 1, 1975. The words were precisely those of Leonid Brezhnev in his speech at Helsinki.

9. The citations from the communist rulers are in Stephen J. Roth, *The Helsinki "Final Act" and Soviet Jewry*, (London: Institute of Jewish Affairs, 1976), p. 3. For background, see Department of State, *The Conference on Security and Cooperation in Europe*, Historical Issues, No. 22 (Washington, DC, July 1985), pp. 1-5.

10. *23 S'ezd kommunisticheskoi partii Sovetskogo Soiuza, stenograficheskii otchet*, (Moscow: Political Literature Publishing House, 1966), Vol. 1, p. 456. This is a stenographic report of the 23rd Congress of the CPSU.

11. For a succinct review and evaluation of the Helsinki accord, see Stephen Lehne, *The Vienna Meeting of the Conference on Security and Cooperation in Europe 1986-1989: A Turning Point in East-West Relations* (Boulder: Westview Press, 1991), pp. 1-5; also Maresca, *To Helsinki*, pp. 3-7.

12. Maresca, *To Helsinki*, pp. 211-26.

13. *Ibid.*, pp. 227-83.

14. For details, see Russell, "The Helsinki Declaration," pp. 251-53.

15. *Ibid.*, p. 252, note 33.

16. A summary of the author's treatment of the subject presented in his paper to the Woodrow Wilson International Center can be found in William Korey, *Human Rights and the Helsinki Accord* (New York: Foreign Policy Association, 1983), pp. 15-16.

17. For details, see Maresca, *To Helsinki*, pp. 119-54.

18. Russell, "The Helsinki Declaration," pp. 268-69.

19. Cited in Roth, *The Helsinki "Final Act" and Soviet Jewry*, p. 14.

20. *Izvestiia*, August 8, 1975.

21. *New Times*, November 1975, as cited in Roth, *The Helsinki "Final Act" and Soviet Jewry*, p. 15.

22. *Ibid.*

23. *International Herald Tribune* (Paris), August 16, 1975.

24. *International Herald Tribune* (Paris), August 19, 1975.

25. *Pravda*, December 9, 1975.

26. Alexandre Charles Kiss and Mary Francis Dominick, "The International Legal Significance of the Human Rights Provisions of the Helsinki Final Act," *Vanderbilt Journal of Transnational Law*, Vol. 13, No. 2-3, Spring-Summer 1980, pp. 314-15.

27. Jordan J. Paust, "Transnational Freedom of Speech: Legal Aspects of the Helsinki Final Act," *Law and Contemporary Problems*, Vol. 45, 1982, pp. 53-70. Another Helsinki legal expert, Professor Thomas Buergenthal, has recently posited that legally non-binding agreements such as the Final Act may nonetheless have "a substantial effect on legal rights and obligations." See his article, "The CSCE Rights System," *The George Washington Journal of International Law and Economics*, Vol. 25, No. 2, 1991, pp. 333-86, especially pp. 379-80.

28. Korey, *Human Rights and the Helsinki Accord*, pp. 21-2.

29. Kissinger's conflict with Congress over human rights is described in Sandy Vogelgesang, *American Dream, Global Nightmare: The Dilemma of US Human Rights Policy* (New York: Norton, 1980), pp. 124-33.

30. Kissinger, *White House Years*. For a brief summary of his view, see Department of State, *The Conference on Security and Cooperation in Europe*, p. 4.

31. Kissinger, *Years of Upheaval*, pp. 1164-65.

32. For background, see Maresca, *To Helsinki*, pp. 45-46.

33. Interview with Albert Sherer, Jr., conducted by phone from Washington, DC, on March 12, 1983.

34. Ferraris, *Report on a Negotiation*.

35. Maresca, *To Helsinki*, pp. 156-59.

NOTES TO CHAPTER 2

1. Maresca, *To Helsinki*, p. xii.

2. Even Jimmy Carter initially held to this view, *NYT*, October 3, 1976. Max Kampelman sought to put the "Yalta Myth" to rest in a speech in Madrid; see his *Three Years at the East-West Divide* (New York: Freedom House, 1983), pp. 89-90.

3. The comment was by George Ball in *Newsweek* (International Edition), August 11, 1975, p. 12.

4. Paul Goldberg, *The Final Act: The Dramatic Revealing Story of the Moscow Helsinki Watch Group* (New York: Morrow, 1988), pp. 62-3.

5. *Ibid.,* p. 61.

6. *Ibid.,* p. 62.

7. *Ibid.,* p. 22.

8. *Ibid.,* pp. 61-62.

9. *Ibid.,* p. 62.

10. Madeleine Albright and Alfred Friendly, *Executive-Legislative Cooperation and East-West Relations: The Birth of the Helsinki Commission* (Washington, DC, December 1984), mimeo, p. 11. Subsequently published as a chapter in Edmund Muskie, Kenneth Rush, and Kenneth Thompson, eds., *The President, the Congress and Foreign Policy: A Joint Policy Project of the Association of Former Members of Congress and the Atlantic Council of the United States* (Lanham: University Press of America, 1986).

11. Paul Goldberg, *The Final Act*, p. 62.

12. *Ibid.,* p. 58.

13. Albright and Friendly, *Executive-Legislative Cooperation*, p. 12. In their work, they chose to underline Senator Case's comment.

14. *Ibid.,* p. 14-7.

15. *Ibid.,* p. 13.

16. US Congress, Senate Committee on Foreign Relations, *Establishing a Commission on Security and Cooperation in Europe*, Report 94-756 (Washington, DC, April 23, 1976), pp. 4-5.

17. Albright and Friendly, *Executive-Legislative Cooperation*, pp. 28-29.

18. *Congressional Record*, May 5, 1976, p. 12691.

19. *Ibid.*

20. *Ibid.*, p. 12692.

21. *Ibid.*, p. 12691.

22. Albright and Friendly, *Executive-Legislative Cooperation*, p. 19.

23. *Ibid.,* p. 29.

24. US Congress, House Committee on International Relations, *Hearings Before the Subcommittee on International Political and Military Affairs* (Washington, DC, May 4, 1976), p. 61.

25. *Ibid.*

26. *Ibid.,* p. 62.

27. Paul Goldberg, *The Final Act*, p. 61.

28. *Ibid.,* p. 60.

29. Vojtech Mastny, *Helsinki, Human Rights and European Security: Analysis and Documentation* (Durham: Duke University Press, 1986), p. 12.

30. Martin Sletzinger, *Executive-Legislative Branch Cooperation in East-West Policy: A Case Study of the Commission on Security and Cooperation in Europe* (Washington, DC, July 1984), mimeo, p. 9.

31. *Ibid.*

32. Joshua L. Dorosin, *The Role and Significance of the Commission on Security and Cooperation in Europe within the Helsinki Process* (Washington, DC, Spring 1989), mimeo (revised version), p. 14. Dorosin served as a research assistant to the author for several months in 1988.

33. This meeting is described in a letter from Dante Fascell to President Gerald Ford (September 27, 1976). A copy is in the Commission files.

34. *Ibid.*

35. *The Washington Star*, September 22, 1976. The commentator was Henry Bradsher.

36. Albright and Friendly, *Executive-Legislative Cooperation*, p. 24.

37. Dorosin, *The Role and Significance of the Commission*, p. 14. The information was based upon the February 26, 1988, interview with Spencer Oliver.

38. Letter from President Ford to Congressman Dante Fascell (October 2, 1976). A copy is in the Commission files.

39. Dorosin, *The Role and Significance of the Commission*, p. 14. This was based upon the formal report of the Commission meeting in August 1976.

40. *Ibid.*, p. 16.

41. Sletzinger, *Executive-Legislative Branch Cooperation in East-West Policy*, p. 13.

42. *Ibid.*, p. 14.

43. *Ibid.*, p. 15.

44. *Ibid.*, p. 16.

45. *Congressional Record*, September 30, 1976, p. 34153.

46. Dorosin, *The Role and Significance of the Commission*, p. 17. This is drawn from a memorandum by Jenkins sent to the Commission in October 1976. The memorandum is in the Commission files.

47. Albright and Friendly, *Executive-Legislative Cooperation*, p. 29.

48. *NYT*, October 7, 1976.

49. Sletzinger, *Executive-Legislative Branch Cooperation in East-West Policy*, p. 18.

50. Albright and Friendly, *Executive-Legislative Cooperation*, p. 31. Cited here is a press release of the Commission dated November 1, 1976.

51. *NYT*, November 2, 1976.

52. Sletzinger, *Executive-Legislative Branch Cooperation in East-West Policy*, p. 19.

53. *Ibid.*

54. TASS, November 4, 1976.

55. Commission, *Report of the Study Mission to Europe* (Washington, DC, 1976), pp. 1-2.

56. *Ibid.*, p. 4.

57. Cited in Dorosin, *The Role and Significance of the Commission*, p. 20. The citation is from the record of the Commission working meeting of January 6, 1977.

58. Paul Goldberg, *The Final Act*, pp. 63-4.

59. *Ibid.*

60. *NYT*, July 16, 1976.

61. *NYT*, October 3, 1976.

62. Albright and Friendly, *Executive-Legislative Cooperation*, p. 30.

63. *NYT*, October 7, 1976.

64. Korey, *Human Rights and Helsinki Accord*, p. 31.

65. *Ibid.* See also Sletzinger, *Executive-Legislative Branch Cooperation in East-West Policy*, p. 21.

66. This is drawn from the interview with Spencer Oliver, February 26, 1988.

67. *Ibid.*

68. Korey, *Human Rights and the Helsinki Accord*, p. 31.

69. Sletzinger, *Executive-Legislative Branch Cooperation in East-West Policy*, pp. 21-2.

70. Letter from Secretary of State Cyrus Vance to Dante Fascell (March 10, 1977). This is from the Commission files.

71. Sletzinger, *Executive-Legislative Branch Cooperation in East-West Policy*, pp. 25-6.

72. Interview with Spencer Oliver, February 26, 1988.

73. *Ibid.*

74. Albert W. Sherer, Jr., "Goldberg's Variation," *Foreign Policy*, No. 39, Summer 1980, p. 157.

75. Sletzinger, *Executive-Legislative Branch Cooperation in East-West Policy*, p. 26.

76. Dorosin, *The Role and Significance of the Commission*, p. 27.

77. Commission, *Hearing on Human Rights* (Washington, DC, February 23-24, 1977), p. 2.

78. Interview with Spencer Oliver, February 26, 1988.

79. Dorosin, *The Role and Significance of the Commission*, p. 32.

80. Memorandum from Meg Donovan to Spencer Oliver (January 25, 1977).

81. Rather, the focus was upon "reunion of families" and travel.

82. Commission, *Report on the Implementation of the Final Act* (Washington, DC, August 1977), p. 194.

83. Albright and Friendly, *Executive-legislative Cooperation*, p. 6.

84. Sletzinger, *Executive-Legislative Branch Cooperation in East-West Policy*, p. 27.

85. Dorosin, *The Role and Significance of the Commission*, p. 33.

86. Memorandum from Matthew Nimetz through Warren Christopher to Cyrus Vance (April 6, 1977). A copy is in the Commission files.

87. Letter from Dante Fascell to President Jimmy Carter (April 27, 1977). A copy of this letter is in the Commission files.

88. Sletzinger, *Executive-Legislative Branch Cooperation in East-West Policy*, p. 30.

89. Thomas Franck and Edward Weisband, *Foreign Policy by Congress* (New York: Oxford University Press, 1979).

90. Margaret E. Galey, "Congress, Foreign Policy and Human Rights: Ten Years After Helsinki," *Human Rights Quarterly*, Vol. 7, No. 3, 1985, pp. 334-372.

NOTES TO CHAPTER 3

1. Ludmilla Alexeyeva, *Soviet Dissent: Contemporary Movements for National, Religious, and Human Rights* (Middletown: Wesleyan University Press, 1985), p. 335.

2. Paul Goldberg, *The Final Act*, p. 42.

3. *Ibid.*, pp. 43-8.

4. *Ibid.*, pp. 33-6, and Yuri Orlov, *Dangerous Thoughts: Memoirs of a Russian Life* (New York: Morrow, 1991), pp. 188-89.

5. Orlov, *Dangerous Thoughts*, p. 188.

6. Paul Goldberg, *The Final Act*, pp. 36-7.

7. *Ibid.*, p. 31, and Alexeyeva, *Soviet Dissent*, p. 336.

8. Alexeyeva, *Soviet Dissent*, p. 336.

9. *Ibid*. She elaborated on this theme in an interview with the author held in her home near Washington, DC, on July 6, 1989.

10. Orlov, *Dangerous Thoughts*, p. 188.

11. *Ibid.*, pp. 188-89.

12. *Ibid.*, p. 194.

13. *Ibid.*, p. 195.

14. *Ibid.*, p. 189; Paul Goldberg, *The Final Act*, p. 38.

15. Paul Goldberg, *The Final Act*, p. 18.

16. *Ibid.*, p. 22.

17. *Ibid.*, p. 18.

18. *Ibid.*, p. 46.

19. *Ibid.*

20. Cited in Secretary of State Baker's speech to the Copenhagen meeting of the Conference on the Human Dimension, June 5, 1990.

21. Paul Goldberg, *The Final Act*, p. 63.

22. TASS, May 15, 1976; *NYT*, May 16, 1976.

23. Cited in Paul Goldberg, *The Final Act*, p. 56.

24. *Ibid.*, p. 66.

25. *Ibid.*, p. 62. The same letter is referred to in Chapter 2, note 59.

26. *Ibid.*, p. 46.

27. Orlov, *Dangerous Thoughts*, p. 195.

28. Alexeyeva, *Soviet Dissent*, p. 339.

29. *Ibid.*, pp. 340-41.

30. *Ibid.* In his June 5, 1990, speech at the Copenhagen meeting of the Conference on the Human Dimension, Baker described the relationship between Solidarity and the Helsinki Final Act.

31. H. Gordon Skilling, ed., *Charter 77 and Human Rights* (London: Allen & Unwin, 1981), pp. 209-13.

32. *Ibid.*, p. 213.

33. Commission, *Hearings* (Washington, DC, 1977), Vol. 3, pp. 389-90.

34. *Ibid.*, pp. 280-87.

35. *Ibid.*

36. Ernst Kux, "Revolution in Eastern Europe—Revolution in the West?" *Problems of Communism*, Vol. XL, May-June 1991, pp. 1-13.

37. The Soviet scholar M. P. Pavlov-Silvanskaia wrote on the subject for *Komsomolskaia pravda*, January 5, 1990.

38. See the comments of Ambassador John J. Maresca in "he American Society of International Law, *Proceedings of the Eighty-fourth Annual Meeting*, "Human Rights: The Helsinki Process" (Washington, DC, March 28-31, 1990), p. 123.

39. See William Korey, *The Soviet Cage: Anti-Semitism in Russia* (New York: Viking, 1973), p. 271; and William Korey, "Sakharov and the Soviet Jewish National Movement," *Midstream*, Vol. XX, No. 2, February 1974, pp. 35-8. Anatoly Shcharansky and one or two of his colleagues were exceptions in that they joined the democratic movement even as they remained active in the Jewish emigration drive.

40. See *Izvestiia*, December 5, 1966. Kosygin was asked about how the Holocaust "separated many Jewish families" and whether Soviet authorities would permit emigration so as to facilitate the "coming together" of these families.

41. Korey, "Sakharov and the Soviet Jewish National Movement," pp. 358 and *The Soviet Cage*, p. 271.

42. *Ibid.*

43. José D. Inglés, *A Study of Discrimination with Respect to the Right of Everyone to Leave Any Country, Including His Own, and to Return to His Own Country* (New York: United Nations, 1963), pp. 1-115.

44. *Ibid.*, pp. 64-73.

45. *Congressional Record*, March 15, 1973, p. 8071.

46. William Korey, "The Future of Soviet Jewry," *Foreign Affairs*, Vol. 58, No. 1, Fall 1979, p. 67.

47. See Evelyn Greenberg, "An 1869 Petition on Behalf of Russian Jews," *American Jewish Historical Quarterly*, Vol. LIV, March 1965, pp. 278-95.

48. Cited in Korey, "The Future of Soviet Jewry," p. 67.

49. Alex Littman, *Principle in Action: America's Outcry Against the Mistreatment of Jews in Russia, 1880-1892* (New York, 1968), mimeo, pp. 1-25. Drawn from his master's thesis at New York University.

50. See Naomi W. Cohen, "The Abrogation of the Russo-American Treaty of 1832," *Jewish Social Studies*, Vol. XXV, January 1963, pp. 3-41.

51. Charlotte Saikowski, "When Russia Let Jews Out, Not In," *The Christian Science Monitor*, April 17, 1973.

52. Cohen, "The Abrogation," p. 37.

53. William Korey, "The Jackson-Vanik Amendment in Perspective," *Soviet Jewish Affairs* (London), Vol. 18, No. 1, 1988, pp. 31-32.

54. *Ibid.*

55. *Ibid.*

56. Korey, "The Future of Soviet Jewry," p. 69.

57. Mark Y. Azbel, *Refusenik: Trapped in the Soviet Union* (Boston: Houghton Mifflin, 1981), p. 300.

58. Korey, "The Jackson-Vanik Amendment in Perspective," pp. 31-32.

59. See William Korey, "Jackson-Vanik and Soviet Jewry," *The Washington Quarterly*, Winter 1984, pp. 116-28.

60. Andrei Sakharov, "Open Letter to the Congress of the United States." It is dated September 14, 1973. A copy is in the author's possession.

61. *Ibid.*

62. *Ibid.*

63. William Korey, "The Struggle over Jackson-Mills-Vanik," *The American Jewish Year Book 1975* (Philadelphia: American Jewish Committee and Jewish Publication Society of America, 1976), pp. 200-10.

64. *Ibid.*

65. *Yediot Achranot*, March 21, 1973.

66. Alan Dowty, *Closed Borders* (New Haven: Yale University Press and the Twentieth Century Fund, 1987), p. 231.

67. See *Petitions, Letters and Appeals from Soviet Jews* (Jerusalem: Hebrew University, 1979), Vols. IX and X. These two sizable volumes were closely examined by the author. The one-third figure is based upon this examination.

68. The former Jewish activists were interviewed by the author in Jerusalem in June 1986. The results of the interviews were presented in William Korey, "The Legacy of Helsinki," *Reform Judaism*, Vol. XVI, No. 3, Spring 1988, pp. 8-9.

69. *Ibid.*

70. *Ibid.*

NOTES TO CHAPTER 4

1. Sakharov's message is to be found in the *International Herald Tribune* (Paris), October 6, 1977.

2. The episode is described in Andrei Sakharov, *Memoirs* (New York: Knopf, 1990), pp. 465-66.

3. Martin Gilbert, *Shcharansky: Hero of Our Time* (New York: Viking, 1986), p. 200.

4. Mastny, *Helsinki, Human Rights and European Security*, p. 155.

5. *Izvestiia*, September 3, 1975.

6. TASS, September 9, 1977.

7. Sakharov, *Memoirs*, pp. 448-49.

8. *Soviet Jewry and the Implementation of the Helsinki Final Act: Report* (London: World Conference on Soviet Jewry, 1977), pp. 7-8.

9. Mastny, *Helsinki, Human Rights and European Security*, p. 155.

10. *Ibid.*

11. *Ibid.*, p. 159.

12. *Ibid.*

13. Albert W. Sherer, "Goldberg's Variations," pp. 154-59.

14. *Fourth Semiannual Report by the President to the Commission on Security and Cooperation in Europe, December 1, 1977–June 1, 1978*, Special Report No. 45 (Washington DC, June 1978), pp. 3-7.

15. Commission, *Hearings*, (Washington, DC), June 6, 1977, pp. 86-7.

16. *Ibid.*, pp. 90-91.

17. *Ibid.*, pp. 96-7.

18. *Ibid.*, pp. 101-02.

19. *Ibid.*, p. 102.

20. *Ibid.*

21. Michael B. Wall, "Design to Avoid Confrontation," *Radio Free Europe Report*, Belgrade, June 16, 1977.

22. *Ibid.*

23. *Ibid.*

24. The "Yellow Book" took on the character of structural bylaws for the Commission. Spencer Oliver underscored its importance in his interview with Dorosin February 26, 1988. The "Yellow Book's" importance is also noted in Jan Sizoo and Rudolph Jurrjens, *CSCE Decision-Making: The Madrid Experience* (The Hague: Martinus Nijhoff, 1984), p. 50.

25. Sletzinger, *Executive-Legislative Branch Cooperation in East-West Policy*, p. 31.

26. Interview with Spencer Oliver, February 26, 1988.

27. The unpublished essay was by Jonathan Greenwald, who served as an aide to Ambassador Arthur Goldberg. The essay had been sent by Greenwald to Dorothy Goldberg and was made available to the author by the secretary to Goldberg, Fran Guilbert.

28. Zbigniew Brzezinski, *Power and Principle* (New York: Farrar Straus Giroux, 1985), p. 297.

29. *Ibid.*

30. This is the theme of Sherer's article in *Foreign Policy*. Also see his wife's essay, Carroll Sherer, "Breakdown at Belgrade," *The Washington Quarterly*, Autumn 1978, pp. 80-5. She writes: ". . . the ambassador [Goldberg] was acting out in his fashion what he perceived to be the chief executive's wishes."

31. Kampelman, *Entering New Worlds*, p. 221.

32. The "subject" of the cable was *Composition of the US CSCE Delegation.* It was dated September 2, 1977. The preparer of the cable was John Kornblum of the State Department's Bureau of European Affairs. A penciled note on the cable said that it was "not sent."

33. How the administration viewed the Goldberg appointment is noted in Sletzinger, *Executive-Legislative Branch Cooperation in East-West Policy*, p. 33.

34. Albert Sherer, "Goldberg's Variations," p. 158.

35. *Ibid.*, p. 159.

36. The draft speech is in the Sherer Archive, which was made available to the author by Sherer's widow, Carroll. It was entitled "The Geneva Negotiations, The Second Stage of the Helsinki Process." The date of the preparation is not clear.

37. *Ibid.* Sherer made the same point in vigorous fashion in his article in *Foreign Policy*.

38. Interview with Spencer Oliver, February 26, 1988. Confirmation can be found in Kampelman, *Entering New Worlds*, p. 221.

39. Dorothy K. Goldberg, *A Personal Journal*, p. 44.

40. *Ibid.*, p. 46.

41. Interview with Spencer Oliver, February 26, 1988.

42. Carroll Sherer, "Breakdown at Belgrade," pp. 84-5.

43. Dorothy K. Goldberg, *A Personal Journal*, p. 188.

44. Statement by President Jimmy Carter, November 18, 1977.

45. Press conference by Ambassador Arthur Goldberg, November 18, 1977.

46. Memorandum from Matthew Nimetz to Non-governmental Organizations (July 29, 1977). A copy is in the files of the Helsinki Commission.

47. Memorandum from Matthew Nimetz to Non-governmental Organizations (August 25, 1977). A copy is in the Commission's files.

48. Memorandum from Matthew Nimetz to Acting Secretary of State Warren Christopher (September 2, 1977). A copy is in the Commission files.

49. The letter of the ten non-governmental organizations to Matthew Nimetz is in the Commission files.

50. See Carroll Sherer, "Breakdown at Belgrade," pp. 80-1.

51. Sletzinger, *Executive-Legislative Branch Cooperation in East-West Policy*, p. 33.

52. *Ibid.*

53. Commission, *Hearing on the Belgrade Conference* (Washington, DC), March 21, 1978, p. 3.

54. *Ibid.*

55. Dorothy K. Goldberg, *A Personal Journal*, p. 91.

56. *Ibid.,* p. 92.

NOTES TO CHAPTER 5

1. Dorothy K. Goldberg, *A Personal Journal*, p. 48.

2. "Special Report on Belgrade," *State Department Bulletin*, No. 43, June 1978, p. 9.

3. Dorothy K. Goldberg, *A Personal Journal*, pp. 26-38.

4. *Ibid.*, p. 37.

5. *Ibid.*, p. 141.

6. *Ibid.*, pp. 54-7.

7. *Ibid.*, p. 99.

8. *Ibid.*

9. *Ibid.*, p. 100.

10. *Ibid.*, pp. 100-104.

11. *Ibid.*, pp. 101-102.

12. *Ibid.*, p. 108.

13. The full episode in presented in *ibid.*, pp. 171-74.

14. The letter carried the heading, "Make Human Rights a Central Issue." See *ibid.*, p. 174.

15. *Ibid.*, p. 213.

16. *The Times* (London), October 6, 1977.

17. *Pravda*, October 23, 1977.

18. *WP*, October 16, 1977.

19. Dorothy K. Goldberg, *A Personal Journal*, p. 214.

20. *WP*, October 16, 1977.

21. Dorothy K. Goldberg, *A Personal Journal*, p. 193.

22. *WP*, October 16, 1977.

23. *Pravda*, October 23, 1977.

24. *The Economist* (London), January 11, 1978.

25. *The Times* (London), November 1, 1977.

26. Dorothy K. Goldberg, *A Personal Journal*, p. 187.

27. *Ibid.*, p. 360.

28. *Ibid.*, p. 276.

29. *Ibid.*, p. 277.

30. *Ibid.*, p. 376.

31. Korey, *Human Rights and the Helsinki Accord*, p. 21.

32. Dorothy K. Goldberg, *A Personal Journal*, p. 376.

33. *Ibid.*, p. 309. This is based upon the US policy statement in "Special Report on Belgrade," referred to in note 2, above.

34. Dorothy K. Goldberg, *A Personal Journal*, pp. 303-11.

35. *Ibid.*, p. 293.

36. *Ibid.*, p. 559.

37. "From Speech by Soviet Delegation Chief," *Radio Free Europe Report*, Belgrade, March 9, 1978.

38. Dorothy K. Goldberg, *A Personal Journal*, p. 416.

39. *Ibid.*, p. 410.

40. *Ibid.*, pp. 515-16.

41. Don Cook, "Making America Look Foolish," *Saturday Review*, No. 5, May 13, 1978, pp. 8-11.

42. Dorothy K. Goldberg, *A Personal Journal*, p. 515.

43. The eight-page "confidential memorandum" is entitled *Trade-offs with the Soviets in the Concluding Document*. The memo was prepared at Goldberg's request. Greenwald notes that it was not cleared by the State Department.

44. Commission, *Hearings*, June 6, 1977, pp. 101-02.

45. Greenwald, *Trade-offs*, p. 2.

46. *Ibid.*, pp. 3-4.

47. *Ibid.*, p. 5.

48. *Ibid.*

49. "Barter Discussed," *Radio Free Europe Report*, Belgrade, November 3, 1977.

50. The comments of Yugoslav Ambassador Milorad Pesic were in *Radio Free Europe Report*, Belgrade, March 9, 1978.

51. Described in Natan Sharansky (Anatoly Shcharansky), *Fear No Evil* (New York: Random House, 1989), pp. 184-209.

52. "The Weary Consensus," *Radio Free Europe Report*, Belgrade, March 8, 1978.

53. Dante B. Fascell, "Did Human Rights Survive Belgrade?" *Foreign Policy*, No. 31, Summer 1978, p. 112.

54. "Soft and Hard Europeans," *Radio Free Europe Report*, Munich, December 1, 1977.

55. *Fourth Semiannual Report by the President*, pp. 3-7.

56. "From Speech by West German State Secretary," *Radio Free Europe Report*, Belgrade, March 9, 1978.

57. Nils Andrea and Karl Birnbaum, eds., *Belgrade and Beyond: The CSCE Process in Perspective* (The Hague: Kluwer Academic, 1981), pp. 161-63.

58. *NYT*, March 20, 1978.

59. *Ibid.*

60. Commission, *The Helsinki Process and East-West Relations: Progress in Perspective; Report on the Positive Aspects of the Implementation of the Helsinki Final Act* (Washington, DC, 1985), pp. 8-10.

NOTES TO CHAPTER 6

1. Fascell, "Did Human Rights Survive Belgrade?" p. 112.

2. Sherer, "Goldberg's Variation."

3. *Ibid.*, p. 158.

4. Mastny, *Helsinki, Human Rights and European Security*; particularly the introduction.

5. For details, see Stephen J. Roth, "The Madrid Follow-Up Conference to Helsinki: A Half-Time Assessment," *IJA Research Report*, No. 25, December 1980, pp. 6-8.

6. See *ibid.*, p. 7.

7. See President Jimmy Carter's Speech on the Fifth Anniversary of the Signing of the Helsinki (July 29, 1980); distributed by the United States Information Agency, August 2, 1980.

8. *Keesing's Contemporary Archives* (London: Longman), 1980, p. 30162.

9. *Ibid.*, p. 30421.

10. "Can We Negotiate with the Russians?" *Encounter*, Pamphlet No. 15, 1985, p. 2. The pamphlet incorporated two separate interviews with Kampelman conducted by George Urban. The interviews were published in February and March 1985 issues of *Encounter*.

11. Sletzinger, *Executive-Legislative Branch Cooperation in East-West Policy*, p. 39.

12. The details are in *ibid.*, pp. 45-46.

13. Interview with Spencer Oliver, February 26, 1988.

14. *Ibid.* Also, see Sletzinger, *Executive-Legislative Branch Cooperation in East-West Policy*, p. 46.

15. The Commission staff memorandum is in the possession of the author. Some of its details are recorded in Korey, *Human Rights and the Helsinki Accord*.

16. *Ibid.*

17. Sletzinger, *Executive-Legislative Branch Cooperation in East-West Policy*, p. 39.

18. *Ibid.*, p. 40.

19. The essentials of the letter are in *ibid.*, p. 47.

20. Commission, *Implementation of the Final Act of the Conference on Security and Cooperation in Europe: Findings and Recommendations Five Years After Helsinki* (Washington, DC, August, 1980).

21. Commission, *Fulfilling Our Promises*, 313 pp.

22. *Ibid.*, pp. 55-61.

23. The details are from the interview with Spencer Oliver, February 26, 1988.

24. Sletzinger, *Executive-Legislative Branch Cooperation in East-West Policy*, p. 49.

25. Brzezinski noted this in a luncheon meeting with the author in Washington, DC, in the spring of 1983. Kampelman confirmed the matter in his memoirs. See Kampelman, *Entering New Worlds* p. 22.

26. See Kampelman, *Entering New Worlds*, p. 218. Kampelman was especially explicit in the February 1985 interview with George Urban published in *Encounter*, as noted in note 10, above.

27. Sletzinger, *Executive-Legislative Branch Cooperation in East-West Policy*, p. 50.

28. Commission, *Hearings* (Washington, DC), March 23, 1982, p. 4.

29. Roland Eggleston, "Canadian Foreign Minister's Speech," *Radio Free Europe Report*, Madrid, November 12, 1980.

30. Michael B. Wall, "Trials Cast Shadow over Bonn Meeting," *Radio Free Europe Report*, Bonn, July 11, 1978.

31. Morton Vonduyke, "The Hamburg Scientific Forum," *Radio Free Europe Report*, Hamburg, February 21, 1980.

32. Philip Handler, "Science and Human Rights," *World Affairs*, 1982, pp. 342-51. The speech was given in Madrid on December 3, 1980. *World Affairs* reproduced it—as it did other speeches—two years later.

33. *Ibid.*, pp. 342-43.

34. *Ibid.*, p. 351.

35. Cited in Stephen J. Roth, "The Hamburg 'Scientific Forum' of the Helsinki Conference," *IJA Research Report*, No. 6, April 1980. Also, see Dorothy K. Goldberg, *A Personal Journal*, pp. 679-85. She carries the key citation on p. 682.

36. Peter Reddaway, *Soviet Policies on Dissent and Emigration: The Radical Change of Course Since 1979* (Washington, DC, August 28, 1984), colloquium paper mimeo, p. 19. The paper was prepared for the Kennan Institute for Advanced Russian Studies.

37. *Ibid.*, pp. 19-20.

38. *A Chronicle of Current Events*, Press No. 63, 1981, p. 58.

39. *Ibid.*, p. 74.

40. Semyon Tsvigun, "Concerning the Intrigues of the Imperialist Intelligence Services," *Kommunist*, No. 14, September 1981, pp. 88-99. This is translated in *Current Digest of the Soviet Press*, Vol. XXXIII, No. 49, pp. 4-5.

41. *A Chronicle of Current Events*, No. 60, 1980, p. 77.

42. Roland Eggleston, "Policy Toward Dissidents Defended," *Radio Free Europe Report*, Madrid, May 9, 1981.

43. The data were made available by the National Conference on Soviet Jewry.

44. Reddaway, *Soviet Policies on Dissent*, p. 24.

45. The comments of Zivs are in *NYT*, June 7, 1983. Also see *The Position of Soviet Jewry, 1983-1986: Report on the Implementation of the Helsinki Final Act Since the Madrid Follow-Up Conference* (London: World Conference on Soviet Jewry, 1986), p. 10.

46. *The Position of Soviet Jewry 1983-1986*, p. 11. As of the end of 1985, 648,423 affidavits had been sent from Israel to relatives in the Soviet Union requesting them. Of these, 265,673 received exit visas. The difference is 382,750.

47. *Ibid.*, p. 35.

48. The crackdown on the Jewish cultural movement is in *ibid.*, pp. 35-6.

49. Reddaway, *Soviet Policies on Dissent*, p. 25.

50. *Ibid.*

51. *Ibid.*, pp. 25-26.

52. *Ibid.*, p. 26.

53. *Ibid.*

54. *The Times* (London), July 27, 1984.

55. Reddaway, *Soviet Policies on Dissent*, p. 26.

56. *Pravda*, July 22, 1990.

57. *Pionerskaia pravda*, October 10, 1980.

58. Korneyev was extraordinarily prolific. His anti-Semitic articles appeared in virtually every Soviet publication. His book was the first to cite openly and favorably the infamous Tsarist anti-Semite, Aleksei Shmakov.

59. Authoritative support and endorsement was not surprising. Korneyev was a staff researcher at the Soviet Academy of Sciences.

60. For background, see William Korey, *Glasnost and Soviet Anti-Semitism* (New York: American Jewish Committee, 1991), p. 26.

61. *Ibid.*, p. 27.

62. For decisions of the Council of Europe and the European Parliament of the EC see *The Position of Soviet Jewry, 1977-1980, Report on the Implementation of the Helsinki Final Act Since the Belgrade Follow-Up Conference* (London: World Conference on Soviet Jewry, 1980), pp. 78-81.

63. On the pattern of discrimination in Soviet higher education, see *The Position of Soviet Jewry, 1983-86*, pp. 58-9.

64. *Ninth Semiannual Report by the President to the Commission on Security and Co-operation in Europe on the Implementation of the Final Act, June 1, 1980-November 30, 1980* (Washington, DC, 1980), pp. 21, especially 3, 5-8.

65. *Ibid.*, p. 6.

66. *Ibid.*

67. *Ibid.*, p. 7.

68. See *Petitions, Letters and Appeals from Soviet Jews, 1976-77-78* (Jerusalem: Hebrew University, 1980), 603 pp. No collection of documents has been published since, but the author has in his possession copies of post-1978 petitions.

69. Commission, *Human Rights in Czechoslovakia: The Documents of Charter 77, 1977-82* (Washington, DC, 1982), p. 16.

NOTES TO CHAPTER 7

1. *Le Monde* (Paris), November 12, 1980.

2. *Ibid.* The author was present at a number of these crowded press conferences with prominent dissidents or their families.

3. William Korey, "The Helsinki/Madrid Meeting," *The Washington Quarterly*, Spring 1982, pp. 195-96.

4. *CSCE Digest*, Washington, DC, September 24, 1982. Also, see *NYT*, September 9, 1982.

5. Cited in Korey, "The Helsinki/Madrid Meeting," p. 197.

6. Susan Ovadia, "French Activists Demand Firmness in Madrid," *Radio Free Europe Report*, Paris, November 11, 1980.

7. Roland Eggleston, "Soviet-Prompted Deadlock," *Radio Free Europe Report*, Madrid, September 12, 1980.

8. *Ibid.*

9. William Korey, "The Helsinki Review: Rattling the Russians in Madrid," *The New Leader*, February 9, 1981, p. 6.

10. Commission, *Implementation of the Final Act; Findings and Recommendations Five Years After Helsinki*, pp. 5-7.

11. Roland Eggleston, "Discussion Reaches Bedrock," *Radio Free Europe Report*, Madrid, September 24, 1980.

12. *Ibid.*

13. *Ibid.*

14. See Korey, "The Helsinki Review," p. 6. Also, see Roland Eggleston, "Three Separate Proposals," *Radio Free Europe Report*, Madrid, November 7, 1980.

15. Roland Eggleston, "Conference Clocks Stopped," *Radio Free Europe Report*, Madrid, November 11, 1980.

16. *Ibid.*

17. Korey, "The Helsinki Review," p. 7.

18. Sizoo and Jurrjens, *CSCE Decision-Making: The Madrid Experience*, p. 140.

19. *Chronicle of Human Rights in USSR*, No. 41, January-February 1981, pp. 21-2.

20. Korey, *Human Rights and the Helsinki Accord*, p. 53.

21. Korey, "The Helsinki Review Meeting," p. 7.

22. *Ibid.* This section was based upon a series of interviews conducted by the author with Ambassador Max Kampelman in November-December 1980 during the Madrid CSCE meeting. They became the basis of *Human Rights and the Helsinki Accord.*

23. *Pravda*, August 1, 1980.

24. The information was made available to the author by Ambassador Kampelman in the Madrid interviews. It is covered, in part, in Korey, "The Helsinki Review Meeting," p. 7.

25. *Ibid.*

26. Roland Eggleston, "The West Has Its Way," *Radio Free Europe Report*, Madrid, November 28, 1980.

27. *International Herald Tribune* (Paris), November 26, 1980.

28. Eggleston, "The West Has Its Way."

29. See Korey, "The Helsinki Review," p. 7. The wide range of the US criticism can be found in an early lengthy presentation by Kampelman on November 17, 1980. See Kampelman, *Three Years at the East-West Divide*, pp. 9-13.

30. Kampelman, *Three Years at the East-West Divide*, p. 10.

31. "Statement by Max M. Kampelman, Madrid, March 3, 1982," *World Affairs*, No. 4, Spring 1982, pp. 497-98.

32. Korey, *Human Rights and the Helsinki Accord*, p. 45.

33. *Ibid.*, p. 46.

34. *Ibid.*

35. Ambassador Kampelman himself gave it detailed attention in a speech on December 1, 1981. See Kampelman, *Three Years at the East-West Divide*, pp. 62-66.

36. Roland Eggleston, "Hostages to Detente," *Radio Free Europe Report*, Madrid, December 3, 1980.

37. See Kampelman's speech of November 17, 1980, in Kampelman, *Three Years at the East-West Divide*, p. 11.

38. Jerome Shestack served as President of the International League for Human Rights. His address was made available to the author.

39. See Korey, *Human Rights and the Helsinki Accord*, p. 54, and Roland Eggleston, "Belgium Charges Soviet Anti-Semitism," *Radio Free Europe Report*, Madrid, November 27, 1980.

40. *Pravda*, February 25, 1981.

41. *Pravda*, July 19, 1965.

42. Commission, *Hearings*, March 23, 1982, p. 8.

43. Korey, *Human Rights and the Helsinki Accord*, p. 55. The information was drawn from the Madrid interviews by the author with Ambassador Kampelman.

44. Cited in *ibid.*, p. 54.

45. *Ibid.*, p. 56.

46. The Lipavsky case is outlined in detail in Paul Goldberg, *The Final Act*, pp. 235-243. The decision of the Kissinger "Committee" was, of course, a blunder and violated a tradition of avoiding any linkage of spying with the human rights movement in the USSR.

47. This was communicated to the author in various interviews with Kampelman during the Madrid meeting and, later, especially August 1, 1986. The author was once asked by Kampelman which, of all the "prisoners of conscience," the United States ought to seek release, assuming such a choice was possible. The author, profoundly aware of the Lipavsky case, had no hesitancy in saying Shcharansky.

48. Peter Wright, *Spycatcher* (New York: Dell, 1988), pp. 255-57.

49. Kampelman informed the author of this detail in the August 1, 1986, interview. Later, he publicly revealed his role in this matter in Max M. Kampelman, *Entering New Worlds*, pp. 269-70.

50. Sharansky, *Fear No Evil*, p. 357.

51. For details of the release, see *ibid.*, pp. 399-416. The official announcement that was read to him said that he was "being expelled from the Soviet Union" on grounds that he was an "American spy" and had engaged in "conduct unworthy of a Soviet Citizen."

52. Congressman Levitas communicated this information to the Helsinki Commission on January 24, 1982. Commission staff members informed the author of the details shortly afterward. The episode is related in Korey, *Human Rights and the Helsinki Accord*, p. 53.

53. *Ibid.*

54. See the interview with Ambassador Kampelman conducted by George Urban in the February and March 1985 issues of *Encounter*, which served as the basis for *Encounter* pamphlet No. 15. The cited quotation from Kampelman is on p. 5 of the pamphlet.

55. *Ibid.*

56. The *Encounter* interviews are especially revealing of the connection between raising the human rights issue and the emplacement of the Pershing II and cruise missiles. Pages 3-5 of the pamphlet are particularly appropriate.

57. *Ibid.*, p. 5.

NOTES TO CHAPTER 8

1. Commission, *Hearings*, March 23, 1982, p. 8.

2. Arthur J. Goldberg, "The Final Act Revisited," *American Foreign Policy Newsletter*, Vol. 5, No. 2, April 1982, p. 3.

3. Korey, *Human Rights and the Helsinki Accord*, p. 26.

4. *Time*, June 30, 1980.

5. See William Safire, "Doing It Ourselves," *NYT*, May 22, 1980.

6. William Safire, "To Deter Invasion of Poland," *NYT*, December 11, 1980.

7. The statement of the Republican Platform Committee is in the author's possession.

8. The Reagan statement is in the author's possession.

9. Kampelman, *Three Years at the East-West Divide*, p. 12.

10. The press conference was attended by the author. The citations are from his notes.

11. The citations are from the author's notes.

12. For several months, however, the Reagan administration lacked a clear and positive human rights policy in general.

13. Commission, *Hearings*, March 23, 1982, p. 8.

14. *Ibid.*

15. Korey, *Human Rights and the Helsinki Accord*, p. 56.

16. *Tenth Semiannual Report by the President to the Commission on Security and Cooperation in Europe, December 1, 1980-May 31, 1981*, Special Report No. 85 (Washington, DC, 1981), pp. 1-23.

17. *Ibid.*, p. 19.

18. The Ford Foundation specialist on East Europe was Felice Gaer. Her comments are in Korey, *Human Rights and the Helsinki Accord*, p. 58.

19. *Ibid.*

20. *Ibid.*

21. *Ibid.*

22. *Document CSCE/RM/PVR.6*, as cited in Roth, "The Madrid Follow-Up Conference," p. 9.

23. *NYT*, November 25, 1980.

24. Roland Eggleston, "Speech by the Head of British Delegation," *Radio Liberty Report*, Madrid, December 3, 1980.

25. Vladimir Lomeiko, "Realities and Prospects of Detente as seen in Moscow after the Belgrade Conference" in Cornelius C. van der Heuvel and Rio D. Pracining, eds., *The Belgrade Conference: Progress or Retrogression* (Leiden: New Rhine, 1987), pp. 33-37; cited in Mastny, *Helsinki, Human Rights and European Security*, p. 211.

26. *Pravda*, August 1, 1980. The interview with Brezhnev took place on the fifth anniversary of the Helsinki Final Act, for which the Soviet leader claimed personal credit.

27. See "Memorandum on a Conference on Disarmament in Europe," *Europa-Archiv*, Vol. 35, No. 18, September 25, 1980, D506; see also *Keesing's*, 1980, p. 30421.

28. Roland Eggleston, "East and West Differ on CBMs," *Radio Free Europe Report*, Madrid, December 3, 1980.

29. *Ibid.*

30. *Ibid.*

31. *Ibid.*

32. Roland Eggleston, "French Delegate on the Polish Situation," *Radio Free Europe Report*, Madrid, December 17, 1980.

33. This Swedish proposal for a disarmament conference is cited in Mastny, *Helsinki, Human Rights and European Security*, pp. 233-35.

34. The initial proposal was carried by TASS, May 15, 1980. It was formally submitted at Madrid on December 8, 1980.

35. The French proposal was advanced at Madrid on December 9, 1980.

36. *Pravda*, February 24, 1981.

37. See Korey, *Human Rights and the Helsinki Accord*, p. 50, footnote 1.

38. See Kampelman, *Three Years at the East-West Divide*, pp. 30-32.

39. *Ibid.*, p. 32.

40. This was communicated by Kampelman to the author in a private interview during early November 1980 in Madrid. It is discussed in Korey, "The Helsinki Review," p. 7.

41. Kampelman's first criticism of Soviet military maneuvers was made in a speech on October 30, 1981. See his *Three Years at the East-West Divide*, pp. 53-57. His culminating speech on the subject, given on December 18, is on pp. 66-68.

42. The extent to which the imposition of martial law involved the USSR is unclear. Jaruzelski's later published memoirs indicates that the decision was his. For Kampelman's cited comments, see Roland Eggleston, "The CSCE's Worst Crisis," *Radio Free Europe Report*, Madrid, January 27, 1982.

43. Mastny, *Helsinki, Human Rights and European Security*, p. 26.

44. Michael Wall, "Western Disagreements," *Radio Free Europe Report*, Bonn, February 2, 1982,

45. The Deputy Foreign Minister's remarks are recorded in William Korey, "The Helsinki/Madrid Meeting," p. 198.

46. The text of the Haig speech was published by the State Department's Bureau of Public Affairs. "Alexander Haig: Europe at the Crossroads," *Current Policy*, No. 367 (Washington, DC, February 9, 1982).

47. *Ibid.*

48. The episode is recounted in Sizoo and Jurrjens, *CSCE Decision Making: The Madrid Experience*, pp. 197-203.

49. *Ibid.*, p. 201.

50. Korey, "The Helsinki/Madrid Meeting," p. 198.

51. Roland Eggleston, "The Eloquent Silences," *Radio Free Europe Report*, Madrid, March 2, 1982.

52. Mastny, *Helsinki, Human Rights and European Security*, p. 27. Oliver's role was described in his interview with Joshua L. Dorosin, February 26, 1988.

53. For a detailed description, see Sizoo and Jurrjens, *CSCE Decision Making: The Madrid Experience*, pp. 203-08.

54. *Ibid.*, p. 206.

55. *Ibid.*, p. 207.

56. The disagreements are discussed in *ibid.*, pp. 237-38. Also, see Roland Eggleston, "New Western Proposals," *Radio Free Europe Report*, Madrid, November 9, 1982.

57. See Eggleston, "New Western Proposals." Also see his *Report* of November 11, 1982, for further details.

58. Research on the subject by the author was noted in William Korey, *Human Rights and the Helsinki Accord*, p. 59.

59. *Ibid.*, p. 61.

60. *Ibid.*

61. Sizoo and Jurrjens, *CSCE Decision Making: The Madrid Experience*, p. 85.

62. *Ibid.*

63. *Ibid.*, pp. 254-55, 260.

64. Roland Eggleston, "Bid for Soviet Concession," *Radio Free Europe Report*, Madrid, December 13, 1982.

65. Roland Eggleston, "Soviets Find Amendments Unacceptable," *Radio Free Europe Report*, Madrid, June 15, 1983.

66. *Ibid.*

67. Roland Eggleston, "Speech by Spanish Premier," *Radio Free Europe Report*, Madrid, June 17, 1983.

68. *Ibid.*

69. The text of the address by Ambassador Jörg Kastl, head of the West German delegation, was filed from Madrid by Roland Eggleston on June 24, 1983.

70. Roland Eggleston, "Qualified US Agreement," *Radio Free Europe Report*, Madrid, June 24, 1983.

71. The text of the Kovalev address was filed by Roland Eggleston from Madrid on July 1, 1983.

72. Sizoo and Jurrjens, *CSCE Decision Making: The Madrid Experience*, p. 255.

73. *Ibid.*, p. 256. The full text of the "Concluding Document" is to be found on pp. 296-317.

74. Eggleston, "Soviets Find Amendments Unacceptable."

75. Roland Eggleston, "Radio Free Europe Defended," *Radio Free Europe Report*, Madrid, February 4, 1981.

76. Roland Eggleston, "Debate on Monitoring Rights," *Radio Free Europe Report*, Madrid, July 1, 1983.

77. Roland Eggleston, "The Remaining Differences," *Radio Free Europe Report*, Madrid, July 1, 1983.

78. Roland Eggleston, "A Fairly Substantial Document," *Radio Free Europe Report*, Madrid, July 15, 1983.

79. Department of State, "George Shultz: The Challenge of the Helsinki Process," *Current Policy* (Washington, DC, September 9, 1983), No. 508.

80. Sizoo and Jurrgens, *CSCE Decision Making: The Madrid Experience*, p. 141.

81. Arthur Goldberg, "The Madrid CSCE Conference—'Twas a Hollow Victory," *American Foreign Policy Newsletter*, Vol. 7, No. 1, February 1984, pp. 1-5.

82. Edward L. Killham, "The Madrid CSCE Conference: A Fourth Opinion," *American Foreign Policy Newsletter*, Vol. 8, No. 2, April 1985, pp. 7-9.

83. Arthur Goldberg, "A Reply," *American Foreign Policy Newsletter*, Vol. 8, No. 2, April 1985, pp. 10-11.

NOTES TO CHAPTER 9

1. Reddaway, *Soviet Policies on Dissent and Emigration*, pp. 25-28.

2. *Ibid.*, p. 26

3. Department of State, "New Soviet Legislation Restricts Rights, Strengthens Internal Security," (Washington, DC, July 1984), p. 2.

4. *The Position of Soviet Jewry: Human Rights and the Helsinki Accords* (London: World Conference on Soviet Jewry, 1985), p. 56

5. Reddaway, *Soviet Policies on Dissent and Emigration*, p. 27.

6. *The Position of Soviet Jewry: Human Rights and the Helsinki Accords*, pp. 55-6.

7. *Ibid.*, pp. 3-12.

8. *International Herald Tribune* (Paris), November 15, 1984.

9. *The Position of Soviet Jewry, 1983-1986*, p. 10.

10. *Ibid.*, pp. 10-13.

11. *Ibid.*, p. 12.

12. *The Position of Soviet Jewry: Human Rights and the Helsinki Accord*, p. 5.

13. Examples are offered in a study of the Committee of Concerned Scientists, *Report on Basket III Violations of the Helsinki Final Act* (New York, February 24, 1986), mimeo, 14 pp.

14. See the report to the National Conference on Soviet Jewry by the international law firm White & Case, *Who May Leave: A Review of Soviet Practice Restricting Emigration on Grounds of Knowledge of "State Security" in Comparison with Standards of International Law and the Policies of Other States* (New York, 1987), pp. 52-111.

15. The UN study is discussed in Chapter 14. Mikhail Gorbachev himself supported a 5-10 year limit in an interview with Paris Television. See *Le Monde* (Paris), October 3, 1985.

16. The comment of Kondrashev is quoted in the *Jewish Chronicle* (London), December 11, 1981.

17. *The Daily Telegraph* (London), June 8, 1985.

18. *NYT*, February 3, 1985. The official was Vladimir S. Alkhimov, Chairman of the Soviet State Bank.

19. *The Position of Soviet Jewry: Human Rights and the Helsinki Accords*, pp. 11-12.

20. *Ibid.*, pp. 12-17.

21. *Ibid.*, pp. 14-15.

22. Cited in Dorothy K. Goldberg, *A Personal Journal*, pp. 715-16.

23. *Ibid.*, p. 719.

24. The action is recalled by Goodby in a later speech. See Roland Eggleston, "Address by the Head of the US Delegation," *Radio Free Europe Report*, Stockholm, September 18, 1984.

25. Cited by Dorothy K. Goldberg, *A Personal Journal*, pp. 719-20.

26. *Ibid.*, p. 722.

27. Eggleston, "Address by the Head of the US Delegation."

28. *Ibid.*

29. "Stockholm CDE Conference Update," *CSCE Digest*, November 2, 1984, p. 3.

30. Cited by Ambassador James Goodby in his "A Report on the First Year of the [Stockholm] Conference," in Mastny, *Helsinki, Human Rights and European Security*, p. 320.

31. *Ibid.*, p. 321.

32. *Ibid.*, pp. 324-25.

33. *Ibid.*, p. 322.

34. Roland Eggleston, "A Fairly Substantial Document," *Radio Liberty Report*, Madrid, July 7, 1983.

35. Commission, *Basket I—Implementation of the Final Act*, p. 10. Also see the "Stockholm CDE Conference Update," p. 2.

36. Cited by Ambassador James Goodby, "A Report on the First Year of the [Stockholm] Conference," p. 325.

37. Closing statement of Sir Anthony Williams, Head of United Kingdom Delegation to the Ottawa Meeting on Human Rights, June 17, 1985.

38. Soviet Committee for European Security and Cooperation, *Ten Years After Helsinki: The Results and Prospects of the Process for European Security*, Supplement to *Moscow News*, No. 30, July 28, 1985.

39. The episode is examined in Ambassador Richard Schifter's opening address at Ottawa on May 10, 1985. It is carried in Mastny, *Helsinki, Human Rights and European Security*, pp. 286-87.

40. The comment was made by the head of the Soviet delegation, Vsevolod Sofinsky, on May 14, 1985. See Roth, "Ten Years After Helsinki," p. 5.

41. The commentator was Ernst Levy. See the *Frankfurter Allgemeine Zeitung*, June 26, 1985. Levy's citation is in Roth, "Ten Years After Helsinki," p. 7.

42. At previous meetings, the Soviet delegates had begun by denouncing Western criticism of Moscow's human rights practices as a violation of Principle VI of the Helsinki accord.

43. The quotation is in Roth, "Ten Years After Helsinki," p. 6.

44. *Ibid.*, p. 5. Sergei Kondrashev, again the second-ranking member of the Soviet delegation, was the KGB major-general with whom Kampelman had worked closely in Madrid.

45. The comment was made by the head of the West German delegation, Ambassador Ekkehard Eickhoff, in an October 1985 article in *Europa-Archiv*. See Mastny, *Helsinki, Human Rights and European Security*, p. 306.

46. Roth, "Ten Years After Helsinki," p. 5.

47. The observation was made by Ambassador Schifter in his opening address on May 10, 1985. See Mastny, *Helsinki, Human Rights and European Security*, p. 285.

48. "US and Soviet Quality of Life Compared by Richard Schifter." May 22, 1985. The text is in *ibid.*, pp. 289-303.

49. Dorothy K. Goldberg, *A Personal Journal*, p. 520.

50. See Schifter's statement, "The US and International Covenants," on June 4, 1985. The text is in Mastny, *Helsinki, Human Rights and European Security*, pp. 287-89. Schifter cites the text of the Polish proposal calling for ratification of the international covenants on human rights.

51. *Ibid.*

52. See Roth, "Ten Years After Helsinki," p. 7.

53. *Ibid.*

54. *Ibid.*, pp. 7-8.

55. Roland Eggleston, "KGB General on Human Rights, *Radio Liberty Report*, Ottawa, May 17, 1985.

56. Roth, "Ten Years After Helsinki," p. 8.

57. *CSCE/OME. 36.* It was submitted by Czechoslovakia, the German Democratic Republic, Hungary and the USSR.

58. *CSCE/OME 47.* It was submitted by Canada, Iceland, Italy, Norway, Portugal, Spain, Turkey, and the United States.

59. Statement by Sir Anthony Williams, June 17, 1985, as cited in Roth, "Ten Years After Helsinki," p. 10.

60. *Izvestiia*, July 12, 1985.

61. TASS, July 19, 1985.

62. *The Economist* (London), July 27, 1985.

63. Roland Eggleston, "Congressmen Dismayed by Soviet Attitudes," *Radio Liberty Report*, Ottawa, May 11, 1985.

64. *Ibid.*

65. This would be articulated to the author by British CSCE veteran Philip Hurr in Bern in April 1986. It is implied in testimony of Assistant Secretary of State Rozanne Ridgway to the Helsinki Commission on June 18, 1986; see Commission, *Hearings: Bern Human Contacts Experts Meeting, June 18, 1986* (Washington, DC, 1986).

66. This is made evident in Dorothy K. Goldberg, *A Personal Journal*, pp. 716-777.

67. *Neue Zürcher Zeitung*, September 20, 1986.

68. Eggleston, "Congressmen Dismayed by Soviet Attitudes."

69. *Ibid.*

70. The message was delivered in a formal press statement on May 14, 1985. It is in Mastny, *Helsinki, Human Rights and European Security*, p. 333.

71. Cited by Roland Eggleston, correspondent of Radio Liberty, in his filed report from Ottawa on October 14, 1985.

72. Richard Pipes, "The Helsinki Accords, Ten Years After: Who Gained?" *NYT*, August 1, 1985.

73. George F. Will, "Iron Curtain, Rubber Words," *Newsweek*, April 1, 1985.

74. Unger's comments are cited in "Can We Negotiate with the Russians?" p. 4.

75. *Ibid.*

76. Roth, "Ten Years After Helsinki," p. 3.

77. Soviet Committee for European Security and Cooperation, *Ten Years After Helsinki*.

78. Ludmilla Alexeyeva, "Why Helsinki Must Stay Afloat," *The Times* (London), July 31, 1985.

79. Commission, *Progress in Perspective*, p. 3.

80. Roth, "Ten Years After Helsinki," p. 4.

81. *Frankfurter Allgemeine Zeitung*, August 12, 1985. French Foreign Minister Roland Dumas' view was not very different from that of Secretary of State George Shultz, who said that everyone was aware that "progress might come slowly." See Commission, *Basket I—Implementation of the Final Act*, p. 13.

NOTES TO CHAPTER 10

1. See Boris Meissner, "Gorbachev's Foreign Policy Programme," *Aussenpolitik*, Vol. 37 2/86, pp. 116-17; and Bohdan Nahaylo "Soviet Foreign Policy During Gorbachev's First Year," *Radio Liberty Research*, RL 78/86, February 17, 1986, pp. 1-2.

2. Nahaylo, "Soviet Foreign Policy," p. 1.

3. The observations were made in one of his major speeches. Richard Schifter, "Glasnost: The Dawn of Freedom," *Public Information Series of US State Department* (Washington, DC, 1989), p. 2. The address was to the American Academy of Political and Social Science in Philadelphia on April 28, 1989. Later, in 1991, Schifter made this same point in an opening statement at a CSCE meeting in Oslo. See Commission, *The Oslo Seminar of Experts on Democratic Institutions* (Washington, DC, 1991), p. 11.

4. Commission, *Basket I—Implementation of the Final Act*, p. 13.

5. *Ibid.*

6. "The Budapest Cultural Forum: Heritage, Diversity, Freedom," *Radio Free Europe Research*, RAD Background Report/117, October 11, 1985, pp. 2-3.

7. Statement by Nathan Glazer, US Delegation to Budapest Cultural Forum, November 12, 1985.

8. Personal letter of Glazer to the author (December 3, 1985).

9. Commission, *Hearings*, (Washington, DC), December 11, 1985, p. 72.

10. *Ibid.*, p. 3.

11. *Subject: Budapest Cultural Forum; November 8 Plenary Statement by Ambassador [Sol] Polansky*. This was a copy of a cable sent to the Department of State and marked unclassified.

12. *Subject: Statement by William Least Heat-Moon at Budapest Cultural Forum*. This was a copy of a cable sent to the Department of State and marked unclassified.

13. Roland Eggleston, "One Europe and Writers' Duty," *Radio Free Europe Report*, Budapest, November 5, 1985.

14. This was a standard device used by Moscow at other Helsinki meetings. Organized exchanges were seen by the USSR as advancing cooperation and peace.

15. Eggleston, "One Europe and Writers' Duty."

16. Commission, *Annual Report of the Commission on Security and Cooperation for the Period Covering January 1 through December 31, 1985* (Washington, DC, 1986), pp. 7-8.

17. Commission, *Hearings*, December 11, 1985, p. 64.

18. *Ibid.*, p. 2.

19. *Ibid.*, p. 3.

20. *Ibid.*

21. Roland Eggleston, "The Budapest Cultural Forum," *Radio Liberty Research*, RL 392/85, November 26, 1985.

22. Commission, *Hearings*, December 11, 1985, p. 66.

23. Stoessel's protests are in his Commission testimony of December 11, 1985, p. 6. Fleischman, in her testimony, details the meetings in private apartments, *ibid.*

24. See Stoessel's testimony, Commission, *Hearings*, December 11, 1985, p. 6.

25. Commission, *Hearings*, December 11, 1985.

26. *Ibid.*

27. See William Korey, "Helsinki, Human Rights and the Gorbachev Style," *Ethics and International Affairs*, Vol. 1, 1987, p. 120. President Reagan reported that human rights was "a subject we went into quite deeply." See Associated Press, November 23, 1985.

28. Radio Moscow, November 18, 1985.

29. *Pravda*, January 16, 1986.

30. Boris Meissner, "Gorbachev's Foreign Policy Programme," p. 117. Also see Gorbachev's February 25 speech to the 27th Party Congress, *Pravda*, February 26, 1986.

31. *Pravda*, February 26, 1986.

32. F.J.M. Feldbrugge, "The Soviet Human Rights Doctrine in the Crossfire Between Dissidents at Home and Critics Abroad," *Vanderbilt Journal of Transnational Law*, Vol. XIII, No. 2-3, Spring-Summer 1980, pp. 451-466.

33. Professor Maurice Friedberg of the University of Illinois-Champaign Slavic Department provided the author with this insight.

34. TASS, July 7, 1986.

35. Anatoly Dobrynin, "Za bez'yadernyi mir, navstrechu XXI veka" ("For a nuclear-free world at the brink of the 21st century"), *Kommunist*, No. 9, 1986, pp. 18-31.

36. *Pravda*, February 26, 1986.

37. Schifter, "Glasnost: The Dawn of Freedom?" p. 3.

38. Sakharov, *Memoirs*, p. 600.

39. In his initial response to Gorbachev's call on December 16, 1985, Sakharov demanded the release of the prisoners of conscience. See *ibid.*, pp. 615-16. The text of the February letter was printed in a special issue of *Human Rights Bulletin* (New York: December 1986), published by the International League of Human Rights.

40. *L'Humanité* (Paris), February 8, 1986.

41. Sakharov, *Memoirs*, p. 607.

42. Commission, *Basket I—Implementation of the Final Act*.

43. *Human Contacts: Reunion of Families and Soviet Jewry* (London: World Conference on Soviet Jewry, 1986), p. 32. Appendices provide detailed information on the refusenik category.

44. For a summary of the report, see *ibid.*, pp. 11-14.

45. *The Times* (London), November 28, 1985.

46. US Postal Service, *Mailing to the Soviet Union* (Washington, DC, September 1985).

47. *The Guardian* (London), February 10, 1976. It correctly noted that mail interference also violated "the spirit of the Final Act."

48. Commission, *Basket I—Implementation of the Final Act*, p. 186.

49. *L'Humanité* (Paris), February 8, 1986.

50. The author has dealt with the subject in William Korey, *Glasnost and Anti-Semitism*, p. 20.

51. *Ibid.*

52. Radio Moscow, May 22, 1987. The broadcast made clear that it was a TASS dispatch.

53. The remark was brought to the author's attention by Radio Liberty research. Unofficial estimate of the Jewish emigration potential was 383,000. See World Conference on Soviet Jewry, *Human Contacts: Reunion of Families and Soviet Jewry*, p. 27.

54. The figures were provided by the National Conference of Soviet Jewry.

55. Committee of Concerned Scientists, *Report on Basket III Violations*, pp. 1-4.

56. "Appeal to the CSCE Experts' Meeting on Human Contacts," (April 1986). A copy of this open letter is in the author's possession.

57. Roland Eggleston, "Private Groups in Bern Seek Exit Permits for Relatives," *Radio Liberty Research*, RL 171/86, April 22, 1986, p. 2.

58. *Ibid.*

59. *Ibid.*

60. *Ibid.*, p. 1.

61. Statement by Yuri B. Kashlev, Soviet Delegation to the Bern CSCE Meeting, April 16, 1986.

62. The Canadian, British and US delegations called attention to the Soviet maneuver. For the details, see William Korey, "The Soviets Get Tougher on the Refuseniks," *WSJ*, June 18, 1986.

63. Roland Eggleston, "West Wants USSR to Honor Existing Accords on Human Contacts," *Radio Liberty Research*, RL 164/85, April 9, 1986, p. 1.

64. *Ibid.*, pp. 1-4.

65. "Ordinary People: The Dream and the Reality," statement by Ambassador Michael Novak, Head of the US Delegation to the Bern CSCE Meeting, April 17, 1986.

66. Roland Eggleston, "The Bern Conference Begins," *Radio Liberty Research*, RL 162/86, April 16, 1986, pp. 1-4.

67. *Ibid.*, p. 2.

68. Quoted in *ibid.*, p. 3.

69. Commission, *Basket I—Implementation of the Final Act*, p. 15.

70. The annex was entitled "Cases of Soviet Denial of Human Contacts in the Area of Family Reunification, Freedom to Choose One's Place of Residence," 7 pp.

71. Statement by Ambassador Michael Novak, April 17, 1986.

72. The intent of the Alexander statement, apparently, was to serve the bargaining purpose of obtaining, if possible, further liberalizing concessions. The report was filed from Bern by Roland Eggleston of Radio Free Europe on May 26, 1986, citing the Associated Press interview.

73. Sir Anthony nonetheless found the neutral/non-aligned document to be, in general, positive.

74. See Michael Novak, "Taking Helsinki Seriously," *WSJ*, June 4, 1986. See also his testimony in Commission, *Hearings*, June 18, 1986, pp. 30-9.

75. Statement by Sir Anthony Williams, Head of the United Kingdom Delegation to the Bern CSCE Meeting, May 27, 1986.

76. Letter to Ambassador Michael Novak from Commission Chairman Alfonse M. D'Amato and Co-chairman Steny H. Hoyer (April 24, 1986). A copy is in the possession of the author.

77. Commission, *Hearings Before the Commission on Security and Cooperation in Europe: Natan Shcharansky to Mark the 10th Anniversary of the Moscow Helsinki Group* (Washington, DC, May 14, 1986), p. 21.

78. Interview with Ambassador Rozanne Ridgway, July 18, 1990. This was conducted by the author in her office at the Atlantic Council in Washington. The point was made to the author earlier in a Washington interview with Julian LeBourgeois, July 21, 1986. He was the key State Department official handling CSCE matters. He described the Ridgway-Novak telephone conversation as leaving the decision entirely in Novak's hands.

79. See his official paper, *Analysis of NNA Final Proposal at Bern Human Contacts Experts Meeting*, July 28, 1986, pp. 1-26. Novak's analysis is entitled *Comparison of Helsinki/Madrid Language with Bern's Final Compromise Proposals and Analytical Comments*. The Commission's own internal study is more positive than the Schifter paper. It is entitled *Comparison of the NNA Draft Document BME.49 with the Helsinki Final Act and Madrid Concluding Document*.

80. This was confirmed by a Commission staff member in a Washington interview with the author on June 9, 1986. He preferred anonymity.

81. *The Los Angeles Times*, June 1, 1986.

82. Communicated to the author in an interview with Edward Alexander, June 21, 1986, in New York.

83. Novak, "Taking Helsinki Seriously."

84. For a perceptive analysis of "who got what" from Helsinki, see the lecture by Warren Zimmermann, "The Helsinki Process: Interests and Prospects" at the National Leadership Forum held in Washington, DC, at the Georgetown University Center for Strategic and International Studies, May 16, 1985. The Germans clearly benefited most.

85. Interview with Ed Alexander, June 21, 1986.

86. *The Times* (London), May 27, 1986.

87. Interview with Ed Alexander, June 21, 1986.

88. *Ibid.* The State Secretary of the Swiss Federal Department of Foreign Affairs, Edouard Brunner, in a personal letter to the author dated July 29, 1986, stated that "all delegations," including the US delegation, by the afternoon of May 26 had said "they could agree" on the document emerging from the neutral/non-aligned proposal.

89. *Neue Zürcher Zeitung*, May 28, 1986. The phrase "vast silence" was emphasized.

90. *The Los Angeles Times*, June 1, 1986. The dispatch was filed from Bern by correspondent Don Cook, who had been critical of the US anti-Soviet policy line since the Belgrade follow-up meeting.

91. Neal Ascherson, "An American Veto Delights a Russian," *Observer* (London), June 1, 1986.

92. *Ibid.*

93. Interview with Ed Alexander, June 21, 1986.

94. Commission, *Testimony on the Bern Human Contact Meeting: Leonard R. Sussman, Executive Director, Freedom House, Before the Commission on Security and Cooperation in Europe* (Washington, DC, June 18, 1986), mimeo, 6 pp.

95. "Breakthrough in Bern," *WSJ*, June 4, 1986.

96. Norman Podhoretz, "A Response to Broken Promises," *WP*, June 8, 1986.

97. *The Economist* article, "The Slow Road from Helsinki," was carried in *The Washington Times*, June 3, 1986.

98. *The Los Angeles Times*, June 1, 1986.

99. The author was present throughout the various activities of Ambassador Kampelman.

100. Interview with Ambassador Max Kampelman, July 23, 1986. The interview was conducted by the author in Washington, DC.

101. Statement by Ambassador William Bauer, Head of the Canadian Delegation to the CSCE meeting on Human Contacts in Bern, May 26, 1986.

102. Delegates from the Netherlands and Belgium made this view clear to the author.

103. Commission, *Hearings*, June 18, 1986, p. 3.

104. Statement by Sir Anthony Williams, May 27, 1986.

105. Interview with anonymous Commission staff member, June 9, 1986.

106. *Neue Zürcher Zeitung*, May 28, 1986. The word "amateurism" was underscored in the article.

107. Interview with Ambassador Warren Zimmermann, July 21, 1986. The interview was conducted in New York by the author. Zimmermann did say that West German officials were "still angry."

108. The figures were provided to the author by the Helsinki Commission.

NOTES TO CHAPTER 11

1. Commission, *Hearings*, June 18, 1985, p. 26.

2. Commission, *Basket I—Implementation of the Final Act*, pp. 24-27.

3. *Ibid.*, p. 24.

4. *Ibid.*, p. 25.

5. *Ibid.*

6. *Ibid.*

7. *Ibid.*, p. 26.

8. Commission, *Hearings*, May 14, 1986, p. 20.

9. *Ibid.*

10. Data are from the National Conference on Soviet Jewry.

11. Commission, *Hearings*, May 14, 1986, p. 21.

12. *Ibid.*

13. *Ibid.*

14. *Ibid.*, p. 22.

15. *Ibid.*, p. 23.

16. *Ibid.*, p. 24.

17. *Ibid.*, p. 27.

18. For a discussion of this development, see Korey, "Helsinki, Human Rights and the Gorbachev Style," p. 123.

19. See Elizabeth Teague, "Yuri Kashlev to Head Soviet Delegation to Helsinki Follow-Up Conference in Vienna," *Radio Liberty Research*, RL 412/86, October 30, 1986.

20. Korey, "Helsinki, Human Rights and the Gorbachev Style," p. 123. Also see William Korey, "Human Rights: It's Time for Pressure," *International Herald Tribune* (Paris), September 25, 1986.

21. *NYT*, July 29, 1986. Broad excerpts from Gorbachev's speech in Vladivostok were reprinted here.

22. Interview with Philip Hurr, May 15, 1986. Conducted by the author in Bern, Switzerland.

23. Commission, *Hearings*, June 18, 1986, p. 26.

24. *The Times* (London), April 19, 1986.

25. "Robert Barry on the Stockholm Accords," Institute for East-West Security Studies Meeting Report, New York, 1986. America's upbeat view was reported in a dispatch from Stockholm by Reuters, September 11, 1986.

26. The text of Gorbachev's speech at the Mitterrand dinner is in TASS, July 7, 1986. Akhromeyev's speech to the Stockholm meeting was given on August 29, 1986, and carried in *RFE/RL* Wireless File FW-147.

27. The text is carried in Commission, *Hearings*, October 1, 1986.

28. Korey, "Helsinki, Human Rights and the Gorbachev Style," p. 131.

29. *NYT*, September 22, 1986.

30. *NYT*, September 25, 1986.

31. *NYT*, September 23, 1986.

32. *Ibid.*

33. Korey, "Helsinki, Human Rights and the Gorbachev Style," p. 132.

34. *Ibid.*, p. 133. Concern about "imbalance" was stressed by Dante Fascell in his article in *The Miami Herald*, August 2, 1987.

35. Korey, "Helsinki, Human Rights and the Gorbachev Style," p. 133.

36. *Ibid.*, p. 122.

37. Roland Eggleston, "Questions about Soviet Openness in Vienna," *Radio Liberty Reports* (FF012), November 10, 1986. The negative press conference was reported in a memo from Commission staffer Orest Deychak to the author dated November 11, 1986.

38. *NYT*, December 10, 1986.

39. *Ibid.*

40. TASS, November 5, 1986. The text was distributed at the Vienna plenary. See statement by Eduard Shevardnadze, Foreign Minister of the USSR, at the Vienna CSCE Meeting, November 5, 1986.

41. Statement by Anatoly Kovalev, First Deputy Minister of Foreign Affairs of the USSR, at the Vienna CSCE Meeting, December 10, 1986.

42. *Ibid.*

43. *Die Presse*, November 8-9, 1986.

44. Statement by Ambassador Warren Zimmermann, Head of the United States Delegation to the Vienna CSCE Meeting, November 14, 1986.

45. Notes on Count Ledebur's intervention, November 14, 1986, taken by the author at the plenary session.

46. Notes on Ambassador Kashlev's intervention, November 14, 1986, taken by the author at the plenary session.

47. Draft cable on bilateral with Soviets, November 11, 1986. The draft of the cable summarizing the meeting was prepared by Commission staffer John Finerty.

48. *NYT*, December 13, 1986. Marchenko's death took place on December 9, and was reported the next day in *NYT*. By a striking coincidence, both his and the author's opinion pieces were published together in *NYT*, September 24, 1986, several months before his death.

49. The episode is recounted in detail in Medvedev and Chiesa, *Time of Change*, pp. 34-5, 92-3.

50. *Ibid.*, p. 92.

51. Letter from Andrei Sakharov to Ambassador Warren Zimmermann (January 25, 1987). A copy is in the possession of the author.

NOTES TO CHAPTER 12

1. Doder and Branson, *Gorbachev: Heretic in the Kremlin*, pp. 209-11.

2. Notes on an address by Assistant Secretary of State Richard Schifter to National Conference on Soviet Jewry, Washington, DC, June 11, 1989.

3. *Ibid.*

4. *Le Monde* (Paris), February 11, 1987.

5. Medvedev and Chiesa, *Time of Change*, pp. 77-91.

6. *Ibid.*, pp. 77-91.

7. Cited in Doder and Branson, *Gorbachev: Heretic in the Kremlin*, p. 193.

8. *Ibid.*, p. 198.

9. Medvedev and Chiesa, *Time of Change*, pp. 68-72.

10. Notes on Schifter's address to National Conference on Soviet Jewry.

11. Interview with Ambassador Warren Zimmermann in New York on January 20, 1988. As late as March 1988, the talks seemed to be stalemated. See *NYT*, March 27, 1988.

12. Warren Zimmermann, "Making Moscow Pay the Price for Rights Abuses," *NYT*, August 1, 1986.

13. According to a top State Department aide, Secretary of State Shultz made the crucial general decision to link all arms reduction negotiations at the ministerial level with human rights discussions in April 1987. From that point on, the frequent Shultz-Shevardnadze meetings were accompanied by US demands for "additional steps in the human rights field." See Richard Schifter, "Democracy's New Converts"; an address to the National Strategy Forum, Chicago, IL, on November 14, 1990.

14. The comments were made in Shultz's address to the Los Angeles World Affairs Council on October 31, 1986. See US Department of State, Bureau of Public Affairs, "Secretary Shultz: Human Rights and Soviet-American Relations," *Current Policy*, No. 882, (Washington, DC, 1986). At the opening session of the Vienna meeting on November 5, he again emphasized the linkage. See State Department, "Vienna CSCE Review Conference Address by Secretary of State George P. Shultz," *Current Policy*, No. 892 (Washington, DC, 1986).

15. Statement by Ambassador Robert H. Frowick to "S" Group Meeting, Vienna, September 1, 1988.

16. See William Korey, "Human Rights and the Policy of Leverage and Linkage: The Lesson of the Helsinki Process," in Vojtech Mastny and Jan Zielonka, eds., *Human Rights and Security: Europe on the Eve of a New Era* (Boulder: Westview Press, 1991), p. 86.

17. See *NYT*, March 27, 1988. The correspondent also quoted Zimmermann as saying that the USSR was "stalling and stonewalling" and hardly acting in the spirit of "glasnost."

18. "Brussels Declaration on Conventional Arms Control by Ministers at North Atlantic Council Session," *NATO Review*, December 1986, pp. 27-8.

19. The US delegate to the Conventional Stability Talks (CST) in Vienna was Ambassador Stephen Ledogar.

20. Letter to Congressman Steny Hoyer from Ambassador Warren Zimmermann (April 9, 1987).

21. Letter to Ambassador Warren Zimmermann from Morris B. Abram, Chairman, National Conference on Soviet Jewry (March 30, 1988).

22. Letter to Morris B. Abram, Chairman, National Conference on Soviet Jewry, from Ambassador Warren Zimmermann (April 21, 1988).

23. Interview with Ambassador Warren Zimmermann, December 14, 1988. Conducted by the author in Zimmermann's office in Vienna.

24. Interview with Ambassador Robert Frowick, December 12, 1988. Conducted by the author in Frowick's office in Vienna.

25. Roland Eggleston, "Question Mark Over Moscow Humanitarian Conference," *Radio Liberty Research* (RL 239/88), June 9, 1988.

26. Eduard Shevardnadze, *The Future Belongs to Freedom* (New York: Pantheon, 1991), p. 86. He refers to "stormy debates" in the Politburo that preceded his decision, and to widespread disagreements.

27. The author, while attending the sessions in July 1987, was informed of the change in wording. "Exemplary" might not even have applied to several NATO states.

28. Statement by Ambassador Warren Zimmermann, Head of the US Delegation to the Vienna CSCE Meeting, July 28, 1987.

29. Roland Eggleston, "The Vienna Debate on the Proposed Moscow Human Rights Meetings," *Radio Liberty Research* (RL 422/87), October 27, 1987.

30. Statement by Ambassador Yuri Kashlev, Head of USSR Delegation to the Vienna CSCE Meeting, July 24, 1977.

31. Shevardnadze, *The Future Belongs to Freedom*, p. 86. He comments that "more people disagreed with me than I had expected."

32. Eggleston, "The Vienna Debate on the Proposed Moscow Human Rights Meetings."

33. *Ibid.*, p. 2.

34. *The Sunday Times* (London), November 1, 1987.

35. Eggleston, "Question Mark Over Moscow Humanitarian Conference."

36. *Ibid.*

37. See Doder and Branson, *Gorbachev: Heretic in the Kremlin*, pp. 305-336.

38. *NYT*, October 13, 1988. In his memoirs, Shevardnadze emphasized that a human rights conference in Moscow would "provide an impetus for democratization" within the USSR. See *The Future Belongs to Freedom*, p. 86.

39. Interview with Ambassador Warren Zimmermann, December 14, 1988.

40. *NYT*, October 13, 1988.

41. *WP*, October 14, 1988.

42. Interview with Ambassador Warren Zimmermann, December 14, 1988. The Ambassador orally provided the author with a summary of the October 1987 conditions. The memorandum itself was kept confidential throughout and only revealed some 14 months later.

43. As subsequently reported in *NYT*, November 21, 1988.

44. Interview with Ambassador Warren Zimmermann, December 14, 1988.

45. US Congress, House Committee on Foreign Affairs, "*Fascell Warns of Human Rights Compromise*" (Washington, DC: August 19, 1988), mimeo. A year earlier, Fascell had written in *The Miami Herald* (August 2, 1987) that the linkage with CST could lead to the CSCE degenerating into the "generalized, propagandist European-security forum that the Soviets have sought all along." The Fascell statement was attached to the release (see Chapter 11, note 34, above).

46. State Department Briefing on Helsinki Process, September 8, 1988. The briefing was for NGOs. Notes were taken by a B'nai B'rith colleague of the author.

47. *Ibid.*

48. *Ibid.*

49. *Ibid.* Assistant Secretary of State Richard Schifter had emphasized the new structure in various speeches and interviews.

50. Interview with Assistant Secretary of State Richard Schifter, July 7, 1989. It was conducted by the author in Washington.

51. Commission, "Helsinki Co-Chairman Warns that Emphasis on Military and Trade Issues Could Endanger Helsinki Process," press release (Washington, DC, September 22, 1988).

52. The letter from President Reagan was sent to the Washington-based Union of Councils, a lobbying group on behalf of Soviet Jewry. The letter was dated October 20, 1988. The Council shared a copy with the author.

53. Interview with Ambassador Warren Zimmermann, December 14, 1988. The same threat was communicated to Assistant Secretary Schifter in September in Moscow by a high Soviet Foreign Ministry official; interview with Assistant Secretary Richard Schifter, July 7, 1989.

54. Interview with Ambassador Warren Zimmermann, December 14, 1988.

55. Interview with Ambassador Warren Zimmermann, October 16, 1988. Conducted in Vienna by the author.

56. *Ibid.*

57. *WP*, October 14, 1988.

58. The contents of the confidential Shultz letter were summarized to the author in the interview with Ambassador Warren Zimmermann, December 14, 1988.

59. US formulation found its way into Annex XI of the "Vienna Concluding Document." See Lehne, *The Vienna Meeting*, p. 292.

60. *Ibid.*, pp. 123-33.

61. Department of State, "The Evolution of Soviet Emigration Policy: Address by Assistant Secretary of State Richard Schifter," Long Island, New York, October 14, 1990, p. 6.

62. This view was expressed by Ambassador Sam Wise in an interview in Vienna with the author on December 12-13, 1988. However, Assistant Secretary of State Schifter told the author in an interview on July 7, 1989, that in his negotiations with Moscow, he pressed for the release of long-term refuseniks. He placed no time limit on their refusenik status. Rather, he told Moscow that the figure of 120 long-term refuseniks would be appropriate for immediate action. That figure was literally pulled out of a hat.

63. UN Sub-Commission on Prevention of Discrimination and Protection of Minorities, *Analysis of the Current Trends and Development Regarding the Right to Leave Any Country Including One's Own and to Return to One's Own Country, and Some Other Rights on Consideration Arising Therefrom*, E/CN. 4/Sub. 2/35 (1988). The study was prepared by special Rapporteur C.L.C. Mubanga-Chipoya. See, especially, Article 7 of his proposed "Draft Declaration" for the five-year limitation.

64. The data was provided by the Committee of Concerned Scientists in New York.

65. Information was made available in mid-December 1988 by Ron McNamara, a Helsinki Commission staff member with the US delegation in Vienna.

66. Roland Eggleston, "Soviet Delegation Will Press for Moscow Conference," *Radio Liberty Reports* (FF 192), December 2, 1988.

67. For a review of the congressional trip to Moscow and its resulting "optimism," see Steny H. Hoyer, "Human Rights in the Era of Glasnost," address to the Baltimore Council on Foreign Affairs, November 29, 1988, 5 pp.

68. *Pravda*, November 27, 1988.

69. *NYT*, December 2, 1988.

70. *Le Monde* (Paris), December 3, 1988.

71. Eggleston, "Soviet Delegation Will Press for Moscow Conference."

72. Information communicated to the author by the President of B'nai B'rith, Seymour M. Reich.

73. Interview with Ambassador Warren Zimmermann, December 14, 1988.

74. *Ibid.* Shultz told Schifter that US leverage was a "wasting asset" which, with time, would become ineffectual. Interview with Assistant Secretary Richard Schifter, July 7, 1989.

75. Interview with Congressman Steny Hoyer, July 31, 1989, in Washington, DC.

76. Remarks of Secretary Shultz to the author on January 16, 1989. The occasion was a small reception held by the Secretary in Vienna for delegation members. The author was an invited guest.

77. Interview with Philip Hurr, March 4, 1989. Hurr was a long-time CSCE "hand" in the UK delegation. The author interviewed him at the British Foreign Office in London.

78. *NYT*, January 5, 1989. The White House spokesman was Roman Popadiuk.

79. US Information Service, *Wireless File*, No. 10, January 18, 1989, p. 8.

80. *Ibid.*, p. 11.

NOTES TO CHAPTER 13

1. Frederick B. Artz, *Reaction and Revolution 1814-1832* (New York: Harper, 1934), p. 112.

2. *Ibid.*

3. Commission, *The Vienna CSCE Follow-up Meeting: Report Prepared by the Staff of the US Commission on Security and Cooperation in Europe* (Washington, DC, 1990), p. 4.

4. Interview with Ambassador Warren Zimmermann, December 14, 1988.

5. *Ibid.* For details, see William Korey, "The Helsinki Accord: A Growth Industry," *Ethics and International Affairs*, No. 4, April 1990, pp. 53-70.

6. Interviews with Ambassadors Bauer and Zimmermann on the significance of the Vienna document were conducted by the author on January 17, 1989, in Vienna.

7. For a summary of the Vienna achievements, see North Atlantic Assembly Papers, *CSCE: The Vienna Conference* (Brussels: NATO, August 1989), pp. 1-39. For the full text itself, see Lehne, *The Vienna Meeting*, pp. 221-92. Ambassador William Bauer's enthusiastic views are captured in an interview with the author in Vienna on December 14, 1988.

8. Stephen Roth, "New Chapter in the Helsinki Process: The Vienna Conference and its Aftermath," *IJA Research Report*, No. 4, July 1989, p. 8.

9. The author was present at US delegation discussions in Vienna on this proposal. The subject is briefly treated in *ibid.*, p. 7, and Lehne, *The Vienna Meeting*, p. 164.

10. The Mubanga-Chipoya study is in UN Doc. E/CN. 4/Sub. 2/35 (1988); see Chapter 12, note 63, above.

11. Foreign Broadcast Information Service, December 1, 1987. The text was also carried in *Sovetskaia Rossiia*, December 2, 1987.

12. The text of the UN General Assembly speech by President Gorbachev was distributed by Novosti, December 7, 1988.

13. *International Herald Tribune* (Paris), December 9, 1988.

14. The Kartashkin interview appeared in *Ogonek* (Moscow), No. 5, January 1989.

15. *Sovetskaia kultura*, February 11, 1989.

16. See Lehne, *The Vienna Meeting*, pp. 164-65; and Roth, "New Chapter in the Helsinki Process," pp. 7-8.

17. Lehne, *The Vienna Meeting*, pp. 159-60.

18. A detailed survey of the problem can be found in a study by Jonathan Eyal, "Recent Developments in the Jamming of Western Radio Stations Broadcasting to the USSR and Eastern Europe," *Radio Liberty Research Bulletin*, Supplement 8/87, No. 38, September 23, 1987, pp. 1-17.

19. *Ibid.*

20. Statement by Ambassador Warren Zimmermann, September 19, 1988.

21. Roland Eggleston, "USSR Rejects Ban on Jamming," *Radio Liberty Reports* (RFE/RL CN130), September 19, 1988.

22. Roland Eggleston, "Jamming of RFE/RL an Issue at Vienna Conference," *Radio Liberty Reports* (FF 130), September 27, 1988.

23. Novosti, December 7, 1988.

24. Reuters, December 16, 1988. The author was present in Vienna at the US delegation offices when the encouraging news about the end of jamming was arriving.

25. Reuters, December 23, 1988.

26. The research was made available to the author for his use. Also see Lehne's analysis, which notes that "roughly two-thirds of the principles section" in the Vienna document is devoted to but one of Helsinki's Decalogue. Lehne, *The Vienna Meeting*, p. 152.

27. Lehne, *The Vienna Meeting*, pp. 154-55.

28. Sian Lewis, "A Step Forward for International Human Rights Protection," *Interights Bulletin*, Vol. 3, No. 4, 1988.

29. Novosti, December 7, 1988.

30. Roth, "New Chapter in the Helsinki Process," p. 12.

31. *Ibid.*

32. See Lehne, *The Vienna Meeting*, p. 292. This carries the "chairman's statement," which constitutes Annex XI of the concluding document.

33. Roth, "New Chapter in the Helsinki Process," p. 11.

34. CSCE/WT. 19, February 4, 1987. For a discussion of the mechanism on the human dimension, see Lehne, *The Vienna Meeting*, pp. 169-70.

35. Interview with Assistant Secretary Richard Schifter, July 7, 1989.

36. Commission, *The Vienna CSCE Follow-up Meeting*, pp. 11-12.

37. The initiative was actually undertaken by US Ambassador Max M. Kampelman. He encouraged the Swedish Ambassador to speak first on the subject.

38. The episode is recounted in William Korey, "Will Little Signs Add Up to Real Soviet Thaw on the Wallenberg Case," *The Los Angeles Times*, February 27, 1989.

39. *Ibid.*

40. Commission, *The Vienna CSCE Follow-up Meeting*, p. 8.

41. *Ibid.*

42. *Ibid.*, p. 23. Bulgaria, Czechoslovakia, and East Germany are singled out for castigation.

43. For a discussion of the subject, see Erika Schlager, "The Procedural Framework of the CSCE: From the Helsinki Consultations to the Paris Charter," *Human Rights Law Journal*, Vol. 12, No. 6-7, July 12, 1991, p. 225.

44. *Ibid.* See also Lehne, *The Vienna Meeting*, p. 132. Romania's "reservations" were officially withdrawn on January 15, 1990, one month after the overthrow of the Ceausescu regime.

45. Lehne, *The Vienna Meeting*. He uses the phrase in the sub-title of his work.

46. Commission, *The Vienna CSCE Follow-up Meeting*, pp. 9-10.

47. *Ibid.*, p. 10.

48. *Ibid.*, p. 17.

49. *Ibid.*

50. *Ibid.*, p. 19.

51. *Ibid.*

52. A sharp dispute between the US and France concerning how to proceed on the conventional arms stability talks, particularly in relation to CSCE, delayed action in Vienna. For details on the resolutions of the dispute, see Lehne, *The Vienna Meeting*, pp. 108-9.

53. See, for example, Dante Fascell's August 2, 1987, warnings in *The Miami Herald*, referred to in Chapter 11, note 34, above.

54. The quoted paragraph appeared on page 6 of the initial draft of the Commission, which was printed up in March 1989 but not released. The author's copy reads: *The Vienna CSCE Follow-up Meeting: Report Prepared by the Staff of the US Commission on Security and Cooperation in Europe.* By the time the final draft appeared a year later—with the same title—the paragraph disappeared. Indeed, "many more words" and documents were yet to come.

NOTES TO CHAPTER 14

1. Novosti, December 7, 1988.

2. US Congress, Senate Committee on Foreign Relations, *Hearings*, January 17 and 18, 1989 (Washington, DC, 1989), p. 112.

3. For an analysis of the ramifications of the "Common European House," see Suzanne Crow, "The Soviet Union Knocks on Europe's Door," *Radio Liberty Report on the USSR* (Munich), November 16, 1990, pp. 5-8.

4. Department of State, Bureau of Public Affairs, "Secretary [James] Baker: New Horizons in Europe," *Current Policy* (Washington, DC, 1989), No. 1154, pp. 1-4.

5. *Ibid.*, p.3.

6. Department of State, Bureau of Public Affairs, "Secretary [James] Baker: Power for Good: American Foreign Policy in the New Era," *Current Policy* (Washington, DC, 1989), No. 1162, pp. 1-4.

7. Department of State, Bureau of Public Affairs, "Secretary [James] Baker: The Challenge of Change in US-Soviet Relations," *Current Policy* (Washington, DC, 1989), No. 1170, pp. 1-4.

8. Department of State, Bureau of Public Affairs, "President George Bush: Proposals for a Free and Peaceful Europe," *Current Policy* (Washington, DC, 1989), No. 1179, pp. 1-3.

9. *Ibid.*, p. 2. A strikingly similar phrase to "whole and free" was enunciated by Secretary of State George Shultz in his concluding speech to the Vienna follow-up meeting on January 17. No doubt a fine State Department speech writer was the source of both addresses.

10. The Bush comment is in *ibid.,* p. 2. The Gorbachev "freedom of choice" phrase is in his UN speech of December 7, 1988. Analysis of its status quo intent is in I. F. Stone, "The Rights of Gorbachev," *The New York Review of Books*, February 16, 1989, pp. 3-7.

11. The letter to Secretary James Baker is from the Helsinki Commission files. It is dated May 3, 1989.

12. The State Department letter to Senator Dennis DeConcini and Congressman Steny Hoyer is in the Helsinki Commission files. It is dated May 14, 1989.

13. Commission, *The Copenhagen Meeting of the Conference on the Human Dimension of the Conference on Security and Cooperation in Europe* (Washington, DC, August 1990), pp. 1, 9.

14. It is cited as the motivating formula of the Paris meeting in Commission, *The Paris Meeting of the Conference on the Human Dimension of the Conference on Security and Cooperation in Europe* (Washington, DC, July 1989), p. 6.

15. Statement by Ambassador Morris Abram, Head of the United States Delegation to Paris CSCE Meeting on the Human Dimension, May 31, 1989.

16. Commission, *From Vienna to Helsinki: Reports on the Intersessional Meetings of the CSCE Process* (Washington, DC, April 1992), pp. 1-8.

17. Statement by Ambassador Morris Abram, June 9, 1989.

18. Statement by Ambassador Morris Abram, June 5, 1989.

19. Morris B. Abram, *Report on the Paris Meeting of the Conference on the Human Dimension of the CSCE May 30-June 23, 1989* (Washington, DC, July 1989), mimeo, p. 4.

20. *Ibid.*

21. *Ibid.*

22. Statement by Ambassador Morris Abram, June 5, 1989.

23. *Ibid.* In his presentation, Abram drew upon the author's article. See William Korey, "The Persistent Plight of Refuseniks," *WSJ/Europe*, February 8, 1989.

24. Background notes on meeting with Soviets, June 7, 1989, together with lists, were provided the author by Helsinki Commission staffers. Interviews with Commission Deputy Staff Director Jane Fisher and with staffer Orest Deychak on June 21, 1989, filled in the details on the other bilaterals.

25. Interview with Jane Fisher, June 21, 1989.

26. See Lehne, *The Vienna Meeting*, p. 249.

27. Statement by Ambassador Morris B. Abram, June 23, 1989.

28. This section is based on the background notes on the meeting which were provided the author by the Commission staff, as well as on interviews with Jane Fisher and Orest Deychak.

29. The meeting with Reshetov was held on June 2. The author was present. Not until 1990 was the new emigration law introduced. Adopted in 1991, it would become operable only in 1993.

30. Interview with Jane Fisher, June 21, 1989.

31. Roland Eggleston, "Paris Human Rights Conference Closes," *RFE/RL Research Reports* (Munich), July 7, 1989.

32. Statement by Ambassador Morris Abram, May 31, 1989.

33. The new thrust for free elections and political pluralism as derived from the Helsinki Final Act itself was intellectually developed in a special memorandum to Ambassador Abram written by Helsinki Commission staffer Bob Hand on June 5, 1989. A copy is in the author's possession.

34. Statement by Ambassador Morris Abram, May 31, 1989.

35. Statement by Ambassador Morris Abram, June 5, 1989.

36. *International Herald Tribune* (Paris), June 7, 1989. Ambassador Abram called attention to this article in remarks made to the plenary on June 8, 1989.

37. *Ibid.*

38. Statement by Ambassador Morris Abram, June 9, 1989.

39. Statement by the Honorable Steny B. Hoyer, June 19, 1989.

40. Statement by Ambassador Morris B. Abram, June 23, 1989.
41. "National Minorities," statement by Paula Dobriansky, June 16, 1989.

42. Shikalov's remarks are summarized in a US delegation telegram to the State Department, *Subject: Paris CSCE/CDH MSG No. 49: US-Soviet Exchange, June 21, on American Human Rights Record.*

43. Hoyer's comments were taken down by the author in written form. Abram's observations on the Shikalov criticism are contained in Abram, *Report on the Paris Meeting*, p. 5.

44. Bob Hand, *Free Elections and Multiple Political Parties in Eastern Europe and the Soviet Union* (memorandum to Ambassador Abram), June 5, 1989. Also, see the State Department cable mentioned in note 42, above.

45. Abram, *Report on the Paris Meeting*, p. 11.

46. *Ibid.*, p. 12.

47. *Ibid.*, p. 2.

48. *Ibid.*, p. 12.

49. The Samoilovich case is dealt with in detail in William Korey, "Helsinki in Paris," *The New Leader*, Vol. 72, No. 11, July 10-24, 1989, pp. 12-14. It is based upon an interview with Philip Hurr in Paris on June 2, 1989. Hurr, a veteran British CSCE official, provided the author with details on the British Foreign Office role on this issue.

50. For details, see Fons Coomans and Liesbeth Lijnzard, "Initiating the CSCE Supervisory Procedure: The Cases of the Netherlands and Czechoslovakia," in A. Bloed and P. van Dijk, eds., *The Human Dimension of the Helsinki Process* (Dordrecht: Kluwer Academic, 1991), pp. 109-27. Later representations were made by Austria and Sweden.

51. Erika Schlager of the Commission staff prepared a detailed analytical chart which, as of July 11, 1989, showed some 50 instances of the use of the mechanism, mainly by the West. However, according to an Austrian authority, the mechanism was used "roughly 70 times." See Lehne, *The Vienna Meeting*, p. 188.

52. The comment by the Swiss delegate, Klaus Jacobi, can be found in a Reuters dispatch from Paris which was published in *The Washington Times*, June 5, 1989.

53. Statement by Jane Fisher, June 7, 1989.

54. *Ibid.*

55. *Ibid.*

56. *Ibid.*

57. *Ibid.*

58. *Ibid.*

59. Interview with Erika Schlager, June 28, 1989. Conducted by the author in Washington, DC.

60. Interview with Assistant Secretary of State Richard Schifter, July 7, 1989.

61. Interview with Erika Schlager, June 28, 1989.

62. Statement by Ambassador Morris Abram, May 31, 1989.

63. Statement by Jane Fisher, June 7, 1989.

64. Statement by Erika Schlager, June 6, 1989.

65. Statement by Jane Fisher, June 6, 1989.

66. Statement by John Evans of the US Delegation to the Paris CSCE Meeting on the Human Dimension, June 6, 1989.

67. *Ibid.*

68. *Ibid.*

69. Statement by Erika Schlager, June 6, 1989.

70. Commission, *The Paris Meeting of the Conference on the Human Dimension of the Conference on Security and Cooperation in Europe* (Washington, DC, July 1989), draft, p. 7.

71. The Swiss proposal was described in detail by Ambassador Abram in Commission, *Report on the Paris Meeting*, p. 3.

72. Statement by Ambassador Morris B. Abram, June 23, 1989.

73. Abram, *Report on the Paris Meeting*, p. 3.

74. Moscow was quickly responsive to the criticism. Gorbachev called upon the Congress of People's Deputies to withdraw the new law on "discrediting" institutions. It did so. See Commission, *Report on the Paris Meeting*, p. 18.

75. *NYT*, June 25, 1989.

76. Notes on the Soviet delegation press conference of June 1, 1989, were taken by the author.

77. *Ibid.*

78. Sakharov, *Memoirs*, pp. 611-12.

79. Richard Schifter in a speech, "The Soviet Union in Transition," given on April 16, 1990, at the Kennan Institute for Advanced Russian Studies in Washington, DC.

NOTES TO CHAPTER 15

1. For the role of Hungary, see *NYT*, September 15, 1989. Emigration of East Germans through Hungary was covered in several NYT articles running from September 10; see especially the *NYT* editorial on the subject on September 19. Concerning the potential size of East German emigration, see *NYT* of August 22, 1989. As for Soviet Jewish and Soviet German emigration sparked by Vienna, see Sidney Heitman, "Soviet Emigration in 1990: A New 'Fourth Wave'?" *Soviet Jewish Affairs*, Vol. 21, No. 2, Winter 1991, pp. 11-21. Additional data came from the National Conference on Soviet Jewry.

2. For a detailed treatment of the dynamics of German unification, see Manfred Görtemaker, *European Revolution and German Unity: 1989-1990* (New York: St. Martin's Press and the Institute for EastWest Studies, forthcoming).

3. Statement by Czechoslovak Deputy Prime Minister and Minister of Foreign Affairs Jiri Dienstbier at the Copenhagen Meeting of the Conference on the Human Dimension, June 4, 1990.

4. Commission, *The Sofia CSCE Meeting on the Protection of the Environment, October 16-November 3, 1989* (Washington, DC, November 1989), draft, p. 11. The final version elaborated more fully on the point. The draft was prepared by Bob Hand of the Commission staff.

5. A copy of the text is in the author's possession. The letter was addressed to "President Nicolai Ceausescu" and is signed by Gheorghe Apostol, Alexandru Birladeanu, Corneliu Manescu, Constantin Pirvulescu, Grigore Raceanu and Silviu Brucan. See *NYT*, March 7, 1989.

6. See Kux, "Revolution in Eastern Europe—Revolution in the West?" p. 6. The significance of the electronic media upon East Europe was emphasized by the Soviet specialist M. P. Pavlova-Silvanskaia in *Komsomolskaia pravda*, January 3, 1990. Details of the Helsinki process were continuously broadcast into Eastern Europe by major Western radio stations. (See Chapter 3, notes 36-7, above.)

7. *WP*, December 1, 1989.

8. *Ibid.*

9. *Ibid.*

10. William Korey, "Challenging Bigotry: Unfinished Helsinki Business," *The New Leader*, Vol. LXXIII, No. 15, November 12-26, 1990, p. 13.

11. *Ibid.*

12. F. Stephen Larrabee, "Moscow and German Unification," *The Harriman Institute Forum*, Vol. 5, No. 9, May 1992, pp. 3-5. See also Richard Ullman, *Securing Europe* (Princeton: Princeton University Press and the Twentieth Century Fund, 1991), pp. 3-4.

13. See *International Herald Tribune* (Paris), December 4 and 7, 1989. For the East European attitude, see also *NYT*, February 5, 1990. The venue was Davos, Switzerland, where a World Economic Forum was in session.

14. That was the title of his address at Copenhagen, June 5, 1990.

15. *NYT*, June 3 and 4, 1990.

16. Commission, *Hearings*, July 18, 1990, p. 39.

17. *Ibid.*, p. 38.

18. The author was a witness to how Kampelman utilized the concentrated legal expertise in his delegation. Long hours were spent on a weekend exploring the development of an all-encompassing draft.

19. *Suddeutsche Zeitung*, June 30-July 1, 1990, as cited in a Thomas Buergenthal mimeo manuscript (Washington, DC, 1990), p. 28. It was later published as "The Copenhagen CSCE Meeting: A New Public Order for Europe," *Human Rights Law Journal*, Vol. 11, 1990.

20. Yuri Reshetov, "The Road to Moscow and Beyond," presentation to University of Copenhagen Colloquium on the CSCE Process, June 11, 1990. The paper is in the author's possession.

21. See Kampelman, *Entering New Worlds*, pp. 119-40. The author was a witness at one of the lengthy, closely argued legal sessions in Copenhagen held by Kampelman with the law professors.

22. This disclosure was communicated to the author later in Moscow. Interview with Max M. Kampelman, September 12, 1991.

23. Commission, *Document of the Copenhagen Meeting of the Conference on the Human Dimension of the CSCE* (Washington, DC, June 1990), pp. 1-29.

24. The author was present at some of these discussions.

25. Commission, *The Copenhagen Meeting* (June 1990), pp. 13-14.

26. *Ibid.*, p. 7.

27. *Ibid.*

28. Commission, *From Vienna to Helsinki*, pp. 53-65.

29. Commission, *Hearings*, July 18, 1990, pp. 4-5.

30. *Ibid.*

31. *Ibid.*, p. 3.

32. Buergenthal, "The Copenhagen CSCE Meeting," p. 2 of the mimeo cited in note 18, above.

33. This technical legal point was made by Erika Schlager. See her article, "The Procedural Framework of the CSCE," pp. 231-2.

34. Commission, *Hearings*, July 18, 1990, p. 20.

35. Commission, *The Copenhagen Meeting* (June 1990), p. 15.

36. Buergenthal, "The Copenhagen CSCE Meeting," mimeo, p. 20.

37. Commission, *The Copenhagen Meeting* (June 1990), pp. 16-20.

38. *Ibid.*, p. 18.

39. Commission, *The Copenhagen Meeting* (August 1990), p. 27.

40. Commission, *The Copenhagen Meeting* (June 1990), p. 19.

41. Stephen J. Roth, "CSCE Outlaws Anti-Semitism," *IJA Research Report*, No. 6, October 1990, p. 8.

42. *Ibid.*

43. *Ibid.*

44. Korey, *Glasnost and Soviet Anti-Semitism*, pp. 32-43.

45. William Korey, "A Fear of Pogroms Haunts Soviet Jews," *NYT*, January 25, 1990.

46. Howard Spier, ed., "Anti-Semitism in Central and Eastern Europe," *IJA Research Report*, November 1991, pp. 1-51.

47. Dominique Moïsi, "A Spectre is Haunting Europe: Its Past," *NYT*, May 29, 1990.

48. Adam Michnik, "Why I Won't Vote for Lech Walesa," *NYT*, November 23, 1990.

49. Statement by Foreign Minister Jiri Dienstbier, June 4, 1990.

50. Statement by Johannes Langhoff, Head of the Delegation of the German Democratic Republic to the Copenhagen CSCE Meeting, June 6, 1990.

51. Cited in Roth, "CSCE Outlaws Anti-Semitism," p. 6.

52. Statement by Max M. Kampelman, Head of the US Delegation to the Copenhagen CSCE Meeting, June 11, 1990.

53. Roth, "CSCE Outlaws Anti-Semitism," p. 7.

54. *Ibid.*

55. *Ibid.*

56. *Ibid.*

57. *Ibid.*

58. Commission, *The Copenhagen Meeting* (June 1990), p. 19.

59. See Roth, "CSCE Outlaws Anti-Semitism," pp. 9-10. At Copenhagen, Roth prepared a paper on the subject which he distributed to all CSCE delegations.

60. Korey, *Glasnost and Anti-Semitism*, p. 1.

61. Reshetov, "The Road to Moscow and Beyond."

62. For a discussion of the case, see William Korey, "Message from Moscow," *Hadassah Magazine*, February 1991, pp. 22-3.

63. Korey, *The Soviet Cage*, pp. 63-97.

64. Statement by Ambassador Max M. Kampelman, June 11, 1990.

65. Korey, *Glasnost and Anti-Semitism*, p. 1.

66. Mikhail Gorbachev, *Perestroika: New Thinking for Our Country and the World* (New York: Harper & Row, 1987), pp. 121-22.

67. Korey, *Glasnost and Anti-Semitism*, pp. 40-2.

68. *Komsomolskaia pravda*, April 12, 1990.

69. Korey, *Glasnost and Anti-Semitism*, p. 42.

70. *Pravda*, July 22, 1990.

71. Interview with Robin Saipe, July 19, 1990, by telephone from Washington, DC. Saipe was a key professional of the National Conference on Soviet Jewry.

72. *Ibid.* A letter to a Jewish organization professional by Max Kampelman, dated July 5, 1990, claims that he "obtained" the "condemnation of anti-Semitism." It somewhat exaggerated.

73. Commission, *Hearings*, July 18, 1990, p. 40.

74. Letter from CSFR President Vaclav Havel to the Copenhagen CSCE Meeting, June 5, 1990.

75. Statement by Danish Foreign Minister Uffe Ellemann-Jensen to the Copenhagen CSCE Meeting, June 5, 1990.

76. Commission, *The Copenhagen Meeting* (August 1990), p. 19.

77. *Ibid.*

78. *Ibid.*

79. Commission, *The Copenhagen Meeting* (June 1990), p. 20.

80. *Ibid.*

81. Statement by Foreign Minister Jiri Dienstbier, June 4, 1990.

82. Commission, *The Copenhagen Meeting* (August 1990), pp. 29-30.

83. Commission, *Hearings*, July 18, 1990, p. 2.

84. Commission, *The Copenhagen Meeting* (June 1990), p. 21.

85. Statement by US Secretary of State James A. Baker to the Copenhagen CSCE Meeting, June 6, 1990.

86. Commission, *Hearings*, July 18, 1990, p. 4.

87. Statement by Ambassador Yuri Reshestov, Head of the USSR Delegation to the Copenhagen CSCE Meeting, June 7, 1990.

88. Statement by Ambassador Max M. Kampelman, June 11, 1990.

89. International Helsinki Federation, "Hearings on Human Rights Situation in the Fifteen Soviet Republics," press release, June 6, 1990.

90. Commission, *Hearings*, July 18, 1990, p. 40.

91. Statement by Ambassador Max M. Kampelman, June 22, 1990.

92. Statement by Secretary of State James A. Baker, June 6, 1990.

93. *Ibid.*

94. Statement by Foreign Minister Uffe Ellemann-Jensen on June 5, 1990.

95. Statement by Eduard E. Shevardnadze, Foreign Minister of the USSR, at the Copenhagen CSCE Meeting, June 5, 1990.

NOTES TO CHAPTER 16

1. As a public member of the US delegation, the author was present in the hall when the announcement by the French head of delegation was made.

2. Schlager, "The Procedural Framework of the CSCE," p. 231.

3. See William Korey, "Challenging Bigotry: Unfinished Helsinki Business," *The New Leader*, Vol. LXXIII, No. 15, November 12-16, 1990, p. 13. See also *NYT*, November 22, 1990.

4. Statement by Margaret Thatcher, Prime Minister of Great Britain, at the Paris CSCE Summit Meeting, November 19, 1990.

5. Conference on Security and Cooperation in Europe (hereafter CSCE), *Charter of Paris for New Europe*, November 16, 1990/Version 2, p. 2.

6. *Ibid.* The new institutions are spelled out in a "Supplementary Document to Give Effect to Certain Provisions Contained in the Charter of Paris for a New Europe."

7. NATO, "London Declaration on a Transformed North Atlantic Alliance," Press Communiqué S-1 (90) 36, Brussels, July 6, 1990, pp. 1-6.

8. Henry Kissinger, "Bad Bargain for the West," *The New York Post*, July 25, 1990.

9. For an analysis, see Ullman, *Securing Europe*, pp. 54, 60-2.

10. See Eduard Shevardnadze's article in *Pravda*, June 26, 1990.

11. Ullman, *Securing Europe*, p. 60.

12. CSCE, "Communiqué of the New York Meeting of CSCE Foreign Ministers," New York, October 2, 1990. President Bush was especially enthusiastic about "Germany's day of celebration . . . ." See the White House, Office of the Press Secretary, "Remarks by the President to CSCE Ministerial," October 1, 1990.

13. Manfred Wörner, "We Still Need a Conventional Forces Treaty," *WP*, March 6, 1990.

14. The substantive elements of the agreement are in *NYT*, October 4-5, 1990.

15. "CSCE Countries Adopt Document on Security-Building Measures: Report by Agence France-Presse," *Radio Free Europe Report*, Vienna, November 18, 1990.

16. Reuters, November 15, 1990. Cited in "Instead of Sealing German Split, CSCE Helped to Overcome It," *Radio Free Europe Report*, Vienna, November 15, 1990.

17. *Ibid.*

18. CSCE, "Statement on the Crisis in the Gulf," New York, October 2, 1990.

19. The White House, Office of the Press Secretary, "Remarks by the President to CSCE Ministerial," New York, October 1, 1990.

20. For an analysis see Erika B. Schlager, "Does CSCE Spell 'Stability' for Europe?" presentation to the Cornell Law Journal Symposium on "Restructuring the European Security Equilibrium—The Role of International Law," March 8-9, 1991, mimeo, p. 23.

21. See *NYT*, November 20 and 22, 1990.

22. CSCE, *Charter of Paris for a New Europe*, pp. 1-3.

23. Statement by Margaret Thatcher, November 19, 1990.

24. Statement by Mikhail S. Gorbachev at the Paris CSCE Summit Meeting, November 19, 1990.

25. For background, see *News from Helsinki Watch: Albania*, April 19, 1991, pp. 1-21.

26. "Hearing Focuses on Recent Events in Albania," *CSCE Digest*, Vol. 14, No. 4, May 1991, p. 4.

27. Commission, *The Elections in Albania: March-April, 1991* (Washington, DC, April 1991), p. 1.

28. International Helsinki Federation, "International Helsinki Federation in Albania," press release, Vienna, March 11, 1991, pp. 1-3.

29. "Hearing Focuses on Recent Events in Albania," p. 4.

30. *Ibid.*

31. CSCE, *Supplementary Document to Give Effect to Certain Provisions Contained in the Charter of Paris for a New Europe.*

32. Schlager, "Does CSCE Spell 'Stability' for Europe?" p. 8.

33. *Ibid.* See especially footnote 7.

34. *Ibid.*, p. 8.

35. *WP*, June 20, 1991.

36. *Ibid.*

37. *Ibid.*

38. "CSCE Parliament Established at Madrid Meeting," *CSCE Digest*, Vol. 14, No. 3, April 1991, p. 3.

39. As an example of congressional anger, see Dante Fascell, "The CSCE: Properly Homeless," *International Herald Tribune* (Paris), September 28, 1990.

40. Joel Blocker, "Council of Europe Asks for Major Role in Future CSCE Process," *Radio Free Europe Report*, Paris, November 20, 1990.

41. *Ibid.*

42. "CSCE Parliament Established at Madrid Meeting," p. 3.

43. *Ibid.*

44. For a favorable view of the Madrid meeting, see Rafael Estrella, "The CSCE and the Creation of a Parliamentary Assembly," *NATO Review*, October 1991, pp. 23-6.

45. Fascell, "The CSCE: Properly Homeless."

46. The American Society of International Law, *Proceedings of Eighty-Fourth Annual Meeting*, p. 119.

47. *Ibid.*, p. 123.

48. *Ibid.*, p. 124. Here Maresca refers to his earlier published work on the subject.

49. See *Position of the Government of Poland on the Idea of 35-Nation CSCE Summit in 1990*. It was made available by the Helsinki Commission.

50. *Ibid.* The Mitterrand "confederation" idea is in *Le Monde* (Paris), January 2, 1990.

51. *NYT*, November 21, 1990; also see statement by Tadeusz Mazowiecki, Prime Minister of Poland, to the Paris CSCE Summit Meeting, November 19, 1990.

52. *Proposal to Establish European Security Commission*, pp. 2-4. The memorandum was dated April 6, 1990.

53. *NYT*, November 21, 1990; also see statement by Vaclav Havel, President of the Czech and Slovak Federal Republic, to the Paris CSCE Summit Meeting, Paris, November 20, 1990.

54. Speech by British Prime Minister Margaret Thatcher, Cambridge, British Information Services, March 29, 1990.

55. *NYT*, November 21, 1990.

56. *NYT*, December 14, 1990. Early the following month, the Council of Europe held a two-day conference to seek to cope with the expected refugee wave. See *NYT*, January 27, 1991.

57. *NYT*, November 21, 1990.

58. *Ibid.*

59. CSCE, *Charter of Paris for a New Europe*, p. 8.

60. *NYT*, November 21, 1990.

61. Reuters, November 21, 1990. Also see an analysis of the summit in *NYT*, November 22, 1990.

62. *NYT*, November 20, 1990.

63. Reuters, November 21, 1990.

64. Statement by the Supreme Council of the Republic of Lithuania to the CSCE (issued in Munich, Germany), November 22, 1990.

65. CSCE, *Supplementary Document*, p. 10. Annex III carries the planned details of the scheduled Geneva "Meeting of Experts on National Minorities."

66. *NYT*, November 22, 1990.

NOTES TO CHAPTER 17

1.   Stephen Rosenfeld, "A Timely Warning," *WP*, November 30, 1990.

2.   Department of State, *President's 29th CSCE Report, Implementation of the Helsinki Final Act, April 1, 1990-March 31, 1991*, Vol. 2, Dispatch Supplement No. 3 (Washington, DC, July 1991), pp. 1-52.

3.   Schlager, "Does CSCE Spell 'Stability' for Europe?"

4.   Department of State, *Dispatch*, October 8, 1990, pp. 154-55.

5.   Steny H. Hoyer, "CSCE and the Blueprint for Europe," speech at Georgetown University, Washington, DC, March 6, 1991.

6.   *Ibid.*

7.   Cited in Anthony Lewis, "Hate Against Hate," *NYT*, November 15, 1991. The article by Sir Isaiah had appeared in the Fall 1991 issue of *New Perspectives Quarterly*.

8.   CSCE, *Recommendations of the Ad Hoc Group of Experts of the Participating States on Administrative, Financial and Personal Arrangements for the CSCE Institutional Structure Created by the Paris Summit*, CSCE/ET.1/Rev.1 (Vienna, January 28, 1991).

9.   CSCE, *Berlin Meeting of the CSCE Council, 19-20 June 1991: Summary of Conclusions*.

10. For a short review, see Commission, *Conference on Security and Cooperation in Europe: An Overview* (Washington, DC, September 1991), p.9.

11. *Ibid.*

12. For the various initiatives undertaken by CSCE, see the documents in Commission, *Activities of the CSCE and Selected US Statements at CSCE Meetings Regarding the Conflict in Yugoslavia* (Washington, DC, 1991).

13. See the testimony of Ralph R. Johnson, Principal Deputy Assistant Secretary of State for European and Canadian Affairs, in Commission, *Hearing on the Conflict in Yugoslavia* (Washington, DC, October 31, 1991).

14. Department of State, *Dispatch*, Vol. 2, No 42. This carries the testimony of Deputy Assistant Secretary Ralph Johnson to Senate Foreign Relations Committee on October 16, 1991.

15. *Ibid.*, p.2.

16. *Ibid.*

17. Interview with Erika B. Schlager, January 14, 1992 by telephone from Washington, DC.

18. *Ibid.*

19. For the Montreux and Athens meetings, see Commission, *Peaceful Settlements of Disputes in the CSCE Process* (Washington, DC, August 1991), pp. 3-5, 42-44.

20. *Ibid.*

21. *Ibid.*

22. The Mechanism is described in *ibid.*, pp. 15-18.

23. *Ibid.*, pp. 18-20.

24. Cited in *ibid.*, p. 1. A similar observation can be found in James Goodby, "A New European Concern: Settling Disputes in CSCE," *Arms Control Today*, January-February 1991, p. 6.

25. Interview with Erika B. Schlager, January 14, 1992. She had been a participant in the Valletta deliberations and provided the author with considerable background material.

26. Citations from Wilson can be found in Karl E. Meyer, "Editorial Notebook, Woodrow Wilson's Dynamite," *NYT*, August 14, 1991.

27. Arthur Schlesinger Jr., "Self-Determination: Yes, But . . . ," *WSJ*, September 27, 1991.

28. Meyer, "Editorial Notebook."

29. Schlesinger, "Self-Determination: Yes."

30. This is noted in Cvijeto Job, "The Next Yugoslavia," *WP*, September 26, 1991.

31. Commission, *National Minorities and Peoples, Their Rights and the Rights to Self-determination Within the Context of CSCE or Helsinki Principles* (Washington, DC, 1991). This unpublished paper was prepared by Bob Hand of the Helsinki Commission staff.

32. Magarditsch Hatschikjan, "Eastern Europe—Nationalist Pandemonium," *Aussenpolitik*, Vol. 42, Quarterly Edition No. 3, 1991, pp. 213.

33. *Financial Times* (London), August 28, 1991.

34. *Ibid.*

35. Commission, *The Cracow Symposium on Cultural Heritage of the CSCE Participating States* (Washington, DC, 1991), pp. 1-41.

36. Interview with Erika B. Schlager, October 16, 1991, was conducted by telephone from Washington, DC.

37. Commission, *The Cracow Symposium*, p. 39.

38. This was noted in the longest and one of the most important resolutions adopted at the All-Union Congress of Jewish Organizations, December 20, 1989.

39. Korey, *The Soviet Cage*, pp. 85-7.

40. The history of the poem and its impact is discussed in *ibid.*, pp. 98-124.

41. Judith Miller, *One By One: Facing The Holocaust* (New York: Simon & Schuster, 1990), pp. 192-93.

42. Cited in detail in Robert D. Kaplan, "Croatianism," *The New Republic*, November 25, 1991.

43. *NYT*, August 2, 1991.

44. See Commission, *The Geneva CSCE Experts Meeting on National Minorities: July 1-July 19, 1991* (Washington, DC, August 1991), p. 4.

45. *Ibid.*, p. 6.

46. *Ibid.*

47. *Ibid.*

48. Statement by Max M. Kampelman, Head of the US Delegation to the Geneva CSCE Meeting, July 1, 1991.

49. *Ibid.*

50. *Ibid.*

51. "The Euro-Atlantic Architecture: From East to West," address by Secretary of State James A. Baker III to the Aspen Institute-Berlin, June 18, 1991.

52. David K. Shipler, "Democracy is a System, Not a Man," *NYT*, January 9, 1991.

53. Statement by Ambassador Max M. Kampelman, July 19, 1991. See also his earlier speech on July 1, 1991.

54. Commission, *Hearings*, July 31, 1991. Thus, after emphasizing the rights of the individual as the very essence of democracy, Kampelman said that it was "not necessary or even desirable to enact special group rights. . . ."

55. United Nations Economic and Social Council, Commission on Human Rights, *Promotion, Protection and Restoration of Human Rights at the National, Regional and International Levels*, E/CN. 4/Sub. 2/1985/31 (May 14, 1985), pp. 3, 11-13, 14, 26, 30.

56. For the text of Article XXVII and an analysis of it, see Mala Tabory, "Minority Rights in the CSCE Context," *Israel Yearbook on Human Rights* (Tel Aviv: Israel Trust Ltd, 1991), Volume 20, pp. 201-03.

57. United Nations Economic and Social Council, Commission on Human Rights, *Report of the Working Group on the Rights of Persons Belonging to National, Ethnic, Religious and Linguistic Minorities*, E/CN. 4/1991-53 (March 5, 1991).

58. *Ibid.*, pp. 3, 20. A leading publication was sharply critical of the US delegation's emphasis on "group rights" and "its stubborn (and lonely) use of the awkward phrase 'rights of persons belonging to national minorities.'" See *The Economist* (London), July 13, 1991.

59. "Minority Questions Prove Difficult in Geneva," *CSCE Digest*, Vol. 14, No. 6, Summer 1991, p. 5.

60. Statement by Ambassador Samuel G. Wise, US Delegation to the Geneva CSCE Meeting, July 4, 1991.

61. Statement by Ambassador Samuel G. Wise, July 9, 1991.

62. Statement by David M. Evans, US Delegation to the Geneva CSCE Meeting, July 12, 1991.

63. Statement by Ambassador Max M. Kampelman, July 19, 1991.

64. Commission, *Report of the CSCE Meeting of Experts on National Minorities* (Geneva, July 1991), pp. 1-11.

65. See "US Legislation Against Hate Crimes," statement by William H. Hill, Deputy Head of US Delegation to Geneva CSCE Meeting, July 5, 1991.

66. Commission, *The Geneva CSCE Experts Meeting* (August 1991), p. 7. Ambassador Kampelman's speeches at Geneva communicated the message clearly.

67. "Minority Questions Prove Difficult in Geneva," p. 5.

68. *RFE/RL Report on the USSR* (Munich), July 26, 1991, p. 42. The Soviet delegate was Georgii Tarazevich.

69. Interview with Erika B. Schlager, October 16, 1991.

70. Statement by Ambassador Max M. Kampelman, July 19, 1991.

71. "Minority Questions Prove Difficult in Geneva," p. 5.

72. *Ibid.* Also see Budapest media interviews with Hungarian delegation in *FBIS-EEU-91-40*, July 22, 1991, pp. 20-1; and *FBIS-EEU-91-141*, July 23, 1991, pp. 14-20.

73. Commission, *The Geneva CSCE Experts Meeting* (August 1991), pp. 7-9.

74. Commission, *Report of the CSCE Meeting of Experts on National Minorities* (July 1991), p. 4.

75. Commission, *The Geneva CSCE Experts Meeting* (August 1991), p. 6.

76. Statement by Ambassador Max M. Kampelman, July 19, 1991.

77. Lloyd N. Cutler, "The Dilemma of Secession," *WP*, July 21, 1991.

78. *NYT*, August 1, 1991.

79. *Izvestiia*, August 20, 1991. The document was headlined, "The Appeal to the Soviet People of August 19, 1991."

80. TASS, December 22, 1990.

81. *Sovetskaia Rossiia*, December 22, 1990.

82. *Literaturnaia Rossiia*, January 10, 1991.

83. *Den*, May 1991; also see *Literaturnaia gazeta*, No. 35, 1991 and *Moscow News*, No. 40, 1991.

84. *NYT*, June 18, 1991.

85. *Sovetskaia Rossiia*, July 23, 1991.

86. TASS, July 30, 1991; for a detailed characterization of Zhironovsky, see Paul Quinn-Judge, "Russia's David Duke," *The New Republic*, November 11, 1991.

87. This is conveyed in Gorbachev's press conference on August 22 and his address to the Russian Parliament the next day.

88. *NYT*, August 24, 1991.

89. Interview with Aleksandr Gelman, September 15, 1991. Gorbachev had singled out Gelman for his integrity and commitment to glasnost during the Soviet leader's press conference of August 21. See *NYT*, August 23, 1991. The author interviewed Gelman in Moscow.

90. Reuters, August 20, 1991.

NOTES TO CHAPTER 18

1. Yakovlev himself warned publicly that a coup was in the making three days before its occurrence. *NYT*, August 17, 1991.

2. *NYT*, August 21, 1991.

3. *Ibid.*

4. The changing information was passed on to the author by US Helsinki Commission staffers.

5. *NYT*, September 6, 1991.

6. Statement by Mikhail Gorbachev, President of the USSR, to the Moscow CSCE Meeting, September 10, 1991.

7. Interview with Ambassador Max M. Kampelman, September 12, 1991, in Moscow. The text of the "Declaration" was published in *Izvestiia*, September 7, 1991.

8. Statement by Mikhail Gorbachev, September 10, 1991.

9. Statement by Danish Foreign Minister Uffe Ellemann-Jensen at the Moscow CSCE Meeting, September 10, 1991.

10. Statement by British Foreign Secretary Douglas Hurd at the Moscow CSCE Meeting, September 10, 1991.

11. "Democracy's Season," statement by US Secretary of State James A. Baker at the Moscow CSCE Meeting, September 11, 1991.

12. Statement by Soviet Foreign Minister Boris D. Pankin at the Moscow CSCE Meeting, September 11, 1991.

13. *Pravda*, June 27, 1991; and TASS, July 2, 8, 9, 1991.

14. These were off-the-cuff remarks which the author, who sat in the gallery, took down in note form.

15. Notes on US Delegation staff meeting, September 13, 1991. The notes are in the author's possession.

16. "Refuseniks and the Soviet Emigration Law," intervention by the British Delegation at the Moscow CSCE Meeting, September 16, 1991. Also, see the statement presented by the World Conference on Soviet Jewry to the Moscow CSCE Meeting, September 16, 1991.

17. Statement by Ambassador Samuel Wise of the US Delegation to the Moscow CSCE Meeting, October 2, 1991.

18. Notes on Sergei Kovalev's speech, September 11, 1991, were taken by the author.

19. The Soviet action had been criticized by the US, and its representative on the Committee of Senior Officials, Ambassador Jack Maresca, denounced it at the Committee's Prague meeting.

20. Ambassador Kampelman elaborated upon the courtesies at the briefing he gave to Helsinki Watch in New York on September 4, 1991. The notes of the briefing are in the author's possession.

21. See, e.g., Congressman Hoyer's opening statement in Commission, *Hearings* (Washington, DC, May 7, 1991), pp. 1-2, 34-39. Hoyer was Commission chairman at the time. *Hearings* carries the full text of the three invited witnesses—the President of Lithuania and the Prime Ministers of Latvia and Estonia.

22. "Baltic Leaders Testify Before Commission," *CSCE Digest*, Vol. 14, No. 4, May 1991, pp. 1-2. The following issue played up the Commission's meeting with then RSFSR President Yeltsin and his positive view of independence for the Baltics; see "Triumphant Yeltsin Visits Congress as RSFSR President," *CSCE Digest*, Vol. 14, No. 5, June 1991, p. 1.

23. See statement by Mikhail Gorbachev, September 10, 1991, and statement by Foreign Minister Boris Pankin, September 11, 1991.

24. Statement by Lithuanian Foreign Minister Algirdis Saudargas to the Moscow CSCE Meeting, September 11, 1991.

25. "CSCE Delegation Visits Independent Baltics," pp. 1-2.

26. Statement by Ambassador Max M. Kampelman, Head of the US Delegation to the Moscow CSCE Meeting, September 16, 1991.

27. "CSCE Delegation Visits Independent Baltics," p. 2.

28. *Ibid.*, p. 2.

29. *NYT*, September 5, 1991.

30. The commitment was, indeed, followed through, at least in part. On October 16, a Lithuania Supreme Court justice halted the pardoning of war crime convictions. See *NYT*, October 17, 1991.

31. Statement by Ambassador Max Kampelman, September 16, 1991.

32. *Ibid.*

33. *Ibid.*

34. *Ibid.*

35. *Ibid.*

36. Statement by World Conference on Soviet Jewry, September 11, 1991.

37. *The Daily Telegraph* (London), August 31, 1991.

38. See Institute for Jewish Affairs, *Intelligence Survey*, No. 1, January 1991. On July 7, 1991, Yazov issued an unusual directive ordering all Soviet Army and Navy units to take out subscriptions to *Nash sovremennik*. See *Moskovskaia pravda*, October 4, 1991.

39. See the interview with Gen. Viktor Filatov, editor of the *Military-Historical Journal*, in *NYT*, January 7, 1991.

40. Statement by J. Kenneth Blackwell of the US Delegation to the Moscow CSCE Meeting, September 27, 1991.

41. *Jewish Telegraphic Agency Daily Bulletin*, October 3, 1991.

42. *Ibid.*

43. For the Gorbachev statement at Babi Yar, see *Jewish Telegraphic Agency Daily Bulletin*, October 8, 1991.

44. *NYT*, August 1, 1991.

45. Commission, *The Moscow Meeting of the Conference on the Human Dimension of the Conference on Security and Cooperation in Europe, 10 September-4 October 1991* (Washington, DC, 1991).

46. *Ibid.*, p. 42.

47. Statement by J. Kenneth Blackwell, September 27, 1991.

48. See, for example, *The German Tribune*, No. 1487, October 6, 1991; *NYT*, October 11, 13, and 14, 1991.

49. *NYT*, November 1, 1991. On the UK action, see *NYT*, November 2, 1991.

50. *NYT*, October 19 and 28, 1991. See also its "News of the Week Section: The World," October 20, 1991.

51. Robert S. Boynton, "Czech Mates," *The New Republic*, August 5, 1991, pp. 14-16.

52. *NYT*, October 20, 1991.

53. From the author's notes at the US Delegation staff meeting held on September 16, 1991.

54. Statement by Ambassador Max M. Kampelman, September 16, 1991.

55. *Ibid.*

56. *Ibid.*

57. Statement by Ambassador Max M. Kampelman, September 23, 1991.

58. *Ibid.*

59. *Ibid.*

60. Kampelman referred to his labor mediation experiences as a source for his views in comments he made to the meeting of US Helsinki Watch in New York on September 4, 1991.

61. Notes on US Delegation staff meeting, September 16, 1991. See also speech by German Foreign Minister Hans-Dietrich Genscher at the Moscow CSCE Meeting, September 10, 1991.

62. Notes on US Delegation staff meeting, September 16, 1991.

63. Statement by US Delegation, September 18, 1991.

64. Commission, *The Moscow Meeting*, pp. 24-8.

65. *Ibid.*, p. 24, item 3.

66. How the Mechanism would work was spelled out in a special paper, *Highlights of the Moscow Concluding Document*, prepared by and distributed to the press by the US Delegation in October 1991.

67. Statement by Ambassador Max M. Kampelman, October 4, 1991.

68. Commission, *The Moscow Meeting*, p. 22.

69. Statement by Ambassador Max M. Kampelman, October 4, 1991.

70. Suzanne Crow, "Soviet Reaction to the Crisis in Yugoslavia," *RFE/RL Report on the USSR* (Munich), No. 31, August 2, 1991.

71. *Financial Times* (London), September 10, 1991.

72. Statement by Ambassador Max M. Kampelman, October 4, 1991.

73. Commission, *The Moscow Meeting*, p. 37.

74. Letter from Secretary of State James A. Baker III to Ambassador Max M. Kampelman (October 12, 1991).

75. Letter from Undersecretary of State for Economic Affairs Robert Zoellick to Ambassador Max M. Kampelman (October 15, 1991).

76. Commission, *The Moscow Meeting*, pp. 29-43.

77. Statement by Ambassador Max M. Kampelman, October 4, 1991.

78. Letter from Professor Thomas Buergenthal to Ambassador Max M. Kampelman (October 15, 1991).

79. Interview with Ambassador Sam Wise, October 10, 1991, by telephone from Washington, DC.

80. Statement by Ambassador Max M. Kampelman, October 4, 1991.

81. *Ibid.*

82. Statement by Sergei Kovalev, Co-chair of the Soviet Delegation to the Moscow CSCE Meeting, October 3, 1991; see also his article "The West Turns Down the Soviet Demand for Control," *New Times*, 40/91, pp. 22-23.

83. Statement by Ambassador Max M. Kampelman, October 4, 1991.

84. *Ibid.*

85. *Ibid.*

86. Leif Mevik, *Underveis Europa* (Oslo: Aventura Forlag, 1990). The excerpt was translated by Mevik and forwarded to Kampelman.

87. Kampelman, *Entering New Worlds*, p. 5.

Bibliography

BOOKS

Ludmilla Alexeyeva, *Soviet Dissent: Contemporary Movements for National, Religious, and Human Rights* (Middletown: Wesleyan University Press, 1985).

Nils Andrea and Karl Birnbaum, eds., *Belgrade and Beyond: The CSCE Process in Perspective* (The Hague: Kluwer Academic, 1981).

Frederick B. Artz, *Reaction and Revolution 1814-1832* (New York: Harper, 1934).

Mark I. Azbel, *Refusenik: Trapped in the Soviet Union* (Boston: Houghton Mifflin, 1981).

Arie Bloed, ed., *From Helsinki to Vienna: Basic Documents of the Helsinki Process* (Dordrecht: Martinus Nijhoff, 1990).

Zbigniew Brzezinski, *Power and Principle* (New York: Farrar Straus Giroux, 1985).

Dusko Doder and Louise Branson, *Gorbachev: Heretic in the Kremlin* (New York: Viking Penguin, 1990).

Alan Dowty, *Closed Borders: The Contemporary Assault on Freedom of Movement* (New Haven: Yale University Press and the Twentieth Century Fund, 1987).

Luigi Vittorio Ferraris, ed., *Report on a Negotiation: Helsinki-Geneva-Helsinki, 1972-1975* (The Hague: Kluwer Academic Publishers, 1981).

Thomas Franck and Edward Weisband, *Foreign Policy by Congress* (New York: Oxford University Press, 1979).

Martin Gilbert, *Shcharansky: Hero of Our Time* (New York: Viking, 1986).

Manfred Görtemaker, *European Revolution and German Unity: 1989-1990* (New York: St. Martin's Press and the Institute for EastWest Studies, forthcoming).

Paul Goldberg, *The Final Act: The Dramatic, Revealing Story of the Moscow Helsinki Watch Group* (New York: William Morrow & Co., 1988).

Mikhail Gorbachev, *Perestroika: New Thinking for Our Country and the World* (New York: Harper & Row, 1987).

Robert Hartmann, *Palace Politics: An Inside Account of the Ford Years* (New York: McGraw-Hill, 1980).

Max M. Kampelman, *Entering New Worlds: The Memoirs of a Private Man in Public Life* (New York: HarperCollins, 1991).

——, *Three Years at the East-West Divide* (New York: Freedom House, 1983).

Henry A. Kissinger, *The White House Years* (Boston: Little, Brown & Co., 1979).

——, *Years of Upheaval* (Boston: Little, Brown & Co., 1982).

William Korey, *The Soviet Cage: Anti-Semitism in Russia* (New York: Viking, 1973).

——, *Human Rights and the Helsinki Accord* (New York: Foreign Policy Association, 1983).

——, *Glasnost and Soviet Anti-Semitism* (New York: American Jewish Committee, 1991).

Stephen Lehne, *The Vienna Meeting of the Conference on Security and Cooperation in Europe, 1986-1989: A Turning Point in East-West Relations* (Boulder: Westview Press, 1991).

John J. Maresca, *To Helsinki: The Conference on Security and Cooperation in Europe 1973-1975* (Durham: Duke University Press, 1985).

Vojtech Mastny, *Helsinki, Human Rights, and European Security: Analysis and Documentation* (Durham: Duke University Press, 1986).

——, *The Helsinki Process and the Reintegration of Europe 1986-1991: Analysis and Documentation* (New York: New York University Press and the Institute for EastWest Studies, 1992).

Roy Medvedev and Giulietto Chiesa, *Time of Change: An Insider's View of Russia's Transformation* (New York: Pantheon, 1989).

Judith Miller, *One By One: Facing the Holocaust* (New York, Simon & Schuster, 1990).

Yuri Orlov, *Dangerous Thoughts: Memoirs of a Russian Life* (New York: Morrow, 1991).

Stephen J. Roth, *The Helsinki "Final Act" and Soviet Jewry* (London: Institute of Jewish Affairs, 1976).

Andrei Sakharov, *Memoirs* (New York: Alfred A. Knopf, 1990).

Natan Sharansky (Anatoly Shcharansky), *Fear No Evil* (New York: Random House, 1989).

Eduard Shevardnadze, *The Future Belongs to Freedom* (New York: Pantheon, 1991).

Arkady N. Shevchenko, *Breaking with Moscow* (New York: Alfred A. Knopf, 1985).

Jan Sizoo and Rudolph Jurrjens, *CSCE Decision-Making: The Madrid Experience* (The Hague: Martinus Nijhoff, 1984).

H. Gordon Skilling, ed., *Charter 77 and Human Rights in Czechoslovakia* (London: Allen & Unwin, 1981).

Richard H. Ullman, *Securing Europe* (Princeton: Princeton University Press and the Twentieth Century Fund, 1991).

Sandy Vogelgesang, *American Dream, Global Nightmare: The Dilemma of US Human Rights Policy* (New York: Norton, 1980).

World Conference on Soviet Jewry, *Soviet Jewry and the Implementation of the Helsinki Final Act: Report* (London: World Conference on Soviet Jewry, 1977).

———, *Human Contacts: Reunion of Families and Soviet Jewry* (London: World Conference on Soviet Jewry, 1986).

SCHOLARLY ARTICLES

Thomas Buergenthal, "The CSCE Rights System," *The George Washington Journal of International Law and Economics*, Vol. 25, No. 2, 1991.

———, "The Copenhagen CSCE Meeting: A New Public Order for Europe," *Human Rights Law Journal*, Vol. 11, 1990.

Naomi W. Cohen, "The Abrogation of the Russo-American Treaty of 1832," *Jewish Social Studies*, Vol. XXV, January 1963.

Fons Coomans and Liesbeth Lijnzard, "Initiating the CSCE Supervisory Procedure: The Cases of the Netherlands and Czechoslovakia," in Arie Bloed and P. van Dijk, eds., *The Human Dimension of the Helsinki Process* (Dordrecht: Kluwer Academic, 1991).

Dante B. Fascell, "Did Human Rights Survive Belgrade?" *Foreign Policy*, No. 31, Summer 1978.

F. J. M. Feldbrugge, "The Soviet Human Rights Doctrine in the Crossfire Between Dissidents at Home and Critics Abroad," *Vanderbilt Journal of Transnational Law*, Vol. 13, No. 2-3, Spring-Summer 1980.

Margaret E. Galey, "Congress, Foreign Policy and Human Rights: Ten Years After Helsinki," *Human Rights Quarterly*, Vol. 7, No. 3, 1985.

James E. Goodby, "A New European Concern: Settling Disputes in CSCE," *Arms Control Today*, January-February 1991.

Evelyn Greenberg, "An 1869 Petition on Behalf of Russian Jews," *American Jewish Historical Quarterly*, Vol. LIV, March 1965.

Magarditsch Hatschikjan, "Eastern Europe—Nationalist Pandemonium," *Aussenpolitik*, Vol. 42, Quarterly Edition No. 3, 1991.

Sidney Heitman, "Soviet Emigration in 1990: A New 'Fourth Wave'?" *Soviet Jewish Affairs*, Vol. 21, No. 2, Winter 1991.

Alexandre Charles Kiss and Mary Francis Dominick, "The International Legal Significance of the Human Rights Provisions of the Helsinki Final Act," *Vanderbilt Journal of Transnational Law*, Vol. 13, No. 2-3, Spring-Summer 1980.

William Korey, "Sakharov and the Soviet Jewish National Movement," *Midstream*, Vol. XX, No. 2, February 1974.

———, "The Struggle over Jackson-Mills-Vanik," *The American Jewish Year Book 1975* (Philadelphia: American Jewish Committee and Jewish Publication Society of America, 1976).

———, "The Future of Soviet Jewry," *Foreign Affairs*, Vol. 58, No. 1, Fall 1979.

———, "Sin of Omission," *Foreign Policy*, No. 39, Summer 1980.

———, "The Helsinki/Madrid Meeting," *The Washington Quarterly*, Spring 1982.

———, "Jackson-Vanik and Soviet Jewry," *The Washington Quarterly*, Winter 1984.

———, "Helsinki, Human Rights and the Gorbachev Style," *Ethics and International Affairs*, Vol. 1, 1987.

———, "The Jackson-Vanik Amendment in Perspective," *Soviet Jewish Affairs*, Vol. 18, No. 1, 1988.

———, "The Legacy of Helsinki," *Reform Judaism*, Vol. XVI, No. 3, Spring 1988.

———, "Human Rights and the Policy of Leverage and Linkage: The Lesson of the Helsinki Process," in Vojtech Mastny and Jan Zielonka, eds., *Human Rights and Security: Europe on the Eve of a New Era* (Boulder: Westview Press, 1991).

Ernst Kux, "Revolution in Eastern Europe—Revolution in the West?" *Problems of Communism*, Vol. XL, May-June 1991.

F. Stephen Larrabee, "Moscow and German Unification," *The Harriman Institute Forum*, Vol. 5, No. 9, May 1992.

Sian Lewis, "A Step Forward for International Human Rights Protection," *Interights Bulletin*, Vol. 3, No. 4, 1988.

Boris Meissner, "Gorbachev's Foreign Policy Programme," *Aussenpolitik*, Vol. 37, Quarterly Edition No. 2, 1986.

Jordan J. Paust, "Transnational Freedom of Speech: Legal Aspects of the Helsinki Final Act," *Law and Contemporary Problems*, Vol. 45, 1982.

Stephen J. Roth, "The Hamburg 'Scientific Forum' of the Helsinki Conference," *IJA Research Report*, No. 6, April 1980.

———, "The Madrid Follow-Up Conference to Helsinki," *IJA Research Report*, No. 25, December 1980.

————, "New Chapter in the Helsinki Process: The Vienna Conference and its Aftermath," *IJA Research Report*, No. 4, July 1989.

————, "CSCE Outlaws Anti-Semitism," *IJA Research Report*, No. 6, October 1990.

Harold S. Russell, "The Helsinki Declaration: Brobdingnag or Lilliput?" *American Journal of International Law*, Vol. 70, April 1976.

Erika Schlager, "The Procedural Framework of the CSCE: From the Helsinki Consultations to the Paris Charter," *Human Rights Law Journal*, Vol. 12, No. 6-7, July 12, 1991.

Albert W. Sherer, Jr., "Goldberg's Variation," *Foreign Policy*, No. 39, Summer 1980.

Carroll Sherer, "Breakdown at Belgrade," *The Washington Quarterly*, Autumn 1978.

Mala Tabory, "Minority Rights in the CSCE Context," *Israel Yearbook on Human Rights*, Vol. 20 (Tel Aviv: Israel Trust Ltd., 1991).

Andrei Zagorsky and Yuri Kashlev, "The Human Dimension of Politics," *International Affairs* (Moscow), No. 3, March 1990.

DOCUMENTS OF THE COMMISSION ON SECURITY AND COOPERATION IN EUROPE

(All published in Washington, DC, unless otherwise noted; listed by year of publication except for transcripts of Commission hearings, which are listed by date of proceedings.)

1976
Report of the Study Mission to Europe.

1977
Hearings on Human Rights (February 3-4).
Hearings on US Policy and the Belgrade Conference (June 6).
Implementation of the Final Act of the CSCE: Findings and Recommendations Two Years After Helsinki (September).

1978
Hearing on the Belgrade Conference (March 21).

1979
Fulfilling Our Promises: The United States and the Helsinki Final Act—A Status Report (November).

1980
Implementation of the Final Act of the Conference on Security and Cooperation in Europe: Findings and Recommendations Five Years After Helsinki (August).

1982
Hearings (March 18).
Hearings on Phase IV of the Madrid CSCE Meeting (March 23).
Human Rights in Czechoslovakia: The Documents of Charter 77, 1977-82 (July).

1985

The Helsinki Process and East-West Relations: Progress in Perspective—Report on the Positive Aspects of the Implementation of the Helsinki Final Act from 1975 through 1984 (March).

Hearings on Restrictions on Artistic Freedom in the Soviet Union and the Budapest Cultural Forum (October 29 and December 11).

Annual Report of the Commission on Security and Cooperation for the Period Covering January 1 through December 31, 1985.

1986

Hearings: Bern Human Contacts Experts Meeting (March 18 and June 18).

Hearings Before the Commission on Security and Cooperation in Europe: Natan Shcharansky to Mark the 10th Anniversary of the Moscow Helsinki Group (May 14).

Hearings on the Stockholm Meeting of the Conference on Confidence- and Security-Building Measures and Disarmament in Europe (October 1).

1987

Basket I—Implementation of the Final Act of the Conference on Security and Cooperation in Europe: Findings Eleven Years After Helsinki (November).

1988

"Helsinki Co-chairman Warns that Emphasis on Military and Trade Issues Could Endanger Helsinki Process" (press release, September 22).

1989

The Paris Meeting of the Conference on the Human Dimension of the Conference on Security and Cooperation in Europe (July).

1990

The Vienna CSCE Follow-up Meeting: Report Prepared by the Staff of the US Commission on Security and Cooperation in Europe (January).

The Copenhagen Meeting of the Conference on the Human Dimension of the Conference on Security and Cooperation in Europe (July).

The Copenhagen Meeting of the Conference on the Human Dimension of the Conference on Security and Cooperation in Europe—June 5 to 29 (August).

1991

The Cracow Symposium on Cultural Heritage of the CSCE Participating States.

The Elections in Albania: March-April 1991 (April).

Hearings—Baltic Leadership on the Status of Independence Movements (May 7).

Report of the CSCE Meeting of Experts on National Minorities (Geneva, July)

The Geneva CSCE Experts Meeting on National Minorities July 1-July 19, 1991 (August).

Peaceful Settlements of Disputes in the CSCE Process (August).

Conference on Security and Cooperation in Europe: An Overview (September).

The Moscow Meeting of the Conference on the Human Dimension of the Conference on Security and Cooperation in Europe, 10 September-4 October 1991.

Hearing on the Conflict in Yugoslavia (October 31).

The Oslo Seminar of Experts on Democratic Institutions.

Activities of the CSCE and Selected US Statements at CSCE Meetings Regarding the Conflict in Yugoslavia.

1992
From Vienna to Helsinki: Reports on the Intersessional Meetings of the CSCE Process (April).

OTHER US GOVERNMENT DOCUMENTS
(All published in Washington, DC.)

Fourth Semiannual Report by the President to the Commission on Security and Cooperation in Europe, December 1, 1977—June 1, 1978, Special Report No. 45 (1978).

Ninth Semiannual Report by the President to the Commission on Security and Cooperation in Europe on the Implementation of the Final Act, June 1, 1980-November 30, 1980 (1980).

Tenth Semiannual Report by the President to the Commission on Security and Cooperation in Europe on the Implementation of the Final Act, December 1, 1980-May 31, 1981, Special Report No. 85 (1981).

Department of State, *The Conference on Security and Cooperation in Europe*, Historical Issues, No. 22 (July 1985).

———, *President's 29th CSCE Report, Implementation of the Helsinki Final Act, April 1, 1990-March 31, 1991*, Vol. 2, Dispatch Supplement No. 3 (July 1991).

———, Bureau of Public Affairs, *Current Policy* (various issues).

———, Office of the Historian, *The Conference on Security and Cooperation in Europe; Public Statements and Documents, 1954-1986* (1986).

Postal Service, *Mailing to the Soviet Union* (September 1985).

US Congress, Senate Committee on Foreign Relations, *Hearings*, January 17-18, 1989.

———, Senate Committee on Foreign Relations, *Establishing a Commission on Security and Cooperation in Europe*, Report 94-756 (April 23, 1976).

———, House Committee on International Relations, *Hearings Before the Subcommittee on International Political and Military Affairs* (May 4, 1976).

CSCE DOCUMENTS

Conference on Security and Cooperation in Europe, *Charter of Paris for New Europe*, November 16,1990/Version 2.

———, *Recommendations of the Ad Hoc Group of Experts of the Participating States on Administrative, Financial and Personal Arrangements for the CSCE Institutional Structure Created by the Paris Summit*, CSCE/ET.1/Rev.1 (Vienna, January 28, 1991).

———, *Berlin Meeting of the CSCE Council, 19-20 June 1991: Summary of Conclusions*.

UNITED NATIONS DOCUMENTS

José D. Inglés, *A Study of Discrimination with Respect to the Right of Everyone to Leave Any Country, Including His Own, and to Return to His Country* (New York: United Nations, 1963).

United Nations Sub-Commission on Prevention of Discrimination and Protection of Minorities, *Analysis of the Current Trends and Development Regarding the Right to Leave Any Country Including One's Own and to Return to One's Own Country, and Some Other Rights on Consideration Arising Therefrom*, E/CN. 4/Sub. 2/35 (New York, 1988). The study was prepared by Special Rapporteur C.L.C. Mubanga-Chipoya.

United Nations Economic and Social Council, Commission on Human Rights, *Promotion, Protection and Restoration of Human Rights at the National, Regional and International Levels*, E/CN. 4/Sub. 2/1985/31 (New York, May 1985), pp. 3, 11-13, 14, 26, 30.

——, *Report of the Working Group on the Rights of Persons Belonging to National, Ethnic, Religious and Linguistic Minorities*, E/CN. 4/1991-53 (New York, March 1991).

UNPUBLISHED MATERIAL

Madeleine Albright and Alfred Friendly, *Executive-Legislative Cooperation and East-West Relations: The Birth of the Helsinki Commission* (Washington, DC: December 1984), mimeo, p. 11. Subsequently published as a chapter in Edmund Muskie, Kenneth Rush, and Kenneth Thompson, eds., *The President, The Congress and Foreign Policy: A Joint Policy Project of the Association of Former Members of Congress and the Atlantic Council of the United States* (Lanham: University Press of America, 1986).

Commission on Security and Cooperation in Europe, *The Sofia CSCE Meeting on the Protection of the Environment, October 16-November 3, 1989* (Washington, DC: November 1989). This was a draft version of the eventual report that was published under the same title later in the year.

——, *National Minorities and Peoples, Their Rights and the Rights to Self-determination Within the Context of CSCE or Helsinki Principles* (1991).
Committee of Concerned Scientists, *Report on Basket III Violations of the Helsinki Final Act* (New York: February 24, 1986).

Joshua L. Dorosin, *The Role and Significance of the Commission on Security and Cooperation in Europe within the Helsinki Process* (Washington, DC: Spring 1989), mimeo (revised version). Dorosin served as a research assistant to the author for several months in 1988.

Dorothy Kurgans Goldberg, *A Personal Journal of International Negotiations About Human Rights* (undated).

Jonathan Greenwald, *Trade-Offs with the Soviets in the Concluding Document* (Belgrade: November 2, 1977). Found in the Sherer Archive, the memo had been prepared at Goldberg's request but never cleared by the State Department.

————, An untitled and undated essay regarding his view of the battle between State Department and Commission officials at the time of the Belgrade meeting. The essay had been sent by Greenwald to Dorothy Goldberg and was made available to the author by the secretary to Goldberg, Fran Guilbert.

Alex Littman, *Principle in Action: America's Outcry Against the Mistreatment of Jews in Russia, 1880-1892* (New York: 1968); drawn from his master's thesis at New York University.

Peter Reddaway, *Soviet Policies on Dissent and Emigration: The Radical Change of Course Since 1979* (Washington, DC: August 28, 1984). The paper was prepared for the Kennan Institute for Advanced Russian Studies.

Erika B. Schlager, *Does CSCE Spell `Stability' for Europe?*; presentation to the Cornell Law Journal Symposium on "Restructuring the European Security Equilibrium—The Role of International Law," March 8-9, 1991.

Albert Sherer, Jr., *The Geneva Negotiations, The Second Stage of the Helsinki Process* (undated).

Martin Sletzinger, *Executive-Legislative Branch Cooperation in East-West Policy: A Case Study of the Commission on Security and Cooperation in Europe* (Washington, DC: July 1984), mimeo.

INTERVIEWS

Edward Alexander
Ludmilla Alexeyeva
Mark Azbel
Mikhail Beizer
Yosef Begun
Zbigniew Brzezinski
Guy Coriden
Yakov Eisenstadt
Ilya Essas
Veniamin Fain
Jane Fisher
Robert Frowick
Aleksandr Gelman
Steny Hoyer
Philip Hurr

Max Kampelman
Julian LeBourgeois
Veniamin Levich
Spencer Oliver
Rozanne Ridgway
Harold Russell
Robin Saipe
Richard Schifter
Erika Schlager
Anatoly Shcharansky (Natan Sharansky)
Albert Sherer, Jr.
George Vest
Aleksandr Voronel
Samuel Wise
Warren Zimmermann

MISCELLANEOUS

American Foreign Policy Newsletter

The American Society of International Law, Proceedings of the 84th Annual Meeting, "Human Rights: The Helsinki Process" (Washington, DC: 1990).

A Chronicle of Current Events

Chronicle of Human Rights in the USSR

Congressional Record

CSCE Digest

Current Digest of the Soviet Press

Current Policy

Encounter

The New Leader

Petitions, Letters and Appeals from Soviet Jews (various publications from Hebrew University, Jerusalem).

The Position of Soviet Jewry (various publications by the World Conference on Soviet Jewry, London).

Radio Free Europe/Radio Liberty (various publications).

Soviet Committee for European Security and Cooperation, *Ten Years After Helsinki: The Results and Prospects of the Process for European Security* (supplement to *Moscow News*, No. 30, July 28, 1985).

State Department Bulletin

White & Case, *Who May Leave: A Review of Soviet Practice Restricting Emigration on Grounds of Knowledge of "State Security" in Comparison with Standards of International Law and the Policies of Other States* (New York: 1987).

Index